Abridged
Dewey Decimal Classification
and Relative Index

Abridged
Dewey Decimal Classification
and Relative Index

Devised by Melvil Dewey

EDITION 13

Edited by

Joan S. Mitchell, Editor

Julianne Beall, Assistant Editor

Winton E. Matthews, Jr., Assistant Editor

Gregory R. New, Assistant Editor

FOREST PRESS

A Division of
OCLC Online Computer Library Center, Inc.
ALBANY, NEW YORK
1997

Library of Congress Cataloging-in-Publication Data

Dewey, Melvil, 1851-1931.
    Abridged Dewey decimal classification and relative index / devised by Melvil Dewey. -- Ed. 13 / edited by Joan S. Mitchell . . . [et al.]
        p.   cm.
    Includes index.
    ISBN 0-910608-59-8 (alk. paper)
    1. Classification, Dewey decimal.   I. Mitchell, Joan S.
II. Title.
Z696.D54   1997   97-10791
025.4'31--dc21   CIP

The paper used in this publication meets the requirements of ANSI/NISO Z39.48-1992 (Permanence of Paper).

 Recycled paper

Dedicated

to

Benjamin A. Custer

Editor

Dewey Decimal Classification

1956-1980

Reaching out to library organizations
and users throughout the world,
he turned the development of the
Dewey Decimal Classification
into a worldwide cooperative
venture.

Contents

Publisher's Foreword

The seven years since the publication of Abridged Edition 12 have been filled with important accomplishments and activities for OCLC Forest Press. These include publication of the first electronic version of the Dewey Decimal Classification in January 1993, and the subsequent release of Dewey for Windows in August 1996; the development of twelve new products for the Forest Press catalog, mostly aids to understanding and using the DDC; an expanded education and training program, with forty-one workshops given in seven years; a vigorous translation program; and the initiation of research efforts to facilitate the use of the Classification as an information retrieval tool in online environments. With the publication of DDC 21 in July 1996, an edition of the Dewey Decimal Classification appeared in two formats for the very first time: in print and on the Dewey for Windows CD-ROM. With the increased use of faceting in DDC 21, the twenty-first edition of the Classification is truly a tool for the 21st century.

To help users, a second and revised edition of the textbook *Dewey Decimal Classification: A Practical Guide* was published at the same time as Edition 21. A workbook for Abridged Edition 13 will be published in 1997, simultaneously with the appearance of the new abridged edition.

Our translation program has been pursued with a view to finding long-term partners in other regions or countries, developing electronic databases of foreign language editions, and making translations available more quickly. At present, there are translations of current editions of DDC (in print or in process) in Italian, French, Spanish, Arabic, Turkish, Greek, Hebrew, and Persian. For the first time ever, a Russian edition of Dewey will be published in 1998, under the aegis of the Russian National Public Library for Science and Technology in Moscow. Negotiations are underway for a Chinese translation of DDC 21.

For all of these activities, we are grateful to many organizations and individuals for their help and support.

Since Forest Press became a division of OCLC Online Computer Library Center in 1988, the staff and management of OCLC have provided a wide range of skills and resources to enable the Press to carry out its expanded programs. Thanks particularly to Dr. K. Wayne Smith, President and CEO; to Don Muccino, Executive Vice-President; and to Vice-Presidents Phyllis Bova Spies and Gary Houk for their continuing encouragement and support. In addition, we have received much help from the OCLC Office of Research, under the direction first of Martin Dillon and later Terry Noreault.

An equally important role in our work is played by the Library of Congress, where editorial work on the Classification is performed under contract between OCLC Forest Press and the Library of Congress.

The American Library Association and the (British) Library Association have been most generous in appointing committees to advise us on specific problems, such as developing priorities in the application of Dewey numbers or reviewing Dewey classes undergoing revision or expansion.

I acknowledge with pleasure the debt of the Dewey world to Joan S. Mitchell, who was appointed editor of the Dewey Decimal Classification in 1993, filling the gap left by the death of John Comaromi, who served as editor from 1980 to 1991. Ms. Mitchell has brought wit, wisdom, patience, vision, and seemingly boundless energy to the task of maintaining high quality and meeting publishing deadlines. We are also grateful to Dewey Decimal Classification Division Chief David A. Smith, and Assistant Editors Julianne Beall, Winton E. Matthews, Jr., and Gregory R. New, who carried forward the work on Edition 21 while the position of editor was vacant between 1991 and 1993.

I thank Forest Press staff: Judith Kramer-Greene, Judith Pisarski, and Elizabeth Hansen for their dedication, skill, and enthusiasm for the wide variety of tasks necessary to publish a new edition.

Lastly, I acknowledge with gratitude the permission given by Margaret Cockshutt to use her words on the dedication page of this book.

Peter J. Paulson
Executive Director
Forest Press

17 March 1997

DECIMAL CLASSIFICATION, ADDITIONS, NOTES AND DECISIONS

To keep users of Dewey Decimal Classification Abridged Edition 13 up-to-date on developments regarding the Classification, OCLC Forest Press publishes *Dewey Decimal Classification, Additions, Notes and Decisions.* Popularly known as *DC&,* it is published annually. All purchasers of Abridged Edition 13 are entitled to subscribe to *DC&* and may be placed on the mailing list for this publication by either returning the enclosed card or by writing to OCLC Forest Press, 6565 Frantz Road, Dublin, Ohio 43017-3395, USA.

Preface by the Decimal Classification Editorial Policy Committee

The intention of the abridged edition of the Dewey Decimal Classification is to provide a scheme for users who do not require the extensive detail set forth in the unabridged edition. The thirteenth abridged edition represents an abridgment of the twenty-first unabridged edition, which was published in 1996.

New editions of the Dewey Decimal Classification are needed to maintain the vigor and usefulness of the scheme. The degree of change varies depending on the priorities identified by Dewey users, trends in publishing, and the need to correct errors, improve classification structure, or ensure currency. The completely revised schedules in Edition 21 and Abridged Edition 13 are 350–354 Public administration and parts of 560–590 Life sciences. The extensive changes in these disciplines necessitated altering the fundamental classification structure. 370 Education was revised in Edition 21 to accommodate current thinking and to correct an outdated structure, but the relatively small number of changes reflected in Abridged Edition 13 converted Edition 21's extensive revision to a routine revision.

Changes to Edition 21 and Abridged Edition 13 also reflect the care and concern for international users and for collections that contain non-Christian and nonwestern materials. Sensitivity to cultural and social issues outside of the United States increases the international usefulness of the Classification.

The publication of Edition 21 and Abridged Edition 13 brings to fruition almost nine years' work of the editors, the Decimal Classification Editorial Policy Committee (EPC), and many advisors representing both subject expertise and the needs of specific user communities.

The Decimal Classification Editorial Policy Committee was established in 1937 to provide advice in determining the direction and policy of the Dewey Decimal Classification. It was reconstituted as a joint committee of the Lake Placid Education Foundation and the American Library Association in 1955. Although the connection with the Lake Placid Education Foundation was dissolved in 1988 with the sale of Forest Press to OCLC Online Computer Library Center, Inc., the Decimal Classification Editorial Policy Committee continues in its advisory role at the request of OCLC Forest Press. EPC works closely with the editors to facilitate changes, innovations, and the general development of the Classification.

Many persons served on the Decimal Classification Editorial Policy Committee during the preparation of Edition 21 and Abridged 13, each bringing his or her particular perspective to the undertaking. The present committee is composed of ten persons from public, special, academic, and government libraries, as well as library education. The members represent the American Library Association, the Library of Congress, OCLC Forest Press (publisher of the Classification), and the Library Association (United Kingdom). Additionally, the committee includes members from Canada and Australia.

The following committee members contributed to the preparation of Abridged 13; each is listed with the position they held or now hold as members: David Balatti, Director,

Bibliographic Services, National Library of Canada; Pamela P. Brown, Information Technology Services Director, Suburban Library System; Jan M. DeSirey, Audiovisual Materials Cataloger, Hennepin County Library; Giles Martin, Auchmuty Library, University of Newcastle, New South Wales, Australia; Peter J. Paulson, Executive Director, OCLC Forest Press; Andrea L. Stamm, Head, Catalog Department, Northwestern University Library; Elaine Svenonius, Professor Emerita, Graduate School of Education and Information Studies, University of California, Los Angeles; Winston Tabb, Associate Librarian for Library Services, Library of Congress; Helena M. Van Deroef, Serials Librarian, Lucent Technologies; Beacher Wiggins, Acting Director for Cataloging, Library of Congress; Susi Woodhouse, Library Association (United Kingdom).

The committee was guided in its work on Abridged 13 by the advice of the American Library Association Subject Analysis Committee Subcommittee to Review Abridged Dewey 13, chaired by Heeja Chung, and the Library Association Dewey Decimal Classification Abridged Edition 13 Subcommittee, chaired by Susi Woodhouse. EPC wishes to express its appreciation to these committees.

The Decimal Classification Editorial Policy Committee commends to you Abridged Edition 13 of the Dewey Decimal Classification. Each edition marks the progress of the Classification at a particular point in time and is a distillation of the best thinking and analysis to date. The Decimal Classification Editorial Policy Committee has begun preparatory work on Edition 22 and Abridged Edition 14. In order for these next editions of the Classification to grow and develop, the suggestions and comments of its users are welcomed by the committee. Communications may be addressed to the chair of the committee, to the editor of the Classification, or via e-mail <dewey@loc.gov>.

David Balatti
Chair, 1996-
Decimal Classification Editorial
Policy Committee

10 March 1997

Acknowledgments

Abridged Edition 13 is a true abridgment of Edition 21. We received invaluable advice on topics for inclusion from the Abridged Edition 13 review committees of the (British) Library Association Dewey Decimal Classification Committee and the Subject Analysis Committee of the American Library Association. I extend my gratitude and thanks to the hard-working members of those committees.

Since the contents of Abridged Edition 13 depend on those of Edition 21, I will repeat my acknowledgments to the primary developers of the full edition. I joined the active work on Edition 21 halfway in its development cycle. The three assistant editors of the Classification, Julianne Beall, Winton E. Matthews, Jr., and Gregory R. New, did the bulk of revision of the schedules and tables. I greatly admire their scholarly work, dedication, and commitment. Some highlights of their contributions follow. Ms. Beall developed the revision and expansion of 297 Islam, prepared numerous expansions for peoples and languages, and updated 004–006 Computer science. Mr. Matthews revised the area numbers for countries of the former Soviet Union, and worked with several national libraries to develop other expansions in Table 2. Mr. New led development efforts on the three major revisions in Edition 21: 350–354 Public administration, 370 Education, and 560–590 Life sciences. Ross Trotter, British Library, joined the editorial team as a guest editor for the revision of 560–590 Life sciences. Mr. Trotter worked closely with Mr. New to shape the final version of this major revision. We are fortunate to have such a knowledgeable and dedicated colleague at the British Library.

Abridged Edition 13 has stayed on course through the support and encouragement of Peter J. Paulson, executive director of OCLC Forest Press. I am also grateful to the Forest Press staff: Elizabeth Hansen, Judith Kramer-Greene, and Judith Pisarski.

The advice and critical review offered by the members of the Decimal Classification Editorial Policy Committee have enabled us to respond to the needs of our users throughout the world and to move the Classification forward with knowledge. I value their wise counsel.

David A. Smith, chief of the Library of Congress Decimal Classification Division, is a constant source of guidance and colleagueship. He and the Decimal Classification Division staff have continuously supported the editorial efforts by offering an expert view of emerging topics and areas requiring revision. In addition to the three assistant editors, present and past staff members who have contributed to the development of Abridged Edition 13 include: Darlene Banks, Victoria Behrens, Frances A. Bold, Michael B. Cantlon, Carletta Cartledge, Rosalee Connor, Eve M. Dickey, Adrian Gore, Keith Harrison, William S. Hwang, Jeannette Jackson, Sterlin S. Johnson, Shirley D. Jones, Sarah Keller, Walter McClughan, Nobuko Ohashi, Letitia J. Reigle, Virginia A. Schoepf, Emily Spears, Cosmo Tassone, Dorothy A. Watson, and Susanne Welsh.

I will close by acknowledging the legacy of my predecessors, John P. Comaromi and Benjamin A. Custer. Dr. Comaromi's commitment to making the Dewey Decimal Classification easier to use and Mr. Custer's vision of the DDC as an international knowledge-organization tool are reflected in the pages of this edition.

Joan S. Mitchell
Editor
Dewey Decimal Classification
OCLC Forest Press

4 March 1997

New Features in Abridged Edition 13

Overview

The Dewey Decimal Classification system is continuously revised to keep pace with knowledge. This means accommodating new topics, as well as revising existing schedules to reflect new views of the field or to reduce bias. Abridged Edition 13 includes major revisions in public administration and the life sciences, significant changes in education and religion, and expansions for numerous popular topics and for several countries.

Some of the special features of Abridged Edition 13 are highlighted below.

User Convenience

The aim of Abridged Edition 12 was user convenience. How is user convenience furthered in Abridged Edition 13? Abridged Edition 13 includes more information located strategically to guide the classifier in decision making.

Numerous captions have been rewritten to eliminate vague headings or headings composed solely of adjectival or prepositional phrases. The note structure in the schedules has been simplified by replacing "example" and "contains" notes with an existing note type, the "including" note. Many notes have been added to provide guidance on which concepts in a multiple term heading may have standard subdivisions applied to them.

The Relative Index has more entries than the index to Abridged Edition 12, including entries for selected built numbers, terms to provide entry vocabulary for international users, and index terms for Manual notes. More interdisciplinary numbers are identified in the schedules and Relative Index.

Abridged Edition 13 has an expanded Manual. Each Manual note is located at the preferred or "if-in-doubt" number. Several notes contain lists of examples or sample titles.

Terminology

Terminology for persons in the schedules and tables has been updated to reflect currency, sensitivity, and international usage. Terminology for persons with disabilities has been changed to reflect a "person first, disability second" viewpoint. For example, the phrase "persons with disabilities " replaces "handicapped persons."

International Needs and Cooperative Development

Since the Dewey Decimal Classification is used by diverse libraries throughout the world, Abridged Edition 13 includes several changes to address international or special needs. Special attention has been given to reduction of U.S. bias and Christian bias in the Classification. For example, the U.S. bias in structure and wording of the new public administration development has been greatly reduced. In religion, the standard subdivisions of Christianity in 201–209 have been relocated to 230–270 as part of a multi-edition plan to reduce Christian bias. The schedule for 297 Islam has been expanded.

Selected List of Changes in Edition 21

Listed below are summaries of the major revisions in Edition 21 and selected other revisions in the tables and schedules. An accompanying booklet contains lists of relocations, reductions, and reused numbers; and comparative and equivalence tables for the major revisions in public administration and the life sciences

MAJOR REVISIONS IN ABRIDGED EDITION 13

297	Islam, Babism, Bahai Faith Expanded
350–354	Public administration Completely revised. Public administration still occupies 351–354, but the subdivisions are entirely different. The preference order has been changed from jurisdiction/topic to topic/jurisdiction, and U.S. bias in wording and structure has been reduced
370	Education Education of women relocated from 376 to 371.822, religious schools relocated from 377 to 371.07, elementary reading expanded in 372.4, and elementary language arts expanded in 372.6. Other changes include the relocation of home schools from 649 to 371.04; relocation of educational sociology from 370.19 to 306.43; adoption of regular notation from Table 1 under 370.7 Education, research, related topics; and updating and internationalization of terminology
560–590	Life sciences 570 (Biology in general) completely revised; 581 and 590 extensively revised. Features of the revision include reversal of preference order from organism/process to process/organisms for internal biological processes in 571–575; collocation of microorganisms, fungi, algae in 579; and more specific numbers for fishes and mammals. The Abridged Edition 12 number for biology (574) was left vacant in the revision to aid library implementation of the new schedule, since samples of library holdings in WorldCat (the OCLC Online Union Catalog) indicated that 70% of the holdings among Dewey libraries on general biology were in 574

Selected Revisions in the Tables

TABLE 1. STANDARD SUBDIVISIONS

—01	Philosophy and theory Communication and terminology added to the meaning of the number
—02	Miscellany The subject for persons in specific occupations added to the meaning of the number

—07   Education, research, related topics
         Research added to the meaning of the number

—071   Education
         Broadened from "Schools and courses" to include education and teaching

—0835   Young people twelve to twenty
         Heading changed, and comprehensive works on young adults relocated to —084

—084   Persons in specific stages of adulthood
         Comprehensive works on young adults relocated from —0835

—086   Persons by miscellaneous social characteristics
         New number

—087   Persons with disabilities and illnesses, gifted persons
         Broadened from "Handicapped and ill persons" to include gifted persons

—088   Occupational and religious groups
         New number

TABLE 2. GEOGRAPHIC AREAS, AND PERSONS

—47   Eastern Europe   Russia
         Expanded

—495   Greece
         Aegean Islands, Crete relocated from —499 (*DC&* 5:3)

—499   Bulgaria
         Relocated from —4977. This number was previously used for the Aegean Islands (relocated to —495 in *DC&* 5:3)

—5693   Cyprus
         Relocated from —5645 (*DC&* 5:3)

Selected Revisions in the Schedules

001.94   Mysteries
         New development, with subdivisions for UFOs and monsters

004.67   Wide area networks
         New number that includes the Internet

006.7   Multimedia systems
         New number; relocated from 006.6

200.1–.9	Standard subdivisions of religion The standard subdivisions of comparative religion relocated from 291.01–291.09, with the exception of philosophy and theory, which have been relocated from 291.01 to 210
[201–209]	Standard subdivisions of Christianity Vacated as part of the move to reduce Christian bias. Standard subdivisions of Christianity have been relocated to appropriate subdivisions of 230–270
210	Philosophy and theory of religion Heading formerly "Natural religion." Philosophy and theory of religion relocated from 200.1; philosophy and theory of comparative religion relocated from 291.01
230	Christianity Christian theology Comprehensive works on Christianity relocated from 200. The development for Christianity is now in one continuous span, 230–280 (with the Bible remaining in 220)
230.071	Education in Christianity, in Christian theology Education in Christianity (formerly 207) has been combined with education in Christian theology
263	Days, times, places of religious observance Pilgrimages relocated from 248.4
280	Denominations and sects of Christian church Ecumenical movement relocated from 270.8
305.23	Young people Expanded
306.43	[Sociology of] Education Relocated from 370.19
320.5	Political ideologies Expanded
331.892	Strikes New number
341.242	European Union New number
342–349	Branches of law; laws (statutes), regulations, cases; law of specific jurisdictions, areas, socioeconomic regions Heading expanded to reflect content of subdivisions

344.01	Labor [law]
	New number
362.28	Suicide
362.292	Alcohol [abuse]
362.76	Abused and neglected children
362.883	Rape [victims]
363.25	Detection of crime (Criminal investigation)
363.34	Disasters
363.738	Pollutants
363.739	Pollution of specific environments
	New numbers for social problems and services
364.15	Offenses against persons
364.16	Offenses against property
	New numbers for kinds of crimes
364.36	Juvenile delinquents
	New number
368.3	Old age insurance and insurance against death, illness, injury
	Expanded to provide numbers for life and health insurance
391	Costume and personal appearance
	Expanded
392	Customs of life cycle and domestic life
	Expanded
394.25	Carnivals
	New number
394.26	Holidays
	New number, with subdivisions for specific holidays
395	Etiquette (Manners)
	Expanded
398.2093–	Treatment [of folk literature] by specific continents, countries, localities
.2099	Tales and lore from specific areas relocated from 398.21–.27 (*DC&* 5:5)
439	Other Germanic (Teutonic) languages
	Yiddish relocated from 437
508.2	Seasons
	New number
523.4	Planets
	Expanded to provide specific numbers for most planets

530.1	Theories and mathematical physics Expanded to provide numbers for relativity theory and quantum mechanics
551.2	Volcanoes, earthquakes, thermal waters and gases Expanded to provide numbers for volcanoes and earthquakes
551.56	Atmospheric electricity and optics New number
551.63 551.64	Weather forecasting and forecasts, reporting and reports Forecasting and forecasts of specific phenomena New numbers
613.2	Dietetics Applied nutrition relocated from 641.1
616.7	Diseases of musculoskeletal system Nonsurgical aspects of and comprehensive works on orthopedics relocated from 617.3
617.4	Surgery by systems Orthopedic surgery of the musculoskeletal system relocated from 617.3
636	Animal husbandry Interdisciplinary works on species of domestic mammals relocated from 599
636.5	Poultry Chickens Interdisciplinary works on species of domestic birds relocated from 598
636.7	Dogs Expanded to provide for specific breeds
636.9	Other mammals New number divided like 599. Animals raised for fur (fur farming) relocated from 636.088 to 636.97
639.34 639.8 639.97	Fish culture in aquariums Aquaculture [Conservation of] Specific kinds of mammals New numbers
660.6	Biotechnology New number
726.5 726.6	Church buildings Cathedrals New numbers

739.3	Clocks and watches New number
745.5928	[Handcrafted] Models and miniatures New number
746.1–.9	[Textile] Products and processes Preference order changed so that process is usually preferred (*DC&* 5:5)
781.646	Reggae New number
782.421649	Rap New number
793.735	Riddles New number
796.04	General kinds of sports and games New number. Intramural sports relocated from 371.8 (*DC&* 5:5)
796.15	Play with remote-control models, kites, similar devices New number
796.21	Roller skating
796.22	Skateboarding (*DC&* 5:4)
796.81	Unarmed combat
796.83	Boxing
796.86	Fencing
796.964	Curling (*DC&* 5:5) New numbers for sports
799.2	Hunting Comprehensive works on commercial and sports hunting relocated from 639
919.904	Travel on extraterrestrial worlds Projected accounts of manned space flight relocated from 629.45
940–990	General history of modern world, of extraterrestrial worlds History of individual countries updated to include new historical periods and to reflect changes in Table 2, e.g., Czech Republic and Slovakia 943.7, Ukraine 947.7

Introduction
to the
Dewey Decimal Classification

About the Introduction

1.1   This Introduction explains the basic principles and structure of the Dewey Decimal Classification.

1.2   The Introduction is meant to be used in conjunction with the Glossary and the Manual. The Glossary defines terms used in the Introduction and elsewhere in the Classification. The Manual contains additional and more detailed information about specific areas of the Classification, offers advice on classifying in difficult areas, and explains how to choose between related numbers.

Classification: What It Is and What It Does

2.1   *Classification* provides a system for organizing knowledge. Classification may be used to organize knowledge represented in any form, e.g., books, documents, electronic records.

2.2   *Notation* is the system of symbols used to represent the classes in a classification system. In the Dewey Decimal Classification system (DDC), the notation is expressed in Arabic numerals. The notation gives at once both the unique meaning of the class and its relation to other classes. No matter how words describing subjects may differ, the notation provides a universal language to identify the class within which the subject belongs and related classes.

2.3   Libraries usually arrange their collections according to the systematic structure of a library classification. Each item is assigned a *call number (shelf mark)*. The call number consists of the Dewey notation for its class, accompanied by a book number or some other device to subarrange the items of a class. The call number provides a unique identifying code that is used as an "address" on the shelf, and as a tag for library recordkeeping in circulation and inventory control.

History and Current Use of the Dewey Decimal Classification

3.1   The DDC was conceived by Melvil Dewey in 1873 and first published in 1876. The Dewey Decimal Classification is the most widely used library classification system in the world. It is used in more than 135 countries, and has been translated into over 30 languages. In the United States, 95% of all public and school libraries, 25% of all college and university libraries, and 20% of special libraries use the DDC.

3.2   The DDC is developed, maintained, and applied in the Decimal Classification Division of the Library of Congress (LC), where annually over 110,000 DDC numbers are assigned to works cataloged by the Library. DDC numbers are incorporated into machine-readable cataloging (MARC) bibliographic records, and distributed to libraries by way of computer media, Cataloging-in-Publication (CIP) data, and LC cards. DDC numbers appear in MARC records issued by countries throughout the world and are used in the national bibliographies of Australia, Botswana, Brazil, Canada, Iceland, India, Indonesia, Italy, Namibia, New Zealand, Norway, Pakistan, Papua New Guinea, the Philippines, South Africa, Turkey, the United Kingdom, Venezuela, Zimbabwe, and other countries. Various bibliographic utilities and services in the United States and elsewhere make DDC numbers available to libraries through online access, publications, and production of catalog cards.

3.3   The Dewey Decimal Classification is published in two editions, full and abridged. The abridged edition is intended for libraries with collections of 20,000 volumes or less. The Classification is kept up-to-date between editions through additions and corrections published in *Dewey Decimal Classification, Additions, Notes and Decisions (DC&)*.

The full edition is also published in an enhanced electronic version, *Dewey for Windows*. Each update disc of *Dewey for Windows* incorporates the changes announced in *DC&*.

Overview of the Dewey Decimal Classification

CONCEPTUAL FRAMEWORK

4.1   In the DDC, basic classes are organized by disciplines or fields of study. No principle is more basic to the DDC than this: the parts of the Classification are arranged by *discipline*, not by *subject*.

4.2   The consequence of this principle is that there is likely to be no single place for a given subject. A subject may appear in any discipline. For example, "clothing" has aspects that fall under several disciplines. Customs associated with clothing belong in 391 as part of the discipline of customs; clothing in the sense of fashion design belongs in 746.9 as part of the discipline of the arts. The Relative Index assembles the disciplinary aspects of the subject of clothing in one place:

Clothing	391
armed forces	355.8
costume	355.1
arts	746.9
commercial manufacturing	687
fur	685
leather	685
customs	391
home economics	646
home sewing	646.4
see Manual at 391 vs. 646, 746.9	

NOTATION

4.3 At the broadest level, the DDC is divided into ten *main classes*, which together cover the entire world of knowledge. Each main class is further divided into ten *divisions,* and each division into ten *sections* (not all the numbers for the divisions and sections have been used).

4.4 The ten main classes are:

000	Generalities
100	Philosophy, paranormal phenomena, psychology
200	Religion
300	Social sciences
400	Language
500	Natural sciences and mathematics
600	Technology (Applied sciences)
700	The arts Fine and decorative arts
800	Literature (Belles-lettres) and rhetoric
900	Geography, history, and auxiliary disciplines

4.5 Main class 000 is the most general class, and is used for works not limited to any one specific discipline, e.g., encyclopedias, newspapers, general periodicals. This class is also used for certain specialized disciplines that deal with knowledge and information, e.g., computer science, library and information science, journalism. Main classes 100–900 consist of major disciplines or groups of related disciplines.

4.6 The first digit in the numbers listed above indicates the main class. Zeros are used to fill out the notation to the minimum required length of three digits.

4.7 Each main class consists of ten divisions, also numbered 0 through 9. The second digit indicates the division. For example, 500 is used for general works on the sciences, 510 for mathematics, 520 for astronomy, 530 for physics.

4.8 Each division has ten sections, again numbered 0 through 9. The third digit in each three-digit number indicates the section. Thus, 530 is used for general works on physics, 531 for classical mechanics, 532 for fluid mechanics, 533 for gas mechanics.

4.9 A *decimal point* follows the third digit, after which division by ten continues to the specific degree of classification needed.

PRINCIPLE OF HIERARCHY

4.10 *Hierarchy* in the DDC is expressed through structure and notation.

4.11 *Structural hierarchy* means that all topics (aside from the ten main classes) are subordinate to and part of the broader topics above them. The corollary is also true: whatever is true of the whole is true of the parts. This important concept is sometimes called *hierarchical force*. Any note regarding the nature of a class holds true for all its subordinate classes, including logically subordinate topics classed at coordinate numbers. (For a discussion of notes with hierarchical force, see paragraphs 7.7–7.14 and 7.17–7.19.)

Because of the principle of hierarchical force, hierarchical notes are usually given only once—at the highest level of application. For example, the scope note at 700 applies to 730, to 737, and to 737.4. The words "Description, critical appraisal . . ." found in the scope note at 700 also govern the critical appraisal of coins in 737.4 Coins. In order to understand the structural hierarchy, the classifier must read up and down the schedules (and remember to turn the page).

4.12   *Notational hierarchy* is expressed by length of notation. As the following example shows, numbers at any given level are usually *subordinate* to a class whose notation is one digit shorter; *coordinate* with a class whose notation has the same number of significant digits; and *superordinate* to a class with numbers one or more digits longer. The underlined digits in the example below demonstrate this notational hierarchy:

<u>6</u>00	Technology (Applied sciences)
<u>63</u>0	Agriculture and related technologies
<u>636</u>	Animal husbandry
<u>636.7</u>	Dogs
<u>636.8</u>	Cats

4.13   "Dogs" and "Cats" are more specific than (i.e., are subordinate to) "Animal husbandry"; they are equally specific as (i.e., are coordinate with) each other; and "Animal husbandry" is less specific than (i.e., is superordinate to) "Dogs" and "Cats."

4.14   Sometimes, other devices must be used to express the hierarchy when it is not possible or desirable to do so through the notation. Relationships among topics that violate notational hierarchy are indicated by special headings, notes, and entries. A dual heading is used when a subordinate topic is the major part of the subject; the subject as a whole and the subordinate topic as a whole share the same number (e.g., 610 Medical sciences   Medicine). A see reference leads the classifier to subdivisions of a subject located outside the notational hierarchy. A centered entry (so called because its numbers, heading, and notes appear in the center of the page) constitutes a major departure from notational hierarchy. A centered entry is used to indicate and relate structurally a span of numbers that together form a single concept for which there is no specific hierarchical notation available. In the DDC, centered entries are always flagged typographically by the symbol > in the number column.

Classifying with the DDC

5.1   Classifying a work with the DDC requires determination of the subject, the disciplinary focus, and, if applicable, the approach or form. (For advice on determining the subject and discipline of a work, see paragraphs 5.2–5.9; for a discussion of approach or form, see paragraph 8.3.)

Please note that works of the imagination are generally classified by literary form rather than by subject in the DDC.

DETERMINING THE SUBJECT OF A WORK

5.2   Classifying a work properly depends first upon determining the subject of the work in hand.

   (A)   The title is often a clue to the subject, but should never be the sole source of analysis. For example, *The Greening of America* is a book about social conditions and social change, not a work on ecology.

   (B)   The table of contents may list the main topics discussed. Chapter headings may substitute for the absence of a table of contents. Chapter subheadings often prove useful.

   (C)   The preface or introduction usually states the author's purpose. If a foreword is provided, it often indicates the subject of the work and suggests the place of the work in the development of thought on the subject. The book jacket or accompanying material may include a summary of the subject content.

   (D)   A scan of the text itself may provide further guidance or confirm preliminary subject analysis.

   (E)   Bibliographical references and index entries are sources of subject information.

   (F)   Cataloging copy from centralized cataloging services is often helpful by providing subject headings, classification numbers, and notes. Such copy appears on the verso of the title page of many U.S., Australian, British, and Canadian books as part of Cataloging-in-Publication (CIP) data. Data from these sources should be verified with the book in hand, since cataloging-in-publication is based on prepublication information.

   (G)   Occasionally, consultation of outside sources such as reviews, reference works, and subject experts may be required to determine the subject of the work.

DETERMINING THE DISCIPLINE OF A WORK

5.3   After determining the subject, the classifier must then select the proper discipline, or field of study, of the work.

5.4   The guiding principle of the DDC is that a work is classed in the discipline for which it is intended, rather than the discipline from which the work derives. This enables works that are used together to be found together. For example, a general work by a zoologist on agricultural pest control should be classed in agriculture, not zoology, along with other works on agricultural pest control.

5.5   Once the subject has been determined, and information on the discipline has been found, the experienced classifier will turn to the schedules. The summaries are a good means of mental navigation for beginners. The headings and notes in the schedules themselves and the Manual provide much guidance. The Relative Index may help by suggesting the disciplines in which a subject is normally treated. (For a discussion of the summaries, see paragraph 7.1; for a discussion of the Manual, see paragraphs 10.1–10.5; for a discussion of the Relative Index, see paragraphs 11.1–11.15.)

5.6   If the Relative Index is used, the classifier must still rely on the structure of the Classification and various aids throughout to arrive at the proper place to classify a work. Even the most promising Relative Index citations must be verified in the schedules; the schedules are the only place where all the information about coverage and use of the numbers may be found.

MORE THAN ONE SUBJECT IN THE SAME DISCIPLINE

5.7   A work may include multiple aspects of one subject, or more than one subject, from the viewpoint of a single discipline. Use the following guidelines in determining the best placement for the work:

(A)   Class a work dealing with interrelated subjects with the subject that is being acted upon. This is called the *rule of application*, and takes precedence over any other rule. For instance, class an analytical work dealing with Shakespeare's influence on Keats with Keats.

(B)   Class a work on two subjects with the subject receiving fuller treatment.

(C)   If two subjects receive equal treatment, and are not used to introduce or explain one another, class the work with the subject whose number comes first in the DDC schedules. This is called the *first-of-two rule*. For example, a history dealing equally with the United States and Japan, in which the United States is discussed first and is given first in the title, is classed with the history of Japan because 952 Japan precedes 973 United States.

Often, specific instructions are given to use numbers that do not come first in the schedules. These instructions may be in the form of a note or table on preference order, an add note with instructions on citation order in number building, or a note identifying the comprehensive number for the subject. For example, at 598, the note "class comprehensive works on warm-blooded vertebrates in 599" tells the classifier to ignore the first-of-two rule and class a work on birds (598) and mammals (599) in 599, which is the comprehensive number for warm-blooded vertebrates.

Also disregard the first-of-two rule when the two topics are the two major subdivisions of a subject. For example, water supply (628.1) and waste technology (628.4) taken together constitute most of 628 Sanitary and municipal engineering; works covering both of these topics are classed in 628 (not 628.1).

(For a discussion of number building, including the addition of standard subdivisions, see paragraphs 8.1–8.15; for a discussion of citation and preference order, see paragraphs 9.1–9.5; for a discussion of comprehensive numbers, see paragraphs 7.14 and 7.17–7.18.)

(D)   Class a work on three or more subjects that are all subdivisions of a broader subject in the first higher number that includes them all (unless one subject is treated more fully than the others). This is called the *rule of three*. For example, a history of Portugal (946.9), Sweden (948.5), and Greece (949.5) is classed with the history of Europe (940).

(E) Subdivisions beginning with zero should be avoided if there is a choice between 0 and 1–9 at the same point in the hierarchy of the notation. Similarly, subdivisions beginning with 00 should be avoided when there is a choice between 00 and 0. This is called the *rule of zero*.

MORE THAN ONE DISCIPLINE

5.8   Treating a subject from the point of view of more than one discipline is different from treating several subjects in one discipline. Use the following guidelines in determining the best placement for the work:

(A) Use the *interdisciplinary number* provided in the schedules or Relative Index if one is given. An important consideration in using such an interdisciplinary number is that the work must contain significant material on the discipline in which the interdisciplinary number is found. For example, 305.231 (a sociology number) is provided for interdisciplinary works on child development. However, if a work that is interdisciplinary with respect to child development gives little emphasis to social development and a great deal of emphasis to the psychological and physical development of the child (155.4 and 612.6, respectively), class it in 155.4 (the first number in the schedules of the next two obvious choices). In short, interdisciplinary numbers are not absolute; they are to be used only when applicable. (For a discussion of interdisciplinary numbers, see paragraphs 7.14, 7.17–7.18, and 11.8–11.9.)

(B) Class works not given an interdisciplinary number in the discipline given the fullest treatment in the work. For example, a work dealing with both the scientific and the engineering principles of electrodynamics is classed in 537.6 if the engineering aspects are introduced primarily for illustrative purposes, but in 621.31 if the basic scientific theories are only preliminary to the author's exposition of engineering principles and practices.

(C) When classifying interdisciplinary works, do not overlook the possibilities of main class 000 Generalities, e.g., 080 for a collection of interviews of famous people from various disciplines.

Any other situation is treated in the same fashion as those found in the instructions at More Than One Subject in the Same Discipline (paragraph 5.7).

TABLE OF LAST RESORT

5.9   When several numbers have been found for the work in hand, and each seems as good as the next, the following table of last resort (in order of preference) may be used as a guideline in the absence of any other rule:

Table of last resort

(1)   Kinds of things

(2)   Parts of things

(3)   Materials from which things, kinds, or parts are made

(4)   Properties of things, kinds, parts, or materials

(5)   Processes within things, kinds, parts, or materials

(6)   Operations upon things, kinds, parts, or materials

(7)   Instrumentalities for performing such operations

Do not apply this table or any other guideline if it appears to disregard the author's intention and emphasis.

How Abridged Edition 13 Is Arranged

6.1   Abridged Edition 13 is composed of eight major parts:

(A)   New Features in Abridged Edition 13: A brief explanation of the special features and changes in Abridged 13

(B)   Introduction: A description of the DDC and how to use it

(C)   Glossary: Short definitions of terms used in the DDC

(D)   Index to the Introduction and Glossary

(E)   Tables: Four numbered tables of notation that can be added to class numbers to provide greater specificity

(F)   Schedules: The organization of knowledge from 000–999

(G)   Relative Index: An alphabetical list of subjects with the disciplines in which they are treated subarranged alphabetically under each entry

(H)   Manual: A guide to classifying in difficult areas, information on new schedules, and an explanation of the policies and practices of the Decimal Classification Division at the Library of Congress. Information in the Manual is arranged by the numbers in the tables and schedules

Key Features of the Schedules and Tables

SUMMARIES

7.1   *Summaries* provide an overview of the structure of classes. Two types of summaries appear in the DDC:

(A)   The summaries of the schedules as a whole are found at the front of the schedules.

(B) Single-level summaries in the schedules and tables provide an overview of classes that have subdivisions covering more than three pages. For example, 380 Commerce, communications, transportation has the following summary:

SUMMARY

380.01–.09	**Standard subdivisions**
.1	**Commerce (Trade)**
381	**Internal commerce (Domestic trade)**
382	**International commerce (Foreign trade)**
383	**Postal communication**
384	**Communications Telecommunication**
385	**Railroad transportation**
386	**Inland waterway and ferry transportation**
387	**Water, air, space transportation**
388	**Transportation Ground transportation**
389	**Metrology and standardization**

ENTRIES

7.2 Entries in the schedules and tables are composed of a DDC number in the number column (the column at the left margin), a heading describing the class that the number represents, and often one or more notes. DDC numbers are printed in groups of three digits for ease of reading and copying. All entries (numbers, headings, and notes) should be read in the context of the hierarchy. (For a discussion of the principle of hierarchy, see paragraphs 4.10–4.14.)

7.3 The first three digits of schedule numbers (main classes, divisions, sections) appear only once in the number column, when first used. They are repeated at the top of each page where their subdivisions continue. Subordinate numbers appear in the number column, beginning with a decimal point, with the initial three digits understood.

7.4 Table numbers are given in full in the number column of the tables, and are never used alone. There are four numbered tables in Abridged Edition 13:

T1	Standard Subdivisions
T2	Geographic Areas, and Persons
T3	Subdivisions for Individual Literatures, for Specific Literary Forms
T4	Subdivisions of Individual Languages

Except for notation from Table 1 (which may be added to any number unless there is an instruction in the schedules or tables to the contrary), table notation may be added only as instructed in the schedules and tables. (For a detailed discussion of the use of the four tables, see paragraphs 8.3–8.10.)

7.5 When a subordinate topic is a major part of a number, it is sometimes given as a part of a dual heading. For example:

—72	Middle America	Mexico
610	Medical sciences	Medicine

7.6   Some numbers in the schedules and tables are enclosed in parentheses or square brackets. Numbers and notes in parentheses provide options to standard practice. Numbers in square brackets represent topics that have been relocated or discontinued, or are unassigned. Square brackets are also used for standard subdivision concepts that are represented in another location. Bracketed numbers should never be used. (For a discussion of options, see paragraphs 12.1–12.6; for a discussion of bracketed standard subdivisions, see paragraph 7.23.)

NOTES

7.7   Notes are important because they supply information that is not obvious in the notational hierarchy or in the heading with regard to order, structure, subordination, and other matters. The notes described below (A) define what is found in the class and its subdivisions; (B) identify topics in *standing room*, i.e., topics with insufficient literature to have their own number; (C) describe what is found in other classes; and (D) explain changes in the schedules and tables. Other notes are described in the sections on number building (paragraphs 8.1–8.15), citation and preference order (paragraphs 9.1–9.5), the Manual (paragraphs 10.1–10.5), and options (paragraphs 12.1–12.4).

7.8   Notes in categories (A) and (C) have hierarchical force (i.e., are applicable to all the subdivisions of a particular number). Those in category (B) do not have hierarchical force.

(A)   Notes That Describe What Is Found in a Class

7.9   *Definition notes* indicate the meaning of the class. For example:

004.7   Peripherals

Input, output, storage devices that work with a computer but are not part of its central processing unit or internal storage

7.10   *Scope notes* indicate whether the meaning of the number is narrower or broader than is apparent from the heading. For example:

700   The arts   Fine and decorative arts

Description, critical appraisal, techniques, procedures, apparatus, equipment, materials of the fine, decorative, literary, performing, recreational arts

7.11   *Former-heading notes* are given only when a heading has been altered to such a degree that the new heading bears little or no resemblance to the old. There is usually no change in the meaning of the number. For example:

153.4   Thought, thinking, reasoning, intuition, value, judgment

Former heading: Knowledge (Cognition)

7.12   *Variant-name notes* are used for synonyms or near synonyms. For example:

> 531   Classical mechanics   Solid mechanics
>
>> Variant names for classical mechanics: mechanics, continuum mechanics

7.13   *Class-here notes* list major topics in a class. These topics may be broader or narrower than the heading, overlap it, or define another way of looking at essentially the same material. Topics in class-here notes are considered to *approximate the whole* of the class. For example:

> 371.04   Alternative schools
>
>> Class here experimental schools, free schools

Standard subdivisions may be added for any topic in a class-here note. (For a detailed discussion of the use of standard subdivisions for concepts that approximate the whole of a class, see paragraphs 8.3–8.5 and the beginning of Table 1.)

7.14   Class-here notes are also used to indicate where interdisciplinary and comprehensive works are classed. In the DDC, *interdisciplinary works* treat a subject from the perspective of more than one discipline. For example:

> 391   Costume and personal appearance
>
>> Class here interdisciplinary works on costume, clothing, fashion

Comprehensive works treat a subject from various points of view within a single discipline. For example:

> 612   Human physiology
>
>> Class here comprehensive works on human anatomy and physiology

(B) Including Notes (Notes That Identify Topics in Standing Room)

7.15   *Including notes* identify topics that have "standing room" in the number where the note is found. Standing room numbers provide a location for topics with relatively few works written about them, but whose literature may grow in the future, at which time they may be assigned their own number. For example:

> 371.102   Teaching
>
>> Including classroom management, classroom discipline

Standard subdivisions cannot be added for topics in standing room, nor are other number-building techniques allowed.

7.16   Including notes are also used for the kinds of information previously found in contains, examples, and common name notes.

(C) Notes on What Is Found in Other Classes

7.17   *Class-elsewhere notes* lead the classifier to interrelated topics, or distinguish among numbers in the same notational hierarchy. They are used to show preference order, to lead to the comprehensive or interdisciplinary number, to override the first-of-two rule, or to lead to broader or narrower topics in the same hierarchical array that might otherwise be overlooked. They may point to a specific number, or to a concept scattered throughout the schedules. All notes that begin with the word "class" are class-elsewhere notes, except when they begin with "class here."

> 370.15   Educational psychology
>
>> Class behavior modification methods of instruction in 371.39; class interdisciplinary works on psychology in 150. Class psychology of a specific topic in education with the topic, plus notation 01 from Table 1, e.g., psychology of adult education 374.001

7.18   *See references* lead from a stated or implied comprehensive number for a concept to the component (subordinate) parts of that concept. See references also lead from the interdisciplinary number for a concept to treatment of the concept in other disciplines. A see reference may point to a specific number, or to a concept scattered throughout the schedules. Each see reference begins with the word "For" and appears in italics. For example:

> 577.7   Marine ecology
>
>> Class here saltwater ecology
>
>> *For salt lake ecology, see 577.63; for saltwater wetland and seashore ecology, see 577.69*

> 305.4   Women
>
>> Class here interdisciplinary works on women, on females
>
>> *For a specific aspect of women not provided for here, see the aspect, e.g., women's suffrage 324.6, education of women 371.822*

7.19   *See-also references* lead the classifier to related topics. They are reminders that minor differences in wording and context can imply differences in classification. Each see-also reference appears in italics. For example:

> 599.65   Deer
>
>> *See also 599.63 for mouse deer*

(D) Notes Explaining Changes or Irregularities in the Schedules and Tables

7.20   *Revision notes* warn users that there have been changes in the subdivisions of a class since the previous edition. A *complete* or *extensive revision* is always introduced by a revision note that appears first under the heading of the class affected. (For an example of a complete revision note, see 570 Life sciences   Biology.)

7.21   *Discontinued notes* indicate that all or part of the contents of a number have been moved to a more general number in the same hierarchy, or have been dropped entirely. For example:

> [289.4]   Church of the New Jerusalem (Swedenborgianism)
>
> > Number discontinued; class in 289
>
> 581   Specific topics in natural history of plants
>
> > Use of this number for comprehensive works on botany, on plants discontinued; class in 580

7.22   *Relocation notes* state that all or part of the contents of a number have been moved to a different number. For example:

> [370.19]   Sociology of education
>
> > Sociology of education relocated to 306.43 . . .
>
> 307.2   Movement of people to, from, within communities
>
> > Population size and composition relocated to 304.6

The former number is usually given at the new number, either in the heading or in the appropriate note. For example:

> 306.43   Education [*formerly* 370.19]
>
> 304.6   Population
>
> > Class here population size and composition [*both formerly also* 307.2] . . .

7.23   *Do-not-use notes* instruct the classifier not to use all or part of the regular standard subdivision notation or an add table provision in favor of a special provision, or standard subdivisions at a broader number. When the whole standard subdivision should not be used, the note appears under a bracketed standard subdivision; when only part of the standard subdivision is *displaced*, the part displaced is specified. For example:

> [374.009]   Historical, geographic, persons treatment
>
> > Do not use; class in 374
>
> 351.09   Historical and persons treatment
>
> > Do not use for treatment by areas, regions, places in general; class in 351.1. Do not use for treatment by specific continents, countries, localities; class in 351.3–351.9

Number Building

8.1   The classifier will often find that to arrive at a precise number for a work it is necessary to build or synthesize a number that is not specifically printed in the schedules. Such *built numbers* allow for greater depth of content analysis. They are used only when instructions in the schedules make them possible (except for standard subdivisions, which are discussed in paragraphs 8.3–8.5). Number building begins with a base number (always stated in the instruction note) to which another number is added.

8.2　　There are four sources of notation from which to build numbers: (A) Table 1 Standard Subdivisions; (B) Tables 2–4; (C) other parts of the schedules; and (D) add tables in the schedules.

(A) Adding Standard Subdivisions from Table 1

8.3　　Notation from Table 1 Standard Subdivisions may be added to any number in the schedules unless there is a specific instruction to the contrary. A *standard subdivision* represents a recurring physical form (such as a dictionary, periodical, or index) or approach (such as history or research) and thus is applicable to any subject or discipline. Here are a few examples with the standard subdivision concept underlined:

150.5	Periodical on psychology
230.003	Dictionary of Christianity
340.025	Directory of lawyers
401	Philosophy of language
507.8	Use of apparatus and equipment in the study and teaching of science, e.g., science fair projects
624.0285	Computer applications in civil engineering
796.962092	Biography of an ice hockey player
808.0071	Teaching of rhetoric

The classifier should never use more than one zero in applying a standard subdivision unless instructed to do so. If more than one zero is needed, the number of zeros is always indicated in the schedules. When using standard subdivisions with numbers built by adding from Tables 2–4 or other parts of the schedules, be sure to check the table or schedule used for the segment preceding the standard subdivision for special instructions on the number of zeros.

8.4　　*Standard-subdivisions-are-added notes* indicate which topics in a multiterm heading may have standard subdivisions added for them because the designated topics are considered to *approximate the whole* of the subject. For example:

> 639.2　　Commercial fishing, whaling, sealing
>
> > Standard subdivisions are added for commercial fishing, whaling, sealing together; for commercial fishing alone

Standard-subdivisions-are-added notes do not have hierarchical force.

8.5　　*The most important caveat with respect to standard subdivisions is that they are added only for works that cover or approximate the whole of the subject of the number.* For example, the management of educational voucher programs for private education should be classed in 379.3, not 379.3068. Notation 068 from

Table 1 may not be added to 379.3 because educational vouchers are in an including note at 379.3; therefore, they do not approximate the whole of the subject of the number.

(B) Adding from Tables 2–4

8.6 The classifier may be instructed to add notation from Tables 2–4 to a base number from the schedules or to a number from a table. A summary of the use of each table follows. Further instructions on using Tables 2–4 are found at the beginning of each table. See also the Manual notes for Tables 2–4.

8.7 *Table 2 Geographic Areas, and Persons.* Notation from Table 2 is added through the use of standard subdivision —09 from Table 1, e.g., reading instruction in the primary schools of Australia is 372.40994 (372.4 reading instruction in primary schools + 09 Historical, geographic, persons treatment from Table 1 + 94 Australia from Table 2).

8.8 Area notation is sometimes added directly to schedule numbers, but only when specified in a note. For example:

373.3–373.9   Secondary education in specific continents, countries, localities

> Add to base number 373 notation 3–9 from Table 2, e.g., secondary schools of Australia 373.94

8.9 *Table 3 Subdivisions for Individual Literatures, for Specific Literary Forms.* These subdivisions are used in class 800 as instructed, following numbers for specific languages in 810–890.

8.10 *Table 4 Subdivisions of Individual Languages.* These subdivisions are used as instructed in class 400, following numbers for designated specific languages in 420–490.

(C) Adding from Other Parts of the Schedules

8.11 There are several instructions to make a direct addition to a number from another part of the schedules. For example:

016   Bibliographies and catalogs of works on specific subjects or in specific disciplines

> Add to base number 016 notation 001–999, e.g., bibliographies of philosophy 016.1, of novels 016.80883

8.12 In many cases, part of a number may be added to another number upon instruction. For example:

636.9   Other mammals

> Add to base number 636.9 the numbers following 599 in 599.2–599.8, e.g., fur-bearing animals (fur farming) 636.97 . . .

In this example, 7 comes from 599.7. Sometimes numbers are taken from more than one place in the schedules; in such cases the procedure for the second addition is the same as for the first.

(D) Adding from Tables Found in the Schedules

8.13   Add tables in the schedules provide numbers to be added to designated schedule numbers (identified by an asterisk and accompanying footnoted instruction); these tables must be used only as instructed. For example:

> 384.54   *Radiobroadcasting

The asterisk in the entry above leads to the following footnote: "Add as instructed under 380." The add table at 380 is used only for topics tagged with an asterisk or for topics in class-here notes under headings tagged with an asterisk.

8.14   *Subdivisions-are-added notes* indicate which terms in a multiterm heading may have subdivisions applied to them. For example:

> 672   Iron, steel, other iron alloys
>
> > Add to base number 672 the numbers following 671 in 671.2–671.8, e.g., welding 672.5.
> >
> > > Subdivisions are added for any or all topics in heading

8.15   *Number-built notes* identify and explain the source of built numbers included in the schedules and tables. Built numbers are occasionally included in the schedules or tables to provide additional information or to indicate exceptions to regular add instructions. For example:

> 919.904   Travel on extraterrestrial worlds
>
> > Number built according to instructions under 913–919
> >
> > Class here projected accounts [*formerly* 629.45]

Citation and Preference Order

9.1   Citation and preference order must be considered when multiple aspects or characteristics of a subject (such as age, area, gender, historical periods, national origin) are provided for in the Classification, and a single work treats more than one of them.

CITATION ORDER

9.2   Citation order allows the classifier to build or synthesize a number using two or more characteristics (*facets*) as specified in instruction notes. Success in building a DDC number requires determining which characteristics apply to a specific work, and then determining from the instructions in the schedule the sequence in which the facets will be ordered.

9.3   The notes at the beginning of Table 3 are an example of number-building instructions that specify the sequence in which characteristics of literature will be shown: first language, then literary form, then (if applicable) collections of history and criticism.

PREFERENCE ORDER

9.4 If there is no provision to show more than one of the aspects or characteristics, it is a matter of preference (because a choice must be made among several characteristics). Preference notes supply either an instruction or table establishing the order in which to make the choice. An example of a preference instruction is found at 302–307:

> 302–307 Specific topics in sociology and anthropology
>
>> Unless other instructions are given, class a subject with aspects in two or more subdivisions of 302–307 in the number coming last, e.g., social deterioration during civil wars 303.6 (*not* 303.45)

9.5 An example of a table indicating preference order is found at the beginning of Table 1.

The Manual

10.1 The Manual gives advice on classifying in difficult areas, provides in-depth information on major revisions, and explains the policies and practices of the Decimal Classification Division at the Library of Congress.

10.2 *See-Manual references* in the schedules and tables refer the classifier to the Manual for additional information about a certain number, range of numbers, or choice among numbers. In some cases, the see-Manual reference refers only to a portion of a longer Manual note, or topic narrower than the numbers in the heading, e.g., "See Manual at 913–919: Add table: 04." The see-Manual reference is repeated in the entries for each of the numbers or number spans covered in the Manual note. For example, "See Manual at 300 vs. 600" is listed in the entries for 300 and 600.

ARRANGEMENT AND FORMAT OF THE MANUAL

10.3 The Manual is arranged by table and schedule numbers, with the broadest span coming before entries for narrower spans or individual numbers. Manual notes are entered under the preferred or "if-in-doubt" number. After the entry number, schedule numbers are listed before table numbers in each part of the heading.

10.4 The terms in the Manual note headings match the terms associated with the same number(s) in the tables and schedules. Additional terms are added in square brackets to provide context. For example:

> 782.1 vs. 792.5
>
>> [Musical aspects of] Dramatic vocal forms Operas vs. [Staging]
>> Dramatic vocal forms Operas

10.5   If the Manual note is very long, or focuses on a topic narrower than the heading, subheadings may be provided. For example:

004.6 vs. 621.382, 621.39

Interfacing and communications [in computer science] vs. Communications engineering vs. [Engineering of] Computers

Digital communications   *(subheading)*

The Relative Index

11.1   The Relative Index is so named because it relates subjects to disciplines. In the schedules, subjects are distributed among disciplines; in the Relative Index subjects are arranged alphabetically, with terms identifying the disciplines in which they are treated subarranged alphabetically under them. An example of the Relative Index entry for Clothing is found in paragraph 4.2.

11.2   The Relative Index is primarily an index to the DDC as a system. It includes most terms found in the schedules and tables, and terms with literary warrant for concepts represented by the schedules and tables. The Relative Index is not exhaustive. If the term sought is not found, the classifier should try a broader term, or consult the schedules and tables directly. The schedules and tables should always be consulted before a number found in the Relative Index is applied.

ARRANGEMENT AND FORMAT OF THE RELATIVE INDEX

11.3   Index entries are arranged alphabetically word by word, e.g., Birth order precedes Birthday. Entries with the same word or phrase but with different marks of punctuation are arranged in the following order:

Term
Term. Subheading
Term (Parenthetical qualifier)
Term, inverted term qualifier
Term as part of phrase

Initialisms and acronyms are entered without punctuation and are filed as if spelled as one word. Hyphens are ignored and treated as a space. Terms indented below the main headings are alphabetized in one group even though they may be a mixture of disciplines, topical subheadings, and, to a limited extent, words that form phrases or inverted phrases when combined with the main heading.

11.4   Class numbers are printed in groups of three digits for ease of reading and copying. The spaces are not part of the numbers and do not represent convenient places to abridge the number.

11.5   See-also references are used for synonyms (but only when two or more new numbers will be found at the synonym), for references to selected broader terms (when the broader term may be unclear), and for references to related terms.

11.6   See-Manual references lead the classifier to relevant discussions in the Manual.

11.7   Numbers drawn from Tables 1–4 are prefixed by T1 through T4. (For a complete listing of table names and abbreviations, see paragraph 7.4.)

INTERDISCIPLINARY NUMBERS

11.8   The first class number displayed in an index entry (the unindented term) is the number for interdisciplinary works. If the term also appears in the tables, the table numbers are listed next, followed by other aspects of the term. The discipline of the interdisciplinary number may be repeated as a subentry if the discipline is not clear. For example:

Adult education	374
	T1—071
public support	379.1

11.9   Interdisciplinary numbers are not provided for all topics in the Relative Index. They are omitted when the index entry is ambiguous, does not have a disciplinary focus, or lacks literary warrant. In such cases, a blank appears opposite the unindented entry.

(For more information on interdisciplinary numbers, see paragraphs 5.8, 7.14, 7.17–7.18.)

TERMS INCLUDED IN THE RELATIVE INDEX

11.10   The Relative Index contains most terms found in the headings and notes of the schedules and tables, and synonyms and terms with literary warrant for concepts represented by the schedules and tables. The Relative Index also contains terms for the broad concepts covered in Manual notes.

Inverted phrases are avoided, except for personal and geographic names (see paragraphs 11.12–11.13). Qualifiers are used for homonyms, ambiguous terms, and most initialisms and abbreviations. The most common use of the term may not be qualified. Disciplinary qualifiers are avoided.

11.11   The following types of names from Table 2 Geographic Areas are included in the Index: (A) names of countries; (B) names of the states and provinces (or equivalent units) of several countries; and (C) names of certain important geographic features.

11.12   Also included in the Relative Index are the personal names of heads of state used to identify historical periods, e.g., Juan Carlos I; and founders or revealers of religions, e.g., Muhammad.

11.13   Place names and other proper names are generally given in the form specified by the second edition, revised, of the *Anglo-American Cataloguing Rules (AACR2R)*, based on the names established in the Library of Congress authority files. If the AACR2R form is not the common English name, an entry is also included under the familiar form of the name.

Plants and animals are indexed under their common names.

11.14   The choice of singular form versus plural form follows BS 3700: 1988, *British Standard Recommendations for Preparing Indexes to Books, Periodicals and Other Documents*. Count nouns are generally in the plural; noncount nouns and abstract concepts are generally in the singular. Parts of the body are in the plural only when more than one occurs in a fully formed organism (e.g., ears, hands, nose). Plants and animals follow scientific convention in choice of singular form versus plural form, with the decision based on whether the taxonomic class has more than one member (e.g., Horses, Lion, Yorkshire terrier). Where usage varies across disciplines, the index entry reflects the form preferred in the discipline where interdisciplinary works are classified.

TERMS NOT INCLUDED IN THE RELATIVE INDEX

11.15   Terms usually not included in the Relative Index are:

(A)   Phrases beginning with the adjectival form of countries, languages, nationalities, religions, e.g., English poetry, French cooking, Italian architecture, Hindu prayer books.

(B)   Phrases that contain general concepts represented by standard subdivisions such as education, statistics, laboratories, and management, e.g., Art education, Educational statistics, Medical laboratories, Bank management.

(C)   Names of literatures whose numbers correspond to the notation in their language numbers, e.g., Efik literature, whose number (896) corresponds to the number (496) for Efik language, which is indexed.

When the phrase heading is a proper name or provides the only form of access to the topic, it may be included, e.g., English Channel, French horns. Literatures with their own number listed in the 800 schedule are included, even if the number corresponds to the 400 number, e.g., English literature 820 (corresponds to English language 420).

Options

12.1   Some devices are required to enable the Classification to serve needs beyond those represented in the standard English-language edition. At a number of places in the schedules and tables, *options* are provided to give emphasis to an aspect in a library's collection not given preferred treatment in the standard notation. In some cases, options are also suggested to provide shorter notation for the aspect.

12.2   Options described in notes appear in parentheses and begin with "Option:". Options that apply to the full entry appear at the end of the entry; options to a specific instruction in the entry are indented under the appropriate note. For example, the following option appears indented under a note in the entry for 810–890:

> (Option: Class translations into a language requiring local emphasis with the literature of that language)

12.3   Some *optional numbers* are enumerated in the schedules and tables and appear in parentheses in the number column.

12.4   *Arrange-alphabetically* and *arrange-chronologically notes* are not placed in parentheses, but are also options. They represent suggestions only; the material need not be arranged alphabetically or chronologically. An example of an arrange-alphabetically note is found at 005.265 Programming for specific microcomputers: "Arrange alphabetically by name of microcomputer or microprocessor, e.g., IBM PC®."

12.5   Some national libraries and central cataloging authorities assign a few optional numbers, e.g., the National Library of Canada uses C810 for Canadian literature in English and C840 for Canadian literature in French. Optional numbers assigned by the Library of Congress are described in the appendix to the Manual.

12.6   Most of the time, however, the responsibility for implementing an option rests with the local library. If options are needed, the library should prefer those described in the Classification rather than attempting local developments.

Close and Broad Classification

13.1   The Dewey Decimal Classification provides the basic option of close versus broad classification. *Close classification* means that the content of a work is specified by notation to the fullest extent possible. *Broad classification* means that the work is placed in a broad class by use of notation that has been logically abridged. For example, a work on French cooking is classed closely at 641.5944 (641.59 Cooking by place + 44 France from Table 2), or broadly at 641.5 (Cooking).

13.2   A library should base its decision on close versus broad classification on the size of its collection and the needs of its users. For example, an engineering library might prefer close classification for works in engineering, but broad classification for disciplines outside science and technology.

13.3   The classifier should never reduce the notation to less than the most specific three-digit number (no matter how small the library's collection). A number also must never be reduced so that it ends in a 0 anywhere to the right of the decimal point.

13.4   One aid to logical abridgment of DDC numbers is the segmentation device provided by the Decimal Classification Division of the Library of Congress and some other centralized cataloging services. A more detailed description of this device is provided in the appendix to the Manual.

Selected Bibliography

14.1   Classifiers desiring a more in-depth introduction to the Dewey Decimal Classification may consult *Dewey Decimal Classification: A Practical Guide*, 2nd ed., by Lois Mai Chan, John P. Comaromi, Joan S. Mitchell, and Mohinder P. Satija (Albany, N.Y.: OCLC Forest Press, 1996). OCLC Forest Press also issues training materials to accompany each new edition of the DDC.

14.2   For the history of the DDC through Edition 18, see John P. Comaromi's *The Eighteen Editions of the Dewey Decimal Classification* (Albany, N.Y.: Forest Press, 1976).

14.3   For a list of book numbers, consult *Cutter-Sanborn Three-Figure Author Table*, Swanson-Swift revision, 1969 (distributed by Libraries Unlimited, Littleton, Colo.). For descriptive works on book numbers, see John P. Comaromi's *Book Numbers: A Historical Study and Practical Guide to Their Use* (Littleton, Colo.: Libraries Unlimited, 1981) and Donald J. Lehnus's *Book Numbers: History, Principles, and Applications* (Chicago: American Library Association, 1980).

Glossary

Add note.   A note instructing the classifier to append digits found elsewhere in the Classification to a given base number.   *See also* **Base number.**

Approximate the whole.   When the topic of a work is nearly coextensive with the topic of a DDC heading, the work is said to "approximate the whole." The term is also used to characterize works that cover more than half the content of the heading, and works that cover representative examples from three or more subdivisions of a class. When a work approximates the whole of a subject, standard subdivisions may be added. Topics that do not approximate the whole are said to be in "standing room" in the number.   *See also* **Class-here note; Standard-subdivisions-are-added note; Standing room; Unitary term.**

Arrange-alphabetically note.   A note suggesting the option of alphabetical subarrangement where identification by specific name or other identifying characteristic is desired.   *See also* **Option.**

Arrange-chronologically note.   A note suggesting the option of chronological subarrangement where identification by date is desired.   *See also* **Option.**

Aspect.   An approach to a subject, or a characteristic (facet) of a subject.   *See also* **Discipline; Facet; Subject.**

Base number.   A number to which other numbers are appended.   *See also* **Add note.**

Book number.   The part of a call number that distinguishes a specific item from other items within the same class number. A library using the Cutter-Sanborn system can have D548d indicate David Copperfield by Dickens (where D stands for the D of Dickens, 548 for "ickens," and d for David Copperfield).   *See also* **Call number; Cutter number.**

Broad classification.   The classification of works in broad categories by logical abridgment, even when more specific numbers are available, e.g., classing a cookbook of Mexican recipes in 641.5 Cooking (instead of in 641.5972 Mexican cooking).

Built number.   A number constructed according to add instructions stated or implied in the schedules and tables.   *See also* **Number building.**

Call number.   A set of letters, numerals, or other symbols (in combination or alone) used by a library to identify a specific copy of a work. A call number may consist of the class number; book number; and other data such as date, volume number, copy number, and location symbol.   *See also* **Book number; Class number.**

Centered entry.   An entry representing a subject covered by a span of numbers, e.g., 372–374 Specific levels of education. The entry is called "centered" because the span of numbers is printed in the center of the page rather than in the number column on the left side of the page. Centered entries are identified by the symbol > in the number column.

Citation order.   The order in which two or more characteristics (facets) of a class are to be combined in number building. When number building is not permitted or possible, instructions on preference order with respect to the choice of facets are provided.   *See also* **Facet; Number Building; Preference order.**

Class. (Noun) (1) A group of objects exhibiting one or more common characteristics, identified by a specific notation. (2) One of the ten major groups of the DDC numbered 0–9. *See also* **Main class.** (3) A subdivision of the DDC of any degree of specificity. (Verb) To assign a class number to an individual work. *See also* **Classify.**

Class-elsewhere note. A note instructing the classifier on the location of interrelated topics. The note may show preference order, lead to the interdisciplinary or comprehensive number, override the first-of-two rule, or lead to broader or narrower numbers in the same hierarchical array that might otherwise be overlooked. *See also* **Comprehensive number; Interdisciplinary number; Preference order.**

Class-here note. An instruction identifying topics that are to be classed in the given number and in its subdivisions. Topics identified in class-here notes, even if broader or narrower than the heading, are said to "approximate the whole" of the number; therefore, standard subdivisions may be added for topics in class-here notes. Class-here notes also may identify the comprehensive or interdisciplinary number for a subject. *See also* **Approximate the whole; Comprehensive number; Interdisciplinary number.**

Class number. Notation that designates the class to which a given item belongs. *See also* **Call number.**

Classification. A logical system for the arrangement of knowledge.

Classification by attraction. The classification of a specific aspect of a subject in an inappropriate discipline, usually because the subject is named in the inappropriate discipline but not mentioned explicitly in the appropriate discipline.

Classify. (1) To arrange a collection of items according to a classification system. (2) To assign a class number to an individual work.

Close classification. The classification of works to the fullest extent permitted by the notation.

Complex subject. A complex subject is a subject that has more than one characteristic. For example, "unemployed bibliographers" is a complex subject because it has more than one characteristic (employment status and occupation). *See also* **Preference order.**

Comprehensive number. A number (often identified by a "Class here comprehensive works" note) that covers all the components of the subject treated within that discipline. The components may be in a span of consecutive numbers or distributed in the Classification. *See also* **Interdisciplinary number.**

Cutter number. The notation in a book number derived from the Cutter-Sanborn tables. *See also* **Book number.**

DDC. Dewey Decimal Classification.

Decimal point. The dot that follows the third digit in a DDC number. In strict usage the word "decimal" is not accurate; however, common usage is followed in this edition's explanatory material.

Definition note. A note indicating the meaning of a term in the heading.

Discipline. An organized field of study or branch of knowledge, e.g., 200 Religion, 530 Physics, 364 Criminology. In the DDC, subjects are arranged by disciplines. *See also* **Subject.**

Discontinued number. A number from the previous edition that is no longer used because the concept represented by the number has been moved to a more general number in the same hierarchy, or has been dropped entirely. Discontinued numbers appear in square brackets. *See also* **Schedule reduction.**

Division. The second level of subdivision in the Classification, represented by the first two digits in the notation, e.g., 62 in 620 Engineering and allied operations. *See also* **Main class; Section.**

Do-not-use note. A note instructing the classifier not to use all or part of a regular standard subdivision notation or an add table provision in favor of a special provision, or standard subdivisions at a broader number.

Dual heading. A heading with two separate terms, the first of which is the main topic and the second of which is a major subordinate topic, e.g., 570 Life sciences   Biology. A dual heading is used when the subject as a whole and the subordinate topic as a whole share the same number. Standard subdivisions may be added for either or both topics in a dual heading.

Entry. (1) In the schedules and tables, a self-contained unit consisting of a number or span of numbers, a heading, and often one or more notes.   (2) In the Relative Index, a term or phrase usually followed by a DDC number.

Facet. Any of the various categories into which a given class may be divided, e.g., division of the class "people" by the categories race, age, education, and language spoken. Each category contains terms based on a single characteristic of division, e.g., children, adolescents, and adults are characteristics of division of the "ages" category. *See also* **Citation order.**

Facet indicator. A digit used to introduce notation representing a characteristic of the subject. For example, "0" is often used as a facet indicator to introduce standard subdivision concepts.

First-of-two rule. The rule instructing that works dealing equally with two subjects not used to introduce or explain one another are classed in the number coming first in the schedules or tables.

Former-heading note. A note listing the heading associated with the class number in the previous edition. The note is used when the heading has changed so much that it bears little or no resemblance to the previous heading, even though the meaning of the number has remained substantially the same.

Heading. The word or phrase used as the caption of a given class.

Hierarchical force. The principle that the attributes of a class as defined in the heading and in certain basic notes apply to all the subdivisions of the class, and to all other classes to which reference is made.

Hierarchy. The arrangement of a classification system from general to specific. In the Dewey Decimal Classification, the degree of specificity of a class is usually indicated by the length of the notation and the corresponding depth of indention of the heading. Hierarchy may also be indicated by special headings, notes, and centered entries.

Including note. A note enumerating topics that are logically part of the class but are less extensive in scope than the concept represented by the class number. These topics do not have enough literature to warrant their own number. Standard subdivisions may not be added to the numbers for these topics. *See also* **Literary warrant; Standing room.**

Interdisciplinary number. A number (often identified by a "Class here interdisciplinary works" note) to be used for works covering a subject from the perspective of more than one discipline, including the discipline where the interdisciplinary number is located, e.g., the interdisciplinary number for marriage is 306.81 in Sociology. *See also* **Comprehensive number.**

Literary warrant. Justification for the development of a class or naming of a topic in the schedules, tables, or Relative Index, based on the existence of a body of published literature on the topic.

Main class. One of the ten major subdivisions of the Dewey Decimal Classification, represented by the first digit in the notation, e.g., the 3 in 300. *See also* **Division; Section.**

Manual. A guide to the use of the DDC that is made up primarily of extended discussions of problem areas in the application of the Classification. In the schedules and tables, see-Manual references indicate where relevant discussions are located in the Manual.

Notation. Numerals, letters, and/or other symbols used to represent the main and subordinate divisions of a classification scheme. In the DDC, Arabic numerals are used to represent the classes, e.g., notation 07 from Table 1 and 511.3 from the schedules.

Number building. The process of constructing a number by adding notation from the tables or other parts of the schedules to a base number. *See also* **Base number; Citation order.**

Number column. The column of numbers printed in the left margin of the schedules and tables, and to the right of the alphabetical entries in the Relative Index.

Option. An alternative to standard notation provided in the schedules and tables to give emphasis to an aspect in a library's collection not given preferred treatment in the standard notation. In some cases, an option may provide shorter notation for the aspect.

Optional number. (1) A number listed in parentheses in the schedules or tables that is an alternative to the standard notation. (2) A number constructed by following an option.

Preference order. The order indicating which one of two or more numbers is to be chosen when different characteristics of a subject cannot be shown in full by number building. A note (sometimes containing a table of preference) indicates which characteristic is to be selected for works covering more than one characteristic. When the notation can be synthesized to show two or more characteristics, it is a matter of citation order. *See also* **Citation order.**

Relative Index. The index to the DDC, called "Relative" because it relates subjects to disciplines. In the schedules, subjects are arranged by disciplines. In the Relative Index, subjects are listed alphabetically; indented under each subject is an alphabetical list of the disciplines in which the subject is found.

Relocation. The shifting of a topic in a new edition of the DDC from one number to another number which differs from the old number in respects other than length.

Reused number. A number with a total change in meaning from one edition to another. Usually numbers are reused only in complete revisions or when the reused number has been vacant for two consecutive editions.

Revision. The result of editorial work that alters the text of any class of the DDC. There are three degrees of revision: *Routine revision* is limited to updating terminology, clarifying notes, and providing modest expansions. *Extensive revision* involves a major reworking of subdivisions but leaves the main outline of the schedule intact. *Complete revision* (formerly called a phoenix) is a new development; the base number remains as in the previous edition, but virtually all subdivisions are changed. Changes for complete and extensive revisions are shown through tables in a separate booklet rather than through relocation notes in the schedule or table affected.

Rule of application. The rule instructing that works about the application of one subject to a second subject are classified with the second subject.

Rule of three. The rule instructing that works that give equal treatment to three or more subjects that are all subdivisions of a broader subject are classified in the first higher number that includes all of them.

Rule of zero. The rule instructing that subdivisions beginning with zero should be avoided if there is a choice between 0 and subdivisions beginning with 1–9 in the same position in the notation. Similarly, subdivisions beginning with 00 should be avoided when there is a choice between 00 and 0.

Scatter note. A class-elsewhere, see-reference, or relocation note that leads to multiple locations in the Classification.

Schedule reduction. The elimination of certain provisions of a previous edition, often resulting in discontinued numbers. *See also* **Discontinued number.**

Schedules. The series of DDC numbers 000–999, their headings, and notes.

Scope note. A note indicating that the use of a class number is broader or narrower than is apparent from the heading.

Section. The third level of subdivision in the Classification, represented by the first three digits in the notation, e.g., 625 in 625 Engineering of railroads, roads, highways. *See also* **Division; Main class.**

See-also reference. (1) In the schedules and tables, a note leading to classes that are tangentially related to the topic and therefore might be confused with it. (2) In the Relative Index, a note leading to a synonym, broader term, or related term.

See-Manual reference. A note leading to additional information about the number in the Manual.

See reference.   A note (introduced by the word "for") that leads from the stated or implied comprehensive or interdisciplinary number for a concept to component parts of the subject located elsewhere.   *See also* **Class-elsewhere note.**

Segmentation.   The indication of logical breaks in a number by a typographical device, e.g., slash marks or prime marks. Segmentation marks indicate the end of an abridged number or the beginning of a standard subdivision.

Standard subdivisions.   Subdivisions found in Table 1 that represent frequently recurring physical forms (dictionaries, periodicals) or approaches (history, research) applicable to any subject or discipline. They may be used with any number in the schedules and tables for concepts that approximate the whole of the number unless there are instructions to the contrary.

Standard-subdivisions-are-added note.   A note indicating which topics in a multiterm heading may have standard subdivisions applied to them. The designated topics are considered to approximate the whole of the number.   *See also* **Approximate the whole.**

Standing room.   A term characterizing a topic without sufficient literature to have its own number, and considerably narrower in scope than the class number in which it is included. Standard subdivisions cannot be added to a topic in standing room, nor are other number-building techniques allowed. Topics listed in including notes have standing room in the class number, as do minor unnamed topics that logically fall in the same place in the Classification. To have standing room is the opposite of approximating the whole.   *See also* **Approximate the whole.**

Subdivisions-are-added note.   A note used where subdivisions are provided by add instructions indicating which topics in a multiterm heading may have subdivisions applied to them. The designated topics are considered to approximate the whole of the number. *See also* **Approximate the whole.**

Subject.   An object of study. Also called topic. It may be a person or a group of persons, thing, place, process, activity, abstraction, or any combination of these. In the DDC, subjects are arranged by disciplines. A subject is often studied in more than one discipline, e.g., marriage is studied in several disciplines such as ethics, religion, sociology, and law. *See also* **Discipline.**

Summary.   A listing of the chief subdivisions of a class that provides an overview of its structure. Summaries are also provided for the main classes, divisions, and sections of the Classification as a whole.

Table.   In the DDC, a table of numbers that may be added to other numbers to make a class number appropriately specific to the work being classified. The numbers found in a table are never used alone. There are two kinds: (1) The four numbered tables (Tables 1–4) representing standard subdivisions, geographic areas, and aspects of literature and languages. (2) Lists of special notation found in add notes under specific numbers throughout the schedules and in Table 3 at —1–8. These lists are called add tables.

Variant-name note.   A note listing synonyms or near synonyms for a topic when they might not be immediately recognized.

Index to the Introduction and Glossary

References to the Introduction are identified by paragraph numbers. References to the alphabetically arranged Glossary are identified by G.

Tables

Use of the Tables

Full instructions on the use of the tables are found in paragraphs 8.3–8.10 of the Introduction to the Dewey Decimal Classification. Instructions for the use of each table precede the table. Important supplemental general instructions for Table 3 are found in the Manual.

These are auxiliary tables, and are to be used only in conjunction with the schedules. In some instances, numbers from one table may be added to those of another table; but in all cases, numbers from one table or a combination of tables are to be used only with appropriate numbers from the schedules.

The dash preceding each number indicates that the number never stands alone. The dash is omitted when the table number is added to a schedule number to make a complete class number.

Numbers in square brackets [ ] are not used. Numbers in parentheses ( ) are options to standard usage.

Table 1. Standard Subdivisions

The following notation is never used alone, but may be used as required with any number from the schedules, e.g., workbooks (—076 in this table) in arithmetic (513): 513.076. When adding to a number from the schedules, always insert a decimal point between the third and fourth digits of the complete number

Standard subdivisions should be added only when the work in hand covers the whole, or approximately the whole, subject of the number in the schedules

When standard subdivision notation from Table 1 is printed in the schedules, all of its subdivisions as given in this table may be used. In addition, other Table 1 notation that is not printed in the schedules may be used. For example, the fact that 610.9 is printed does not exclude the use of 610.92 or 610.8

Do not add one standard subdivision to another standard subdivision unless specifically instructed. Numbers in the schedules that look as though they were built with notation from this table but have headings with broader or different meanings are not considered "standard" subdivisions. Hence notation from Table 1 may be added to such schedule numbers

If the 0 subdivisions of a number in a schedule are used for special purposes, use 001–009 for standard subdivisions. For example, 301–307 is used for sociology; therefore, use 300.1–300.9 for standard subdivisions of social sciences

(continued)

Table 1. Standard Subdivisions (continued)

Unless other instructions are given, observe the following table of preference, e.g., education and research in a specific area —07 (*not* —093–099):

Special topics	—04
Persons	—092
Auxiliary techniques and procedures; apparatus, equipment, materials	—028
Education, research, related topics (*except* —074, —075, —076)	—07
Management	—068
Philosophy and theory	—01
The subject as a profession, occupation, hobby	—023
Directories of persons and organizations	—025
Commercial miscellany	—029
Organizations	—06
History and description with respect to kinds of persons	—08
Treatment by specific continents, countries, localities; extraterrestrial worlds	—093–099
Treatment by areas, regions, places in general	—091
Museums, collections, exhibits	—074
Museum activities and services Collecting	—075
Review and exercise	—076
Illustrations, models, miniatures	—022
Miscellany (without subdivision)	—02
Dictionaries, encyclopedias, concordances	—03
Historical treatment (*not* limited by area)	—09
Serial publications	—05

SUMMARY

—01	**Philosophy and theory**
—02	**Miscellany**
—03	**Dictionaries, encyclopedias, concordances**
—04	**Special topics**
—05	**Serial publications**
—06	**Organizations and management**
—07	**Education, research, related topics**
—08	**History and description with respect to kinds of persons**
—09	**Historical, geographic, persons treatment**

—01　　　**Philosophy and theory**

Including psychology of learning specific subjects [*formerly also* 370.15]; classification, communication, computer modeling and simulation, forecasts and forecasting, language, methodology, psychological and scientific principles, systems, terminology, value

Class here methodology, schools of thought

Class interdisciplinary works on classification in 001.01; class interdisciplinary works on systems (including computer modeling and simulation) in 003; class interdisciplinary works on philosophy in 100; class interdisciplinary works on values in 121; class interdisciplinary works on psychology in 150; class interdisciplinary works on communications in 303.2; class interdisciplinary works on language in 400; class interdisciplinary works on terminology in 401; class interdisciplinary works on natural sciences and mathematics in 500

> *For dictionaries, see —03; for short term forecasts (ten years or less) in a specific historical period, see —09; for forecasts in a specific continent, country, locality, see —093–099*
>
> *See Manual at T1—01 vs. T1—02; also at T1—01 vs. T1—03; also at T1—01 vs. T4—86; also at 302–307 vs. 150, T1—01*

—(016)　　　Bibliographies, catalogs, indexes

(Optional number; prefer 016)

—02　　　**Miscellany**

Including humorous treatment; identification marks, e.g., trademarks; patents, standards, statistics; other tabulated materials, e.g., inventories; the subject for persons in specific occupations; synopses and outlines

Class works called synopses and outlines that are regular treatises or introductions to a subject in 001–999 without adding notation 02 from Table 1; class interdisciplinary collections of statistics in 310; class interdisciplinary works on patents in 346.04; class interdisciplinary collections of patents in 608; class interdisciplinary works on standardization in 389; class interdisciplinary collections of standards in 602

> *See Manual at T1—02; also at T1—01 vs. T1—02; also at T1—02 vs. T3—7, T3—8*

—022   Illustrations, models, miniatures

> Including atlases, cartoons, charts, designs; maps, plans, diagrams; pictures; drafting illustrations

> Class simulation models in —01; class humorous cartoons, statistical graphs in —02; class model and miniature educational exhibits in —074; class comprehensive works on historical maps and atlases in 911; class interdisciplinary works on drafting illustrations in 604.2; class interdisciplinary works on illustrations in 760; class interdisciplinary works on models and miniatures in 688; class interdisciplinary works on cartoons in 741.5; class interdisciplinary works on maps, plans, diagrams; on maps, plans, diagrams of geography and travel in general and in specific areas in 912

> *See Manual at 912 vs. T1—022*

—023   The subject as a profession, occupation, hobby

> Class here vocational guidance, choice of vocation, career opportunities, occupational specialties, professional relationships; the subject as a profession, occupation, hobby for specific kinds of persons

> Class interdisciplinary works on vocational guidance, choice of vocation, career opportunities, occupational specialties, professional relationships in 331.7; class interdisciplinary works on hobbies in 790.1

—025   Directories of persons and organizations

> Class here directories of public officials and employees; membership lists containing directory information, e.g., employment and education

> Class directories giving biographical information in —092

> *See also —029 for directories of products and services, 016.02506 for directories of databases on specific subjects*

> *See Manual at 338 vs. 060, 381, 382, 670.29, 910, T1—025, T1—029*

—(026)   Law

> (Optional number: prefer 341–347)

—028   Auxiliary techniques and procedures; apparatus, equipment, materials

Including environmental engineering, waste technology; instruments, instrumentation; maintenance and repair, conservation, preservation, restoration; personal safety and safety engineering; testing and measurement

Class use of apparatus and equipment in study and teaching in —078; class interdisciplinary works on safety in 363.1; class interdisciplinary works on personal safety in 613.6; class interdisciplinary works on safety engineering in 620.8; class interdisciplinary works on measurement in 530.8; class interdisciplinary works on maintenance and repair, on testing in 620; class interdisciplinary works on environmental engineering in 628; class interdisciplinary works on technology of testing and measuring instruments in 681; class interdisciplinary works on artistic conservation, preservation, restoration in 702.8

For drafting illustrations, see —022; for educational testing, see —076

See Manual at 363.1

—028 5   Data processing   Computer applications

Class here data processing in research

Class computer modeling and simulation in —01; class interdisciplinary works on data processing in 004

See Manual at T1—0285

—029   Commercial miscellany

Including advertisements, price lists, product directories, trade catalogs and directories; buyers' guides and consumer reports; evaluation and purchasing manuals, price trends; estimates of time, labor, materials

Class here listings of products and services offered for sale, lease, or free distribution

Class house organs in —05; class noncurrent offers for sale used primarily to illustrate civilization and customs of an earlier period in 900; class interdisciplinary commercial miscellany in 380.1029; class interdisciplinary evaluation and purchasing manuals in 381.3

For price trends for collectors, see —075; for catalogs of bibliographic materials on specific subjects, see 016

See also —074 for listings of noncommercial collections and exhibits

See Manual at 338 vs. 060, 381, 382, 670.29, 910, T1—025, T1—029

—03   **Dictionaries, encyclopedias, concordances**

Class interdisciplinary encyclopedias in 030; class interdisciplinary dictionaries in 413

See Manual at T1—01 vs. T1—03

—04 **Special topics**

Use this subdivision only when it is specifically set forth in the schedules. Add other standard subdivisions —01–09 to it and its subdivisions as required, e.g., technical drawing as a profession 604.2023

—05 **Serial publications**

Regardless of frequency

Class here house organs, magazines, newspapers, yearbooks

Class monographic series in 001–999 without adding notation 05 from Table 1; class interdisciplinary serial publications in 050; class interdisciplinary newspapers in 071–079

> *For a special kind of serial publication, see the kind, e.g., directories in serial form —025, administrative reports of organizations —06*

—06 **Organizations and management**

Including Greek-letter societies, other student organizations [*formerly* 371.8]; history, charters, regulations, membership lists, administrative reports

Class directories of organizations, membership lists with directory information in —025; class organizations engaged in education, research, related topics in —07; class business enterprises in 338.7; class government administrative and military organizations in 350; class nonadministrative reports and proceedings of organizations in 001–999 without adding notation 06 from Table 1; class interdisciplinary works on organizations in 060

—068 **Management**

The science and art of conducting organized enterprises and projects

Including executive management; management of distribution (marketing), e.g., sales management; management of materials; management of production; organization and financial management, e.g., fund raising, initiation of business enterprises; personnel (human resource) management; plant management

Class management in the sense of carrying out ordinary activities of a subject in 001–999 without adding notation 068 from Table 1, e.g., management of patients 616 (*not* 616.0068); class interdisciplinary works in 658

> *See also —079 for fund raising for competitions, festivals, awards, financial support*

> *See Manual at T1—068 vs. 353–354; also at 658 and T1—068; also at 658.4 and T1—068; also at 658.8, T1—068 vs. 659*

(Option: Class management of specific enterprises in 658)

—07   **Education, research, related topics**

Including programmed texts

Class here subject-oriented study programs; comprehensive works on education and research, on resources for education and research

Class results of research in 001–999 without adding notation 07 from Table 1; class interdisciplinary works on research in 001.4

For modeling, simulation, mathematical techniques for research, see —01; for testing in research, see —028; for data processing in research, see —0285. For a specific resource not provided for here, see the resource, e.g., directories —025, bibliographies 016, libraries 026

See Manual at 016 vs. 026, T1—07

—071   Education

Including adult education, e.g., on-the-job training; higher education, secondary education

Class here curricula in specific subjects or directed toward specific subject objectives [*formerly* 375], study (education), teaching, vocational education

Class student organizations in —06; class textbooks and school activities in a subject in 001–999 without adding notation 071 from Table 1; class religious education to inculcate religious faith and values in 291.7 (*not* 200.71); class religious education to inculcate Christian faith and values in 268 (*not* 230.071); class comprehensive works on education and research in —07; class interdisciplinary works on on-the-job training in 331.25; class interdisciplinary works on education in 370; class interdisciplinary works on teaching in 371.1

For review and exercise, see —076; for use of apparatus and equipment in education, see —078; for competitions, festivals, awards, financial support in education, see —079; for special education in specific subjects, see 371.9; for education in specific subjects at elementary level, see 372.3–372.8

See Manual at 407.1, T1—071 vs. 401, 410.71, 418.0071, T4—80071

—074   Museums, collections, exhibits

Class here collections located in specific areas; catalogs and lists regardless of whether or not articles are offered for sale; guidebooks, history and description

Class comprehensive works on museology of a subject in —075; class interdisciplinary works on museums, collections, exhibits in 069

For collections representing a specific time period or area, see —09; for collections of books and related informational materials in specific subjects, see 016

—075   Museum activities and services   Collecting

> Class here museology, collectibles, memorabilia, price trends for collectors

> Class interdisciplinary works on museum activities and services, on museum collecting in 069; class interdisciplinary works on recreational collecting in 790.1

>> *For maintenance and repair of collected objects, see —028; for activities and services of or relating to specific museums, collections, exhibits, see —074*

—076   Review and exercise

> Including workbooks with problems, questions, answers; civil service examinations; testing, test construction and evaluation

> Class programmed texts with problems, questions, answers in —07; class interdisciplinary works on civil service examinations in 351.076; class interdisciplinary works on examinations and tests in 371.26

>> *For review and exercise using apparatus and equipment, see —078*

> (Option: Class civil service examinations in specific subjects in 351.076)

—078   Use of apparatus and equipment in study and teaching

> Including computer-assisted instruction

> Class here laboratory manuals, student projects and experiments

> Class laboratory manuals used in research in —07

>> *For laboratory manuals used in testing, see —028*

—079   Competitions, festivals, awards, financial support

> Including fund raising to support such activities; judging competitions

> Class here fellowships and scholarships, grants-in-aid, honorary titles, prizes

> Class description of works that are entered into competitions and festivals, that receive awards, or that result from financial support in 001–999 without adding notation 079 from Table 1; class interdisciplinary works on awards in 929.8

>> *See also —068 for fund raising*

—08   History and description with respect to kinds of persons

> Class here minorities

> Unless other instructions are given, class a subject with aspects in two or more subdivisions of —08 in the number coming last, e.g., children with disabilities —087 (*not* —083)

> Class racial, ethnic, national minorities in —089; class treatment of specific kinds of persons as individuals in —092, e.g., collected biography of a specific racial, ethnic, national group —092 (*not* —089)

—081   **Men**

        Class here males

          See Manual at T1—081 and T1—082

—082   **Women**

        Class here females; feminist views of a subject, e.g., feminist Christian theology 230.082

          See Manual at T1—081 and T1—082

—083   **Young people**

        Including infants

        Class here children

—083 5   **Young people twelve to twenty**

        Variant names: adolescents, teenagers, young adults, youth

        Comprehensive works on young adults relocated to —084

        Class youth twenty-one and over in —084

—084   **Persons in specific stages of adulthood**

        Aged twenty-one and above

        Including comprehensive works on young adults [*formerly* —0835], persons in late adulthood

        Class comprehensive works on adults in 001–999 without adding notation 084 from Table 1

          For young adults under twenty one, see —0835

—085   **Relatives   Parents**

        Including brothers, sisters, grandparents

        Class here adoptive and foster parents, stepparents

—086   **Persons by miscellaneous social characteristics**

        Not provided for elsewhere

        Including gay men and lesbians, married and divorced persons, offenders, retired persons, social classes, socially disadvantaged persons, unemployed persons, unmarried mothers, veterans

—087   **Persons with disabilities and illnesses, gifted persons**

—088   **Occupational and religious groups**

        Including homemakers, students

—089   Racial, ethnic, national groups

Class here racial, ethnic, national minorities

Class treatment with respect to miscellaneous kinds of persons of a specific racial, ethnic, national group in —081–088, e.g., Chinese children —083; class treatment with respect to specific racial, ethnic, national groups in places where they predominate in —09

See Manual at T1—09 vs. T1—089

—09   **Historical, geographic, persons treatment**

Class historical and geographic treatment of museums, collections, exhibits representing the whole subject in —074; class historical and geographic treatment of museum activities and services representing the whole subject in —075

See Manual at T1—09; also at T1—09 vs. T1—089

—091   Treatment by areas, regions, places in general

History and description

Add to base number —091 the numbers following —1 in notation 11–19 from Table 2, e.g., torrid zone —0913

Class history and description with respect to kinds of persons in —08; class persons regardless of area, region, place in —092; class treatment by specific continents, countries, localities in —093–099

—092   Persons

Biography, autobiography, description and critical appraisal of work, diaries, reminiscences, correspondence of persons regardless of area, region, or place who are part of the subject or who study the subject, e.g., biographers, collectors, leaders and followers, practitioners and clients, scholars

Class history and description with respect to kinds of persons in —08; class biography not clearly related to any specific subject in 920; class literary diaries, reminiscences, correspondence in 800

See Manual at T1—092

(Option A: Class biography in 920.1–928)

(Option B: Class individual biography in 92, or B)

(Option C: Class individual biography of men in 920.71, of women in 920.72)

—093–099   Treatment by specific continents, countries, localities; extraterrestrial worlds

History and description by place, by specific instance of the subject

Add to base number —09 notation 3–9 from Table 2, e.g., the subject in North America —097, United States —0973, Brazil —0981

Class history and description with respect to kinds of persons regardless of continent, country, locality in —08; class treatment by areas, regions, places not limited by continent, country, locality in —091; class persons regardless of continent, country, locality in —092

Table 2. Geographic Areas, and Persons

The following numbers are never used alone, but may be used as required (either directly when so noted or through the interposition of notation 09 from Table 1) with any number from the schedules, e.g., public libraries (027.4) in Japan (—52 in this table): 027.452; railroad transportation (385) in Japan: 385.0952. When adding to a number from the schedules, always insert a decimal point between the third and fourth digits of the complete number

Except where instructed otherwise, further subdivisions may be added when the number from this table is added directly to a schedule number, e.g., international relations (327) between Brazil (—81 in this table) and France (—44 in this table): 327.81044; history (—09 from Table 1) of the international relations of Brazil: 327.81009

SUMMARY

—001–009	Standard subdivisions
—1	Areas, regions, places in general
—2	Persons
—3	The ancient world
—4	Europe Western Europe
—5	Asia Orient Far East
—6	Africa
—7	North America
—8	South America
—9	Other parts of world and extraterrestrial worlds Pacific Ocean islands

—001–008	Standard subdivisions
—009	Historical treatment

       If "historical" appears in the heading for the number to which notation 009 could be added, this notation is redundant and should not be used

—[009 01–009 9]	Geographic and persons treatment

       Do not use; class in —1–9

—1   Areas, regions, places in general

Not limited by continent, country, locality

Unless other instructions are given, class an area with aspects in two or more subdivisions of —1 in the number coming last in the table, e.g., forested valleys in north temperate zone —15 (*not* —12 or —14)

Class persons regardless of area, region, place in —2; class specific continents, countries, localities in —3–9

—11   **Frigid zones**

Class here polar regions

—12   **Temperate zones (Middle latitude zones)**

—13   **Torrid zone (Tropics)**

—14   **Land and landforms**

Including beaches, caves, coastal regions, continents, islands, mountains, plains, shorelines, steppes, valleys; soil

—15   **Regions by type of vegetation**

Including deserts, forests, grasslands

—16   **Air and water**

Including inland seas, lagoons, lakes, rivers

Class specific inland seas in —4–9

—161   Atmosphere

—162   Oceans and seas

Class special oceanographic forms and inland seas in —16

For Atlantic Ocean, see —163; for Pacific Ocean, see —164; for Indian Ocean, see —165; for Antarctic waters, see —167

See also —182 for ocean and sea basins

See Manual at T2—162

—163   Atlantic Ocean

Including Arctic Ocean, Baltic Sea, Black Sea, Caribbean Sea, Chesapeake Bay, English Channel, Gulf of Mexico, Mediterranean Sea, North Sea

For Bering Strait, see —164; for Suez Canal, see —165; for Atlantic sector of Antarctic waters, see —167

See Manual at T2—162; also at T2—163, T2—164, T2—165 vs. T2—182

—164   Pacific Ocean

Including Arafura Sea, Bering Sea, East China Sea, Java Sea, Sea of Japan, Sea of Okhotsk, South China Sea

Panama Canal relocated to —7287

For Pacific sector of Antarctic waters, see —167

See Manual at T2—162; also at T2—163, T2—164, T2—165 vs. T2—182

—165   Indian Ocean

> Including Andaman Sea, Persian Gulf, Red Sea, Suez Canal, Timor Sea
>
> *For Arafura Sea, Singapore Strait, see —164; for Indian Ocean sector of Antarctic waters, see —167*
>
> *See Manual at T2—162; also at T2—163, T2—164, T2—165 vs. T2—182*

—167   Antarctic waters

> *See Manual at T2—162; also at T2—163, T2—164, T2—165 vs. T2—182*

—17   **Socioeconomic regions**

> Including regions where specific racial, ethnic, national groups predominate; regions where specific languages predominate; where specific religions predominate; nations belonging to specific international organizations, e.g., nations belonging to Organization of Petroleum Exporting Countries

—171   Socioeconomic regions by political orientation

> Including blocs, noncontiguous empires and political unions, non-self-governing territories
>
> Class Roman Empire in —37

—172   Socioeconomic regions by degree of economic development

> Including developed and developing regions

—173   Socioeconomic regions by concentration of population

> Including urban, suburban, rural regions

—18   **Other kinds of terrestrial regions**

—181   Hemispheres

> Class zonal, physiographic, socioeconomic regions in a specific hemisphere in —11–17
>
> *See Manual at T2—7 vs. T2—181*

—182   Ocean and sea basins

> The totality of continents facing and islands in specific major bodies of water
>
> Including Atlantic, Indian Ocean, Mediterranean, Pacific region; Occident
>
> Class ocean and sea waters in —162; class zonal, physiographic, socioeconomic regions in a specific ocean or sea basin in —11–17
>
> *See also —729 for Caribbean Area*
>
> *See Manual at T2—163, T2—164, T2—165 vs. T2—182*

—19   **Space**

> Class extraterrestrial worlds in —99
>
> *See Manual at T2—99 vs. T2—19*

—2   **Persons**

> Regardless of area, region, place
>
> Class here description and critical appraisal of work, biography, autobiography, diaries, reminiscences, correspondence of persons associated with the subject, e.g., elementary educators 372.92
>
> All schedule and Manual notes for notation 092 from Table 1 are applicable here

---

>   **—3–9   Specific continents, countries, localities; extraterrestrial worlds**

> Class here specific instances of the subject
>
> An area is classed in its present number even if it had a different affiliation at the time under consideration, e.g., Arizona under Mexican sovereignty —791 (*not* —72)
>
> Class areas, regions, places not limited by continent, country, locality in —1; class parts of oceans and non-inland seas limited by country or locality in —16; class persons regardless of area, region, place in —2; class comprehensive works in 001–999, without adding notation from Table 2
>
> *See Manual at T2—162; also at T2—3 vs. T2—4–9*

—3   **The ancient world**

> Class a specific part of ancient world not provided for here in —4–9
>
> *See Manual at T2—3 vs. T2—4–9*
>
> (Option: Class specific parts in —4–9 as detailed below)

—31   **China**

> (Option: Class in —51)

—32   **Egypt**

> (Option: Class in —62)

—33   **Palestine**

> Including Israel, Samaria
>
> (Option: Class Palestine, Israel in —5694; class Jordanian part of Palestine, Samaria in —5695)

—34   **India**

> (Option: Class in —54)

—35   **Mesopotamia and Iranian Plateau**

Class central Asia in —39

(Option: Class Iranian Plateau in —55; class Mesopotamia in —567)

—36   **Europe north and west of Italian Peninsula**

Class here comprehensive works on Europe

For a specific part of Europe not provided for here, see the part, e.g., Greece —38

(Option: Class in —4)

—361   British Isles   Northern Britain and Ireland

For southern Britain, see —362

(Option: Class British Isles in —41; class northern Britain in —411; class Ireland in —415)

—362   Southern Britain   England

Class comprehensive works on British Isles in —361

(Option: Class in —42)

—363   Germanic regions

For British Isles, see —361

(Option: Class in —43)

—364   Celtic regions

Class here Gaul

For British Isles, see —361

(Option: Class in —44)

—366   Iberian Peninsula and adjacent islands

(Option: Class in —46)

—37   **Italian Peninsula and adjacent territories**

Including Etruria, Malta, Sardinia, Sicily, Corsica, Istria

Class here Roman Empire

For a specific part of Roman Empire provided for here, see the part, e.g., Britain —361

(Option: Class Corsica in —44; class Italian Peninsula, Etruria, Malta, Sardinia, Sicily, Roman Empire in —45; class Istria in —4972)

—38   **Greece**

Including Macedonia

Class here comprehensive works on Greece and the Roman Empire; the Hellenistic World; southern Europe

> *For Roman Empire, see —37. For a specific part of Greece, Hellenistic World, southern Europe not provided for here, see the part, e.g., Ptolemaic Egypt —32, Aegean Islands —39*

(Option: Class southern Europe in —4; class Greece in —495)

—39   **Other parts of ancient world**

Including southeastern Europe, e.g., Aegean Islands, Crete, Illyria, Moesia, Thrace; Middle East, e.g., Arabia, Arabia Deserta, Asia Minor, Cyprus, Phoenicia, Sinai Peninsula, Syria; Black Sea and Caucasus regions, e.g., Armenia, Albania, Colchis, Iberia, Sarmatia; central Asia; North Africa, e.g., Algerian and Moroccan parts of North Africa, Cush, Ethiopia, Nubia

> *For Egypt, see —32; for Palestine, see —33; for Mesopotamia and Iranian Plateau, see —35; for Greece, see —38*

(Option: Class Caucasus in —475; class Albania in —4754; class Colchis, Iberia in —4758; class Black Sea region, Sarmatia in —477; class Aegean Islands, Crete, Thrace in —495; class southeastern Europe in —496; class Illyria in —497; class Moesia in —499; class Arabia, Sinai Peninsula in —53; class Middle East in —56; class Asia Minor in —561; class Armenia in —566; class Arabia Deserta in —567; class Syria in —5691; class Phoenicia in —5692; class Cyprus in —5693; class central Asia in —58; class North Africa in —61; class Cush, Ethiopia, Nubia in —625; class Moroccan part of North Africa in —64; class Algerian part of North Africa in —65)

\>   **—4–9   The modern world; extraterrestrial worlds**

Class comprehensive works on specific jurisdictions, regions, or features extending over more than one country, state or other unit and identified by * with the unit where noted in this table, e.g., Scottish Highlands —411. For works on a part of such a jurisdiction, region, or feature, see the specific unit where the part is located, e.g., Scottish Highlands in Grampian region —412

Class comprehensive works in 001–999, without adding from Table 2

> *See Manual at T2—4–9; also at T2—3 vs. T2—4–9*

(Option: Class here specific parts of the ancient world; prefer —3)

—4   **Europe   Western Europe**

Class here southern Europe

Class Eurasia in —5

(Option: Class here ancient Europe, western Europe, southern Europe; prefer —36 for ancient Europe, western Europe, —38 for ancient southern Europe)

SUMMARY

—41	**British Isles**
—42	**England and Wales**
—43	**Central Europe Germany**
—44	**France and Monaco**
—45	**Italian Peninsula and adjacent islands Italy**
—46	**Iberian Peninsula and adjacent islands Spain**
—47	**Eastern Europe Russia**
—48	**Scandinavia**
—49	**Other parts of Europe**

—41   **British Isles**

Class here Great Britain, United Kingdom

For England and Wales, see —42

(Option: Class here ancient British Isles; prefer —361)

—411   Scotland

Including Highland Region, Islands authorities; *Scottish Highlands

For northeastern Scotland, see —412; for southeastern Scotland, see —413; for southwestern Scotland, see —414

(Option: Class here ancient northern Britain; prefer —361)

—412   Northeastern Scotland

Including Fife, Grampian, Tayside regions

—413   Southeastern Scotland

Including Borders, Central, Lothian regions; *Forth River

Class here *Central Lowlands

—414   Southwestern Scotland

Including Dumfries and Galloway, Strathclyde Regions; *Clyde River

—415   Ireland

For divisions of Ireland, see —416–419

(Option: Class here ancient Ireland; prefer —361)

>   —416–419 Divisions of Ireland

Class comprehensive works in —415

—416   Ulster   Northern Ireland

—416 9   Counties of Republic of Ireland in Ulster

Including Cavan, Donegal, Monaghan

*For a specific part of this jurisdiction, region, or feature, see the part and follow instructions under —4–9

—417   Republic of Ireland (Eire)

Including Connacht, consisting of Galway, Leitrim, Mayo, Roscommon, Sligo counties

Class here *Shannon River

For counties in Ulster, see —4169; for Leinster, see —418; for Munster, see —419

—418   Leinster

Including Carlow, Dublin, Kildare, Kilkenny, Laois, Longford, Louth, Meath, Offaly, Westmeath, Wexford, Wicklow counties

—419   Munster

Including Clare, Cork, Kerry, Limerick, Tipperary, Waterford counties

—42   England and Wales

(Option: Class here ancient southern Britain, England; prefer —362)

\>   —421–428 England

Class comprehensive works in —42

—421   Greater London

—422   Southeastern England

Including Berkshire, East Sussex, Hampshire, Isle of Wight, Kent, Surrey, West Sussex

Class here *Home Counties; *Thames River

For Greater London, see —421

—423   Southwestern England and Channel Islands

Including Avon, Cornwall, Devon, Dorset, Somerset, Wiltshire

—424   Midlands of England

Including Gloucestershire, Hereford and Worcester, Shropshire, Staffordshire, Warwickshire, West Midlands Metropolitan County

For East Midlands, see —425

—425   East Midlands of England

Including Bedfordshire, Buckinghamshire, Derbyshire, Hertfordshire, Leicestershire, Lincolnshire, Nottinghamshire, Northamptonshire, Oxfordshire

---

*For a specific part of this jurisdiction, region, or feature, see the part and follow instructions under —4–9

—426   Eastern England   East Anglia

  Including Cambridgeshire, Essex, Norfolk, Suffolk

  Class here *The Fens

  Class London boroughs created from Essex in —421

—427   Northwestern England and Isle of Man

  Including Cheshire, Cumbria, Greater Manchester Metropolitan County, Lancashire, Merseyside Metropolitan County, Lake District

  Class here comprehensive works on northern England

   For northeastern England, see —428

—428   Northeastern England

  Including Cleveland, Durham, Humberside, North Yorkshire, Northumberland, Tyne and Wear Metropolitan County, South Yorkshire Metropolitan County, West Yorkshire Metropolitan County

  Class here the *Pennines

—429   Wales

—43   Central Europe   Germany

  Including former German Democratic Republic (East Germany)

  Class here Federal Republic of Germany, *Holy Roman Empire

   For Switzerland, see —494

  (Option: Class here ancient Germanic regions; prefer —363)

—[431–432]   Northeastern Germany, and Saxony and Thuringia

  Numbers discontinued; class in —43

—436   Austria and Liechtenstein

—436 4   Liechtenstein

  Subdivisions may not be added

—437   Czech Republic and Slovakia

  Class here Czechoslovakia

—437 1   Czech Republic

  Class here Bohemia

   For Moravia, see —4372

—437 2   Moravia

---

*For a specific part of this jurisdiction, region, or feature, see the part and follow instructions under —4–9

—437 3	Slovakia
—438	Poland
—439	Hungary
—44	**France and Monaco**

Including Corsica

> *For a specific overseas department of France, see the department, e.g., Martinique —7298*

(Option: Class here ancient Celtic regions, Gaul, Corsica; prefer —364 for ancient Celtic regions, Gaul, —37 for ancient Corsica)

—449	Monaco

Subdivisions may not be added

—45	**Italian Peninsula and adjacent islands** **Italy**

Including Sicily, Sardinia

Class here Apennines

(Option: Class here ancient Italian Peninsula and adjacent islands, Roman Empire; prefer —37)

—454	San Marino

Subdivisions may not be added

—456	Vatican City

Subdivisions may not be added

—458	Malta

Subdivisions may not be added

—46	**Iberian Peninsula and adjacent islands** **Spain**

Including Balearic Islands; *Pyrenees Mountains

> *For Canary Islands, see —64*

(Option: Class here ancient Iberian Peninsula and adjacent islands; prefer —366)

—467	Andorra

Subdivisions may not be added

—468	Gibraltar

Subdivisions may not be added

---

*For a specific part of this jurisdiction, region, or feature, see the part and follow instructions under —4–9

—469   Portugal

         Including Madeira, Azores

—47   **Eastern Europe   Russia**

         Class here Commonwealth of Independent States, former Union of Soviet Socialist Republics (Soviet Union)

         For Balkan Peninsula, see —496; for Siberia (Asiatic Russia), see —57; for Commonwealth of Independent States in Asia, see —58; for Franz Josef Land, Novaya Zemlya, see —98

—475   Caucasus

         Including Caucasus area of Russia

         Class here *Caspian Sea

         (Option: Class here ancient Caucasus; prefer —39)

\>   —475 4–475 8   Transcaucasus

         Class comprehensive works in —475

—475 4   Azerbaijan

            Class comprehensive works on Azerbaijan region in —55

            (Option: Class here ancient Albania; prefer —39)

—475 6   Armenia

            Class comprehensive works on Armenia region in —566

—475 8   Georgia

            (Option: Class here ancient Colchis, Iberia; prefer —39)

—476   Moldova

         Class comprehensive works on Moldavia in —498

—477   Ukraine

         Class here *Black Sea area of Commonwealth of Independent States

         (Option: Class here ancient Black Sea region, Sarmatia; prefer —39)

—478   Belarus

         Variant name: Belorussia, Byelarus

—479   Lithuania, Latvia, Estonia

         Class here Baltic States

---

*For a specific part of this jurisdiction, region, or feature, see the part and follow instructions under —4–9

—479 3	Lithuania
—479 6	Latvia
—479 8	Estonia

       Class here Livonia

        For Latvia, see —4796

—48   **Scandinavia**

       Class here northern Europe

        For northwestern islands, see —491

—481   Norway

        *For divisions of Norway, see —482–484; for Jan Mayen Island,
Svalbard, see —98*

\>   **—482–484 Divisions of Norway**

       Class comprehensive works in —481

—482   Southeastern Norway (Østlandet)

       Including Oslo

       Aust-Agder, Vest-Agder counties (fylker) relocated to —483

—483   Southwestern Norway (Sørlandet and Vestlandet)

       Including Aust-Agder, Vest-Agder counties (fylker) [*formerly* —482]

—484   Central and northern Norway (Trøndelag and Nord-Norge)

—485   Sweden

        For divisions of Sweden, see —486–488

\>   **—486–488 Divisions of Sweden**

       Class comprehensive works in —485

—486   Southern Sweden (Götaland)

—487   Central Sweden (Svealand)

       Including Stockholm

—488   Northern Sweden (Norrland)

—489   Denmark and Finland

—489 7   Finland

—49	**Other parts of Europe**
—491	Northwestern islands
—491 2	Iceland
—491 5	Faeroes
—492	Netherlands (Holland)

Class here comprehensive works on Low Countries, on Benelux countries

> *For southern Low Countries, see —493; for Netherlands Antilles, see —7298*

—493	Southern Low Countries	Belgium
—493 5	Luxembourg	
—494	Switzerland	

Including *Alps

—495	Greece

Including Aegean Islands, Crete [*both formerly* —499]; comprehensive works on Macedonia region, Thrace

> *For Turkish Thrace, see —4961; for country of Macedonia, see —4976; for Bulgarian Thrace, Macedonia in Bulgaria, see —499*

(Option: Class here ancient Greece, Aegean Islands, Crete, Thrace; prefer —38 for ancient Greece, —39 for ancient Aegean Islands, Crete, Thrace)

—496	*Balkan Peninsula

Class here *Danube River

> *See also —56 for Ottoman Empire*

(Option: Class here ancient southeastern Europe; prefer —39)

—496 1	Turkey in Europe (Turkish Thrace)

Including Edirne (Adrianople), İstanbul, Kırklareli, Tekirdağ provinces (illeri); European portion of Çanakkale Province (İli)

> *For Asian portion of İstanbul Province, see —563*

—496 5	Albania
—497	Yugoslavia, Croatia, Slovenia, Bosnia and Hercegovina, Macedonia

Class here Yugoslavia (1918–1991)

Class Yugoslavia (1991–   ) in —4971

(Option: Class here ancient Illyria; prefer —39)

---

*For a specific part of this jurisdiction, region, or feature, see the part and follow instructions under —4–9

—497 1   Serbia

> Class here Yugoslavia (1991–   )
>
> *For Montenegro, see —49745*

—497 2   Croatia

> (Option: Class here ancient Istria; prefer —37)

—497 3   Slovenia

—497 4   Bosnia and Hercegovina, Montenegro

—497 42   Bosnia and Hercegovina

—497 45   Montenegro

—497 6   Macedonia

> Class comprehensive works on Macedonia region in —495

—[497 7]   Bulgaria

> Relocated to —499

—498   Romania

—499   Bulgaria [*formerly* —4977]

> Aegean Islands and Crete relocated to —495
>
> (Option: Class here ancient Moesia; prefer —39)

—5 Asia Orient Far East

> Class here Eurasia
>
> *For Europe, see —4*

SUMMARY

—51	China and adjacent areas
—52	Japan
—53	Arabian Peninsula and adjacent areas
—54	South Asia India
—55	Iran
—56	Middle East (Near East)
—57	Siberia (Asiatic Russia)
—58	Central Asia
—59	Southeast Asia

—51   China and adjacent areas

> Including Tibet
>
> Class here People's Republic of China
>
> (Option: Class here ancient China; prefer —31)

—512	Taiwan, Hong Kong, Macao
	Subdivisions may not be added
—512 4	Taiwan (Formosa) and adjacent islands
	Republic of China (Nationalist China)
	Subdivisions may not be added
—512 5	Hong Kong
	British crown colony
—512 6	Macao
	Overseas territory of Portugal
—517	Outer Mongolia (Mongolian People's Republic)
	Including *Gobi Desert
	Subdivisions may not be added
—519	Korea
—519 3	North Korea (People's Democratic Republic of Korea)
—519 5	South Korea (Republic of Korea)
—52	**Japan**
—53	**Arabian Peninsula and adjacent areas**
	Including Gaza Strip, Sinai Peninsula
	(Option: Class here ancient Arabia, Sinai Peninsula; prefer —39)
—533	Yemen
	Class here Republic of Yemen
—533 2	Northern Yemen
	Class here Yemen Arab Republic
—533 5	Southern Yemen
	Class here Federation of South Arabia, People's Democratic Republic of Yemen
—535	Oman and United Arab Emirates
—535 3	Oman
—535 7	United Arab Emirates
—536	Persian Gulf States
	For Oman and United Arab Emirates, see —535

*For a specific part of this jurisdiction, region, or feature, see the part and follow instructions under —4–9

—536 3	Qatar	
—536 5	Bahrain	
—536 7	Kuwait	
—538	Saudi Arabia	

—54   **South Asia   India**

> *For southeast Asia, see —59*
>
> (Option: Class here ancient India; prefer —34)

—549   Other jurisdictions

> Class here Pakistan (West and East, 1947–1971)

—549 1   Pakistan

> Former name: West Pakistan
>
> Class here *Indus River

—549 2   Bangladesh

> Former names: East Bengal, East Pakistan
>
> Class here comprehensive works on Brahmaputra River
>
> Class Brahmaputra River in India in —54

—549 3   Sri Lanka

> Former name: Ceylon

—549 5   Maldives

—549 6   Nepal

> Class here *Himalaya Mountains

—549 8   Bhutan

—55   **Iran**

> Including Azerbaijan region
>
> *For country of Azerbaijan, see —4754*
>
> (Option: Class here ancient Iranian Plateau; prefer —35)

—56   ***Middle East (Near East)***

> Class here *Ottoman Empire
>
> (Option: Class here ancient Middle East; prefer —39)

---

*For a specific part of this jurisdiction, region, or feature, see the part and follow instructions under —4–9

—561   Turkey

Class here Asia Minor

For divisions of Turkey, see —562–566

(Option: Class here ancient Asia Minor; prefer —39)

>   —562–566 Divisions of Turkey

Class comprehensive works in —561

For Turkey in Europe, see —4961

—562   Western Turkey

Including Afyon, Aydın, Balıkesir, Burdur, Çanakkale, Denizli, İzmir, Kütahya, Manisa, Muğla, Uşak provinces (illeri)

For European portion of Çanakkale Province, see —4961

—563   North central Turkey

Including Amasya, Ankara, Bilecik, Bolu, Bursa, Çankırı, Çorum, Eskişehir, Kastamonu, Kocaeli, Sakarya, Samsun, Sinop, Yozgat, Zonguldak provinces (illeri); Asian portion of İstanbul Province (İli)

—564   South central Turkey

Including Adana, Antalya, Gaziantep, Hatay, İçel, Isparta, Kayseri, Kırşehir, Konya, Nevşehir, Niğde provinces (illeri)

—[564 5]   Cyprus

Relocated to —5693

—565   East central Turkey

Including Adıyaman, Giresun, Gümüşhane, Kahraman Maraş, Malatya, Ordu, Şanlıurfa, Sivas, Tokat, Trabzon provinces (illeri)

—566   Eastern Turkey

Including Ağrı, Artvin, Bingöl, Bitlis, Diyarbakır, Elazığ, Erzincan, Erzurum, Hakkâri, Kars, Mardin, Muş, Rize, Siirt, Tunceli, Van provinces (illeri); comprehensive works on Armenia, on Kurdistan

For country of Armenia, see —4756; for Iranian Kurdistan, see —55; for Iraqi Kurdistan, see —567

(Option: Class here ancient Armenia; prefer —39)

—567   Iraq

Class here Mesopotamia

(Option: Class here ancient Mesopotamia, Arabia Deserta; prefer —35 for ancient Mesopotamia, —39 for Arabia Deserta)

—569   Syria, Lebanon, Cyprus, Israel, Jordan

—569 1   Syria

                (Option: Class here ancient Syria; prefer —39)

—569 2   Lebanon

                (Option: Class here ancient Phoenicia; prefer —39)

—569 3   Cyprus [*formerly* —5645]

                (Option: Class here ancient Cyprus; prefer —39)

—569 4   Palestine   Israel

                Palestine: area covering Israel, Gaza Strip, and West Bank of Jordan River

                Including *Jordan River, *Dead Sea

                    For Gaza Strip, see —53; for West Bank, see —5695

                (Option: Class here ancient Palestine, Israel; prefer —33)

—569 5   West Bank and Jordan

                (Option: Class here Jordanian part of ancient Palestine, ancient Samaria; prefer —33)

—57   **Siberia (Asiatic Russia)**

—58   **Central Asia**

                (Option: Class here ancient central Asia; prefer —39)

—581   Afghanistan

—584   Turkestan

                Class Sinkiang in —51

                    For Turkmenistan, see —585; for Tajikistan, see —586; for Uzbekistan, see —587

—584 3   Kyrgyzstan

—584 5   Kazakhstan

—585   Turkmenistan

—586   Tajikistan

—587   Uzbekistan

---

*For a specific part of this jurisdiction, region, or feature, see the part and follow instructions under —4–9

—59	**Southeast Asia**

Class here *Indochina (southeast peninsula of Asia)

Class works about "Indochina" when used to equate with French Indochina in —597

—591	Myanmar (Burma)
—593	Thailand
—594	Laos
—595	Commonwealth of Nations territories Malaysia

Including Malay Peninsula

> *For Myanmar (Burma), see —591; for Thailand, see —593*

—595 5	Brunei
—595 7	Singapore
—596	Cambodia (Khmer Republic, Kampuchea)
—597	Vietnam

Class here *French Indochina (Indochina)

Class works about "Indochina" when used to equate with the southeast peninsula of Asia in —59

—598	Indonesia

Including Borneo

Class here Malay Archipelago

> *For northern Borneo, see —595; for Philippines, see —599; for Irian Jaya, see —951*

—599	Philippines
—6	**Africa**

SUMMARY

—61	**Tunisia and Libya**
—62	**Egypt and Sudan**
—63	**Ethiopia and Eritrea**
—64	**Northwest African coast and offshore islands** **Morocco**
—65	**Algeria**
—66	**West Africa and offshore islands**
—67	**Central Africa and offshore islands**
—68	**Southern Africa** **Republic of South Africa**
—69	**South Indian Ocean islands**

*For a specific part of this jurisdiction, region, or feature, see the part and follow instructions under —4–9

—61   **Tunisia and Libya**

       Class here *Barbary States, *North Africa

       (Option: Class here ancient North Africa; prefer —39)

—611   Tunisia

—612   Libya

—62   **Egypt and Sudan**

       Class here *Nile River

         For Sinai, see —53

       (Option: Class here ancient Egypt; prefer —32)

—624   Sudan

         For provinces of Sudan, see —625–629

>   **—625–629**   Provinces of Sudan

       Class comprehensive works in —624

—625   Eastern and Northern regions of Sudan

         (Option: Class here ancient Cush, Ethiopia, Nubia; prefer —39)

—626   Khartoum province and Central region of Sudan

         Including *Blue Nile River

—627   Darfur region of Sudan

—628   Kordofan region of Sudan

—629   Southern regions of Sudan

         Including Baḥr al Ghazāl, Buḥayrāh, Equatoria, Upper Nile regions; *White Nile River

—63   **Ethiopia and Eritrea**

       Class here Horn of Africa

         For Djibouti and Somalia, see —677

—635   Eritrea

—64   **Northwest African coast and offshore islands**   **Morocco**

       Including Canary Islands

       (Option: Class here Moroccan part of ancient North Africa; prefer —39)

---

*For a specific part of this jurisdiction, region, or feature, see the part and follow instructions under —4–9

—648	Western Sahara
—65	**Algeria**

(Option: Class here Algerian part of ancient North Africa; prefer —39)

—66	**West Africa and offshore islands**

Class here *Sahara Desert, *Sahel

—661	Mauritania
—662	Mali, Burkina Faso, Niger
—662 3	Mali
—662 5	Burkina Faso

Former name: Upper Volta

—662 6	Niger
—663	Senegal

Class here Senegambia

For Gambia, see —6651

—664	Sierra Leone
—665	Gambia, Guinea, Guinea-Bissau, Cape Verde

Class here *Upper Guinea area

—665 1	Gambia
—665 2	Guinea
—665 7	Guinea-Bissau
—665 8	Cape Verde

Class here Cape Verde Islands

—666	Liberia and Côte d'Ivoire
—666 2	Liberia
—666 8	Côte d'Ivoire (Ivory Coast)
—667	Ghana
—668	Togo and Benin
—668 1	Togo
—668 3	Benin

Former name: Dahomey

*For a specific part of this jurisdiction, region, or feature, see the part and follow instructions under —4–9

—669	Nigeria
—67	**Central Africa and offshore islands**

Class here *Black Africa, *Sub-Saharan Africa (Africa south of the Sahara)

—671	Cameroon, Sao Tome and Principe, Equatorial Guinea

Class here Islands of Gulf of Guinea, *Lower Guinea area

—671 1	Cameroon
—671 5	Sao Tome and Principe
—671 8	Equatorial Guinea
—672	Gabon and Republic of the Congo
—672 1	Gabon
—672 4	Republic of the Congo

See also —6751 for Democratic Republic of the Congo (Zaire)

—673	Angola
—674	Central African Republic and Chad
—674 1	Central African Republic
—674 3	Chad
—675	Zaire, Rwanda, Burundi
—675 1	Zaire

Former names: Democratic Republic of the Congo, Belgian Congo

Class here *Congo (Zaire) River

See also —6724 for Republic of the Congo

—675 7	Rwanda and Burundi

Class here former Ruanda-Urundi

—675 71	Rwanda
—675 72	Burundi
—676	Uganda and Kenya

Class here *East Africa, *Great Rift Valley

—676 1	Uganda
—676 2	Kenya

---

*For a specific part of this jurisdiction, region, or feature, see the part and follow instructions under —4–9

—677	Djibouti and Somalia
	Class here Somaliland
—677 1	Djibouti
—677 3	Somalia
—678	Tanzania
	Including Tanganyika
—679	Mozambique
—68	**Southern Africa** **Republic of South Africa**

>	—682–687 Republic of South Africa
	Class comprehensive works in —68
—682	Transvaal
—684	Natal
—685	Orange Free State
—687	Cape of Good Hope
—688	Namibia, Botswana, Lesotho, Swaziland
—688 1	Namibia
—688 3	Botswana
—688 5	Lesotho
—688 7	Swaziland
—689	Zimbabwe, Zambia, Malawi
—689 1	Zimbabwe
	Former name: Zimbabwe Rhodesia
—689 4	Zambia
—689 7	Malawi
—69	**South Indian Ocean islands**
	Including Réunion
—691	Madagascar
—694	Comoros (Federal and Islamic Republic of the Comoros)
	Subdivisions may not be added

—696   Seychelles

—698   Mauritius

       Subdivisions may not be added

—7   North America

Class Western Hemisphere in —181

See Manual at T2—7 vs. T2—181

SUMMARY

—71	Canada
—72	Middle America Mexico
—73	United States
—74	Northeastern United States (New England and Middle Atlantic states)
—75	Southeastern United States (South Atlantic states)
—76	South central United States Gulf Coast states
—77	North central United States Lake states
—78	Western United States
—79	Great Basin and Pacific Slope region of United States Pacific Coast states

—71   Canada

See Manual at T2—73 vs. T2—71

—711   British Columbia

       Class here *Rocky Mountains in Canada

—712   Prairie Provinces

       Class here *western Canada

—712 3   Alberta

—712 4   Saskatchewan

—712 7   Manitoba

—713   Ontario

       Class here *eastern Canada, Great Lakes in Canada

—714   Quebec

       Class here *Canadian Shield; *Saint Lawrence River

—715   Atlantic Provinces   Maritime Provinces

       Including New Brunswick

          For Nova Scotia, see —716; for Prince Edward Island, see —717; for Newfoundland and Labrador, see —718

---

*For a specific part of this jurisdiction, region, or feature, see the part and follow instructions under —4–9

—716	Nova Scotia
—717	Prince Edward Island
—718	Newfoundland and Labrador, Saint-Pierre and Miquelon
—719	Northern territories

> Including Yukon Territory; Northwest Territories, consisting of Baffin, Fort Smith, Inuvik, Keewatin, Kitikmeot regions
>
> Class here Canadian Arctic

—72	**Middle America Mexico**
—728	Central America
—728 1	Guatemala
—728 2	Belize
—728 3	Honduras
—728 4	El Salvador
—728 5	Nicaragua
—728 6	Costa Rica
—728 7	Panama

> Including Panama Canal [*formerly* —164]

—729	West Indies (Antilles) and Bermuda

> Class here *Caribbean Area

>	—729 1–729 5 Greater Antilles

> Class comprehensive works in —729

—729 1	Cuba
—729 2	Jamaica and Cayman Islands
—729 3	Dominican Republic

> Class here comprehensive works on Hispaniola
>
> *For Haiti, see* —7294

—729 4	Haiti
—729 5	Puerto Rico
—729 6	Bahama Islands

*For a specific part of this jurisdiction, region, or feature, see the part and follow instructions under —4–9

> —729 7–729 8 Lesser Antilles (Caribbees)

Class comprehensive works in —729

—729 7 Leeward Islands

Including Guadeloupe, Montserrat, Saba, Saint Eustatius, Saint Martin, Virgin Islands

For Dominica, see —729841

—729 73 Anguilla and Saint Kitts-Nevis

—729 74 Antigua and Barbuda

—729 8 Windward and other southern islands

Including Aruba, Bonaire, Curaçao, Martinique

For Nueva Esparta, Venezuela, see —87

—729 81 Barbados

—729 83 Trinidad and Tobago

—729 84 Windward Islands

—729 841 Dominica

—729 843 Saint Lucia

—729 844 Saint Vincent and the Grenadines

For Carriacou, see —729845

—729 845 Grenada and Carriacou

—729 9 Bermuda

—73 United States

For specific states, see —74–79

See Manual at T2—73 vs. T2—71

> **—74–79 Specific states of United States**

Class comprehensive works in —73

For Hawaii, see —969

—74 Northeastern United States (New England and Middle Atlantic states)

Class here United States east of Allegheny Mountains, east of Mississippi River; *Appalachian Mountains; *Connecticut River

For southeastern United States, see —75; for south central United States, see —76; for north central United States, see —77

---

*For a specific part of this jurisdiction, region, or feature, see the part and follow instructions under —4–9

>	—741–746 New England

Class comprehensive works in —74

—741	Maine
—742	New Hampshire
—743	Vermont
—744	Massachusetts
—745	Rhode Island
—746	Connecticut

>	—747–749 Middle Atlantic states

Class comprehensive works in —74

—747	New York

Including *Lake Ontario

—748	Pennsylvania
—749	New Jersey
—75	**Southeastern United States (South Atlantic states)**

Class here southern states, *Piedmont, *Atlantic Coastal Plain

For south central United States, see —76

—751	Delaware
—752	Maryland

Class here *Potomac River

—753	District of Columbia (Washington)
—754	West Virginia
—755	Virginia

Class here *Blue Ridge

—756	North Carolina
—757	South Carolina
—758	Georgia
—759	Florida

*For a specific part of this jurisdiction, region, or feature, see the part and follow instructions under —4–9

—76   **South central United States   Gulf Coast states**

>   Class here Old Southwest

>   —761–764   Gulf Coast states

          Class comprehensive works in —76

          For Florida, see —759

—761   Alabama

—762   Mississippi

—763   Louisiana

—764   Texas

          Including *Rio Grande

—766   Oklahoma

—767   Arkansas

—768   Tennessee

          Class here *Tennessee River and Valley

—769   Kentucky

—77   **North central United States   Lake states**

          Class here *Middle West, *Mississippi River and Valley, *Ohio River and Valley, *Great Lakes

---

>   —771–776   Lake states

          Class comprehensive works in —77

          For New York, see —747; for Pennsylvania, see —748

—771   Ohio

          Including *Lake Erie

—772   Indiana

—773   Illinois

—774   Michigan

          Including *Lake Superior

          Class here Lakes *Huron, *Michigan

---

*For a specific part of this jurisdiction, region, or feature, see the part and follow instructions under —4–9

—775	Wisconsin
—776	Minnesota
—777	Iowa
—778	Missouri
—78	**Western United States**

Class here the West; *Great Plains; *Rocky Mountains; *Missouri River

> For Great Basin and Pacific Slope region, see —79

—781	Kansas
—782	Nebraska
—783	South Dakota
—784	North Dakota

>	—786–789 Rocky Mountain states

Class comprehensive works in —78

> For Idaho, see —796

—786	Montana
—787	Wyoming
—788	Colorado
—789	New Mexico
—79	**Great Basin and Pacific Slope region of United States Pacific Coast states**

Class here new Southwest

—791	Arizona

Including *Colorado River

—792	Utah
—793	Nevada
—794	California
—795	Oregon

Class here Pacific Northwest; *Cascade and *Coast Ranges

> For British Columbia, see —711; for Idaho, see —796; for Washington, see —797

---

*For a specific part of this jurisdiction, region, or feature, see the part and follow instructions under —4–9

—796	Idaho
—797	Washington
—798	Alaska

—8   South America

Class here Latin America, Spanish America; the *Andes

For Middle America, see —72

—81   Brazil

Including *Amazon River

—82   Argentina

—83   Chile

—84   Bolivia

—85   Peru

—86   Colombia and Ecuador

—861	Colombia
—866	Ecuador

—87   Venezuela

—88   Guiana

—881	Guyana
	Former name: British Guiana
—882	French Guiana (Guyane)
	Overseas department of France
—883	Surinam (Suriname)
	Former name: Dutch Guiana

—89   Paraguay and Uruguay

—892	Paraguay
—895	• Uruguay

—9   Other parts of world and extraterrestrial worlds   Pacific Ocean islands

---

*For a specific part of this jurisdiction, region, or feature, see the part and follow instructions under —4–9

> —93–96 *Pacific Ocean islands

Class comprehensive works in —9

—93 New Zealand

—[931] Specific islands

Number and its subdivisions discontinued; class in —93

—94 Australia

—941 Western Australia

—942 Central Australia

—942 3 South Australia

—942 9 Northern Territory

Class here northern Australia

For Western Australia, see —941; for Queensland, see —943

—943 Queensland

Class here Great Barrier Reef

—944 New South Wales

Class here *Murray River

—945 Victoria

—946 Tasmania

—947 Australian Capital Territory

—95 Melanesia   New Guinea

Class here Oceania

Class Polynesia, Micronesia in —96

> —951–957 New Guinea

Class comprehensive works in —95

—951 Irian Jaya

—953 Papua New Guinea   New Guinea region

For Papuan region, see —954; for Highlands region, see —956; for Momase region, see —957; for Bismarck Archipelago, see —958; for North Solomons Province, see —9592

*For a specific part of this jurisdiction, region, or feature, see the part and follow instructions under —4–9

—954   Papuan region

         Including Central, Gulf, Milne Bay, Northern (Oro), Western (Fly River) provinces; National Capital District

—956   Highlands region

         Including Eastern Highlands, Enga, Simbu (Chimbu), Southern Highlands, Western Highlands provinces

—957   Momase (Northern coastal) region

         Including East Sepik, Madang, Morobe, West Sepik (Sandaun) provinces

—958   Bismarck Archipelago

         Part of Papua New Guinea

         Including East New Britain, Manus, New Ireland, West New Britain provinces

—959   Other parts of Melanesia

—959 2   North Solomons Province

         Part of Papua New Guinea

—959 3   Solomon Islands

         Independent nation

         Former name: British Solomon Islands

—959 5   Vanuatu

         Former name: New Hebrides

—959 7   New Caledonia

—96   **Other parts of Pacific Ocean   Polynesia**

—961   Southwest central Pacific Ocean islands, and isolated islands of southeast Pacific Ocean

         Including Easter, Pitcairn, Tokelau Islands; comprehensive works on Samoa

         Class Western Samoa in —9614

—961 1   Fiji

—961 2   Tonga (Friendly Islands)

—961 4   Western Samoa

—961 6   Wallis and Futuna Islands

—962	South central Pacific Ocean islands
	Including Cook Islands, Tahiti
	Class here French Polynesia
	For Marquesas, Tuamotu Islands, see —963
—963	Southeast central Pacific Ocean islands
	Including Marquesas, Tuamotu Islands
	For isolated islands of southeast Pacific Ocean, see —961
—964	Line Islands (Equatorial Islands)
	For Palmyra Island, see —969
—965	*West central Pacific Ocean islands (Micronesia) *Trust Territory of the Pacific Islands
—966	Federated States of Micronesia and Republic of Palau
	Class here Caroline Islands
—967	Mariana Islands
	Class here Commonwealth of the Northern Mariana Islands
—968	Islands of eastern Micronesia
	Including Marshall Islands
—968 1	Kiribati
	For Line Islands, see —964
—968 2	Tuvalu
—968 5	Nauru (Pleasant Island)
—969	North central Pacific Ocean islands Hawaii
	Including Palmyra Island
—97	***Atlantic Ocean islands**
	Including Bouvet Island, Falkland Islands, Saint Helena
—98	***Arctic islands and Antarctica**
	Including Franz Josef Land, Jan Mayen Island, Novaya Zemlya, Severnaya Zemlya, Spitsbergen Island, Svalbard
—982	Greenland

*For a specific part of this jurisdiction, region, or feature, see the part and follow instructions under —4–9

—99   **Extraterrestrial worlds**

Worlds other than earth

Class space in —19

See Manual at T2—99 vs. T2—19

Table 3. Subdivisions for Individual Literatures, for Specific Literary Forms

Notation from Table 3 is never used alone, but may be used as required by add notes under subdivisions of individual literatures in 810–890. It is never used for individual literatures that lack instructions to add from Table 3; the number for works by or about such literatures ends with the language notation, e.g., Inuit poetry 897

Procedures for building numbers for works by or about more than one author, limited to literatures of specific languages, and for works by individual authors:

1.   Look in the schedule 810–890 to find the base number for the language. The base number is identified in an add note, e.g., at 820.1–828 ("Add to base number 82"). If there is a specific literary form, go to step 2; if not, skip to step 4

2.   In Table 3 find the subdivision for the literary form, e.g., poetry —1. Add this to the base number, e.g., English poetry 821, Portuguese poetry 869.1. If the work is by an individual author, or deals with or falls within a limited time period, the class number is complete. For other works, go to step 3

3.   Go to the subdivisions under the particular form in Table 3, e.g., under —1 for poetry go to —1001–1009. If the work deals with specific kinds of poetry, drama, fiction, speeches, or miscellaneous writings, check the add note; if further adding is not permitted, the number is complete. If adding is permitted, follow the add instructions, which will lead to the table under —1–8. For example, the number for a collection of English poetry is 821.008. Also follow the add instructions leading to the add table under —1–8 for works *not* dealing with specific kinds of poetry, drama, fiction, speeches, or miscellaneous writings

4.   If the work is not limited to a specific literary form, consult —01–09 in Table 3, and follow the instructions at the number selected. For example, the number for history and criticism of Swedish literature is 839.709
    (Option: Where two or more countries share the same language, either [1] use initial letters to distinguish the separate countries, or [2] for English-language works, use the special number designated for literatures of those countries that are not preferred, e.g., 20th-century drama in English by New Zealand authors NZ822 or 828.99, collections of 20th-century Australian writings in English A820.8 or 828.99. Full instructions appear under 810, 819, 820.1–828, 828.99)

See Manual at Table 3; also at 800

SUMMARY

—01–09   [Standard subdivisions; collections; history, description, critical appraisal]
—1   Poetry
—2   Drama
—3   Fiction
—4   Essays
—5   Speeches
—6   Letters
—7   Humor and satire
—8   Miscellaneous writings

—01–07   Standard subdivisions

Standard subdivisions are used for general works consisting equally of literary texts and history, description, critical appraisal, e.g., a serial consisting equally of literary texts and history, description, critical appraisal of a variety of literature in English 820.5. Works limited to specific topics are classed in —08

Class collections of literary texts in —08; class history, description, critical appraisal in —09

—08   Collections of literary texts in more than one form

Works by more than one author

Works limited to a specific topic and consisting equally of literary texts and history, description, critical appraisal of a specific literature are classed here, e.g., texts and criticism of English-language literary works about war 820.8

Class history, description, critical appraisal of a specific literature in —09; class collections by individual authors in —1–8

—09   History, description, critical appraisal of more than one form

Works by more than one author

Class here collected biography

—090 001–090 009   Standard subdivisions

> ## —1–8 Specific forms

Unless other instructions are given, observe the following table of preference for works combining two or more literary forms, e.g., poetic drama —2 (*not* —1):

Drama	—2
Poetry	—1
Class epigrams in verse in —8	
Fiction	—3
Essays	—4
Speeches	—5
Letters	—6
Miscellaneous writings	—8
Humor and satire	—7

When told to add as instructed under —1–8, add as follows:

1–7   Standard subdivisions

Standard subdivisions are used for general works consisting equally of literary texts and history, description, critical appraisal, e.g., a serial consisting equally of literary texts and history, description, critical appraisal of poetry in English 821.005. Works limited to specific topics are classed in 8

Class collections of literary texts in 8; class history, description, critical appraisal in 9

8   Collections of literary texts

General works consisting equally of literary texts and history, description, critical appraisal are classed in —1–7, in the number for the specific form. Works consisting equally of literary texts and history, description, critical appraisal are classed here if limited to specific topics

8001–8007   Standard subdivisions

[8008]   History and description with respect to kinds of persons
           Do not use; class in 8

[8009]   Historical, geographic, persons treatment
           Do not use; class in 9

9   History, description, critical appraisal

Class here collected biography

Follow the instructions under 8 for works consisting equally of literary texts and history, description, critical appraisal

901–907   Standard subdivisions

[908–909]   History and description with respect to kinds of persons; historical, geographic, persons treatment
           Do not use; class in 9

Class comprehensive works on two or more forms in the base number for the individual literature, plus notation 01–09 from Table 3 if applicable, adding 0 when required to make a three-figure number, e.g., comprehensive works on English poetry and fiction 820; however, class comprehensive works on prose literature in —8

—1   Poetry

Including works by and about individual authors

See Manual at T3—2 vs. T3—1

—100 1–100 9   Standard subdivisions; collections; history, description, critical appraisal

Works by and about more than one author

Add to —100 as instructed under —1–8, e.g., collections of poetry —1008; however, do not add for poetry of specific genres or periods, e.g., collections of epic poetry, of lyric poetry, of 20th century poetry —1 (*not* —1008)

—2   Drama

Including works by and about individual authors

See Manual at T3—2 vs. T3—1

—200 1–200 9   Standard subdivisions; collections; history, description, critical appraisal

Works by and about more than one author

Add to —200 as instructed under —1–8, e.g., collections of drama —2008; however, do not add for drama for mass media (radio, television, motion pictures), drama of restricted scope (including monologues), drama of specific genres or periods, e.g., collections of radio plays, of one-act plays, of historical drama, of religious and morality plays, of farces, of 20th century drama —2 (*not* —2008)

—3   Fiction

Including works by and about individual authors

Class here novels, novelettes

Class graphic novels (cartoon or comic strip novels) in 741.5

—300 1–300 9   Standard subdivisions; collections; history, description, critical appraisal

Works by and about more than one author

Add to —300 as instructed under —1–8, e.g., collections of fiction —3008; however, do not add for short stories or for fiction of specific genres or periods, e.g., collections of historical and period fiction, of romances and love stories, of science fiction, of 20th century fiction —3 (*not* —3008)

—4   Essays

Including works by and about individual authors

—400 1–400 9   Standard subdivisions; collections; history, description, critical appraisal

> Works by and about more than one author

> Add to —400 as instructed under —1–8, e.g., collections of essays —4008; however, do not add for essays of specific periods, e.g., collections of 20th century essays —4 (*not* —4008)

—5   Speeches

> Including works by and about individual authors

—500 1–500 9   Standard subdivisions; collections; history, description, critical appraisal

> Works by and about more than one author

> Add to —500 as instructed under —1–8, e.g., collections of speeches —5008; however, do not add for speeches of specific kinds (e.g., after-dinner, platform, television speeches, speeches and toasts for specific occasions) or speeches of specific periods, e.g., collections of debates, of 20th century speeches —5 (*not* —5008)

—6   Letters

> Including works by and about individual authors

> *See Manual at T3—6*

—600 1–600 9   Standard subdivisions; collections; history, description, critical appraisal

> Works by and about more than one author

> Add to —600 as instructed under —1–8, e.g., collections of letters —6008; however, do not add for letters of specific periods, e.g., collections of 20th century letters —6 (*not* —6008)

—7   Humor and satire

> Limited to collections and criticism of works in two or more literary forms, including both verse and prose, and by and about more than one author

> Including collections of humor to be read for pleasure

> Class here parody

> Works by and about individual authors of satire and humor in more than one form relocated to —8; works by and about individual authors of satire and humor in a single form relocated to the form, e.g., satirical poetry —1

> Class textbooks and teaching collections showing the development of manifestations of comedy in literature of a specific form with the form, e.g., comedy as an aspect of drama —2008

> *See Manual at T1—02 vs. T3—7, T3—8*

—700 1–700 9   Standard subdivisions; collections; history, description, critical appraisal

> Add to —700 as instructed under —1–8, e.g., collections of satire and humor —7008; however, do not add for satire and humor of specific periods, e.g., collections of 20th century satire and humor —7 (*not* —7008)

—8   Miscellaneous writings

> Including anecdotes, diaries, epigrams, graffiti, jokes, journals, quotations, reminiscences, riddles that are jokes, prose literature in more than one form, works without identifiable form

> Including works by and about individual authors of satire and humor in more than one form [*formerly* —7], works by and about individual authors of miscellaneous writings, works by and about individual authors not limited to or chiefly identified with one specific form

> Class a specific identifiable form of literature with the form, e.g., essays —4

> *See Manual at T3—8; also at T1—02 vs. T3—7, T3—8*

—800 1–800 9   Standard subdivisions; collections; history, description, critical appraisal

> Works by and about more than one author

> Add to —800 as instructed under —1–8, e.g., critical appraisal of miscellaneous writings from more than one period —8009; however, do not add for miscellaneous writings of specific kinds or periods, e.g., collections of jokes, of reminiscences, of 20th century miscellaneous writings —8 (*not* —8008)

Table 4. Subdivisions of Individual Languages

The following notation is never used alone, but may be used as required by add notes under subdivisions of specific languages or with the base numbers for individual languages identified by * as explained under 420–490, e.g., Portuguese (base number 469) phonology (—1 in this table): 469.1. A point is inserted following the third digit of any number thus constructed that is longer than three digits. Notation from Table 1 is added to the notation in Table 4 when appropriate, e.g., —509 history of grammar, 469.509 history of Portuguese grammar

See Manual at 410

SUMMARY

—01–09	Standard subdivisions
—1	Writing systems, phonology, phonetics of the standard form of the language
—2	Etymology of the standard form of the language
—3	Dictionaries of the standard form of the language
—5	Grammar of the standard form of the language
—7	Historical and geographic variations, modern nongeographic variations
—8	Standard usage of the language (Prescriptive linguistics) Applied linguistics

—01   **Philosophy and theory**

Including content analysis, semantics, semiotics; lexicology, terminology

For history of word meanings, see —2; for dictionaries, see —3; for lexicography, see —3028; for discursive works on terminology intended to teach vocabulary, see —81. For terminology of a specific subject or discipline, see the subject or discipline, plus notation 01 from Table 1, e.g., terminology of accounting 657.01

—02   **Miscellany**

—03   **Encyclopedias and concordances**

Do not use for dictionaries of standard form of language; class in —3. Do not use for dictionaries of historical and geographic variations, of modern nongeographic variations in the language; class in —7

—05–08   **Standard subdivisions**

See Manual at 407.1, T1—071 vs. 401, 410.71, 418.0071, T4—80071

—09   **Historical, geographic, persons treatment**

Do not use for works that stress distinctive characteristics of historical and geographic variations from the standard form of the language; class in —7

> **—1–5   Description and analysis of the standard form of the language**

Class writing systems, phonology, etymology, dictionaries, grammar of historical and geographic variations, of modern nongeographic variations of the language in —7; class standard usage, prescriptive and applied linguistics in —8; class comprehensive works in the base number for the language (adding 0 when required to make a three-digit number), e.g., comprehensive works on phonology, etymology, dictionaries, grammar of standard French 440

See Manual at T4—1–5, T4—8 vs. T4—7

—1   Writing systems, phonology, phonetics of the standard form of the language

Including abbreviations, acronyms; alphabets, ideographs; braille; paleography (in narrow sense of study of ancient and medieval handwriting); punctuation; spelling

Class dictionaries of abbreviations and acronyms, specialized spelling and pronouncing dictionaries in —3; class paleography in the broad sense of all aspects of early writings in the base number for the language (adding 0 when required to make a three-digit number), e.g., Latin paleography 470; class paleography (in both broad and narrow senses) of historical and geographic variations, of modern nongeographic variations of the language in —7, e.g., paleography of postclassical Latin 477; class training in standard spelling and pronunciation in —81; class finger spelling and manual alphabets regardless of language in 419; class speech training for public speaking, debating, conversation in 808.5; class comprehensive works on phonology and morphology, on phonology and syntax, or on all three in —5

—2   Etymology of the standard form of the language

Including foreign elements

—3   Dictionaries of the standard form of the language

Including bilingual dictionaries; specialized dictionaries, e.g., dictionaries of abbreviations, picture dictionaries, thesauri (synonym dictionaries)

A bilingual dictionary with entry words in only one language is classed with that language, e.g., an English-French dictionary 423. A bilingual dictionary with entry words in both languages is classed with the language in which it will be the more useful; for example, most libraries in English-speaking regions will find English-French, French-English dictionaries most useful classed with French in 443, Chinese-French, French-Chinese dictionaries with Chinese in 495.1. If classification with either language is equally useful, give priority to the language coming later in the sequence 420–490, e.g., French-German, German-French dictionaries 443

Class etymological dictionaries in —203; class spellers in —81

See Manual at T4—3; also at T4—3 vs. T4—81

—302 8   Techniques, procedures, apparatus, equipment, materials

              Class here lexicography

—5   Grammar of the standard form of the language

Descriptive study of morphology and syntax

Including generative grammar

Class here parts of speech; comprehensive works on phonology and morphology, on phonology and syntax, or on all three

Class derivational etymology in —2

For phonology, see —1; for prescriptive grammar, including inflectional schemata designed for use as aids in learning languages, see —8

—7   Historical and geographic variations, modern nongeographic variations

Including early forms; dialects, pidgins, creoles; slang

Use notation 7 only for works that stress differences among the forms of a language

Topics classed in —1–5 and —8 when applied to standard forms of the language are classed here when applied to historical and geographic variations, to modern nongeographic variations, e.g., the distinctive grammatical characteristics of a particular dialect

See Manual at T4—7; also at T4—1–5, T4—8 vs. T4—7

—8   Standard usage of the language (Prescriptive linguistics)   Applied linguistics

General, formal, informal usage

Including standard usage in composition; translation and interpretation to and from other languages

When classing translation and interpretation, use the base number for the language being translated into, e.g., translation from French into English 428, translation from English into French 448

Class here works for persons learning a second language, works for native speakers who are learning the acceptable patterns of their own language

Class purely descriptive linguistics in —1–5; class prescriptive and applied linguistics applied to historical and geographic variation, to modern nongeographic variations of the language in —7

For dictionaries, see —3; for rhetoric, see 808

See Manual at T4—1–5, T4—8 vs. T4—7; also at 410

—800 1–800 9   Standard subdivisions

              See Manual at 407.1, T1—071 vs. 401, 410.71, 418.0071, T4—80071

—81   **Words**

Meaning, pronunciation, spelling

Including spellers

Class formal presentation of vocabulary in —82; class audio-lingual presentation of vocabulary in —83

> *See also —1 for nonprescriptive treatment of spelling and pronunciation, —3 for dictionaries*
>
> *See Manual at T4—3 vs. T4—81*

—82   **Structural approach to expression**

Formal (traditional) presentation of grammar, vocabulary, reading selections

Class here verb tables and inflectional schemata designed for use as aids in learning a language

> *For words, see —81; for reading, see —84*

—83   **Audio-lingual approach to expression**

Informal presentation through practice in correct usage

Class here the "hear-speak" school of learning a language

> *For pronunciation, see —81*

—84   **Reading**

Including developmental and remedial reading

> *For readers, see —86*

—840 1   Philosophy and theory

Class psychology of reading in 418 unless there is emphasis on the specific language being read

—86   **Readers**

Graded selections with emphasis on structure and vocabulary as needed

Including readers compiled for training college students in reading comprehension, readers for new literates

Class here texts intended primarily for practice in reading a language

> *See Manual at T4—86; also at T1—01 vs. T4—86*

(Option: Class elementary readers in 372.41)

Summaries

First Summary*
The Ten Main Classes

000	**Generalities**
100	**Philosophy & psychology**
200	**Religion**
300	**Social sciences**
400	**Language**
500	**Natural sciences & mathematics**
600	**Technology (Applied sciences)**
700	**The arts Fine & decorative arts**
800	**Literature & rhetoric**
900	**Geography & history**

*Consult schedules for complete and exact headings

Second Summary*
The Hundred Divisions

000 Generalities
010 Bibliography
020 Library & information sciences
030 General encyclopedic works
040
050 General serial publications
060 General organizations & museology
070 News media, journalism, publishing
080 General collections
090 Manuscripts & rare books

100 Philosophy & psychology
110 Metaphysics
120 Epistemology, causation, humankind
130 Paranormal phenomena
140 Specific philosophical schools
150 Psychology
160 Logic
170 Ethics (Moral philosophy)
180 Ancient, medieval, Oriental philosophy
190 Modern western philosophy

200 Religion
210 Philosophy & theory of religion
220 Bible
230 Christianity   Christian theology
240 Christian moral & devotional theology
250 Christian orders & local church
260 Social & ecclesiastical theology
270 History of Christianity & Christian church
280 Christian denominations & sects
290 Comparative religion & other religions

300 Social sciences
310 Collections of general statistics
320 Political science
330 Economics
340 Law
350 Public administration & military science
360 Social problems & services; associations
370 Education
380 Commerce, communications, transportation
390 Customs, etiquette, folklore

400 Language
410 Linguistics
420 English & Old English
430 Germanic languages   German
440 Romance languages   French
450 Italian, Romanian, Rhaeto-Romanic
460 Spanish & Portuguese languages
470 Italic languages   Latin
480 Hellenic languages   Classical Greek
490 Other languages

500 Natural sciences & mathematics
510 Mathematics
520 Astronomy & allied sciences
530 Physics
540 Chemistry & allied sciences
550 Earth sciences
560 Paleontology   Paleozoology
570 Life sciences   Biology
580 Plants
590 Animals

600 Technology (Applied sciences)
610 Medical sciences   Medicine
620 Engineering & allied operations
630 Agriculture & related technologies
640 Home economics & family living
650 Management & auxiliary services
660 Chemical engineering
670 Manufacturing
680 Manufacture for specific uses
690 Buildings

700 The arts   Fine & decorative arts
710 Civic & landscape art
720 Architecture
730 Plastic arts   Sculpture
740 Drawing & decorative arts
750 Painting & paintings
760 Graphic arts   Printmaking & prints
770 Photography & photographs
780 Music
790 Recreational & performing arts

800 Literature & rhetoric
810 American literature in English
820 English & Old English literatures
830 Literatures of Germanic languages
840 Literatures of Romance languages
850 Italian, Romanian, Rhaeto-Romanic
860 Spanish & Portuguese literatures
870 Italic literatures   Latin
880 Hellenic literatures   Classical Greek
890 Literatures of other languages

900 Geography & history
910 Geography & travel
920 Biography, genealogy, insignia
930 History of ancient world to ca. 499
940 General history of Europe
950 General history of Asia   Far East
960 General history of Africa
970 General history of North America
980 General history of South America
990 General history of other areas

*Consult schedules for complete and exact headings

Third Summary*
The Thousand Sections

000	**Generalities**	**050**	**General serial publications**
001	Knowledge	051	American English-language
002	The book	052	In English
003	Systems	053	In other Germanic languages
004	Data processing Computer science	054	In French, Provençal, Catalan
005	Computer programming, programs, data	055	In Italian, Romanian, Rhaeto-Romanic
006	Special computer methods	056	In Spanish & Portuguese
007		057	In Slavic languages
008		058	In Scandinavian languages
009		059	In other languages
010	**Bibliography**	**060**	**General organizations & museology**
011	Bibliographies	061	In North America
012	Bibliographies of individuals	062	In British Isles In England
013	Of works by specific classes of authors	063	In central Europe In Germany
014	Of anonymous & pseudonymous works	064	In France & Monaco
015	Of works from specific places	065	In Italy & adjacent territories
016	Of works on specific subjects	066	In Iberian Peninsula & adjacent islands
017	General subject catalogs	067	In eastern Europe In Russia
018	Catalogs arranged by author, date, etc.	068	In other geographic areas
019	Dictionary catalogs	069	Museology (Museum science)
020	**Library & information sciences**	**070**	**News media, journalism, publishing**
021	Library relationships	071	Journalism & newspapers in North America
022	Administration of the physical plant	072	In British Isles In England
023	Personnel administration	073	In central Europe In Germany
024		074	In France & Monaco
025	Library operations	075	In Italy & adjacent territories
026	Libraries for specific subjects	076	In Iberian Peninsula & adjacent islands
027	General libraries	077	In eastern Europe In Russia
028	Reading & use of other information media	078	In Scandinavia
029		079	In other geographic areas
030	**General encyclopedic works**	**080**	**General collections**
031	American English-language	081	American English-language
032	In English	082	General collections in English
033	In other Germanic languages	083	In other Germanic languages
034	In French, Provençal, Catalan	084	In French, Provençal, Catalan
035	In Italian, Romanian, Rhaeto-Romanic	085	In Italian, Romanian, Rhaeto-Romanic
036	In Spanish & Portuguese	086	In Spanish & Portuguese
037	In Slavic languages	087	In Slavic languages
038	In Scandinavian languages	088	In Scandinavian languages
039	In other languages	089	In Italic, Hellenic, other languages
040		**090**	**Manuscripts & rare books**
041		091	Manuscripts
042		092	Block books
043		093	Incunabula
044		094	Printed books
045		095	Books notable for bindings
046		096	Books notable for illustrations
047		097	Books notable for ownership or origin
048		098	Prohibited works, forgeries, hoaxes
049		099	Books notable for format

*Consult schedules for complete and exact headings

Philosophy and psychology

100	**Philosophy & psychology**	150	**Psychology**
101	Theory of philosophy	151	
102	Miscellany	152	Perception, movement, emotions, drives
103	Dictionaries & encyclopedias	153	Mental processes & intelligence
104		154	Subconscious & altered states
105	Serial publications	155	Differential & developmental psychology
106	Organizations & management	156	Comparative psychology
107	Education, research, related topics	157	
108	Kinds of persons treatment	158	Applied psychology
109	Historical & collected persons treatment	159	
110	**Metaphysics**	**160**	**Logic**
111	Ontology	161	Induction
112		162	Deduction
113	Cosmology (Philosophy of nature)	163	
114	Space	164	
115	Time	165	Fallacies & sources of error
116	Change	166	Syllogisms
117	Structure	167	Hypotheses
118	Force & energy	168	Argument & persuasion
119	Number & quantity	169	Analogy
120	**Epistemology, causation, humankind**	**170**	**Ethics (Moral philosophy)**
121	Epistemology (Theory of knowledge)	171	Ethical systems
122	Causation	172	Political ethics
123	Determinism & indeterminism	173	Ethics of family relationships
124	Teleology	174	Occupational ethics
125		175	Ethics of recreation & leisure
126	The self	176	Ethics of sex & reproduction
127	The unconscious & the subconscious	177	Ethics of social relations
128	Humankind	178	Ethics of consumption
129	Origin & destiny of individual souls	179	Other ethical norms
130	**Paranormal phenomena**	**180**	**Ancient, medieval, Oriental philosophy**
131	Parapsychological & occult methods	181	Oriental philosophy
132		182	Pre-Socratic Greek philosophies
133	Parapsychology & occultism	183	Sophistic & Socratic philosophies
134		184	Platonic philosophy
135	Dreams & mysteries	185	Aristotelian philosophy
136		186	Skeptic & Neoplatonic philosophies
137	Divinatory graphology	187	Epicurean philosophy
138	Physiognomy	188	Stoic philosophy
139	Phrenology	189	Medieval western philosophy
140	**Specific philosophical schools**	**190**	**Modern western philosophy**
141	Idealism & related systems	191	Philosophy of United States & Canada
142	Critical philosophy	192	Philosophy of British Isles
143	Bergsonism & intuitionism	193	Philosophy of Germany & Austria
144	Humanism & related systems	194	Philosophy of France
145	Sensationalism	195	Philosophy of Italy
146	Naturalism & related systems	196	Philosophy of Spain & Portugal
147	Pantheism & related systems	197	Philosophy of former Soviet Union
148	Eclecticism, liberalism, traditionalism	198	Philosophy of Scandinavia
149	Other philosophical systems	199	Philosophy in other geographic areas

Religion

200	**Religion**		**250**	**Christian orders & local church**
201			251	Preaching (Homiletics)
202			252	Texts of sermons
203			253	Pastoral office (Pastoral theology)
204			254	Parish administration
205			255	Religious congregations & orders
206			256	
207			257	
208			258	
209			259	Pastoral care of families & persons
210	**Philosophy & theory of religion**		**260**	**Social & ecclesiastical theology**
211	Concepts of God		261	Social theology
212	Existence, knowability, attributes of God		262	Ecclesiology
213	Creation		263	Days, times, places of observance
214	Theodicy		264	Public worship
215	Science & religion		265	Sacraments, other rites & acts
216			266	Missions
217			267	Associations for religious work
218	Humankind		268	Religious education
219			269	Spiritual renewal
220	**Bible**		**270**	**History of Christianity & Christian church**
221	Old Testament (Tanakh)		271	Religious orders in church history
222	Historical books of Old Testament		272	Persecutions in church history
223	Poetic books of Old Testament		273	Doctrinal controversies & heresies
224	Prophetic books of Old Testament		274	History of Christianity in Europe
225	New Testament		275	History of Christianity in Asia
226	Gospels & Acts		276	History of Christianity in Africa
227	Epistles		277	History of Christianity in North America
228	Revelation (Apocalypse)		278	History of Christianity in South America
229	Apocrypha & pseudepigrapha		279	History of Christianity in other areas
230	**Christianity Christian theology**		**280**	**Christian denominations & sects**
231	God		281	Early church & Eastern churches
232	Jesus Christ & his family		282	Roman Catholic Church
233	Humankind		283	Anglican churches
234	Salvation (Soteriology) & grace		284	Protestants of Continental origin
235	Spiritual beings		285	Presbyterian, Reformed, Congregational
236	Eschatology		286	Baptist, Disciples of Christ, Adventist
237			287	Methodist & related churches
238	Creeds & catechisms		288	
239	Apologetics & polemics		289	Other denominations & sects
240	**Christian moral & devotional theology**		**290**	**Comparative religion & other religions**
241	Moral theology		291	Comparative religion
242	Devotional literature		292	Classical (Greek & Roman) religion
243	Evangelistic writings for individuals		293	Germanic religion
244			294	Religions of Indic origin
245			295	Zoroastrianism (Mazdaism, Parseeism)
246	Use of art in Christianity		296	Judaism
247	Church furnishings & articles		297	Islam, Babism, Bahai Faith
248	Christian experience, practice, life		298	
249	Christian observances in family life		299	Other religions

Social sciences

300	**Social sciences**	**350**	**Public administration & military science**
301	Sociology & anthropology	351	Public administration
302	Social interaction	352	General considerations
303	Social processes	353	Specific fields of public administration
304	Factors affecting social behavior	354	Administration of economy & environment
305	Social groups	355	Military science
306	Culture & institutions	356	Foot forces & warfare
307	Communities	357	Mounted forces & warfare
308		358	Air & other specialized forces
309		359	Sea (Naval) forces & warfare
310	**Collections of general statistics**	**360**	**Social problems & services; associations**
311		361	General social problems & welfare
312		362	Social welfare problems & services
313		363	Other social problems & services
314	General statistics of Europe	364	Criminology
315	General statistics of Asia	365	Penal & related institutions
316	General statistics of Africa	366	Associations
317	General statistics of North America	367	General clubs
318	General statistics of South America	368	Insurance
319	General statistics of other areas	369	Miscellaneous kinds of associations
320	**Political science**	**370**	**Education**
321	Systems of governments & states	371	Schools & activities; special education
322	Relation of state to organized groups	372	Elementary education
323	Civil & political rights	373	Secondary education
324	The political process	374	Adult education
325	International migration & colonization	375	Curricula
326	Slavery & emancipation	376	
327	International relations	377	
328	The legislative process	378	Higher education
329		379	Public policy issues in education
330	**Economics**	**380**	**Commerce, communications, transportation**
331	Labor economics	381	Internal commerce (Domestic trade)
332	Financial economics	382	International commerce (Foreign trade)
333	Economics of land & energy	383	Postal communication
334	Cooperatives	384	Communications Telecommunication
335	Socialism & related systems	385	Railroad transportation
336	Public finance	386	Inland waterway & ferry transportation
337	International economics	387	Water, air, space transportation
338	Production	388	Transportation Ground transportation
339	Macroeconomics & related topics	389	Metrology & standardization
340	**Law**	**390**	**Customs, etiquette, folklore**
341	International law	391	Costume & personal appearance
342	Constitutional & administrative law	392	Customs of life cycle & domestic life
343	Military, tax, trade, industrial law	393	Death customs
344	Labor, social, education, cultural law	394	General customs
345	Criminal law	395	Etiquette (Manners)
346	Private law	396	
347	Civil procedure & courts	397	
348	Law (Statutes), regulations, cases	398	Folklore
349	Law of specific jurisdictions & areas	399	Customs of war & diplomacy

Language

400	**Language**		**450**	**Italian, Romanian, Rhaeto-Romanic**
401	Philosophy & theory		451	Italian writing system & phonology
402	Miscellany		452	Italian etymology
403	Dictionaries & encyclopedias		453	Italian dictionaries
404	Special topics		454	
405	Serial publications		455	Italian grammar
406	Organizations & management		456	
407	Education, research, related topics		457	Italian language variations
408	Kinds of persons treatment		458	Standard Italian usage
409	Geographic & persons treatment		459	Romanian & Rhaeto-Romanic
410	**Linguistics**		**460**	**Spanish & Portuguese languages**
411	Writing systems		461	Spanish writing system & phonology
412	Etymology		462	Spanish etymology
413	Dictionaries		463	Spanish dictionaries
414	Phonology & phonetics		464	
415	Grammar		465	Spanish grammar
416			466	
417	Dialectology & historical linguistics		467	Spanish language variations
418	Standard usage Applied linguistics		468	Standard Spanish usage
419	Verbal language not spoken or written		469	Portuguese
420	**English & Old English**		**470**	**Italic languages Latin**
421	English writing system & phonology		471	Classical Latin writing & phonology
422	English etymology		472	Classical Latin etymology
423	English dictionaries		473	Classical Latin dictionaries
424			474	
425	English grammar		475	Classical Latin grammar
426			476	
427	English language variations		477	Old, Postclassical, Vulgar Latin
428	Standard English usage		478	Classical Latin usage
429	Old English (Anglo-Saxon)		479	Other Italic languages
430	**Germanic languages German**		**480**	**Hellenic languages Classical Greek**
431	German writing system & phonology		481	Classical Greek writing & phonology
432	German etymology		482	Classical Greek etymology
433	German dictionaries		483	Classical Greek dictionaries
434			484	
435	German grammar		485	Classical Greek grammar
436			486	
437	German language variations		487	Preclassical & postclassical Greek
438	Standard German usage		488	Classical Greek usage
439	Other Germanic languages		489	Other Hellenic languages
440	**Romance languages French**		**490**	**Other languages**
441	French writing system & phonology		491	East Indo-European & Celtic languages
442	French etymology		492	Afro-Asiatic languages Semitic
443	French dictionaries		493	Non-Semitic Afro-Asiatic languages
444			494	Altaic, Uralic, Hyperborean, Dravidian
445	French grammar		495	Languages of East & Southeast Asia
446			496	African languages
447	French language variations		497	North American native languages
448	Standard French usage		498	South American native languages
449	Provençal & Catalan		499	Austronesian & other languages

Natural sciences and mathematics

500	**Natural sciences & mathematics**	**550**	**Earth sciences**
501	Philosophy & theory	551	Geology, hydrology, meteorology
502	Miscellany	552	Petrology
503	Dictionaries & encyclopedias	553	Economic geology
504		554	Earth sciences of Europe
505	Serial publications	555	Earth sciences of Asia
506	Organizations & management	556	Earth sciences of Africa
507	Education, research, related topics	557	Earth sciences of North America
508	Natural history	558	Earth sciences of South America
509	Historical, geographic, persons treatment	559	Earth sciences of other areas
510	**Mathematics**	**560**	**Paleontology Paleozoology**
511	General principles of mathematics	561	Paleobotany; fossil microorganisms
512	Algebra, number theory	562	Fossil invertebrates
513	Arithmetic	563	Fossil marine & seashore invertebrates
514	Topology	564	Fossil mollusks & mollusk-like animals
515	Analysis	565	Fossil arthropods
516	Geometry	566	Fossil chordates
517		567	Fossil cold-blooded vertebrates
518		568	Fossil birds
519	Probabilities & applied mathematics	569	Fossil mammals
520	**Astronomy & allied sciences**	**570**	**Life sciences Biology**
521	Celestial mechanics	571	Physiology & related subjects
522	Techniques, equipment, materials	572	Biochemistry
523	Specific celestial bodies & phenomena	573	Specific systems in animals
524		574	
525	Earth (Astronomical geography)	575	Specific parts of & systems in plants
526	Mathematical geography	576	Genetics & evolution
527	Celestial navigation	577	Ecology
528	Ephemerides	578	Natural history of organisms
529	Chronology	579	Microorganisms, fungi, algae
530	**Physics**	**580**	**Plants**
531	Classical mechanics Solid mechanics	581	Specific topics in natural history
532	Fluid mechanics Liquid mechanics	582	Plants noted for characteristics & flowers
533	Pneumatics (Gas mechanics)	583	Dicotyledons
534	Sound & related vibrations	584	Monocotyledons
535	Light & paraphotic phenomena	585	Gymnosperms Conifers
536	Heat	586	Seedless plants
537	Electricity & electronics	587	Vascular seedless plants
538	Magnetism	588	Bryophytes
539	Modern physics	589	
540	**Chemistry & allied sciences**	**590**	**Animals**
541	Physical & theoretical chemistry	591	Specific topics in natural history
542	Techniques, equipment, materials	592	Invertebrates
543	Analytical chemistry	593	Marine & seashore invertebrates
544	Qualitative analysis	594	Mollusks & mollusk-like animals
545	Quantitative analysis	595	Arthropods
546	Inorganic chemistry	596	Chordates
547	Organic chemistry	597	Cold-blooded vertebrates Fishes
548	Crystallography	598	Birds
549	Mineralogy	599	Mammals

Technology (Applied sciences)

600	**Technology (Applied sciences)**		**650**	**Management & auxiliary services**
601	Philosophy & theory		651	Office services
602	Miscellany		652	Processes of written communication
603	Dictionaries & encyclopedias		653	Shorthand
604	Special topics		654	
605	Serial publications		655	
606	Organizations		656	
607	Education, research, related topics		657	Accounting
608	Inventions & patents		658	General management
609	Historical, geographic, persons treatment		659	Advertising & public relations
610	**Medical sciences Medicine**		**660**	**Chemical engineering**
611	Human anatomy, cytology, histology		661	Technology of industrial chemicals
612	Human physiology		662	Explosives, fuels, related products
613	Promotion of health		663	Beverage technology
614	Incidence & prevention of disease		664	Food technology
615	Pharmacology & therapeutics		665	Industrial oils, fats, waxes, gases
616	Diseases		666	Ceramic & allied technologies
617	Surgery & related medical specialties		667	Cleaning, color, coating technologies
618	Gynecology & other medical specialties		668	Technology of other organic products
619	Experimental medicine		669	Metallurgy
620	**Engineering & allied operations**		**670**	**Manufacturing**
621	Applied physics		671	Metalworking & metal products
622	Mining & related operations		672	Iron, steel, other iron alloys
623	Military & nautical engineering		673	Nonferrous metals
624	Civil engineering		674	Lumber processing, wood products, cork
625	Engineering of railroads & roads		675	Leather & fur processing
626			676	Pulp & paper technology
627	Hydraulic engineering		677	Textiles
628	Sanitary & municipal engineering		678	Elastomers & elastomer products
629	Other branches of engineering		679	Other products of specific materials
630	**Agriculture & related technologies**		**680**	**Manufacture for specific uses**
631	Techniques, equipment, materials		681	Precision instruments & other devices
632	Plant injuries, diseases, pests		682	Small forge work (Blacksmithing)
633	Field & plantation crops		683	Hardware & household appliances
634	Orchards, fruits, forestry		684	Furnishings & home workshops
635	Garden crops (Horticulture)		685	Leather, fur goods, related products
636	Animal husbandry		686	Printing & related activities
637	Processing dairy & related products		687	Clothing & accessories
638	Insect culture		688	Other final products & packaging
639	Hunting, fishing, conservation		689	
640	**Home economics & family living**		**690**	**Buildings**
641	Food & drink		691	Building materials
642	Meals & table service		692	Auxiliary construction practices
643	Housing & household equipment		693	Specific materials & purposes
644	Household utilities		694	Wood construction Carpentry
645	Household furnishings		695	Roof covering
646	Sewing, clothing, personal living		696	Utilities
647	Management of public households		697	Heating, ventilating, air-conditioning
648	Housekeeping		698	Detail finishing
649	Child rearing & home care of persons		699	

The arts   Fine and decorative arts

700	**The arts Fine & decorative arts**	**750**	**Painting & paintings**
701	Philosophy of fine & decorative arts	751	Techniques, equipment, materials, forms
702	Miscellany of fine & decorative arts	752	Color
703	Dictionaries of fine & decorative arts	753	Symbolism, allegory, mythology, legend
704	Special topics in fine & decorative arts	754	Genre paintings
705	Serial publications of fine & decorative arts	755	Religion
706	Organizations & management	756	
707	Education, research, related topics	757	Human figures
708	Galleries, museums, private collections	758	Other subjects
709	Historical, geographic, persons treatment	759	Historical, geographic, persons treatment
710	**Civic & landscape art**	**760**	**Graphic arts Printmaking & prints**
711	Area planning (Civic art)	761	Relief processes (Block printing)
712	Landscape architecture	762	
713	Landscape architecture of trafficways	763	Lithographic (Planographic) processes
714	Water features	764	Chromolithography & serigraphy
715	Woody plants	765	Metal engraving
716	Herbaceous plants	766	Mezzotinting, aquatinting, related processes
717	Structures in landscape architecture	767	Etching & drypoint
718	Landscape design of cemeteries	768	
719	Natural landscapes	769	Prints
720	**Architecture**	**770**	**Photography & photographs**
721	Architectural structure	771	Techniques, equipment, materials
722	Architecture to ca. 300	772	Metallic salt processes
723	Architecture from ca. 300 to 1399	773	Pigment processes of printing
724	Architecture from 1400	774	Holography
725	Public structures	775	
726	Buildings for religious purposes	776	
727	Buildings for education & research	777	
728	Residential & related buildings	778	Fields & kinds of photography
729	Design & decoration	779	Photographs
730	**Plastic arts Sculpture**	**780**	**Music**
731	Processes, forms, subjects of sculpture	781	General principles & musical forms
732	Sculpture to ca. 500	782	Vocal music
733	Greek, Etruscan, Roman sculpture	783	Music for single voices The voice
734	Sculpture from ca. 500 to 1399	784	Instruments & instrumental ensembles
735	Sculpture from 1400	785	Ensembles with one instrument per part
736	Carving & carvings	786	Keyboard & other instruments
737	Numismatics & sigillography	787	Stringed instruments (Chordophones)
738	Ceramic arts	788	Wind instruments (Aerophones)
739	Art metalwork	789	
740	**Drawing & decorative arts**	**790**	**Recreational & performing arts**
741	Drawing & drawings	791	Public performances
742	Perspective in drawing	792	Stage presentations
743	Drawing & drawings by subject	793	Indoor games & amusements
744		794	Indoor games of skill
745	Decorative arts	795	Games of chance
746	Textile arts	796	Athletic & outdoor sports & games
747	Interior decoration	797	Aquatic & air sports
748	Glass	798	Equestrian sports & animal racing
749	Furniture & accessories	799	Fishing, hunting, shooting

Literature and rhetoric

800	**Literature & rhetoric**		**850**	**Italian, Romanian, Rhaeto-Romanic**
801	Philosophy & theory		851	Italian poetry
802	Miscellany		852	Italian drama
803	Dictionaries & encyclopedias		853	Italian fiction
804			854	Italian essays
805	Serial publications		855	Italian speeches
806	Organizations & management		856	Italian letters
807	Education, research, related topics		857	Italian humor & satire
808	Rhetoric & collections of literature		858	Italian miscellaneous writings
809	History, description, criticism		859	Romanian & Rhaeto-Romanic literatures
810	**American literature in English**		**860**	**Spanish & Portuguese literatures**
811	American poetry in English		861	Spanish poetry
812	American drama in English		862	Spanish drama
813	American fiction in English		863	Spanish fiction
814	American essays in English		864	Spanish essays
815	American speeches in English		865	Spanish speeches
816	American letters in English		866	Spanish letters
817	American humor & satire in English		867	Spanish humor & satire
818	American miscellaneous writings		868	Spanish miscellaneous writings
819			869	Portuguese literature
820	**English & Old English literatures**		**870**	**Italic literatures Latin**
821	English poetry		871	Latin poetry
822	English drama		872	Latin dramatic poetry & drama
823	English fiction		873	Latin epic poetry & fiction
824	English essays		874	Latin lyric poetry
825	English speeches		875	Latin speeches
826	English letters		876	Latin letters
827	English humor & satire		877	Latin humor & satire
828	English miscellaneous writings		878	Latin miscellaneous writings
829	Old English (Anglo-Saxon)		879	Literatures of other Italic languages
830	**Literatures of Germanic languages**		**880**	**Hellenic literatures Classical Greek**
831	German poetry		881	Classical Greek poetry
832	German drama		882	Classical Greek dramatic poetry & drama
833	German fiction		883	Classical Greek epic poetry & fiction
834	German essays		884	Classical Greek lyric poetry
835	German speeches		885	Classical Greek speeches
836	German letters		886	Classical Greek letters
837	German humor & satire		887	Classical Greek humor & satire
838	German miscellaneous writings		888	Classical Greek miscellaneous writings
839	Other Germanic literatures		889	Modern Greek literature
840	**Literatures of Romance languages**		**890**	**Literatures of other languages**
841	French poetry		891	East Indo-European & Celtic
842	French drama		892	Afro-Asiatic literatures Semitic
843	French fiction		893	Non-Semitic Afro-Asiatic literatures
844	French essays		894	Altaic, Uralic, Hyperborean, Dravidian
845	French speeches		895	Literatures of East & Southeast Asia
846	French letters		896	African literatures
847	French humor & satire		897	North American native literatures
848	French miscellaneous writings		898	South American native literatures
849	Provençal & Catalan literatures		899	Austronesian & other literatures

Geography and history

900	**Geography & history**	**950**	**General history of Asia Far East**
901	Philosophy & theory	951	China & adjacent areas
902	Miscellany	952	Japan
903	Dictionaries & encyclopedias	953	Arabian Peninsula & adjacent areas
904	Collected accounts of events	954	South Asia India
905	Serial publications	955	Iran
906	Organizations & management	956	Middle East (Near East)
907	Education, research, related topics	957	Siberia (Asiatic Russia)
908	Kinds of persons treatment	958	Central Asia
909	World history	959	Southeast Asia
910	**Geography & travel**	**960**	**General history of Africa**
911	Historical geography	961	Tunisia & Libya
912	Graphic representations	962	Egypt & Sudan
913	Geography of & travel in ancient world	963	Ethiopia & Eritrea
914	Geography of & travel in Europe	964	Northwest African coast & offshore islands
915	Geography of & travel in Asia	965	Algeria
916	Geography of & travel in Africa	966	West Africa & offshore islands
917	Geography of & travel in North America	967	Central Africa & offshore islands
918	Geography of & travel in South America	968	Southern Africa Republic of South Africa
919	Geography of & travel in other areas	969	South Indian Ocean islands
920	**Biography, genealogy, insignia**	**970**	**General history of North America**
921		971	Canada
922		972	Middle America Mexico
923		973	United States
924		974	Northeastern United States
925		975	Southeastern United States
926		976	South central United States
927		977	North central United States
928		978	Western United States
929	Genealogy, names, insignia	979	Great Basin & Pacific Slope region
930	**History of ancient world to ca. 499**	**980**	**General history of South America**
931	China to 420	981	Brazil
932	Egypt to 640	982	Argentina
933	Palestine to 70	983	Chile
934	India to 647	984	Bolivia
935	Mesopotamia & Iranian Plateau to 637	985	Peru
936	Europe north & west of Italy to ca. 499	986	Colombia & Ecuador
937	Italy & adjacent territories to 476	987	Venezuela
938	Greece to 323	988	Guiana
939	Other parts of ancient world to ca. 640	989	Paraguay & Uruguay
940	**General history of Europe**	**990**	**General history of other areas**
941	British Isles	991	
942	England & Wales	992	
943	Central Europe Germany	993	New Zealand
944	France & Monaco	994	Australia
945	Italian Peninsula & adjacent islands	995	Melanesia New Guinea
946	Iberian Peninsula & adjacent islands	996	Other parts of Pacific Polynesia
947	Eastern Europe Russia	997	Atlantic Ocean islands
948	Scandinavia	998	Arctic islands & Antarctica
949	Other parts of Europe	999	Extraterrestrial worlds

Schedules

Use of the Schedules

Full instructions on the use of the schedules are found in the Introduction to the Dewey Decimal Classification.

The first three digits of a DDC number are found in the number column, or at the top of the page.

Numbers in square brackets [ ] are not used. Numbers in parentheses ( ) are options to standard usage.

000 Generalities

SUMMARY

001–006	[Knowledge, the book, systems, data processing]
010	Bibliography
020	Library and information sciences
030	General encyclopedic works
050	General serial publications
060	General organizations and museology
070	Documentary media, educational media, news media; journalism; publishing
080	General collections
090	Manuscripts, rare books, other rare printed materials

SUMMARY

001	Knowledge
002	The book
003	Systems
004	Data processing Computer science
005	Computer programming, programs, data
006	Special computer methods

001 Knowledge

Including history, description, critical appraisal of intellectual activity in general; increase, modification, dissemination of information and understanding

Class here discussion of ideas from many fields

Class epistemology in 121. Class a compilation of knowledge in a specific form with the form, e.g., encyclopedias 030

See Manual at 500 vs. 001

.01 Theory of knowledge

Do not use for philosophy of knowledge, philosophical works on the theory of knowledge; class in 121

.1 Intellectual life

Nature and value

For scholarship and learning, see 001.2

See also 900 for broad description of intellectual situation and condition

.2 Scholarship and learning

Intellectual activity directed toward increasing knowledge

Class methods of study and teaching in 371.3. Class scholarship and learning in a specific discipline or subject with the discipline or subject, e.g., scholarship in the humanities 001.3, in history 900

For research, see 001.4

See Manual at 500 vs. 001

.3 Humanities

Including relative value of science versus the humanities

.4 Research; statistical methods

Including descriptive, experimental, historical methods; support of and incentives for research, e.g., fellowships, grants, prizes

Class here works discussing what research is

Class computer modeling, operations research in 003; class student finance in higher education in 378.3. Class research in a specific discipline or subject with the discipline or subject, plus notation 07 from Table 1, e.g., research in linguistics 410.7; class works embodying the results of research in a specific discipline or subject with the subject of the research, but without notation 07 from Table 1, e.g., results of research in linguistics 410 (*not* 410.7); class awards granted in a specific discipline with the discipline, plus notation 079 from Table 1, e.g., prizes for research in linguistics 410.79

See also 310.7 for methods of collecting general social statistical data, 929.8 for awards for general achievements

.9 Controversial knowledge

Including well established phenomena for which explanations are controversial; the end of the world; hoaxes, delusions, superstitions

Class here interdisciplinary works on controversial knowledge and paranormal phenomena

Class a hoax that influenced history with the hoax in 900, e.g., False Dmitri 947

For paranormal phenomena, see 130. For controversial knowledge concerning a specific discipline or subject, see the discipline or subject, e.g., superstitions as a subject of folklore 398, Piltdown man hoax 569.9, controversial medical remedies 615.8, an alleged conspiracy to assassinate John F. Kennedy 973.922

See Manual at 001.9 and 130

.94 Mysteries

Reported phenomena not explained, not fully verified

Including Atlantis, Bermuda Triangle, pyramid power

Class here nonastronomical extraterrestrial influences on earth

See also 900 for Atlantis as a subject of archaeology

.942 Unidentified flying objects (UFOs, Flying saucers)

.944 Monsters and related phenomena

Including abominable snowman, Loch Ness monster

See also 590 for animals whose reality is not controversial

002 The book

Class here historical bibliography, interdisciplinary works on the book

Class comprehensive works on historical and analytical bibliography in 010

For book publishing, see 070.5; for rare books, see 090; for social aspects of the book, see 302.23; for book arts, see 686

.02 Miscellany

Do not use for lists, inventories; class in 010

.029 Commercial miscellany

Do not use for price lists, trade catalogs, directories; class in 010

.07 Education, research, related topics

.074 Museums, collections, exhibits

Do not use for catalogs and lists; class in 010

003 Systems

Including bionics, coding theory, computer implementation of mathematical models of systems, cybernetics, data processing and computer science applied to systems, decision theory, information theory, perception theory, theory of communication in systems; large-scale systems, linear systems, self-organizing systems; interdisciplinary works on forecasting, on control and stability of systems, on computer modeling and simulation (on computer implementation of mathematical models of systems)

Class here operations research; systems theory, analysis, design; models (simulation) applied to real-world systems

Class computer vision in 006.3; class psychology of human perception in 153.7; class simulation in education in 371.39; class perception in animals in 573.8; class automatic control of man-made physical systems in 629.8; class coding for purpose of limiting access to information (cryptography) in 652; class social aspects of and interdisciplinary works on communication in systems in 302.2. Class systems in a specific subject or discipline with the subject or discipline, plus notation 01 from Table 1, e.g., systems theory in the social sciences 300.1; class information theory in communications engineering of a specific kind of communications with the kind, without using notation 01 from Table 1, e.g., radio 621.384; class information theory in any other specific subject with the subject, plus notation 01 from Table 1, e.g., information theory in economics 330.01

> *For artificial intelligence, see 006.3; for forecasting by parapsychological and occult means, see 133.3; for social forecasting, see 303.49; for control theory in automation engineering, see 629.8. For computer modeling and simulation applied to a specific subject, see the subject, plus notation 01 from Table 1, e.g., computer modeling in economics 330.01; for control and stability of systems in a specific subject, see the subject, plus notation 01 from Table 1, e.g., control and stability of systems in general engineering 620.001*

> *See also 511 for mathematical models not applied to real-world systems, 519.7 for mathematical programming not applied to real-world systems*

> *See Manual at 003; also at 003 vs. 004.2*

[.028 5]   Data processing   Computer applications

Do not use; class in 003

004 Data processing   Computer science

Including parallel processing, multiprocessing; distributed processing, client-server computer systems; specific types of computers, processors, computer systems distinguished by their processing modes, e.g., multiprocessors, parallel processors

Class here selection and use of computer hardware; electronic computers; electronic digital computers; computer systems (computers, their peripheral devices, their operating systems); central processing units; computer reliability; interactive, online processing; comprehensive works on hardware and programs in electronic data processing

Unless other instructions are given, class a subject with aspects in two or more subdivisions of 004 in the number coming last, e.g., external storage for microcomputers 004.5 (*not* 004.16)

Class computer modeling and simulation in 003. Class data processing and computer science applied to a specific subject or discipline with the subject or discipline, plus notation 0285 from Table 1, e.g., data processing in banking 332.10285

> *For computer programming, programs, data, see 005; for special computer methods, see 006; for engineering of computers, see 621.39*

> *See also 025.04 for automated information storage and retrieval; 303.48 for computers as a cause of social change; 343.09 for computer law; 364.1 for financial and business computer crimes; 371.33 for computer-assisted instruction (CAI); 652.5 for word processing; 658 for data processing in management; 794.8 for computer games*

> *See Manual at 004–006; also at 004–006 vs. 621.39; also at 004 vs. 005*

.01   Philosophy and theory

Including computer mathematics, human-computer interaction, psychological principles and human factors in data processing and computer science

Class ergonomic engineering of computer peripherals in 621.39

.02   Miscellany

.028   Auxiliary techniques and procedures; apparatus, equipment, materials

Do not use for testing and measurement; class in 004.2

.1   General works on specific types of computers

Including digital supercomputers, mainframe computers, minicomputers; analog computers

Class specific types of computers, processors, computer systems distinguished by their processing modes, such as multiprocessors, in 004; class programmable calculators in 510.285; class comprehensive works on minicomputers and microcomputers in 004.16

.16 Digital microcomputers

Class here computer systems based on microcomputers; laptop, notebook, palmtop, pen, personal, pocket computers; personal digital assistants, workstations; microprocessors; comprehensive works on minicomputers and microcomputers

Class minicomputers in 004.1

.165 Specific digital microcomputers

Arrange alphabetically by name of microcomputer or microprocessor, e.g., Macintosh®

See Manual at 004.165

.2 Systems analysis and design, computer architecture, performance evaluation

Including performance measurement and evaluation to aid in designing or improving performance of a computer system

Class performance evaluation as a consideration in purchasing a specific item with the item in 004, plus notation 029 from Table 1, e.g., evaluating microcomputers for purchase 004.16029

See Manual at 003 vs. 004.2

.5 Storage

Including hardware aspects of virtual memory; internal storage (main memory), e.g., random-access memory (RAM); external (auxiliary) storage, e.g., CD-ROM (compact disc read-only memory), floppy disks and floppy disk drives, hard disks and hard disk drives, magnetic tapes and tape drives

Class comprehensive works on virtual memory in 005.4

.6   Interfacing and communications

Equipment and techniques linking computers to peripheral devices or to other computers

Standard subdivisions are added for either or both topics in heading

Including communications network architecture; data transmission modes and data switching methods, e.g., packet switching, multiplexing; interfacing and communications protocols (standards); local-area networks, e.g., baseband and broadband networks, high-speed local networks; modems, optical-fiber cable, peripheral control units

Class here interdisciplinary works on computer communications

Interdisciplinary works on telecommunication relocated to 384

Class peripheral control units controlling a specific kind of peripheral with the peripheral, e.g., printer controllers 004.7; class protocols for specific aspects of interfacing and communications with the aspect, e.g., protocols for error-correcting codes 005.7

For data, programs, programming in interfacing and communications, see 005.7; for social aspects of computer communications, see 302.23; for economic and related aspects of providing computer communications to the public, see 384.3

See also 004 for distributed processing

See Manual at 004.6 vs. 005.7; also at 004.6 vs. 384.3; also at 004.6 vs. 621.382, 621.39

.602   Miscellany

Do not use for standards; class in 004.6

.67   Wide-area networks

Including Internet

See Manual at 004.67 vs. 025.04, 384.3

.69   Specific kinds of computer communications

Including videotex

.692   Electronic mail

.693   Electronic bulletin boards

.7 **Peripherals**

Input, output, storage devices that work with a computer but are not part of its central processing unit or internal storage

Including keyboards, printers, terminals, monitors (video display screens)

Class peripheral storage in 004.5. Class a peripheral devoted to a special purpose with the purpose, e.g., communications devices 004.6, input devices that utilize pattern recognition methods 006.4, graphics output devices 006.6

See also 005.7 for data entry

005 Computer programming, programs, data

Class here text processing; software reliability, compatibility, portability, reusability, usability

Unless other instructions are given, class a subject with aspects in two or more subdivisions of 005 in the number coming last, e.g., writing database management programs in C 005.74 (*not* 005.13)

Class computer programming, programs, data for special computer methods in 006

See also 652.5 for word processing

See Manual at 005; also at 004–006; also at 004–006 vs. 621.39; also at 004 vs. 005

SUMMARY

005.1	Programming
.2	Programming for specific types of computers, for specific operating systems, for specific user interfaces
.3	Programs
.4	Systems programming and programs
.6	Microprogramming and microprograms
.7	Data in computer systems
.8	Data security

> **005.1–005.6 Computer programming and programs**

Class comprehensive works in 005

.1 **Programming**

Including software systems analysis and design, e.g., analysis of a user's problem preparatory to developing a software system to solve it; special programming techniques, e.g., object-oriented, structured, visual programming; debugging, preparation of software documentation, software maintenance

Class here application programming, software engineering

Class software systems analysis and design in relation to programming languages, special programming techniques in relation to programming languages (e.g., object-oriented programming with a specific program language) in 005.13. Class a specific application of programming within computer science with the application in 005.4–006.7, e.g., programming computer graphics 006.6

> *For programming for specific types of computers, for specific operating systems, for specific user interfaces, see 005.2*

> *See Manual at 005.1–005.2 vs. 005.4; also at 005.1 vs. 005.3; also at 005.1 vs. 510*

.101 Philosophy and theory

Do not use notation 01 from Table 1 here or with subdivisions of 005.1–005.2 for general discussions of logic in programming

> *See also 005.13 for the symbolic (mathematical) logic of programming languages*

.102 Miscellany

.102 8 Auxiliary techniques and procedures; apparatus, equipment, materials

Do not use for maintenance, repair, measurement, testing, special programming techniques; class in 005.1

.13 *Programming languages

Including machine and assembly languages; mathematical principles of programming languages

Class here coding of programs

Specific machine and assembly languages relocated to 005.2

Class mathematical principles of programming in 005.101; class microprogramming languages in 005.6

> *See also 005.1 for general works about logic in programming, 005.4 for programming-language interpreters and compilers*

.130 1 Philosophy and theory

Do not use for mathematical principles; class in 005.13

*Do not add notation 01 from Table 1 for general discussions of logic in programming

.2   **Programming for specific types of computers, for specific operating systems, for specific user interfaces**

Including specific machine and assembly languages [*formerly* 005.13]; programming for supercomputers, mainframe computers, minicomputers; programming for distributed computer systems, for real-time computer systems; programming for multiprocessor computers, e.g., parallel programming; programming for specific operating systems, e.g., programming for Unix®; programming for specific user interfaces, e.g., programming for Motif®

Class programming for digital microcomputers, for specific operating systems that run on microcomputers, for specific user interfaces that run on microcomputers in 005.26; class specific microcomputer machine and assembly languages, programming for specific microcomputers in 005.265

See Manual at 005.1–005.2 vs. 005.4

.26   *Programming for digital microcomputers

Including writing programs that run on specific operating systems, e.g., MS-DOS®; writing programs that run on specific user interfaces, e.g., Microsoft Windows®

Class here programming for microprocessors, for personal computers, for microcomputer workstations; comprehensive works on programming for minicomputers and microcomputers

Class programming for minicomputers in 005.2; class programming for a specific operating system where the operating system is the only operating system that runs on a specific computer in 005.265

.265   Programming for specific microcomputers

Class here programming for specific microprocessors, for computer systems based on specific microcomputers; programming for a specific operating system where the operating system is the only operating system that runs on a specific computer

Arrange alphabetically by name of microcomputer or microprocessor, e.g., IBM PC®

Class programming for a specific operating system or specific user interface where more than one operating system or user interface is available for a specific computer in 005.26

See Manual at 004.165

*Do not add notation 01 from Table 1 for general discussions of logic in programming

.3   **Programs**

Software and firmware

Collections of programs, systems of interrelated programs, individual programs having interdisciplinary applications

Including online help; programs for supercomputers, mainframe computers, minicomputers; programs for real-time computer systems, for multiprocessor computers; programs for distributed computer systems, e.g., groupware; programs for specific operating systems, e.g., programs that run on Unix®; programs for specific user interfaces, e.g., programs that run on Motif®; specific programs, e.g., SAS®

Class here application programs, electronic spreadsheets, integrated programs, software documentation; comprehensive works on software and firmware, on applications and systems programs

Class programs for digital microcomputers in 005.36; class programs for specific microcomputers in 005.365; class programs for specific operating systems that run on microcomputers, for specific user interfaces that run on microcomputers in 005.368; class specific programs for microcomputers in 005.369. Class programs for a specific application in computer science with the application in 005–006, e.g., programs for computer graphics 006.6; class online help in specific kinds of programs with the kind, e.g., online help in programs for microcomputers 005.36

For systems programs, see 005.4; for firmware, see 005.6

See also 005.1 for preparation of program documentation

See Manual at 005.3; also at 005.1 vs. 005.3; also at 005.3 vs. 005.4

.302 8   Auxiliary techniques and procedures; apparatus, equipment, materials

Do not use for testing and measurement, maintenance and repair of programs; class in 005.1

.302 9   Commercial miscellany

See Manual at 011 vs. 005.3029

.36   Programs for digital microcomputers

.362   Programs in specific programming languages

Arrange alphabetically by name of programming language, e.g., BASIC

See Manual at 005.362

.365   Programs for specific microcomputers

Class here programs for specific microprocessors, for systems based on specific microcomputers

Arrange alphabetically by name of microcomputer or microprocessor, e.g., Macintosh®

See Manual at 004.165; also at 005.368 vs. 005.365

.368   Programs for specific operating systems and for specific user
                  interfaces

                        Including programs for specific graphical user interfaces

                        Class programs for a specific operating system where the operating
                        system is the only operating system that runs on a specific computer in
                        005.365

                        See Manual at 005.368 vs. 005.365

.369   Specific programs

                        Class here specific computer software systems (organized sets of
                        programs that work together)

                        Arrange alphabetically by name of program or software system, e.g.,
                        Lotus 1–2–3®

                        See Manual at 005.369

.4   Systems programming and programs

                        Including programming to produce operating systems, memory management
                        programming, programming of user interfaces; assemblers, code generators,
                        compilers, interpreters, macro processors, parsers, translators; operating
                        systems; multiprogramming (multitasking); memory management programs,
                        file system management programs; user interfaces, e.g., graphical user
                        interfaces; utility programs; comprehensive works on virtual memory

                        Class translators for microprogramming languages in 005.6; class
                        programming and programs for interfacing and data communications in 005.7;
                        class for management of files and databases in 005.74; class text editors in
                        652.5. Class a specific application of systems programs with the application,
                        e.g., computer interfacing and device drivers 005.7, computer security 005.8

                        *For hardware aspects of virtual memory, see 004.5; for data backup and
                        recovery, see 005.8*

                        *See also 418 for programs to translate natural languages into other natural
                        languages*

                        *See Manual at 005.1–005.2 vs. 005.4; also at 005.3 vs. 005.4; also at
                        005.74 vs. 005.4*

.6   Microprogramming and microprograms

                        Including firmware viewed as microprograms, firmware development,
                        microcode

                        Class firmware viewed as hardware in 004

.7   **Data in computer systems**

Including programming and programs for data communications, for interfacing; device drivers; data preparation and representation, record formats, e.g., conversion to machine-readable form, data entry and validation, digital codes, error-correcting codes; data structures

Class computer input devices in 004.7; class data validation in file processing, data structures in data files and databases in 005.74

For data security, see 005.8

See also 004.6 for hardware for interfacing and data communications

See Manual at 005.7; also at 004.6 vs. 005.7

.74   Data files and databases

Including data dictionaries, data directories; data compression; file organization and access methods, e.g., data file formats, merging, search algorithms, sort algorithms, sorting; validation in file processing

Class here data file processing, data file and database management systems, database design and architecture

Class comprehensive works on data validation in 005.7; class interdisciplinary works on computer science and information science aspects of databases in 025.04. Class data files and databases related to a specific computer method with the method in 006, e.g., expert systems 006.3; class data files and databases with regard to their subject content with the subject, e.g., encyclopedic databases 030, nonbibliographic medical databases 610

For specific types of data files and databases, see 005.75

See Manual at 005.74; also at 005.74 vs. 005.4

.75   Specific types of data files and databases

Including flat-file, hierarchical, network, object-oriented, relational databases; distributed data files and databases; full-text database management systems, e.g., hypertext databases

.8   **Data security**

Including cryptography used for security in computer systems; computer viruses, e.g., Trojan horses, worms; data backup and recovery

Class here access control

Class interdisciplinary works on cryptography in 652

See also 658.4 for data security in management

006 Special computer methods

Not otherwise provided for

Including automatic data collection, virtual reality

Class here programs, programming, selection and use of hardware in relation to special computer methods

Unless other instructions are given, class a subject with aspects in two or more subdivisions of 006 in the number coming last, e.g., computer graphics in expert systems 006.6 (*not* 006.3)

> *See also 003 for computer modeling and simulation; notation 01 from Table 1 for computer modeling and simulation in a specific discipline or subject; 004.6 for computer communications; 005.74 for file and database management; 005.8 for data security; 629.8 for special methods in automatic control engineering*

> *See Manual at 004–006; also at 004–006 vs. 621.39*

.3 Artificial intelligence

Including computer vision; knowledge-based systems, e.g., expert systems, programming and programming languages for knowledge-based systems; machine learning; natural language processing, neural nets (neural networks)

Class here question-answering systems

> *See also 006.4 for pattern recognition not used as a tool of artificial intelligence*

> *See Manual at 006.3 vs. 006.4, 621.36, 621.39; also at 153 vs. 006.3; also at 410.285 vs. 006.3*

.4 Computer pattern recognition

Including optical pattern recognition, e.g., optical character recognition (OCR); speech recognition; comprehensive works on optical pattern recognition and computer graphics, on speech recognition and speech synthesis; interdisciplinary works on bar coding

Class pattern recognition as a tool of artificial intelligence in 006.3; class optical engineering aspects of optical pattern recognition in 621.36

> *For speech synthesis, see 006.5; for computer graphics, see 006.6; for use of bar coding in materials management, see 658.7*

> *See also 006.3 for computer vision*

> *See Manual at 006.3 vs. 006.4, 621.36, 621.39*

.5 Computer sound synthesis

Including speech synthesis

> *See also 786.7 for computer music*

.6 **Computer graphics**

Including computer graphics hardware, both equipment specifically designed for computer graphics and works treating use of equipment for computer graphics even if the equipment was not specifically designed for that purpose; computer graphics programs and programming; three-dimensional graphics, e.g., ray tracing; computer animation, e.g., morphing

Multimedia systems, interactive video, comprehensive works on computer graphics and computer sound synthesis relocated to 006.7

Class works that treat equally the use of equipment for graphics and nongraphics tasks in 004; class use of computers in video production in 778.590285

> *For a specific product of computer animation techniques, see the product, e.g., animated cartoons 741.5*

> *See also 760 for computer graphic art*

.7 **Multimedia systems [*formerly* 006.6]**

Including interactive video [*formerly* 006.6]

Class here comprehensive works on computer graphics and computer sound synthesis [*formerly* 006.6]

Class use of computers in video production in 778.590285

> *For computer sound synthesis, see 006.5; for computer graphics, see 006.6*

> *See also 384.3 for interactive videotex*

010 Bibliography

History, identification, description of printed, written, audiovisual, machine-readable materials

Including preparation and compilation of bibliographies

Class descriptive cataloging in 025.3. Class preparation and compilation of a specific kind of bibliography with the kind, plus notation 028 from Table 1, e.g., preparation and compilation of biobibliographies 012.028; class catalogs and lists of art works with the subject, plus notation 074 from Table 1, e.g., a catalog of prints 769.074

> *For historical bibliography, see 002*

> *See also 028.1 for reviews*

SUMMARY

011	**Bibliographies**
012	**Bibliographies and catalogs of individuals**
013	**Bibliographies and catalogs of works by specific classes of authors**
014	**Bibliographies and catalogs of anonymous and pseudonymous works**
015	**Bibliographies and catalogs of works from specific places**
016	**Bibliographies and catalogs of works on specific subjects or in specific disciplines**
017	**General subject catalogs**
018	**Catalogs arranged by author, main entry, date, or register number**
019	**Dictionary catalogs**

[.28]   Auxiliary techniques and procedures; apparatus, equipment, materials

Do not use; class in 010

[.74]   Museums, collections, exhibits

Do not use; class in 011–019

011   Bibliographies

Including bibliographies of best books, of computer programs, of dissertations and theses; general bibliographies and catalogs of works published in specific historical periods; general bibliographies of reference works, of free materials, of works published in specific forms (e.g., audiovisual media, microforms, newspapers), of rare books, of reprints, of works in series, of works issued by specific kinds of publishers (e.g., government publications)

Class here general bibliographies (in any form) in which the items are books or other written or printed works

Class catalogs in 012–019; class bibliographies of music scores and discographies of music in 016.78026; class bibliographies of dramatic and entertainment motion pictures and videotapes in 016.79143; class bibliographies of maps in 016.912

For bibliographies of individuals, of works by specific classes of authors, of anonymous and pseudonymous works, of works from specific places, of works on specific subjects or in specific disciplines, see 012–016

See Manual at 011 vs. 005.3029

.001–.007   Standard subdivisions

.008   Bibliographies with respect to kinds of persons

Class bibliographies of works for specific kinds of users in 011.6

.009   Historical, geographic, persons treatment

Class bibliographies of works published in specific historical periods in 011; class bibliographies of works from specific places in 015

.6   *General bibliographies of works for specific kinds of users

---

*Do not add notation 091–099 from Table 1 for bibliographies of works from specific places; class in 015

.62   *Works for children and young adults

Standard subdivisions are added for works for children and young adults together, for works for children alone

.63   *Works for persons with disabilities and illnesses

Including braille, large-type publications

Class here works for persons with physical disabilities

Class talking and cassette books for persons with physical disabilities in 011

> ## 012–016 Bibliographies and catalogs of individuals, of works by specific classes of authors, of anonymous and pseudonymous works, of works from specific places, of works on specific subjects or in specific disciplines

Unless other instructions are given, observe the following table of preference, e.g., bibliographies of scientific works by women published in France 016.5 (*not* 013 or 015.44):

Bibliographies and catalogs of works on specific subjects or in specific disciplines	016
Bibliographies and catalogs of individuals	012
Bibliographies and catalogs of anonymous and pseudonymous works	014
Bibliographies and catalogs of works by specific classes of authors	013
Bibliographies and catalogs of works from specific places	015

Class comprehensive works in 011

012   Bibliographies and catalogs of individuals

Works by or about persons not clearly associated with a specific subject

Class here biobibliographies

For biobibliographies of persons associated with a specific subject, see the biography of the subject, e.g., biobibliographies of psychologists 150.92

---

*Do not add notation 091–099 from Table 1 for bibliographies of works from specific places; class in 015

013   Bibliographies and catalogs of works by specific classes of authors

> Works not dealing with a specific subject
>
> Including authors resident in specific regions, continents, countries, localities; authors adherent to specific religions, following specific vocations, of specific sexes and ages
>
> *For bibliographies and catalogs of individuals, see 012*
>
> *See also 011 for bibliographies of dissertations and theses*

014   Bibliographies and catalogs of anonymous and pseudonymous works

015   Bibliographies and catalogs of works from specific places

> Works issued or printed in specific regions, continents, countries, localities, or by specific publishers
>
> Class here bibliographies and catalogs of theses and dissertations for degrees awarded at specific institutions and at institutions in specific places, publishers' catalogs, sales catalogs of specific college and university presses
>
> Add to base number 015 notation 1–9 from Table 2, e.g., works issued in Canada 015.71; however, do not add notation 01–09 from Table 1; class in number for area

016   Bibliographies and catalogs of works on specific subjects or in specific disciplines

In list or essay form

Class here annotated subject bibliographies with descriptive annotations that do not give substantive information about the subject; indexes

Add to base number 016 notation 001–999, e.g., bibliographies of philosophy 016.1, of novels 016.80883

Add to the various subdivisions of 016 notation 01–09 from Table 1 as required for works listed in the bibliographies and catalogs, but not for the bibliographies and catalogs being classed, e.g., bibliographies of serial publications on philosophy 016.105, but serially published bibliographies on philosophy that include monographs 016.1 (*not* 016.105)

Class bibliographies and catalogs of literature in more than two languages in 016.8088. Class biobibliographies of persons associated with a specific subject with the biography of the subject, e.g., biobibliographies of psychologists 150.92; class bibliographies with abstracts giving substantive information about the subject with the subject, e.g., bibliographies with substantive abstracts about chemistry 540

> *See also 011 for general bibliographies arranged by subject and general bibliographies of works published in specific forms, e.g., audiovisual materials, computer software, manuscripts, serials; 017–019 for general subject catalogs and general catalogs of serial publications; 050 for general indexes of specific serial publications not limited by subject*
>
> *See Manual at 016 vs. 026, T1—07*

(Option: Class with the specific discipline or subject, plus notation 016 from Table 1, e.g., bibliographies of medicine 610.16)

>   017–019   General catalogs

Lists of works held in a specific collection or group of collections, or offered for sale by specific organizations other than publishers or at auction, and not restricted to specific subjects, to individuals or specific types of authorship, or to specific places of publication

Class here general catalogs of serial publications and their indexes, union catalogs

Class general catalogs of works published in specific historical periods in 011; class catalogs of individuals, of works by specific classes of authors, of anonymous and pseudonymous works, of works from specific places, of works on specific subjects or in specific disciplines in 012–016; class comprehensive works in 017

> *See also 011 for general bibliographies*

017 ***General subject catalogs**

Including alphabetically arranged subject catalogs, classified catalogs

Class here comprehensive works on catalogs

For catalogs on specific subjects, see 016. For a specific kind of nonsubject catalog, see the kind of catalog, e.g., catalogs of works by specific classes of authors 013

018 ***Catalogs arranged by author, main entry, date, or register number**

019 ***Dictionary catalogs**

020 Library and information sciences

Standard subdivisions are added for either or both topics in heading

Class here archives and archival techniques

For bibliography, see 010

See also 003 for information theory, 651.5 for records management as a managerial service

See Manual at 020

SUMMARY

[.68] Management

Do not use; class in 025.1

.7 **Education, research, related topics**

.71 Education

Do not use for in-service training; class in 023

.9 **Historical, geographic, persons treatment**

Class here comparative librarianship; historical, geographic, persons treatment of librarianship

For historical and persons treatment of libraries, see 027.009; for geographic treatment of libraries, see 027.01–027.09

---

*Do not add notation 091–099 from Table 1 for catalogs of works from specific places; class in 015

021 Relationships of libraries, archives, information centers

Standard subdivisions are added for any or all topics in heading

Class here libraries, archives, information centers as social forces

See also 027 for comprehensive works on libraries, archives, information centers

.2 Relationships with the community

Including clearinghouse for information on community action programs, sponsorship of community cultural programs

.6 Cooperation and networks

Including consortia

Class networks, systems, consortia for a specific kind of institution in 026–027. Class cooperation in and networks, systems, consortia for a specific function with the function, e.g., cooperative cataloging 025.3, interlibrary loan networks 025.6

See also 017–019 for specific union catalogs

.7 Promotion of libraries, archives, information centers

Standard subdivisions are added for any or all topics in heading

Including friends of the library organizations

Class here public relations

Class advertising in 659.1

.8 Relationships with government

Regardless of governmental level

Including library commissions and governing boards, financial support by government

022 Administration of the physical plant

Including bookmobiles

Class here library quarters in buildings devoted primarily to other activities, e.g., physical plant of school libraries; maintenance of physical plant

See also 025.8 for physical security of collections, closed versus open stacks; 727 for library architecture

023 Personnel administration

Including in-service training

025 Operations of libraries, archives, information centers

Standard subdivisions are added for any or all topics in heading

Including technical processing

Class here documentation (systematic collection, organization, storage, retrieval, dissemination of recorded information)

Class comprehensive works on operations in specific kinds of institutions in 026–027. Class a specific technical process with the process, e.g., acquisitions 025.2

.001–.009   Standard subdivisions

.04   Information storage and retrieval systems

Class here search and retrieval in information storage and retrieval systems; front-end systems; comprehensive works on online catalogs integrated with information storage and retrieval systems, on storage, search, and retrieval of information; interdisciplinary works on databases

Class information storage in 025.3

For computer science aspects of automated information storage and retrieval systems, of databases, see 005.74; for automated information storage and retrieval systems devoted to specific disciplines and subjects, see 025.06. For a specific kind of information storage and retrieval system, see the kind, e.g., online catalogs 025.3

See also 658.4 for management use of automated information storage and retrieval systems

See Manual at 004.67 vs. 025.04, 384.3; also at 005.74

.06   Information storage and retrieval systems devoted to specific disciplines and subjects

Class here documentation of specific disciplines and subjects

[.060 001–.060 009]   Standard subdivisions

Do not use; class in 025.0401–025.0409

.1   **Administration**

Including photocopying, finance, comprehensive works on user fees

Class government financial support in 021.8; class publishing by libraries, archives, information centers in 070.5; class interdisciplinary works on photoduplication in 686.4. Class administration of a specific function with the function, plus notation 068 from Table 1, e.g., administration of cataloging 025.3068

For administration of physical plant, see 022; for personnel administration, see 023. For user fees for a specific service, see the service, plus notation 068 from Table 1, e.g., user fees for automated search and retrieval 025.04068

.17 Administration of collections of special materials

Including audiovisual materials, machine-readable materials

Class here nonbook materials, comprehensive works on treatment of special materials

For a specific kind of treatment of special materials, see the kind of treatment, e.g., cataloging, classification, indexing of special materials 025.3

.2 **Acquisitions and collection development**

Standard subdivisions are added for acquisitions and collection development together, for acquisitions alone

Including selection policies and procedures; collection analysis, evaluation, management; weeding; censorship, comprehensive works on library policies and practices relating to intellectual freedom

Class interdisciplinary works on censorship in 363.3

For policies and practices relating to intellectual freedom in a library operation other than collection development, see the operation, e.g., circulation services 025.6

See also 098 for prohibited works, 303.3 for sociological studies of censorship, 323.44 for intellectual freedom as a civil right, 342 for law on intellectual freedom, 344 for laws of censorship

.3 **Bibliographic analysis and control**

Including the catalog and its maintenance, machine-readable catalog record formats, retrospective conversion, descriptive cataloging, cataloging and classification of special materials, cooperative cataloging and classification, recataloging, reclassification; name and title authorities, comprehensive works on authority files

Class here comprehensive works on cataloging and classification, on indexing, on information storage

For subject analysis and control, see 025.4

See also 025.04 for comprehensive works on information storage and retrieval systems

.302 Miscellany

Do not use for standards; class in 025.3

.4 **Subject analysis and control**

Including subject cataloging, subject indexing; classification, specific classification systems, e.g., Dewey Decimal Classification; assignment of book numbers (shelflisting)

Class classification and subject cataloging of special materials, cooperative classification and subject cataloging, reclassification and subject recataloging in 025.3

.402		Miscellany

> Do not use for standards; class in 025.4

.402 8		Abstracting techniques; auxiliary techniques and procedures; apparatus, equipment, materials

> Class techniques and style in writing abstracts in 808

.5 Services to users

Including information and referral services, information search and retrieval, reference services, selective dissemination of information; library orientation; library use studies

Class library services to special groups and organizations in 027.6; class use of books and other media as sources of information in 028.7; class comprehensive works on the creation and use of information storage and retrieval systems in 025.04; class comprehensive works on the creation and use of specific tools for bibliographic control in 025.3. Class a specific service not provided for here with the service, e.g., circulation services 025.6, storytelling for children 027.62

.6 Circulation services

Including interlibrary loans

Class here document delivery

Class circulation services for special groups and organizations in 027.6

.7 Physical preparation for storage and use

Including binding, repair

Class conservation and preservation in 025.8

.8 Maintenance and preservation of collections

Including access to collections, e.g., access to stacks; security against theft and other hazards, taking of inventory, conservation

Class repair in 025.7

> ## 026–027 Specific kinds of institutions

Class here specific libraries, archives, informations centers and their collections; systems and networks for specific kinds of institutions; comprehensive works on operations in specific kinds of institutions

Class comprehensive works in 027. Class a specific operation in a specific kind of institution with the operation, e.g., reference and information services in college libraries 025.5

026 Libraries, archives, information centers devoted to specific disciplines and subjects

Class here information organizations and library departments and collections in specific disciplines and subjects; comprehensive works on archives, on special libraries

Class special libraries not devoted to specific disciplines and subjects in 027.6, e.g., general museum libraries, general libraries in newspaper offices, patients' libraries

See Manual at 016 vs. 026, T1—07

.000 1–.000 5	Standard subdivisions
.000 6	Organizations
[.000 68]	Management
	Do not use; class in 025.1
.000 7–.000 9	Standard subdivisions

027 General libraries, archives, information centers

Standard subdivisions are added for any or all topics in heading

In the subdivisions of this number, the term *libraries* is used as a short way of saying libraries, archives, information centers, media centers

Class here comprehensive works on libraries, on information centers, on libraries and information centers devoted to special materials

For libraries, archives, information centers devoted to specific disciplines and subjects, see 026

.001–.005	Standard subdivisions
.006	Organizations
[.006 8]	Management
	Do not use; class in 025.1
.007–.008	Standard subdivisions
.009	Historical and persons treatment
	Do not use for geographic treatment; class in 027.01–027.09
.01–.09	*Geographic treatment
	Add to base number 027.0 notation 1–9 from Table 2, e.g., libraries in France 027.044

*Do not add notation 068 from Table 1; class in 025.1

.4   *Public libraries

Institutions that provide free service to all residents of a community, district, region, usually supported in whole or in part from public funds

Class here public library branches, use of bookmobiles (mobile libraries) in public librarianship

Class physical plant management of bookmobiles (mobile libraries) in 022; class public library units devoted to specific disciplines and subjects in 026; class public library units for special groups and organizations in 027.6

[.409 3–.409 9]   Treatment by specific continents, countries, localities

Do not use; class in 027.43–027.49

.43–.49   *Treatment by specific continents, countries, localities

Add to base number 027.4 notation 3–9 from Table 2, e.g., public libraries in France 027.444

.5   *Government libraries

National, state, provincial, local

For government libraries for special groups, see 027.6

.509 3–.509 9   Treatment by specific continents, countries, localities

Class specific institutions in 027.53–027.59

.53–.59   *Specific institutions

Add to base number 027.5 notation 3–9 from Table 2 for area served, e.g., Library of Congress 027.573

.6   *Libraries for special groups and organizations

Including libraries for persons in late adulthood, for minorities, for persons with disabilities; patients' libraries; prison libraries; libraries for religious organizations, for nonprofit organizations, for business and industrial organizations

Class here library and information services to special groups and organizations, to the socially disadvantaged

Class libraries for special groups and organizations but devoted to specific disciplines and subjects in 026

For libraries for educational institutions, see 027.7–027.8

.62   Libraries for children and young people aged twelve to twenty

Including storytelling

Class libraries for children and young people who are also members of other special groups and organizations, e.g., libraries for children with disabilities, in 027.6

*Do not add notation 068 from Table 1; class in 025.1

[.620 1–.620 9]   Standard subdivisions

Do not use; class in 027.62

> **027.7–027.8 Libraries for educational institutions**

Class here instructional media centers

Class comprehensive works in 027.7; class libraries for educational institutions but devoted to specific disciplines and subjects in 026

.7   ***College and university libraries**

Standard subdivisions are added for either or both topics in heading

Including comprehensive works on instructional materials centers [*formerly* 027.8]

Class here comprehensive works on libraries for educational institutions, college and university library branches

For branches devoted to specific disciplines and subjects, see 026; for elementary and secondary school libraries, see 027.8

.709 3–.709 9   Treatment by specific continents, countries, localities

Class specific institutions in 027.73–027.79

.73–.79   *Specific institutions

Add to base number 027.7 notation 3–9 from Table 2, e.g., Perkins Library of Duke University 027.7756

.8   ***School libraries**

Comprehensive works on instructional materials centers relocated to 027.7

.809 3–.809 9   Treatment by specific continents, countries, localities

Class specific institutions in 027.8

028   Reading and use of other information media

Reading interests and habits, use of books and other media as sources of recreation and self-development are classed in 028, without use of 028.01–028.09; reading interest and habits of children and young adults, use of books and other media as sources of recreation and self-development by children and young adults are classed with children and young adults in 028.5

*Do not add notation 068 from Table 1; class in 025.1

.1   **Reviews**

Including reviews of reference works, of audiovisual materials

Class here general collections of book reviews

Class reviews of computer programs in 005.3029; class techniques of reviewing in 808. Class reviews of works on a specific subject or in a specific discipline with the subject or discipline, e.g., reviews of works on chemistry 540, reviews of entertainment films 791.43, critical appraisal of literature 800

.5   **Reading and use of other information media by children and young people**

Standard subdivisions are added for either or both topics in heading

See also 028.1 for reviews of materials for children and young people

.7   **Use of books and other media as sources of information**

Standard subdivisions are added for either or both topics in heading

Class here use of reference works

For reading and use of other information media by children and young people, see 028.5

030   General encyclopedic works

Class here books of miscellaneous facts (e.g., almanacs), encyclopedia yearbooks, general works about curiosities

.9   **Historical, geographic, persons treatment**

Class historical, geographic, persons treatment of general encyclopedic works in specific languages and language families in 031–039

> ## 031–039   General encyclopedic works in specific languages and language families

By language in which originally written

Class here specific encyclopedias and books of miscellaneous facts, works about them

Class comprehensive works, encyclopedic works originally written in two or more languages or language families without any language or language family being preponderant in 030. Class encyclopedic works originally written in two or more languages or language families with one language or language family being preponderant with the preponderant language or language family, e.g., encyclopedic work written in Spanish with some articles in French 036

031   American English-language encyclopedias

English-language encyclopedias and books of miscellaneous facts originating in Western Hemisphere

.02   Books of miscellaneous facts

> Do not use for other types of miscellany; class in 031

> Including almanacs with general information, believe-it-or-not books, other books of curious and unusual facts

032   General encyclopedic works in English

> *For American English-language encyclopedic works, see 031*

.02   Books of miscellaneous facts

> Do not use for other types of miscellany; class in 032

> Including almanacs with general information, believe-it-or-not books, other books of curious and unusual facts

033   General encyclopedic works in other Germanic languages

> Class here comprehensive works on Germanic-language general encyclopedias

> *For English-language encyclopedias, see 032; for Scandinavian-language encyclopedias, see 038*

034   General encyclopedic works in French, Provençal, Catalan

035   General encyclopedic works in Italian, Sardinian, Dalmatian, Romanian, Rhaeto-Romanic

036   General encyclopedic works in Spanish and Portuguese

037   General encyclopedic works in Slavic languages

038   General encyclopedic works in Scandinavian languages

039   General encyclopedic works in Italic, Hellenic, other languages

050   General serial publications

> Class here periodicals; indexes to general serial publications

> Class books of miscellaneous facts (even if published annually, e.g., almanacs), encyclopedia yearbooks in 030; class administrative reports and proceedings of general organizations in 060. Class indexes that focus on a specific subject or discipline in general serial publications with the subject or discipline in 016, e.g., an index to information on medicine in general serial publications 016.61

> *For newspapers, see 070*

> *See also 011 for bibliographies of general serial publications and bibliographies of directories, 017–019 for catalogs of general serial publications*

.9 **Historical, geographic, persons treatment**

Class historical, geographic, persons treatment of general serial publications in specific languages and language families, and their indexes in 051–059

> **051–059 General serial publications in specific languages and language families**

By language in which originally written

Class here specific serial publications and works about them

Class comprehensive works, serials originally written in two or more language families without any language or language family being preponderant in 050. Class serials originally written in two or more languages or language families with one language or language family being preponderant with the preponderant language or language family, e.g., serial written in Spanish with some articles in French 056

(Option: Arrange serial publications alphabetically under 050)

051 **American English-language serial publications**

English-language serial publications of Western Hemisphere

052 **General serial publications in English**

For American English-language serial publications, see 051

053 **General serial publications in other Germanic languages**

Class here comprehensive works on general serial publications in Germanic languages

For English-language serial publications, see 052; for Scandinavian-language serial publications, see 058

054 **General serial publications in French, Provençal, Catalan**

055 **General serial publications in Italian, Sardinian, Dalmatian, Romanian, Rhaeto-Romanic**

056 **General serial publications in Spanish and Portuguese**

057 **General serial publications in Slavic languages**

058 **General serial publications in Scandinavian languages**

059 **General serial publications in Italic, Hellenic, other languages**

060 General organizations and museology

General organizations: associations, conferences, congresses, foundations, societies whose activity is not limited to a specific field

Including history, charters, regulations, membership lists, administrative reports and proceedings

Class here interdisciplinary works on organizations; interdisciplinary works on licensing, certification, accreditation by nongovernmental organizations

Class history, charters, regulations, membership lists, administrative reports and proceedings of a specific organization in 061–068; class interdisciplinary works on licensing, certification, accreditation by governmental and nongovernmental bodies in 352.8

> *For interdisciplinary works on international governmental organizations, see 341.2. For organizations devoted to a specific discipline or subject, see the discipline or subject, plus notation 06 from Table 1, e.g., organizations devoted to library and information sciences 020.6*

> *See Manual at 338 vs. 060, 381, 382, 670.29, 910, T1—025, T1—029*

.4 **General rules of order (Parliamentary procedure)**

Including *Robert's Rules of Order*

> *For rules and procedures of legislative bodies, see 328*

> *See also 658.4 for conduct of meetings of business organizations*

[.401–.409] Standard subdivisions

Do not use; class in 060.4

.9 **Historical and persons treatment**

Do not use for geographic treatment of general organizations; class in 061–068

> ## 061–068 General organizations

Class comprehensive works in 060

061 General organizations in North America

Class general organizations in Middle America in 068

062 General organizations in British Isles   In England

063 General organizations in central Europe   In Germany

Including general organizations in Austria, Czech Republic, Slovakia, Poland, Hungary

> *For general organizations in Switzerland, see 068*

064   **General organizations in France and Monaco**

065   **General organizations in Italy and adjacent territories**

066   **General organizations in Iberian Peninsula and adjacent islands**   **In Spain**

067   **General organizations in eastern Europe**   **In Russia**

068   **General organizations in other geographic areas**

069   **Museology (Museum science)**

> Including collecting, preparing, maintaining, repairing museum objects; identifying forgeries and preventing thefts; collections and exhibits of museum objects; management of museums; services to patrons

> *For collections of a specific kind of object or objects that pertain to a specific subject or discipline, see the subject or discipline, plus notation 074 from Table 1, e.g., collections of fossils 560.74; for museum activities and services limited to a specific subject or discipline, collecting a specific kind of object or objects that pertain to a specific subject or discipline, see the subject or discipline, plus notation 075 from Table 1, e.g., activities and services of an aerospace museum 629.1075*

[.068]   Management of museums

> Do not use; class in 069

.09   Historical, geographic, persons treatment

> Class here specific museums not limited to a specific discipline or subject

> Class historical, geographic, persons treatment of museum buildings in 069. Class museums devoted to specific subjects and disciplines with the subject or discipline, plus notation 074 from Table 1, e.g., natural history museums 508.074

070   Documentary media, educational media, news media; journalism; publishing

> Standard subdivisions are added for documentary media, educational media, news media, journalism, publishing together; for newspapers and journalism together

.01–.08   Standard subdivisions of documentary media, educational media, news media; journalism; publishing

.09   Historical, geographic, persons treatment of documentary media, educational media, news media; journalism; publishing

> Class historical and persons treatment of journalism and newspapers in 070.9; class geographic treatment of journalism and newspapers in 071–079

.1 Documentary media, educational media, news media

Including documentary, educational films; educational, expository radio and television programs; radio and television news; newspapers, periodicals

Class here comprehensive works on journalism and production of specific kinds of educational, expository, news media

Class the book in 002; class specific general periodicals in 050; class photography aspects of motion pictures in 778.5; class comprehensive works on documentary, educational, news, and dramatic or entertainment films, radio, television programs in 791.4; class interdisciplinary works on mass media in 302.23; class interdisciplinary works on motion pictures in 384; class interdisciplinary works on radio in 384.54; class interdisciplinary works on television in 384.55. Class documentary, educational, news works themselves and discussion of them with the kind of general work or subject, e.g., general periodicals 050, recorded television programs on investing 332.6

> For specific journalistic activities and types of journalism, see 070.4; for expository writing and editorial techniques, see 808

> See also 371.33 for use of motion pictures, radio, television in teaching

.4 Journalism

Collecting, writing, editing information and opinion of current interest for presentation in newspapers, periodicals, films, radio, television

Including journalism directed to special groups, e.g., religious groups, ethnic groups; persons in a specific type of journalism, e.g., editors, foreign correspondents; specific types of journalism, e.g., photojournalism; radio and television sports programs

Class journalism of specific kinds of news media in 070.1; class journalists whose careers span many activities in 070.92; class school journalism in 371.8; class journalistic composition and editorial mechanics in 808; class comprehensive works on journalism and information media in 070

> See also 050 for general periodicals, 070.5 for newspaper publishing, 071–079 for specific newspapers, 174 for ethics of journalism, notation 05 from Table 1 for journals on a specific discipline or subject

.401–.407   Standard subdivisions

.408   Journalism with respect to groups of persons

Class journalism directed to special groups in 070.4

[.409]   Historical, geographic, persons, treatment

Do not use for historical and persons treatment; class in 070.9. Do not use for geographic treatment; class in 071–079

.5   **Publishing**

Including selection and editing of manuscripts, relations with authors, literary agents; kinds of publications, e.g., newspapers, paperback books, maps, music; kinds of publishers, e.g., academic, commercial, governmental publishers

Class here book publishing; publishers regardless of their field of activity; book clubs, e.g., Book-of-the-Month Club®; comprehensive works on publishing and printing

Class works on desktop publishing that emphasize typography in 686.2; class editorial techniques in 808

For printing, see 686.2

See Manual at 808.001–808.7 vs. 070.5

.502 9   Commercial miscellany

Class publishers' catalogs in 015

.509   Historical, geographic, persons treatment

Class here comprehensive works on specific publishers, using the area number for the location of the publisher's main office, e.g., U.S. Government Printing Office 070.509753

.9   **Historical and persons treatment of journalism and newspapers**

Class geographic treatment in 071–079

.92   Persons regardless of area, region, place

>   **071–079   Geographic treatment of journalism and newspapers**

Class here specific general newspapers, indexes to them, other works about them

Class comprehensive works in 070

(Option: Arrange newspapers alphabetically under 070)

071   **Journalism and newspapers in North America**

Standard subdivisions are added for either or both topics in heading

Class journalism and newspapers in Middle America in 079

072   **Journalism and newspapers in British Isles**   **In England**

073   Journalism and newspapers in central Europe   In Germany

Standard subdivisions are added for either or both topics in heading

Including journalism and newspapers in Austria, Czech Republic, Slovakia, Poland, Hungary

For journalism and newspapers in Switzerland, see 079

074   Journalism and newspapers in France and Monaco

Standard subdivisions are added for journalism, newspapers, or both

075   Journalism and newspapers in Italy and adjacent territories

Standard subdivisions are added for journalism, newspapers, or both

076   Journalism and newspapers in Iberian Peninsula and adjacent islands   In Spain

Standard subdivisions are added for journalism, newspapers, or both

077   Journalism and newspapers in eastern Europe   In Russia

Standard subdivisions are added for journalism, newspapers, or both

078   Journalism and newspapers in Scandinavia

Standard subdivisions are added for either or both topics in heading

079   Journalism and newspapers in other geographic areas

Standard subdivisions are added for either or both topics in heading

080   General collections

Class here addresses, lectures, essays, interviews, graffiti, quotations

Class essays as literary form, collections gathered for their literary quality in 800

See Manual at 080 vs. 800

.9   Historical, geographic, persons treatment

Class historical, geographic, persons treatment of collections in specific languages and language families in 081–089

>   081–089   General collections in specific languages and language families

Class comprehensive works in 080

See Manual at 081–089

(Option: Arrange collections alphabetically under 080)

081 American English-language general collections

English-language collections of Western Hemisphere

082 General collections in English

For American English-language general collections, see 081

083 General collections in other Germanic languages

Class here comprehensive works on Germanic-language collections

For English-language collections, see 082; for Scandinavian-language collections, see 088; for Old-English-language (Anglo-Saxon-language) collections, see 089

084 General collections in French, Provençal, Catalan

085 General collections in Italian, Sardinian, Dalmatian, Romanian, Rhaeto-Romanic

086 General collections in Spanish and Portuguese

087 General collections in Slavic languages

088 General collections in Scandinavian languages

089 General collections in Italic, Hellenic, other languages

Including Old English (Anglo-Saxon)

090 Manuscripts, rare books, other rare printed materials

Class interdisciplinary works on books in 002. Class a manuscript or rare book on a specific subject with the subject, e.g., a book of hours 242; class an artistic aspect of a manuscript or rare book with the aspect, e.g., illumination 745.6

See also 011 for bibliographies of manuscripts, rare books, other rare printed materials

091 Manuscripts

092 Block books

093 Incunabula

Books printed before 1501

094 Printed books

Including early books to 1700; first editions, limited editions, typographic masterpieces

For block books, see 092; for incunabula, see 093

095   Books notable for bindings

> *See also 686.3 for bookbinding*

096   Books notable for illustrations and materials

> Class illustrated manuscripts in 091

097   Books notable for ownership or origin

> Standard subdivisions are added for either or both topics in heading

098   Prohibited works, forgeries, hoaxes

099   Books notable for format

> Including miniature editions

100 Philosophy, paranormal phenomena, psychology

Class philosophy of a specific discipline or subject with the discipline or subject, plus notation 01 from Table 1, e.g., philosophy of history 901

See Manual at 170; also at 190 vs. 100, 109: also at 200 vs. 100

SUMMARY

101–109	**Standard subdivisions of philosophy**
110	**Metaphysics**
120	**Epistemology, causation, humankind**
130	**Paranormal phenomena**
140	**Specific philosophical schools and viewpoints**
150	**Psychology**
160	**Logic**
170	**Ethics (Moral philosophy)**
180	**Ancient, medieval, Oriental philosophy**
190	**Modern western and other non-Oriental philosophy**

101 Theory of philosophy

Class here works on the concept of philosophy, on the nature of the philosophical task, on the method of philosophy

Class schools of philosophical thought in 140; class ancient, medieval, Oriental schools in 180

102–108 Standard subdivisions of philosophy

109 Historical and collected persons treatment of philosophy

Do not use for geographic treatment; class in 180–190

Not limited by period or place

See Manual at 190 vs. 100, 109

.2 Collected treatment of persons

Do not use for individual persons; class in 180–190

110 Metaphysics

For epistemology, causation, humankind, see 120

111　Ontology

Including being, essence, existence, substance, nonbeing and nothingness, interdisciplinary works on aesthetics

> *For aesthetics of a specific subject, see the subject, e.g., aesthetics of fine arts 701*

113　Cosmology (Philosophy of nature)

Including origin of universe (cosmogony), origin and nature of life

Class origin and nature of human life in 128; class cosmology as a topic in astronomy in 523.1

> *For specific topics of cosmology not provided for here, see 114–119*

114　Space

Class here relation of space and matter

Class matter in 117

115　Time

Including eternity, space and time, relation of time and motion

> *For space, see 114*

116　Change

Including cycles, evolution, motion, process

Class relation of time and motion in 115

117　Structure

Including matter, form, order, chaos

Class relation of space and matter in 114

118　Force and energy

Standard subdivisions are added for either or both topics in heading

119　Number and quantity

120　Epistemology, causation, humankind

121   Epistemology (Theory of knowledge)

Including belief and faith; certainty; doubt and denial; evidence; meaning, interpretation, hermeneutics; philosophy of language; probability; semantics, semiotics; worth and theory of values (axiology)

Class here comprehensive works on truth

Class knowledge and its extension in 001; class reason as a human attribute in 128; class ethical values in 170; class religious faith in 200; class interdisciplinary works on semiotics in 302.2

For truth in logic, see 160

See also 149 for linguistic philosophies as schools of philosophy, 401 for semantics and semiotics in linguistics

122   Causation

Class here chance versus cause

For determinism and indeterminism, see 123; for teleology, see 124

123   Determinism and indeterminism

Standard subdivisions are added for either or both topics in heading

Including chance, fate, freedom, freedom of will, necessity

Class chance versus cause in 122

124   Teleology

126   The self

Class here consciousness, personality

Class the unconscious and the subconscious in 127

127   The unconscious and the subconscious

Standard subdivisions are added for either or both topics in heading

128   Humankind

Including emotion, imagination, memory, will; death; human action, experience; human body; love; mind, mind-body relationship; rationality and reason; soul

Class here philosophical anthropology; comprehensive works on philosophy of human life, on philosophy and psychology of human life

Class reason as an instrument of knowledge in 121; class interdisciplinary works on death in 306.9

For freedom of will, see 123; for the self, see 126; for origin and destiny of individual souls, see 129; for psychology, see 150; for science of reasoning (logic), see 160

129 Origin and destiny of individual souls

Including immortality, reincarnation

Class accounts of previous incarnations in 133.9

> *See Manual at 133.9 vs. 129*

130 Paranormal phenomena

Class phenomena of religious experience in 200; class interdisciplinary works on controversial knowledge and paranormal phenomena in 001.9

> *See Manual at 001.9 and 130*

.1 Philosophy and theory

Do not use for forecasting and forecasts; class comprehensive works on parapsychological and occult forecasting and forecasts in 133.3. Class a specific type with the type, without adding notation 01 from Table 1, e.g., astrological methods of forecasting 133.5

131 Parapsychological and occult techniques for achieving well-being, happiness, success

Standard subdivisions are added for any or all topics in heading

Class interdisciplinary works limited to psychological and parapsychological or occult techniques for achieving personal well-being, happiness, success in 158; class interdisciplinary works on successful living, on management of personal and family living in 646.7. Class specific methods of parapsychology and occultism for achieving well-being with the method in 133–139, e.g., spells and charms 133.4

133 Parapsychology and occultism

Standard subdivisions are added for either or both topics in heading

Including specific things used for more than one purpose, in more than one branch of parapsychology and occultism, e.g., occult use of crystals for healing, personality analysis, fortune-telling

Class here frauds in occultism

> *For cabalistic, hermetic, Rosicrucian traditions, see 135. For a specific parapsychological or occult use of a specific thing, see the use in 131–139, e.g., fortune-telling by crystals 133.3; for use of a specific thing in a specific branch of parapsychology and occultism, see the branch in 131–139, e.g., astrological aspects of planets 133.5*

> *See Manual at 133 vs. 200*

.1   **Apparitions**

Including works that treat one specific haunted place, e.g., old Monterey's Hotel del Monte

Class here ghosts

Class ghosts as subjects of folklore in 398; class folkloristic ghost stories in 398.25; class literary accounts of ghosts in 808.8; class interdisciplinary works on spirits (discarnate beings) in 133.9

.109   Historical, geographic, persons treatment

Do not use for a single haunted place; class in 133.1

Class here two or more haunted places, e.g., haunted places in Wales 133.109429

.3   **Divinatory arts**

Including crystal gazing, dowsing, numerology, oracles, tarot

Class here works on the symbolism of divinatory arts and objects, comprehensive works on occult methods of foretelling the future

Class use of extrasensory perception for divination in 133.8; class interdisciplinary works on forecasting in 003

For astrology, see 133.5; for palmistry, see 133.6; for dream books, see 135; for divinatory graphology, see 137; for physiognomy, see 138

See also 291.3 for divination as a religious practice, 303.49 for social forecasting

.4   **Demonology and witchcraft**

Including demoniac possession, evil spirits, exorcism, magic, satanism (devil worship), spells and charms

Class here black arts

For divinatory arts, see 133.3

See also 291.2 for religious beliefs about demons; 235 for Christian beliefs; 299 for satanic cults regarded as religions by their adherents, for voodooism

.5   **Astrology**

Class here works on the symbolism of astrology

.501   Philosophy and theory

Do not use for forecasting and forecasts; class in 133.5

.508   History and description with respect to kinds of persons

.508 8	Occupational and religious groups

Do not use for types or schools of astrology originating in or associated with a specific religious group; class in 133.5

Including astrology in general with respect to specific religious groups

.508 9	Racial, ethnic, national groups

Do not use for types or schools of astrology originating in or associated with a specific racial, ethnic, national group; class in 133.5

Class here astrology in general with respect to specific racial, ethnic, national groups

.509	Historical, geographic, persons treatment

.509 3–.509 9	Treatment by specific continents, countries, localities

Do not use for types or schools of astrology originating in or associated with a specific area; class in 133.5

Class here astrology in general in a specific area

.6	**Palmistry**

.601	Philosophy and theory

Do not use for forecasting and forecasts; class in 133.6

.8	**Psychic phenomena**

Including clairvoyance, precognition, psychokinesis, telepathy

Class here psi phenomena, psychic communication, psychic talents and gifts; comprehensive works treating extrasensory perception (ESP), spiritualism, and ghosts together

Class comprehensive works on divination in 133.3

For ghosts, see 133.1; for spiritualism, see 133.9

.801	Philosophy and theory

Do not use for forecasting and forecasts; class in 133.8

.9 **Spiritualism**

The phenomena and systems of ideas connected with belief in communication with spirits (discarnate beings)

Including astral projection, channeling, mediumship; mediumistic phenomena, e.g., ectoplasm, spirit photography, table tipping; nature of spiritual world and life after death; personal recollections of previous incarnations; personal survival; psychic messages (method and content of communications purporting to come from discarnate entities)

Class here communication with extraterrestrial spirits, necromancy, interdisciplinary works on spirits (discarnate beings)

For ghosts, see 133.1; for psychic messages on religious subjects, see 200

See Manual at 133.9 vs. 129

135 Dreams and mysteries

Including cabalistic, hermetic, Rosicrucian traditions; dream books

Class mysteries of magic and witchcraft in 133.4; class interdisciplinary works on mysteries in the sense of reported phenomena not explained, not fully verified in 001.9; class interdisciplinary works on psychological and parapsychological aspects of dreams in 154.6

See also 296.1 for cabala in Judaism

137 Divinatory graphology

Class interdisciplinary works on graphology and use of graphology in analyzing character in 155.2

138 Physiognomy

Class here comprehensive works on determination of character or divination from analysis of physical features

For palmistry, see 133.6; for phrenology, see 139

139 Phrenology

Determination of mental capacities from skull structure

140 Specific philosophical schools and viewpoints

Including the concept of ideology, of a world view, of a system of beliefs

Class development, description, critical appraisal, collected writings, biographical treatment of individual philosophers regardless of viewpoint in 180–190; class comprehensive works on modern western and ancient, medieval, Oriental viewpoints in 100; class comprehensive works on modern western viewpoints in 190. Class a specific topic or branch of philosophy treated from a specific philosophical viewpoint with the topic or branch, e.g., existentialist ontology 111, realist epistemology 121; class ideologies concerning a specific discipline with the discipline, e.g., political ideologies 320.5

For ancient, medieval, Oriental schools, see 180

See also 171 for systems and schools of ethics

See Manual at 140; also at 140 vs. 180–190

141 Idealism and related systems and doctrines

Standard subdivisions are added for idealism and related systems and doctrines together, for idealism alone

Including individualism, modern Platonism and Neoplatonism, personalism, romanticism, spiritualism, subjectivism, transcendentalism

Class comprehensive works on Platonism in 184; class comprehensive works on Neoplatonism in 186

142 Critical philosophy

Including existentialism, Kantianism, phenomenology

Class critical realism in 149

143 Bergsonism and intuitionism

144 Humanism and related systems and doctrines

Standard subdivisions are added for humanism and related systems and doctrines together, for humanism alone

Including pragmatism, utilitarianism

145 Sensationalism

146 Naturalism and related systems and doctrines

Standard subdivisions are added for naturalism and related systems and doctrines together, for naturalism alone

Including empiricism, evolutionism, materialism, dialectical materialism, mechanism, positivism, process philosophy, comprehensive works on the analytical movement

Class philosophic foundations of Marxism in 335.4

For linguistic philosophies, see 149

147   Pantheism and related systems and doctrines

Standard subdivisions are added for pantheism and related systems and doctrines together, for pantheism alone

Including dualism, monism, pluralism

148   Dogmatism, eclecticism, liberalism, syncretism, traditionalism

149   Other philosophical systems and doctrines

Including deconstruction, fatalism, linguistic philosophies, neo-Aristotelianism, neo-scholasticism, neo-Thomism, nihilism, nominalism, optimism, pessimism, postmodernism, rationalism, realism, relativism, skepticism, structuralism

Class semantics, semiotics as philosophical topics in 121; class ancient Aristotelianism in 185; class medieval scholasticism, medieval Thomism in 189; class comprehensive works on the analytical movement in 146. Class postmodernism in relation to a specific discipline with the discipline, e.g., in relation to literary criticism 801

> *See also 302.2 for interdisciplinary works on semiotics; 401 for philosophy of language*

150   Psychology

Unless other instructions are given, observe the following table of preference, e.g., emotions of children 155.4 (*not* 152.4):

[Aptitude and vocational interest tests]	153.9
Comparative psychology	156
Subconscious and altered states and processes	154
Differential and developmental psychology	155
Sensory perception, movement, emotions, physiological drives	152
Conscious mental processes and intelligence (*except* aptitude and vocational interest tests 153.9)	153
Applied psychology	158

Class testing for aptitude in a specific discipline or subject in 153.9; class social psychology in 302

> *For psychological principles (other than the principles of aptitude and vocational interest testing) of a specific discipline or subject, see the discipline or subject, plus notation 01 from Table 1, e.g., psychological principles of advertising 659.101*

> *See Manual at 302–307 vs. 150, T1—01*

SUMMARY

.1   **Philosophy and theory**

.19   Systems, schools, viewpoints

> Standard subdivisions are added for any or all topics in heading

> Including functionalism; Gestalt psychology; psychoanalysis, e.g., Freudian, Jungian systems; reductionism, e.g., behaviorism; existential psychology

.2   **Miscellany**

.28   Auxiliary techniques and procedures; apparatus, equipment, materials

> Do not use for comprehensive works on intelligence testing and personality testing; class in 153.9

.8   **History and description with respect to kinds of persons**

> Do not use for psychology of specific kinds of persons; class in 155

.9   **Historical, geographic, persons treatment**

> Class national psychology of specific countries in 155.8

152   Sensory perception, movement, emotions, physiological drives

> Class here comprehensive works on psychology and neurophysiology of sensory perception, movement, emotions, physiological drives

> *For neurophysiology of sensory perception, movement, emotions, physiological drives, see 612.8*

> *See Manual at 612.8 vs. 152*

.1   **Sensory perception**

> Including senses of hearing, smell, taste, touch; pain; biofeedback

> *See Manual at 153.7 vs. 152.1*

.14   Visual perception

> Including color, movement, pattern, space perception; interdisciplinary works on optical illusions

> *For a specific aspect or use of optical illusions, see the aspect or use, e.g., physiological aspects 612.8, use of optical illusions in art 701*

.3   **Movements and motor functions**

Standard subdivisions are added for either or both topics in heading

Including coordination, handedness, laterality, locomotion, motor learning, reflexes, vocal and graphic expressions, comprehensive works on habits

Class meaning of movements (as in body language) in 153.6

> *For reaction-time studies, see 152.8; for conscious mental habits, see 153*
>
> *See also 362.29 for substance abuse*

.4   **Emotions and feelings**

Standard subdivisions are added for either or both topics in heading

Including aggressive moods and feelings, anger, embarrassment, envy, fear, grief, guilt, love and affection

Class here affects, attitudes, moods, sentiments; complexes of emotions and feelings

Class character traits such as bashfulness, comprehensive works on psychology of aggression in 155.2; class grief associated with bereavement by death, loneliness in 155.9; class depression in 616.85

.5   **Physiological drives**

Class motivation, comprehensive works on drives in 153.8

.8   **Quantitative threshold, discrimination, reaction-time studies**

153   **Conscious mental processes and intelligence**

Standard subdivisions are added for conscious mental processes and intelligence together, for conscious mental processes alone

Class here cognitive science, intellectual processes

> *For artificial intelligence, see 006.3; for emotions and feelings, see 152.4*
>
> *See also 121 for epistemology, 128 for mind-body problem in philosophy*
>
> *See Manual at 153 vs. 006.3; also at 153 vs. 153.4*

.028   Auxiliary techniques and procedures; apparatus, equipment, materials

Do not use for testing and measurement; class in 153.9

.1   **Memory and learning**

Including Pavlovian (classical) conditioning, operant conditioning

Class memory with respect to a specific topic with the topic, e.g., memory and dreams 154.6

> *See Manual at 153.1 vs. 370.15; also at 155.4–155.6 vs. 153.1*

.2   **Formation and association of ideas**

.3 **Imagination, imagery, creativity**

Standard subdivisions are added for imagination, imagery, creativity together; for imagination alone

Class here daydreams, fantasies, reveries considered as aspects of the imagination

Class comprehensive works on daydreams, fantasies, reveries in 154.3

For creativity in a specific field, see the field, plus notation 01 from Table 1, e.g., creativity in the arts 700.1

.4 **Thought, thinking, reasoning, intuition, value, judgment**

Former heading: Knowledge (Cognition)

Including problem solving

For formation and association of ideas, see 153.2; for moral judgment, see 155.2

See Manual at 153 vs. 153.4; also at 153.4 vs. 160

.402 8 Auxiliary techniques and procedures; apparatus, equipment, materials

Do not use for testing and measurement; class in 153.9

.6 **Communication**

Including listening; nonverbal communication, e.g., body language

Class here individual aspects of interpersonal communication

Class sociolinguistics in 306.44; class psychology of language and language processing (psycholinguistics), speech perception in 401; class psychology of reading in 418.01; class social psychology of, interdisciplinary works on communication in 302.2

.7 **Perceptual processes**

Perceptual apprehension and understanding

Including attention, errors, subliminal perception; perception of space, time, rhythm, movement

For extrasensory perception, see 133.8; for sensory perception, see 152.1

See Manual at 153.7 vs. 152.1

.8 **Will (Volition)**

Including choice, decision; modification of will, e.g., brainwashing, persuasion; self-control

Class here intentionality, motivation, comprehensive works on drives

For physiological drives, see 152.5

See also 155.2 for modification of character and personality

.9 **Intelligence and aptitudes**

Including aptitude, intelligence, vocational interest tests and testing; comprehensive works on testing and measurement of cognition, of conscious mental processes, of intelligence and personality

Class factors in differential and developmental psychology that affect intelligence and aptitudes in 155; class comprehensive works on vocational interests in 158.6

For personality tests, see 155.2; for educational tests and measurement, see 371.26; for tests to diagnose neuropsychiatric conditions, see 616.8

See Manual at 153.9

.902 8 Auxiliary techniques and procedures; apparatus, equipment, materials

Do not use for testing and measurement; class in 153.9

154 Subconscious and altered states and processes

.2 **The subconscious**

Including id, ego, superego; complexes, sublimation, transference

.3 **Daydreams, fantasies, reveries**

Standard subdivisions are added for any or all topics in heading

Class here secondary consciousness

For daydreams, fantasies, reveries considered as aspects of imagination, see 153.3

.4 **Altered states of consciousness**

Including altered states due to use of drugs; hallucinations

.6 **Sleep phenomena**

Including sleepwalking, interdisciplinary works on dreams

For parapsychological aspects of dreams, see 135; for physiological aspects of dreams, see 612.8

See Manual at 612.8 vs. 154.6

.7 **Hypnotism**

Class here interdisciplinary works on hypnotism

For psychic aspects of hypnotism, see 133.8; for medical applications of hypnotism, see 615.8

155 Differential and developmental psychology

Including role of play in development

Unless other instructions are given, observe the following table of preference, e.g., influence of social environment on children 155.4 (*not* 155.9):

Psychology of specific ages	155.4–155.6
Ethnopsychology and national psychology	155.8
Evolutional psychology	155.7
Environmental psychology	155.9
Sex psychology and psychology of the sexes	155.3
Individual psychology	155.2

Class role of play in relation to a specific topic with the topic, e.g., role of play in child development 155.4

.2 Individual psychology

Including defense mechanisms; development and modification of personality; personality appraisals and tests, e.g., handwriting analysis, Rorschach test; personality traits, e.g., altruism, bashfulness, extroversion, introversion; personality determinants, e.g., environment versus heredity; typology, e.g., classification scheme of Jung; comprehensive works on the psychology of aggression; interdisciplinary works on graphology

Class here the self; character, identity, individuality, personality

Class general application of topics of individual psychology in 158; class use of personality tests to diagnose psychiatric disorders in 616.89; class use of personality tests to determine vocational interests and comprehensive works on appraisals and tests for intelligence and personality in 153.9; class interdisciplinary works on aggression, aggressive social interactions in 302.5. Class defense mechanisms in relation to a specific topic with the topic, e.g., defense mechanisms and reactions to death 155.9

For divinatory graphology, see 137; for aggressive emotions and feelings, see 152.4; for aggressive drives, see 153.8; for handwriting analysis for the examination of evidence, see 363.25; for handwriting analysis for screening of prospective employees, see 658.3

See Manual at 158 vs. 155.2

.202 8 Auxiliary techniques and procedures; apparatus, equipment, materials

Do not use for testing and measurement; class in 155.2

.3 Sex psychology and psychology of the sexes

Including erogeneity and libido; sex and personality; sex differences, e.g., masculinity, femininity, bisexuality; sexual relations

Class interdisciplinary works on and social psychology of sexual relations in 306.7

See Manual at 306.7 vs. 155.3

> **155.4–155.6 Psychology of specific ages**

Class here developmental psychology

Class influence of specific situations (e.g., death, accidents) on specific ages in 155.9; class comprehensive works in 155

See Manual at 155.4–155.6 vs. 153.1

.4 **Child psychology**

Through age eleven

Class socialization in 303.3; class interdisciplinary works on child development in 305.23

See also 649 for child rearing

> **155.42–155.45 Specific groupings**

Unless other instructions are given, observe the following table of preference, e.g., boys aged three to five 155.42 (*not* 155.43):

Exceptional children	155.45
Children by status, type, relationships	155.44
Children in specific age groups	155.42
Children by sex	155.43

Class comprehensive works in 155.4

.42 Children in specific age groups

Including infants, preschool children, school children

.43 Children by sex

Class here sex psychology of children

.44 Children by status, type, relationships

Including adopted, institutionalized children; siblings, twins

Class here psychology of temporary or permanent separation from parents

.45 Exceptional children

Including children with disabilities, gifted children

.5 **Psychology of young people twelve to twenty**

Comprehensive works on psychology of young adults relocated to 155.6

Class vocational tests for young people twelve to twenty in 153.9; class interdisciplinary works on the development of people twelve to twenty in 305.235

.6	**Psychology of adults**

Including comprehensive works on psychology of young adults [*formerly* 155.5]

.67	Persons in late adulthood

.7	**Evolutional psychology**

Evolution of basic human mental and psychological characteristics

Including behavioral genetics

Class here comprehensive works on environment versus heredity in psychology

> *For environment versus heredity in determining traits of character and personality, see 155.2; for environmental psychology, see 155.9*

.8	**Ethnopsychology and national psychology**

Class here cross-cultural psychology

Class cultural influence, influence of specific situations (e.g., death, accidents) on specific ethnic and national groups in 155.9

.9	**Environmental psychology**

Including influence and effect of diseases, physical disabilities; of physical environments, e.g., climate, noise; of social environments, e.g., community and housing, family, loneliness; of specific situations, e.g., accidents, disasters, death and dying, reaction to death of others; stress

> *For job stress, see 158.7*

> *See Manual at 302–307 vs. 155.9, 158.2*

156 Comparative psychology

Comparison of human psychology and the psychology of other organisms; study of other organisms to elucidate human behavior

Class behavior of nonhuman organisms in 591.5

158   Applied psychology

Including negotiation, counseling and interviewing, leadership; systems and schools of applied psychology

Class here application of individual psychology in general; comprehensive works on how to better oneself and how to get along with other people; comprehensive works on psychological and parapsychological or occult techniques for achieving personal well-being, happiness, success

Class aptitude and vocational interest tests (both general and applied to specific subjects) in 153.9; class interdisciplinary works on successful living, on management of personal and family living in 646.7; class interdisciplinary works on success in business and other public situations in 650.1. Class a specific application of psychology with the application, e.g., educational guidance and counseling 371.4; class application of a specific branch of psychology (other than individual psychology in general 155.2) with the branch, e.g., how to improve one's memory 153.1, how to be creative 153.3; class application of systems and schools of applied psychology with the application, e.g., application of transactional analysis to industrial psychology 158.7

> *For parapsychological and occult techniques for achieving personal well-being, happiness, success, see 131*

> *See Manual at 158 vs. 155.2*

.1   Personal improvement and analysis

Standard subdivisions are added for either or both topics in heading

Including meditation, collections of thoughts for use in meditation; personality analysis and improvement

Class here works intended to make one a better person or to stave off failure, to solve problems or to adjust to a life that does not meet one's expectations; works on specific systems and schools of applied psychology written for persons who wish to be improved or analyzed

Class works on how to get along with other people in 158.2; class works on specific systems and schools of applied psychology written for advisors and counselors to help them assist others, comprehensive works on how to better oneself and how to get along with other people in 158

> *See Manual at 616.86 vs. 158.1, 248.8, 291.4, 362.29*

.2   Interpersonal relations

Relations between an individual and other people

Class here dominance, intimacy; overcoming loneliness; applications of assertiveness training, sensitivity training, transactional analysis

Class individual aspects of interpersonal communication in 153.6; class interpersonal relations in counseling, interviewing, leadership, negotiation in 158; class social psychology of communication in 302.2; class interactions within groups in 302.3; class comprehensive works on loneliness in 155.9

> *See Manual at 302–307 vs. 155.9, 158.2*

.6   **Vocational interests**

Class aptitudes in 153.9; class interdisciplinary works on choice of vocation in 331.7

.602 8   Auxiliary techniques and procedures; apparatus, equipment, materials

Do not use for testing and measurement; class in 153.9

.7   **Industrial psychology**

Works focusing on the psychology of the individual employee in relation to work or taking a broad view that encompasses the concerns of individual employees, union leaders, management

Including job stress

Class here psychology of work

Class workaholism as a personality trait in 155.2. Class industrial psychology applied to a specific subject outside psychology with the subject, plus notation 01 from Table 1, e.g., psychological principles of personnel management 658.3001

See also 158.2 for psychology of interpersonal relations with work associates

160   Logic

Science of reasoning

Class psychology of reasoning in 153.4; class symbolic (mathematical) logic in 511.3

See Manual at 153.4 vs. 160

161   Induction

For hypotheses, see 167; for analogy, see 169

162   Deduction

For syllogisms, see 166

165   Fallacies and sources of error

Standard subdivisions are added for either or both topics in heading

Including contradictions, fictions, paradoxes

166   Syllogisms

167   Hypotheses

168   Argument and persuasion

Standard subdivisions are added for either or both topics in heading

169   Analogy

170 Ethics (Moral philosophy)

Class here ethics of specific subjects and disciplines

> *For religious ethics, see 291.5; for social ethics as a method of social control, see 303.3. For ethics of a specific religion, see the religion, e.g., Christian moral theology 241*
>
> *See Manual at 170; also at 170 vs. 303.3*

[.88] Occupational and religious groups

> Do not use for ethics of occupational groups; class in 174. Do not use for ethics of religious groups; class in 291.5

.92 Persons

> *See Manual at 170.92 vs. 171*

171 Ethical systems

Regardless of time or place

Including altruism, hedonism, relativism, utilitarianism, situation ethics; systems based on evolution, on moral sense, on natural law, on reason, on self-realization, on social factors

Class a specific topic in ethics, regardless of the system within which it is treated, with the topic in 172–179, e.g., professional ethics 174

> *See Manual at 170.92 vs. 171*

> ## 172–179 Applied ethics (Social ethics)
>
> Ethics of specific human qualities, relationships, activities
>
> Class comprehensive works in 170

172 Political ethics

Including duties of citizens, of states and governments, of officeholders and officials; ethics of civil war, espionage, international relations, nuclear weapons, revolution, war and peace

173 Ethics of family relationships

Including ethics of marriage, divorce, separation, parent-child relationships

Class ethics of sex and reproduction in 176

174 Occupational ethics

Including business ethics, legal ethics, medical ethics, occupational ethics of clergy; ethics of gambling business, genetic engineering, human experimentation, industrial espionage

Class here economic, professional ethics; ethics of work

For experimentation on animals, see 179

See also 175 for gambling

See Manual at 174

175 Ethics of recreation, leisure, public performances, communication

Including ethics of dancing, gambling, music, television; sportsmanship

Ethics of hunting relocated to 179

Class occupational ethics for those involved in the recreation industry in 174

176 Ethics of sex and reproduction

Including artificial insemination, celibacy, chastity, contraception, homosexuality, in vitro fertilization, obscenity, pornography, premarital and extramarital relations, prostitution, surrogate motherhood

Class abortion in 179.7

For obscenity in speech, see 179

177 Ethics of social relations

Limited to benevolence, caring, charity, conversation, courtesy, courtship, discriminatory practices, flattery, friendship, gossip, hospitality, kindness, liberality, love, lying, personal appearance, philanthropy, politeness, slander, slavery, truthfulness

Class sexual ethics in courtship in 176; class etiquette in 395

178 Ethics of consumption

Including abstinence, gluttony, greed, overindulgence, temperance

Class here ethics of use of natural resources, of wealth

Class environmental and ecological ethics, respect for nature, consumption of meat in 179

179 Other ethical norms

Including ethics of hunting [*formerly* 175]; blasphemy; environmental and ecological ethics; courage, cowardice; profanity, obscenity in speech; respect for life and nature; treatment of children, of animals; vegetarianism; vices and virtues not otherwise provided for

Class here cruelty

[.01–.09]   Standard subdivisions

> Do not use; class in 170

.7   Respect and disrespect for human life

> Standard subdivisions are added for either or both topics in heading
>
> Including abortion, capital punishment, dueling, euthanasia, genocide, homicide, suicide
>
> Class here comprehensive works on ethics of violence, of nonviolence
>
> Class medical ethics in 174; class ethics of contraception in 176; class treatment of children in 179
>
> *For ethics of violence, of nonviolence in political activity, ethics of war, see 172*

> ## 180–190   Historical, geographic, persons treatment of philosophy
>
> Class here development, description, critical appraisal, collected writings, biographical treatment of individual philosophers regardless of viewpoint
>
> Class comprehensive works on geographic treatment in 100; class comprehensive works on historical treatment in 109; class comprehensive works on collected persons treatment in 109.2. Class critical appraisal of an individual philosopher's thought on a specific topic with the topic, plus notation 092 from Table 1, e.g., critical appraisal of Kant's theory of knowledge 121.092
>
> *See Manual at 180–190; also at 140 vs. 180–190*

180   Ancient, medieval, Oriental philosophy

[.01–.09]   Standard subdivisions of ancient, medieval, Oriental philosophy

> Do not use; class in 180

.1–.8   Standard subdivisions of ancient philosophy

.9   Historical and geographic treatment of ancient philosophy

> Do not use for ancient Oriental philosophy; class in 181
>
> Class treatment of specific schools of ancient western philosophy in 182–188

[.938]   Greece

> Do not use; class in 180

181   Oriental philosophy

Ancient, medieval, modern

Including philosophy of Arabia, China, Egypt, India, Palestine; philosophies based
on specific religions of Oriental origin, e.g., on Judaism, on Islam;
interdisciplinary works on the practice of yoga and yoga as a philosophical school

*For Christian philosophy, see 190; for yoga as a religious and spiritual
discipline, see 291.4; for Hindu yoga as a religious and spiritual discipline, see
294.5; for physical (hatha) yoga, see 613.7*

.001–.008   Standard subdivisions

.009   Historical treatment

Do not use for geographic treatment; class in 181

> ### 182–188 Ancient western philosophy

Class comprehensive works in 180

182   *Pre-Socratic Greek philosophies

183   *Sophistic, Socratic, related Greek philosophies

184   *Platonic philosophy

Class here comprehensive works on ancient and modern Platonism

For modern Platonism, see 141

185   *Aristotelian philosophy

Class here comprehensive works on Aristotelian and Neo-Aristotelian philosophy

For neo-Aristotelianism, see 149

186   *Skeptic and Neoplatonic philosophies

Including comprehensive works on ancient and modern Neoplatonism

For modern Neoplatonism, see 141

187   *Epicurean philosophy

188   *Stoic philosophy

189   †Medieval western philosophy

Including mystic, patristic, scholastic philosophy

Class here early Christian philosophy

For neo-scholasticism, neo-Thomism, see 149

---

*Do not add notation 092 from Table 1
†Do not add notation 09 from Table 1

190 Modern western and other non-Oriental philosophy

Class here comprehensive works on Christian philosophy, on modern philosophy, on modern western philosophy, on western philosophy, on European philosophy

Modern philosophy of areas not provided for in 180 is classed here, even if not in the western tradition, e.g., North American native philosophy 191.089, traditional African philosophy 199

Class Oriental philosophy in 181

> *For ancient western and European philosophy, see 180; for early and medieval Christian philosophy, medieval western and European philosophy, see 189*
>
> *See Manual at 190 vs. 100, 109*

[.94–.99] Treatment by continent, country, locality

Do not use; class in 191–199

191 †United States and Canada

Standard subdivisions are added for either or both topics in heading

Class here North American philosophy

> *For Middle American and Mexican philosophy, see 199*

192 †British Isles

193 †Germany and Austria

Standard subdivisions are added for either or both topics in heading

194 †France

195 †Italy

196 †Spain and Portugal

197 †Former Soviet Union

Class philosophy of former Soviet Asia in 181

198 †Scandinavia

Including Finland

199 †Other geographic areas

> *For Asian philosophy, see 181*

†Do not add notation 09 from Table 1

200   Religion

Beliefs, attitudes, practices of individuals and groups with respect to the ultimate nature of existences and relationships within the context of revelation, deity, worship

Including public relations for religion [*formerly* 659.2]

Comprehensive works on Christianity relocated to 230

Class comparative religion, works dealing with various religions in 291

> *See also 306.6 for sociology of religion*
>
> *See Manual at 133 vs. 200; also at 200 vs. 100*

SUMMARY

200.1–.9	**Standard subdivisions of religion**
210	**Philosophy and theory of religion**
220	**Bible**
230	**Christianity Christian theology**
240	**Christian moral and devotional theology**
250	**Local Christian church and Christian religious orders**
260	**Christian social and ecclesiastical theology**
270	**Historical, geographic, persons treatment of Christianity Church history**
280	**Denominations and sects of Christian church**
290	**Comparative religion and religions other than Christianity**

.1   **Systems, value, scientific principles, psychological principles [*all formerly also* 210.1, 291.01]**

Class here psychology of religion

Philosophy and theory of religion relocated to 210

.2–.5   **Standard subdivisions [*formerly also* 291.02–291.05]**

[.6]   **Organizations and management**

Relocated to 291.6

.7   **Education, research, related topics [*formerly also* 291.07]**

.71		Education

Class here religion as an academic subject

Class religious education to inculcate religious life and practice, comprehensive works on religious education in 291.7

See also 379.2 for place of religion in public schools

See Manual at 291.7 vs. 200.71

.8 **History and description with respect to kinds of persons [*formerly also* 291.08]**

.9 **Historical, geographic, persons treatment [*formerly also* 291.09]**

See Manual at 200.9 vs. 294, 299

.92 Persons

Class here persons not associated with one specific religious activity or religion

Class a person associated with one religious activity with the activity in 291, e.g., a theologian 291.2092; class a person associated with a specific religion with the religion, e.g., an Islamic religious leader 297.092

[201]   Philosophy and theory of Christianity

Relocated to 230.01

[202–203]Standard subdivisions of Christianity

Relocated to 230.002–230.003

[204]   Christian mythology

Relocated to 230

[205]   Serial publications of Christianity

Relocated to 230.005

[206]   Organizations of Christianity

Relocated to 260

[207]   Education, research, related topics of Christianity

Education relocated to 230.071; research, related topics relocated to 230.007

[208]   Christianity with respect to kinds of persons

Relocated to 270.08

[209]   Historical, geographic, persons treatment of Christianity

Relocated to 270

210 Philosophy and theory of religion [*formerly* 200.1, 291.01]

Religious beliefs and attitudes attained through observation and interpretation of evidence in nature, through speculation, through reasoning, but not through revelation or appeal to authoritative scriptures

Class here natural theology, philosophical theology

Class a specific topic treated with respect to religions based on revelation or authority with the topic in 291, e.g., concepts of God in world religions 291.2; class a specific topic with respect to a specific religion with the religion, e.g., Christian concepts of God 231

.1 Theory of philosophy of religion

Including language and communication of religion

Systems, value, scientific principles, psychological principles relocated to 200.1

211 Concepts of God

Including agnosticism, atheism, deism, humanism, rationalism, secularism, skepticism, theism, e.g., monotheism, pantheism, polytheism

Class here comprehensive works on God, on The Holy

For existence, knowability, attributes of God, see 212

212 Existence, knowability, attributes of God

Including miracles, proofs

213 Creation

Including creation of life and human life, evolution versus creation, evolution as method of creation

See Manual at 231.7 vs. 213, 500, 576.8

214 Theodicy

Vindication of God's justice and goodness in permitting existence of evil and suffering

Including providence

Class here good and evil [*formerly* 216]

215 Science and religion

Including technology and religion

Class religion and scientific theories of creation in 213

[216] Good and evil

Relocated to 214

218   Humankind

Including body and soul, immortality

For creation of humankind, human evolution, see 213

220   Bible

Holy Scriptures of Judaism and Christianity

Class Christian Biblical theology in 230; class Biblical precepts in Christian codes of conduct in 241.5; class Jewish Biblical theology, Biblical precepts in Jewish codes of conduct in 296.3

See Manual at 220

SUMMARY

220.01–.09	**Standard subdivisions**
.1–.9	**Generalities**
221	**Old Testament**
222	**Historical books of Old Testament**
223	**Poetic books of Old Testament**
224	**Prophetic books of Old Testament**
225	**New Testament**
226	**Gospels and Acts**
227	**Epistles**
228	**Revelation (Apocalypse)**
229	**Apocrypha, pseudepigrapha, intertestamental works**

.01–.02   Standard subdivisions

[.03]   Dictionaries, encyclopedias, concordances

Do not use for dictionaries and encyclopedias; class in in 220.3. Do not use for concordances; class in 220.4–220.5

.05–.08   Standard subdivisions

.09   Historical, geographic, persons treatment of Bible

Class the canon in 220.1

For geography, history, chronology, persons of Bible lands in Bible times, see 220.9

>   **220.1–220.9   Generalities**

Class comprehensive works in 220. Class generalities applied to a specific part of the Bible with the part, e.g., a commentary on Job 223

.1   **Origins and authenticity**

Including canon, inerrancy, inspiration, Biblical prophecy and prophecies

Class Christian messianic prophecies in 232; class Christian eschatological prophecies in 236; class Jewish messianic and eschatological prophecies in 296.3

.3   **Encyclopedias and topical dictionaries**

> *For dictionaries of specific texts, see 220.4–220.5*

> **220.4–220.5   Texts, versions, translations**

Class here critical appraisal of language and style; concordances, indexes, dictionaries of specific texts; complete texts; selections from more than one part; paraphrases

Class texts accompanied by commentaries in 220.7; class comprehensive works in 220.4. Class selections compiled for a specific purpose with the purpose, e.g., selections for daily meditations 242

.4   **Original texts, early versions, early translations**

Including textual (lower) criticism (use of scientific means to ascertain the actual original texts)

Class here original texts accompanied by modern translations, comprehensive works on texts and versions

> *For modern versions and translations, see 220.5*

.5   **Modern versions and translations**

In any language

.6   **Interpretation and criticism (Exegesis)**

Including authorship, harmonies, literary (higher) criticism, symbolism and typology; mythology in Bible, demythologizing

Class Christian meditations based on Biblical passages and intended for devotional use in 242; class material about the Bible intended for use in preparing Christian sermons in 251; class Christian sermons based on Biblical passages in 252; class material for preparation of Jewish sermons and text of Jewish sermons in 296.4; class Jewish meditations based on Biblical passages and intended for devotional use in 296.7

> *For textual (lower) criticism, see 220.4; for commentaries, see 220.7*

> *See also 809 for the Bible as literature*

.601   Philosophy and theory

Class here hermeneutics

.7   **Commentaries**

Criticism and interpretation arranged in textual order with or without text

.8   **Nonreligious subjects treated in Bible**

Including sciences in Bible, position of women in Bible

Class a religious subject treated in Bible with the specific religion and topic, e.g., Christian theology 230, Jewish theology 296.3

[.801–.809]   Standard subdivisions

> Do not use; class in 220.8

.9   Geography, history, chronology, persons of Bible lands in Bible times

Including Bible stories retold

Class general history of Bible lands in the ancient world in 930. Class an individual person with the part of the Bible in which the person is chiefly considered, e.g., Abraham 222

See Manual at 220.9; also at 230–280

>   **221–228   Specific parts of Bible**

Class comprehensive works in 220

For Apocrypha, see 229

221   Old Testament (Tanakh)

Holy Scriptures of Judaism, Old Testament of Christianity

For historical books, Torah, see 222; for poetic books, Ketuvim, see 223; for prophetic books, Nevi'im, see 224

[.03]   Dictionaries, encyclopedias, concordances

> Do not use for dictionaries and encyclopedias; class in in 221.3. Do not use for concordances; class in 221.4–221.5

.09   Historical, geographic, persons treatment of Old Testament

Class the canon in 221.1

For geography, history, chronology, persons of Old Testament lands in Old Testament times, see 221.9

.1–.9   Generalities

Add to base number 221 the numbers following 220 in 220.1–220.9, e.g., commentaries 221.7

See Manual at 220.9; also at 230–280

222   *Historical books of Old Testament

Including Pentateuch (Torah: Genesis, Exodus, Leviticus, Numbers, Deuteronomy), Joshua, Judges, Ruth, Samuel, Kings, Chronicles, Ezra, Nehemiah, Esther

(Option: Class here Tobit [Tobias], Judith, deuterocanonical part of Esther; prefer 229)

---

*Do not use standard subdivisions

223 ***Poetic books of Old Testament**

Including Job, Psalms, Proverbs, Ecclesiastes (Qohelet), Song of Solomon (Canticle of Canticles, Song of Songs)

Class here wisdom literature, Ketuvim (Hagiographa, Writings)

> *For Apocryphal wisdom literature, see 229. For a specific book of Ketuvim not provided for here, see the book, e.g., Ruth 222*

(Option: Class here Wisdom of Solomon [Wisdom], Ecclesiasticus [Sirach]; prefer 229)

224 ***Prophetic books of Old Testament**

Including Isaiah, Jeremiah, Lamentations, Ezekiel, Daniel, Hosea, Joel, Amos, Obadiah, Jonah, Micah, Nahum, Habakkuk, Zephaniah, Haggai, Zechariah, Malachi

Class here Major Prophets, Nevi'im

> *For a specific book of Nevi'im not provided for here, see the book, e.g., Joshua 222*

(Option: Class here Baruch, Song of the Three Children, Susanna, Bel and the Dragon, Maccabees 1 and 2 [Machabees 1 and 2]; prefer 229)

225 **New Testament**

> *For Gospels and Acts, see 226; for Epistles, see 227; for Revelation, see 228*

[.03]   Dictionaries, encyclopedias, concordances

Do not use for dictionaries and encyclopedias; class in in 225.3. Do not use for concordances; class in 225.4–225.5

.09   Historical, geographic, persons treatment of New Testament

Class the canon in 225.1

> *For geography, history, chronology, persons of New Testament lands in New Testament times, see 225.9*

.1–.9   **Generalities**

Add to base number 225 the numbers following 220 in 220.1–220.9, e.g., commentaries 225.7

> *For Jesus Christ and his family, Mary, John the Baptist, see 232*

> *See Manual at 220.9; also at 230–280*

226 ***Gospels and Acts**

*Do not use standard subdivisions

> **226.2–226.5 Specific Gospels**

Class comprehensive works in 226

For miracles, see 226.7; for parables, see 226.8

.2 *Matthew

Class Golden Rule as code of conduct in 241.5

For Sermon on the Mount, see 226.9

.3 *Mark

.4 *Luke

Class Golden Rule as code of conduct in 241.5

For Sermon on the Mount, see 226.9

.5 *John

Class here comprehensive works on Johannine literature

For Epistles of John, see 227; for Revelation (Apocalypse), see 228

.6 *Acts of the Apostles

.7 *Miracles

Class miracles in the context of Jesus' life in 232.9

.8 *Parables

Class parables in the context of Jesus' life in 232.9

.9 *Sermon on the Mount

Including beatitudes, Lord's Prayer

Class Sermon on the Mount as code of conduct in 241.5

227 *Epistles

Including Epistles of Paul to Romans, Corinthians, Galatians, Ephesians, Philippians, Colossians, Thessalonians, Timothy, Titus, Philemon, Hebrews; Epistles of James, Peter, John, Jude

228 *Revelation (Apocalypse)

*Do not use standard subdivisions

229   *Apocrypha, pseudepigrapha, intertestamental works

Apocrypha: works accepted as deuterocanonical in some Bibles

Pseudepigrapha, intertestamental works: works from intertestamental times connected with the Bible but not accepted as canonical

Including pseudo gospels

(Option: Class Tobit [Tobias], Judith, deuterocanonical part of Esther in 222; Wisdom of Solomon [Wisdom], Ecclesiasticus [Sirach] in 223; Baruch, Song of the Three Children, Susanna, Bel and the Dragon, Maccabees 1 and 2 [Machabees 1 and 2] in 224)

> ## 230–280   Christianity

Unless other instructions are given, observe the following table of preference for the history of Christianity and the Christian church (except for biography, explained in Manual at 230–280: Biography), e.g., Jesuit missions 266 (*not* 271); persecution of Jesuits by Elizabeth I 272 (*not* 271, 274.2, or 282):

Specific topics	220–260
Persecutions in general church history	272
Doctrinal controversies and heresies in general church history	273
Religious congregations and orders in church history	271
Denominations and sects of Christian church	280
Treatment of Christianity and Christian church by continent, country, locality	274–279
General historical, geographic, persons treatment of Christianity and Christian church (*except* 271–279)	270

Class comprehensive works in 230

For Bible, see 220

See Manual at 230–280

> ## 230–270   Specific elements of Christianity

Class here specific elements of specific denominations and sects
    (Option: Class specific elements of specific denominations and sects in 280)

Class comprehensive works in 230

*Do not use standard subdivisions

230   Christianity [*formerly* 200]   Christian theology

Including Christian mythology [*formerly* 204]; Biblical, evangelical, fundamentalist, liberation theology

Class doctrinal controversies in general church history in 273. Class theology of a specific part of Old or New Testament with the part, e.g., theology of Pauline epistles 227; class biblical theology of a specific topic with the topic, e.g., New Testament writers' view of war and peace 261.8

> *For Christian moral and devotional theology, see 240; for local Christian church and Christian religious orders, see 250; for Christian social and ecclesiastical theology, see 260; for historical, geographic, persons treatment of Christianity and Christian church, see 270; for denominations and sects of Christian church, see 280*

> *See Manual at 220*

SUMMARY

230.002–.007		**Standard subdivisions of Christianity**
.01–.09		**Standard subdivisions of Christian theology**
231		**God**
232		**Jesus Christ and his family** **Christology**
233		**Humankind**
234		**Salvation (Soteriology) and grace**
235		**Spiritual beings**
236		**Eschatology**
238		**Creeds, confessions of faith, covenants, catechisms**
239		**Apologetics and polemics**

[.001]   Philosophy and theory of Christianity

> Do not use; class in 230.01

.002–.003   Standard subdivisions of Christianity [*formerly* 202–203]

.005   Serial publications of Christianity [*formerly* 205]

[.006]   Organizations and management of Christianity

> Do not use; class in 260

.007   Research, related topics of Christianity [*formerly* 207]

[.007 1]   Education

> Do not use; class in 230.071

[.008]   Christianity with respect to kinds of persons

> Do not use; class in 270.08

[.009]   Historical, geographic, persons treatment of Christianity

> Do not use; class in 270

.01   Philosophy and theory of Christianity [*formerly* 201], of Christian theology

.02–.06   Standard subdivisions of Christian theology

.07   Education, research, related topics of Christian theology

.071   Education in Christianity [*formerly* 207], in Christian theology

> Including Bible colleges, divinity schools, theological seminaries, graduate and undergraduate faculties of theology; education of ministers, pastors, priests, theologians
>
> Class here Christianity as an academic subject
>
> Class comprehensive works on Christian religious education, religious education to inculcate Christian faith and practice, catechetics in 268. Class training for clergy in a specialized subject with the subject, plus notation 071 from Table 1, e.g., education in pastoral counseling 253.5071
>
> *See Manual at 268 vs. 230.071*

.08   Christian theology with respect to kinds of persons

.09   Historical, geographic, persons treatment of Christian theology

.092   Theologians

> Class here theologians not connected with any specific type of theology
>
> Class theologians who are connected with a specific denomination, Protestant theologians in 230. Class critical appraisal of an individual theologian's thought on a specific topic with the topic, e.g., on eschatology 236.092
>
> *See Manual at 230–280*

>   **231–239   Christian doctrinal theology**

> Class specific types of Christian doctrinal theology (e.g., evangelical, fundamentalist, liberation theologies), comprehensive works on doctrines of specific denominations and sects, comprehensive works on Christian doctrinal theology in 230
>
> *See Manual at 261.5 vs. 231–239*

231   God

> Including attributes, e.g., goodness, justice, love, wisdom; Holy Trinity (God the Father, God the Son, God the Holy Spirit); non-Trinitarian concepts of God; providence; ways of knowing God, e.g., faith, reason; theodicy (vindication of God's justice and goodness in permitting existence of evil and suffering)
>
> *For Jesus Christ, see 232*

.7   Relation to the world

> Including covenant relationship, Kingdom of God, miracles, prophecy, revelation, sovereignty; creation, creationism, relation of scientific and Christian viewpoints of origin of universe
>
> Class here God's relation to individual believers
>
> Class providence in 231; class redemption in 234; class Kingdom of God to come in 236; class believers' experience of God in 248
>
> > *For Biblical prophecy and prophecies, see 220.1; for messianic prophecies, see 232; for miracles of Jesus, see 232.9; for miracles associated with Mary, see 232.91; for creation of humankind, see 233; for eschatological prophecies, see 236*
> >
> > *See Manual at 231.7 vs. 213, 500, 576.8*

232   Jesus Christ and his family   Christology

> Including divinity, humanity, incarnation, messiahship of Christ; offices as Prophet, Priest, King; atonement, intercession, resurrection of Christ; typology
>
> > *See Manual at 232*

.9   Family and life of Jesus

> Including character, personality, historicity of Jesus; resurrection, appearances, ascension; John the Baptist
>
> Class here non-Trinitarian concepts of Jesus
>
> > *See Manual at 230–280*

.900 1–.900 9   Standard subdivisions

.91   Mary, mother of Jesus

> Including apparitions, miracles of Mary
>
> Class here Mariology

.92   Birth, infancy, childhood of Jesus

> Including Holy Family
>
> Class Joseph in 232.9
>
> > *For Mary, see 232.91*

.96   Passion and death of Jesus

233   Humankind

> Including creation, fall, original sin; nature; humankind as image and likeness of God, as child of God; body, soul, spirit; freedom of choice between good and evil
>
> Class salvation in 234; class sins in 241; class comprehensive works on creation in 231.7
>
> > *For death, immortality, see 236*

234   Salvation (Soteriology) and grace

Including speaking in tongues (glossolalia) [*formerly also* 248.2], other spiritual gifts, e.g., healing; baptism in the Holy Spirit; forgiveness, free will, holiness, justification, obedience, predestination, redemption, regeneration, repentance, sanctification; faith and hope; sacraments, e.g., baptism, Eucharist (Lord's Supper), matrimony

Class liturgy and ritual of sacraments in 265

> *See Manual at 615.8 vs. 234, 291.3*

235   Spiritual beings

Including angels, devils, saints

Class miracles associated with saints in 231.7

> *For God, see 231; for Jesus Christ and his family, see 232*

> *See Manual at 230–280*

236   Eschatology

Including Antichrist, death, heaven, hell, immortality, life after death, purgatory, resurrection of the dead; Last Judgment and related events, e.g., end of the world, Second Coming of Christ, millennium, rapture

Class here Kingdom of God to come

Class interdisciplinary works on end of the world in 001.9

238   Creeds, confessions of faith, covenants, catechisms

Class catechetics in 268. Class catechisms on a specific doctrine with the doctrine, e.g., attributes of God 231

239   Apologetics and polemics

Standard subdivisions are added for either or both topics in heading

Apologetics: systematic argumentation in defense of the divine origin and authority of Christianity

Class apologetics of specific denominations in 230. Class apologetics and polemics on a specific doctrine with the doctrine, e.g., on the doctrine of the Holy Trinity 231; class attacks on doctrines of a specific religion with the religion, e.g., attacks on doctrines of Judaism 296.3

> *See also 273 for doctrinal controversies and heresies in general church history*

[.001–.009]   Standard subdivisions

> Relocated to 239.01–239.09

.01–.09   Standard subdivisions [*formerly* 239.001–239.009]

240   Christian moral and devotional theology

241   Moral theology

Including conscience, divine law, sins, vices; virtues, e.g., faith; specific moral issues, e.g., abortion, birth control, sexual ethics

Class original sin in 233; class faith and hope as means of salvation in 234

See Manual at 241 vs. 261.8

.5   Codes of conduct

Including Golden Rule, Sermon on the Mount, Ten Commandments

242   Devotional literature

Including prayers and meditations based on passages from Bible; specific prayers, prayers to Mary

Class here texts of meditations, contemplations, prayers for individuals and families, religious poetry intended for devotional use

Class devotional literature on a specific subject with the subject, e.g., meditations on passion and death of Jesus 232.96

For evangelistic writings, see 243; for hymns, see 264

.08   History and description with respect to kinds of persons

Do not use for devotional literature for specific classes of persons; class in 242

243   Evangelistic writings for individuals and families

Works designed to convert readers, promote repentance

Class evangelistic sermons in 252

[245]   Texts of hymns for devotional use of individuals and families

Relocated to 264

246   Use of art in Christianity

Religious meaning, significance, purpose

Including Christian symbolism, icons, crosses and crucifixes; dramatic, musical, rhythmic arts; architecture

Class attitude of Christianity and Christian church toward secular art, the arts in 261.5; class creation, description, critical appraisal as art in 700

For church furnishings and related articles, see 247

247   Church furnishings and related articles

248   Christian experience, practice, life

Class here spirituality

See Manual at 230–280

.06 Organizations and management

> Pious societies, sodalities, confraternities relocated to 267

.2 Religious experience

> Including conversion, mysticism
>
> Speaking in tongues (glossolalia) relocated to 234
>
> Class spiritual gifts in 234
>
> > *For conversion of Christians to another religion, see the religion, e.g., conversion of Christians to Judaism 296.7*

.3 Worship

> Including meditation, prayer
>
> Class here comprehensive works on worship
>
> Class texts of prayers and devotions in 242
>
> > *For observances in family life, see 249; for public worship, see 264*

.4 Christian life and practice

> Including asceticism, observance of restrictions and limitations
>
> Class here Christian marriage and family
>
> Pilgrimages relocated to 263
>
> > *For moral theology, see 241; for worship, see 248.3; for Christian observances in family life, see 249; for clerical celibacy, see 253; for practices of religious congregations and orders, see 255*

.408 History and description with respect to kinds of persons

> > Do not use for guides to Christian life for specific classes of persons; class in 248.8

.8 Guides to Christian life for specific classes of persons

> Including guides for children, men, women, mothers, parents, physicians, bereaved persons; Christian child rearing, Christian religious training of children in the home
>
> Class here guides to Christian life for specific classes of persons who are adherents of specific denominations and sects
>
> Class guides to a specific aspect of Christian life with the aspect, e.g., prayer 248.3
>
> > *See Manual at 616.86 vs. 158.1, 248.8, 291.4, 362.29*

249 Christian observances in family life

> Class here family prayer; family observance of religious restrictions, rites, ceremonies

> ## 250–280 Christian church

Class comprehensive works in 260

250 Local Christian church and Christian religious orders

Standard subdivisions are added for local Christian church and Christian religious orders together, for local Christian church alone

Class public worship in 264; class missions in 266; class religious education in 268

[.68]   Management

Do not use; class in 254

.9   **Historical, geographic, persons treatment**

Class general historical treatment of the church in specific localities in 274–279; class historical, geographic, persons treatment of specific denominations in 280

> ### 251–254 Local church

Class here basic Christian communities

Class the local church in overall church organization in 262; class comprehensive works in 250

For pastoral care of specific kinds of persons, see 259

See Manual at 260 vs. 251–254, 259

251 Preaching (Homiletics)

Class texts of sermons in 252

.001–.009   Standard subdivisions

252 Texts of sermons

Class sermons on a specific subject with the subject, e.g., God's providence 231

.001–.009   Standard subdivisions

253   Pastoral office and work (Pastoral theology)

Including professional and personal qualifications; families of clergy; clerical celibacy; pastoral methods, e.g., group work

Class here the work of ministers, pastors, priests, chaplains, deacons, laity in relation to the work of the church at the local level

Class education of clergy in 230.071; class guides to Christian life for clergy in 248.8; class local clergy and laity in relation to the government, organization and nature of the church as a whole, the ordination of women (unless the work treats the ordination of women only in relation to its effect on the local parish) in 262; class the role of clergy in religious education in 268

For preaching, see 251; for parish administration, see 254

.08   History and description with respect to kinds of persons

Do not use for pastoral care of kinds of persons; class in 259

Class here pastoral care performed by kinds of persons

.09   Historical, geographic, persons treatment

.092   Persons treatment

Do not use for biography of clergy in the period prior to 1054; class in 270.1–270.3. Do not use for biography of clergy in the period subsequent to 1054; class in 280

See Manual at 230–280

.5   **Counseling and spiritual direction**

Including pastoral psychology

Class counseling, spiritual direction of specific kinds of persons in 259

254   Parish administration

Including membership, programs; initiation of new churches; buildings, equipment, grounds

.001–.009   Standard subdivisions

[.3–.8]   **Use of communications media, public relations and publicity, finance**

Numbers discontinued; class in 254

255   Religious congregations and orders

Class here monasticism, comprehensive works on Christian religious congregations and orders

For guides to Christian life for persons in religious orders, see 248.8; for religious congregations and orders in church organization, see 262; for religious congregations and orders, monasticism in church history, see 271. For a specific type of activity of religious congregations and orders, see the activity, e.g., pastoral counseling 253.5, missionary work 266

.001–.009 Standard subdivisions

259 Pastoral care of specific kinds of persons

Former heading: Activities of the local church

Pastoral care for specific kinds of persons performed by clergy or laity

Including pastoral care of families, e.g., family, marriage, premarital counseling; pastoral care of persons with disabilities, with physical or mental illness; campus ministry, hospital chaplaincy, prison chaplaincy

Class here pastoral counseling of specific kinds of persons

Class comprehensive works on pastoral care of specific kinds of persons in 253

> *See also 361.7 for works limited to social welfare work by religious organizations*

> *See Manual at 260 vs. 251–254, 259*

[.01–.07] Standard subdivisions

Do not use; class in 253.01–253.07

.08 History and description with respect to kinds of persons

Do not use for bereaved persons; class in 259

Class pastoral care performed by kinds of persons in 253.08; class comprehensive works on pastoral care of specific kinds of persons in 253

[.083] Young people

Do not use; class in 259

[.084] Persons in specific stages of adulthood

Do not use; class in 259

.086 Persons by miscellaneous social characteristics

Do not use for antisocial and asocial persons, delinquents, criminals; class in 259

.087 Gifted persons

Do not use for persons with disabilities and illnesses; class in 259

.088 Occupational and religious groups

Do not use for students; class in 259

[.09] Historical, geographic, persons treatment

Do not use; class in 253.09

260   Christian social and ecclesiastical theology

Institutions, services, observances, disciplines, work of Christianity and Christian church

Class here organizations of Christianity [*formerly* 206], comprehensive works on Christian church

> For local church and religious orders, see 250; for denominations and sects, see 280

> See Manual at 260 vs. 251–254, 259

SUMMARY

.9   Historical, geographic, persons treatment

Do not use for historical, geographic, persons treatment of Christian church; class in 270

261   Social theology and interreligious relations and attitudes

Attitude of Christianity and Christian church toward and influence on secular matters, attitude toward other religions, interreligious relations

Class here Christianity and culture

Class sociology of religion in 306.6

.2   Christianity and other systems of belief

Including Christianity and irreligion

.5   Christianity and secular disciplines

Including art, literature, philosophy, science; comprehensive works on attitude toward and use of communications media

> For a specific use of communications media by the church, see the use, e.g., television evangelism 269

> See Manual at 261.5; also at 261.5 vs. 231–239

.7 **Christianity and political affairs**

Including religious freedom

Class here Christianity and civil rights

For Christianity and international affairs, see 261.8

See Manual at 322 vs. 261.7, 291.1

.8 **Christianity and socioeconomic problems**

Including attitude toward and influence on social problems, the economic order, international affairs, war and peace

Class here comprehensive works on the Christian view of socioeconomic and political affairs

For Christianity and political affairs, see 261.7

See also 361.7 for welfare services of religious organizations

See Manual at 241 vs. 261.8

262 Ecclesiology

Church government, organization, nature

Including authority, function, role of governing leaders, e.g., papacy, bishops, clergy; ordination of clergy; parishes and religious congregations and orders in church organization; specific forms of church organization, e.g., episcopal; general councils; church and ministerial authority and its denial

Class persons treatment of church leaders in 270; class persons treatment of leaders of specific denominations in 280. Class nonlegal decrees of church councils on a specific subject with the subject, e.g., statements on original sin 233

For parish administration, see 254; for government and administration of religious congregations and orders, see 255

See Manual at 230–280; also at 260 vs. 251–254, 259

.001 Philosophy and theory

Including church renewal, ecumenism

Do not use for the history of the ecumenical movement; class in 280

.002–.005 Standard subdivisions

[.006] Organizations and management

Do not use; class in 262

.007–.009 Standard subdivisions

.9   **Church law and discipline**

Including Acts of the Holy See, e.g., encyclicals

Class here canon (ecclesiastical) law

Class civil law relating to church or religious matters in 340. Class Acts of the Holy See on a specific subject with the subject, e.g., on the nature of the church 262

> *See also 364.1 for offenses against religion as defined and penalized by the state*

263   Days, times, places of religious observance

Including pilgrimages [*formerly* 248.4]; Sabbath, Sunday; church year, saints' days; shrines; specific holy places, e.g., Jerusalem

> *For works treating miracles and the shrines associated with them, see 231.7; for miracles of Jesus and shrines associated with them, see 232.9; for miracles associated with Mary and the shrines associated with them, see 232.91*

> *See Manual at 263, 291.3 vs. 394.265*

264   Public worship

Ceremonies, rites, services (liturgy and ritual)

Including texts of hymns for devotional use of individuals and families [*formerly* 245]; Eucharist, Holy Communion, Lord's Supper, Mass; music, prayers, scripture readings

Including works limited by denomination or sect about sacraments, other rites and acts

Class works not limited by denomination or sect about sacraments, other rites and acts in 265; class Sunday school services in 268; class comprehensive works on worship in 248.3; class interdisciplinary works on Christian sacred music in 781.71; class interdisciplinary works on sacred vocal music in 782.2; class hymnals containing both text and music, interdisciplinary works on hymns in 782.27

.001   Philosophy and theory

       Class here liturgical renewal

.002–.009   Standard subdivisions

265   Sacraments, other rites and acts

Standard subdivisions are added for sacraments and other rites and acts together, for sacraments alone

Not limited by denomination or sect

Including baptism, matrimony, funerals, ceremonies of joining a church, exorcism

Class works limited by denomination or sect about sacraments, other rites and acts in 264

> *For Eucharist, Holy Communion, Lord's Supper, Mass, see 264*

266   Missions

Class here missionary societies, religious aspects of medical missions

Class medical services of medical missions in 362.1

> *For mission schools, see 371.071*

.001–.008   Standard subdivisions

.009   Historical, geographic, persons treatment

Do not use for foreign missions originating in specific continents, countries, localities; for historical, geographic, persons treatment of missions of specific denominations and sects; class in 266

Class here joint and interdenominational missions; foreign missions by continent, country, locality served

267   Associations for religious work

Including Young Men's and Young Women's Christian Associations

Class here pious societies, sodalities, confraternities [*all formerly* 248.06]

> *For religious congregations and orders, see 255; for missionary societies, see 266*

> *See Manual at 230–280*

268   Religious education

Class here catechetics (the science or art devoted to organizing the principles of religious teaching), curricula, comprehensive works on Christian religious education

Class Christian religious schools providing general education in 371.071; class place of religion in public schools in 379.2. Class textbooks on a specific subject with the subject, e.g., on missions 266

> *For religious education at the university level and study of Christianity in secular secondary schools, see 230.071*

> *See Manual at 268 vs. 230.071*

[.068]	Management
	Do not use; class in 268
.08	History and description with respect to kinds of persons
	Do not use for students, education of specific groups; class in 268
	Class here education, teaching performed by kinds of persons

269 Spiritual renewal

Including camp meetings, retreats, revivals; evangelism, television evangelism

Class history of pentecostal movement in 270.8

See also 243 for evangelistic writings for individuals and families, 252 for texts of evangelistic sermons, 266 for missionary evangelization

---

> ## 270–280 Historical, geographic, persons treatment of Christianity; Church history; Christian denominations and sects

Unless other instructions are given, observe the following table of preference for the history of Christianity and the Christian church (except for biography, explained in Manual at 230–280: Biography), e.g., persecution of Jesuits by Elizabeth I 272 (*not* 271, 274.2, or 282.):

Persecutions in general church history	272
Doctrinal controversies and heresies in general church history	273
Religious congregations and orders in church history	271
Denominations and sects of Christian church	280
Treatment of Christianity and Christian church by continent, country, locality	274–279
General historical, geographic, persons treatment of Christianity and Christian church (*except* 271–279)	270

Class comprehensive works in 270

See Manual at 230–280

270 Historical, geographic, persons treatment of Christianity [*formerly* 209]   Church history

Class here collected writings of apostolic and church fathers (patristics)

Observe table of preference under 230–280

For historical, geographic, persons treatment of specific denominations and sects, see 280

See Manual at 230–280

.01–.07	Standard subdivisions
.08	Christianity with respect to kinds of persons [*formerly* 208], church history with respect to kinds of persons
.09	Areas, regions, places in general, persons
[.093–.099]	Treatment by continent, country, locality

> Do not use; class in 274–279

> ## 270.1–270.8 Historical periods

Class historical periods in specific continents, countries, localities in 274–279; class comprehensive works in 270

.1 **Apostolic period to 325**

.2 **Period of ecumenical councils, 325–787**

.3 **787–1054**

Class here comprehensive works on Middle Ages

For a specific part of Middle Ages, see the part, e.g., late Middle Ages 270.5

.4 **1054–1200**

.5 **Late Middle Ages through Renaissance, 1200–1517**

.6 **Period of Reformation and Counter-Reformation, 1517–1648**

Including 17th century

For 1648–1699, see 270.7

.7 **Period from Peace of Westphalia to French Revolution, 1648–1789**

.8 **Modern period, 1789–**

Including comprehensive works on evangelicalism, fundamentalism, pentecostalism, charismatic movement

Ecumenical movement relocated to 280

Class evangelical, fundamentalist, pentecostal churches that are independent denominations in 289.9

For evangelicalism, fundamentalism, pentecostalism, charismatic movement in a specific branch or denomination, see the branch or denomination, e.g., Protestant fundamentalism 280

> ## 271–273 Special topics of church history

Class comprehensive works in 270

271   Religious congregations and orders in church history

Class here history of monasticism, history of specific monasteries and convents even if not connected with a specific order

Class persecutions involving religious congregations and orders in 272; class doctrinal controversies and heresies involving congregations and orders in 273

.001–.009   Standard subdivisions

272   Persecutions in general church history

Regardless of denomination

Including Inquisition, persecution of Albigenses

Class here martyrs

Class relation of state to church in 322

273   Doctrinal controversies and heresies in general church history

Including Albigensianism, Arianism, Catharism, Christian gnosticism, Jansenism, modernism, Pietism, Waldensianism

Class persecutions resulting from controversies and heresies in 272; class churches founded on specific doctrines in 280; class comprehensive works and non-Christian gnosticism in 299

See also 239 for apologetics and polemics

274–279 Treatment by continent, country, locality

Add to base number 27 notation 4–9 from Table 2, e.g., Christian church in Europe 274, in France 274.4

Class geographic treatment of a specific subject with the subject, plus notation 09 from Table 1, e.g., persecutions in France 272.0944

280 Denominations and sects of Christian church

Including ecumenical movement [*formerly* 270.8]; relations between denominations; Protestantism; works on Protestant evangelicalism, fundamentalism, pentecostalism, charismatic movement

Class here general historical and geographic treatment of, comprehensive works on specific denominations and sects and their individual local churches

Class persecution of or by specific churches in 272; class comprehensive works on evangelicalism, fundamentalism, pentecostalism, charismatic movement in general church history in 270.8

> For specific elements of specific denominations and sects, see the element, e.g., doctrines 230

> See also 273 for doctrines of specific churches considered as heresies

> See Manual at 230–280

(Option: Class here specific elements of specific denominations and sects; prefer 230–270)

SUMMARY

280.01–.09	Standard subdivisions
281	Early church and Eastern churches
282	Roman Catholic Church
283	Anglican churches
284	Protestant denominations of Continental origin and related bodies
285	Presbyterian churches, Reformed churches centered in America, Congregational churches, Puritanism
286	Baptist, Disciples of Christ, Adventist churches
287	Methodist churches; churches related to Methodism
289	Other denominations and sects

.01–.09   Standard subdivisions

281 Early church and Eastern churches

Including Coptic, Monophysite, Nestorian churches

Class general history of the early church in 270.1–270.3

> See Manual at 281

.9 Eastern Orthodox churches

[.909 3]   Geographic treatment in the ancient world

> Do not use; class early church in 270

[.909 4–.909 9]   Treatment by specific continents, countries, localities in the modern world

> Do not use; class in 281.9

282 Roman Catholic Church

Class here the Catholic traditionalist movement, comprehensive works on Roman Catholic Church and Eastern rite churches in communion with Rome

Class modern schisms in Roman Catholic Church in 284

For Eastern rite churches in communion with Rome, see 281

See Manual at 281

[.093]   Geographic treatment in the ancient world

Do not use; class early church in 270

[.094–.099]   Treatment by specific continents, countries, localities in the modern world

Do not use; class in 282

283   Anglican churches

[.094–.099]   Treatment by specific continents, countries, localities in the modern world

Do not use; class in 283

284   Protestant denominations of Continental origin and related bodies

Including Anabaptist, Arminian, Catharist, Huguenot, Hussite, Moravian, Waldensian churches; modern schisms in Roman Catholic Church, e.g., Jansenism; comprehensive works on Calvinistic churches, on Reformed churches

For Protestant denominations of Continental origin not provided for here, see the denomination, e.g., Baptists 286

.1   Lutheran churches

[.109 4–.109 9]   Treatment by specific continents, countries, localities in the modern world

Do not use; class in 284.1

285   Presbyterian churches, Reformed churches centered in America, Congregational churches, Puritanism

Standard subdivisions are added for Presbyterian churches, Reformed churches centered in America, Congregational churches together; for Presbyterian churches alone

.7   Reformed churches centered in America

[.709 4–.709 9]   Treatment by specific continents, countries, localities in the modern world

Do not use; class in 285.7

.8 **Congregationalism**

Class Evangelical and Reformed Church in 285.7; class United Church of Canada, Uniting Church in Australia in 287.9

[.809 4–.809 9] Treatment by specific continents, countries, localities in the modern world

Do not use; class in 285.8

286 Baptist, Disciples of Christ, Adventist churches

Standard subdivisions are added for Baptist, Disciples of Christ, Adventist churches together; for Baptist churches alone

.6 **Disciples of Christ (Campbellites)**

[.609 4–.609 9] Treatment by specific continents, countries, localities in the modern world

Do not use; class in 286.6

.7 **Adventist churches**

[.709 4–.709 9] Treatment by specific continents, countries, localities in the modern world

Do not use; class in 286.7

287 Methodist churches; churches related to Methodism

Standard subdivisions are added for Methodist churches and churches related to Methodism together; for Methodist churches alone

For Evangelical United Brethren Church, see 289.9

.9 **Churches related to Methodism**

Limited to Church of the Nazarene [*formerly* 289.9], Church of North India, Church of South India, Salvation Army, United Church of Canada, Uniting Church in Australia

289 Other denominations and sects

Including Church of the New Jerusalem (Swedenborgianism), Shakers (United Society of Believers in Christ's Second Appearing)

.1 **Unitarian and Universalist churches**

Class here Anti-Trinitarianism, Socinianism, Unitarianism

[.109 4–.109 9] Treatment by specific continents, countries, localities in the modern world

Do not use; class in 289.1

(.2) **(Permanently unassigned)**

(Optional number used to provide local emphasis or a shorter number for a specific denomination or sect; prefer the number for the specific denomination or sect in 281–289)

.3   Latter-Day Saints (Mormons)

[.309 4–.309 9]   Treatment by specific continents, countries, localities in the modern world

> Do not use; class in 289.3

[.4]   Church of the New Jerusalem (Swedenborgianism)

> Number discontinued; class in 289

.5   Church of Christ, Scientist (Christian Science)

[.509 4–.509 9]   Treatment by specific continents, countries, localities in the modern world

> Do not use; class in 289.5

.6   Society of Friends (Quakers)

[.609 4–.609 9]   Treatment by specific continents, countries, localities in the modern world

> Do not use; class in 289.6

.7   Mennonite churches

> Including Amish, Church of God in Christ, Hutterian Brethren

[.709 4–.709 9]   Treatment by specific continents, countries, localities in the modern world

> Do not use; class in 289.7

.9   Denominations and sects not provided for elsewhere

> Including African independent churches, Churches of God, Evangelical United Brethren Church, independent fundamentalist and evangelical churches, Jehovah's Witnesses, New Thought; Pentecostal churches, e.g., Assemblies of God, United Pentecostal Church; Unification Church, United Brethren in Christ, Unity School of Christianity

> Church of the Nazarene relocated to 287.9

> Class nondenominational and interdenominational Christian churches in 280; class eclectic New Thought, comprehensive works in 299

> (Option: Class a specific denomination or sect requiring local emphasis in 289.2)

290   Comparative religion and religions other than Christianity

> *See Manual at 290*

SUMMARY

291   Comparative religion

Including prehistoric religions, religions of nonliterate peoples

Class here works dealing with various religions, with religious topics not applied to specific religions; syncretistic religious writings of individuals expressing personal views and not claiming to establish a new religion or to represent an old one

Class treatment of religious topics with respect to philosophy of religion, natural theology in 210; class treatment with respect to Christianity in 220–280; class treatment with respect to a specific religion other than Christianity in 292–299

See Manual at 291

[.01]   Philosophy and theory

Relocated to 210

Systems, value, scientific principles, psychological principles relocated to 200.1

[.02–.05]   Standard subdivisions

Relocated to 200.2–200.5

[.06]   Organizations and management

Do not use for management; class in 291.6

Organizations relocated to 291.6

[.07–.09]   Standard subdivisions

Relocated to 200.7–200.9

.1   Religious mythology, social theology, interreligious relations and attitudes

Including general classes of religions, e.g., shamanism; attitudes of religions toward secular disciplines, e.g., science; religions and political affairs, e.g., international affairs, war and peace; religions and socioeconomic problems, e.g., ecology, treatment of children

Class written sources of religion, of mythology in 291.8. Class myths on a specific subject with the subject, e.g., creation myths 291.2

See also 361.7 for welfare work of religious organizations

See Manual at 322 vs. 261.7, 291.1; also at 398.2 vs. 291.1

.2   Doctrines

Including gods and goddesses, angels, devils, nature, persons, images as objects of worship and veneration; relation of deity to the world, e.g., miracles, prophecy, revelation; humankind, e.g., repentance, salvation, soul; cosmology, creation; eschatology, e.g., death, immortality, reincarnation, end of the world

Class here beliefs, apologetics, polemics, comprehensive works on theology

For social theology, see 291.1; for moral theology, see 291.5

.3   Public worship and other practices

Practices predominantly public or collective in character

Including pilgrimages [*formerly* 291.4]; ceremonies, rites; sacrifices, penances; symbolism, symbolic objects; religious use, significance of the arts; religious healing; sacred places and times; divination, witchcraft

Class leaders and organization, monasteries in 291.6; class comprehensive works on worship in 291.4; class interdisciplinary works on sacred music in 781.7; class interdisciplinary works on sacred vocal music in 782.2

See Manual at 263, 291.3 vs. 394.265; also at 615.8 vs. 234, 291.3

.4   Religious experience, life, practice

Practices predominantly private or individual in character

Including asceticism, celibacy, contemplation, conversion, devotional texts; guides to religious life, e.g., marriage and family life, religious training of children in the home; meditation, mysticism, observances of restrictions and limitations, prayer, sermons, worship, yoga

Pilgrimages relocated to 291.3

For public worship, see 291.3; for moral theology, see 291.5

See Manual at 291; also at 616.86 vs. 158.1, 248.8, 291.4, 362.29

.5   Moral theology

Including conscience, sins, vices, virtues; specific moral issues, e.g., abortion, sexual ethics, morality of war

.6   **Leaders and organization**

Including organizations and management [*both formerly also* 200.6, 291.06]; congregations, monasteries; role, function, duties of leaders, e.g., clergy, gurus, martyrs, saints; ordination of clergy

Class persons treatment of religious leaders in 200.92; class theologians in 291.2. Class a specific activity of a leader with the activity, e.g., religious healings by priests 291.3

.7   **Missions and religious education**

Including comprehensive works on religious education and religion as an academic subject

For education in and teaching of comparative religion, religion as an academic subject, see 200.71

See Manual at 291.7 vs. 200.71

.8   **Sources**

Including sacred books and scriptures, e.g., original texts, translations, interpretation and criticism; oral traditions, laws and decisions

Class civil law relating to religious matters in 340

.9   **Sects and reform movements**

Class specific aspects of sects and reform movements in 291.1–291.8

See Manual at 291: Denominations and sects

>   **292–299   Religions other than Christianity**

Class comprehensive works in 291

See Manual at 291

292   **Classical (Greek and Roman) religion**

See also 299 for modern revivals of classical religions

.001–.005   Standard subdivisions

[.006]   Organizations and management

Do not use for management; class in 292.6

Organizations relocated to 292.6

.007   Education, research, related topics

.007 1   Education

Class here classical religion as an academic subject

Class comprehensive works on religious education, religious education to inculcate religious life and practice in 292.7

See Manual at 291.7 vs. 200.71

.008–.009   Standard subdivisions

>   292.07–292.08 Classical religion by specific culture

Class specific elements regardless of culture in 292.1–292.9; class comprehensive works in 292

.07   Roman religion

.08   Greek religion

.1–.9   Specific elements

Add to base number 292 the numbers following 291 in 291.1–291.9, e.g., organizations 292.6 [*formerly* 292.006]

Class classical religion as an academic subject in 292.0071

293   Germanic religion

See also 299 for modern revivals of Germanic religion

[.06]   Organizations and management

Do not use for management; class in 293

Use of this number for organizations discontinued; class in 293

.07   Education, research, related topics

.071   Education

Class here Germanic religion as an academic subject

Class comprehensive works on religious education, religious education to inculcate religious life and practice in 293

See Manual at 291.7 vs. 200.71

294   Religions of Indic origin

See Manual at 200.9 vs. 294, 299

.3   **Buddhism**

See Manual at 291

[.306]	Organizations and management

Do not use for management; class in 294.3

Use of this number for organizations discontinued; class in 294.3

.307   Education, research, related topics

.307 1   Education

Class here Buddhism as an academic subject

Class comprehensive works on religious education, religious education to inculcate religious life and practice in 294.3

See Manual at 291.7 vs. 200.71

.4   **Jainism**

See Manual at 291

[.406]   Organizations and management

Do not use for management; class in 294.4

Use of this number for organizations discontinued; class in 294.4

.407   Education, research, related topics

.407 1   Education

Class here Jainism as an academic subject

Class comprehensive works on religious education, religious education to inculcate religious life and practice in 294.4

See Manual at 291.7 vs. 200.71

.5   **Hinduism**

Including Vedic literature, Vishnuism

Class here Brahmanism

See Manual at 291

[.506]   Organizations and management

Do not use for management; class in 294.5

Use of this number for organizations discontinued; class in 294.5

.507   Education, research, related topics

.507 1   Education

Class here Hinduism as an academic subject

Class comprehensive works on religious education, religious education to inculcate religious life and practice in 294.5

See Manual at 291.7 vs. 200.71

.6 Sikhism

See Manual at 291

[.606] Organizations and management

Do not use for management; class in 294.6

Use of this number for organizations discontinued; class in 294.6

.607 Education, research, related topics

.607 1 Education

Class here Sikhism as an academic subject

Class comprehensive works on religious education, religious education to inculcate religious life and practice in 294.6

See Manual at 291.7 vs. 200.71

295 Zoroastrianism (Mazdaism, Parseeism)

Class Mithraism in 299

[.06] Organizations and management

Do not use for management; class in 295

Use of this number for organizations discontinued; class in 295

.07 Education, research, related topics

.071 Education

Class here Zoroastrianism as an academic subject

Class comprehensive works on religious education, religious education to inculcate religious life and practice in 295

See Manual at 291.7 vs. 200.71

296 Judaism

See Manual at 291

[.06] Organizations and management

Do not use for management; class in 296.6

Organizations relocated to 296.6

.07 Education, research, related topics

.071   Education

Including Jewish theological faculties, rabbinical seminaries, yeshivot, education of rabbis

Class here Judaism as an academic subject

Class comprehensive works on Jewish religious education, religious education to inculcate religious faith and practice in 296.6

See Manual at 291.7 vs. 200.71

.09   Historical, geographic, persons treatment

Class here history of specific synagogues [*formerly* 296.8]

See also 320.54095694 for Zionism, 909 for world history of Jews

.092   Persons

Class here persons not associated with one activity or denomination

Class a person associated with one activity or denomination with the activity or denomination with which the person is associated, e.g., a theologian 296.3092, a Reform rabbi 296.8

.1   Sources

Including Talmudic literature; Midrash; cabala; Halakhah (legal literature), e.g., work of Maimonides, Responsa; Aggadah; sources of specific sects and movements, e.g., Qumran community (Dead Sea Scrolls)

Class Jewish theology based on these sources in 296.3; class Jewish mystical experience in 296.7; class modern Jewish mystical movements in 296.8; class works proposing or treating Jewish law as the law of a country, or comparing Jewish and other Oriental systems of law in 340.5. Class Jewish law on a specific religious topic with the topic elsewhere in 296, e.g., laws of marriage 296.4

For Torah and sacred scripture (Tanakh, Old Testament), see 221; for pseudepigrapha in Dead Sea Scrolls, see 229

.3   Theology, ethics, views of social issues

Standard subdivisions are added for theology, ethics, social issues together; for theology alone

Including apologetics and polemics, Judaism and secular disciplines, Judaism and other systems of belief

Class here Biblical theology, the Thirteen Articles of Faith

Class guides to conduct of life in 296.7

See Manual at 220; also at 322 vs. 296.3, 320.54095694

.4   Traditions, rites, public services

Including comprehensive works on worship [*formerly* 296.7]; festivals, holy days, fasts; rites and customs for occasions that occur generally once in a lifetime, e.g., bar mitzvah, marriage, divorce, burial; liturgy and prayers; use of arts and symbolism; sermons; pilgrimages and sacred places

Class individual observances not provided for here in 296.7; class works containing both text and music, interdisciplinary works on Jewish liturgical music in 782.3. Class sermons on a specific subject with the subject, e.g., social theology 296.3

See Manual at 263, 291.3 vs. 394.265

.6   Leaders, organization, religious education, outreach activity

Including organizations [*formerly also* 296.06]; management

Including role, function, duties of leaders, e.g., ordination, work of rabbis; pastoral care; synagogues and congregations

Class persons treatment of religious leaders in 296.092; class laws and decisions in 296.1

.7   Religious experience, life, practice

Standard subdivisions are added for religious experience, life, practice together; for religious life and practice together

Practices which continue throughout life

Including conversion, devotional texts, meditation, mysticism, observance of dietary laws (kosher observance), marriage and family life

Class here guides to religious life, spirituality

Comprehensive works on worship relocated to 296.4

Class cabalistic literature in 296.1; class Jewish mystical movements in 296.8

For ethics, see 296.3; for traditions, rites, public services, see 296.4

.8   Denominations and movements

Including orthodox, conservative, reform Judaism; mystical Judaism, e.g., Hasidism

History of specific synagogues relocated to 296.09

Class specific aspects of denominations and movements in 296.1–296.7

See Manual at 291: Denominations and sects

297   Islam, Babism, Bahai Faith

Standard subdivisions are added for Islam, Babism, Bahai Faith together; for Islam alone

[.06]   Organizations and management

                 Do not use for management; class in 297.6

                 Organizations relocated to 297.6

.07   Education, research, related topics

.071   Education

                 Class here Islamic religion as an academic subject

                 Class comprehensive works on Islamic religious education, religious
                 education to inculcate religious faith and practice in 297.7

                 See Manual at 291.7 vs. 200.71

.09   Historical, geographic, persons treatment

                 Class here comprehensive religious works on Islamic fundamentalism

                 Class political science aspects of Islam in 320

                 *For Islamic fundamentalism in a specific sect or reform movement, see
                 297.8*

                 See also 909 for Islamic civilization

                 See Manual at 320.5 vs. 297.09, 322

.092   Persons

                 Class here persons not associated with one activity, sect or reform
                 movement

                 Class Muslims primarily associated with a specific religious activity in
                 297.1–297.7; class Sufis in 297.4; class Muḥammad the Prophet and his
                 family and companions in 297.6; class Muslims primarily associated
                 with a specific sect or reform movement in 297.8. Class interdisciplinary
                 works on caliphs as civil and religious heads of state with the subject in
                 940–990, e.g., Abu Bakr 953

>   **297.1–297.8 Islam**

                 Class comprehensive works in 297

.1   **Sources of Islam**

                 Including Koran, Hadith; religious and ceremonial laws and decisions; stories,
                 legends, parables, proverbs, anecdotes told for religious edification

                 Class theology based on Koran and Hadith in 297.2; class Islamic law relating
                 to secular matters, interdisciplinary works on Islamic law in 340.5. Class
                 religious law on a specific topic with the topic, e.g., religious law concerning
                 pilgrimage to Mecca 297.3; class a religious subject treated in the Koran with
                 the subject, e.g., Islamic ethics 297.5

                 See Manual at 340.5 vs. 297.1

.2   **Islamic doctrinal theology ('Aqā'id and Kalām); Islam and secular disciplines; Islam and other systems of belief**

Standard subdivisions are added for Islamic doctrinal theology, Islam and secular disciplines, Islam and other systems of belief together; for Islamic doctrinal theology alone

Class Islamic moral theology in 297.5; class doctrines concerning Muḥammad the Prophet in 297.6

See Manual at 322 vs. 261.7, 291.1

.3   **Islamic worship**

Public and private

Including Pillars of Islam (Pillars of the Faith), e.g., annual fast of Ramadan, hajj (pilgrimage to Mecca); mosques, sacred places, pilgrimages; prayer and meditation; sermons and preaching; use of arts and symbolism in worship

Class zakat (almsgiving), comprehensive works on fasting in 297.5

For Sufi worship, see 297.4

.4   **Sufism (Islamic mysticism)**

See Manual at 297.4

.5   **Islamic moral theology and religious experience, life, practice**

Standard subdivisions are added for moral theology and religious experience, life, practice together; for moral theology alone

Including conscience; general works on duty, sin, vices, virtues; zakat (almsgiving); comprehensive works on fasting

Class annual fast of Ramadan in 297.3

For jihad, see 297.7

.6   **Islamic leaders and organization**

Including organizations [*formerly* 297.06]; role, function, duties of leaders; Muḥammad the Prophet; Muḥammad's family and companions

Class persons treatment of Islamic religious leaders (except for Muḥammad the Prophet and Muḥammad's family and companions) in 297.092

.7   **Protection and propagation of Islam**

Including da'wah, e.g., call to Islam; jihad, missionary work; Islamic religious education

Class Islam as an academic subject in 297.071

See Manual at 291.7 vs. 200.71

.8   **Islamic sects and reform movements**

Including Black Muslim movement

Class specific aspects of sects and reform movements in 297.1–297.7; class secular view of relation of state to religious organizations and groups in 322; class secular view of religious political parties in 324.2

For Sufism, see 297.4

See Manual at 291: Denominations and sects

.9   **Babism and Bahai Faith**

(298)   **(Permanently unassigned)**

(Optional number used to provide local emphasis and a shorter number to a specific religion; prefer the number for the specific religion elsewhere in 292–299)

299   **Other religions**

Including religions of Chinese origin, e.g., Confucianism, Taoism; religions of Japanese origin, e.g., Shintoism; religions originating among Black Africans and people of Black African descent, e.g., Santeria, voodooism; religions of North and South American native origin; religions of other ethnic origin, e.g., ancient Egyptian, Celtic, Polynesian

Including religions of eclectic and syncretistic origin, e.g., anthroposophy, gnosticism, Manicheism, New Age religions, New Thought, scientology, theosophy; modern revivals of long dormant religions

Class Four Books of Confucius, interdisciplinary works on Confucianism in 181; class Christian gnosticism, Christian Manicheism in 273; class syncretistic religious writings of individuals expressing personal views and not claiming to establish a new religion or to represent an old one in 291

For Black Muslim movement, see 297.8

See Manual at 291; also at 200.9 vs. 294, 299

(Option: Class a specific religion requiring local emphasis in 298)

300

---

300 Social sciences

Class here behavioral sciences, social studies

Class a specific behavioral science with the science, e.g., psychology 150; class military, diplomatic, political, economic, social, welfare aspects of a war with the history of the war, e.g., diplomatic efforts to end the Vietnamese War 959.704

For language, see 400; for history, see 900

See Manual at 300, 320 vs. 352–354; also at 300 vs. 600

SUMMARY

300.1–.9	**Standard subdivisions**
301–307	**[Sociology and anthropology]**
310	**Collections of general statistics**
320	**Political science (Politics and government)**
330	**Economics**
340	**Law**
350	**Public administration and military science**
360	**Social problems and services; associations**
370	**Education**
380	**Commerce, communications, transportation**
390	**Customs, etiquette, folklore**

SUMMARY

300.1–.9	**Standard subdivisions**
301	**Sociology and anthropology**
302	**Social interaction**
303	**Social processes**
304	**Factors affecting social behavior**
305	**Social groups**
306	**Culture and institutions**
307	**Communities**

.1 **Philosophy and theory**

.2 **Miscellany**

Do not use for statistics; class in 310

.3–.9 **Standard subdivisions**

301 Sociology and anthropology

Standard subdivisions are added for either or both topics in heading

Class here interdisciplinary works on society, humans

Class social problems and social welfare in 361–365

> *For a specific topic in sociology and anthropology, see 302–307; for criminal anthropology, see 364.2; for physical anthropology, see 599.9. For a specific aspect of society not provided for in 302–307, see the aspect, e.g., general history 900*
>
> *See Manual at 301–307 vs. 361–365*

.01 Philosophy and theory

Do not use for psychological principles; class in 302

> ## 302–307 Specific topics in sociology and anthropology

Unless other instructions are given, class a subject with aspects in two or more subdivisions of 302–307 in the number coming last, e.g., social deterioration during civil wars 303.6 (*not* 303.45)

Class comprehensive works in 301. Class effect of one factor on another with the factor affected, e.g., effect of climate on social change 303.4

> *See Manual at 302–307 vs. 150, T1—01; also at 302–307 vs. 155.9, 158.2; also at 302–307 vs. 320*

302 Social interaction

Including social dysfunction, e.g., apathy, mass hysteria; social participation, e.g., competition, cooperation; social role (role theory); social skills

Class here interpersonal relations, psychological principles of sociology, social psychology

Class social psychology of a specific situation with the situation, e.g., social psychology of ethnic groups 305.8

> *See also 155.9 for effect of social environment on individuals, 158 for individual aspects of interpersonal relations*

.01 Philosophy and theory

Do not use for psychological principles; class in 302

.2   Communication

Including body language; literacy; verbal, nonverbal, oral, written communication; semiotics; interdisciplinary works on nonlinguistic communication, e.g., symbols, symbolism

Class here mass communication, interdisciplinary works on communication

Class manual language for the deaf in 419

> *For information theory, see 003; for Christian religious symbols, see 246; for religious symbolism, see 291.3; for conversation, see 302.3; for censorship, see 303.3; for language, see 400; for iconography, see 704.9; for insignia, see 929.9*

.23   Media (Means of communication)

Including books, newspapers, motion pictures, radio, television, telephone; the electronic media; signs

Class here mass media

Interdisciplinary works on a specific medium relocated to the medium, e.g., newspapers 070.1, television 384.55

Class effect of media on a subject other than social groups with the subject, e.g., the effect of media on elections 324.7

.230 8   History and description with respect to kinds of persons

Class here the effect of mass media on specific groups

.3   Social interaction within groups

Including committees, crowds, gangs, mobs, play groups; bureaucracy, organizational behavior; conversation

Class here group decision-making processes, group dynamics, negotiation

> *See also 362.74 for predelinquent gangs, 364.106 for gangs engaging in crime*

.4   Social interaction between groups

Including ingroups

Class social interaction between a specific social group and other social groups in 305

.5   Relation of the individual to society

Including aggression, alienation, ambition, individualism, isolation; reference groups

> *See also 155.9 for psychological effects of the social environment upon the individual*

303   Social processes

> *For social interaction, see 302; for factors affecting social behavior, see 304*

.3　**Coordination and control**

Including attitudes, authority, censorship, coercion, conformity, leadership, peer group, play groups, prejudice, propaganda, public opinion, social learning, socialization; social norms, e.g., belief systems, values; stereotypes; interdisciplinary works on persuasion

Class here policy formulation, power

Class coordination and control in and through specific social institutions in 306; class interdisciplinary works on child development in 305.231. Class public opinion on a specific subject with the subject, e.g., on racial stereotypes 305.8, on the political process 324

> *For socialization by education, see 370. For a specific aspect of persuasion, see the aspect, e.g., individual psychology of persuasion 153.8*
>
> *See Manual at 170 vs. 303.3; also at 363.3 vs. 303.3, 791.4*

.4　**Social change**

Class social changes in a specific aspect of society with the aspect in 302–307, e.g., changes in religious institutions 306.6

.401　Philosophy and theory

Do not use for forecasting and forecasts; class in 303.49

.44　Growth and development

Standard subdivisions are added for either or both topics in heading

Class here progress, specialization

.45　Deterioration and decay

Standard subdivisions are added for either or both topics in heading

.48　Causes of change

Including acculturation, assimilation, commerce, contact between cultures, development of science and technology, disasters, social reform, war

Class political aspects of reform movements in 322.4; class role of reform movements in addressing social problems in 361–365

> *See Manual at 303.48 vs. 306.4*

.49　Social forecasts

Class here futurology, social forecasting

Class interdisciplinary works on forecasting in 003. Class forecasting in and forecasts of a specific subject with the subject, plus notation 01 from Table 1, e.g., future of Olympic games in the 21st century 796.4801

.490 9　Historical and persons treatment

Do not use for geographic treatment; class in 303.491–303.499

.491–.499   Forecasts for specific areas

> Add to base number 303.49 notation 1–9 from Table 2, e.g., Eastern Europe in the year 2000 303.4947

.6   **Conflict**

> Including civil disobedience, civil disorder, civil war, militarism, nonviolence, pacifism, peace movements, protest, revolution, riots, terrorism, war; resolution of conflicts, of disputes

> Class war as a cause of social change in 303.48; class prevention of war in 327.1; class the art and science of warfare in 355–359; class interdisciplinary works on war in 355.02. Class conflict in a specific social relation with the relation, e.g., racial conflict 305.8; class military, diplomatic, political, economic, social, welfare aspects of a specific war with the history of the war, e.g., World War II 940.53; class a specific conflict considered an historical event with the event in 900, e.g., disturbances of May-June 1968 in France 944.083

> *See also 363.3 for the prevention of terrorism*

304   Factors affecting social behavior

.2   **Human ecology**

> Including greenhouse effect, influence of weather and climate; environmental abuse, pollution

> Class here human geography

> Class interdisciplinary works on pollution in 363.73

> *See Manual at 333.7 vs. 304.2, 363.7; also at 578 vs. 304.2, 508, 910*

.5   **Genetic factors**

> Class here sociobiology (biosociology), study of genetic bases of human social behavior

> Class a specific aspect of sociobiology with the aspect in 302–307, e.g., sociobiology of conflict 303.6

> *For sociobiology of plants and animals, see 577.8*

.6   **Population**

> Including births, deaths, family size, life expectancy; abortion, birth control, genocide

> Class here population size and composition [*both formerly also* 307.2], demography, population geography; comprehensive works on population

> Class interdisciplinary works on population control in 363.9

> *For movement of people, see 304.8*

> *See also 363.9 for family planning programs*

> *See Manual at 363.9 vs. 304.6*

.8 **Movement of people**

Including emigration, immigration

For movement to, from, within communities, see 307.2

.809 Historical, geographic, persons treatment

Class here internal movement, emigration from specific areas

Class emigration to specific areas in 304.8

305 Social groups

Including interactions, problems, role, social status of social groups; discrimination against and conflict involving social groups

Class here culture and institutions of specific groups other than indigenous racial, ethnic, national groups; consciousness-raising groups; subcultures of specific groups; social stratification, equality, inequality

Unless other instructions are given, observe the following table of preference, e.g., black Roman Catholic middle-class male youths 305.235 (*not* 305.31, 305.5, 305.6, or 305.896):

Persons by physical and mental characteristics	305.9
Age groups	305.2
Groups by sex	305.3–305.4
Social classes	305.5
Religious groups	305.6
Racial, ethnic, national groups	305.8
Language groups	305.7
Occupational and miscellaneous groups	305.9
(*except* persons by physical and mental characteristics 305.9)	

Class effect of mass media on specific groups, on social stratification in 302.2308; class opinions of specific social groups in 303.3; class interactions, problems, role, social status of specific groups, discrimination against and conflict involving specific social groups in 305.2–305.9; class specific problems of, welfare services to social groups in 362. Class the role of specific groups in a specific institution with the institution in 306, e.g., women in political institutions 306.2082; class a specific aspect of discrimination with the aspect, e.g., discrimination in housing 363.5

See Manual at 305; also at 305 vs. 306, 909, 930–990

SUMMARY

305.2	Age groups
.3	Men and women
.4	Women
.5	Social classes
.6	Religious groups
.7	Language groups
.8	Racial, ethnic, national groups
.9	Occupational and miscellaneous groups

.2   **Age groups**

Class here comprehensive works on generation gap

For generation gap within families, see 306.874

.23   Young people

Through age twenty

Class here interdisciplinary works on children

For a specific aspect of children, see the aspect, e.g., social welfare of children 362.7

.231   Child development

Class here interdisciplinary works on child development

Class socialization in 303.3

For psychological development of children, see 155.4; for physical development of children, see 612.6

.232   Infants

Children from birth through age two

.233   Children three to five

Class here preschool children

.234   Children six to eleven

Class here school children

For school children over eleven, see 305.235

.235   Young people twelve to twenty

Variant names: adolescents, teenagers, young adults, youth

Including interdisciplinary works on the development of young people twelve to twenty

Comprehensive works on young adults relocated to 305.242

Class young people twenty-one and over in 305.242

For psychological development, see 155.5; for physical development, see 612.6

.24   Adults

Class adults of specific sexes in 305.3–305.4

For late adulthood, see 305.26

.242   Young adults

Aged twenty-one and above

Class here comprehensive works on young adults [*formerly* 305.235]

For young adults under twenty-one, see 305.235

.244   Persons in middle adulthood

Class here middle age

.26   Late adulthood

Class sociology of retirement in 306.3

See also 646.7 for retirement guides

.3   Men and women

Class here interdisciplinary works on sex role, the sexes, gender identity; adult men and women

Class sex psychology and the psychology of the sexes in 155.3. Class relations between the sexes and within the sexes with the institution in 306, e.g., husband-wife relationship 306.872; class the relation of a specific sex to a specific subject with the subject, plus notation 081–082 from Table 1, e.g., women in U.S. history 973.082

For men and women in late adulthood, see 305.26; for women, see 305.4. For a specific aspect of sex role and gender identity, see the aspect, e.g., psychology of gender identity 155.3

.31   Men

Class here interdisciplinary works on men, on males

For specific aspects of sociology of men, see 305.32–305.38. For a specific aspect of men not provided for in 305.3, see the aspect, e.g., legal status of men 346.01

[.310 8]   History and description with respect to kinds of men

Do not use; class in 305.33–305.38

>   305.32–305.38 Specific aspects of sociology of men

Class comprehensive works in 305.31

.32   Social role and status of men

Standard subdivisions are added for either or both topics in heading

Class here discrimination against men, men's movements, e.g., men's liberation movement

Class social role and status of specific kinds of men with the kind of men in 305.33–305.38, e.g., role and status of widowers 305.38

.33 Men's occupations

.38 Specific kinds of men

Including men belonging to specific religious, language, racial, ethnic, national groups; men by kinship characteristics, cultural level, marital status, sexual orientation

Class kinds of men defined by occupation in 305.33

[.380 1–.380 9] Standard subdivisions

Do not use; class in 305.3101–305.3109

.4 Women

Class here interdisciplinary works on women, on females

For a specific aspect of women not provided for here, see the aspect, e.g., women's suffrage 324.6, education of women 371.822

[.408] History and description with respect to kinds of women

Do not use; class in 305.43–305.48

.42 Social role and status of women

Standard subdivisions are added for either or both topics in heading

Class here discrimination against women, women's movements, e.g., women's liberation movement

Class social role and status of specific kinds of women with the kind of women in 305.43–305.48, e.g., role and status of widows 305.48

.43 Women's occupations

.48 Specific kinds of women

Including women belonging to specific religious, language, racial, ethnic, national groups; women by kinship characteristics, cultural level, marital status, sexual orientation

Class kinds of women defined by occupation in 305.43

[.480 1–.480 9] Standard subdivisions

Do not use; class in 305.401–305.409

.5   **Social classes**

> Including upper, middle, lower classes; white collar, blue collar classes; elites, intellectuals, professionals; the poor; hippies, hoboes, homeless persons, peasants, slaves, tramps, untouchables; minorities, nondominant groups; social mobility
>
> Class here class struggle
>
> Class a specific minority or nondominant group with the group, e.g., nondominant ethnic groups 305.8
>
> > *For theory of class struggle in Marxism, see 335.4*
> >
> > *See Manual at 305.9 vs. 305.5*

.6   **Religious groups**

.7   **Language groups**

> Racial, ethnic, national groups associated with a specific language relocated to 305.8

.8   **Racial, ethnic, national groups**

> Including ancient Romans, Osco-Umbrians
>
> Class here racial, ethnic, national groups associated with a specific language [*formerly* 305.7]; ethnology, cultural ethnology, ethnography; race relations
>
> Except where instructed otherwise, give preference to ethnic group over nationality, e.g., United States citizens of Irish descent 305.891 (*not* 305.813), British citizens of African descent 305.896 (*not* 305.82)
>
> Except where instructed otherwise, when choosing between two ethnic groups, give preference to the group for which the notation is different from that of the nationality of the people, e.g., a work treating equally the Hispanic and native American heritage of bicultural Spanish-Quechua mestizos of Peru 305.898 (*not* 305.868)
>
> Except where instructed otherwise, when choosing between two national groups, give preference to the former or ancestral group, e.g., people from Russia who have become United States citizens 305.891 (*not* 305.813)
>
> Class unassimilated indigenous racial, ethnic, national groups in 306.08; class physical ethnology in 599.97. Class a specific aspect of racial, national, ethnic groups with the aspect, e.g., ethnopsychology 155.8
>
> > *See also 909 for comprehensive history of specific widely distributed racial, ethnic, national groups; 930–990 for history of specific groups in specific continents, countries, localities*
> >
> > *See Manual at 305.8 vs. 306.08*

SUMMARY

305.800 1–.800 9	Standard subdivisions
.81	North Americans
.82	British, English, Anglo-Saxons
.83	Nordic (Germanic) people
.84	Modern Latin peoples
.85	Italians, Romanians, related groups
.86	Spanish and Portuguese
.88	Greeks and related groups
.89	Other racial, ethnic, national groups

.800 1–.800 9   Standard subdivisions

.81   *North Americans

Class national groups of predominantly African descent, e.g., Haitians, in 305.896

For Spanish Americans, see 305.868; for North Americans of Celtic (e.g., Irish, Scots, Welsh) origin, see 305.891; for North American native peoples, see 305.897

See Manual at 305.81

.811   Canadians

Including Canadians of British and French origin

For Canadians not of British or French origin, see the racial or ethnic group of origin, e.g., Canadians of German origin 305.83, Inuit 305.897

.811 001–.811 009   Standard subdivisions

.813   People of United States ("Americans")

Class here United States citizens of British origin, people of the United States as a national group

For United States citizens of other origins, see the racial or ethnic group of origin, e.g., German Americans 305.83, African Americans 305.896

.813 001–.813 009   Standard subdivisions

*Do not use standard subdivisions

.82 British, English, Anglo-Saxons

Standard subdivisions are added for British, English, Anglo-Saxons together; for British as ethnic group; for English people as ethnic group

Including people of the British Isles, Australians, New Zealanders, South Africans of British origin

Class South Africans as a national group in 305.896

For North Americans of British origin, see 305.81; for Anglo-Indians (Indian citizens of British origin), people of Celtic (e.g., Irish, Scots, Welsh) origin, see 305.891. For United Kingdom citizens, Australians, New Zealanders of other origins, see the racial or ethnic group of origin, e.g., Australians of Italian origin 305.85, Australian native peoples 305.89

.820 01–.820 09   Standard subdivisions

.83 *Nordic (Germanic) people

Including Afrikaners, Dutch, Germans, Scandinavians; comprehensive works on Belgians, people of Switzerland

Class South Africans as a national group in 305.896

For English, Anglo-Saxons, see 305.82; for Walloons and French-speaking Swiss, see 305.84; for Italian-speaking and Romansh-speaking Swiss, see 305.85

See also 305.89 for Finns and Sami

.84 *Modern Latin peoples

Including Catalans, French, Walloons

For Canadians of French origin, see 305.811; for Corsicans, Italians, Romanians, related groups, see 305.85; for Spanish and Portuguese, see 305.86; for Basques, see 305.89

.85 *Italians, Romanians, related groups

Including Corsicans

.86 *Spanish and Portuguese

Including Spaniards, Brazilians

For Catalans, see 305.84; for Basques, see 305.89

.868 Spanish Americans

Class here comprehensive works on Latin Americans

Class non-Spanish Latin Americans with the specific ethnic or national affiliation, e.g., Brazilians 305.86, South American native peoples 305.898

.868 001–.868 009   Standard subdivisions

*Do not use standard subdivisions

.88   *Greeks and related groups

Including modern Greeks; comprehensive works on people of Cyprus, on ancient Greeks and Romans

Class ancient Romans in 305.8

For Turkish Cypriots, see 305.89

See also 305.891 for Slavic Macedonians

.89   *Other racial, ethnic, national groups

Including Australian native peoples; Basques; Dravidians, e.g., Tamil, Telugu; people who speak, or whose ancestors spoke, Malayo-Polynesian languages; peoples of North and West Asian origin or situation other than Indo-European and Semitic groups, e.g., Finns, Hungarians, Turks, Sami; non-Semitic Afro-Asiatic peoples, e.g., Berbers, Hausa

.891   *Other Indo-European peoples

Including Celts, e.g., Irish, Scots, Welsh; Indic peoples, e.g., Bengali, Hindis, Romanies; Afghans, Persians; Slavs, e.g., Poles, Russians, Ukrainians

Including comprehensive works on people of India, of South Asia

Class ancient Romans, Osco-Umbrians in 305.8; class Dravidians and Scytho-Dravidians in 305.89

For South Asians who speak, or whose ancestors spoke, languages closely related to East and Southeast Asian languages, see 305.895

.892   *Semites

Including Arabs, Ethiopians; Israelis, Jews

Class non-Semitic Afro-Asiatic peoples of Arab countries and Ethiopia, e.g., Berbers, in 305.89

For Mauritanians as a national group, see 305.896

.895   *East and Southeast Asian peoples; Mundas

Including Asian Americans, Chinese, Japanese, Koreans, Vietnamese; the Bhutia as an ethnic group

Class here comprehensive works on Asian peoples

Class Aeta, Ainu, Andamanese, Malays in 305.89

For a specific Asian people not provided for here, see the people, e.g., Pakistanis 305.891

See also 305.891 for Bhutanese as a national group

*Do not use standard subdivisions

.896   *Africans and people of African descent

Including African Americans

Class here African Negro races

Class North Africans and non-Semitic Afro-Asiatic peoples in 305.89

For Arabs, Ethiopians, Eritreans, see 305.892

.897   *North American native peoples

Including Inuit of Siberia and Greenland

Class here North American native races; people who speak, or whose ancestors spoke, North American native languages; comprehensive works on North and South American native peoples, on North and South American native races

Class national groups of modern Central America where Spanish is an official language in 305.868 even if the majority of their population is of North American native origin, e.g., Guatemalans as a national group

For South American native peoples and races, see 305.898

.898   *South American native peoples

Including Quechua

Class here South American native races; people who speak, or whose ancestors spoke, South American native languages

Class national groups of modern South America where Spanish is an official language in 305.868 even if the majority of their population is of South American native origin, e.g., Peruvians as a national group

.9   Occupational and miscellaneous groups

Including groups of persons with respect to kinship, cultural level, marital status, sexual orientation, physical and mental characteristics; persons with respect to special social status, e.g., socially disadvantaged persons

Class here occupational mobility

Class men's occupations in 305.33; class women's occupations in 305.43

See Manual at 305.9 vs. 305.5

[.901–.909]   Standard subdivisions

Do not use; class in 305.9

*Do not use standard subdivisions

306 Culture and institutions

Culture: the aggregate of a society's beliefs, folkways, mores, science, technology, values, arts

Institutions: patterns of behavior in social relationships

Including subcultures, e.g., counterculture, drug culture

Class here mass culture (popular culture), cultural and social anthropology

Class cultural exchanges in 303.48; class subcultures of specific groups in 305; class drug usage considered a social problem in 362.29; class physical anthropology in 599.9; class history of a specific ethnic group in 900

For customs and folklore, see 390

See Manual at 305 vs. 306, 909, 930–990

SUMMARY

306.08	**Indigenous racial, ethnic, national groups**
.2	**Political institutions**
.3	**Economic institutions**
.4	**Specific aspects of culture**
.6	**Religious institutions**
.7	**Institutions pertaining to relations of the sexes**
.8	**Marriage and family**
.9	**Institutions pertaining to death**

.08   Indigenous racial, ethnic, national groups

Do not use for culture and institutions of a specific kind of person not provided for here; class in 305. Do not use for nonindigenous racial, ethnic, national groups; class in 305.8

Class here culture and institutions, ethnology, race relations of indigenous groups living in distinct communities not integrated in the economic and social life of a nation

See Manual at 305.8 vs. 306.08

[.089]   Racial, ethnic, national groups

Do not use for nonindigenous racial, ethnic, national groups; class in 305.8. Do not use for indigenous racial, ethnic, national groups; class in 306.08

.2   **Political institutions**

Institutions maintaining internal and external peace

Including military institutions

Class here political sociology

Class political science in 320; class law in 340; class public administration and military science in 350

See Manual at 320 vs. 306.2

.3   **Economic institutions**

Social arrangements for production, distribution

Including division of labor, industrial sociology, retirement, slavery, socialism, unemployment, work ethic

Class here economic anthropology, economic sociology, sociology of consumption

Class specific occupational groups in 305.9; class interdisciplinary works on socialism in 335

> *For economic institutions related to housing, see 307.3*

> *See also 305.5 for social classes, 330 for economics*

> *See Manual at 335 vs. 306.3, 320.53*

.4   **Specific aspects of culture**

Not provided for elsewhere

Including arts, medicine; recreation, e.g., gambling, leisure, play, sports; science, technology

> *See Manual at 303.48 vs. 306.4*

.43   Education [*formerly* 370.19]

Including interdisciplinary works on relations of teachers and society [*formerly* 371.1], school and society

Class here educational anthropology

> *For community-school relations in education, see 371.19*

> *See also 370.11 for education for social responsibility*

.44   Language

Including biculturalism, bilingualism, multiculturalism, multilingualism

Class here sociolinguistics

Class biculturalism and multiculturalism in which difference in language is not a central element in 306

> *See also 400 for linguistic aspects of bilingualism*

.440 89   History and description with respect to racial, ethnic, national groups

Class here ethnolinguistics

.6   **Religious institutions**

Religious institutions considered from a secular, nonreligious viewpoint

Class here sociology of religion

> *See also 261 for Christian social theology, 291.1 for social theology*

.7	**Institutions pertaining to relations of the sexes**

Class here interdisciplinary works on sex, sexual love, sexual relations

For sexual ethics, see 176; for problems and controversies concerning various sexual relations, see 363.4; for sex offenses, see 364.15; for customs pertaining to relations between the sexes, see 392.6; for sexual hygiene and techniques, see 613.9

See Manual at 306.7 vs. 155.3

.73	General institutions

Including celibacy, courtship, premarital sexual relations, adultery, extramarital relations

Class here dating behavior

For marriage, see 306.81

.74	Prostitution

See also 363.4 for prostitution as a social problem

[.740 8]	History and description with respect to kinds of persons

Do not use; class in 306.74

.76	Sexual orientation

Including bisexuality, homosexuality, heterosexuality

Class practices associated with specific orientations in 306.77

.77	Sexual practices

Including transvestism

For sexual practices viewed as medical disorders, see 616.85

.8	**Marriage and family**
.81	Marriage

Class here interdisciplinary works on marriage

Class patterns of mate selection in 306.82; class alteration of marriage arrangements in 306.88

For types of marriage, see 306.84. For other aspects of marriage, see the aspect, e.g., marriage counseling 362.82

.82	Patterns in mate selection

Class courtship in 306.73

.83	Types of kinship systems
.84	Types of marriage

Including common-law, mixed marriage; polygamy; remarriage

.85   Family

                Including single-parent family, unwed parenthood

                Class here interdisciplinary works on the family

> *For kinship systems, see 306.83; for intrafamily relationships, see 306.87; for alteration of family arrangements, see 306.88. For a specific aspect of family, see the aspect, e.g., achieving harmonious family relations 646.7*

.87   Intrafamily relationships

                Including abuse within family, birth order, childlessness; in-law relationships

                Class incest in 306.877. Class abuse in a specific family relationship with the relationship, e.g., spouse abuse 306.872

> *For alteration of family arrangements, see 306.88*

> *See also 646.7 for guides to harmonious family relationships*

.872   Husband-wife relationship

                Class sexual practices in 306.77

> *See also 613.9 for sexual techniques*

.874   Parent-child relationship

                Including adopted children, children born out of wedlock, only child; stepparent-stepchild relationship; surrogate motherhood; teenage parenthood

                Class here generation gap in families

                Class comprehensive works on the generation gap in 305.2

> *See also 649 for child rearing (parenting)*

.875   Sibling relationships

.877   Incest

.88   Alteration of family arrangements

                Including death, desertion

> *For separation and divorce, see 306.89*

.89   Separation and divorce

                Standard subdivisions are added for either or both topics in heading

                Including shared custody

                Class divorced families with single-parent custody in 306.85; class parent-child relationship in divorced families in 306.874

.9 **Institutions pertaining to death**

Class here interdisciplinary works on death

For a specific aspect of death, see the aspect, e.g., psychology of death 155.9

307 Communities

See Manual at 307

.1 **Planning and development**

See also 711 for the physical aspect of area planning

.2 **Movement of people to, from, within communities**

Population size and composition relocated to 304.6

Class comprehensive works on population in 304.6

.3 **Structure**

Including land use, neighborhoods, redevelopment, residential patterns, sociology of housing

Class movement within communities in 307.2

See also 363.5 for housing programs

.7 **Specific kinds of communities**

Class a specific aspect of specific kinds of communities in 307.1–307.3

.72 Rural communities

Class here rural sociology

.74 Suburban communities

.740 9 Historical and persons treatment

Do not use for geographic treatment; class in 307.7609

.76 Urban communities

Class here urban sociology, interdisciplinary works on cities

For suburban communities, see 307.74. For a specific aspect of cities, see the aspect, e.g., public administration of cities 352.16

.760 9 Historical, geographic, persons treatment

Class here specific suburban communities, specific urban communities regardless of size or kind

.77 Self-contained communities

Including communes, kibbutzim, tribal communities

310 Collections of general statistics

Class works on collecting statistical data in 001.4. Class statistics of a specific subject, other than general statistics of a place, with the subject, plus notation 02 from Table 1, e.g., statistics on criminal offenses 364.102

See also 001.4 for analysis and presentation of statistical data

[.94–.99]   Treatment by specific continents, countries, localities in modern world

Do not use; class in 314–319

314–319 General statistics of specific continents, countries, localities in modern world

Add to base number 31 notation 4–9 from Table 2, e.g., statistics of France 314.4

320 Political science (Politics and government)

Including policy making

Class sociology of political institutions and processes in 306.2

For law, see 340; for public administration and military science, see 350

See Manual at 320; also at 300, 320 vs. 352–354; also at 302–307 vs. 320; also at 320 vs. 306.2; also at 909, 930–990 vs. 320

SUMMARY

320.01–.09	**Standard subdivisions**
.1–.9	**[Structure and functions of government, ideologies, political situation and conditions, related topics]**
321	**Systems of governments and states**
322	**Relation of the state to organized groups and their members**
323	**Civil and political rights**
324	**The political process**
325	**International migration and colonization**
326	**Slavery and emancipation**
327	**International relations**
328	**The legislative process**

.01   Philosophy and theory

Including nature, legitimacy, role of government; decision making; political change, political justice, theory of liberty; political persuasion and propaganda

Class specific theories in the sense of ideologies in 320.5; class personal liberty in 323.44; class interdisciplinary works on persuasion and propaganda in 303.3. Class theories on a specific aspect of political science with the aspect, e.g., theories of origin of the state 320.1

.02–.08   Standard subdivisions

.09   Historical, geographic, persons treatment

Do not use for political situation and conditions, for forecasting and forecasts in a specific period or area; class in 320.9

.092   Persons

Class here political philosophers and scientists

Do not use for biography of political thinkers identified with specific ideologies; class in 320.5

.1   The state

Including sovereignty, territory, theories of origin; geopolitics

Class systems of government and states, states with restricted sovereignty in 321; class acquisition of territory in 325; class territory in international law in 341.4; class history of territorial changes in 911

For geopolitics in international relations, see 327.101

See Manual at 320

.101   Philosophy and theory

Do not use for theory of origin of the state; class in 320.1

.3   Comparative government

Class comparison of a specific aspect of government with the aspect, e.g., comparison of legislatures 328

.4   Structure and functions of government

Including separation of powers, interdisciplinary works on branches of government

Class here civics

Class analysis of systems by which government is structured, systems of selecting chief executives in 321; class separation of powers in specific areas in 320.41–320.49; class legislative control and oversight of executive branch in 328.3

For comparative government, see 320.3; for relation of local government to higher levels of government, see 320.8; for relation of federal to state and provincial governments, see 321.02; for legislative branch, see 328; for judicial branch, see 347; for executive branch, see 351

See Manual at 320.9, 320.4 vs. 351; also at 909, 930–990 vs. 320.4, 321, 321.09

.409   Historical and persons treatment

Do not use for geographic treatment; class in 320.41–320.49

.41–.49   Geographic treatment

Class here systems of state and government in specific jurisdictions

Add to base number 320.4 notation 1–9 from Table 2, e.g., structure of government in Cuba 320.47291

.5   Political ideologies

Including anarchism, racism, religiously oriented ideologies

Class Christian socialism, Nazism in 320.53; class Zionism in 320.54095694; class interdisciplinary works on anarchism in 335. Class ideologies with respect to a specific aspect of political science with the aspect, e.g., ideologies with respect to change in system of government 321.09

See Manual at 320.5 vs. 297.09, 322; also at 324 vs. 320.5, 320.9

.51   Liberalism

Including modern liberalism, traditional liberalism (ideologies and theories stressing rationalism, individualism, limited government, e.g., libertarianism)

See also 320.52 for conservatism

.52   Conservatism

Ideologies and theories stressing limits of human reason and virtue, value of tradition, caution in effecting social change

See also 320.51 for traditional liberalism

.53   Collectivism and fascism

Standard subdivisions are added for collectivism and fascism together, for collectivism alone

Including communism, Marxism, socialism; national socialism, e.g., Nazism

Class here new left, radicalism, totalitarianism, comprehensive works on authoritarianism

Class religiously oriented authoritarianism in 320.5; class interdisciplinary works on socialism and related systems in 335

See Manual at 335 vs. 306.3, 320.53

.54   Nationalism

Class here ethnic nationalism, "pan" movements

.540 956 94   Palestine   Israel

Class here Zionism

See Manual at 322 vs. 296.3, 320.54095694

.8 **Local government**

Including provinces

Class here relation of local governments to higher levels of government

For provinces as state-level units, see 321.02; for local administration, see 352.14

See also 321 for city-states

See Manual at 352.13 vs. 352.15

.9 **Political situation and conditions**

Class general political history in 900

See Manual at 320.9, 320.4 vs. 351; also at 324 vs. 320.5, 320.9; also at 909, 930–990 vs. 320

.900 1–.900 8   Standard subdivisions

[.900 9]   Historical, geographic, persons treatment

Do not use for historical treatment; class in 320.9. Do not use for geographic and persons treatment; class in 320.91–320.99

.91–.99   Geographic and persons treatment

Add to base number 320.9 notation 1–9 from Table 2, e.g., political conditions in Egypt 320.962

321   Systems of governments and states

Including empires, ideal states, nation-states, small states, states with restricted sovereignty, proposed regional and world unions; heads of state and administration

Class here kinds of states

Unless other instructions are given, use 321 only for consideration of "system" or "kind," and only for areas broader than a specific state. Use 320.4 for the structure and functions of governments of any system or kind, and for the system or systems of any specific state

Selecting chief executives relocated to 324

Class a national state or nation in the sense of a sovereign state in 320.1. Class a kind of head of state or administration characteristic of a specific system of government with the system, e.g., prime ministers responsible to legislatures, constitutional monarchs 321.8

See Manual at 909, 930–990 vs. 320.4, 321, 321.09

.001–.009   Standard subdivisions

.02   Federations

> Including systems of relating federal to state, regional, provincial governments; states and provinces in federal systems
>
> Class here confederations
>
> Class relation of federal to state, regional, provincial governments in specific nations in 320.43–320.49; class proposed world and regional federations in 321

.09   Change in system of government

> Including coups d'état, revolution
>
> Class change in system of government in specific nations in 321.09093–321.09099; class interdisciplinary works on revolution in 303.6
>
> *See Manual at 909, 930–990 vs. 320.4, 321, 321.09*

[.4]   **Pure democracy**

> Relocated to 321.8

.5   **Elitist systems**

> Including aristocracy, oligarchy, plutocracy, theocracy

.8   **Democratic government**

> Including pure democracy [*formerly* 321.4], cabinet system, limited monarchy, republics

.9   **Authoritarian government**

> Including communist and fascist systems
>
> Class here dictatorship, totalitarian government
>
> Class absolute monarchy in 321
>
> *For elitist systems, see 321.5*

322   Relation of the state to organized groups and their members

Relation of the state to groups other than political parties

Including armed services, business and industry, labor movements and groups, religious organizations and groups

> *For groups organized for a specific purpose not provided for here, see the purpose, e.g., groups organized to promote political rights 323.5*
>
> *See also 323.3 for relation of the state to the working class*
>
> *See Manual at 320.5 vs. 297.09, 322; also at 322 vs. 261.7, 291.1; also at 322 vs. 296.3, 320.54095694*

.4   Political action groups

Including pressure groups, reform movements, revolutionary and subversive groups, e.g., revolutionary and subversive activities and branches of political parties

Class here protest groups; nonelectoral tactics used by political action groups, e.g., civil disobedience, passive resistance; specific kinds of conflicts between political action groups and constituted authorities, e.g., riots

Class political action committees (United States fund-raising groups) in 324; class comprehensive works on parties and international party organizations engaged in both nonviolent activity and revolutionary activity in 324.2; class interdisciplinary works on social reform in 303.48; class interdisciplinary works on conflicts and their resolution in 303.6. Class a pressure group or movement working for a specific goal with the goal, e.g., suffrage movements 324.6, welfare reform 361.6

323   Civil and political rights

Standard subdivisions are added for civil and political rights together, for civil rights alone

Including citizen participation, repression, resistance

Class here civil liberties, human rights, individual freedom, rights of mankind; relation of the state to its residents

Class limitation and suspension of civil rights in 323.4; class welfare aspects of human rights in 361.6. Class citizen participation in a specific issue with the issue, e.g., participation in control of public education 379.1

For relation of the state to organized groups other than political parties and related organizations, see 322; for relation of the state to political parties and related organizations, see 324; for civil rights laws, see 342

[.08]   History and description with respect to kinds of persons

Do not use for civil and political rights of nondominant groups; class in 323.1. Do not use for civil and political rights of other social groups; class in 323.3

.1   Civil rights and political rights of nondominant groups

Standard subdivisions are added for either or both topics in heading

Including racial, ethnic, national groups

Class specific civil rights of nondominant groups in 323.4; class specific political rights of nondominant groups in 323.5

For specific nondominant groups other than members of racial, ethnic, national groups, see 323.3

See also 305.5 for interdisciplinary works on social aspects of nondominant groups, 305.8 for social aspects of nondominant ethnic groups

(Option: Class civil and political rights of North American native races in 970.5)

[.109 3–.109 9]	Treatment by continent, country, locality

Do not use; class in 323.1

.3   Civil and political rights of other social groups

Groups other than racial, ethnic, national groups

Including women, socioeconomic classes

Class a specific civil right of social groups in 323.4; class a specific political right of social groups in 323.5

See also 305 for interdisciplinary works on social aspects of specific groups, e.g., 305.4 for women

[.301–.309]   Standard subdivisions

Do not use; class in 323.01–323.09

.4   Specific civil rights; limitation and suspension of civil rights

Including right of assembly and association, right of petition, right to bear arms, right to life and property

Class interdisciplinary works on economic rights in 330

[.401–.409]   Standard subdivisions

Do not use; class in 323.01–323.09

.42   Equal protection of law

Including procedural rights

Specific procedural rights relocated to 340, e.g., trial by jury 345

.44   Freedom of action (Liberty)

Including freedom of conscience and religion, of information, of speech, of the press; right to privacy

Class here intellectual freedom

Class right of assembly, of association, of petition in 323.4

.5   Political rights

Including right to hold office, right to representation

Class right of assembly, of petition in 323.4; class exercise of political rights in 324

For citizenship and related rights, see 323.6; for voting rights, see 324.6

[.508]   History and description with respect to kinds of persons

Do not use for political rights of nondominant groups; class in 323.1. Do not use for political rights of other social groups; class in 323.3

.6   Citizenship and related topics

> Standard subdivisions are added for citizenship and related topics together, for citizenship alone

> Including aliens, asylum, expatriation and repatriation, naturalization, passports and visas, stateless persons

324   The political process

> Including interest and pressure groups; auxiliary party organizations, e.g., youth groups; comprehensive works on lobbying

> Class here selecting chief executives [*formerly also* 321], elections

> Class auxiliary organizations of international party organizations in 324.1; class auxiliary organizations of specific parties in 324.24–324.29; class comprehensive works on interest and pressure groups, political action groups in 322.4

> > *For legislative-branch lobbying, see 328.3. For lobbying for a specific goal, see the goal, e.g., lobbying for penal reform 364.6*

> > *See Manual at 324 vs. 320.5, 320.9; also at 909, 930–990 vs. 320*

SUMMARY

324.09	**Historical, geographical, persons treatment**
.1	**International party organizations, auxiliaries, activities**
.2	**Political parties**
.5	**Nomination of candidates**
.6	**Election systems and procedures; suffrage**
.7	**Conduct of election campaigns**
.9	**Historical and geographic treatment of elections**

.09   Historical, geographic, persons treatment

> Do not use for historical and geographic treatment of elections; class in 324.9

.1   International party organizations, auxiliaries, activities

> Not directly controlled by specific national parties

> Class revolutionary and subversive activities of party organizations in 322.4

.2   Political parties

> Including campaign literature, platforms, programs; finance, leadership, relation of political parties to the state and government

> Class comprehensive works on auxiliary party organizations in 324; class campaign literature, platforms, programs; finance, leadership, relation of political parties to the state and government in specific countries and localities in 324.24–324.29

> > *For revolutionary and subversive activities and branches of parties, see 322.4; for international organizations and activities of parties, see 324.1; for nomination of candidates, see 324.5. For campaign literature on a specific subject, see the subject, e.g., campaign literature on United States participation in Vietnamese War 959.704*

[.202 3]	Politics as a profession, occupation, hobby
	Do not use; class in 324.2
.209 4–.209 9	Treatment by specific continents

Do not use for parties in specific countries and localities in modern world; class in 324.24–324.29

See Manual at 324.2094–324.2099 and 324.24–324.29

.24–.29   Parties in specific countries in modern world

Class here nomination of party candidates [*formerly* 324.5094–324.5099], auxiliary party organizations

Except where specifically instructed to the contrary below, for a specific country or for localities within a country add to base number 324.2 notation 4–9 from Table 2 for the specific country, e.g., parties in France 324.244; then add further as follows:
    001–009   Standard subdivisions

See Manual at 324.2094–324.2099 and 324.24–324.29

Special developments follow for selected specific countries

.241	Parties in United Kingdom
.241 001–.241 009	Standard subdivisions
.241 04	Conservative Party
.241 06	Liberal Party
.241 07	Labour Party
.271	Parties in Canada
.271 001–.271 009	Standard subdivisions
.271 04	Progressive Conservative Party
.271 06	Liberal Party
.271 07	New Democratic Party
.271 1–.271 9	Parties in provinces and territories of Canada

Add to base number 324.271 the numbers following —71 in notation 711–719 from Table 2 for province or territory, e.g., parties in Quebec 324.2714; then add further as follows:
    001–009   Standard subdivisions

.273   Parties in United States

For parties in specific states and District of Columbia, see 324.274–324.279

.273 01–.273 09   Standard subdivisions

.273 2	Historical parties

Parties existing prior to 1945 and no longer in existence

Including Federalist, Jeffersonian Republican parties

.273 4	Republican Party
.273 6	Democratic Party

Including Democratic-Republican Party

.274–.279	Parties in states of United States and District of Columbia

Add to base number 324.27 the numbers following —7 in notation 74–79 from Table 2 for state or District of Columbia, e.g., parties in California 324.2794; then add further as follows:
001–009   Standard subdivisions

Class comprehensive works in 324.273

For political parties of Hawaii, see 324.2969

.294	Parties in Australia
.294 001–.294 009	Standard subdivisions
.294 1–.294 7	Parties in states and territories of Australia

Add to base number 324.294 the numbers following —94 in notation 941–947 from Table 2 for province or territory, e.g., parties in New South Wales 324.2944; then add further as follows:
001–009   Standard subdivisions

.296 9	Parties in Hawaii
.296 900 1–.296 900 9	Standard subdivisions

.5   Nomination of candidates

Including nominations by conventions, by primaries

Class here campaigns for nomination; results of campaigns, e.g., delegate counts

Class comprehensive works on nomination and election campaigns in 324.9

See also 324.2 for convention finance

.509 4–.509 9	Treatment by specific continents

Nomination of party candidates in specific countries and localities relocated to 324.24–324.29

.6   Election systems and procedures; suffrage

Including electoral systems; qualifications for voting, voting rights; registration of voters; voting procedures, e.g., procedures for contested elections; election fraud; recall

Class here comprehensive works on systems and procedures for nominations and elections

Class conduct of election campaigns, irregularities in campaign finance in 324.7; class comprehensive works on political rights in 323.5

> *For nomination of candidates, see 324.5; for electoral basis of representation in legislative bodies, see 328.3*

.7   Conduct of election campaigns

Variant name: practical politics

Including campaign finance, citizen participation

Class party finance in 324.2; class conduct of campaigns for nomination in 324.5

.9   Historical and geographic treatment of elections

Class here campaigns, election returns and results, studies of voting behavior

Class platforms, campaign literature in 324.2; class nomination by primary elections in 324.5

.900 1–.900 8   Standard subdivisions

[.900 9]   Historical, geographic, persons treatment

Do not use for historical treatment; class in 324.9. Do not use for geographic treatment; class in 324.91–324.99

[.900 92]   Persons

Do not use; class in 324.092

.91–.99   Geographic treatment

Add to base number 324.9 notation 1–9 from Table 2, e.g., election campaigns in United Kingdom 324.941; then add further as follows:
001–009   Standard subdivisions

325   International migration and colonization

Standard subdivisions are added for international migration and colonization together, for international migration alone

Including involuntary population transfer and exchange, political refugees, imperialism

Administration of colonies relocated to 353.1

Class comprehensive works on foreign policy in 327.1

[.094–.099]   Treatment by specific continent, country, locality in modern world

Do not use; class in 325.4–325.9

.4–.9   International migration to and colonization in specific continents, countries, localities in modern world

Add to base number 325 notation 4–9 from Table 2, e.g., migration to Israel 325.5694
Subdivisions are added for either or both topics in heading

Class emigration from specific continents, countries, localities in modern world to specific continents, countries, localities; colonization by specific continents, countries, localities in modern world; comprehensive works on colonization by and in specific continents, countries, localities in modern world in 325

326   Slavery and emancipation

Standard subdivisions are added for slavery and emancipation together, for slavery alone

Including abolitionism, antislavery movements

Class interdisciplinary works on slavery in 306.3

327   International relations

Class military science in 355; class interdisciplinary works on relations among countries in 303.48

For international relations with respect to a specific subject, see the subject, e.g., trade relations of Germany 382.0943

See Manual at 341 vs. 327

[.01]   Philosophy and theory

Do not use; class in 327.101

.06   Organizations

For international governmental organizations, see 341.2

[.068]   Management

Do not use; class in 353.1

.09   Historical, geographic, persons treatment

Class here diplomatic history, international relations of or in specific areas or blocks, e.g., international relations in Middle East 327.0956, foreign relations of former Communist bloc 327.09171

.092   Persons

Do not use for diplomats; class in 327.2092

.093–.099   Treatment by specific continents

Do not use for foreign relations and diplomatic history of specific nations; class in 327.3–327.9

.1   Foreign policy and specific topics in international relations

Standard subdivisions are added for foreign policy alone

Including specific topics in international relations of specific nations [*formerly* 327.3–327.9], disarmament [*formerly also* 355] and arms control, alliances and collective security, balance of power, boycotts and sanctions, foreign aid, promotion of peace, propaganda and war of nerves, spheres of influence; international conflict; international cooperation

Class here imperialism in international relations, international politics, power politics

Class international governmental organizations in 341.2; class war in 355.02; class comprehensive works on political propaganda in 320.01; class comprehensive works on imperialism, imperialism as national policy in 325; class comprehensive works on specific topics in international relations in 327; class interdisciplinary works on propaganda in 303.3

> *For diplomacy, see 327.2; for law of international cooperation, see 341.7*

.101   Philosophy and theory of international relations, of foreign policy

Including role and position of small states, economic bases of international relations

Class here geopolitics in international relations, nature of power in international relations

Class comprehensive works on geopolitics in 320.1

.109   Historical, geographic, persons treatment of foreign policy

.109 2   Persons

Do not use for diplomats; class in 327.2092

.109 3–.109 9   Treatment by specific continents

Do not use for foreign policy of specific nations; class in 327.3–327.9

.12   Espionage and subversion

Standard subdivisions are added for either or both topics in heading

Class here interdisciplinary works on espionage, subversion, intelligence gathering

> *For military espionage and subversion, see 355.3*

.120 93–.120 99   Treatment by specific continents, countries, localities

Do not use for espionage and subversion by specific nations; class in 327.123–327.129

.123–.129   Espionage and subversion by specific nations

> Add to base number 327.12 notation 3–9 from Table 2, e.g., espionage by France 327.1244; then add further as follows:
> 001–008   Standard subdivisions
> 009   Historical and persons treatment
> > Do not use for espionage of a specific nation in a specific area; class in the number for the nation without adding notation 009

.2   Diplomacy

> Including protocol

> Use 327.2 for methods and style of diplomacy; 327 for substance and content of diplomatic relations

> *For law of diplomacy, see 341.3*

.209 2   Persons

> Do not use for persons treatment of diplomats of specific nations; class in 327.3–327.9

.3–.9   Foreign relations of specific nations

> Add to base number 327 notation 3–9 from Table 2, e.g., foreign relations of Brazil 327.81; then, for relations between that nation and another nation or region, add 0* and to the result add notation 1–9 from Table 2, e.g., relations between Brazil and France 327.81044, between Brazil and Arab world 327.81017

> Give priority in notation to the nation emphasized. If emphasis is equal, give priority to the one coming first in the sequence of area numbers
> > (Option: Give priority in notation to the nation requiring local emphasis, e.g. libraries in United States class foreign relations between United States and France in 327.73044)

> Specific topics in international relations of specific nations relocated to 327.1

328   The legislative process

> Including rules and procedures of legislative bodies

> Class here legislative branch, legislative bodies

> Class rules and procedures of legislative committees in 328.3; class rules and procedures of specific legislative bodies in modern world in 328.4–328.9; class comprehensive rules of order in 060.4

> *See Manual at 909, 930–990 vs. 320*

.094–.099   Treatment by specific continents

> Do not use for legislative process in specific jurisdictions in modern world; class in 328.4–328.9

---

*Add 00 for standard subdivisions; see instructions at beginning of Table 1

.2   Initiative and referendum

.209 4–.209 9   Treatment by specific continents

>   Do not use for treatment in specific jurisdictions in modern world; class in 328.24–328.29

.24–.29   Initiative and referendum in specific jurisdictions in modern world

>   Add to base number 328.2 notation 4–9 from Table 2, e.g., initiative in California 328.2794
>   Subdivisions are added for either or both topics in heading

.3   Specific topics of legislative bodies

>   Including procedures for legislative enactment of budgets [*formerly* 351.72]; committees, electoral basis of representation, enactment of legislation, legislative powers, lobbying, ombudsmen; compensation, privileges and immunities, terms of members

>   Use of this number for legislative bodies discontinued; class in 328

>   Class rules and procedures of legislative bodies in 328; class specific topics of legislative bodies of specific jurisdictions in modern world in 328.4–328.9; class interdisciplinary works on ombudsmen in 352.8. Class committee hearings and reports on a specific subject that emphasize proposed legislation with the subject in 340, e.g., hearing on bills governing armed services 343; class committee hearings and reports on a specific subject that do not emphasize proposed legislation with the subject in 001–999, e.g., general reports on military affairs 355

>   *For enactment of budgets, see 352.4*

[.301–.309]   Standard subdivisions

>   Do not use; class in 328.01–328.09

.4–.9   The legislative process in specific jurisdictions in modern world

>   Add to base number 328 notation 4–9 from Table 2, e.g., the legislative process in Canada 328.71; however, do not add notation 01–09 from Table 1; class in number for jurisdiction

>   *For initiative and referendum in specific jurisdictions in modern world, see 328.24–328.29*

330   Economics

Including interdisciplinary works on economic rights

Class here comprehensive works on economics and management

Unless other instructions are given, observe the following table of preference, e.g., the role of labor in agricultural production 331.7 (*not* 338.1):

Cooperatives	334
Public finance	336
Economics of labor, finance, land, energy	331–333
Production, Commerce (381–382), Transportation (385–388)	338
Macroeconomics and related topics	339
International economics	337
Socialism and related systems	335

For management, see 658. For a specific kind or aspect of economic rights, see the kind or aspect, e.g., political aspects of property rights 323.4

See Manual at 330 vs. 650

SUMMARY

330.01–.09	**Standard subdivisions**
.1–.9	**[Systems, schools, theories; economic situation and conditions]**
331	**Labor economics**
332	**Financial economics**
333	**Economics of land and energy**
334	**Cooperatives**
335	**Socialism and related systems**
336	**Public finance**
337	**International economics**
338	**Production**
339	**Macroeconomics and related topics**

.01   Philosophy and theory

Do not use for theories; class in 330.1

Including econometrics

.02–.08   Standard subdivisions

.09   Historical, geographic, persons treatment of economics as a discipline

Do not use for economic situation and conditions; class in 330.9

.1   **Systems, schools, theories**

Including theories of wealth and property

For socialist and related systems and schools, see 335; for macroeconomic aspects of wealth, see 339

.12 Systems

> Including free enterprise economy (usually synonymous with capitalism); mixed economies, e.g., welfare state systems; planned economies

> Class laissez-faire economic theory in 330.15

.15 Schools of economic thought

> Including classical economics, Keynesianism, Chicago school of economics, supply-side economics

.9 Economic situation and conditions

> Standard subdivisions are added for either or both topics in heading

> Class here works describing situation and conditions at both the macroeconomic level (the economy viewed as a whole) and the microeconomic level (level of the individual unit, such as the household or firm)

> Class policies to promote economic growth and development in 338.9; class macroeconomic policies in 339.5

.900 1–.900 8 Standard subdivisions

.900 9 Historical and persons treatment

> Do not use for specific historical periods; class in 330.9

[.900 91] Treatment by areas, regions, places in general

> Do not use; class in 330.91

[.900 93–.900 99] Treatment by specific continents, countries, localities

> Do not use; class in 330.93–330.99

.91 Geographic treatment (Economic geography) by areas, regions, places in general

> Add to base number 330.91 the numbers following — 1 in notation 11–19 from Table 2, e.g., economic situation and conditions in developing countries 330.9172; however, do not add notation from Table 1 for standard subdivisions

.93–.99 Geographic treatment (Economic geography) by specific continents, countries, localities

> Add to base number 330.9 notation 3–9 from Table 2, e.g., economic situation and conditions in France 330.944; however, do not add notation from Table 1 for standard subdivisions

---

> **331–333 Economics of labor, finance, land, energy**

> Class comprehensive works on economics of labor, finance, land, energy in 330; class comprehensive works on labor, capital, land considered as factors of production in 338

331 Labor economics

Class here industrial relations, interdisciplinary works on labor

Unless other instructions are given, observe the following table of preference, e.g., compensation of women 331.4 (*not* 331.2):

Labor force by personal characteristics	331.3–331.6
Labor force and market	331.1
Conditions of employment	331.2
Labor unions (Trade unions), labor-management (collective) bargaining and disputes	331.8
Labor by industry and occupation	331.7

Class economic conditions of laboring classes in 330.9; class full employment policies in 339.5

For noneconomic aspects of labor, see the aspect, e.g., relation of labor movements to the state 322, managerial views of labor 658.3

See also 305.5 for sociology of laboring classes, 306.3 for sociology of labor

See Manual at 331 vs. 331.8; also at 331 vs. 658.3

SUMMARY

331.01–.09	**Standard subdivisions**
.1	**Labor force and market**
.2	**Conditions of employment**
.3	**Workers by age group**
.4	**Women workers**
.5	**Special categories of workers other than by age or sex**
.6	**Categories of workers by racial, ethnic, national origin**
.7	**Labor by industry and occupation**
.8	**Labor unions (Trade unions), labor-management (collective) bargaining and disputes**

.01 Philosophy and theory

Do not use for systems of labor; class in 331.11

Including employment rights; industrial democracy (determination of a company's policies affecting the welfare of its workers by joint action of management and worker representatives)

Class producer cooperatives in 334; class worker control of industry in 338.6; class employee representation in management discussed from the managerial viewpoint in 658.3

For role of labor unions in industrial democracy, see 331.88

[.08] History and description with respect to kinds of persons

Do not use for comprehensive works; class in 331.11. Do not use for labor force by specific personal characteristics; class in 331.3–331.6

.1   **Labor force and market**

Class labor force and market in relation to choice of vocation in 331.7

See Manual at 331.1 vs. 331.11, 331.12

.11   Labor force

All who are employed or available for employment

Including qualifications of labor force; labor productivity; systems of labor; comprehensive works on labor force by personal characteristics

Class here human resources, manpower and womanpower, labor supply, size of labor force

Class industrial productivity in 338

For workers with specific personal characteristics, see 331.3–331.6

See also 331.12 for demand for labor, 331.87 for union membership

See Manual at 331.1 vs. 331.11, 331.12

.12   Labor market

The activities of and opportunities for buying and selling labor

Including demand for labor, job vacancies; government policy on the labor market; labor actively employed; labor mobility (geographic, e.g., brain drain, and interoccupational), turnover; placement

Class here supply of labor in relation to demand

For maladjustments in labor market, see 331.13

See Manual at 331.1 vs. 331.11, 331.12; also at 331.12 vs. 331.13

.13   Maladjustments in labor market

Including unemployment and its prevention and relief; labor shortages and surpluses; discrimination in employment, equal employment opportunity programs

Class personnel aspects of discrimination in government employment in 352.608; class comprehensive works about personnel policies on discrimination in 658.3008

For a specific measure of prevention or relief, see the measure, e.g., job sharing 331.25, economic stabilization 339.5, welfare 362.85; for discrimination in relation to a specific aspect of industrial relations, see the aspect, e.g., discrimination as a factor affecting compensation 331.2, discrimination by unions 331.87

See Manual at 331.12 vs. 331.13

.2 **Conditions of employment**

Including compensation, pay equity, wages; guaranteed-wage plans; comprehensive works on wage-price policy

Class conditions of employment in relation to choice of vocation in 331.7; class guaranteed minimum income in 362.5; class conditions of employment discussed from the managerial viewpoint in 658.3

For wage-price controls to combat inflation, see 332.4; for price policy, see 338.5; for wage-price policy as a factor in economic stabilization, see 339.5

See Manual at 331.2 vs. 331.89

.25 Conditions of employment other than compensation

Including compressed work week, flexible working hours, job sharing, leave, overtime work, part-time employment; employee discipline; pensions, unemployment compensation; telecommuting; worker security; interdisciplinary works on fringe benefits, on on-the-job vocational training, on vocational training provided by industry, on apprenticeship

Class stock ownership and purchase plans in 331.2; class apprentices as a special class of workers in 331.5; class work experience as part of education in 371.2; class interdisciplinary works on vocational education conducted by an educational institution in 370.11

For fringe benefits provided by unions, see 331.87; for fringe benefits for veterans of military service and their survivors, see 362.86; for benefits provided through insurance, see 368.3; for benefits provided through government-sponsored social insurance, see 368.4; for managerial aspects of training by the employer and comprehensive works on administration of employee benefits, see 658.3. For on-the-job training in a specific occupation, see the occupation, plus notation 071 from Table 1, e.g., on-the-job apprenticeship of carpenters 694.071

> **331.3–331.6 Labor force by personal characteristics**

Including labor force and market, conditions of employment, specific industries and occupations, labor unions, labor-management bargaining with respect to workers with specific personal characteristics

Unless other instructions are given, class a subject with aspects in two or more subdivisions of 331.3–331.6 in the number coming first in the schedule, e.g., young North American native women 331.3 (*not* 331.4 or 331.6)

Class choice of vocation for persons with specific personal characteristics in 331.7; class comprehensive works in 331.11. Class employment services as a form of social service to persons with specific personal characteristics with the kind of person in 362.6–362.8, e.g., sheltered employment for older persons 362.6

.3 **Workers by age group**

Class apprentices in 331.5

.4   **Women workers**

Including married women, maternity leave, sex discrimination against women

.5   **Special categories of workers other than by age or sex**

Including apprentices; contract, casual, migrant workers; gay workers; prisoners, ex-convicts; veterans; workers with physical and mental disabilities

Class training of apprentices in 331.25

For categories of workers by racial, ethnic, national origin, see 331.6

.6   **Categories of workers by racial, ethnic, national origin**

Including immigrants

See also 331.5 for migrant workers

.7   **Labor by industry and occupation**

Standard subdivisions are added for either or both topics in heading

Including professional, service, industrial, agricultural, unskilled occupations; government employment, choice of vocation, interdisciplinary works describing vocations and occupational specialties, interdisciplinary works on career opportunities and vocational counseling

Class studies of vocational interest in 158.6; class job hunting in 650.14

For vocational counseling in schools, see 371.4. For professional relationships in, descriptions of, career opportunities in, choice of vocation with regard to a specific occupation, see the occupation, plus notation 023 from Table 1, e.g., career opportunities in accounting 657.023

.700 1–.700 9   Standard subdivisions

.8   **Labor unions (Trade unions), labor-management (collective) bargaining and disputes**

Class here interdisciplinary works on labor movements

Class comprehensive works on industrial democracy in 331.01; class labor unions and labor-management bargaining in relation to choice of vocation in 331.7

For a specific aspect of labor movements, see the aspect, e.g., political activities of labor movements 322

See Manual at 331 vs. 331.8

.87   Labor union organization

Including constitutions, bylaws, rules; levels of organization, e.g., locals, nationals, federations; membership policies, discrimination by unions; officers, elections, conventions; benefits

Class comprehensive works about labor unions in 331.88

.88   Labor unions (Trade unions)

Including company, craft, industrial unions; open and closed shop, right to work; preferential hiring, sole bargaining rights; control of hiring and layoffs, dues checkoff, control of grievance procedures, make-work arrangements (featherbedding)

Class here unions organized along religious lines, e.g., Christian trade unions

Class managerial viewpoint on labor unions in 658.3

For labor union organization, see 331.87

See also 322 for political activities of labor unions

.880 9   Historical, geographic, persons treatment of labor unions

.880 91   Treatment by areas, regions, places in general

Class here international unions

Class international unions with members from only two countries in 331.88094–331.88099, using the comprehensive notation from Table 2 for the two countries, e.g., unions with United States and Canadian workers 331.880973

.89   Labor-management (Collective) bargaining and disputes

Standard subdivisions are added for either or both topics in heading

Including organizing, winning recognition, contracts; arbitration, mediation; labor measures other than strikes, e.g., boycotts; management measures, e.g., lockouts, strikebreaking, yellow-dog contracts; government measures, e.g., right-to-work policy, strike requirements

See Manual at 331.2 vs. 331.89

.892   Strikes

Including picketing, sit-down strikes

Class conciliation measures, management and government measures to deal with strikes in 331.89

[.892 09]   Historical, geographic, persons treatment

Do not use; class in 331.892

332 Financial economics

Including capital, international finance

Class capital and international finance in relation to a specific topic of financial economics with the topic, e.g., role of banks in international finance 332.1

> *For public finance, see 336; for capital formation discussed in relation to production in specific kinds of industries, see 338.1–338.4; for financing of firms, see 338.6; for savings and investments as a factor affecting national income, see 339.4; for balance of payments, see 382*

> *See Manual at 332, 336 vs. 339; also at 332 vs. 338, 658.15*

.02 Miscellany

.024 Personal finance

Including increasing income, net worth, financial security; planning for retirement, e.g., annuities, individual retirement accounts (IRAs); estate planning; debt management; coping with depression and inflation

> *For management of personal expenditure, see 640. For a specific aspect of personal finance not provided for here, see the aspect, e.g., investing in stocks 332.63, consumer information 381.3*

> *See Manual at 332.024 vs. 640*

.024 001–.024 007 Standard subdivisions

[.024 008] Personal finance with respect to kinds of persons

Do not use; class in 332.024

.024 009 Historical, geographic, persons treatment

.06 Organizations and management

Do not use for financial institutions and their management; class in 332.1

.1 Banks

Including central, chartered, commercial, development, international banks; credit and debit cards issued by banks; deposits, e.g., checking accounts, savings accounts, NOW (negotiable order of withdrawal) accounts; savings departments, trust services of commercial banks

Class here banking; bank failures; government guaranty of deposits; comprehensive works on money and banking, on financial institutions and their functions

> *For development banks serving one country, specialized banking institutions, see 332.2; for credit and loan institutions, see 332.3; for money, see 332.4; for credit, see 332.7; for credit unions, see 334*

> *See also 332.7 for credit functions not limited to a specific type of financial institution*

> *See Manual at 332.7 vs. 332.1*

.2   **Specialized banking institutions**

Including development banks serving one country, savings banks, trust companies

For international banks, see 332.1; for agricultural institutions, see 332.3; for investment banks, see 332.66; for banking cooperatives, see 334

.3   **Credit and loan institutions**

Standard subdivisions are added for either or both topics in heading

Including agricultural institutions, e.g., land banks; consumer and sales finance organizations; industrial banks; savings and loan associations (building and loan associations, home loan associations, mortgage institutions); credit and loan functions of enterprises whose primary function is not credit and loan, e.g., credit function of insurance companies, retail stores; comprehensive works on thrift institutions

Class interdisciplinary works on insurance companies in 368.006

For savings banks, see 332.2; for credit unions, see 334

.4   **Money**

Including devaluation; gold standard, foreign exchange; inflation, stagflation, deflation; wage-price controls to combat inflation; comprehensive works on monetary policy

Class here comprehensive works on mediums of exchange

Class mediums of exchange other than money in 332; class fiscal policy in 336.3; class comprehensive works on wage-price policy in 331.2; class comprehensive works on money and banking in 332.1; class comprehensive works on economic stabilization policies in 339.5; class comprehensive works on balance of payments in 382

For International Monetary Fund, relation of central banks to monetary policy, see 332.1; for use of monetary policy for economic stabilization, see 339.5

See Manual at 339.4 vs. 332.4

[.409]   Historical, geographic, persons treatment

Do not use; class in 332.4

.6   **Investment and investments**

Standard subdivisions are added for either or both topics in heading

Including brokerage firms, investment counselors, international exchange of securities, investment for specific purposes (e.g., for tax advantages)

Class here portfolio analysis and management

Class real estate brokerage in 333.33; class description and analysis of business enterprises issuing securities in 338.7–338.8. Class investment for specific purposes in relation to another specific aspect of investment with the aspect, e.g., reducing tax liability by investing in municipal bonds 332.63

.601 Philosophy and theory

Do not use for forecasting and forecasts; class in 332.67

.63 Forms of investment

Including art, coins; real estate, mortgages; stock options, commodity futures; stocks, bonds, commodities

Class here speculation in specific forms of investment

Class buying and selling procedures for securities and commodities, speculation in multiple forms of investment in 332.64; class investment in specific kinds of businesses regardless of form in 332.67; class buying and selling procedures for real estate in 333.33

For foreign exchange futures, see 332.4

See also 332.7 for real estate finance

.64 Exchange of securities and commodities

Including over-the-counter market; speculation in multiple forms of investment

Class here buying and selling of securities and commodities; organization, procedures, activities of organized exchanges

Class brokerage firms, international exchange of securities in 332.6; class speculation in specific forms of investment in 332.63; class guides to speculation in 332.67

.66 Investment banks

Class here investment banking (underwriting and sale of security issues), issuing houses

For international investment banks, see 332.1

.67 Investments by field of investment, kind of enterprise, kind of investor; investment guides

Class international exchange of securities in 332.6; class investment in specific forms of securities, e.g., investment in railroad stocks, in 332.63; class exchange of securities and commodities, speculation in multiple forms of investment, e.g., speculation by pension funds, in 332.64; class investment banks in 332.66

.7 **Credit**

Including agricultural, commercial, mercantile, industrial credit; real estate finance and mortgages; small business loans, personal loans, consumer credit; bankruptcy; checks, credit cards, debit cards, money orders

Class credit functions of banks in 332.1; class credit functions of specialized banking institutions in 332.2; class credit functions of credit and loan institutions in 332.3; class interest and discount in 332.8

See also 332.63 for mortgages as an investment

See Manual at 332.7 vs. 332.1

.8 **Interest and discount**

Including usury

See also 332.63 for interest rate futures

333 Economics of land and energy

Land: all natural and man-made resources over which possession of the earth gives control

Including absentee ownership, interdisciplinary works on land surveys

Class here land as a factor of production

Class a specific kind of land surveys with the kind, e.g., land use surveys 333.73

For land surveying techniques, see 526.9

See also 631.4 for surveys that focus on agricultural use of soils

See Manual at 333.7–333.9 vs. 333; also at 333.73–333.78 vs. 333, 333.1–333.5

SUMMARY

333.001–.009	Standard subdivisions	
.01	Theories	
.1	Public ownership of land	
.2	Ownership of land by nongovernmental groups	
.3	Individual (Private) ownership of land	
.5	Renting and leasing land	
.7	Natural resources and energy	
.8	Subsurface resources	
.9	Other natural resources	

.001 Philosophy and theory

Do not use for theories; class in 333.01. Do not use for land classification; class in 333.7301

.002–.009 Standard subdivisions

.01 Theories

Including theory of economic rent (return produced by ownership of land after deduction of all outlays for labor and capital)

See also 333.5 for renting and leasing land and natural resources

> **333.1–333.5 Ownership of land**

Ownership: right to possession and use; right to transfer of possession and use

Land: all natural and man-made resources over which possession of the earth gives control

Class here the kind of control that stems from ownership; ownership of natural resources

Class comprehensive works in 333.3

See also 333.7–333.9 for usage of natural resources, for control of such usage not stemming from ownership

See Manual at 333.73–333.78 vs. 333, 333.1–333.5

.1 **Public ownership of land**

Including nationalization

Class public control of privately owned lands in 333.7; class comprehensive works on land policy in 333.73

See also 333.2 for ownership and control of land by peoples subordinate to another jurisdiction, 343 for law of public property

.2 **Ownership and control of land by nongovernmental groups**

Including common lands; enclosure of common lands; open-field system

For corporate ownership, see 333.3

.3 **Individual (Private) ownership of land**

Including corporate ownership, land reform, land settlement

Class here comprehensive works on ownership of land

Class absentee ownership in 333

For public ownership, see 333.1; for ownership by nongovernmental groups, see 333.2

.33   Transfer of possession and of right to use

Standard subdivisions are added for either or both topics in heading

Including real estate market; value and price, valuation (appraisal), sale and gift of land; rights to use of minerals, water, air space; sharecropping

Class here comprehensive works on real estate business

Class land reform in 333.3; class valuation for tax purposes in 352.4

For government acquisition and disposal, see 333.1; for rental and leasing, see 333.5; for real estate development, see 333.7

See also 332.63 for real estate investment, 332.7 for real estate finance

.5   **Renting and leasing land**

Including tenancy, landlord-tenant relations; types of renting, e.g., cash renting, share renting

Class renting and leasing specific kinds of land in 333.33

For sharecropping, see 333.33

.7   **Natural resources and energy**

Standard subdivisions are added for natural resources and energy together, for natural resources alone

Aspects other than ownership

Including reserves (stock, supply), shortages; requirements (need, demand); consumption (utilization), abuse, wastage; impact studies; development, e.g., reclamation, restoration, subsidies; conservation, protection; works on national parks that emphasize conservation; public control of privately owned lands and other natural resources, other control of usage

Class here raw materials; interdisciplinary works on the environment

Class ownership of land in 333.1–333.5; class economic geology in 553; class interdisciplinary works on consumption in 339.4. Class reserves (stock, supply), shortages; requirements (need, demand); consumption (utilization), abuse, wastage; impact studies; development, reclamation, restoration, subsidies; conservation, protection; works on national parks that emphasize conservation; public control of privately owned lands and other natural resources, other control of usage in relation to energy or a specific kind of natural resource with the energy or kind of resource, e.g., conservation of water 333.91

For subsurface resources, see 333.8; for natural resources other than land, energy, subsurface resources, see 333.9. For other aspects of the environment, see the aspect, e.g., environmental protection 363.7

See Manual at 333.7–333.9 vs. 333; also at 333.7–333.9 vs. 363.1, 363.73, 577; also at 333.7–333.9 vs. 363.6; also at 333.7–333.9 vs. 508, 913–919, 930–990; also at 333.7 vs. 304.2, 363.7; also at 363

.73   **Land**

Aspects other than ownership

Including kinds of land by physical condition, e.g., arid and semiarid lands, mountainous lands, sand dunes; comprehensive works on natural areas established for land conservation

Class here river basins

Class ownership aspects of land in 333.1–333.5

> *For kinds of land by use, see 333.74–333.78; for shorelands and related areas, submerged lands, wetlands, see 333.91. For a specific type of natural area established for conservation, see the type, e.g., wilderness areas 333.78*
>
> *See Manual at 333.73–333.78 vs. 333, 333.1–333.5*

>   **333.74–333.78   Kinds of land by use**

Class comprehensive works in 333.73

.74   **Pasture (Grazing) lands**

> *See Manual at 333.73–333.78 vs. 333, 333.1–333.5*

.75   **Forest lands**

Class here national forests; jungles, rain forests; timber resources

Class parks, recreational and wilderness areas in 333.78

> *See also 333.95 for wood as a fuel*
>
> *See Manual at 333.73–333.78 vs. 333, 333.1–333.5; also at 338.1 vs. 333.75*

.76   **Rural lands   Agricultural lands**

Including mined lands

Class rural lands of a specific physical condition not devoted to a specific use in 333.73

> *For pasture lands, see 333.74; for forest lands, see 333.75; for rural recreational lands, see 333.78*
>
> *See Manual at 333.73–333.78 vs. 333, 333.1–333.5*

.77   **Urban lands**

Including commercial, industrial, residential lands

Class urban mined lands in 333.76; class urban recreational lands in 333.78

> *See Manual at 333.73–333.78 vs. 333, 333.1–333.5*

.78   Recreational and wilderness areas

Standard subdivisions are added for recreational and wilderness areas together, for recreational areas alone

Including forests, mountains, parks; recreational use of water and land adjoining it, e.g., rivers, beaches

Class wildlife and wildlife refuges in 333.95; class comprehensive works on uses of water and land adjoining it in 333.91

See also 363.6 for park and recreation services

See Manual at 333.73–333.78 vs. 333, 333.1–333.9

.79   Energy

Including alternative, renewable energy resources; energy for specific uses, e.g., use in transportation

Class here power resources, production of energy, interdisciplinary works on energy

Class electric power in 333.793; class extraction of energy resources and comprehensive works on the economics of mineral fuels in 338.2; class interdisciplinary works on mineral fuels in 553. Class a specific renewable or alternative resource with the resource, e.g., solar energy 333.792

For a specific form of energy, a specific energy resource not provided for here, see the form or resource, e.g., fossil fuels, geothermal energy 333.8, wind energy 333.9, hydroelectricity 333.91, biomass as an energy resource 333.95; for a noneconomic aspect of energy, see the aspect, e.g., energy management 658.2, fuel technology 662

.791   Energy conservation

[.791 01–.791 09]   Standard subdivisions

Do not use; class in 333.79

.792   Primary forms of energy

Resources used directly to perform work, to produce other forms of energy

Including solar and nuclear energy; electricity derived from solar energy, from nuclear energy

Class distribution of electricity derived from solar energy, from nuclear energy in 333.793; class nuclear fuels in 333.8

.793   Secondary forms of energy

Energy produced through use of other resources

Including electric power, electric utilities; cogeneration of electric power and heat, district heating; energy from waste materials

Class economics of synthetic fuel production in 338.4

For secondary forms of energy derived from a specific resource, see the resource, e.g., electricity derived from nuclear energy 333.792

.8   **Subsurface resources**

Including fossil fuels, nuclear fuels; geothermal energy, electricity derived from geothermal energy, thermal waters; other minerals

Including supply in storage, shortages, surpluses; requirements (need, demand); consumption (utilization), abuse, wastage; impact studies; conservation, protection; control of usage

Class here strategic materials

Class mined lands in 333.76; class energy derived from nuclear fuels in 333.792; class electricity derived from fossil fuels, distribution of electricity derived from geothermal energy in 333.793; class development of, extraction of subsurface resources and comprehensive works on the economics of subsurface resources in 338.2; class supplies of subsurface resources in nature and interdisciplinary works on subsurface resources in 553; class interdisciplinary works on metals in 669

For ownership aspects of subsurface resources, see 333.1–333.5; for groundwater, see 333.91

See Manual at 333.7–333.9 vs. 333; also at 333.7–333.9 vs. 363.1, 363.73, 577; also at 333.7–333.9 vs. 363.6; also at 333.7–333.9 vs. 508, 913–919, 930–990; also at 553 vs. 333.8, 338.2

.9   **Other natural resources**

Including wind energy

Including reserves (stock, supply), shortages; requirements (need, demand); consumption (utilization), abuse, wastage; impact studies; development, e.g., reclamation, restoration, subsidies; conservation, protection; control of usage

Class distribution of electricity in 333.793. Class reserves (stock, supply), shortages; requirements (need, demand); consumption (utilization), abuse, wastage; impact studies; development, e.g., reclamation, restoration, subsidies; conservation, protection; control of usage in relation to a specific natural resource with the resource, e.g., wildlife conservation 333.95

See Manual at 333.7–333.9 vs. 333; also at 333.7–333.9 vs. 363.1, 363.73, 577; also at 333.7–333.9 vs. 363.6; also at 333.7–333.9 vs. 508, 913–919, 930–990

.91   Water

Including beaches, coasts; groundwater; hydroelectricity; lakes, rivers, oceans; submerged lands, wetlands

Class here aquatic resources, land adjoining water, comprehensive works on the economics of water resources

Class interdisciplinary works on water in 553.7

> *For a specific aquatic resource, see the resource, e.g., minerals 333.8, fishes 333.95; for a specific aspect of water resources not provided for here, see the aspect, e.g., recreational use of water and land adjoining it 333.78, distribution of hydroelectricity 333.793, water supply service 363.6*

> *See Manual at 363.6*

.910 01–.910 09   Standard subdivisions

.95   Biological resources

Including endangered species; game reserves, wildlife, wildlife refuges; fuelwood; interdisciplinary works on biomass as an energy resource

Class here biodiversity, biosphere

Class forests, comprehensive works on timber resources in 333.75

> *For biomass fuel engineering, see 662*

> *See Manual at 333.95 vs. 639.9; also at 338.3 vs. 333.95*

334   Cooperatives

Voluntary organizations or enterprises owned by and operated for the benefit of those using the services

Including banking cooperatives, credit unions; benefit societies; consumer, housing, producer cooperatives

Class comprehensive works on thrift institutions in 332.3; class management of consumer cooperatives in 658.8

335 Socialism and related systems

Standard subdivisions are added for socialism and related systems together, for socialism alone

Including anarchism, syndicalism; Christian, Fabian, utopian socialism; voluntary anarchist and socialist communities

Class here state socialism, interdisciplinary works on socialism and related systems

Class socialism in the sense of communism, comparisons of Communism (Marxism-Leninism) with other systems in 335.43; class socialism in the sense of democratic socialism in 335.5; class interdisciplinary studies of communes, of kibbutzim in 307.77

> For socialism and communism as political ideologies, see 320.5; for socialist and communist political parties, see 324.2. For a specific topic of economics treated from a socialist point of view, see the topic in economics, e.g., interest 332.8

> See Manual at 335 vs. 306.3, 320.53

.001–.009   Standard subdivisions

.4 Marxian systems

Including dialectical materialism, historical materialism; Marxian doctrines and systems characteristic of period before 1917

Class here Marxism

> For democratic Marxian systems, see 335.5

.401   Philosophy and theory

Do not use for philosophical foundations of Marxian systems and general works on theory of Marxian systems; class in 335.4

[.42]   Early period

Number discontinued; class in 335.4

.43   Communism (Marxism-Leninism)

Communism of post-1917 period

Including national variants as schools of thought, e.g., Cuban communism (Castroism) as a school of thought; Trotskyite doctrines; comparison of communism with capitalism, democratic socialism, other forms of collectivism

Class here former Soviet communism, communist theory and practice of democratic socialism

> For communism as a political ideology, see 320.53

.430 9 Historical, geographic, persons treatment

> Do not use for national variants of communism as schools of thought, e.g., Castroism, Maoism; class in 335.43

> Class here geographic treatment of communism as an economic system

.5 Democratic socialism

Marxian and non-Marxian socialism pursued through persuasion and consent of the electorate in a nonauthoritarian state

Class Fabian socialism, Christian socialism, voluntary socialist communities in 335

.6 Fascism

Including falangism, national socialism

> *For fascism as a political ideology, see 320.53*

336 Public finance

Including finance of associations of sovereign states (e.g., United Nations) and public finance by governmental level (multiple jurisdictions at the same level, e.g., municipal finance in the United States)

Class here intergovernmental fiscal relations, comprehensive works on public finance and financial administration of governments

Class a specific aspect of finance of associations of sovereign states and public finance by governmental level with the aspect in 336.1–336.3, e.g., public borrowing by governmental level 336.3

> *For financial administration and budgets, see 352.4*

> *See Manual at 332, 336 vs. 339; also at 336 vs. 352.4*

.001–.005 Standard subdivisions

.006 Organizations and management

> Do not use for finance of associations of sovereign states (e.g., United Nations); class in 336

.007–.008 Standard subdivisions

[.009] Historical, geographic, persons treatment

> Do not use for treatment by government level; class in 336. Do not use for areas, regions, places in general, persons, ancient world; class in 336.09

[.009 4–.009 9] Treatment by specific continents, countries, localities

> Do not use; class in 336.4–336.9

.02 Revenue

> *For specific forms of revenue, see 336.1–336.2*

[.020 91]	Treatment by areas, regions, places in general
	Do not use; class in 336.02
[.020 93–.020 99]	Treatment by specific continents, countries, localities
	Do not use; class in 336.02

.09   Historical, geographic, persons treatment

Class treatment by specific continents, countries, localities in modern world in 336.4–336.9

.091   Areas, regions, places in general

.091 7   Socioeconomic regions

Add to base number 336.0917 the numbers following —17 in notation 171–173 from Table 2, e.g., public finance in developing countries 336.09172

Class public finance in socioeconomic regions by governmental level in 336

.092   Persons

.093   The ancient world

Add to base number 336.093 the numbers following —3 in notation —31–39 from Table 2, e.g., public finance in the Roman Empire 336.0937

Class public finance in ancient world by government level in 336

>   **336.1–336.2 Revenues**

Class comprehensive works in 336.02

.1   **Nontax revenues**

Including revenue from franchises, lotteries, mineral rights, public industries and services; intergovernmental and intragovernmental revenues, e.g., grants-in-aid

For public borrowing, see 336.3

.2   **Taxes and taxation**

Standard subdivisions are added for either or both topics in heading

Including customs, estate, excise, gift, inheritance, personal property, sales, value-added taxes

Including principles of taxation; taxes by governmental level (multiple jurisdictions at the same level); tax reform; provisions that allow tax avoidance, e.g., tax credits, deductions, loopholes; business taxes

Class here interdisciplinary works on taxes and taxation

Class principles of taxation, taxes by governmental level, tax reform, provisions that allow tax avoidance, business taxes in relation to a specific kind of taxes with the kind, e.g., reform of social security taxes 336.249

For tax law, see 343.04; for tax administration, see 352.4

See Manual at 343.04 vs. 336.2, 352.4

.200 1–.200 8   Standard subdivisions

.200 9   Historical, geographic, persons treatment

Do not use for treatment by governmental level; class in 336.2

.22   Real property taxes

Class here rates (United Kingdom), comprehensive works on property taxes

Class personal property taxes in 336.2; class comprehensive works on taxes on personal wealth in 336.24

.24   Income taxes

Including reform of income taxes, provisions that allow avoidance of income taxes (e.g., tax credits), taxes on business income, personal (individual) income taxes

Class here comprehensive works on taxes on personal wealth

Class estate, inheritance, gift, personal property taxes in 336.2

For real property taxes, see 336.22

See also 362.5 for negative income tax

.249   Social security taxes

See also 368.4 for social security benefits

See Manual at 336.249 vs. 368.4

.3   Public borrowing, debt, expenditure

Including government securities, international borrowing, limitation of public indebtedness, public insolvency

Class here fiscal policy, comprehensive works on monetary and fiscal policy

Class investment in government securities in 332.63

> *For role of banks in international borrowing, see 332.1; for monetary policy, see 332.4; for use of fiscal and monetary policy in economic stabilization, see 339.5*

.4–.9   Public finance of specific continents, countries, localities in modern world

Add to base number 336 notation 4–9 from Table 2, e.g., public finance of Australia 336.94

337   International economics

Class here international economic planning; comprehensive works on international economic relations, on international economic cooperation

International development and growth relocated to 338.91

> *For a specific aspect of international economics not provided for here, see the aspect, e.g., international (multinational) business enterprises 338.8, international economic law 341.7, foreign trade 382*

[.093–.099]   Treatment by specific continents, countries, localities

Do not use; class in 337.3–337.9

.1   Multilateral economic cooperation

Including European Union

Class here economic integration, multilateral agreements and multistate organizations for economic cooperation

Class bilateral economic cooperation in 337.3–337.9; class interdisciplinary works on international governmental organizations in 341.2

> *For trade agreements, see 382*

> *See Manual at 337.3–337.9 vs. 337.1*

.109   Historical and persons treatment

Do not use for geographic treatment; class in 337.1

.3–.9 **Foreign economic policies and relations of specific jurisdictions and groups of jurisdictions**

Class here bilateral economic cooperation

Add to base number 337 notation 3–9 from Table 2, e.g., economic policy of United Kingdom 337.41; then, for foreign economic relations between two jurisdictions or groups of jurisdictions, add 0* and to the result add notation 1 or —3–9 from Table 2, e.g., economic relations between United Kingdom and France 337.41044

Give priority in notation to the jurisdiction or group of jurisdictions emphasized. If the emphasis is equal, give priority to the one coming first in the sequence of area numbers
(Option: Give priority in notation to the jurisdiction or group of jurisdictions requiring local emphasis, e.g., libraries in United States class foreign economic relations between United States and France in 337.73044)

Class multilateral economic cooperation in 337.1

See Manual at 337.3–337.9 vs. 337.1

338 **Production**

Including entrepreneurship; products and services; comprehensive works on factors of production, on industrial productivity, on production efficiency (e.g., effect of technological innovations)

Class here interdisciplinary works on industry, on production

Class products and services of specific kinds of industry in 338.1–338.4; class consumption of products and services in 339.4. Class a specific aspect of entrepreneurship with the aspect, e.g., portion of national income distributed to entrepreneurship 339.2

For specific factors of production, see 331–333; for labor productivity, see 331.11; for production economics of financial industries, see 332; for production economics of real estate business, see 333.33; for production of energy, see 333.79; for economics of cooperative production, see 334; for production economics of insurance industry, see 368; for commerce, communications, transportation, see 380. For effect of technological innovations on a specific aspect of the economy, see the aspect, e.g., effect on working conditions 331.25; for a noneconomic aspect of industry and production, see the aspect, e.g., law of industry 343, production technology 620–690

See Manual at 332 vs. 338, 658.15; also at 338 vs. 060, 381, 382, 670.29, 910, T1—025, T1—029; also at 363.5, 363.6, 363.8 vs. 338

*Add 00 for standard subdivisions; see instructions at beginning of Table 1

SUMMARY

.001   Philosophy and theory

> Do not use for forecasting and forecasts of products and services; class in 338. Do not use for general production forecasting and forecasts; class in 338.5

.002–.008   Standard subdivisions

.009   Historical, geographic, persons treatment of general principles and theories

> Do not use for historical, geographic, persons treatment of production; class in 338.09

.09   Historical, geographic, persons treatment of production

> Class here existing and potential resources for production, industrial conditions and situation, industrial surveys, location of industry

> Add to base number 338.09 notation 1–9 from Table 2, e.g., industrial surveys of Canada 338.0971

> Class a specific resource with the resource, e.g., water for power 333.91

> *See also 338.6 for the rationale for and process of locating business enterprises*

> *See Manual at 338.092*

> ### 338.1–338.4 Specific kinds of industry

Including entrepreneurship, finance, other factors of production, industrial productivity, production efficiency, products and services in specific kinds of industry

Class results of market surveys; supply and demand in relation to trade, to marketing opportunities in 380.1–382; class comprehensive works in 338; class interdisciplinary works on capital formation in 332

> *For financial industries, see 332; for credit for specific kinds of industries, see 332.7; for real estate business, see 333.33; for energy production, see 333.79; for cooperatives in specific kinds of industries, see 334; for organization of production in specific kinds of industries, see 338.6; for business enterprises other than cooperatives in specific kinds of industries, see 338.7–338.8; for commerce, communications, transportation, see 380. For biographies of entrepreneurs in a specific kind of industries, see the kind of industry in 338.6–338.8, e.g., biographies of owners of small businesses 338.6, biographies of entrepreneurs in textile manufacturing 338.7; for biographies of people known for their contributions in a specific type of technology, see the type of technology in 600, e.g., biographies of mining engineers 622.092*

> ### 338.1–338.3 Primary (Extractive) industries

Class comprehensive works in 338

.1 Agriculture

Including surpluses and shortages of farm products, forecasts and projections of supply and demand, government farm policies; comprehensive works on the economics of production, storage, distribution of food

Class agricultural cooperatives in 334; class specific producers in 338.7; class hunger as a social problem, interdisciplinary works on food supply in 363.8

> *For agricultural credit, see 332.7; for food processing, see 338.4; for distribution of food, see 380.1*

> *See Manual at 338.1 vs. 333.75; also at 338.1 vs. 631.5; also at 363.8 vs. 338.1*

.2 **Extraction of minerals**

Class here extraction of energy resources, comprehensive works on the economics of extraction and processing of minerals and energy resources

Class industrial credit in 332.7; class conservation of mineral and energy resources in 333.7–333.9; class mined lands, surface-mined lands in 333.76; class supply in storage, shortages, surpluses, demand and projections of mineral and energy resources in 333.8; class specific producers in 338.7; class reserves in nature in 553

For processing of minerals and raw materials of energy, see 338.4

See Manual at 553 vs. 333.8, 338.2

.3 **Other extractive industries**

Including fishing, whaling, hunting, culture of invertebrates and cold-blooded vertebrates

Class insect culture in 338.1; class specific producers in 338.7

See Manual at 338.3 vs. 333.95

.4 **Secondary industries and services**

Standard subdivisions are added for either or both topics in heading

Including construction, manufacturing, service industries; professional services; quantities of goods and services produced, shortages, surpluses, stockpiles, forecasts and projections of supply and demand

Class financial industries in 332; class industrial credit in 332.7; class real estate business in 333.33; class specific producers in 338.7; class insurance industry in 368; class commerce, communications, transportation in 380

.5 **General production economics**

Including business cycles, depressions, other economic fluctuations; business forecasting; costs, prices and their determination; law of supply and demand; risk; theories of value

Class here microeconomics (economics of the firm)

Class effect of money on prices in 332.4; class Marxian labor theory of value in 335.4; class production economics of specific kinds of industries in 338.1–338.4; class effects of prices on the economy as a whole in 339.4; class economic stabilization in 339.5

For organization of production, see 338.6

.501 **Philosophy and theory**

Do not use for forecasting and forecasts; class in 338.5

.6   **Organization of production**

Including competition (fair and unfair), restraint; finance; location; specialization, comparative advantage; systems of production, e.g., cottage industry, factory system; big business, small business, minority enterprises, private and public enterprise; worker control of industry

Class here organization of production in specific kinds of industries

Class finance of specific kinds of industries in 338.1–338.4; class relation of size of enterprise to cost of production in 338.5; class specific types of enterprises of specific sizes in 338.7–338.8; class monopoly and monopolies in 338.8

For role of unions in achieving worker control of industry, see 331.88; for guild socialism, syndicalism, see 335; for business enterprises and their structure, see 338.7

.7   **Business enterprises**

Not limited to private or capitalist enterprises

Including formation and dissolution of business enterprises; individual proprietorships, partnerships, corporations; business enterprises in specific industries and groups of industries, specific individual business enterprises, biographies of entrepreneurs in specific fields

Class here structure of business enterprises; interdisciplinary works on business enterprises, on organizations for production

Class government corporations as part of the public administrative process in 352.2

For financial institutions, see 332.1–332.6; for real estate business enterprises, see 333.33; for enterprises engaged in production of energy, see 333.79; for cooperatives, see 334; for combinations, see 338.8; for insurance companies, see 368.006; for enterprises engaged in commerce, communications, transportation, see 380. For biographies of people known for their contribution to technology, see the kind of contribution in 600, plus notation 092 from Table 1, e.g., biographies of mining engineers 622.092

See Manual at 338 vs. 060, 381, 382, 670.29, 910, T1—025, T1—029

.8 **Combinations**

Organization and structure for massive production and control of production

Including cartels, holding companies, mergers, trusts; conglomerate enterprises; monopolies; multinational enterprises

Class here antitrust policies, economic concentration, comprehensive works on combinations and their practices

To be classed here, works about specific individual enterprises must stress that they are combinations; otherwise, the works are classed in 338.7

Class price determination by combinations in 338.5

> *For combinations of financial institutions, see 332.1–332.6; for combinations of real estate business enterprises, see 333.33; for combinations of enterprises engaged in energy production, see 333.79; for combinations of cooperatives, see 334; for combinations of enterprises in the insurance industry, see 368.006; for combinations of enterprises engaged in commerce, communications, transportation, see 380*

> *See Manual at 338.092*

.9 **Economic development and growth**

Standard subdivisions are added for either or both topics in heading

Including appropriate technology, information and science policy, nationalization, subsidies

Class here economic planning, government programs and policies

Class appropriate technology, information and science policy, nationalization, subsidies in specific continents, countries, localities in 338.93–338.99

> *For economic development and growth with respect to specific kinds of industries, see 338.1–338.4. For economic development and growth with respect to a specific subject not provided for here, see the subject, e.g., international development banks 332.1*

> *See Manual at 338.9 vs. 352.7, 500*

.900 1–.900 8   Standard subdivisions

.900 9   Historical, geographic, persons treatment

[.900 93–.900 99]   Treatment by specific continents, countries, localities

Do not use; class in 338.93–338.99

.91   International development and growth [*formerly also* 337]

Standard subdivisions are added for either or both topics in heading

Foreign economic assistance (foreign aid)

Class here assistance (aid) by international organizations, technical assistance

Class foreign economic policies and relations of specific jurisdictions and groups of jurisdictions in 337.3–337.9

.910 91   Treatment by areas, regions, places in general

> Do not use for assistance given by specific jurisdictions and groups of jurisdictions to other jurisdictions; class in 338.91
>
> Class here assistance to specific jurisdictions and groups of jurisdictions

.910 93–.910 99   Treatment by specific continents, countries, localities

> Do not use for assistance given by specific jurisdictions and groups of jurisdictions to other jurisdictions; class in 338.91
>
> Class here assistance to specific jurisdictions and groups of jurisdictions

.93–.99   Economic development and growth in specific continents, countries, localities

> Add to base number 338.9 notation 3–9 from Table 2, e.g., economic planning in United Kingdom in 338.941; however, do not add notation from Table 1 for standard subdivisions
> Subdivisions are added for either or both topics in heading

339   Macroeconomics and related topics

> Standard subdivisions are added for macroeconomics and related topics together, for macroeconomics alone
>
> *For economic fluctuations, see 338.5*
>
> *See Manual at 332, 336 vs. 339*

.01   Philosophy and theory [*formerly* 339.3]

.2   **Distribution of income and wealth**

> Standard subdivisions are added for either or both topics in heading
>
> Including division of nation's income among factors of production, among families and individuals; consumer income, household income; flow-of-funds accounts, interindustry accounts
>
> Class national wealth and income accounts and accounting in 339.3; class specific aspects of income distribution in 339.4; class transfer payments, redistribution of income in 339.5

.3 **National product, wealth, income accounts and accounting**

Standard subdivisions are added for accounts, accounting, or both

Including gross national product (GNP), net national product, national income

Class here product, wealth, income accounts and accounting of other types of areas, e.g., states, provinces; interdisciplinary works on national product, wealth, income

Philosophy and theory of macroeconomics relocated to 339.01

Class macroeconomic policy in 339.5

> *For distribution of income and wealth, see 339.2; for factors affecting national product, wealth, income, see 339.4*

.309 3–.099 Treatment by specific continents

> Do not use for treatment by specific countries and localities; class in 339.33–339.39

.33–.39 Product, wealth, income accounts and accounting of specific countries and localities

> Add to base number 339.3 notation 3–9 from Table 2, e.g., gross national product of the United States 339.373

.4 **Factors affecting national product, wealth, income**

Standard subdivisions are added for for any or all topics in heading

Including conservation of national resources; economic causes and economic effects of poverty; consumption, cost of living, income, investment, savings, standard of living, and their interrelationships, e.g., relation of income and consumption; consumption of specific products and services, of specific groups of products and services; interdisciplinary works on consumption

Class price statistics and indexes in 338.5; class government spending in 339.5

> *For social aspects of consumption, see 306.3; for conservation of natural resources, consumption viewed in light of its effect on the future supply of natural resources and energy, see 333.7; for consumption as a factor in shortages and surpluses of products, see 338; for economic stabilization, see 339.5; for works discussing consumption as sales or marketing opportunities (e.g., results of market studies) or as a measure of the volume, value, or kind of trade, see 380.1–382*
>
> *See also 362.5 for social causes and social effects of poverty, 658.8 for consumer research in marketing management*
>
> *See Manual at 339.4 vs. 332.4*

.5   **Macroeconomic policy**

Including use of fiscal policy, e.g., income redistribution, government
spending, budget surpluses and deficits, taxation; use of monetary policy

Class here economic stabilization and growth, equilibrium, full employment
policies, income policies

Class comprehensive works on relation of central banks to monetary policy in
332.1; class comprehensive works on monetary policy in 332.4

> *For measures to combat inflation, see 332.4; for measures to control*
> *economic fluctuations, see 338.5; for measures to promote growth and*
> *development, see 338.9*

340   Law

Including comparative law, justice, law and society, law reform, legal reasoning,
natural law

Class here jurisprudence

See Manual at 340; also at 363 vs. 340, 353–354

SUMMARY

340.02–.09   **Standard subdivisions**
　　.5–.9   **[Legal systems, conflict of laws]**
341   **International law**
342   **Constitutional and administrative law**
343   **Military, defense, public property, public finance, tax, trade (commerce),**
                industrial law
344   **Labor, social service, education, cultural law**
345   **Criminal law**
346   **Private law**
347   **Civil procedure and courts**
348   **Laws (Statutes), regulations, cases**
349   **Law of specific jurisdictions, areas, socioeconomic regions**

[.01]   Philosophy and theory

Do not use; class in 340

>   340.02–340.09   Standard subdivisions

Class comprehensive works in 340

See Manual at 340.02–340.09 vs. 349

.02–.08   Standard subdivisions

.09   Historical, geographic, persons treatment

Do not use for historical and geographic treatment of the law of traditional
societies; class in 340.5. Do not use for comprehensive works on the law of
specific jurisdictions and areas in the modern world; class in 349

[.093]	Treatment in the ancient world

Do not use; class in 340.5

.5 Legal systems

Including law of traditional societies regardless of time or place; ancient, Roman, medieval, common law; civil law systems (systems derived from Roman law); indigenous systems of Oriental law

Class comprehensive works on the law of specific jurisdictions and areas in the modern world in 349. Class a specific subject in a specific system of law with the subject in 340.9–347, e.g., ancient criminal law of Rome 345.37; class religious and ceremonial laws of a specific religious body with the body, e.g., Christian canon law 262.9

See Manual at 340.5 vs. 297.1; also at 340.5 vs. 342–347

.9 Conflict of laws

Body of rules governing choice of jurisdiction in cases in private law that fall under laws of two or more jurisdictions

Class here private international law

For domestic conflict of laws, see 342

341 International law

Including texts of more than one treaty

Class the law of a nation or lesser jurisdiction that carries out the provisions of an international agreement in 342–347; class comprehensive works on public law in 342. Class treaties and their texts on a specific subject with the subject in 341, e.g., a disarmament treaty between Russia and the United States 341.7

See also 340.9 for private international law

See Manual at 341 vs. 327

(Option: Class international law of a specific discipline or subject with the discipline or subject, plus notation 026 from Table 1, e.g., international transportation law 388.026, *not* 341.7)

.2 The world community

Including world government; non-self-governing territories, e.g., colonies; areas having special status in international law, e.g., Antarctica

Class here international persons and personality

> 341.22–341.24 International governmental organizations

Class here legal responsibilities of officials, privileges and immunities, interdisciplinary works on international governmental organizations

Personnel administration in international governmental organizations relocated to 352.6

Class comprehensive works on international governmental organizations in 341.2; class interdisciplinary works on international organizations in 060

For administration of international governmental organizations, see 352.11. For a specialized international governmental organization, see the subject with which it deals, plus notation 06 from Table 1, e.g., Interpol 363.206; for legal aspects of a specialized international governmental organization, see the subject with which it deals in 341.2–341.7, e.g., Interpol 341.7

See Manual at 341.22–341.24

.22   League of Nations

[.220 68]   Management

Relocated to 352.11

.23   United Nations

Management relocated to 352.11

[.230 68]   Management

Do not use; class in 352.11

.24   Regional associations and organizations

Including League of Arab States, Organization of American States

.242   European Union

Class here European Common Market, European Community, European Economic Community

Class laws promulgated by European Union with the subject in 341.2–341.7, e.g., economic enactments 341.7

[.242 01–.242 09]   Standard subdivisions

Do not use; class in 341.242

.26 States

Including recognition of states and governments; mergers, sovereignty of states

Class here liability of states

Class liability of states with respect to a specific subject with the subject in 341.2–341.7, e.g., liability for the safety of diplomatic personnel 341.3

For semisovereign states, see 341.27; for relations between states, see 341.3; for jurisdiction of states, see 341.4

.27 Semisovereign states

Including protectorates

.3 Relations between states

Including delegations to international organizations and their staffs, treaties

Class texts of more than one treaty in 341; class officials and employees of international organizations in 341.22–341.24; class interdisciplinary works on diplomacy in 327.2. Class treaties and their texts on a specific subject with the subject in 341, e.g., a disarmament treaty between Russia and the United States 341.7

For jurisdictional relations, see 341.4; for disputes and conflicts, see 341.5; for international cooperation, see 341.7

See Manual at 341.3

.4 Jurisdiction and jurisdictional relations of states

Standard subdivisions are added for either or both topics in heading

Including jurisdiction over airspace, extraterrestrial space, territory; jurisdiction over persons, e.g., aliens and their property, citizenship, civil rights, double taxation, extradition, immigration, refugees, right of asylum; comprehensive works on international law of ocean and sea waters

Class here extraterritoriality, right of innocent passage

Class private international law in 340.9; class mergers of states in 341.26; class international crimes in 341.7

For liability of states for aliens, see 341.26; for enemy aliens and their property, see 341.6; for development and conservation of sea resources, oceanographic research, see 341.7

.5 Disputes and conflicts between states

Including courts and court procedure, role of international organizations, role of domestic courts in adjudicating matters of public international law; sanctions, e.g., boycotts, embargoes

Class peace conferences in 341.7. Class disputes, interpretation on a specific subject with the subject in 341.2–341.7, e.g., interpretation of human rights, jurisdictional disputes 341.4

For law of war, see 341.6

.6   Law of war

Including enemy aliens and their property, noncombatants, prisoners of war; military occupation, neutrality, war crimes

For war claims by private individuals of one country against another country, see 340.9

.7   International cooperation

Including defense and mutual security, disarmament, military assistance, peace; conservation and development of natural resources, pollution; copyright, patents, trademarks; international communications, criminal, transportation law; international economic law, e.g., finance, foreign aid, labor, trade (commerce) law; public health, welfare services

Class right to use airspace and bodies of water in 341.4; class peaceful settlement of disputes in 341.5; class interdisciplinary works on international mutual security pacts in 355

For double taxation, extradition, see 341.4; for war crimes, see 341.6

> ## 342–349   Branches of law; laws (statutes), regulations, cases; law of specific jurisdictions, areas, socioeconomic regions

Class comprehensive works in 340; class comprehensive works on law of specific ancient jurisdictions, areas, socioeconomic regions in 340.5; class comprehensive works on law of specific jurisdictions, areas, socioeconomic regions in 349

See Manual at 342–349

> ## 342–347 Branches of law

Class here comprehensive works on specific subjects in law

Any subject in a branch of law limited to a specific jurisdiction is classed with the jurisdiction. The subject may be given or implied in the heading, in an including note, or in an entry in a zero subdivision of the three-digit number for the branch of law. For example, private and business law of Australia 346.94, property law of Australia 346.9404

Class general laws, regulations, cases in 348; class comprehensive works in 340

> *For a specific subject in international law, see the subject in 341, e.g., international criminal law 341.7*

> *See Manual at 340.5 vs. 342–347*

(Option A: Class courts and procedure in specific fields in 347

(Option B: Class laws, regulations, cases on specific subjects in 348

(Option C: Class the law of a specific discipline or subject with the discipline or subject, plus notation 026 from Table 1, e.g., law of education 370.26, *not* 344)

342 Constitutional and administrative law

Including impeachment [*formerly* 351.9]; administrative agencies and regulatory agencies; administrative procedure, e.g., ombudsmen; civil service, elections, martial law; government liability; jurisdiction over persons, e.g., citizenship, civil rights, freedom of speech, immigration, maintenance of privacy, right of asylum; comprehensive works on abortion, individual rights

Class here comprehensive works on public law

Class government corporations in 346; class interdisciplinary works on civil and individual rights in 323. Class constitutional provisions and amendments, departments, ministries, regulatory agencies, administrative courts dealing with a specific subject in law with the subject in 342–347, e.g., agencies regulating civil aeronautics 343.09

> *For international law, see 341; for social service law aspects of abortion, see 344; for criminal abortion, see 345. For a right associated with a branch of law other than constitutional and administrative law, see the right, e.g., right to education 344, trial by jury 347; for constitutional and administrative aspects of another branch of law, see the branch, e.g., constitutional aspects of criminal law 345*

[.001–.009]   Standard subdivisions

>   Do not use; class in 342

.3–.9 **Specific jurisdictions and areas**

> Add to base number 342 notation 3–9 from Table 2, e.g., constitutional law of the United States 342.73; however, do not add notation 01–09 from Table 1; class in number for the jurisdiction or area

343 Military, defense, public property, public finance, tax, trade (commerce), industrial law

> Including armed forces, military courts and legal procedure; military manpower procurement, e.g., selective service; emergency legislation, national security; veterans' law

> Including fiscal policy, monetary law, revenue law; regulation of economic activity, e.g., antitrust law, economic assistance; regulation of specific industries and services, e.g., agriculture; regulation of trade, e.g., regulation of advertising, marketing, prices

> Class international war crime trials in 341.6; class international law of monetary exchange in 341.7; class military assistance to foreign nations, civilian employees of military services in 342; class public health and safety law in 344; class law of sale, trade regulation of businesses engaged in banking, insurance, securities in 346; class trade regulation of real estate business, comprehensive works on control and use of public and private real property, on control of natural resources in 346.04. Class a specific aspect of military or defense law not provided for here with the aspect in 342–347, e.g., civil rights of soldiers 342, military prisons 344; class an industrial regulation aspect of another branch of law with the branch, e.g., wages 344

> *For war claims, see 341.6; for acquisition and cession of territory, martial law, see 342; for government securities, see 346*

> *See also 346.07 for commercial law*

[.001–.009] Standard subdivisions

> Do not use; class in 343

.04 Tax law

> Class here internal revenue law, tax planning

> Class fiscal policy in 343; class tax planning applied to a specific kind of tax in 343.05–343.06; class tax evasion in 345; class interdisciplinary works on taxes in 336.2

> *For specific kinds of taxes, see 343.05–343.06*

> *See Manual at 343.04 vs. 336.2, 352.4*

> 343.05–343.06 Specific kinds of taxes

Class comprehensive works in 343.04

.05   Kinds of taxes by base

> Including social security taxes [*formerly* 344]; customs, income, inheritance, property, sales taxes; duties
>
> Class internal revenue law in 343.04

.06   Kinds of taxes by incidence

> Including taxes on individuals, on business enterprises
>
> Class taxes on specific bases regardless of incidence in 343.05

.07   Consumer protection

> Class a specific aspect of consumer protection with the aspect in 342–347, e.g., protection against negligence 346.02

[.070 1–.070 9]   Standard subdivisions

> Do not use; class in 343.07

.09   Control of public utilities

> Including communications, electric power, nuclear energy, transportation, water supply; transportation safety; admiralty, maritime, press law; comprehensive works on computer law
>
> Class international maritime law in 341.7; class freedom of the press in 342; class censorship in 344; class criminal tort, traffic offenses in 345; class libel as a tort, private law of transportation accidents in 346.03. Class admiralty and maritime law aspects of another branch of law with the branch, e.g., maritime contracts 346.02
>
> > For a specific aspect of computer law, see the aspect in 342–347, e.g., invasion of privacy 342

.3–.9   Specific jurisdictions and areas

> Add to base number 343 notation 3–9 from Table 2, e.g., military, tax, industrial law of Canada 343.71, of South American countries 343.8; then add further as follows:
>
> [001–009]   Standard subdivisions
> > Do not use; class in number for the jurisdiction or area
>
> 04–09   Tax law, consumer protection, control of public utilities
> > Add to base number 0 the numbers following 343.0 in 343.04–343.09, e.g., transportation law 09, transportation law of Canada 343.7109
> > > If the jurisdiction or area does not have its own number in Table 2, do not add 04–09, e.g., transportation ordinances of Toronto 343.713 (*not* 343.71309)

344 Labor, social service, education, cultural law

Including environmental protection, e.g., pollution and waste control; police services, prisons; public health, e.g., disease control, euthanasia, medical malpractice, services to substance abusers; public housing; safety, e.g., disasters, product safety; social insurance, e.g., government-sponsored health insurance; social security; veterinary public health

Including abortion, censorship, gambling, gun control, liquor and smoking laws, sports law

Social security taxes relocated to 343.05

Class military medicine in 343; class criminal investigation and law enforcement in 345; class conservation of natural resources in 346.04; class comprehensive works on insurance in 346

> *For veterans' welfare, see 343; for transportation safety, see 343.09; for adoption, see 346.01*

[.001–.009]   Standard subdivisions

Do not use; class in 344

.01   Labor

Class medical personnel, certification and licensing of teachers in 344

> *For government officials and employees, see 342; for military personnel, see 343*

.3–.9   Specific jurisdictions and areas

Add to base number 344 notation 3–9 from Table 2, e.g., social law of the United States 344.73, of Pennsylvania 344.748; then add further as follows
[001–009]   Standard subdivisions
Do not use; class in number for the jurisdiction or area
01   Labor law
If the jurisdiction or area does not have its own number in Table 2, do not add 01, e.g., labor law of Pittsburgh 344.748 (*not* 344.74801)

345 Criminal law

Including crimes, evidence, extradition, law enforcement, punishment; criminal courts and trials, juvenile procedure and courts

Class military courts in 343; class comprehensive works on civil and criminal courts and procedures in 347; class interdisciplinary works on criminal justice in 364

> *See Manual at 345 vs. 346.03*

[.001–.009]   Standard subdivisions

Do not use; class in 345

.3–.9   Specific jurisdictions and areas

Add to base number 345 notation 3–9 from Table 2, e.g., criminal law of the United States 345.73, of Pennsylvania 345.748; however, do not add notation 01–09 from Table 1; class in number for the jurisdiction or area

346   Private law

Including banking, insurance, negotiable instruments, securities; organizations (associations), e.g., corporations, foundations

Class organization of labor unions in 344.01. Class regulation of a specific general administrative function of organizations engaged in banking, insurance, securities with the function in 342–347, e.g., wages 344.01; class operation of organizations engaged in a specific type of enterprise with the type of enterprise, e.g., operation of railroad companies 343.09

For social insurance, see 344

See also 340.9 for private international law

[.001–.009]   Standard subdivisions

Do not use; class in 346

.01   Persons and domestic relations

Including marital property [*formerly* 346.04], adoption, child support, divorce, marriage; ethnic and religious groups

Class civil and individual rights in 342

.02   Contracts and agency

Standard subdivisions are added for contracts and agency together, for contracts alone

Class here comprehensive works on liability

Class loan, sale in 346.07. Class contracts dealing with a specific legal aspect with the aspect in 342–347, e.g., law of marriage contracts 346.01; class contracts concerning a specific nonlegal subject with the subject, plus notation 068 from Table 1, e.g., construction contracts 624.068

For government liability, see 342; for liability of schools, of school officials, of school districts, see 344; for criminal liability, see 345; for extracontractual liability, see 346.03

.03   Torts (Delicts)

Including invasion of privacy, libel, malpractice, negligence, product liability

Malpractice pertaining to a specific profession relocated to the profession in 342–347, e.g., medical malpractice 344

Class torts as crimes in 345; class remedies in 347

For personal liability of government officials, see 342

See Manual at 345 vs. 346.03

.04 Property

Including conveyancing, land, mortgages, real estate business; tenancy, e.g., eviction, rent; city planning, e.g., zoning; control of natural resources, e.g., fishing and hunting laws, mineral rights; copyright, patents

Marital property relocated to 346.01

Class inheritance and succession in 346.05

For public property, see 343

.05 Inheritance, succession, fiduciary trusts, trustees

Including estate planning, probate practice, wills

For estate planning to avoid taxes, see 343.05

.07 Commercial law

Including bankruptcy, credit, debtor, liens, loans, sales

Class here laws of a specific jurisdiction governing business investment by foreign nationals, e.g., laws of China governing the conduct of business in China by foreign nationals 346.5107; comprehensive works on business law

For a specific subject of commercial law, of business law not provided for here, see the subject in 342–347, e.g., tax law 343.04

.3–.9 Specific jurisdictions and areas

Add to base number 346 notation 3–9 from Table 2, e.g., private law of the United States 346.73, of South American countries 346.8; then add further as follows:

[001–009] Standard subdivisions
　　　　Do not use; class in number for the jurisdiction or area

01–07 Persons and domestic relations, contracts and agency, torts (delicts), property, inheritance, succession, fiduciary trusts, trustees, commercial law
　　　　Add to 0 the numbers following 346.0 in 346.01–346.05, e.g., marriage law 01, marriage law of New York state 346.74701
　　　　　　If the jurisdiction or area does not have its own number in Table 2, do not add 01–07, e.g, marriage law of New York City 346.747 (*not* 346.74701)

347 Civil procedure and courts

Including arbitration, evidence, legal aid, remedies, trials

Class here comprehensive works on civil and criminal procedure and courts, judicial branch of government, administration of justice, legal services

Class legal aid in criminal cases in 345; class medical jurisprudence, forensic medicine in 614; class interdisciplinary works on legal aid in 362.5. Class courts, procedures, trials dealing with a specific subject with the subject in 342–347, e.g., tax courts 343.04

> For administrative procedure, see 342; for criminal and juvenile procedure and courts, see 345

(Option: Class here courts and procedure in a specific field; prefer the specific field in 342–347)

[.001–.009]   Standard subdivisions

> Do not use; class in 347

.3–.9   Specific jurisdictions and areas

Add to base number 347 notation 3–9 from Table 2, e.g., civil procedure in the United States, United States Supreme Court 347.73, civil procedure in Pennsylvania 347.748; however, do not add notation 01–09 from Table 1; class in number for the jurisdiction or area

348 Laws (Statutes), regulations, cases

Including codes, digests

Class codes, digests of a specific jurisdiction or area in 348.3–348.9; class treatises on the whole law of a specific jurisdiction in 349. Class original materials and their guides limited to a specific branch or subject with the branch or subject in 342–347, e.g., a digest of tax laws 343.04

(Option: Class here laws, regulations, cases on specific subjects; prefer specific subject in 342–347)

[.001–.009]   Standard subdivisions

> Do not use; class in 348

.3–.9   Specific jurisdictions and areas

Add to base number 348 notation 3–9 from Table 2, e.g., U.S. Federal Code 348.73, statutes of Pennsylvania 348.748; however, do not add notation 01–09 from Table 1; class in number for the jurisdiction or area

349 Law of specific jurisdictions, areas, socioeconomic regions

Add to base number 349 notation 4–9 from Table 2, e.g., works on the law of the United States 349.73, of Pennsylvania 349.748

For law of specific ancient jurisdictions, areas, socioeconomic regions, see 340.5; for specific branches of the law of a specific jurisdiction, area, socioeconomic region, see 342–347; for original materials and their guides on the law of a specific jurisdiction, area, socioeconomic region, see 348

See Manual at 340.02–340.09 vs. 349

350 Public administration and military science

Except for military science (355–359), this schedule is new and has been prepared with little or no reference to previous editions. Most numbers have been reused with new meanings

A comparative table giving both old and new numbers for a substantial list of topics and equivalence tables showing the numbers in the old and new schedules are available in a separate booklet

In addition, procedures for legislative enactment of budgets relocated from 351.72 to 328.3; management of police services relocated from 351.74 to 363.2068; impeachment relocated from 351.9 to 342

SUMMARY

351	Public administration
352	General considerations of public administration
353	Specific fields of public administration
354	Public administration of economy and environment
355	Military science
356	Foot forces and warfare
357	Mounted forces and warfare
358	Air and other specialized forces and services; engineering and related services
359	Sea (Naval) forces and warfare

351 Public administration

Class here executive branch of government, programs administered by executive branch, civil service in the sense of all units of public administration outside armed services

Class relation of executive branch to other branches, works that deal comprehensively with more than one branch of government in 320.4; class civil service in the sense of merit system in 352.6; class interdisciplinary works on management in 658. Class management of government-owned enterprises operating a service with the service, plus notation 068 from Table 1, e.g., management of nationalized railroads 385.068

For administration of legislative branch, see 328.068; for administration of judicial branch, see 347; for specific topics of public administration, see 352–354

See Manual at 351; also at T1—068 vs. 353–354; also at 320.9, 320.4 vs. 351

.025		Directories of persons and organizations

Class directories of elected public officials in 324.025

.05		Serial publications

Class here official gazettes, serial administrative reports of government organizations

.06		Nongovernmental organizations

Do not use for governmental organizations; class in 351. Do not use for serial administrative reports of governmental organizations; class in 351.05

[.068]		Management

Do not use; class in 351

.07		Education, research, related topics

.076		Review and exercise

Class here interdisciplinary works on civil service examinations

For civil service examinations in specific subjects, see the subject in 001–999, plus notation 076 from Table 1, e.g., examinations in accounting 657.076

(Option: Class here civil service examinations in specific subjects; prefer the subject in 001–999, plus notation 076 from Table 1. If option is chosen, add to base number 351.076 notation 001–999, e.g., civil service examinations in accounting 351.076657)

.08		History and description with respect to kinds of persons

Do not use for programs directed to kinds of persons; class in 353.53

See Manual at 353.53 vs. 351.08

.09		Historical and persons treatment

Do not use for treatment by areas, regions, places in general; class in 351.1. Do not use for treatment by specific continents, countries, localities; class in 351.3–351.9

.1		**Administration in areas, regions, places in general**

Not limited by continent, country, locality

Add to base number 351.1 the numbers following 1 in notation 11–19 from Table 2, e.g., administration in developing regions 351.172; however, for urban administration, see 352.16; for rural administration, see 352.17

.3–.9   Administration in specific continents, countries, localities

Class here administration in specific jurisdictions, practical works on administration of specific subordinate jurisdictions, e.g., provinces

Add to base number 351 notation 3–9 from Table 2, e.g., public administration in Germany 351.43

Class theoretical works on specific kinds of subordinate jurisdictions in 352.13–352.19

See Manual at 351.3–351.9 vs. 352.13–352.19

> **352–354   Specific topics of public administration**

Class here administration of specific departments and agencies

Except for modifications shown under specific entries, add to each subdivision identified by * as follows:

01–07	Standard subdivisions
	Notation from Table 1 as modified under 351.01–351.07, e.g., serial administrative reports 05
08	History and description with respect to kinds of persons
	Class here programs directed to kinds of persons, equal opportunity programs
	See Manual at 353.53 vs. 351.08
09	Historical, geographic, persons treatment

Unless other instructions are given, class a subject with aspects in two or more subdivisions of 352–354 in the number coming last, e.g., organization of a department of agriculture 354.5 (*not* 352.2)

Class misconduct in office regardless of topic in 353.4; class comprehensive works in 351

See Manual at 352–354; also at 300, 320 vs. 352–354

352   General considerations of public administration

Class here general considerations of public administration applying to two or more branches of government, e.g., financial administration of the legislative and judicial branches 352.4

Class general considerations of public administration applied to a specific field with the field in public administration, e.g., local administration of public safety 353.9

See Manual at 352–354

SUMMARY

[.01–.09]   Standard subdivisions

> Do not use; class in 351.01–351.09

.1   Jurisdictional levels of administration

> Class programs directed to specific kinds of persons at specific levels of administration in 353.53. Class a specific topic in administrative management, support, control at a specific jurisdictional level with the topic in 352.2–352.8, e.g., financial administration and budgets of international agencies 352.4, regulation by local government 352.8
>
> Use 351 for combined treatment of national and other levels of administration except for works that emphasize differences between administration at different levels
>
> *For administration at national level, see 351*

.105   Serial publications

> Class here official gazettes, serial administrative reports of governmental organizations

.106   Nongovernmental organizations

> Do not use for governmental organizations; class in 351. Do not use for serial administrative reports of governmental organizations; class in 352.105

[.106 8]   Management

> Do not use; class in 352.1

.108   History and description with respect to kinds of persons

> Do not use for programs directed to kinds of persons; class in 353.53

.11   International administration

> Including management of League of Nations [*formerly also* 341.22068], management of United Nations [*formerly also* 341.23]
>
> Class here administration of international governmental organizations
>
> Class interdisciplinary works on international governmental organizations in 341.2

.110 5   Serial publications

> Class here official gazettes, serial administrative reports of government organizations

.110 6   Nongovernmental organizations

> Do not use for governmental organizations; class in 351.11. Do not use for serial administrative reports of governmental organizations; class in 352.1105

[.110 68]   Management

> Do not use; class in 352.11

.110 8   History and description with respect to kinds of persons

> Do not use for programs directed to kinds of persons; class in 353.53

.110 9   Historical, geographic, persons treatment

[.110 94–.110 99]   Treatment by specific continents, countries, localities in modern world

> Do not use; class in 352.11

>   352.13–352.19   Administration of subordinate jurisdictions

> Except for modifications shown under specific entries, add to each subdivision identified by † as follows:
> 01–07   Standard subdivisions
>   Notation from Table 1 as modified under 351.01–351.07, e.g., serial administrative reports 05
> 08   History and description with respect to kinds of persons
>   Do not use for programs directed to kinds of persons; class in 353.53
> 09   Historical, geographic, persons treatment

> Class administration in or of a specific subordinate jurisdiction in 351.3–351.9; class comprehensive works on administration of subordinate jurisdictions in 352.14

> *See Manual at 351.13–351.9 vs. 352.13–352.19*

.13   †State and provincial administration

> States and provinces: regularly constituted territorial subdivisions of large countries, with responsibilities cutting across several fields of administration, and usually encompassing many local units

> Standard subdivisions are added for either or both topics in heading

> *See Manual at 352.13 vs. 352.15*

---

†Add standard subdivisions as instructed under 352.13–352.19

.14 †Local administration

Limited to comprehensive and comparative treatment, e.g., local administration in Germany 352.140943

Class here comprehensive works on administration of subordinate jurisdictions

Class local government, combined treatment of local government and local administration in 320.8. Class administration in or of a specific subordinate jurisdiction with the jurisdiction in 351.3–351.9, e.g., administration of Nuremberg 351.43

> *For state and provincial administration, see 352.13; for administration of specific kinds of local jurisdictions, see 352.15–352.19; for support and control of subordinate jurisdictions by higher jurisdictions, see 353.3*

> *See Manual at 351.3–351.9 vs. 352.13–352.19*

> 352.15–352.19 Administration of specific kinds of local jurisdictions

Class comprehensive works in 352.14

.15 †Intermediate units of local administration

Intermediate units: regularly constituted relatively local territorial subdivisions, with responsibilities cutting across several fields of administration, and usually containing few component units

Class here arrondissements, counties, territorial departments; provinces of small countries

See Manual at 352.13 vs. 352.15

.16 †Urban administration

Class here city administration

See also 354.2 for administration of urban development

.17 †Rural administration

See also 354.2 for administration of rural development

.19 †Administration of special service districts

Local districts or authorities established to provide one or a few services

Class regional divisions of state and national agencies in 352.2. Class administration of a specific special service district with the service it administers, e.g., a metropolitan district to coordinate administration of health services 353.6, a local rail transit authority that operates trains 388.4

---

†Add standard subdivisions as instructed under 352.13–352.19

>   **352.2–352.6   Specific topics of management in public administration**

Class here specific topics of management in public administration at specific jurisdictional levels

Class comprehensive works on administrative aspects in 351; class interdisciplinary works on management, on specific topics in management in 658

.2   *Organization of administration

Including kinds of administrative agencies, departments, boards, commissions, and their organization and structure; government corporations; regional field offices

Class government corporations engaged in finance in 332.1–332.6; class government corporations engaged in real estate in 333.33; class government corporations engaged in insurance in 368; class government corporations engaged in commerce, communications, transportation in 380; class government corporations engaged in economic enterprises other than commerce, communication, finance, insurance, real estate in 338.7; class comprehensive works on executive management in public administration in 352.3; class interdisciplinary works on organization in management in 658.1

For a government agency, department, board, commission engaged in a specific activity, see the activity in 352–354, e.g., advisory bodies 352.7, regulatory agencies 352.8, advisory and regulatory agencies concerned with transportation 354.76

.23   *Chief executives

Including deputy chief executives; executive messages, speeches, writings, e.g., inaugural addresses

Class here presidents, prime ministers, monarchs

Class governing boards and commissions, heads of departments and agencies in 352.2

For messages, speeches, writings on a specific subject, see the subject, e.g., budget messages 352.4, executive messages on economic conditions 330.9

.24   *Cabinets and cabinet-level committees

Standard subdivisions are added for either or both topics in heading

Class here councils of ministers, executive councils

For a cabinet-level committee charged with a specific activity, see the activity in 352–354, e.g., cabinet councils on the economy 354

---

*Add standard subdivisions as instructed under 352–354

.3 ***Executive management**

Including accountability, decision making, information management, leadership, managing executive personnel, oversight, planning, policy making

Class here interdisciplinary works on public administrators

Class interdisciplinary works on executive management in 658.4

> *For internal organization, see 352.2; for leadership role of chief executives, see 352.23; for specific aspects of managing executive personnel, see 352.6; for oversight by outside agencies, see 352.8. For a specific aspect of public administrators, see the aspect, e.g., biography 351.092, law 342*

.4 ***Financial administration and budgets**

Standard subdivisions are added for financial administration and budgets together, for financial administration alone

Including management audits, payroll administration, revenue administration

Class here treasury departments and ministries; works covering both government financial administration and administration of financial institutions, money, credit

Class interdisciplinary works on public finance in 336; class interdisciplinary works on financial management in 658.15

> *For procedures for legislative enactment of budgets, see 328.3; for financial assistance, see 352.73; for administration of financial institutions, money, credit, see 354.8*
>
> *See also 332.4 for monetary policy, 336.3 for fiscal policy, 352.6 for wages and salary scales of government workers*
>
> *See Manual at 336 vs. 352.4; also at 343.04 vs. 336.2, 352.4*

.5 ***Property administration and related topics**

Standard subdivisions are added for property administration and related topics together, for property administration alone

Including procurement, public lands, comprehensive works on public contracts

Class here general services agencies

Class records management in 352.3; class comprehensive works on land resources in 354.3

> *For public contracts not related to property, see the subject, e.g., personnel contracts 352.6*

---

*Add standard subdivisions as instructed under 352–354

.6 ***Personnel administration (Human resource administration)**

Including personnel administration in international governmental organizations [*formerly also* 341.22–341.24], civil service (merit) system, government service, government workers, specific aspects of management of executive personnel

Class civil service in the sense of all units of public administration outside armed services in 351; class civil service examinations in 351.076; class contracting out in 352.5; class interdisciplinary works on personnel management in 658.3

> *For general management of executive personnel, see 352.3. For a specific aspect of government service and government workers, see the aspect, e.g., labor economics 331.7*

.602 5 Directories of persons and organizations

Class directories of public officials and employees in 351.025

.608 History and description with respect to kinds of persons

Class here equal employment opportunity programs for government employees

Class comprehensive works on equal employment opportunity programs in 354.908

> **352.7–352.8 Administration of supporting and controlling functions of government**

Class comprehensive works in 351. Class administration of support and control of a specific topic of management with the topic in 352–354, e.g., support of commerce 354.73

*Add standard subdivisions as instructed under 352–354

.7 ***Administration of general forms of assistances**

Including public relations [*formerly* 659.2]; assistance to cities and rural areas; census and surveys; consumer protection; fact-finding and advisory bodies and commissions; promoting libraries, museums, exhibitions; protecting intellectual property; comprehensive works on public works

Class here the promotional and supporting role of administration when considered apart from its restraining and limiting role; administration of research and development in noneconomic fields

Class comprehensive works on administration of culture and related activities in 353.7; class comprehensive works on administration of research and development in 354.2; class interdisciplinary works on public relations in 659.2

For administration of agencies supporting public libraries, see 353.7. For a specific aspect of consumer protection, see the the aspect, e.g., price and cost controls 352.8; for a specific program of public works, see the program, e.g., transportation public works 354.76

See also 352.2 for governing boards and commissions, 352.8 for the restraining and limiting role of administration

See Manual at 338.9 vs. 352.7, 500

.73 ***Financial assistance**

Financial assistance to subordinate jurisdictions or to private parties

Including loans

Class here grants, grants-in-aid, revenue sharing

Class comprehensive works on support and control of subordinate jurisdictions in 353.3

For price supports, see 352.8

.8 ***Administration of general forms of control**

Including grievances against government, inspection, licensing and registration, price and cost controls, rationing, standardization, watchdog agencies, interdisciplinary works on ombudsmen

Class here the restraining and limiting role of administration when considered apart from its promotional and supporting role; regulation, regulatory agencies, quasi-judicial agencies

Class internal control of administrative activities in 352.3

For licensing by nongovernmental agencies, see 060; for ombudsman role in legislative bodies, see 328.3; for government-employee grievances, see 352.6

See also 342 for administrative law, 352.7 for promotional and supporting role of administration

*Add standard subdivisions as instructed under 352–354

353   Specific fields of public administration

For public administration of economy and environment, see 354

See Manual at T1—068 vs. 353–354; also at 352–354; also at 363 vs. 340, 353–354

SUMMARY

353.1	Administration of external and national security affairs
.3	Administration of services related to domestic order
.4	Administration of justice
.5	Administration of social welfare
.6	Administration of health services
.7	Administration of culture and related activities
.8	Administration of agencies supporting and controlling education
.9	Administration of safety, sanitation, waste control Safety administration

[.01–.09]   Standard subdivisions

> Do not use; class in 351.01–351.09

.1   *Administration of external and national security affairs

Standard subdivisions are added for external and national security affairs together, for national security affairs alone

Including administration of colonies [*formerly* 325], other non-self-governing territories, foreign relations, intelligence and counterintelligence, subversion

Class administration of specific non-self-governing territories in 351.3–351.9; class military government of occupied territories in 355.4; class interdisciplinary works on foreign relations in 327; class interdisciplinary works on intelligence, counterintelligence subversion in 327.12; class interdisciplinary works on national security in 355

> *For military and defense administration, see 355.6*

(.2)   Military and defense administration

(Optional number; prefer 355.6 for military, defense, army administration; 358.4 for air force administration; 359.6 for naval administration)

Including air force administration, naval administration

Class here army administration

> *For specific topics in military and defense administration, see 355.6; for specific topics in air force administration, see 358.4; for specific topics in naval administration, see 359.6*

---

*Add standard subdivisions as instructed under 352–354

> **353.3–353.9   Public administration in domestic fields not related to economy and environment**

Many works classed here will concern activities of national or state and provincial governments to regulate, control, or support services provided by local government agencies. These activities are in contrast to those of local governments that provide the actual services. Works on managing local agencies that directly serve the ultimate recipients are normally classed with the service outside public administration, e.g., management of city police departments 363.2068 (*not* 353.3), of local school systems 371.2 (*not* 353.8)

Class comprehensive works in 351

See Manual at T1—068 vs. 353–354

.3   ***Administration of services related to domestic order**

Including corrections, prisons; police services, regulating personal conduct, support and control of subordinate jurisdictions by higher jurisdictions

Class here home departments and ministries, European style interior ministries

Class personal liberty in 323.44; class police control of personal conduct in 363.2; class operational management of police services in 363.2068; class comprehensive works on administration of subordinate jurisdictions in 352.14; class interdisciplinary works on controversies relating to public morals and customs in 363.4; class interdisciplinary works on administration of correctional activities in 364.6068

For control of special service districts, see 352.19; for support of urban, suburban, rural areas, see 352.7; for financial support of subordinate jurisdictions, see 352.73; for administration of justice, see 353.4

See also 354.30973 for United States Department of the Interior

.4   ***Administration of justice**

Including immigration and naturalization services; misconduct in office regardless of area of public administration; promotion of civil rights

Class here administration of criminal justice, departments of justice

For administration of courts, see 347; for correctional activities and police services, see 353.3

---

*Add standard subdivisions as instructed under 352–354

.5   ***Administration of social welfare**

Including birth and death certificates, birth control, housing, nutrition, pensions, social security in the sense of retirement income, unemployment insurance, comprehensive works on government-sponsored insurance

Class here human services, social security in the sense of social welfare

Class employment services in 354.9

For administration of health services, government-sponsored health insurance, see 353.6

See Manual at 361–365 vs. 353.5

.508   History and description with respect to kinds of persons

Do not use for programs directed to kinds of persons; class in 353.53

See Manual at 353.53 vs. 351.08

.53   ***Programs directed to kinds of persons**

Including families, poor people, victims of crime

Class here equal opportunity programs; programs for minorities, for socially disadvantaged groups; comprehensive works on programs in public administration directed to kinds of persons

Class a program directing a specific kind of service to kinds of persons with the kind of service, plus notation 08 from Table 1, e.g., personnel programs directed to minorities 352.608, administrative support for children's cultural activities 353.7083

For programs directed to labor and professional groups, see 354.9

See Manual at 353.35 vs. 351.08

.534   Specific racial, ethnic, national groups

[.534 01–.534 09]   Standard subdivisions

Do not use; class in 353.53

.535   *Women

.536   *Young people to age twenty

Class here children

.537   *Persons in late adulthood

.538   *Veterans

*Add standard subdivisions as instructed under 352–354

.539   *Persons with disabilities and illnesses

> Standard subdivisions are added for either or both topics in heading
>
> Programs not predominantly health related, e.g., access for persons with disabilities
>
> Class health programs for persons with disabilities and illness in 353.6

.6   ***Administration of health services**

> Including health insurance, workers' compensation insurance
>
> Class here rehabilitation services, services for physical illness
>
> Class comprehensive works on administration of social welfare in 353.5

.7   ***Administration of culture and related activities**

> Standard subdivisions are added for culture and related activities together, for culture alone
>
> Including language programs, programs to support and control religion, support of public libraries; parks and recreation, sports
>
> Class administration of public libraries and library systems in 025.1; class support of libraries in general in 352.7
>
> *For promoting museums and exhibitions, see 352.7; for administration of education, see 353.8*

.8   ***Administration of agencies supporting and controlling education**

> Class here agencies supporting and controlling elementary education, supporting and controlling secondary education
>
> Class school administration and management in 371.2; class public policy issues in education in 379; class comprehensive works on promotion and dissemination of knowledge in 352.7
>
> *See Manual at 371 vs. 353.8, 371.2, 379*

.9   ***Administration of safety, sanitation, waste control   Safety administration**

> Including civil defense, disaster and emergency planning, occupational safety
>
> Class management of disaster relief in 363.34; class management of fire departments in 363.37068; class operational management of sanitary services in 363.72068; class comprehensive administrative works on pollution in 354.3
>
> *For police services, see 353.3; for contagious diseases, see 353.6*

---

*Add standard subdivisions as instructed under 352–354

354   *Public administration of economy and environment

Standard subdivisions are added for administration of economy and environment together, for administration of economy alone

Class administration of safety in economy and environment in 353.9

See Manual at T1—068 vs. 353–354; also at 352–354; also at 363 vs. 340, 353–354

.08   History and description with respect to kinds of persons

Class here equal economic opportunity programs

.2   **General forms of assistance**

Including assistance to small business; community, rural, urban development; comprehensive works on administration of development, of research and development

Class comprehensive works on administration of research and development in noneconomic fields in 352.7; class interdisciplinary works on research and development in 338.9

For administration of research and development of a specific economic activity, see the activity in 354, e.g., development of agriculture 354.5

[.201–.209]   Standard subdivisions

Do not use; class in 354.2

> **354.3–354.8 Administration of specific fields of economic and environmental activity**

Class here industries associated with specific fields of economic and environmental activity

Class administration of labor and professions in specific fields of economic and environmental activity in 354.9; class comprehensive works in 354

---

*Add standard subdivisions as instructed under 352–354

.3   *Administration of environment and natural resources

Standard subdivisions are added for either or both topics in heading

Including conservation, environmental protection, hunting, land, pollution, real property, water supply, weather bureaus, zoning

Class here departments of natural resources, primary industries

Class administration of cleanup of pollution in 353.9; class interdisciplinary works on natural resources, on conservation in 333.7; class interdisciplinary works on zoning in 333.73; class interdisciplinary works on environmental protection in 363.7; class interdisciplinary works on pollution in 363.73

For public lands, see 352.5; for recreational use of environment, sports hunting, see 353.7; for sanitation and waste control, see 353.9; for administration of energy and energy-related resources, see 354.4; for administration of agriculture, see 354.5

.4   *Administration of energy and energy-related industries

Standard subdivisions are added for either or both topics in heading

Including control of public utilities supplying energy

Class here departments of energy; energy resources, mineral energy resources

Class comprehensive works on control of public utilities in 354.72

For development of water power, see 354.3

.5   *Administration of agriculture

Including aquatic biological resources, fishing and fisheries, forestry; commodity programs, e.g., marketing services

Class nutrition and food programs in 353.5; class rural development in 354.2; class hunting, irrigation projects, soil conservation in 354.3; class agricultural credit in 354.8

.6   *Administration of construction, manufacturing, service industries

Class here administration of secondary industries

For administration of commerce, communications, transportation, see 354.7; for financial services, see 354.8

.7   *Administration of commerce, communications, transportation

.72   General forms of control

Including comprehensive works on control of public utilities

For control of a specific kind of public utility, see the kind of utility in 354, e.g., control of energy utilities 354.4

[.720 1–.720 9]   Standard subdivisions

Do not use; class in 354.72

---

*Add standard subdivisions as instructed under 352–354

.73   *Commerce

      Including tourist trade regardless of origin

      Class here domestic commerce

      For foreign commerce, see 354.74

.74   *Foreign commerce

      Class foreign tourism in 354.73

.75   *Communications

      Including postal service

      Class here telecommunications

      Class postal organization in 383; class operational management of postal service in 383.068; class management, business organizations, and description of facilities of publicly owned communications systems in 384, e.g., business organization of a publically owned telephone system 384.6

.76   *Transportation

      Including automotive transportation

      Class here ground transportation

      Class transportation safety in 353.9

      For road transportation, see 354.77; for water transportation, see 354.78; for air and space transportation, see 354.79

.77   *Road transportation

      Including traffic control

.78   *Water transportation

      Class here inland water transportation, ocean transportation

.79   *Air and space transportation

      Standard subdivisions are added for air and space transportation together, for air transportation alone

*Add standard subdivisions as instructed under 352–354

.8 ***Administration of financial institutions, money, credit**

Standard subdivisions are added for financial institutions, money, credit together; for financial institutions alone

Including insurance, securities

Class works covering administration of both financial system and government finances in 352.4

> *For government-sponsored insurance, see 353.5; for government-sponsored health insurance, see 353.6*
>
> *See also 332.4 for monetary policy, 336.3 for fiscal policy*

.9 ***Administration of labor and professions**

Standard subdivisions are added for labor and professions together, for labor alone

Including collective bargaining, employment services

Class here departments of labor

Class pensions, unemployment insurance in 353.5; class workers' compensation insurance in 353.6; class occupational safety in 353.9

> *For administration of government workers, see 352.6*

.908 History and description with respect to kinds of persons

Class here affirmative action programs, equal employment opportunity programs

Class affirmative action programs for a government's own employees in 352.608

355 Military science

Including military research and development; military situation and policy, e.g., combat readiness, military assistance

Class here armed forces and services, ground forces and services

Disarmament relocated to 327.1

Class combat readiness of specific units in 355.3

> *For specific kinds of military forces and warfare, see 356–359*
>
> *See also 306.2 for sociology of military institutions; 322 for relation of the state to military organizations; 343 for military and defense law*
>
> *See Manual at 355 vs. 623*

---

*Add standard subdivisions as instructed under 352–354

SUMMARY

.001   Philosophy and theory

.002   Miscellany

[.002 8]   Auxiliary techniques and procedures; apparatus, equipment, materials

> Do not use; class in 355.8

.003–.005   Standard subdivisions

.006   Organizations

[.006 8]   Management

> Do not use; class in 355.6

.007   Education and related topics

> Do not use for research; class in 355

.007 1   Education

> Do not use for reserve training; class in 355.2. Do not use for on-the-job training; class in 355.5

> *See Manual at 378 vs. 355.0071*

.008   History and description with respect to kinds of persons

.009   Historical, geographic, persons treatment

> *See Manual at 930–990 vs. 355.009*

.009 3–.009 9   Treatment by specific continents, countries, localities

> Class organization of specific national armies in 355.3093–355.3099

> *For military history of a specific war, see the war in 930–990, e.g., military history of Vietnamese War 959.704*

.02 War and warfare

Including limited war, nuclear warfare, revolutionary warfare; causes of war; aftermath of war, e.g., occupation, reconstruction; antimilitarism, militarism; interdisciplinary works on military-industrial complex

Class here conventional warfare, total war

For economic aspects of military-industrial complex, see 338.4

See also 341.6 for law of war

See Manual at 355.02 vs. 355.4

.1 Military life and customs

Including housing administration [*formerly* 355.6], ceremonies, colors and standards, deserters, discipline, punishment, military police, morale, prisoners of war, promotion, uniforms and medals, comprehensive works on military housing

Class here conditions of military employment

Class issue and use of uniforms in 355.8

For social and welfare services provided to soldiers and dependents, see 355.3; for quarters for military personnel at military installations, see 355.7

See also 364.1 for war crimes

.2 Military resources

Including all-volunteer army, conscientious objectors, draft, mobilization, recruiting, reserve training; human resources, industrial resources, raw materials

.3 Organization and personnel of military forces

Standard subdivisions are added for organization and personnel together, for organization alone

Including public relations [*formerly also* 659.2]; expeditionary forces, foreign legions, frontier troops, home guards, international forces, mercenary troops, regiments, reserves, women's units; unconventional warfare; medical services, supply-issuing services; religious and counseling services, e.g., chaplain services

Class here national armies, combat readiness of specific units

Class women in armed forces in 355.0082; class persons treatment of soldiers in 355.0092; class promotion and demotion of personnel in 355.1; class training of reserves in 355.2; class interdisciplinary works on espionage and subversion in 327.1

For a specific kind of unit limited to a specific service, see the service, e.g., armored units 358

.4   **Military operations**

Including camouflage, logistics, military geography, occupation and military government of conquered territory, reconnaissance, tactics, war gaming

Class here attack and defense operations, strategy

Class occupation as an aftermath of war in 355.02

See Manual at 355.02 vs. 355.4

.409   Historical and persons treatment

Do not use for geographic treatment; class in 355.4

.5   **Military training**

Training of individuals and units

Including basic training, e.g., drill, self-defense; maneuvers

Class university service academies in 355.0071; class training through war games in 355.4

For reserve training, universal military training, see 355.2

.6   **Military administration**

Including administration of specific kinds of equipment and supplies [*formerly* 355.8], supply management [*formerly also* 355.8068]; executive management; financial, personnel, supply administration; graves registration, military mail, comprehensive works on military contracts

Class here defense administration, departments of defense

Housing administration relocated to 355.1

Class command and control systems in 355.3. Class administration of a function not provided for here with the function, plus notation 068 from Table 1, e.g., administration of installations 355.7068

> *For service periods, promotion and demotion, termination, see 355.1; for managing executive personnel, organization of military forces, personnel and their hierarchy, supply issuing and related services, see 355.3; for supply depots and installations, see 355.7. For contracts for a specific nonsupply item, see the item, plus notation 068 from Table 1, e.g., contracts for real property 355.7068*

(Option: Class comprehensive works in 353.2. If option is chosen, change heading to "Specific topics in military administration," and do not add standard subdivisions)

[.606 8]   Management

Do not use; class in 355.6

.609 1   Treatment by areas, regions, places in general

Class here international military and defense administration

Class administration of international peacekeeping troops in 355.3

.7   **Military installations**

Including barracks, prisoner-of-war camps

Class here military bases, forts, posts, reservations

Class an installation of a specific military force with the force, e.g., army artillery installations 358

.709 3–.709 9   Treatment in specific continent, country, locality

Class here specific forts or systems of forts, installations having two or more functions

Use notation for area of installation, not country maintaining it, e.g., United States bases in Panama Canal Area 355.7097287

.8   **Military equipment and supplies (Matériel)**   **Weapons (Ordnance)**

Limited to equipment and supplies common to two or more land forces, or to at least two of the three major defense forces, e.g., missiles and tanks, supplies of land and sea forces

Including auxiliary techniques and procedures, clothing, vehicles

Class here apparatus, equipment, materials; military aspects of research and development (other than procurement and contracting) of specific kinds of equipment and supplies

Administration of specific kinds of equipment and supplies relocated to 355.6

Class mobilization of military industrial resources in 355.2; class weapons limited to a specific land force in 356–357; class comprehensive works on research and development of supplies, of weapons in 355; class interdisciplinary works on research and development of a specific kind of equipment and supplies in 338.4

[.806 8]   Supply management

Relocated to 355.6

.807   Education and related topics

Do not use for research; class in 355

>   **356–359   Specific kinds of military forces and warfare**

Class here history of specific military forces not limited to any one war, services and units dedicated to specific forces, countermeasures against specific forces

Class comprehensive works in 355. Class a specific countermeasure with the force wielding it, e.g., coast artillery 358 (*not* 359)

See Manual at 355 vs. 623

> ### 356–357   Land forces and warfare

Class comprehensive works in 355

For armored and artillery forces; biological, chemical, radiological warfare, see 358; for missile forces, see 358.1

356   Foot forces and warfare

Including infantry, e.g., commandos, paratroops, rangers, ski troops

357   Mounted forces and warfare

Including horse cavalry; mechanized cavalry, e.g. motorcycle troops

For armored cavalry, see 358

358   Air and other specialized forces and warfare; engineering and related services

Including armored, artillery, space forces; communications, demolition, transportation services; chemical, biological, radiological warfare

Class naval artillery forces in 359.9

.1   Guided missile forces

Including antimissile defense, Strategic Defense Initiative (SDI, star wars); nuclear missile forces, strategic missile forces

Class a specific antimissile defense other than surface-to-air missiles with the defense, e.g., beam weapons 358, air-to-air missiles 358.4

For air guided missile forces, see 358.4; for naval guided missile forces, see 359.9

[.101–.109]   Standard subdivisions

Do not use; class in 358.1

.4   Air forces and warfare

For naval air forces, see 359.9

(Option: Class comprehensive works on air force administration in 353.2. If option is chosen, use 358.4 for specific topics in air force administration)

.400 1–.400 9   Standard subdivisions

Notation from Table 1 as modified under 355.001–355.009, e.g., air forces administration 358.4 (*not* 358.40068)

359   Sea (Naval) forces and warfare

.001–.009   Standard subdivisions

Notation from Table 1 as modified under 355.001–355.009, e.g., naval administration 359.6 (*not* 359.0068)

.1–.5	**Naval life, resources, organization and personnel, operations, training**

Add to base number 359 the numbers following 355 in 355.1–355.5, e.g., naval organization and personnel, ships as naval units 355.3; however, for ships as units of specialized combat services, e.g., aircraft carriers, see 359.9

Class comprehensive works on ships in the navy in 359.8

.6   Naval administration

Including administration of specific kinds of equipment and supplies [*formerly* 359.8], supply management [*formerly also* 359.8068]

(Option: Class comprehensive works in 353.2. If option is chosen, change heading to "Specific topics in naval administration," and do not add standard subdivisions)

.7   Naval installations

.8   Naval equipment and supplies (Naval matériel)   Naval weapons (ordnance)

Including auxiliary techniques and procedures

Class here apparatus, equipment, materials; naval aspects of research and development (other than procurement and contracting) of specific kinds of supplies and equipment

Administration of specific kinds of equipment and supplies relocated to 359.6

Class mobilization of naval industrial resources in 359.2; class comprehensive works on naval aspects of research and development of equipment and supplies, of weapons in 359; class interdisciplinary works on research and development of naval supplies and equipment in 338.4

[.806 8]   Supply management

Relocated to 359.6

.807   Education and related topics

Do not use for research; class in 359

.9   Specialized combat forces; engineering and related forces

Including coast guard as a military service; guided missile forces, marines, naval air forces, submarine forces; communications, demolition, transportation services

Class chemical, biological, radiological warfare in 358; class coast guard as a police service, interdisciplinary works on coast guard in 363.28

360   Social problems and services; associations

SUMMARY

> ## 361–365   Social problems and services

Class here work and policy of government agencies that enforce the law in matters of social problems and services

Class law of social services, including draft laws, enforcement of the law by courts, in 341–346; class the internal administration of governmental agencies dealing with social services, including their administrative annual reports, in 353.5; class insurance in 368; class comprehensive works in 361

For social services in armed forces, see 355–359; for school social services, see 371.7; for social services in specific wars, see 900

See Manual at 361–365; also at 301–307 vs. 361–365; also at 361–365 vs. 353.5

361   Social problems and social welfare in general

Social welfare: social assistance, either free or paid for in part or in full by recipients, to enable individuals to cope with situations usually beyond their individual capacities to overcome

Including counseling, guidance; material assistance, e.g., financial aid

Class here comprehensive works on socioeconomic planning and development, on programs and services encompassing several branches of social sciences, on social problems and services

Class description of present or past social conditions in 930–990. Class assistance with respect to a specific problem with the problem, e.g., financial aid to persons in late adulthood 362.6

For social problems considered purely as social phenomena, see 301–307; for community planning and development, see 307.1; for economic planning and development, see 338.9; for specific problems and services, see 362–365

See Manual at 361 vs. 362

.001–.008   Standard subdivisions

[.009]   Historical, geographic, persons treatment

     Do not use; class in 361.9

.1   Social problems

History, description, appraisal of areas and kinds of social breakdown, of problems endemic to human society

For specific problems, see 362–363

.2   Social action

Including dissent and protest, international action, planning, reform movements

Class change as a social phenomenon in 303.4

For social work, see 361.3; for governmental action, see 361.6; for private action, see 361.7; for combined governmental and private community action, see 361.8

.3   Social work

Including casework, interviewing, volunteer social work

Use of this number for counseling discontinued; class in 361

For group work, see 361.4

.4   Group work

Class counseling in group work in 361

.6   Governmental action

Including welfare and human rights, welfare state, welfare reform

Class here intergovernmental assistance and planning, governmental international action, interdisciplinary works on government-sponsored socioeconomic planning and development

Class economics of welfare state in 330.12; class combined public and private action in 361.2; class public social work in 361.3; class combined public and private community action in 361.8; class interdisciplinary works on human rights in 323

For management of public agencies regulating social welfare services, see 353.5

See Manual at 361.6 vs. 361.7, 361.8

.7   Private action

Including individual philanthropy; business organizations; labor unions; nonprofit organizations, e.g., CARE; private international organizations, e.g., International Red Cross; religious organizations

Class combined public and private action in 361.2; class private social work in 361.3; class relation of government and private sectors in 361.6; class combined public and private community action in 361.8; class programs of employers for employees in 658.3

See Manual at 361.6 vs. 361.7, 361.8

.706	Organizations and management

Do not use for a specific kind of organization, e.g., nonprofit organizations; class in 361.7

.706 8	Management

Including fund raising

.8   Community action

Coordination of public and private action to promote welfare of individuals in the community

Class community development in 307.1; class governmental community action in 361.6; class private community action in 361.7

See Manual at 361.6 vs. 361.7, 361.8

.9   Historical, geographic, persons treatment

Add to base number 361.9 notation 1–9 from Table 2, e.g., welfare work in Arizona 361.9791

Class historical, geographic, persons treatment of specific kinds of social action in 361.2–361.8

> ## 362–363 Specific social problems and services

Including social causes and effects; incidence, distribution, severity; control through standards, monitoring, surveillance, reporting, inspection, testing, certification; preparedness, prevention; remedial measures and forms of assistance, e.g., counseling, guidance, employment services, financial assistance, rescue operations, residential care

Comprehensive works on effects that occur either after the problem has ceased or when the person is no longer close to the person with the problem are classed with the problem, e.g., effects on adult victims of child abuse 362.76. A specific aftereffect is classed with the aftereffect, e.g., social aspects of alcoholism in victims of child abuse 362.292, medical aspects of adult victims of child abuse 616.85

Class discrimination in 305; class safety measures in 363.1; class comprehensive works in 361

For criminology, see 364

See Manual at 362–363 vs. 364.1

362   Social welfare problems and services

Class here social security

Unless other instructions are given, observe the following table of preference, e.g., mentally ill veterans 362.2 (*not* 362.86):

Physical illness	362.1
Mental and emotional illnesses and disturbances	362.2
Mental retardation	362.3
Problems of and services to people with physical disabilities	362.4
Victims of oppression	362.87
Victims of crimes	362.88
Veterans	362.86
Problems of and services to persons in late adulthood	362.6
Problems of and services to young people	362.7
Laboring classes	362.85
Women	362.83
Members of racial, ethnic, national groups	362.84
Problems of and services to the poor	362.5
Families	362.82
Historical, geographic, persons treatment	362.9

To indicate the relation of a specific kind of problem to a specific kind of person, add notation 08 from Table 1 to the number for the problem, e.g., substance abuse among young adults 362.29084. However, persons close to those with a problem, e.g., family members, co-workers, are classed in the number for the problem without use of notation 08, e.g., persons close to substance abusers 362.29 (*not* 362.9208)

For social security as a form of social insurance, see 368.4

See Manual at 361 vs. 362; also at 362–363 vs. 364.1; also at 362 vs. 368.4

SUMMARY

362.1	**Physical illness**
.2	**Mental and emotional illnesses and disturbances**
.3	**Mental retardation**
.4	**Problems of and services to people with physical disabilities**
.5	**Problems of and services to the poor**
.6	**Problems of and services to persons in late adulthood**
.7	**Problems of and services to young people**
.8	**Problems of and services to other groups**
.9	**Historical, geographic, persons treatment**

[.08]   Social welfare problems and services with respect to kinds of persons

Do not use; class in 362.1–362.8

[.09]   Historical, geographic, persons treatment

Do not use; class in 362.9

> **362.1–362.4 Problems of and services to persons with illnesses and disabilities**

Including services of general and special hospitals, clinics, dispensaries, sanatoriums; extended care facilities, e.g., nursing homes; medical and psychiatric social work; professional home care, e.g., visiting nurses' services

Class incidence of and public measures to prevent physical diseases in 614.4–614.5; class comprehensive works in 362.1

See also 649.8 for home care by family members

See Manual at 362.1–362.4 vs. 610; also at 614.4–614.5 vs. 362.1–362.4

.1   **Physical illness**

Including living with a physical illness

Class here interdisciplinary works on illness and disability, on medical care and treatment, on medical missions, on public health

Class accident and health insurance in 368.38; class government-sponsored accident and health insurance in 368.4

For religious aspects of medical missions, see 266; for sociology of medicine, of health, of illness, see 306.4; for mental and emotional illness, see 362.2; for mental retardation, see 362.3; for problems of and services to persons with a specific physical disability regardless of cause, see 362.4; for technology of medicine, see 610

See Manual at 362.1 vs. 368.38; also at 610 vs. 362.1

.102 3   Services to persons with physical illnesses; as a profession, occupation, hobby

Class here interdisciplinary works on health occupations peripheral to the medical and paramedical professions

Class works covering both the medical and peripheral occupations in 610

For a specific peripheral profession, see the profession, e.g., hospital secretaries 651.3

.108   Services to specific kinds of persons with physical illnesses

Do not use for services rendered by groups of persons to persons with physical illnesses; class in 362.1

Class physical illness among groups of persons in 616.008

.108 3   Services to young people

Do not use for services to infants and children up to puberty; class in 362.1

.108 4   Services to persons in specific stages of adulthood

Do not use for services to persons in late adulthood; class in 362.1

.109	Historical, geographic, persons treatment
.109 173	Socioeconomic regions by concentration of population

Do not use for rural regions; class in 362.1

.18   Emergency services

Including ambulance services

.2   Mental and emotional illnesses and disturbances

Standard subdivisions are added for any or all topics in heading

Class here mental disabilities that consist of mental retardation combined with mental illness

Class life with a psychiatric disorder in 616.890092

For mental retardation, see 362.3

.28   Suicide

.29   Substance abuse

Including narcotics abuse

Class here drug abuse; interdisciplinary works on substance abuse, addiction, habituation, intoxication

For subculture of substance abusers, see 306; for drug traffic, see 363.45; for illegal sale, possession, use of drugs, see 364.1; for drug use as a custom, see 394.1; for medical aspects of substance abuse, see 616.86

See also 362.2 for food addiction

See Manual at 616.86 vs. 158, 248.8, 291.4, 362.29

.292   Alcohol

Class here interdisciplinary works on alcoholism

For a specific aspect of alcoholism, see the aspect, e.g., public drunkenness 364.1, medical aspects 616.86

.3   Mental retardation

Class comprehensive works on problems of and services to persons with developmental disabilities (those who have neurological diseases combined with mental retardation and whose problems exhibit themselves before age 18) in 362.1; class comprehensive works on treatment of mental retardation and mental illness in 362.2

.4 Problems of and services to people with physical disabilities

Regardless of cause

Including persons with hearing, mobility, visual impairments

Class here comprehensive works on problems of and services to people with disabilities, to people with mental and physical disabilities

Class comprehensive medical works in 617

For problems of and services to people with mental disabilities, see 362.3

.5 Problems of and services to the poor

Including guaranteed minimum income, negative income tax, interdisciplinary works on legal aid

Class here services to homeless people

Class economic causes and effects of, and measures to prevent poverty in 339; class aid to families with dependent children (AFDC) in 362.71; class housing in 363.5; class birth control as a remedy of poverty in 363.9; class assistance to the poor under social security in 368.4

For law of legal aid, see 347; for food programs, see 363.8

.6 Problems of and services to persons in late adulthood

Including elder abuse

Class here social gerontology

Class parent abuse in 362.82; class elder abuse as a crime in 364.15. Class elder abuse in a specific situation with the situation, e.g., elder abuse in nursing homes 362.1

.7 Problems of and services to young people

Through age seventeen

Class here children

.708 3 Young people twelve to seventeen

Do not use for children; class in 362.7

Class young people eighteen and over in 362

[.708 35] Young people twelve to seventeen

Do not use; class in 362.7083

.708 6 Persons by miscellaneous social characteristics

Do not use for abandoned children, orphans; class in 362.73. Do not use for predelinquents; class in 362.74. Do not use for abused children; class in 362.76. Do not use for juvenile delinquents; class in 364.36

> 362.71–362.73 Specific kinds of services to young people

Class services to maladjusted young people in 362.74; class services to abused and neglected children in 362.76; class comprehensive works in 362.7

.71 Direct relief

Including aid to families with dependent children (AFDC), day care services

.73 Institutional and related services

Including adoption, foster home care

Class here abandoned children, orphans

> 362.74–362.76 Specific kinds of young people

Class comprehensive works in 362.7

For abandoned children, orphans, see 362.73

.74 Maladjusted young people

Including predelinquents, runaways

Class here specific services to maladjusted young people, halfway houses for young people who have not committed any crimes

Class young people with mental and emotional illnesses in 362.2083; class families with missing children in 362.82; class halfway houses for the transition from reform school to society in 365

For juvenile delinquents, see 364.36

.76 Abused and neglected children

Standard subdivisions are added for either or both topics in heading

Class child abuse as a crime in 364.15

.8 Problems of and services to other groups

.82 Families

Including abuse within the family, marriage counseling, missing children, parental kidnapping, single-parent family

Class here parents

Class family welfare when synonymous with general welfare in 362; class aid to families with dependent children (AFDC), day care in 362.71; class adoption in 362.73; class runaway children in 362.74; class abused and neglected children in 362.76; class family planning programs in 363.9; class abuse as a crime in 364.15

.83		Women

Including unmarried mothers

Class wife abuse in 362.82; class rape in 362.883

.84		Members of racial, ethnic, national groups
.840 01–.840 09		Standard subdivisions
.85		Laboring classes

Including migrant workers

.86	Veterans

Class here veterans' rights and benefits

Veterans' higher education benefits relocated to 378.3

Class veterans pensions in 331.25

.87	Victims of oppression

Class here refugees

.88	Victims of crimes

Including crime prevention for the individual

Class here victimology

Class services to abused family members in 362.82; class crime prevention for society as a whole in 364.4

For works on why persons become victims of specific crimes, see 364.1

.880 83	Young people

Class services to abused and neglected children in 362.76

.883	Rape

Including rape prevention for individuals

.9	**Historical, geographic, persons treatment**

Add to base number 362.9 notation 1–9 from Table 2, e.g., social welfare in France 362.944

Class historical, geographic, persons treatment of specific social problems in 362.1–362.8

363   Other social problems and services

Standard subdivisions are added for comprehensive treatment of environmental and safety problems of society, e.g., assuring a safe and secure environment for Japan 363.0952

Class here public works

For communication facilities, see 384; for transportation facilities, see 388

See Manual at 363; also at 362–363 vs. 364.1; also at 363 vs. 340, 353–354

SUMMARY

363.1	Public safety programs
.2	Police services
.3	Other aspects of public safety
.4	Controversies related to public morals and customs
.5	Housing
.6	Public utilities and related services
.7	Environmental problems
.8	Food supply
.9	Population problems

.1   Public safety programs

Including interdisciplinary works on safety investigation

Class here safety measures, interdisciplinary works on safety

Unless other instructions are given, observe the following table of preference, e.g., use of hazardous materials in health care facilities 363.17 (*not* 363.15):

Hazardous materials	363.17
Hazards in sports and recreation	363.14
Transportation hazards	363.12
Hazardous machinery	363.18
Product hazards	363.19
Domestic hazards	363.13
Hazards in health care facilities	363.15
Occupational and industrial hazards	363.11

Class managerial response to safety requirements, comprehensive works on safety management in 658.4. Class safety management in a specific industry with the industry, plus notation 068 from Table 1, e.g., safety management in petroleum industry 665.5068

For police services, see 363.2; for aspects of public safety not provided for here, see 363.3. For a specific kind of remedial measure other than rescue operations, see the measure, e.g., medical care for the injured 362.1; for safety technology of a specific subject, see the subject, plus notation 028 from Table 1, e.g., safety technology in hydraulic engineering 627.028; for a technical or engineering aspect of safety investigations, see the aspect in 600, e.g., safety engineering 620.8, wreckage studies of automobile accidents 629.28; for accounts of a specific incident that affected general social life and history, see the incident in 900, e.g., San Francisco earthquake of 1906 979.4

See Manual at 363.1; also at 333.7–333.9 vs. 363.1, 363.73, 577; also at 363.1 vs. 620.8

.100 1–.100 9   Standard subdivisions [*formerly* 363.101–363.109]

[.101–.109]   Standard subdivisions

Relocated to 363.1001–363.1009

.11   Occupational and industrial hazards

Standard subdivisions are added for either or both topics in heading

Including school safety programs [*formerly* 371.7]

See Manual at 363.11 vs. 613.6

.12   Transportation hazards

Class here accidents, fires resulting from accidents

Class comprehensive works on fires in transportation facilities, e.g., fires caused by deficient electrical wiring in a railroad car, in 363.37

.120 01–.120 09   Standard subdivisions [*formerly* 363.1201–363.1209]

[.120 1–.120 9]   Standard subdivisions

Relocated to 363.12001–363.12009

.13   Domestic hazards

.14   Hazards in sports and recreation

Standard subdivisions are added for either or both topics in heading

.15   Hazards in health care facilities

.17   Hazardous materials

Manufacture, transportation, use

Including nuclear accidents

Class here interdisciplinary works on hazardous materials, on the control of such materials in their ordinary commercial setting (manufacture, sale, commercial and industrial use, disposal)

For hazardous materials as components of articles that become hazardous products, see 363.19; for hazardous materials as impurities in the water supply, see 363.6; for hazardous wastes, see 363.72; for hazardous materials as environmental pollutants, see 363.738; for hazardous materials technology, see 604.7

See Manual at 363.17; also at 363.17 vs. 604.7

.18   Hazardous machinery

.19   Product hazards

Adulteration, contamination, safety, adequacy, effectiveness of products offered for human consumption and use

Including cosmetics, drugs, foods, household appliances, toys

Class here hazards due to containers and applicators that accompany products

.2   Police services

Including crime prevention, law enforcement; patrol, surveillance, pursuit, apprehension; enforcement of civil laws, e.g., traffic control; location of missing persons; auxiliary services, e.g., police records

Class police services in control of factors affecting public morals in 363.4; class police committing a crime in 364.1; class comprehensive works on traffic control in 363.12. Class a social service function of police with the function in 362, e.g., counseling of rape victims 362.883

For control of violence and terrorism, see 363.3

.206 8   Management [*formerly* 351.74]

.25   Detection of crime (Criminal investigation)

Class here forensic science (criminalistics)

Class detection of a specific crime with the crime in 364.1, e.g., detection of a murder 364.15

For forensic medicine, see 614

.28   Services of special kinds of security and law enforcement agencies

Including border and harbor patrols; interdisciplinary works on coast guards

Class agencies to carry out specific police functions in 363.2; class agencies to investigate specific kinds of crime in 363.25

For coast guards as a military service, see 359.9; for narcotics agents, see 363.45; for postal inspectors, see 383

.3   Other aspects of public safety

Including civil defense; control of explosives and firearms; control of violence and terrorism, e.g., crowd control, quelling riots; control of information, press control, censorship as routine government function; interdisciplinary works on censorship, on gun control

Class control of explosives as ordinary hazardous materials in 363.17

For gun control as a civil rights issue, see 323.4. For a specific aspect of censorship not provided for here, see the aspect, e.g., civil rights aspects 323.44, legal aspects in 342

See Manual at 363.1; also at 363.3 vs. 303.3, 791.4

.34   Disasters

Including floods, war

Class prevention of war in 327.1; class problems of war refugees when not treated directly in context of the war in 362.87; class civil defense in 363.3; class technology of flood control in 627. Class a specific kind of remedial measure other than those applied immediately at the time and site of the disaster with the measure, e.g., medical care for injured 362.1

For epidemics and pandemics, see 362.1; for fires, see 363.37. For a specific kind of disaster resulting from one of the hazards listed in 363.1, see the disaster in 363.1, e.g., transportation accidents 363.12

See also 303.6 for sociology of war

See Manual at 900: Historic events vs. nonhistoric events

.37   Fire hazards

Class fire fighting and fire safety technology in 628.9

.4   **Controversies related to public morals and customs**

Treated as social problems

Including gambling, homosexuality, obscenity, pornography, premarital and extramarital relations, prostitution, sale of alcoholic beverages

Class problems of and services to alcoholics in 362.292; class censorship and control of information in 363.3; class a controversy treated as a crime, e.g., gambling as a crime, in 364.1; class interdisciplinary works on homosexuality in 306.76. Class a controversy treated other than as a social problem with the aspect of the controversy, e.g., ethics of gambling 175

.45   Drug traffic

Class here narcotics agents

Class problems of and services to drug addicts in 362.29; class illegal sale, possession, use of drugs in 364.1

See also 363.4 for sale of alcoholic beverages

.46   Abortion

.5   **Housing**

Including discrimination in housing, public housing, urban homesteading

Class here housing as a social problem, interdisciplinary works on housing

For a specific aspect of housing, see the aspect, e.g., sociological aspects 307.3, economic aspects 333.33

See Manual at 363.5, 363.6, 363.8 vs. 338; also at 363.5 vs. 643

[.508]   Housing of specific kinds of persons

Do not use; class in 363.5

.6   **Public utilities and related services**

Standard subdivisions are added for public utilities and related services together, for public utilities alone

Including historic preservation, park and recreation services, gas supply, comprehensive works on water supply

Class here problems of allocation among end users, measures to assure abundance of immediately available supplies and services

Class park policy and park development in 333.78; class technology of building restoration and preservation in 721.028; class recreational centers in 790.06. Class a specific cultural institution maintained by park and recreation services with the institution, e.g., museums 069, theaters 792

For electrical utilities, see 333.79; for flood control, see 363.34; for communication, see 384; for transportation, see 388

See Manual at 363.6; also at 333.7–333.9 vs. 363.6; also at 363.5, 363.6, 383.8 vs. 338; also at 913–919: Historic sites and buildings; also at 930–990: Historic preservation

.7 **Environmental problems**

Including disposal of the dead, removal of animal carcasses, interdisciplinary works on pest control

Class here environmental protection; impact of wastes, of pollution, of actions to control waste and pollution

Class death customs in 393; class technology of disposal of the dead in 614; class interdisciplinary works on the environment in 333.7

> *For control of disease-carrying pests, see 614.4; for comprehensive works on the technology of pest control, see 628.9; for control of agricultural pests, see 632; for control of household pests, see 648*
>
> *See Manual at 333.7 vs. 304.2, 363.7*

.700 1–.700 9   Standard subdivisions [*formerly* 363.701–363.709]

[.701–.709]   Standard subdivisions

Relocated to 363.7001–363.7009

.72 Sanitation

Including recycling, wastes

Class pollution by waste disposal in 363.73; class dangerous wastes that have escaped both safety and sanitary controls in 363.738

.73 Pollution

Class works that discuss waste and sanitation problems as well as pollution in 363.7; class sanitation, waste disposal as a method of pollution prevention in 363.72; class noise in 363.74; class technology of pollution prevention in 628.5; class management responsibilities and measures with respect to protection and preservation of the environment in 658.4

> *See Manual at 333.7–333.9 vs. 363.1, 363.73, 577; also at 363.73 vs. 571.9, 577.27*

.738 Pollutants

Including acid rain; interdisciplinary works on greenhouse effect (global warming), on ozone layer depletion

Class here chemical pollutants

> *For an aspect of greenhouse effect (global warming), of ozone layer depletion outside of social services, see the aspect, e.g., changes in earth's ozone layer or temperature 551.51, effect of global warming on ecology 577.27*

.739   Pollution of specific environments

> Including air, soil pollution; comprehensive works on water pollution
>
> Class specific pollutants in specific environments in 363.738
>
> *For assurance of clean water supply, see 363.6*
>
> *See Manual at 363.6*

.74   Noise

.8   **Food supply**

> Including food stamp programs
>
> Class here hunger, famine; interdisciplinary works on food supply, on nutrition
>
> *For economics of food supply, see 338.1; for problems of malnutrition, see 362.1; for prevention of malnutrition, see 614.5*
>
> *See Manual at 363.5, 363.6, 363.8 vs. 338; also at 363.8 vs. 338.1; also at 363.8 vs. 613.2, 641.3*

.9   **Population problems**

> Including overpopulation and underpopulation, sterilization; interdisciplinary works on eugenics, on birth control, on family planning programs
>
> Class here interdisciplinary works on population problems
>
> Class abortion in 363.46; class interdisciplinary works on population in 304.6
>
> *For family planning techniques, see 613.9. For a specific manifestation of a population problem, see the manifestation, e.g., pressure on food supply leading to famine 363.8; for a specific aspect of eugenics, see the aspect, e.g., civil rights 323.4, eugenic measures to reduce crime 364.4*
>
> *See Manual at 363.9 vs. 304.6*

364   Criminology

Crime and its alleviation

Including extent and incidence of crime

Class here comprehensive works on criminology and criminal law, on criminal justice that includes criminology, police services, and criminal law

Unless other instructions are given, observe the following table of preference, e.g., punishment of specific types of offenders 364.6 (*not* 364.3):

Penology	364.6
Discharged offenders	364.8
Offenders	364.3
Prevention of crime and delinquency	364.4
Causes of crime and delinquency	364.2
Criminal offenses	364.1
Historical, geographic, persons treatment of crime and its alleviation	364.9

Class social services to victims of crimes and self-protection from criminals in 362.88

For criminal law, see 345; for police services, see 363.2

.08	**History and description with respect to kinds of persons**
.086	**Persons by miscellaneous social characteristics**

Do not use for predelinquents; class in 362.74. Do not use for victims of crimes; class in 362.88. Do not use for offenders; class in 364.3. Do not use for juvenile delinquents; class in 364.36. Do not use for convicts; class in 365

.09   **Historical, geographic, persons treatment of criminology as a discipline**

Do not use for historical, geographic, persons treatment of crime and its alleviation; class in 364.9

.1   Criminal offenses

Including political and related offenses, e.g., war crimes; offenses against public morals, e.g., pornography

Class here conspiracy to and incitement to commit an offense, individuals identified with a specific offense or type of offense, investigation of specific crimes, crimes without victims, terrorism as a crime

Class offenses against church law in 262.9; class sociology of terrorism in 303.6; class social services aspects of victims of crimes in 362.88; class investigation of specific types of offenses in 363.25; class a crime as an event in history in 900

See also 341.6 for war crime trials, 363.4 for controversies related to public morals and customs, e.g., pornography

See Manual at 362–363 vs. 364.1; also at 900: Historic events vs. nonhistoric events

.106　　　　　　Organized crime

　　　　　　　　Do not use for organizations dealing with criminal offenses; class in 364.06

　　　　　　　　Class here Mafia

.15　　　　　　Offenses against persons

　　　　　　　　Including abuse, assault and battery, murder, rape, robbery, slander

　　　　　　　　Class elder abuse as a social problem in 362.6; class child abuse as a social problem in 362.76; class abuse within the family as a social problem, parental kidnapping in 362.82

.16　　　　　　Offenses against property

　　　　　　　　Including arson, burglary, fraud, theft, vandalism, white collar crime

.2　　　　　　Causes of crime and delinquency

　　　　　　　　Class here criminal anthropology

　　　　　　　　Class victimology in 362.88

.3　　　　　　Offenders

　　　　　　　　Including offenders with mental illnesses and disabilities

　　　　　　　　Class here criminal psychology

　　　　　　　　Class a specific aspect of the justice system for specific types of offenders with the aspect, e.g., determination of sentences for juvenile offenders 364.6, offenders as prisoners in 365

　　　　　　　　For individuals chiefly identified with a specific offense or type of offense, see 364.1

[.308 1–.308 2]　Men and women

　　　　　　　　Do not use; class in 364.3

[.308 3]　　　　Young people

　　　　　　　　Do not use; class in 364.36

.308 6　　　　Persons by miscellaneous social characteristics

　　　　　　　　Do not use for offenders; class in 364.3. Do not use for juvenile delinquents; class in 364.36

.308 7　　　　Persons with disabilities and illnesses, gifted persons

　　　　　　　　Do not use for persons with mental illnesses and disabilities; class in 364.3

[.308 9]　　　　Racial, ethnic, national groups

　　　　　　　　Do not use; class in 364.3

.36   Juvenile delinquents

Class here comprehensive works on juvenile delinquency, juvenile delinquents, juvenile justice system

Class comprehensive works on maladjusted young people in 362.74

For legal aspects of juvenile delinquents, see 345

.4   **Prevention of crime and delinquency**

Including counseling, guidance, environmental design; welfare services, e.g., recreational services; identification of potential offenders, e.g., through genetic screening; curfew

Class here what society does to prevent crime

Class penalties as a deterrent in 364.6

For law enforcement, prevention of crime by police, see 363.2. For a specific aspect of prevention by a potential victim, see the aspect, e.g., crime prevention for the individual 362.88, household security 643

.6   **Penology**

Including amnesty, pardon; corporal punishment, fines; parole, probation

Class here welfare services to offenders, reform of penal system

Class welfare services to prisoners, reform of penal institutions in 365

For discharged offenders, see 364.8; for institutions for correction of offenders, see 365

.66   Capital punishment

.8   **Discharged offenders**

.9   **Historical, geographic, persons treatment of crime and its alleviation**

Add to base number 364.9 notation 1–9 from Table 2, e.g., persons associated with crime and its alleviation 364.92; however, for victims, see 362.88; for police, see 363.2; for criminologists, see 364.092; for offenders associated with specific kinds of crime, see 364.1; for comprehensive works on offenders, see 364.3; for penologists, see 364.6

365 Penal and related institutions

Institutions for correction of offenders and for incarceration of other groups considered socially undesirable

Standard subdivisions are added for penal and related institutions together, for penal institutions alone

Including concentration camps, jails, military prisons, penal colonies, penitentiaries, prerelease guidance centers, prison farms, reformatories, work camps; institutions for specific classes of inmates, e.g., criminally insane persons, juveniles, political prisoners

Including discipline, security; prison labor; reform of penal institutions

Class here imprisonment and detention

Class institutions for prisoners of war in 355.7; class parole, probation, indeterminate and suspended sentence, reform of penal system in 364.6; class prison architecture in 725. Class penal colonies as a part of history of a place with the place in 930–990, e.g., penal colony of Botany Bay as founding settlement of New South Wales 994.4

> *For concentration camps associated with a specific war, see the war, e.g., World War II concentration camps 940.53*

.068 Management

Do not use for management of plant and equipment; class in 365

[.09] Historical, geographic, persons treatment

Do not use; class in 365

366 Associations

Organizations formed for fraternizing or for mutual assistance

Including Benevolent and Protective Order of Elks, Freemasonry, Independent Order of Odd Fellows, Knights of Pythias

> *For general clubs, see 367; for miscellaneous kinds of associations, see 369; for orders of knighthood, see 929.7. For associations dealing with a specific subject, see the subject, plus notation 06 from Table 1, e.g., mathematical associations 510.6*

> *See also 200 for religious associations, 368.36 for fraternal insurance*

.001–.009 Standard subdivisions

367 General clubs

Including social clubs, study clubs

Class here social clubs for specific types of people, e.g., social clubs for actors

Class clubs dealing with a specific subject with the subject, plus notation 06 from Table 1, e.g., chess clubs 794.106

[.09]   Historical, geographic, persons treatment

Do not use; class in 367

368   Insurance

Including actuarial science, claims, underwriting; conventional comprehensive sales grouping, e.g., automobile, aviation, business, real property insurance

Class here risk, insurance industry

Class risk management as a part of management in 658.15. Class a single line with the line, e.g., business liability insurance 368.8

See Manual at 368 vs. 658.15

.001   Philosophy and theory

Do not use for mathematical principles; class in 368

.002–.005   Standard subdivisions

.006   Organizations and management

Including insurance companies

For credit and loan functions of insurance companies, see 332.3

.007–.008   Standard subdivisions

.009   Historical, geographic, persons treatment

[.009 4–.009 9]   Treatment by specific continents, countries, localities in modern world

Do not use; class in 368

.1   Insurance against damage to and loss of property

Standard subdivisions are added for either or both topics in heading

Including civil commotion, disaster, fire, riot, war risk insurance

Class war risk life insurance in 368.36. Class property damage (liability) insurance as part of a specific type of liability insurance with the type, e.g., property damage insurance as part of public liability 368.5

For insurance against damage to and loss of property in transit, see 368.2; for casualty insurance, see 368.5–368.8

.100 1–.100 9   Standard subdivisions

.2   Insurance against damage to and loss of property in transit (Marine insurance, Transportation insurance)

Class here insurance against damage to and loss of instrumentalities of transportation, e.g., trucks

Class a combination of transportation property insurance and transportation liability insurance in 368

.200 1–.200 9   Standard subdivisions

.3 **Old-age insurance and insurance against death, illness, injury**

Including annuities

Class here comprehensive works on private and government-sponsored old-age insurance and insurance against death, illness, injury; comprehensive works on group insurance, on industrial insurance, on old-age and survivors' insurance, on survivors' insurance

Class personnel management of insurance as a fringe benefit in 658.3; class comprehensive works on insurance as a fringe benefit in 331.25

> *For government-sponsored insurance, see 368.4. For a specific type of group insurance, of industrial insurance, of old-age and survivors' insurance, of survivors' insurance not provided for here, see the type, e.g., group credit insurance 368.8*

.300 1–.300 9 Standard subdivisions

.32 Life insurance

> *For special fields of life insurance, see 368.36*

.320 01–.320 09 Standard subdivisions

.36 Special fields of life insurance

Including burial, fraternal, industrial life insurance; life insurance for members of armed services, e.g., war risk life insurance

.360 01–.360 09 Standard subdivisions

.38 Health insurance, accident insurance, disability income insurance

> *See Manual at 362.1 vs. 368.38*

.380 01–.380 09 Standard subdivisions

.4 **Government-sponsored insurance**

Including accident, health, maternity, old-age and survivors', unemployment, workers' compensation insurance; insurance against crimes of violence; social security in United States

Class here social insurance, social security as a form of social insurance

Class employers' liability insurance in 368.5; class comprehensive works on accident and health insurance in 368.3

> *For a type of government-sponsored insurance not provided for here, see the type, e.g., bank deposit insurance 368.8*
>
> *See also 362.10973 for United States' Medicaid health services*
>
> *See Manual at 336.249 vs. 368.4; also at 362 vs. 368.4*

.400 1–.400 9 Standard subdivisions

> **368.5–368.8 Insurance against casualties (Casualty insurance)**

Class comprehensive works in 368.5

.5 Liability insurance

Including automobile and aviation liability, malpractice insurance

Class here comprehensive works on casualty insurance

For glass insurance, see 368.6; for insurance against industrial casualties, see 368.7; for other casualty insurance, see 368.8

.500 1–.500 9   Standard subdivisions

.6 Glass insurance

.600 1–.600 9   Standard subdivisions

.7 Insurance against industrial casualties (accidents)

.700 1–.700 9   Standard subdivisions

.8 Other casualty insurance

Including business liability, strike insurance; burglary, robbery, theft insurance; bonds; investment guarantees; bank deposit, credit, mortgage, title insurance

Use of this number for comprehensive works on business insurance discontinued; class in 368

369 Miscellaneous kinds of associations

Including hereditary, military, patriotic societies; nationality clubs

.4 Young people's societies

Class a specific aspect of young people's societies with the aspect, e.g., Boy Scout camps 796.54

.42 Boys' societies

For Boy Scouts, see 369.43

.43 Boy Scouts

Including Cub Scouts, Explorers

.46 Girls' societies

For Explorers, see 369.43; for Camp Fire, see 369.47

.463 Girl Scouts and Girl Guides

.47 Camp Fire

.5 Service clubs

Including Lions International, Rotary International

370   Education

Class here basic education, public education

Unless other instructions are given, observe the following table of preference, e.g., special education at elementary level 371.9 (*not* 372):

Public policy issues in education	379
Special education	371.9
Specific levels of education	372–374
Higher education	378
Schools and their activities (*except* 371.9)	371
Education for specific objectives	370.11
Curricula	375
Standard subdivisions, educational psychology (*except* 370.11)	370.1–370.9

Class special education in a specific subject in 371.9; class elementary education in a specific subject in 372.3–372.8. Class comprehensive works on education in a specific subject and on secondary, higher, and adult education in a specific subject with the subject, plus notation 071 from Table 1, e.g., mathematics education 510.71

SUMMARY

370.1–.9	Standard subdivisions, education for specific objectives, educational psychology
371	Schools and their activities; special education
372	Elementary education
373	Secondary education
374	Adult education
375	Curricula
378	Higher education
379	Public policy issues in education

.1   **Philosophy and theory, education for specific objectives, educational psychology**

Including philosophical foundations, e.g., idealism, realism, pragmatism

.11 Education for specific objectives

Including fundamental education (preparation of educationally disadvantaged students for participation in community life) [*formerly* 370.19]; compensatory education [*formerly* 371.96]; humanistic education; moral, ethical, character education; vocational education, vocational schools, occupational training; education for creativity, for effective use of leisure, for social responsibility

Class here curricula directed toward specific educational objectives [*formerly* 375]

Class on-the-job training, vocational training provided by industry in 331.25; class fundamental education of adults in 374; class moral, ethical, character training of children at home in 649

For vocational education at secondary level, see 373.246; for adult vocational education, see 374

See also 306.43 for sociology of education, 331.7 for choice of vocation, 371.4 for vocational guidance in schools

.116 Education for international understanding [*formerly* 370.19]

Including exchange of students, of teachers

Class here educational exchanges, foreign study

Class grants for student exchanges in 371.2

.117 Multicultural (Intercultural) education [*formerly* 370.19] and bilingual education [*formerly* 371.97]

Multicultural education: programs to promote mutual understanding among cultures

Standard subdivisions are added for multicultural education and bilingual education together, for multicultural education alone

.15 Educational psychology

Including behavior modification, creativity and imagination, learning, memory, problem solving

Class here psychology of teaching [*formerly* 371.1]

Psychology of learning specific subjects relocated to specific subject, plus notation 01 from Table 1, e.g., psychology of learning mathematics 510.1

Class behavior modification methods of instruction in 371.39; class interdisciplinary works on psychology in 150. Class psychology of a specific topic in education with the topic, plus notation 01 from Table 1, e.g., psychology of adult education 374.001

See also 370.11 for education to promote creativity

See Manual at 153.1 vs. 370.15

[.19]   Sociology of education

Sociology of education relocated to 306.43; fundamental education relocated to 370.11; education for international understanding relocated to 370.116; multicultural (intercultural) education relocated to 370.117; comparative education relocated to 370.9; community-school relations, e.g., parent-teacher associations, relocated to 371.19; educational equalization (equal education opportunity), affirmative action, right to education, school desegregation, busing to achieve desegregation relocated to 379.2

.28   Auxiliary techniques and procedures [*formerly also* 371.20028]

Do not use for testing and measurement; class in 371.26

Apparatus, equipment, materials, maintenance and repair relocated to 371.6

[.68]   Management

Do not use; class in 371.2

.7   Education, research, related topics

Class here education, research, related topics in teaching [*formerly also* 371.1]

Education of school administrators relocated to 371.20071, education of elementary school teachers relocated to 372.071; education of secondary school teachers relocated to 373.071; education of college and university teachers relocated to 378.0071

.71   Education

Including in-service training of teachers [*formerly* 371.1]

Class here practice teaching

.8   History and description with respect to kinds of persons

Do not use for students; class in 371.8. Do not use for education of a specific kind of student; class in 371.82, e.g., education of ethnic minorities 371.829

.82   Women in education

Do not use for education of women; class in 371.822

.9   Historical, geographical, persons treatment

Class here comparative education [*formerly* 370.19]

371 Schools and their activities; special education

Standard subdivisions are added for schools and their activities, special education together; for schools and their activities together; for schools alone

Class here school systems, school policy

Class auxiliary techniques and procedures in 370.28; class schools and their activities in elementary, secondary, and adult levels in 372–374; class schools and their activities in higher education in 378; class public policy issues in education in 379

> *For curricula, see 375*

> *See Manual at 371 vs. 353.8, 371.2, 379; also at 371 vs. 372–374, 378*

SUMMARY

371.009	**Historical, geographic, persons treatment**
.01–.07	**Specific kinds of schools**
.1	**Teachers and teaching, and related activities**
.2	**School administration; administration of student academic activities**
.3	**Methods of instruction and study**
.4	**Student guidance and counseling**
.5	**Student discipline and related activities**
.6	**Physical plant; materials management**
.7	**Student welfare**
.8	**Students**
.9	**Special education**

[.001–.008]   Standard subdivisions

> Do not use; class in 371

.009   Historical, geographic, persons treatment

.009 4–.009 9   Treatment by specific continents, countries, localities in modern world

> Class here specific all-age schools and school systems

> 371.01–371.07 Specific kinds of schools

Class here specific kinds of school systems; types of education characteristic of specific kinds of schools other than public and community schools

Class comprehensive works in 371. Class a specific kind of school defined by characteristics of student body with the kind in 371.82, e.g., schools for ethnic minorities 371.829

.01   Public schools

> Class public education in 370; class public community schools in 371.03; class public alternative schools in 371.04; class public policy issues concerning public schools in 379

.02   Private schools

Class here publicly supported private schools, schools not under government control

Class private community schools in 371.03; class private alternative schools in 371.04; class public policy issues in private education in 379.3

For religious schools, see 371.07

.03   Community schools

.04   Alternative schools

Including home schools and home schooling [*formerly* 649]

Class here experimental schools, free schools

See also 371.39 for home instruction by visiting teachers

.07   Religious schools [*formerly* 377]

Class religious education to encourage belief and to promote religious life and practice in 291.7

.071   Christian religious schools

Class Christian education to encourage belief and to promote religious life and practice in 268

.072–.079   Other religious schools

Add to base number 371.07 the numbers following 29 in 292–299, e.g., Jewish day schools 371.076

>   **371.1–371.8 Schools and their activities**

Class schools and their activities in special education in 371.9; class public policy issues relating to schools and their activities taken as a whole in 379; class comprehensive works in 371

For specific kinds of schools, see 371.01–371.07

See Manual at 371 vs. 372–374, 378

.1   **Teachers and teaching, and related activities**

Standard subdivisions are added for a combination of two or more topics in heading, for teachers alone

Including academic freedom, tenure; performance contracting; teacher participation in management

Interdisciplinary works on relations of teachers and society relocated to 306.43; psychology of teaching relocated to 370.15; education, research, related topics of teaching relocated to 370.7; in-service training of teachers relocated to 370.71

.100 1–.100 6	Standard subdivisions
.100 7	Education, research, related topics
[.100 71]	Education of teachers

                        Do not use; class in 370.71

| .100 8–.100 9 | Standard subdivisions |

.102   **Teaching**

Including classroom management, classroom discipline

Class here mentoring

Class evaluation of teachers, substitute teaching, team teaching in 371.14; class classroom techniques of instruction in 371.3; class comprehensive works on school discipline in 371.5

For practice teaching, see 370.71; for methods of instruction, see 371.3

.102 01   Philosophy and theory

                Do not use for psychology of teaching; class in 370.15

[.102 07]   Education, research, related topics in teaching

                Do not use; class in 370.7

.103   **Teacher-parent conferences**

One-on-one teacher-parent relations

Class comprehensive works on teacher-parent relations in 371.19

.12   **Professional qualifications of teachers**

Class here teacher certification [*formerly* 379.1]

.14   **Organization of teaching force**

Including differentiated staffing, substitute teaching, team teaching, teacher turnover, teacher workload, use of teacher aides (teachers' assistants); accountability, evaluation, probation of teachers

Class teacher participation in management in 371.1

See also 371.1 for performance contracting, 379.1 for overall school accountability

.19   Community-school relations [*formerly* 370.19]

> Including teacher-community relations, industry-school relations, parent-school relations, parent-teacher associations

> Class here community involvement in schools, community-school partnerships, school involvement in community

> Class interdisciplinary works on relations of schools and society, teachers and society in 306.43

> *For teacher-parent conferences, see 371.103*

> *See also 370.11 for vocational education, 371.2 for student employment in connection with ongoing academic work*

.2   **School administration; administration of student academic activities**

> Standard subdivisions are added for either or both topics in heading

> Including truancy [*formerly also* 371.5]; tuition, financial administration of public schools [*formerly* 379.1]; personnel management, school staff; admission, credits, entrance requirements, school enrollment; grouping students for instruction; promotion and failure, e.g. underachievers; schedules, school day, school year; student aid, e.g., scholarships, student employment; cooperative education, apprenticeship programs, work-study plan; student mobility, e.g., dropouts, graduation; school attendance

> School standards and accreditation relocated to 379.1

> Class methods of instruction in 371.3; class student participation in administration in 371.5; class apprenticeship programs without school sponsorship, interdisciplinary works on apprenticeship in 331.25. Class management of a specific function with the function in 371, plus notation 068 from Table 1, e.g., management of student welfare 371.7068

> *For teachers, see 371.1; for educational and vocational guidance, see 371.4; for plant management, materials management, see 371.6; for school boards, see 379.1*

> *See Manual at 371 vs. 353.8, 371.2, 379*

.200 1   Philosophy and theory

.200 2   Miscellany

[.200 28]   Auxiliary techniques and procedures; apparatus, equipment, materials

> Auxiliary techniques and procedures relocated to 370.28; apparatus, equipment, materials, maintenance and repair relocated to 371.6

.200 3–.200 5   Standard subdivisions

.200 6   Organizations

[.200 68]   Management

> Do not use; class in 371.2

.200 7   Education, research, related topics

.200 71   Education

Including education of school administrators [*formerly* 370.7]

.200 8   History and description with respect to kinds of persons

.200 9   Historical, geographic, persons treatment

.200 92   Persons

Class here collected persons treatment of school administrators and persons treatment of specific administrators not associated with a specific level of education or school

Class persons treatment of school administrators best known as leaders in education in 370.92; class persons treatment of administrators best known as leaders in elementary education in 372.92; class persons treatment of administrators best known as leaders of adult education in 374. Class persons treatment of administrators best known as leaders at a specific level of education other than elementary and adult limited to a specific area or school in the geographic notation for the area or school under the specific level, e.g., a biography of a president of University of California at Berkeley 378.794

.26   Examinations and tests; academic prognosis and placement

Standard subdivisions are added for examinations and tests, academic prognosis and placement together; for examinations alone; for tests alone

Including accreditation of prior learning (APL), advanced placement, standardized tests, test construction, test-taking skills

Class use of examinations and tests in guidance in 371.4; class interdisciplinary works on aptitude and intelligence tests in 153.9. Class standardized tests for a specific subject in elementary school with the subject in 372.3–372.8, plus notation 076 from Table 1, e.g., mathematics tests for elementary school 372.7076; class standardized tests for a specific subject in secondary or higher level with the subject in 001–999, plus notation 076 from Table 1, e.g., mathematics tests for secondary school 510.76

For classroom and school examinations and tests, see 371.27

.260 1   Philosophy and theory

Including test bias; validity and reliability of tests, of standardized tests

Class validity and reliability of specific kinds of standardized tests in 371.26

.27   Classroom and school examinations and tests; marking systems

Classroom and school examinations and tests: tests devised by individual teacher or school

.3   Methods of instruction and study

Including laboratory method, field trips; project methods (that emphasize student direction of group projects), e.g., group work; recitation and discussion; correspondence courses, teleconferencing, use of textbooks, comprehensive works on distance education

Class here classroom techniques, creative activities, seatwork

Class distance education by computer, radio, television; laboratory methods with electronic and visual materials and equipment in 371.33; class group teaching (in which class is divided into groups but activity is still directed by teacher) in 371.39; class public control of textbooks in 379.1; class classroom management, comprehensive works on teaching in 371.102. Class methods of instruction in a specific subject at elementary level with the subject in 372.3–372.8, e.g., methods of teaching mathematics in elementary school 372.7; class methods of instruction in a specific subject at secondary or higher level with the subject in 001–999, plus notation 071 from Table 1, e.g., methods of teaching mathematics in secondary schools 510.71; class textbooks on a specific subject with the subject in 001–999, e.g., textbooks on mathematics 510

.302 8   Auxiliary techniques and procedures; techniques of study, lesson plans

Do not use for apparatus, equipment, materials; class in 371.33

Including techniques of study for parents [*formerly* 649], book reports, homework, note taking, report writing, study skills

Use of this number for classroom techniques discontinued; class in 371.3

[.302 85]   Data processing   Computer applications

Do not use; class in 371.33

[.307 8]   Use of apparatus, equipment, materials for study and teaching

Do not use; class in 371.33

Teaching aids, equipment, materials relocated to 371.33

.33   Teaching aids, equipment, materials [*formerly* 371.3078]

Including audiovisual materials, bulletin boards, computers, educational games and toys, radio, television, videoconferencing

Class here educational media, educational technology

Class instructional materials centers in 027.7; class school resource centers in 028.8; class use of textbooks in 371.3; class public control of teaching materials in 379.1. Class teaching aids, equipment, materials used in a specific method of instruction with the method, e.g., materials used in Montessori method 371.39

For computer modeling and simulation, see 371.39

.39 Other methods of instruction

Limited to behavior modification; gaming and simulation, computer modeling and simulation; group teaching (in which class is divided into groups, but activity is still directed by teacher); home instruction by visiting teachers; lecture method; Montessori method; use of drama (theater); monitorial system of education; Morrison plan; rote learning; Waldorf method of education; individualized instruction, e.g., honors work, independent study, open classroom instruction, programmed instruction, tutoring

Class use of behavior modification in classroom discipline in 371.102; class grouping of students for open classroom instruction in 371.2; class group work that emphasizes student direction of group projects in 371.3; class comprehensive works on instructional use of computers in 371.33; class Montessori method in elementary education in 372.139

For electronic programmed instruction, see 371.33

.4 **Student guidance and counseling**

Standard subdivisions are added for either or both topics in heading

Including educational and vocational guidance; peer counseling (counseling by other students); personal counseling (counseling of students with emotional, personal, social problems by staff other than psychologists and medical personnel)

Class here student personnel services, services of deans of students

Class student welfare programs in 371.7; class interdisciplinary works on vocational guidance in 331.7. Class vocational guidance in a specific occupation with the occupation, plus notation 023 from Table 1, e.g., guidance in law 340.023

For a specific student personnel service not provided for here, see the service, e.g., student employment 371.2

.5 **School discipline and related activities**

Standard subdivisions are added for school discipline and related activities together, for school discipline alone

Including student expulsion, probation, suspension; student government, student participation in administration, student monitors

Truancy relocated to 371.2

Class comprehensive works on crime, delinquency, violence in schools in 371.7

For classroom discipline, see 371.102

.6   Physical plant; materials management

Standard subdivisions are added for physical plant and materials management together, for physical plant alone

Including apparatus, equipment, materials, maintenance and repair [*all formerly also* 370.28, 371.20028]; classrooms, laboratories

Class here plant management, educational buildings, school facilities

Instructional facilities for teaching a specific subject relocated to the subject, e.g., physical education facilities 796.06; facilities for specific noninstructional objective relocated to the objective within 370, e.g., dormitories 371.8

See also 727 for architecture of educational buildings

.602 8   Auxiliary techniques and procedures

Do not use for maintenance and repair; class in 371.6

Use of this number for apparatus, equipment, materials discontinued; class in 371.6

.7   Student welfare [*formerly also* 371.8]

Including food services, e.g., school cafeterias, school lunch programs; student health programs; programs related to crime, substance abuse, delinquency, violence; sex hygiene and related programs

Class here school social services

School safety programs relocated to 363.11

Class campus police in 363.28; class crime, substance abuse, delinquency, violence as school discipline problems in 371.5; class interdisciplinary works on victims of crime in 362.88; class interdisciplinary works on crime prevention in 364.4

For a specific provision for student welfare not provided for here, see the provision, e.g., personal counseling 371.4, student housing 371.8

.8 Students

Including student competitions; student housing and transportation; student journalism; student movements, activism, protest; student organizations, e.g., Greek-letter societies

Class here extracurricular activities, student life

Student welfare relocated to 371.7; intramural sports relocated to 796.04; Greek-letter societies, other student organizations in specific fields relocated to the specific field, plus notation 06 from Table 1, e.g., student literary societies 806

Class interdisciplinary student journals in 050; class busing for school integration in 379.2. Class a student journal on a specific subject with the subject, plus notation 05 from Table 1, e.g., a journal on student life and extracurricular activities 371.805, a student literary journal 805; class a specific competition with the competition, plus notation 079 from Table 1, e.g., a photographic competition 770.79; class student movements to achieve a specific objective with the objective, e.g., movements to achieve electoral reform 324.6

> *For a specific aspect of students not provided for here, see the aspect, e.g., student discipline 371.5*

.801 Philosophy and theory

Including student psychology

Class educational psychology in 370.15

.805 Serial publications

Limited to serials about students, student life, extracurricular activities

Class student journalism in 371.8

.806 Organizations and management

Do not use for student organizations; class in 371.8

[.808] History and description with respect to kinds of students

Do not use; class in 371.82

.82 Specific kinds of students; schools for specific kinds of students

Class here comprehensive works on education of specific kinds of students

Add to base number 371.82 the numbers following —08 in notation 081–089 from Table 1, e.g., education of women 371.822 [*formerly* 376], education of students by social and economic characteristics 371.826 [*formerly* 371.96], education of students by racial, ethnic, national origin 371.829 [*formerly* 371.97]; however, for students who are the focus of special education, see 371.9

> *For a specific aspect of education of specific kinds of students, see the aspect, e.g., counseling for women students 371.4082*

.9   **Special education**

Including mainstreaming, programs in specific subjects, special education by level

Class here exceptional students, learning disabilities, underachievers in special education; schools and school activities pertaining to special education

Except for modifications shown under specific entries, add to each subdivision identified by * as follows:

     028   Auxiliary techniques and procedures
                     Do not use for apparatus, equipment, materials, maintenance and repair; class in base number
     068   Management
                     Do not use for plant management; class in base number

Unless other instructions are given, observe the following table of preference, e.g., emotionally-disturbed deaf retarded students 371.92 (*not* 371.91 or 371.94):

Gifted students	371.95
Students with mental disabilities	371.92
Students with emotional disturbances	371.94
Students with physical disabilities	371.91
Delinquent and problem students	371.93

Public policy issues relating to special education as a whole relocated to 379

Class mainstreaming, programs in specific subjects, special education by level for specific group in 371.91–371.95

.902 8   Auxiliary techniques and procedures

Do not use for apparatus, equipment, materials, maintenance and repair; class in 371.9

.906 8   Management

Do not use for plant management; class in 371.9

.908   History and description with respect to kinds of persons

Do not use for kinds of students requiring special education; class in 371.9

.91   Students with physical disabilities

Including blindness and visual impairments; hearing impairments; linguistic disorders, e.g., reading disorders; mobility impairments; general works on brain damage

Class students with a specific disorder caused by brain damage with the disorder, e.g., students with emotional disturbances caused by brain damage 371.94

See also 372.43 for remedial reading in elementary education

.92   Students with mental disabilities

Including students with learning disabilities, mental retardation; slow learners

Class here students with developmental disabilities

.93   *Delinquent and problem students

Standard subdivisions are added for either or both topics in heading

Not suffering severe emotional disturbances

Including disruptive, hyperactive, maladjusted students

Class delinquent and problem students suffering severe emotional disturbances in 371.94

.94   *Students with emotional disturbances

Including autistic students

Class here students with mental illness

> For delinquent and problem students not suffering severe emotional disturbances, see 371.93

.95   *Gifted students

[.96]   Students by social and economic characteristics

Compensatory education relocated to 370.11; education of students by social and economic characteristics relocated to 371.826

[.97]   Students by racial, ethnic, national origin

Bilingual education relocated to 370.117; education of students by racial, ethnic, national origin relocated to 371.829

> ## 372–374   Specific levels of education

Public policy issues relating to a specific level of education taken as a whole relocated to 379

Unless other instructions are given, class works treating two sublevels of education that are not subdivisions of the same number with the higher level, e.g., kindergarten and first grade 372.24 (*not* 372.21)

Class special education at any level in 371.9; class comprehensive works on education and works dealing comprehensively with elementary and secondary education, with secondary and higher education in 370; class comprehensive works on schools in 371

> For higher education, see 378

> See Manual at 371 vs. 372–374, 378

*Add standard subdivisions as instructed under 371.9

372   Elementary education

Class here elementary schools, grade schools, grammar schools (United States), junior schools (United Kingdom), primary schools (United Kingdom); lower sections of all-age schools

For adult elementary education, see 374

SUMMARY

372.01–.08	**Standard subdivisions, elementary education for specific objectives**
.1	**Organization and activities in elementary education**
.2	**Specific levels of elementary education**
.3	**Computers, science, technology, health**
.4	**Reading**
.5	**Creative and manual arts**
.6	**Language arts (Communication skills)**
.7	**Mathematics**
.8	**Other studies**
.9	**Historical, geographic, persons treatment of elementary education**

.01   Philosophy and theory; elementary education for specific objectives

Including curricula directed toward specific educational objectives

.02   Miscellany

.028   Auxiliary techniques and procedures

Testing and measurement relocated to 372.126, apparatus, equipment, materials relocated to 372.16

.06   Organizations

[.068]   Management

Do not use; class in 372.12

.07   Education, research, related topics

.071   Education

Including education of elementary school teachers [*formerly* 370.7]

.08   History and description with respect to kinds of persons

Do not use for students; class in 372.18. Do not use for education of a specific kind of student; class in 372.182, e.g., education of ethnic minorities 372.1829

[.09]   Historical, geographic, persons treatment

Do not use; class in 372.9

.1   **Organization and activities in elementary education**

Use of this number for comprehensive works on organization and activities in elementary education discontinued; class in 372

For elementary education for specific objectives, see 372.01; for specific levels of elementary education, see 372.2

[.101–.108]   Standard subdivisions

Do not use; class in 372.01–372.08

[.109]   Historical, geographic, persons treatment

Do not use; class in 372.9

.11–.18   School organization and activities in elementary education

Add to base number 372.1 the numbers following 371 in 371.1–371.8, e.g., testing and measurement 372.126 [*formerly also* 372.028], apparatus, equipment, materials 372.16 [*formerly also* 372.028]; however, for use of drama as a method of instruction, see 372.66

.19   Elementary education in subject areas

Class here curricula

For elementary education in a specific subject, see 372.3–372.8

.2   **Specific levels of elementary education**

Class specific topics of education at a specific level in 372.1; class specific schools at a specific level in 372.9

[.201–.208]   Standard subdivisions

Do not use; class in 372.01–372.08

[.209]   Historical, geographical, persons treatment

Do not use; class in 372.9

.21   Preschool education

Including kindergarten, nursery school

Class here early childhood education, head start programs, preschool education in day-care centers

Class preschool education by parents in the home as part of child-rearing in 649

.24   Specific levels of elementary school

Including primary grades (1–3), infant schools (United Kingdom), primary schools (United States); intermediate grades (4–6)

Class elementary education covering grades 1–4, junior schools (United Kingdom) in 372; class middle schools (grades 5–8), junior high schools in 373.236

See Manual at 372.24 and 373.23

[.240 1–.240 8]   Standard subdivisions

                       Do not use; class in 372.01–372.08

[.240 9]   Historical, geographic, persons treatment

                       Do not use; class in 372.9

> ### 372.3–372.8   Elementary education in specific subjects

Class comprehensive works in 372.19

(Option: Class here elementary textbooks; prefer the subject in 001–999, e.g., elementary textbooks on arithmetic 513)

.3   Computers, science, technology, health

Including environmental studies, nature study, nutrition, sex education

Class family life education in 372.82

> *For mathematics, see 372.7; for home economics, see 372.82; for physical education, see 372.86*

.4   Reading

Class here reading instruction in home schools [*formerly* 649]

Unless other instructions are given, class a subject with aspects in two or more subdivisions of 372.4 in the number coming last, e.g., vocabulary building by phonetic methods 372.46 (*not* 372.44)

.402 8   Auxiliary techniques and procedures, apparatus and equipment

             Materials relocated to 372.41; testing and measurement relocated to 372.48

.41   Instructional materials [*formerly* 372.4028], reading readiness, methods of instruction and study

             Including individualized, small-group, whole-class reading instruction

             See also 372.45 for independent reading

             (Option: Including readers; prefer language in 420–490, plus notation 86 from Table 4, e.g., English language readers 428.6)
             (If this number is used for readers, class readers on a specific subject with the subject in elementary education, e.g., science readers 372.3)

.42   Reading motivation

             Including school-based library reading programs, Reading is Fundamental

.43   Remedial reading

             Including reading failure

             Class reading difficulties treated in special education in 371.91

.44   Vocabulary development

.45   Reading-skill strategies

Including independent reading, oral reading, speed reading

For word-attack strategies, see 372.46; for reading comprehension strategies, see 372.47

.46   Word-attack (Decoding) strategies

Including part-word (phonetic) methods, phonetics in elementary education; whole-word (sight) methods, word-recognition method

Class pronunciation in a specific communication skill with the skill, e.g., pronunciation in speech 372.62

.47   Reading comprehension strategies

Including cognitive strategies, e.g., critical thinking; reading in content areas; strategies using standardized materials, e.g., SQ3R; whole language approach

Class a strategy using standardized materials in a specific subject with the subject in 372.3–372.8, e.g., use of SQ3R in social studies 372.83

.48   Evaluation of reading skills

Including diagnostic testing, standardized testing

Class here testing and measurement [*formerly* 372.4028]

Class evaluation of reading readiness in 372.41

.5   **Creative and manual arts**

Standard subdivisions are added for either or both topics in heading

Including design, drawing, handicrafts, modeling, painting, sculpture, sewing

For literature, see 372.64; for theater, see 372.66; for dance, see 372.86

.6   **Language arts (Communication skills)**

Class here literacy education

Dance relocated to 372.86

For reading, see 372.4

.61   Grammar

Including language usage, word study

.62   Written and spoken expression

Including speech, e.g., pronunciation; composition, comprehensive works on written expression

Class here whole-language approach

Class oral presentations other than public speaking in 372.66

For whole-language approach in reading, see 372.47; for spelling and handwriting, see 372.63

See also 372.46 for phonetic methods of reading instruction, 372.66 for drama

.63   Spelling and handwriting (penmanship)

.64   Literature appreciation

Storytelling relocated to 372.67

Class plays taught as theater in 372.66

.65   Foreign languages and bilingual instruction

Standard subdivisions are added for foreign languages and bilingual instruction together, for foreign languages alone

Add to base number 372.65 the numbers following 4 in 420–490 for language only, e.g., Spanish 372.656, English as a second language 372.652

Class comprehensive works on bilingual education in 370.11

.66   Drama (Theater)

Class here school plays, comprehensive works on oral presentations

Class plays taught as literature in 372.64

For public speaking, see 372.62; for other oral presentations, see 372.67. For use of drama as a method of instruction in a specific subject in elementary education, see the subject in 372.3–372.8, e.g., use of drama in teaching history 371.89

.67   Other oral presentations

Other than drama and public speaking

Including storytelling [*formerly* 372.64], choral speaking, media production and presentation, puppet theater, puppetry, readers' theater

Class here activities related to oral presentation

Class media production of drama in 372.66; class interdisciplinary works on puppetry in 791.5

.69   Listening

.7   **Mathematics**

Including arithmetic

.8   **Other studies**

[.801–.809]   Standard subdivisions

Do not use; class in 372.1901–372.1909

.82   Home economics

Class here family life education, family living

For sewing, see 372.5

.83   Social studies

Including civics (citizenship)

Class family life education in 372.82

For environmental studies, see 372.3; for history and geography, see 372.89

.84   Religion

Class religious education of children under church auspices to inculcate Christian faith and practice in 268; class religious education of children under auspices of other religious bodies to inculcate religious faith and practice in 291.7

.86   Dance [*formerly* 372.6] and physical education

Standard subdivisions are added for dance and physical education together, for physical education alone

Including movement education

.87   Music

See also 372.86 for dance

.89   History and geography

Standard subdivisions are added for history and geography together, for history alone

Class here civilization

.9   **Historical, geographic, persons treatment of elementary education**

Class here specific schools and school systems

Add to base number 372.9 notation 1–9 from Table 2, e.g., elementary education in Brazil 372.981

373   Secondary education

Class here upper sections of all-age schools

Class secondary education in a specific subject with the subject, plus notation 071 from Table 1, e.g., secondary education in agriculture 630.71

.01 **Philosophy and theory, secondary education for specific objectives**

Including curricula directed toward specific educational objectives

For vocational education, see 373.246

.02 **Miscellany**

.028 **Auxiliary techniques and procedures**

Testing and measurement relocated to 373.126, apparatus, equipment, materials relocated to 373.16

.06 **Organizations**

[.068] **Management**

Do not use; class in 373.12

.07 **Education, research, related topics**

.071 **Education**

Including education of secondary school teachers [*formerly* 370.7]

.08 **History and description with respect to kinds of persons**

Do not use for students; class in 373.18. Do not use for schools and education for a specific kind of student; class in 373.182, e.g., secondary schools for ethnic minorities 373.1829

.082 **Women in secondary education**

Do not use for secondary education of young women; class in 373.18235

.09 **Historical, geographic, persons treatment**

[.093–.099] **Treatment by specific continents, countries, localities**

Do not use; class in 373.3–373.9

.1 Organization and activities in secondary education

Use of this number for comprehensive works on organization and activities in secondary education discontinued; class in 373

For secondary education for specific educational objectives, see 373.01; for schools and programs of specific kinds, levels, curricula, focus, see 373.2

[.101–.109] **Standard subdivisions**

Do not use; class in 373.01–373.09

.11–.18 **School organization and activities in secondary education**

Add to base number 373.1 the numbers following 371 in 371.1–371.8, e.g., testing and measurement 373.126 [*formerly also* 373.028], apparatus, equipment materials 373.16 [*formerly also* 373.028]; however, for cooperative education, see 373.2

.19 Curricula

Class curricula directed toward specific secondary educational objectives in 373.01; class education in secondary schools identified by specific types of curricula in 373.2. Class curricula in a specific subject with the subject in 001–999, plus notation 071 from Table 1, e.g., ethnic studies curricula 305.80071

.2 **Secondary schools and programs of specific kinds, levels, curricula, focus**

Including comprehensive secondary schools (schools offering academic, vocational, general programs when considered distinct from undifferentiated secondary schools); general secondary schools (schools offering nonvocational, general terminal education when considered distinct from undifferentiated secondary schools); private secondary schools (preparatory schools); apprenticeship programs, cooperative education, work-study plan; comprehensive works on boarding schools

Class here types of education (other than public education in general) provided by schools and programs of a specific kind, level, curricula, focus

Class a specific topic relating to schools and programs of a specific kind, level, curriculum, focus in 373.11–373.18; class a specific school regardless of kind, level, curriculum, focus in 373.3–373.9; class continuation schools, folk high schools in 374; class apprenticeship programs offered by industry in 331.25; class apprenticeship training as part of personnel management in 658.3; class comprehensive works on sixth-form colleges in 378.1

For a specific kind of boarding school (other than private secondary schools), see the kind, e.g., private elementary boarding schools 372.1, military boarding schools 373.24

[.201–.209] Standard subdivisions

Do not use; class in 373.01–373.09

.23 Specific levels of secondary education

Class private schools, comprehensive secondary schools, general secondary schools regardless of level in 373.2; class academic, military, vocational schools regardless of level in 373.24; class comprehensive works on levels of secondary schools, four-year high schools not of a specific type in 373

See Manual at 372.24 and 373.23

[.230 1–.230 9] Standard subdivisions

Do not use; class in 373.01–373.09

.236 Lower level

Including grades above 6 in elementary schools, forms above the equivalent level in junior schools (United Kingdom)

Class here junior high schools, middle schools

For lower grades of middle schools, see 372.24

.238   Upper level

Including high school equivalency programs

Class here senior high schools; high school postgraduate programs; lower years of four-year and three-year junior colleges, sixth form colleges

Class comprehensive works on sixth-form colleges in 378.1

.24   Academic, military, vocational schools

Military schools: secondary schools offering professional military education but remaining basically academic in nature

Including classical schools (schools emphasizing Latin and Greek), gymnasiums (Europe), lycées, modern academic schools, modern grammar schools (United Kingdom), comprehensive works on magnet schools

Class private modern academic schools in 373.2; class schools concentrating on professional military education in 355.0071

For a specific type of magnet school other than modern academic schools, see the type, e.g., magnet elementary schools 372.1, magnet schools for science 507.1, magnet schools for arts 700.71

.246   Vocational schools

Class here technical high schools, vocational education

Class comprehensive works on vocational education in 370.11

.3–.9   **Secondary education in specific continents, countries, localities**

Class here specific schools, school systems

Add to base number 373 notation 3–9 from Table 2, e.g., secondary schools of Australia 373.94

374   **Adult education**

Including adult basic education, fundamental education, literacy programs, study groups; distance education, correspondence schools, open learning

Class here continuing, further, lifelong, permanent, recurrent education

Class on-the-job training in 331.25; class adult high school equivalency programs in 373.238. Class adult education in a specific subject with the subject, plus notation 071 from Table 1, e.g., sculpture courses for adults 730.71

For alternative colleges and universities as agencies for adult education, see 378; for university extension services as agencies for adult education, see 378.1

.001   Philosophy and theory

.002   Miscellany

.002 8   Auxiliary techniques and procedures

                                    Use of this number for apparatus, equipment, materials, testing and measurement discontinued; class in 374

.003–.005   Standard subdivisions

.006   Organizations

[.006 8]   Management

                                    Do not use; class in 374

.007   Education, research, related topics

.008   History and description with respect to kinds of persons

                                    Do not use for students, education of specific kinds of students; class in 374

[.009]   Historical, geographic, persons treatment

                                    Do not use; class in 374

375   Curricula

Curricula directed toward specific educational objectives relocated to 370.11; curricula for specific subject objectives, comprehensive works on curricula and courses in specific subjects relocated to specific subjects in 001–999, plus notation 071 from Table 1, e.g., history curricula 907.1

Class curricula of a specific subject at elementary level in 372.3–372.8. Class curricula for a specific level with the level, e.g., secondary-school curricula 373.19; class curricula of a specific subject for a specific level other than elementary level and for more than one level with the subject, plus notation 071 from Table 1, e.g., curricula for health 613.071

.000 1–.000 9   Standard subdivisions

[376]   Education of women

Relocated to 371.822

[377]   Schools and religion

Religious schools relocated to 371.07; place of religion in public schools relocated to 379.2

378   Higher education

Including professional education; specific kinds of colleges and universities, e.g., private, state, church-related colleges

Class here college education, university education; universities

Class four-year colleges in 378.1. Class higher education in a specific subject with the subject, plus notation 071 from Table 1, e.g., medical schools 610.71

See Manual at 371 vs. 372–374, 378; also at 378 vs. 355.0071

.001	Philosophy and theory
.002	Miscellany
.002 8	Auxiliary techniques and procedures

> Apparatus, equipment, materials, testing and measurement relocated to 378.1

.003–.005	Standard subdivisions
.006	Organizations
[.006 8]	Management

> Do not use; class in 378.1

.007	Education, research, related topics
.007 1	Education

> Class here education of college and university teachers [*formerly* 370.7]

.008	History and description with respect to kinds of persons

> Do not use for students, higher education of specific kinds of students; class in 378.1

.009	Historical, geographic, persons treatment
.009 2	Persons

> Class here administrators

> Class persons associated with specific colleges and universities in 378.4–378.9

[.009 4–.099]	Treatment by specific continents, countries, localities in modern world

> Do not use; class in 378.4–378.9

.1 Organization and activities in higher education

Including apparatus, equipment, materials, testing and measurement [*formerly also* 378.0028]; academic freedom, sabbatical leave, tenure; college entrance examinations; financial management, tuition; specific levels of higher education, e.g., junior colleges, four-year colleges, graduate schools;

Class higher education for specific objectives; specific kinds of colleges and universities, e.g., private, state, church-related universities in 378; class specific institutions in 378.4–378.9

> *For academic degrees and related topics, see 378.2; for student aid and related topics, see 378.3*

[.100 1–.100 9]	Standard subdivisions

> Do not use; class in 378.001–378.009

.2 **Academic degrees and related topics**

Standard subdivisions are added for academic degrees and related topics together, for academic degrees alone

Including academic costume; requirements for earned degrees, e.g., dissertations; honorary degrees

.3 **Student aid and related topics**

Standard subdivisions are added for student aid and related topics, for student aid alone

Including veterans' higher education benefits [*formerly also* 362.86]; student employment, e.g., work-study programs; cooperative education, e.g., work-study plan

Class student aid in a specific field with the field, plus notation 079 from Table 1, e.g., student aid in medical education 610.79

.4–.9 **Higher education in specific continents, countries, localities in modern world**

Class here specific schools

Add to base number 378 notation 4–9 from Table 2, e.g., higher education in Mexico 378.72

Class a school or department of a college or university devoted to a specific subject with the subject, plus notation 071 from Table 1, e.g., Harvard Law School 340.071

379 Public policy issues in education

Class here public policy issues relating to special education as a whole [*formerly also* 371.9]; public policy issues relating to specific levels of education as a whole [*formerly also* 372–374]

Class public administration of education in 353.8; class school administration in 371.2

For public policy issues on a topic not provided for here, see the topic, e.g., policy on school admissions 371.2, on medical schools 610.71

See Manual at 371 vs. 353.8, 371.2, 379

[.094–.099] Treatment by specific continents, countries, localities in modern world

Do not use; class in 379.4–379.9

.1 **Specific elements of support and control of public education**

Including support of public education; support by specific levels of government and international support; support of specific levels of education and special education; financial support, e.g., educational vouchers; school choice; revenue sources

Including school standards and accreditation [*formerly also* 371.2]; control of public education; control by specific levels of government, e.g., school boards and districts; control of specific levels of education and special education; control of curriculum; control of teachers and administrators; control of teaching materials, e.g., textbooks; school accountability and evaluation; school centralization and consolidation

Use of this number for comprehensive works on support and control of public education discontinued; class in 379

Teacher certification relocated to 371.12, tuition, financial administration of public schools relocated to 371.2

Class support and control of activities involved in specific policy issues in 379.2

For use of educational vouchers in private education, see 379.3

[.101–.109] Standard subdivisions

Do not use; class in 379.01–379.09

.2 **Specific policy issues in public education**

Not otherwise provided for

Including place of religion in public schools [*formerly* 377], e.g., teaching creationism; compulsory education, school-leaving age; literacy policies, right to read

Including educational equalization (equal education opportunity), affirmative action, right to education; school desegregation, busing to achieve desegregation [*all formerly* 370.19]

Use of this number for comprehensive works on public education and state discontinued; class in 379

[.201–.209] Standard subdivisions

Do not use; class in 379.01–379.09

.3 **Public policy issues in private education**

Including public support, financial support, educational vouchers; public control

.4–.9 **Public policy issues in specific continents, countries, localities in modern world**

Add to base number 379 notation 4–9 from Table 2, e.g., public educational policies in United States 379.73

380   Commerce, communications, transportation

Except for modifications shown under specific entries, add to each subdivision identified by * as follows:

06   Organization and management
           Including business organizations, e.g., individual proprietorships, partnerships, companies, public and private corporations, combinations
           See Manual at 380: Add table: 09 vs. 06

068   Management
           Public and private

09   Historical, geographic, persons treatment
           Class specific business organizations in 06
           See Manual at 380: Add table: 09 vs. 06

Class public regulation and control in 354.7

See Manual at 380

SUMMARY

380.01–.09	**Standard subdivisions**
.1	**Commerce (Trade)**
381	**Internal commerce (Domestic trade)**
382	**International commerce (Foreign trade)**
383	**Postal communication**
384	**Communications Telecommunication**
385	**Railroad transportation**
386	**Inland waterway and ferry transportation**
387	**Water, air, space transportation**
388	**Transportation Ground transportation**
389	**Metrology and standardization**

.01–.09   Standard subdivisions

.1   *Commerce (Trade)*

Including commercial policy

Class here warehousing, interdisciplinary works on marketing

Class supply and demand in 338.1–338.5; class restrictive practices in business organizations engaged in commerce in 338.8; class comprehensive works on warehousing in 388; class interdisciplinary works on consumption in 339.4. Class cooperative, labor, finance, land, energy economics in relation to commerce with the branch of economics in 330, e.g., cooperative marketing 334

For internal commerce, see 381; for international commerce, see 382; for management of marketing, see 658.8

See Manual at 380.1 and 381, 382; also at 380.1 vs. 658.8; also at 709.2 vs. 380.1

*Add as instructed under 380

.102 9   Commercial miscellany

> Do not use for evaluation and purchasing manuals; class in 381.3
>
> Class here interdisciplinary works on commercial miscellany
>
> *For commercial miscellany respecting specific goods and services, see the goods and services, plus notation 029 from Table 1, e.g., buyers' guides for tools 621.90029*
>
> *See Manual at 338 vs. 060, 381, 382, 670.29, 910, T1—025, T1—029*

> ## 381–382   Internal and international commerce (trade)

Class here marketing

Class supply and demand in 338.1–338.5; class comprehensive works in 380.1. Class cooperative, labor, finance, land, energy economics in relation to internal and international commerce with the branch of economics in 330, e.g., cooperative marketing 334

381   *Internal commerce (Domestic trade)

Including interregional and interstate commerce; retail trade, e.g., chain stores, garage sales; wholesale trade

See Manual at 338 vs. 060, 381, 382, 670.29, 910, T1—025, T1—029; also at 380.1 and 381, 382; also at 381 vs. 658.8

.029   Commercial miscellany

> Do not use for evaluation and purchasing manuals; class in 381.3

.3   **Commercial policy**

Including consumer protection, comprehensive works on evaluation of commodities to be purchased, interdisciplinary evaluation and purchasing manuals

Class here consumer problems and their alleviation, consumerism

Class product hazards in 363.19; class fraud in 364.16; class commercial policy with respect to specific kinds of domestic trade, to specific commodities and services, to specific groups of commodities and services in 381

> *For evaluation and purchasing guides and consumer education for household and personal products and services, see 640.73. For evaluation and purchasing manuals for a specific product or service, see the product or service, plus notation 029 from Table 1, e.g., manual on evaluating tools 621.90029*

*Add as instructed under 380

382   *International commerce (Foreign trade)

Including import and export trade

Including balance of trade, commercial and tariff policy, customs and duties, import quotas; embargoes on, licensing of imports; export controls and restrictions, e.g., licensing, inspection; export policy, e.g., subsidies; trade agreements, e.g., European Union (European Common Market, Economic Community), World Trade Organization

Class here trade between nations and their colonies, protectorates, trusts

Class tax aspects of custom duties in 336.2; class interdisciplinary works on international finance in 332; class interdisciplinary works on international economics in 337

See Manual at 338 vs. 060, 381, 382, 670.29, 910, T1—025, T1—029; also at 380.1 and 381, 382

.01   Philosophy and theory

Do not use for theories; class in 382

> ## 383–388   Communications and transportation

Class comprehensive works on communications in 384; class comprehensive works on communications and transportation together, on transportation alone in 388

383   Postal communication

Class collection and delivery of mail within the military services in 355.6; class comprehensive works on communications in 384

See also 769.56 for philately

.06   Organizations and management

Do not use for postal organizations; class in 383

[.09]   Historical, geographic, persons treatment

Do not use; class in 383

*Add as instructed under 380

384   *Communications   Telecommunication

Including motion pictures

Class here interdisciplinary works on telecommunication [*formerly also* 004.6]

Class comprehensive works on communications and transportation in 388

> For postal communication, see 383
>
> See also 302.2 for sociology of communication
>
> See Manual at 384 vs. 791.4

.1   *Telegraphy

Including Morse and other code telegraphy; printing telegraphy; facsimile transmission; stock tickers, teletype, telex

Class here submarine cable telegraphy

Class comprehensive works on electronic mail in 384.3

> For radiotelegraphy, see 384.5

.102 8   Auxiliary techniques and procedures, materials

Do not use for apparatus and equipment; class in 384.1

.3   *Computer communication

Transfer of computer-based information by any of various media (e.g., coaxial cable or radio waves) from one computer to another or between computers and terminals

Including electronic bulletin boards, teletex; videotex, e.g., teletext, viewdata; comprehensive works on electronic mail

Class here computer communications networks; links between computers via telephone lines

Class interdisciplinary works on computer communications in 004.6; class interdisciplinary works on electronic mail in 004.692

> For a specific kind of electronic mail, see the kind, e.g., telex 384.1
>
> See Manual at 004.6 vs. 384.3; also at 004.6 vs. 025.04, 384.3

.302 85   Data processing   Computer applications

Class here computer science applied to economic and related aspects of providing computer communication to the public

.5   *Wireless communication

Including radiotelegraphy, satellite communication; radiotelephony, e.g., citizens band radio, portable telephones

> For a specific form of satellite communication, see the form, e.g., television transmission by satellite 384.55

---

*Add as instructed under 380

.54   *Radiobroadcasting

Class here public (noncommercial) broadcasting, public aspects of amateur radio, interdisciplinary works on radiobroadcasting and television broadcasting

Class techniques of producing radio programs in 791.44. Class a specific type of program with the type, e.g., news broadcasts 070.1

For television broadcasting, see 384.55

See Manual at 384 vs. 791.4

.55   *Television

Including general broadcasting (free television), community antenna television (CATV) systems; cable, closed-circuit, public (noncommercial) television; pay television, e.g., premium (subscription) television; video cassette recorders (VCRs), videotapes

Class techniques of producing television programs in 791.45. Class a specific type of television program with the type, e.g., news broadcasts 070.1

See Manual at 384 vs. 791.4

.6   **Telephony**

Class here comprehensive works on wire and cable communication

For telegraphy, see 384.1; for radiotelephony, portable telephones, see 384.5; for cable television, see 384.55

385   *Railroad transportation

Including interurban, monorail, ship railroads; unitized cargo transportation, e.g., piggyback operations

Class here standard-gage and broad-gage railroads

Class comprehensive works on transportation, on ground transportation in 388

For railroad mail, see 383; for container-ship operations, see 387.5; for local rail transit systems, see 388.4

See Manual at 629.04 vs. 388

.3   **Stationary facilities**

Including stations, tunnels, yards

Class use of stationary facilities in specific activities and services in 385

[.301–.309]   Standard subdivisions

Do not use; class in 385.3

*Add as instructed under 380

.5 ***Narrow-gage and industrial railroads**

386 ***Inland waterway and ferry transportation**

Including transportation via rivers, canals, lakes; ports

Class comprehensive works on water transportation in 387; class comprehensive works on transportation in 388

See Manual at 386 vs. 387.1; also at 629.04 vs. 388

387 **Water, air, space transportation**

Class here comprehensive works on water transportation

Class comprehensive works on transportation in 388

For inland waterway and ferry transportation, see 386

.001–.009 Standard subdivisions of water transportation

Notation from Table 1 as modified under 380, e.g., water transportation business organizations 387.006

.1 **Ports**

Including navigational aids, e.g., lighthouses

For inland ports, see 386

See Manual at 386 vs. 387.1

.2 **Ships**

Class use of ships in inland waterway transportation in 386; class use of ships in specific activities and services in 387.5

See Manual at 629.04 vs. 388

.5 ***Ocean (Marine) transportation**

Including coastwise and intercoastal routes, salvage

For sea mail, see 383; for seaports, see 387.1; for ships, see 387.2

See Manual at 629.04 vs. 388

.7 ***Air transportation**

Including airports

See Manual at 629.04 vs. 388; also at 629.136 vs. 387.7

.8 ***Space transportation**

See Manual at 629.04 vs. 388

*Add as instructed under 380

388   *Transportation   Ground transportation

Including mass transportation, passenger and freight services, comprehensive works on warehousing

Class here comprehensive works on communications and transportation, interdisciplinary works on transportation

Class services designed to facilitate the use of transportation by persons with disabilities in 362.4; class services designed to facilitate the use of transportation by older persons in 362.6. Class mass transportation, passenger and freight services in relation to a kind of ground transportation with the kind in 388.1–388.4, e.g., subways 388.4

For transportation safety and safety measures, see 363.12; for transportation security, see 363.2; for commerce aspects of warehousing, see 380.1; for postal transportation, see 383; for communications, see 384; for railroad transportation, see 385; for water, air, space transportation, see 387; for transportation technology, see 629.04

See also 385 for railroads combined with other transportation systems

See Manual at 629.04 vs. 388

.1   *Roads

Including bicycle and pedestrian paths

Class here highways

For highway services and use, see 388.3; for urban roads, see 388.4

.3   *Vehicular transportation

Including traffic flow and maintenance, e.g., lighting, traffic control, traffic signs; vehicular activities and services; vehicles, e.g., automobiles, buses, motorcycles, off-road vehicles, snowmobiles, stagecoaches, trucks, wagons; stations, stops, terminals; comprehensive works on air-cushion vehicles

Class urban vehicular transportation in 388.4

For traffic control by police, see 363.2; for air-cushion ships for inland waterways, see 386; for air-cushion ships for ocean transportation, see 387.2

See Manual at 629.04 vs. 388

*Add as instructed under 380

.4   ***Local transportation**

Including vehicular and pedestrian traffic; urban roads and streets, bicycle paths, sidewalks; services of automobiles, buses, trucks; local rail transit systems, e.g., subways, tramways; stations, stops, terminals and their services; interdisciplinary works on parking

Class here urban and suburban transportation, rapid transit, mass transit, commuter services

Class vehicles in 388.3

For traffic control by police, see 363.2. For a specific aspect of parking, see the aspect, e.g., city planning for parking facilities 711

See also 385 for interurban railways

.5   ***Pipeline transportation**

389   Metrology and standardization

Metrology: social use of systems of measurement

Including metric system; time systems and standards, e.g., daylight saving time

Class interdisciplinary works on chronology in 529; class interdisciplinary works on measurement in 530.8

390   Customs, etiquette, folklore

Class here folkways

For customs of military life, see 355.1

SUMMARY

390.001–.009	**Standard subdivisions**
.01–.09	**Standard subdivisions of customs**
391	**Costume and personal appearance**
392	**Customs of life cycle and domestic life**
393	**Death customs**
394	**General customs**
395	**Etiquette (Manners)**
398	**Folklore**
399	**Customs of war and diplomacy**

.001–.009   Standard subdivisions

.01–.07   Standard subdivisions of customs

.08   History and description of customs with respect to kinds of persons

.086   Persons by miscellaneous social characteristics

Do not use for persons by social and economic levels; class in 390

*Add as instructed under 380

.088   Religious groups

> Do not use for occupational groups; class in 390

.09   Historical, geographic, persons treatment of customs

> ## 391–394   Customs

Class comprehensive works on customs, customs of specific economic, social, occupational classes in 390

For customs of war and diplomacy, see 399

391   Costume and personal appearance

Standard subdivisions are added for costume and personal appearance together, for costume alone

Class here interdisciplinary works on costume, clothing, fashion

Class costumes and clothing associated with a specific occasion with the occasion in 392–394, e.g., wedding apparel 392.5

For fashion design, see 746.9. For a specific aspect of costume and clothing, see the aspect, e.g., military uniforms 355.1, clothing construction 646.4, stage costuming 792

See Manual at 391 vs. 646, 746.9

.001–.007   Standard subdivisions

.008   History and description with respect to kinds of persons

[.008 1–.008 4]   Sex and age groups

> Do not use; class in 391

.008 6   Persons by miscellaneous social characteristics

> Do not use for persons by social and economic levels; class in 391

.008 8   Religious groups

> Do not use for occupational groups; class in 391

.009   Historical, geographic, persons treatment

.4   Auxiliary garments and accessories

Including hats, gloves, hosiery, masks, shoes; purses, umbrellas

For jewelry, see 391.7

.5   Hair styles

Including beards, wigs

.6 **Personal appearance**

Including body contours, personal cleanliness and hygiene, tattooing, use of cosmetics and perfume

For hair styles, see 391.5

.7 **Jewelry**

Class here interdisciplinary works on jewelry

For making jewelry, see 739.27

392 Customs of life cycle and domestic life

For death customs, see 393

.1 **Customs of birth, puberty, majority**

Including child rearing, name giving

.3 **Customs relating to dwelling places and domestic arts**

Including cooking, furnishings

Class comprehensive works on food and meals in 394.1

.4 **Courtship and engagement customs**

.5 **Wedding and marriage customs**

See also 395.2 for etiquette of weddings

.6 **Customs of the relations between sexes**

Including chaperonage

For courtship and engagement customs, see 392.4; for wedding and marriage customs, see 392.5

393 Death customs

Including burial, mourning

394 General customs

Including games, dances; coronations, inaugurations; pageants, processions, parades; fairs, customs of chivalry, dueling, suicide

Class pageants, processions, parades associated with a specific activity with the activity, e.g., Thanksgiving Day parade 394.2649

See also 355.1 for military ceremonies

See Manual at 394 vs. 791.6

.1   **Eating, drinking; using drugs**

> Situations and methods of use, prohibited uses
>
> Including drinking of alcoholic beverages; specific meals, e.g., tea
>
> Class here food and meals
>
> *For cooking, see 392.3*

.2   **Special occasions**

> Including birthdays
>
> Class official ceremonies, pageants, parades, processions in 394

.25   Carnivals

> Including Mardi Gras

.26   Holidays

> Class here festivals; independence days; patriotic, seasonal, secular holidays
>
> Class a season associated with the holiday with the holiday, e.g., the Christmas season 394.2663; class the technology or craft associated with holidays with the technology or craft, e.g., making fireworks 662, decorating Easter eggs 745.594
>
> *For Mardi Gras, see 394.25*

[.260 9]   Historical, geographic, persons treatment

> Do not use; class in 394.269

\>   394.261–394.264   Secular holidays

> Class here patriotic, seasonal holidays
>
> Class religious holidays of a specific season in 394.265; class comprehensive works in 394.26

.261   Holidays of December, January, February

> Class here wintertime holidays of the northern hemisphere, summertime holidays of the southern hemisphere

.261 4   New Year

.261 8   Valentine's Day

.262   Holidays of March, April, May

> Including Mother's Day
>
> Class here springtime holidays of the northern hemisphere, autumn holidays of the southern hemisphere

.262 7   May Day

.263 Holidays of June, July, August

Class here summertime holidays of the northern hemisphere, wintertime holidays of the southern hemisphere

.263 4 Fourth of July

.263 5 Bastille Day

.264 Holidays of September, October, November

Class here autumn holidays of the northern hemisphere, springtime holidays of the southern hemisphere

.264 4 Oktoberfest

.264 6 Halloween

.264 9 Thanksgiving

.265 Religious holidays

Class secular holidays with a religious or quasi-religious origin in 394.261–394.264

For Christian holidays, see 394.266; for Jewish holidays, see 394.267

See Manual at 263, 291.3 vs. 394.265

.266 Christian holidays

Holidays of the church year

.266 3 Christmas

.266 7 Easter

.267 Jewish holidays

.269 Historical, geographic, persons treatment

Add to base number 394.269 notation 1–9 from Table 2, e.g., holidays of Mexico 394.26972

Class historical, geographic, persons treatment of specific holidays and of specific kinds of holidays in 394.261–394.267

395 Etiquette (Manners)

Prescriptive and practical works on social behavior

Class military etiquette in 355.1; class customs in 391–394

For protocol of diplomacy, see 327.2

[.081–.084] Etiquette with respect to sex and age groups

Do not use; class in 395.1

.1 Etiquette for age groups and sexes

Including children, young adults

.2   **Etiquette for stages in life cycle**

Including bar mitzvahs, funerals, weddings

.3   **Etiquette for social occasions**

Including dances

Class here hospitality and entertainment

Class etiquette for stages in life cycle in 395.2; class invitations in 395.4

.4   **Social correspondence**

Including invitations

Class here written and spoken styles and forms of address and greeting

.5   **Etiquette by situations**

Including business, school etiquette; conversation, e.g., telephone etiquette; table manners, tipping

398   Folklore

Including origin, role, function of themes and subjects of folklore and superstitions as cultural and social phenomena; chapbooks

See also 291.1 for religious mythology, 800 for literature by identifiable authors, anonymous literary classics

See Manual at 398, 398.27 vs. 615.8; also at 398.2 vs. 398

.09   Historical, geographic, persons treatment of folklore

For historical, geographic, persons treatment of folk literature, see 398.209

.2   **Folk literature**

Folklore as literature

Class here fairy tales, literary appraisal and criticism of folk literature, interdisciplinary works on mythology

For religious mythology, see 291.1; for minor forms of folk literature, see 398.6–398.9

See Manual at 398.2; also at 398.2 vs. 291.1; also at 398.2 vs. 398; also at 800 vs. 398.2

.209 3–.209 9   Treatment by specific continents, countries, localities

Class here collections of tales and lore on a specific topic from a specific continent, country, locality; individual tales and lore [*both formerly* 398.21–398.27]; collections of tales and lore from a specific continent, country, locality; works consisting equally of the tales and lore and criticism of them

Add to base number 398.209 notation 3–9 from Table 2, e.g., folk literature of France 398.20944; however, do not add notation from Table 1

Class comprehensive works on history and criticism of a specific topic, e.g., witches, in 398

(Option: Class collections of tales and lore on a specific topic from a specific continent, country, locality; individual tales and lore in 398.21–398.27)

\>   398.21–398.27   Tales and lore on a specific topic

Add to each subdivision identified by * as follows:
01–08   Standard subdivisions
09   Historical, geographical, persons treatment
           Class here literary criticism
           Class comprehensive works on history and criticism of a
           specific topic, e.g., witches, in 398
[093–099]   Collections of tales and lore from a specific continent, country,
           locality; individual tales and lore
              Relocated to 398.2093–398.2099
              (Option: Continue to use 093–099; prefer
              398.2093–398.2099)

Class comprehensive works in 398.2

.21   *Tales and lore of paranatural beings of human and semihuman form

Class here witches [*formerly* 398.22], centaurs, fairies, gods and goddesses, mermaids, vampires, wizards

Use of this number for comprehensive works on fairy tales (tales of paranatural beings) discontinued; class in 398.2

For werewolves, see 398.24; for ghosts, see 398.25

.22   *Tales and lore of legendary or mythological persons

Persons without paranormal powers

Class here heroes, kings, ordinary persons

Witches relocated to 398.21, comprehensive works on historical and quasi-historical events relocated to 398.27

*Add as instructed under 398.21–398.27

.23   *Tales and lore of places and times

Class historical and quasi-historical events in 398.27

See also 398.209 for tales originating in specific places

.24   *Tales and lore of plants and animals

Real and legendary

See Manual at 800 vs. 398.24, 590, 636

.25   *Ghost stories

.26   *Tales and lore involving physical phenomena

Real and legendary

Class here fire, heavenly bodies, minerals, water, weather

.27   *Tales and lore of everyday human life

Class here comprehensive works on historical and quasi-historical events [*formerly* 398.22]; birth, love, marriage, death; occupations, recreation; dwellings, food

See Manual at 398, 398.27 vs. 615.8

>   **398.6–398.9   Minor forms of folk literature**

Class here literary appraisal and criticism

Class comprehensive works in 398.2

.6   **Riddles**

Class here interdisciplinary works

For riddles as amusements, see 793.735; for riddles as literature, see 808.88

.8   **Rhymes and rhyming games**

Including counting-out and jump rope rhymes, lullabies, street cries and songs, tongue twisters

Class here nursery rhymes

.9   **Proverbs**

Class here folk aphorisms

399   **Customs of war and diplomacy**

Including peace pipe

Class protocol of diplomacy in 327.2; class customs of military life in 355.1; class cannibalism in 394

*Add as instructed under 398.21–398.27

400

---

400 Language

Including bilingualism

Class here interdisciplinary works on language and literature

Class specific instances of bilingualism in 420–490 with the language dominant in the country in which the linguistic interaction occurs, without use of notation 01–09 from Table 1, e.g., a discussion of Spanish-English bilingualism in the United States 420

> *For literature, see 800; for rhetoric, see 808. For the language of a specific discipline or subject, see the discipline or subject, plus notation 01 from Table 1, e.g., language of science 501*
>
> *See also 306.44 for sociology of bilingualism*
>
> *See Manual at 400 vs. 800; also at T1—01 vs. T4—86*

SUMMARY

401–409	Standard subdivisions
410	Linguistics
420	English and Old English (Anglo-Saxon)
430	Germanic (Teutonic) languages German
440	Romance languages French
450	Italian, Sardinian, Dalmatian, Romanian, Rhaeto-Romanic languages
460	Spanish and Portuguese languages
470	Italic languages Latin
480	Hellenic languages Classical Greek
490	Other languages

401 Philosophy and theory

Including content analysis; general discussions of international languages, universal languages; language acquisition, psycholinguistics, pragmatics in psycholinguistics; semantics, semiotics; lexicology, interdisciplinary works on terminology

Class sociolinguistics, pragmatics in sociolinguistics, sociology of language in 306.44; class psychology of bilingualism in 400; class artificial languages in 499; class interdisciplinary works on semiotics in 302.2. Class a specific international language with the language in 420–490, e.g., Latin as a diplomatic language 470; class a semiotic study of a specific subject or discipline with the subject or discipline, plus notation 01 from Table 1, e.g., a semiotic study of science 501

> *For dictionaries of linguistics, see 410.3; for history of word meanings, see 412; for general polyglot dictionaries, see 413; for applied linguistics treatment of terminology, see 418. For terminology of a specific subject or discipline, see the subject or discipline, plus notation 01 from Table 1, e.g., terminology of accounting 657.01*

> *See also 121 for semantics and semiotics as topics in philosophy, 149 for general semantics as a philosophical school*

> *See Manual at 407.1, T1—071 vs. 401, 410.71, 418.0071, T4—80071*

402 Miscellany

.85   Data processing   Computer applications

    Computational linguistics relocated to 410.285

403 Dictionaries, encyclopedias, concordances

Class here dictionaries, encyclopedias, concordances that treat comprehensively both language and literature

> *For dictionaries, encyclopedias, concordances of linguistics, see 410.3; for general polygot dictionaries, see 413; for dictionaries, encyclopedias, concordances of literature, see 803*

405–406 Standard subdivisions

407 Education, research, related topics

> *See Manual at 407.1, T1—071 vs. 401, 410.71, 418.0071, T4—80071*

408 Treatment of language with respect to kinds of persons

.9   **Treatment of language with respect to racial, ethnic, national groups**

    Class ethnolinguistics in 306.44089

409 Geographic and persons treatment

Do not use for language history not limited by area; class in 417

Class specific languages and groups of languages in 420–490

> *See also 410.9 for geographic and persons treatment of linguistics*

410   Linguistics

Science and structure of spoken and written language

Class here descriptive, synchronic linguistics; comprehensive works on Indo-European languages

Class linguistics of specific languages in 420–490

> *For sociolinguistics, see 306.44; for lexicology, semiotics, see 401; for specific Indo-European languages, see 420–491*
>
> *See Manual at 410*

.1   Philosophy and theory

Do not use for psycholinguistics, for philosophy and theory of language and languages; class in 401

Including schools and theories of linguistics

> *For works on schools and theories of linguistics that stress syntax, or syntax and phonology, see 415*

.2   Miscellany

Do not use for miscellany of language and languages; class in 402

.285   Data processing   Computer applications

> Class here computational linguistics [*formerly also* 402.85]
>
> *See Manual at 410.285 vs. 006.3*

.3–.9   Standard subdivisions

Do not use for standard subdivisions of language and languages; class in 403–409

> *See Manual at 407.1, T1—071 vs. 401, 410.71, 418.0071, T4—80071*

411   Writing systems

Including abbreviations, acronyms; alphabets, ideographs; braille; paleography (study of ancient and medieval handwriting)

Class paleography in the broad sense of all aspects of early writings in 417

412   Etymology

Class comprehensive works on historical linguistics in 417; class interdisciplinary works on onomastics in 929.9. Class a specific aspect of etymology with the aspect, e.g., phonetic development of words 414

413   Dictionaries

Including specialized dictionaries, e.g., dictionaries of abbreviations, picture dictionaries, thesauri (synonym dictionaries)

Class here polyglot dictionaries

.028   Techniques, procedures, apparatus, equipment, materials

Class here lexicography

414   Phonology and phonetics

Standard subdivisions are added for phonology and phonetics together, for phonology alone

Class comprehensive works on phonology and morphology, on phonology and syntax, or on all three in 415

415   Grammar

Descriptive study of morphology and syntax

Including generative grammar

Class here parts of speech; comprehensive works on phonology and morphology, on phonology and syntax, or on all three

Class derivational etymology in 412

> *For phonology, see 414; for prescriptive grammar, including inflectional schemata for use as aids in learning languages, see 418*

417   Dialectology and historical (diachronic) linguistics

Historical (diachronic) linguistics: study of the development of language over time

Including language history not limited by area, language change, paleography in the broad sense of all the aspects of early writings; pidgins and creoles

> *For change in and history of a specific element of language, see the element, e.g., grammar 415*

> *See also 409 for geographic treatment of language history, 410.9 for the history of linguistics*

> *See Manual at T4—7; also at 410*

418   Standard usage (Prescriptive linguistics)   Applied linguistics

Including interpretation, translation; listening; literacy, reading; multilingual phrase books; standard usage in composition

Class dictionaries in 413; class lexicography in 413.028

.001–.009   Standard subdivisions

> *See Manual at 407.1, T1—071 vs. 401, 410.71, 418.0071, T4—80071*

419   Structured verbal language other than spoken and written

Including finger spelling; specific sign languages, e.g., American Sign Language

Class here sign languages

Class nonlinguistic (nonstructured) communication in 302.2

> (

420–490 Specific languages

Class here comprehensive works on specific languages and their literatures

Except for modifications shown under specific entries, add to base number for each language identified by * notation 01–8 from Table 4, e.g., Portuguese grammar 469.5. The base number is the number given for the language unless the schedule specifies a different number

The numbers used in this schedule for individual languages do not necessarily correspond exactly with those in 810–890

Class comprehensive works in 410

> *For specific sign languages, see 419; for literatures of specific languages, see 810–890*

> *See Manual at 420–490*

> ## 420–491 Specific Indo-European languages

Class comprehensive works in 410

420 English and Old English (Anglo-Saxon)

> ### 420.1–428 Subdivisions of English language

Class here comprehensive works on English and Old English (Anglo-Saxon)

Except for modifications shown under specific entries, add to base number 42 notation 01–8 from Table 4, e.g., grammar of English language 425

Class comprehensive works in 420

> *For Old English (Anglo-Saxon), see 429*

421–425 Description and analysis of standard English

Numbers built according to instructions under 420.1–428

427 Historical and geographic variations, modern nongeographic variations

Number built according to instructions under 420.1–428

Including Middle English

For Old English (Anglo-Saxon), see 429

.001–.008   Standard subdivisions

.009	Historical, geographic, persons treatment

Do not use for historical and geographic variations; class in 427

428 Standard English usage (Prescriptive linguistics) Applied linguistics

Number built according to instructions under 420.1–428

Class here Basic English

429 Old English (Anglo-Saxon)

See also 427 for Middle English

430 Germanic (Teutonic) languages   German

For English and Old English (Anglo-Saxon), see 420

.01–.09	Standard subdivisions of Germanic (Teutonic) languages

---

> ### 430.1–438 Subdivisions of German language

Except for modifications shown under specific entries, add to base number 43 notation 01–8 from Table 4, e.g., grammar of German language 435

Class comprehensive works in 430

431–435 Description and analysis of standard German

Numbers built according to instructions under 430.1–438

437 Historical and geographic variations, modern nongeographic variations

Number built according to instructions under 430.1–438

Yiddish relocated to 439

Class Low German in 439

.001–.008	Standard subdivisions
.009	Historical, geographic, persons treatment

Do not use for historical and geographic variations; class in 437

438 Standard German usage (Prescriptive linguistics) Applied linguistics

Number built according to instructions under 430.1–438

439 Other Germanic (Teutonic) languages

Including Yiddish [*formerly* 437]; Low German; Scandinavian languages, e.g., Icelandic, Old Norse

Class Swedish in 439.7; class Danish and Norwegian in 439.8

.3 Netherlandish languages

Including Afrikaans

.31 Dutch

Class here Flemish

.7 *Swedish

.8 Danish and Norwegian

440 Romance languages   French

Class comprehensive works on Italic languages in 470

For Italian, Sardinian, Dalmatian, Romanian, Rhaeto-Romanic, see 450; for Spanish and Portuguese, see 460

.01–.09 Standard subdivisions of Romance languages

> ### 440.1–448 Subdivisions of French language

Except for modifications shown under specific entries, add to base number 44 notation 01–8 from Table 4, e.g., grammar of French language 445

Class comprehensive works in 440

441–445 Description and analysis of standard French

Numbers built according to instructions under 440.1–448

447 Historical and geographic variations, modern nongeographic variations

Number built according to instructions under 440.1–448

See also 449 for Provençal and Franco-Provençal

.001–.008 Standard subdivisions

.009 Historical, geographic, persons treatment

Do not use for historical and geographic variations; class in 447

448 Standard French usage (Prescriptive linguistics) Applied linguistics

Number built according to instructions under 440.1–448

---

*Add to base number as instructed under 420–490

449   Provençal (Langue d'oc), Franco-Provençal, Catalan

.001–.009   Standard subdivisions

450   Italian, Sardinian, Dalmatian, Romanian, Rhaeto-Romanic languages

Class Sardinian, Dalmatian in 457; class comprehensive works on Romance languages in 440; class comprehensive works on Italic languages in 470

.01–.09   Standard subdivisions

> **450.1–458 Subdivisions of Italian language**

Except for modifications shown under specific entries, add to base number 45 notation 01–8 from Table 4, e.g., grammar of Italian language 455

Class comprehensive works in 450

451–455 Description and analysis of standard Italian

Numbers built according to instructions under 450.1–458

457   Historical and geographic variations, modern nongeographic variations

Number built according to instructions under 450.1–458

Including Sardinian, Dalmatian

.001–.008   Standard subdivisions

.009   Historical, geographic, persons treatment

Do not use for historical and geographic variations; class in 457

458   Standard Italian usage (Prescriptive linguistics) Applied linguistics

Number built according to instructions under 450.1–458

459   Romanian and Rhaeto-Romanic

.001–.009   Standard subdivisions

460   Spanish and Portuguese languages

Class comprehensive works on Romance languages in 440

.01–.09   Standard subdivisions for comprehensive works on Spanish and Portuguese

> **460.1–468 Subdivisions of Spanish language**

Except for modifications shown under specific entries, add to base number 46 notation 01–8 from Table 4, e.g., grammar of Spanish language 465

Class comprehensive works in 460

461–465 Description and analysis of standard Spanish

Numbers built according to instructions under 460.1–468

467 Historical and geographic variations, modern nongeographic variations

Number built according to instructions under 460.1–468

Including Papiamento dialect

.001–.008	Standard subdivisions
.009	Historical, geographic, persons treatment

Do not use for historical and geographic variations; class in 467

468 Standard Spanish usage (Prescriptive linguistics) Applied linguistics

Number built according to instructions under 460.1–468

469 *Portuguese

.7 Historical and geographic variations, modern nongeographic variations

Number built according to instructions under 420–490

.700 1–.700 8	Standard subdivisions
.700 9	Historical, geographic, persons treatment

Do not use for historical and geographic variations; class in 469.7

470 Italic languages   Latin

Class comprehensive works on Latin and Greek in 480

For Romance languages, see 440

.01–.09   Standard subdivisions of Italic languages

---

*Add to base number as instructed under 420–490

> **470.1–478 Subdivisions of Latin language**

Except for modifications shown under specific entries, add to base number 47 notation 01–8 from Table 4, e.g., grammar of Latin language 475

Class comprehensive works in 470

471–475 Description and analysis of classical Latin

Numbers built according to instructions under 470.1–478

Class here classical revival (medieval and modern) Latin

477 Old (Preclassical), Postclassical, Vulgar Latin

Number built according to instructions under 470.1–478

478 Classical Latin usage (Prescriptive linguistics)   Applied linguistics

Number built according to instructions under 470.1–478

Class here classical-revival Latin usage during medieval or modern times

479 Other Italic languages

Including Osco-Umbrian languages

480 Hellenic languages   Classical Greek

Classical Greek: the Greek that flourished between 750 and 350 B.C.

Class here comprehensive works on classical (Greek and Latin) languages

For Latin, see 470

.01–.09   Standard subdivisions of classical languages

.1–.9   Standard subdivisions of Hellenic languages, of classical Greek

> **481–488 Subdivisions of classical, preclassical, postclassical Greek**

Except for modifications shown under specific entries, add to base number 48 notation 1–8 from Table 4, e.g., grammar of classical Greek language 485

Dialects of classical Greek are classed in the numbers for classical Greek (480.1–485, 488)

Class comprehensive works in 480

For standard subdivisions of classical Greek, see 480.1–480.9

481–485 Description and analysis of classical Greek

Numbers built according to instructions under 481–488

487 Preclassical and Postclassical Greek

Number built according to instructions under 481–488

Including Biblical, Byzantine Greek; Koine (Hellenistic Greek)

488 Classical Greek usage (Prescriptive linguistics)   Applied linguistics

Number built according to instructions under 481–488

489 Other Hellenic languages

Including modern Greek, e.g., Demotic and Katharevusa

490 Other languages

491 East Indo-European and Celtic languages

Including Albanian, Armenian; Baltic languages, e.g., Latvian, Lithuanian; Iranian languages, e.g., Pashto (Afghan), Persian; Sanskrit, middle Indic languages, comprehensive works on Indo-Aryan (Indic), Prakrit languages

Class modern Indic, modern Prakrit languages in 491.4

.4   Modern Indic languages

Including Bengali, Hindi, Gujarati, Marathi, Panjabi, Romany, Urdu

Class here modern Prakrit languages

Class comprehensive works on Prakrit languages in 491

.6   Celtic languages

Including Breton, Cornish, Irish and Scottish Gaelic, Welsh

.7   East Slavic languages   Russian

Including Belarusian, Ukrainian

Class comprehensive works on Slavic (Slavonic) languages in 491.8

.700 1–.700 9   Standard subdivisions of East Slavic languages

.701–.75   Standard subdivisions, writing systems, phonology, phonetics, etymology, dictionaries, grammar of Russian

Add to base number 491.7 notation 01–5 from Table 4, e.g., grammar of Russian 491.75

.77   Historical and geographic variations, modern nongeographic variations of Russian

All notes under notation 7 from Table 4 are applicable here

.770 01–.770 08   Standard subdivisions

.770 09   Historical, geographic, persons treatment

> Do not use for historical and geographic variations; class in 491.77

.78   Standard Russian usage (Prescriptive linguistics)   Applied linguistics

> Add to base number 491.78 the numbers following —8 in notation 8001–86 from Table 4, e.g., reading Russian 491.784

.8   **Slavic (Slavonic) languages**

> Including Bulgarian, Czech, Polish, Serbo-Croatian, Slovak, Slovenian
>
> Class here comprehensive works on Balto-Slavic languages
>
> Class Baltic languages in 491
>
> *For East Slavic languages, see 491.7*

492   Afro-Asiatic (Hamito-Semitic) languages   Semitic languages

> Including Aramaic, Ethiopian languages, South Arabian languages
>
> *For non-Semitic Afro-Asiatic languages, see 493*

.4   **Hebrew**

.7   **Arabic**

> Class here Classical Arabic
>
> Class South Arabian languages in 492

493   Non-Semitic Afro-Asiatic languages

> Including Berber languages; Chadic languages, e.g., Hausa; Cushitic languages, e.g., Oromo; Egyptian, Coptic; Omotic languages
>
> Including Egyptian hieroglyphics, Rosetta stone

494   Altaic, Uralic, Hyperborean, Dravidian languages

> Including Azerbaijani, Mongolian, Turkish, Uzbek; Estonian, Finnish, Hungarian, Sami

.8   **Dravidian languages**

> Including Kannada, Malayalam, Tamil, Telugu

495 Languages of East and Southeast Asia Sino-Tibetan languages

Including Burmese, Tibetan

Here are classed South Asian languages related to the languages of East and Southeast Asia

For Austronesian languages of East and Southeast Asia, see 499

.1 Chinese

Class here Mandarin (Putonghua) (standard written Chinese)

.6 Japanese

.7 Korean

.9 Miscellaneous languages of Southeast Asia; Munda languages

Limited to language families named here

Including Austroasiatic languages, e.g., Khmer (Cambodian), Vietnamese; Hmong-Mien languages, e.g., Hmong (Miao); Tai languages, e.g., Lao, Thai (Siamese)

496 African languages

Including Fulani, Ibo, Yoruba; Bantu languages, e.g., Swahili, Zulu

Class Afrikaans in 439.3; class Malagasy in 499. Class African creoles that have a non-African primary source language with the source language, plus notation 7 from Table 4, e.g., Krio 427

For Ethiopian languages, see 492; for non-Semitic Afro-Asiatic languages, see 493

497 North American native languages

Including Aleut, Inuit (Inuktitut), Maya, Nahuatl (Aztec)

Class here comprehensive works on North and South American native languages

For South American native languages, see 498

498 South American native languages

Including Guaraní, Quechua

499 Non-Austronesian languages of Oceania, Austronesian languages, miscellaneous languages

Miscellaneous languages limited to Basque, Elamite, Etruscan, Hurrian, Sumerian; Caucasian languages, e.g., Georgian; artificial languages, e.g., Esperanto

Including Australian languages; Malayo-Polynesian languages, e.g., Bahasa Indonesia, Bahasa Malaysia, Javanese, Malagasy, Maori, Tagalog (Filipino); Papuan languages

500

500   Natural sciences and mathematics

Natural sciences: sciences that deal with matter and energy, or with objects and processes observable in nature

Class here interdisciplinary works on natural and applied sciences

Class natural history in 508. Class scientific principles of a discipline or subject with the discipline or subject, plus notation 01 from Table 1, e.g., scientific principles of photography 770.1

> *For applied sciences, see 600*

> *See Manual at 231.7 vs. 213, 500, 576.8; also at 338.9 vs. 352.7, 500; also at 500 vs. 001; also at 500 vs. 600*

SUMMARY

500.2–.8	[Physical and space sciences, history and description with respect to kinds of persons]
501–509	Standard subdivisions and natural history
510	Mathematics
520	Astronomy and allied sciences
530	Physics
540	Chemistry and allied sciences
550	Earth sciences
560	Paleontology Paleozoology
570	Life sciences Biology
580	Plants
590	Animals

.2   **Physical sciences**

> *For astronomy and allied sciences, see 520; for physics, see 530; for chemistry and allied sciences, see 540; for earth sciences, see 550*

.5   **Space sciences**

> *For astronomy, see 520; for earth sciences in other worlds, see 550. For space science aspects of a specific subject, see the subject, plus notation 0919 from Table 1, e.g., physical chemistry in space 541.30919*

> *See Manual at 520 vs. 500.5, 523.1, 530.1, 919.9*

.8   **History and description with respect to kinds of persons**

Add to base number 500.8 the numbers following —08 in notation 081–089 from Table 1, e.g., women scientists 500.82

501 Philosophy and theory

Class scientific method as a general research technique in 001.4; class scientific method applied in natural sciences in 507

502 Miscellany

.8 Auxiliary techniques and procedures; apparatus, equipment, materials

Including interdisciplinary works on microscopes, microscopy

For manufacture of microscopes, see 681

503–506 Standard subdivisions

507 Education, research, related topics

Class research covering science in general, scientific method as a general research technique in 001.4

.8 Use of apparatus and equipment in study and teaching

Class here science fair projects, science projects in schools

508 Natural history

Do not use for the history and description of the natural sciences and mathematics with respect to groups of persons; class in 500.8

Class here description and surveys of phenomena in nature

Class natural history of organisms in 578

See Manual at 333.7–333.9 vs. 508, 913–919, 930–990; also at 578 vs. 304.2, 508, 910

.09 Historical and persons treatment

Do not use for geographic treatment; class in 508.3–508.9

.2 Seasons

Class here interdisciplinary works on seasons

For a specific aspect of seasons, see the aspect, e.g., effect of seasons on organisms 577.2

.3 Treatment by areas, regions, places in general; by specific continents, countries, localities in the ancient world

.31 Treatment by areas, regions, places in general

Add to base number 508.31 the numbers following — 1 in notation 11–19 from Table 2, e.g., natural history of the sea 508.3162

.33	Treatment by specific continents, countries, localities in the ancient world

Add to base number 508.33 the numbers following —3 in notation 31–39 from Table 2, e.g., natural history of ancient Greece 508.338

.4–.9   Treatment by specific continents, countries, localities in the modern world

Add to base number 508 notation 4–9 from Table 2, e.g., natural history of Brazil 508.81

509   Historical, geographic, persons treatment

Class historical, geographic, persons treatment of natural phenomena in 508

510   Mathematics

Class here finite mathematics

See Manual at 510; also at 005.1 vs. 510

.1   Philosophy and theory

Class mathematical logic in 511.3

511   General principles of mathematics

Including algorithms, approximations, combinatorial analysis, graph theory, mathematical models (mathematical simulation)

Class general principles applied to a specific branch of mathematics with the branch, e.g., mathematical models of probabilities 519.2

.3   Mathematical (Symbolic) logic

Including automata theory, Boolean algebra, formal languages, functions, machine theory, recursion theory, sequential machines, set theory, sets

See also 515 for theory of functions

512   Algebra, number theory

Standard subdivisions are added for algebra and number theory together, for algebra alone

Including groups, fields, rings; linear, multilinear, topological algebras

Class here universal algebra, modern algebra (abstract algebra combined with number theory)

Class foundations of algebra in 512.9

For arithmetic and algebra, see 513; for algebraic topology, see 514

.001–.009   Standard subdivisions

.9   Foundations of algebra

Including algebraic operations; theory of equations; matrices, determinants

.900 1–.900 9   Standard subdivisions

513   Arithmetic

.2   Arithmetic operations

Including addition, subtraction, multiplication, division; counting; fractions, percentage; exponents, logarithms; root extraction

.5   Numeration systems

Including binary (base 2), decimal (base 10), sexadecimal (hexadecimal, base 16) systems

514   Topology

Including global analysis in analysis and comprehensive works on global analysis [*formerly also* 515]; algebraic, differential topology; catastrophes; fractals

Class here analysis situs, mappings

For topological vector spaces, see 515

See also 512 for topological algebras

515   Analysis

Including differential and integral calculus and equations, functional analysis, sequences and series, topological vector spaces

Class here calculus, numerical analysis, comprehensive works on the theory of functions

Global analysis and comprehensive works on global analysis relocated to 514

Class differential topology in 514; class integral and differential geometry in 516.3; class probabilities in 519.2. Class theory of a specific function or group of functions with the function or group, e.g., functions in algebra 512

For topological algebras, see 512; for applied numerical analysis, see 519.4

516   Geometry

Including affine, descriptive, projective geometries; geometric shapes

Class here geometry combined with topology

Class geometric probability in 519.2

For topology, see 514

.001–.009   Standard subdivisions

.2   Euclidean geometry

Including famous geometry problems, e.g., trisecting an angle, squaring the circle

Class a specific type of Euclidean geometry with the type, e.g., Euclidean analytic geometry 516.3

.200 1–.200 9   Standard subdivisions

.22   Plane geometry

       Including Pythagorean theorem

.23   Solid geometry

.24   Trigonometry

.3   **Analytic geometries**

       Including algebraic, differential, integral geometry; analytic trigonometry

.9   **Non-Euclidean geometries**

       Class a specific type of non-Euclidean geometry with the type, e.g., non-Euclidean analytic geometries 516.3

519   Probabilities and applied mathematics

       Class a specific application with the application, e.g., game theory in gambling 795.01

.2   **Probabilities**

       Including probabilistic processes, e.g., Markov processes; random (stochastic) processes; Monte Carlo method, random walks

       Class here games of chance, geometric probability

       Class probabilities applied to statistical mathematics in 519.5

       See Manual at 795.01 vs. 519.2

.3   **Game theory**

       Class here mathematical optimization

       Class control theory in 515; class games of chance in 519.2

       For a specific mathematical optimization technique, see the technique, e.g., mathematical programming 519.7

.4   **Applied numerical analysis**

.5   **Statistical mathematics**

       Including mean, median, mode; measures of deviation; multivariate analysis; analysis of variance and covariance; regression analysis; statistical inference, e.g., decision theory, hypothesis testing; theory of sampling; time-series analysis

       Class obtaining, arranging, interpreting statistical data in 001.4

.7   **Programming**

       Including linear and nonlinear programming

.700 1–.700 9   Standard subdivisions

.8 **Special topics**

Including quality control, queuing

520 Astronomy and allied sciences

See Manual at 520 vs. 500.5, 523.1, 530.1, 919.9; also at 520 vs. 523.1, 523.8

SUMMARY

520.1–.9	**Standard subdivisions**
521	**Celestial mechanics**
522	**Techniques, procedures, apparatus, equipment, materials**
523	**Specific celestial bodies and phenomena**
525	**Earth (Astronomical geography)**
526	**Mathematical geography**
527	**Celestial navigation**
528	**Ephemerides**
529	**Chronology**

.1 **Philosophy and theory**

Do not use for chemical principles; class in 523. Do not use for physical principles; class in 523.01

.2 **Miscellany**

[.28] Auxiliary techniques and procedures; apparatus, equipment, materials

Do not use; class in 522

> ### 521–525 Astronomy

Class comprehensive works in 520

For geodetic astronomy, see 526

521 Celestial mechanics

Including gravity, orbits

Class here motion

Class application to specific celestial bodies and phenomena in 523

522 Techniques, procedures, apparatus, equipment, materials

Including observatories, telescopes; infrared and radio astronomy

Class here astrometry, positional and practical astronomy

Class positional astronomy as an aspect of mathematical geography in 526

For practical astronomy of specific celestial bodies and phenomena, see 523

[.028] Auxiliary techniques and procedures; apparatus, equipment, materials

Do not use; class in 522

523 Specific celestial bodies and phenomena

Including cosmochemistry, zodiac

Class phenomena of celestial bodies directly comparable to terrestrial phenomena with the terrestrial phenomena in 550, e.g., volcanic activity on Mars 551.210999

[.001–.009]   Standard subdivisions

> Do not use; class in 520.1–520.9

.01   Astrophysics

> *For celestial mechanics, see 521*

.1   The universe, galaxies, quasars

Standard subdivisions are added for the universe, galaxies, quasars together; for the universe alone

Including cosmic dust, dark matter, interstellar matter; Milky Way

Class here cosmology

Use of this number for space discontinued; class in 520

> *See also 523.8 for black holes*

> *See Manual at 520 vs. 500.5, 523.1, 919.9; also at 520 vs. 523.1, 523.8*

.2   Solar system

> *For specific parts, see 523.3–523.7*

> **523.3–523.7   Specific parts of solar system**

Class comprehensive works in 523.2

.3   Moon

.4   Planets

Class here comprehensive works on planets, satellites, rings

> *For satellites and rings, transits, occultations, see 523.9; for earth, see 525*

.41   Mercury

.42   Venus

.43   Mars

.44   Asteroids (Planetoids)

> Class comprehensive works on meteors and asteroids in 523.5

.45   Jupiter

.46   Saturn

.47	Uranus
.48	Trans-Uranian planets

Including Neptune, Pluto

.5 Meteors, solar wind, zodiacal light

Including meteoroids, meteorites

Class here interplanetary matter, comprehensive works on meteors and asteroids

For asteroids, see 523.44

.6 Comets

.7 Sun

See also 523.5 for solar wind, zodiacal light

.8 Stars

Including black holes, pulsars

Class here comprehensive works on stars and galaxies

For galaxies, see 523.1; for sun, see 523.7

See also 523.1 for quasars

See Manual at 520 vs. 523.1, 523.8

.802 8 Auxiliary techniques and procedures; apparatus, equipment, materials

Do not use for testing and measurement; class in 523.8

.9 Satellites (Moons) and rings; eclipses, transits, occultations

For earth's moon, see 523.3

525 Earth (Astronomical geography)

Including dawn, twilight; astronomical causes of seasons; Foucault's pendulum, orbits

Class determination of size and shape of earth in 526; class climatology in 551.6; class interdisciplinary works on seasons in 508.2

For magnetic properties, see 538

526   Mathematical geography

Including geodesy, latitude, longitude

Class here cartography (map making)

Class map making for a specific purpose with the purpose, e.g., military map making 623

> *For astronomical geography, see 525; for latitude and longitude in celestial navigation, see 527*

> *See also 912 for map reading*

.022   Illustrations, models, miniatures

Including map drawing

.3   Geodetic surveying

Surveying in which curvature of the earth is considered

Including leveling, triangulation

.9   Surveying

Including topographic surveying, e.g., photogrammetry

Class here plane surveying (surveying in which curvature of the earth is disregarded), land surveying

Class engineering surveys in 622–629; class interdisciplinary works on land surveys in 333

> *For geodetic surveying, see 526.3*

527   Celestial navigation

> *For celestial navigation of a specific craft, see the craft, e.g., navigation of nautical craft 623.89*

528   Ephemerides

Variant names: astronomical and nautical almanacs

Class tables of specific celestial bodies in 523

.093–.099   Treatment in ancient world, treatment by specific continent

Use of these numbers for treatment by specific country and locality discontinued; class in 528

529   Chronology

Including calendars; horology; intervals of time, e.g., days, months, years

Class time systems and standards in 389; class instruments for measuring time in 681.1

> *For sidereal month, see 523.3*

> *See also 525 for seasons*

530 Physics

Class here energy, matter, antimatter, classical physics, comprehensive works on classical and quantum mechanics

Class quantum mechanics, energy in quantum mechanics in 530.12; class classical mechanics, energy in classical mechanics in 531; class physical chemistry in 541.3

> *For astrophysics, see 523.01*

> *See Manual at 530 vs. 540; also at 530 vs. 621*

SUMMARY

530.01–.09	**Standard subdivisions**
.1–.8	**[Theories, mathematical physics, states of matter, measurement]**
531	**Classical mechanics Solid mechanics**
532	**Fluid mechanics Liquid mechanics**
533	**Pneumatics (Gas mechanics)**
534	**Sound and related vibrations**
535	**Light and paraphotic phenomena**
536	**Heat**
537	**Electricity and electronics**
538	**Magnetism**
539	**Modern physics**

.01   Philosophy and theory

> Do not use for theories; class in 530.1. Do not use for mathematical physics; class in 530.15

.02   Miscellany

.028   Auxiliary techniques and procedures; materials

> Do not use for apparatus and equipment; class in 530. Do not use for testing and measurement; class in 530.8

.03–.09   Standard subdivisions

.1   Theories and mathematical physics

Standard subdivisions are added for theories and mathematical physics together, for theories alone

Including space

Measurement theory relocated to 530.801

Class applications to specific states of matter in 530.4

> *See Manual at 520 vs. 500.5, 523.1, 530.1, 919.9*

.11   Relativity theory

> Including fourth dimension

> Class here conservation of mass-energy, equivalence of mass-energy ($E=mc^2$), space-time

.12   Quantum mechanics (Quantum theory)

Including matrix mechanics, wave mechanics

Class here relativistic, nonrelativistic quantum mechanics

For quantum statistics, see 530.13; for quantum field theory, see 530.14; for quantum electronics, see 537.5; for quantum electrodynamics, see 537.6

See Manual at 530.12 vs. 531

.13   Statistical mechanics

Including quantum statistics

Class here relativistic, nonrelativistic statistical mechanics

.14   Field and wave theories

Theories accounting for fundamental particles and interactions

Standard subdivisions are added for field and wave theories together, for field theories alone

Including electromagnetic theory, problem of few bodies, problem of many bodies, theory of continuum physics, unified field theory, comprehensive works on supergravity and supersymmetry

Class here quantum, classical, relativistic, nonrelativistic field and wave theories

Class electromagnetic spectrum and waves in 539.2

For wave mechanics, see 530.12; for supersymmetry, see 539.7

See also 537 for theories of electricity, 538.01 for theories of magnetism

.15   Mathematical physics

Class mathematical description of physical phenomena according to a specific theory with the theory in 530.1, e.g., statistical mechanics 530.13

.4   States of matter

Including Brownian motion, bubbles, capillarity, diffusion, ionized gases, liquid crystals, phase transformations, plasma physics, surface physics, surface tension, thin films, transport phenomena

Class here quantum mechanics of specific states of matter; sound, light, heat, electricity, magnetism as properties of specific states of matter

For heat transfer, see 536; for superconductivity and superconductors, see 537.6; for crystallography, see 548

.8 **Measurement**

Including testing; physical units and constants; systems of measurement, e.g., metric system; weights and measures; interdisciplinary works on size

Class here interdisciplinary works on measurement, on mensuration

Class instrumentation for measurement in 530

For social aspects of systems of measurement, see 389; for horology, see 529. For a specific aspect of size, see the aspect, e.g., size of business enterprise 338.6; for measurement, mensuration in a specific subject, see the subject, plus notation 028 from Table 1, e.g., psychological measurement 150.28

See also 516 for geometric mensuration

.801 Philosophy and theory

Class here measurement theory [*formerly* 530.1]

.802 Miscellany

Do not use for tabulated and related material; class in 530.8

531 **Classical mechanics   Solid mechanics**

Variant names for classical mechanics: mechanics, continuum mechanics

Including dynamics, e.g., deformation, vibrations, waves; energy, e.g., momentum, work; mass and gravity; particle mechanics; statics

Class geodetic gravity determination in 526; class mechanics of molecular, atomic, and subatomic particles (quantum mechanics) in 530.12; class comprehensive works on energy in physics in 530; class interdisciplinary works on energy in 333.79

For gravity in celestial mechanics, see 521; for fluid mechanics, see 532

See also 530.12 for waves considered as fundamental properties of matter; 539.7 for fundamental gravitational interaction, 620 for fine particle technology

See Manual at 530.12 vs. 531

.01 Philosophy and theory

Class statistical mechanics in 530.13

532 **Fluid mechanics   Liquid mechanics**

Including boundary layers, buoyancy, cavitation, flow, vortex motion, waves

Class here hydraulics (hydromechanics)

For pneumatics, see 533

.001–.009 Standard subdivisions

533   Pneumatics (Gas mechanics)

Including aerodynamics, supersonic flow, vacuums

> ### 534–538 Specific forms of energy

Class here transformations into specific forms of energy

Class specific forms of energy as properties of specific states of matter in 530.4; class comprehensive works in 530; class comprehensive works on transformation of energy in 531

For mechanical energy, see 531

534   Sound and related vibrations

Standard subdivisions are added for sound and related vibrations together, for sound alone

.5   Vibrations related to sound

Including subsonic and ultrasonic vibrations

Class here vibrations that can not be heard by the human ear

535   Light and paraphotic phenomena

Standard subdivisions are added for light and paraphotic phenomena together, for light alone

Including luminescence, prisms

Class here optics

For chemiluminescence, see 541.3; for bioluminescence, see 572. For a specific aspect of prisms, see the aspect, e.g., geometry of prisms 516

See also 537.5 for electron and ion optics

.01   Spectral regions; philosophy and theory of light and paraphotic phenomena

Including infrared and ultraviolet radiations

Class here paraphotic phenomena, radiations of nonvisible spectral regions

.010 1–.010 9   Standard subdivisions of spectral regions

.02   Miscellany

.028   Auxiliary techniques and procedures; apparatus, equipment, materials

Class spectroscopy in 535.8

.5   Beams

Including polarization

.6   **Color**

.8   **Spectroscopy**

Class here comprehensive works on spectroscopy in physics

Class interdisciplinary works on spectroscopy in 543

For a specific kind of spectroscopy in physics other than optical and paraphotic, see the kind, e.g., microwave spectroscopy 537.5

[.801–.809]   Standard subdivisions

Do not use; class in 535.8

536   **Heat**

Including cryogenics; effect of heat on matter, e.g., expansion and contraction, melting and freezing, evaporation and condensation; temperature; thermodynamics, e.g., entropy

.01   Philosophy and theory

Do not use for theories; class in 536

537   **Electricity and electronics**

Standard subdivisions are added for electricity and electronics together, for electricity alone

Class here electromagnetism

Class electromagnetic theory of matter in 530.14; class interdisciplinary works on electricity in 333.793

For magnetism, see 538

.01   Philosophy and theory

Do not use for theories; class in 537

.5   **Electronics**

Including microwaves, radio waves; photoelectricity

Class here quantum electronics

For semiconductors, see 537.6

.6   **Electrodynamics (Electric currents) and thermoelectricity**

Standard subdivisions are added for electrodynamics and thermoelectricity together, for electrodynamics alone

Including semiconductors, superconductivity

Class dielectrics in 537

538   **Magnetism**

Including auroras, northern lights; geomagnetism, ionosphere, magnetosphere, natural magnets

539   Modern physics

Including atomic and molecular structure, molecular physics

Class here quantum physics

Class nuclear structure in 539.7

For theories of modern physics, see 530.1; for states of matter, see 530.4; for modern physics of specific forms of energy, see 534–538

.01   Philosophy and theory

Do not use for theories; class in 530.1. Do not use for mathematical principles; class in 530.15

.2   **Radiation (Radiant energy)**

Class here electromagnetic radiation, spectrum, waves

For a specific kind of radiation, see the kind, e.g., ultraviolet radiation 535.01, ionizing radiation 539.7

.7   **Atomic and nuclear physics**

Standard subdivisions are added for either or both topics in heading

Including cyclotrons, high-energy physics, ionizing radiations; particle physics, electrons, protons, quarks; radioactivity, supercolliders, superstrings, supersymmetry

Class atomic structure in 539

For field and wave theories accounting for fundamental particles, supergravity, comprehensive works on supergravity and supersymmetry, see 530.14; for ionization of gases, see 530.4; for magnetic properties of particles, see 538

540   Chemistry and allied sciences

Standard subdivisions are added for chemistry and allied sciences together, for chemistry alone

Class cosmochemistry in 523

See Manual at 530 vs. 540

SUMMARY

.1 **Philosophy and theory**

> Do not use for theoretical chemistry; class in 541.2
>
> Including ancient and medieval theories, e.g., alchemy

.2 **Miscellany**

[.28] Auxiliary techniques and procedures; apparatus, equipment, materials

> Do not use; class in 542

.7 **Education, research, related topics**

> Do not use for laboratories; class in 542

> ## 541–547 Chemistry

Class comprehensive works in 540

> ## 541–545 General chemistry

Inorganic and combined inorganic-organic

Class comprehensive works in 540

> *For general topics of specific inorganic chemicals and groups of chemicals,
> see 546; for general topics in organic chemistry, see 547*

541 Physical and theoretical chemistry

Class physical and theoretical chemistry of specific elements, compounds,
mixtures, groupings in 546; class physical and theoretical crystallography in 548

See Manual at 541 vs. 546

.2 **Theoretical chemistry**

Including atomic structure, periodic law; molecular structure, e.g., chemical
bonds, coordination chemistry, inorganic polymers, inorganic stereochemistry,
quantum chemistry, radicals

Comprehensive works on isomers, stereochemistry relocated to 547

Class molecular structure studied without reference to chemical characteristics
in 539; class radiochemistry in 541.3; class periodic table in 546; class
comprehensive works on polymers in 547

.3   Physical chemistry

Including chemical reactions e.g., catalysis, oxidation, reduction; electrochemistry; photochemistry, e.g., chemiluminescence; radiochemistry; solution chemistry, e.g., colloids (foams, fogs, gels), solvents; surface chemistry; thermochemistry, e.g., combustion

Class optical activity in 541; class quantum chemistry in 541.2

For bioluminescence, see 572

542   Techniques, procedures, apparatus, equipment, materials

Standard subdivisions are added for any or all topics in heading

Class techniques, procedures, apparatus, equipment, materials used in a specific application with the application, e.g., techniques and equipment for chemical analysis 543

543   Analytical chemistry

Including interdisciplinary works on spectroscopy

Class analytical chemistry of specific elements, compounds, mixtures, groupings in 546

For spectroscopy in physics, see 535.8; for spectroscopic interpretation of chemical structure, see 541.2; for qualitative analysis, see 544; for quantitative analysis, see 545

See Manual at 543 vs. 544–545

.001   Philosophy and theory

.002   Miscellany

.002 8   Auxiliary techniques and procedures; materials

Do not use for apparatus and equipment, reagents; class in 543

.003–.009   Standard subdivisions

544   Qualitative analysis

Class qualitative analysis of specific elements, compounds, mixtures, groupings in 546

See Manual at 543 vs. 544–545

.001   Philosophy and theory

.002   Miscellany

.002 8   Auxiliary techniques and procedures; materials

Do not use for apparatus and equipment, reagents; class in 544

.003–.009   Standard subdivisions

545 Quantitative analysis

Class quantitative analysis of specific elements, compounds, mixtures, groupings in 546

See Manual at 543 vs. 544–545

.001 Philosophy and theory

.002 Miscellany

.002 8 Auxiliary techniques and procedures; materials

Do not use for apparatus and equipment, reagents; class in 545

.003–.009 Standard subdivisions

546 Inorganic chemistry

Including chemistry of metals; inorganic carbon compounds; periodic table; general topics in chemistry applied to specific elements, compounds, mixtures, groupings

Class here comprehensive works on inorganic and organic chemistry of specific elements, compounds, mixtures, groupings

Class general topics of chemistry applied to inorganic chemistry as a whole in 541–545; class carbon compounds not specifically treated as inorganic compounds in 547; class physical and chemical metallurgy, interdisciplinary works on metals in 669

For organometallic compounds, organic chemistry of specific elements, compounds, mixtures, groupings, see 547

See Manual at 541 vs. 546; also at 549 vs. 546

547 Organic chemistry

Including comprehensive works on isomers, stereochemistry [*both formerly* 541.2]; analytical, physical, and theoretical organic chemistry; macromolecules; comprehensive works on polymers

Class here biochemicals when not considered in their biological context

Class interdisciplinary works on biochemicals, on macromolecules in 572

For inorganic isomers, polymers, stereochemistry, see 541.2; for biochemistry, see 572

.001 Philosophy and theory

Do not use for theoretical organic chemistry; class in 547

.002–.009 Standard subdivisions

[.1–.8] Subdivisions of organic chemistry

Numbers discontinued; class in 547

548 Crystallography

Class crystallographic mineralogy in 549; class comprehensive works on solid-state physics in 530.4

See Manual at 549 vs. 548

549 Mineralogy

Occurrence, description, classification, identification of naturally occurring minerals

Class crystallography in 548; class economic geology in 553

See Manual at 549 vs. 546; also at 549 vs. 548; also at 552 vs. 549

.09 Historical, geographic, persons treatment

Do not use for geographic treatment of minerals; class in 549.9

.9 **Geographic distribution of minerals**

Add to base number 549.9 notation 1–9 from Table 2, e.g., minerals of Mexico 549.972

550 Earth sciences

Class here geophysics; phenomena of celestial bodies that are directly comparable to terrestrial phenomena, e.g., volcanic activity on Mars 551.210999

Use 550 and its standard subdivisions for works that deal comprehensively with geology, hydrology, and meteorology; for works about geology that deal with all earth sciences. Use 551 and its standard subdivisions for works on geology in the sense limited to properties and phenomena of the solid earth

See Manual at 550 vs. 910; also at 559.9

SUMMARY

550.1–.9	**Standard subdivisions**
551	**Geology, hydrology, meteorology**
552	**Petrology**
553	**Economic geology**
554–559	**Earth sciences by specific continents, countries, localities in modern world; extraterrestrial worlds**

.1 **Philosophy and theory**

Do not use for chemical principles; class in 551.9

.9 **Historical, geographic, persons treatment**

[.94–.99] Treatment by specific continent, country, locality in modern world; extraterrestrial worlds

Do not use; class in 554–559

551   **Geology, hydrology, meteorology**

Geology: science that deals with properties and phenomena of the solid earth (lithosphere)

Use 550 and its standard subdivisions for works that deal comprehensively with geology, hydrology, and meteorology; for works about geology that deal with all earth sciences. Use 551 and its standard subdivisions for works on geology in the sense limited to properties and phenomena of the solid earth

> *For astronomical geography, see 525; for geodesy, see 526; for petrology, see 552; for economic geology, see 553; for physical geography, see 910*

SUMMARY

551.01–.09	Standard subdivisions of geology
.1	Gross structure and properties of the earth
.2	Volcanoes, earthquakes, thermal waters and gases
.3	Surface and exogenous processes and their agents
.4	Geomorphology and hydrosphere
.5	Meteorology
.6	Climatology and weather
.7	Historical geology
.8	Structural geology
.9	Geochemistry

.01   Philosophy and theory of geology

Do not use for chemical principles; class in 551.9

.02–.08   Standard subdivisions of geology

.09   Historical, geographic, persons treatment of geology

[.091 62–.091 67]   Treatment in oceans and seas

Do not use; class in 551.46

[.094–.099]   Treatment by specific continent, country, locality in modern world; extraterrestrial worlds

Do not use; class in 554–559

.1   **Gross structure and properties of the earth**

Including core, crust, mantle, plate tectonics (continental drift)

> *For geomagnetism, see 538; for structural geology, see 551.8*

.2   **Volcanoes, earthquakes, thermal waters and gases**

Including fumaroles, hot springs

> *See also 363.34 for volcanic and earthquake disasters*

.21 Volcanoes

> Class here comprehensive works on craters

> Class volcanic thermal waters and gases in 551.2; class petrology of volcanic rocks in 552

> *For meteorite craters, see 551.3*

.22 Earthquakes

> Class here seismology

> Class seismic sea waves in 551.47

.3 Surface and exogenous processes and their agents

> Standard subdivisions are added for any or all topics in heading

> Including geologic work of water, landforms created by water, landslides, mass movement, meteorite craters, sand dunes, soil formation, weathering, comprehensive works on frost, interdisciplinary works on erosion

> Class here sedimentology as study of surface processes

> Class comprehensive works on landforms in 551.41; class comprehensive works on sedimentology in 552

> *For specific landforms created by water, see 551.42–551.45; for frost as a cold spell, see 551.5; for condensation of frost, see 551.57. For a specific aspect of erosion, see the aspect, e.g., erosion engineering 627, control of agricultural erosion 631.4*

.300 1–.300 9 Standard subdivisions

.31 Geologic work of ice Glaciology

> Including moraines

> Class here interdisciplinary works on ice

> Class geologic work of frost in 551.3

> *For ice in water and other forms of ice, see 551.34. For a specific aspect of ice, see the aspect, e.g., ice manufacture 621.5*

.34 Ice in water and other forms of ice

> Standard subdivisions are added for ice in water and other forms of ice together, for ice in water alone

> Including icebergs, sea ice

> *For snow, see 551.57*

.4 Geomorphology and hydrosphere

.41 Geomorphology

Creation and modification of topographical landforms by erosional and depositional processes

Including desert geomorphology

Class here geomorphology of continents, comprehensive works on landforms

For specific landforms, see 551.42–551.45; for submarine geomorphology, see 551.46

See also 551.1 for continental drift

[.410 916 2–.410 916 7] Treatment in oceans and seas

Do not use; class in 551.46

> 551.42–551.45 Specific landforms

Class here specific landforms created by water; comprehensive works on specific kinds of topographical features, on present and past examples of specific landforms

Class comprehensive works in 551.41

For landforms created by tectonic deformations, see 551.8. For a specific landform created by plutonic action, see the landform in 551.2, e.g., volcanic mountains 551.21; for a specific landform created primarily by exogenous agents other than water or living organisms, see the landform in 551.3, e.g., glacial moraines 551.31

.42 Islands and reefs

Standard subdivisions are added for islands and reefs together, for islands alone

Including atolls

.43 Elevations

Including mountains, plateaus, slopes

.44 Depressions and openings

Including canyons, caves, floodplains, sink holes, valleys

For craters, see 551.21; for deltas, see 551.45; for rift valleys, see 551.8

.45 Plane and coastal regions

Including plains, prairies, steppes, tundras; beaches, deltas, seashores, shorelands, tidelands; comprehensive works on grasslands

For floodplains, see 551.44. For a specific kind of grassland not in a plane region, see the kind, e.g., alpine meadows 551.43

.46 Hydrosphere Oceanography

Including deep-sea surveys, estuaries, inland seas, lagoons, ocean bottom, salt lakes, submarine geology

Class here hydrography, marine science, oceans and seas

Class geologic work of water in 551.3; class ice in 551.31; class interdisciplinary works on water in 553.7

> *For dynamic oceanography, see 551.47; for hydrology, see 551.48; for marine ecology, see 577.7; for marine biology, see 578.77*

> *See also 620 for oceanographic engineering*

> *See Manual at 578.76–578.77 vs. 551.46*

.460 01–.460 06 Standard subdivisions

.460 07 Education, research, related topics

> Do not use for deep-sea surveys and explorations; class in 551.46

.460 08–.460 09 Standard subdivisions

.47 Dynamic oceanography

Including ocean currents, e.g., Gulf Stream; tides; waves, e.g., tidal waves

> *See also 551.3 for geologic work of waves*

.470 01–.470 09 Standard subdivisions

.48 Hydrology

Including floods, lakes, ponds, rivers, runoff, streams, waterfalls

Class here hydrologic cycle, limnology, water balance

Class inland seas, salt lakes, comprehensive works on oceanography and hydrology in 551.46; class water resources, interdisciplinary works on water in 553.7

> *For fumaroles, see 551.2; for groundwater, see 551.49; for hydrometeorology, see 551.57*

.49 Groundwater (Subsurface water)

Including artesian wells, springs, water table

Class here aquifers

> *For thermal waters, hot springs, see 551.2*

.5   **Meteorology**

Including atmospheric pressure, radiations, temperature, thermodynamics; atmosphere interactions with earth's surface; frost as a cold spell

Class here atmosphere

Class micrometeorology in 551.6; class forecasts of specific meteorological phenomena in 551.64; class forecasts of specific phenomena in specific areas in 551.65; class comprehensive works on frost in 551.3

> *For climatology and weather, see 551.6*

> *See Manual at 551.5 vs. 551.6*

.501   Philosophy and theory

Do not use for forecasting and forecasts; class in 551.63

.51   Composition, regions, dynamics of atmosphere

Including circulation, winds, monsoons; dust; magnetosphere, ozone layer, stratosphere, troposphere

Class magnetic phenomena in magnetosphere, comprehensive works on magnetosphere in 538

> *For atmospheric disturbances and formations, see 551.55*

.55   Atmospheric disturbances and formations

Standard subdivisions are added for atmospheric disturbances and formations together, for atmospheric disturbances alone

Including blizzards, cold fronts, cyclones, hailstorms, hurricanes, snowstorms, thunderstorms, tornadoes, typhoons

Class here storms

Class precipitation from storms in 551.57

> *See also 363.34 for storms as disasters*

.56   Atmospheric electricity and optics

Including cloud colors, lightning, mirages, rainbows

.57   Hydrometeorology

Including acid rain, clouds, droughts, frost, rain, snow; factors affecting precipitation

Class geologic work of precipitation, comprehensive works on frost in 551.3; class comprehensive works on atmosphere interactions with earth's surface in 551.5; class interdisciplinary work on acid rain in 363.738

.6 **Climatology and weather**

Standard subdivisions are added for either or both topics in heading

Including micrometeorology

Class specific micrometeorological phenomena other than hydrodynamics, comprehensive works on atmosphere interactions with earth's surface in 551.5

See Manual at 551.5 vs. 551.6

.601 Philosophy and theory

Do not use for forecasting and forecasts; class in 551.63

.609 Historical, geographic, persons treatment

Do not use for geographic treatment of weather; class in 551.65. Do not use for geographic treatment of climate, of climate and weather taken together; class in 551.69

.63 Weather forecasting and forecasts, reporting and reports

Standard subdivisions are added for weather forecasting and forecasts, reporting and reports together; for weather forecasting alone; for weather forecasts alone

Including weather lore, weather satellites; use of radar

For forecasting and forecasts of specific phenomena, see 551.64

.630 28 Auxiliary techniques and procedures, materials

Do not use for apparatus and equipment; class in 551.63

.630 9 Historic and persons treatment

Do not use for geographic treatment; class in 551.65

.64 Forecasting and forecasts of specific phenomena

Class here methods of forecasting specific phenomena for specific areas

Class flood forecasting and forecasts in 551.48; class forecasts of specific phenomena for specific areas in 551.65

[.640 1–.640 9] Standard subdivisions

Do not use; class in 551.6301–551.6309

.65 Geographic treatment of weather

Class here geographic treatment of weather forecasts and reports, of forecasts of specific phenomena

[.650 1–.650 9] Standard subdivisions

Do not use; class in 551.601–551.609

.651–.659   Specific regions and areas

> Class here forecasts of specific phenomena for specific regions and areas
>
> Add to base number 551.65 notation 1–9 from Table 2, e.g., forecasts for South Africa 551.6568

.68   Artificial modification and control of weather

.69   Geographic treatment of climate

> Class here paleoclimatology of specific areas
>
> Add to base number 551.69 notation 1–9 from Table 2, e.g., climate of Australia 551.6994
>
> Class general types of climate, microclimatology of specific areas in 551.6; class comprehensive works on paleoclimatology in 551.609

.7   Historical geology

> Including geologic time, ice age
>
> Class here paleogeography, stratigraphy
>
> Class history of a specific kind of geologic phenomenon with the kind of phenomena, e.g., history of Jurassic volcanism in Pacific Northwest 551.2109795, Devonian reefs 551.42, paleozoic orogeny 551.8
>
> *For paleontology, see 560*
>
> *See Manual at 551.7 vs. 560*

.700 1–.700 8   Standard subdivisions

.700 9   Historical, geographic, persons treatment

> Do not use for geographic treatment of historical geology during a specific period; class in 551.7

[.700 94–.700 99]   Historical geology of specific continents, countries, localities in modern world; extraterrestrial worlds

> Do not use; class in 554–559

.8   Structural geology

> Including faults, e.g., rift valleys; folds; intrusions; orogeny (mountain building); stratifications
>
> Class here deformation, tectonics
>
> Class geomorphology in 551.41; class stratifications in specific areas in 554–559; class comprehensive works on elevations in 551.43. Class a specific aspect of orogeny with the aspect, e.g., volcanism 551.21
>
> *For plate tectonics, see 551.1*

.9   Geochemistry

> *For geochemistry of a specific subject in earth sciences or mineralogy, see the subject, e.g., organic geochemistry 553.2*

552 Petrology

Including igneous, metamorphic, sedimentary, volcanic rocks; comprehensive works on sedimentology

Class here petrography, lithology, rocks

Class structural geology in 551.8

> *For mineralogy, see 549; for sedimentology as study of surface processes, see 551.3; for petrology of geologic materials of economic importance other than structural and sculptural stone, see 553*

> *See Manual at 552 vs. 549*

.001–.008 Standard subdivisions

.009 Historical, geographic, persons treatment

> Do not use for geographic distribution of rocks; class in 552.09

.09 Geographic distribution of rocks

> Add to base number 552.09 notation 1–9 from Table 2, e.g., rocks of Sahara Desert 552.0966

> Class rocks studied in their stratigraphic setting in 554–559

553 Economic geology

Quantitative occurrence and distribution of geologic materials of economic utility

Class here interdisciplinary works on nonmetallic materials

Class economic aspects other than reserves of geologic materials in 333.7; class interdisciplinary works on metals in 669

> *For a specific aspect of nonmetallic geologic materials other than economic geology, see the aspect, e.g., prospecting 622*

> *See Manual at 553 vs. 333.8, 338.2*

.2 **Carbonaceous materials**

> Including coal, oil, natural gas

> Class here fossil fuels, organic geochemistry

> Amber and jet relocated to 553.8

> *For diamonds, see 553.8*

.3 **Iron**

.4 **Metals and semimetals**

> Standard subdivisions are added for metals and semimetals together, for metals alone

> *For iron, see 553.3*

.5 **Structural and sculptural stone**

Standard subdivisions are added for either or both topics in heading

Including flagstones, granite, marble

Class petrology of structural and sculptural stone in 552

For semiprecious sculptural stone, see 553.8

.6 **Other economic materials**

Including abrasives, asbestos, clay, gypsum, lime, mineral fertilizers, sand and gravel, sulfur

Class here earthy materials, industrial minerals

Class inorganic gases in 553

For soils, see 631.4

.7 **Water**

Including groundwater, mineral waters, ice

Class interdisciplinary works on thermal waters in 333.8; class interdisciplinary works on ice in 551.31

For geology of thermal waters, see 551.2

See Manual at 363.6

.8 **Gems**

Including amber, jet [*both formerly* 553.2]; diamonds

Class here comprehensive works on stones that are both gems and abrasives

For gemstones treated as abrasives, e.g., industrial diamonds, see 553.6

554–559 Earth sciences by specific continents, countries, localities in modern world; extraterrestrial worlds

Class here geology, geological surveys, stratifications

Add to base number 55 notation 4–9 from Table 2, e.g., geology of Japan 555.2, of moon 559.9

Class historical geology and stratifications of specific continents, countries, localities during a specific geologic period in 551.7; class geological surveys of specific areas emphasizing materials of economic importance in 553.094–553.099; class comprehensive works on earth sciences in 550; class comprehensive works on geology in 551. Class a specific geologic topic (other than historical geology taken as a whole) in a specific area with the topic, e.g., geomorphology of Japan 551.410952, tectonics of Japan 551.80952

See Manual at 559.9

>   **560–590   Life sciences**

        Class comprehensive works in 570

          See Manual at 560–590

560   Paleontology   Paleozoology

       Including stratigraphic paleontology and paleozoology, paleoecology

       Class comprehensive works on paleontology and historic geology in 551.7

        See Manual at 551.7 vs. 560; also at 576.8 vs. 560

.9   **Historical, geographic, persons treatment**

[.909]   Treatment by areas, regions, places in general

           Use of this number for treatment by areas, regions, places in general other than polar, temperate, tropical regions discontinued; class in 560

           Treatment in polar, temperate, tropical regions relocated to 560.91

.91   Treatment in polar, temperate, tropical regions [*formerly* 561.909]

[.914–.919]   Treatment by areas, regions, places in general other than polar, temperate, tropical regions

           Do not use; class in 560

.92   Persons treatment

           Use of this number for aquatic paleontology discontinued; class in 560

561   Paleobotany; fossil microorganisms

       Standard subdivisions are added for paleobotany and fossil microorganisms together, for paleobotany alone

       Including protozoa [*formerly* 563]

       Class here fossil spermatophytes, angiosperms

.09   Historical, geographic, persons treatment

           Do not use for geographic treatment of fossils; class in 561

[.091 4–.091 9]   Treatment by areas, regions, places in general other than polar, temperate, tropical regions

           Do not use; class in 561

>   **562–569   Specific taxonomic groups of animals**

       Class here taxonomic paleozoology

       Class comprehensive works in 560

562 **Fossil invertebrates**

Including fossil worms and related animals [*formerly* 565], conodonts

For protozoa, see 561; for miscellaneous fossil marine and seashore invertebrates, see 563; for fossil mollusks and mollusk-like animals, see 564; for fossil arthropods, see 565

563 **Miscellaneous fossil marine and seashore invertebrates**

Including Anthozoa, Archaeocyatha, coelenterates, corals, Ctenophora, echinoderms, hemichordates, Porifera (sponges), starfish

Protozoa relocated to 561

[.01–.09] Standard subdivisions

Do not use; class in 562.01–562.09

564 **Fossil mollusks and mollusk-like animals**

Including clams, oysters

565 **Fossil arthropods**

Including crustaceans, insects, trilobites

Fossil worms and related animals relocated to 562

566 **Fossil chordates**

Class here fossil vertebrates

For fossil cold-blooded vertebrates, see 567; for fossil birds, see 568; for fossil mammals, see 569

567 **Fossil cold-blooded vertebrates** **Fossil fishes**

Including amphibians

.9 **Reptiles**

Class here archosaurs, dinosaurs

.91 Specific dinosaurs and other archosaurs

Including Thecodontia

Class crocodiles and "dinosaurs" of orders not considered archosaurs in 567.9

[.910 1–.910 9] Standard subdivisions

Do not use; class in 567.901–567.909

> 567.912–567.915 Specific dinosaurs

Class comprehensive works in 567.9

.912   Saurischia

Including Allosaurus, Oviraptor, Tyrannosaurus

Class here carnivorous dinosaurs

For herbivorous Saurischia, see 567.913

.913   Herbivorous Saurischia

Including Apatosaurus (Brontosaurus), Diplodocus, Seismosaurus

.914   Ornithischia

Including duck-billed dinosaurs; Iguanodon, Maiasaura

Class here Ornithopoda

For armored and horned dinosaurs, see 567.915

.915   Armored and horned dinosaurs

Standard subdivisions are added for armored and horned dinosaurs together, for armored dinosaurs alone

Including Ankylosauria, Ceratopsia, Stegosaurus, Triceratops

.918   Flying reptiles

Including pterodactyls

Class comprehensive works on flying and marine reptiles in 567.9

568   Fossil birds

569   Fossil mammals

.9   Hominids (Humans and forebears)

Class here prehistoric humans [*formerly* 573.3]

Class progenitors of contemporary races in 599.97

570 Life sciences Biology

This schedule is new and has been prepared with little or no reference to previous editions. Most numbers have been reused with new meanings

A comparative table giving both old and new numbers for a substantial list of topics and equivalence tables showing the numbers in the old and new schedules are available in a separate booklet

In addition, human races relocated from 572 to 599.97; specific races relocated from 572 to 599.98; physical anthropology relocated from 573 to 599.9; prehistoric humans relocated from 573.3 to 569.9; behavior relocated from 574.5 to 591.5; genetic engineering relocated from 575.1 to 660.6; microscopy of plants relocated from 578 to 580.28; microscopy of animals relocated from 578 to 590.28; collecting and preserving botanical specimens relocated from 579 to 580.75; collecting and preserving zoological specimens relocated from 579 to 590.75

> *For paleontology, see 560; for plants, see 580; for animals, see 590; for medical sciences, see 610*
>
> *See Manual at 560–590*

SUMMARY

570.1–.9	**Standard subdivisions**
571	**Physiology and related subjects**
572	**Biochemistry**
573	**Specific physiological systems in animals, regional histology and physiology**
575	**Specific parts and physiological systems in plants**
576	**Genetics and evolution**
577	**Ecology**
578	**Natural history of organisms and related subjects**
579	**Microorganisms, fungi, algae**

.1 Philosophy and theory

Do not use for taxonomic classification; class in 578.01

Class here nature of life, differences between living and nonliving substances

Class origin of life, conditions needed for life to begin in 576.8

.2 Miscellany

.28 Auxiliary techniques and procedures; apparatus, equipment, materials; microscopy

Including slide preparation

Class interdisciplinary works on microscopy in 502.8

.9 Historical, geographic, persons treatment

Do not use for geographic treatment of organisms; class in 578.09

.919 Space

Do not use for space biology; class in 571.0919

.999   Extraterrestrial worlds

                Do not use for extraterrestrial life; class in 576.8

> ## 571–575 Internal biological processes and structures

Class here internal processes and structures in plants and animals [*formerly* 580–590]

Unless other instructions are given, class a subject with aspects in two or more subdivisions of 571–575 in the number coming last, e.g., cell biology of animal circulatory system 573.1 (*not* 571.1 or 571.6)

Class comprehensive works in 571

See Manual at 571–575; also at 571–575 vs. 630; also at 571–573 vs. 610

> ## 571–572 General internal processes common to all organisms

Class comprehensive works in 571

571 Physiology and related subjects

Standard subdivisions are added for for physiology and related subjects, for physiology alone

Class here comprehensive works on internal biological processes

For biochemistry, see 572; for specific physiological systems in animals, regional histology and physiology, see 573; for specific parts of and physiological systems in plants, see 575; for genetics, see 576.5

.028   Auxiliary techniques and procedures; apparatus, equipment, materials; microscopy

.09   Historical, geographic, persons treatment

.091 9   Space

                    Class here space biology

.099 9   Extraterrestrial worlds

                    Class extraterrestrial life in 576.8

.1   **Animals**

Class here comparative physiology

Class comprehensive works on animals in 590

For protozoa, comparative physiology of plants and microorganisms, see 571.2; for physiology and related subjects in humans, see 612; for physiology and related subjects in domestic animals, see 636.089

.2   **Plants and microorganisms**

Standard subdivisions are added for plants and microorganisms together, for plants alone

Class here comparative physiology of plants and microorganisms, physiology of agricultural plants

Class comprehensive works on microorganisms, fungi, algae in 579; class comprehensive works on plants in 580

See Manual at 571.6 vs. 571.2

.3   **Anatomy and morphology**

Standard subdivisions are added for either or both topics in heading

Class here comparative anatomy

For anatomy and morphology of microorganisms, see 571.6

.4   **Biophysics**

Class here effects of physical forces on organisms

Class bioenergetics, physical biochemistry, comprehensive works on biophysics and biochemistry in 572

.5   **Tissue biology and regional physiology**

Standard subdivisions are added for tissue biology and regional physiology together, for tissue biology alone

Including biophysics of specific tissues

Class here histology, comprehensive works on tissue and cell biology

Class biophysics of tissues in general in 571.4

For cell biology, see 571.6; for histogenesis, see 571.8; for tissues of specific physiological systems in animals, see 573; for regional histology and physiology of animals, see 573.9; for tissues of specific parts of or physiological systems in plants, see 575; for regional histology and physiology of plants, see 575.4

.6   **Cell biology**

Including anatomy and morphology of microorganisms, biological transport

Class here cell physiology, cytology, eukaryotic cells, protoplasm

For reproduction and growth of cells, see 571.8; for cytopathology, see 571.9; for cytochemistry, see 572

See Manual at 576.6 vs. 571.2

.7   Biological control and secretions

Biological control: control of an organism's own physiological processes

Standard subdivisions are added for biological control and secretions together, for biological control alone

Including biorhythms, body temperature, physiological balance; comprehensive works on glands, on hormones

For animal hormones, endocrine glands, see 573.4

See also 632 for biological control of agricultural pests

See Manual at 573.4 vs. 571.7

.8   Reproduction, development, growth

Standard subdivisions are added for any or all topics in heading

Including aging, embryology, maturation, pollination, regeneration, reproduction and growth of cells, sex cells, sex differentiation, vegetative and asexual reproduction

Class here life cycle, sexual reproduction

Class pathological aging and death in 571.9

For reproduction in animals, see 573.6; for reproduction in plants, see 575.6

See Manual at 571.8 vs. 573.6, 575.6

.9   Diseases   Pathology

Including death, immunity, toxicology

Class here histopathology

For diseases of specific physiological systems in animals, see 573; for diseases of specific parts of and physiological systems in plants, see 575; for human diseases, results of experimental research on human diseases in animals, see 616; for diseases of agricultural plants, see 632; for diseases in domestic animals, see 636.089

See Manual at 363.73 vs. 571.9, 577.27; also at 616.07 vs. 571.9

572   Biochemistry

Including bioelectricity, bioluminescence, cell digestion, metabolism, nutrition, photosynthesis, thermobiology; comprehensive works on respiration

Class here cytochemistry, histochemistry; comprehensive works on biochemistry and biophysics; interdisciplinary works on biochemicals, on macromolecules

Class interdisciplinary works on human nutrition in 363.8

> *For chemistry of biochemicals, of macromolecules, see 547; for biophysics, see 571.4; for biochemistry of control processes, see 571.7; for immunochemistry and pathological biochemistry, see 571.9; for biochemistry of a specific physiological system in animals, see 573; for animal respiration, see 573.2; for bioluminescent organs, electric organs, see 573.9; for biochemistry of reproductive organs of or a specific physiological system in plants, see 575.6–575.9; for biochemistry of origin of life, see 576.8; for industrial biochemistry, see 660.6. For a specific aspect of biology of nutrition, see the aspect, e.g., digestive system 573.3*

.8   Biochemical genetics

Including chromosomes, genes; DNA, RNA

Class here cytogenetics, molecular biology, molecular genetics, physiological genetics, nucleic acids

Class developmental genetics in 571.8; class comprehensive works on genetics in 576.5

> *See Manual at 576.5 vs. 572.8*

573   Specific physiological systems in animals, regional histology and physiology

Class here comprehensive works on specific physiological systems

Class comprehensive works on physiological systems in 571

> *For specific physiological systems in plants, see 575; for specific physiological systems in humans, see 612; for specific physiological systems in domestic animals, see 636.089*

> *See Manual at 571–573 vs. 610*

[.01–.09]   Standard subdivisions

Do not use; class in 571.101–571.109

.1   Circulation system

Including blood, heart, lymphatic system

Class here cardiovascular system

> *For circulation in a specific organ or system, see the organ or system, e.g., circulation in brain 573.8*

.2   **Respiratory system**

Including lungs, nose

Class here comprehensive works on respiration in animals

For cell and tissue respiration in animals, see 572

.3   **Digestive system**

Including intestines, liver, stomach

Class here digestion

Class comprehensive works on biology of nutrition in 572; class interdisciplinary works on human nutrition in 363.8

For cellular digestion, see 572

.4   **Endocrine and excretory systems**

Standard subdivisions are added for endocrine and excretory systems together, for endocrine system alone

Including kidneys, urinary system, comprehensive works on animal hormones

Class here endocrinology

Class comprehensive works on endocrine and nervous system in 571.7

For hormones of a specific process or organ, see the process or organ, e.g., growth hormones 571.8, digestive hormones 573.3

See Manual at 573.4 vs. 571.7

.5   **Integument**

Including color, feathers, fur, hair, horns

Class here hide, skin

Class exoskeleton in 573.7

For integument of a specific system or organ, see the system or organ, e.g., pericardium 573.1

.6   **Reproductive system**

Including eggs, pregnancy

Class here genital organs, reproduction, sexual reproduction, comprehensive works on urogenital system

Class comprehensive works on reproduction, development, growth of animals in 571.8

For urinary system, see 573.4

See Manual at 571.8 vs. 573.6, 575.6

.7 **Musculoskeletal system**

Including bones, connective tissues, joints, muscles, skeleton; physiology of flying, locomotion, work

Class here physiology of movement

For bone marrow, see 573.1; for horns, see 573.5. For muscles of a specific system or organ, see the organ or system, e.g., heart muscles 573.1

.8 **Nervous and sensory systems**

Standard subdivisions are added for nervous and sensory systems together, for nervous system alone

Including brain, ears, eyes, nerves; hearing, smell, taste, touch, vision

Class comprehensive works on regulation and control in animals, on endocrine and nervous systems in 571.7

For neural control of a specific system or organ, see the system or organ, e.g., neural control of muscles 573.7

.9 **Miscellaneous systems and organs, regional histology and physiology**

Miscellaneous systems and organs limited to communication systems, bioluminescent organs, electric organs

For receiving sensory systems, see 573.8

[.901–.909]   Standard subdivisions

Do not use; class in 571.101–571.109

[574]   [Unassigned]

Most recently used in Edition 12

575   Specific parts of and physiological systems in plants

For physiological systems in fungi and algae, see 571; for specific parts of fungi and algae, see 571.5; for external description of plant parts and organs and their configurations, see 581.4

[.01–.09]   Standard subdivisions

Do not use; class in 571.201–571.209

.4 **Stems**

Including asexual and vegetative reproduction, wood, xylem

Class here comprehensive works on regional physiology, on shoots

Class comprehensive works on reproduction of plants in 575.6

For leaves, regional physiology of roots, see 575.5

.5 **Roots and leaves**

.6   Reproductive organs   Flowers

Including fruits, seeds

Class here reproduction, sexual reproduction

Class pollination, comprehensive works on reproduction, development, growth in plants in 571.8; class interdisciplinary works on flowers in 582.13

> *For asexual and vegetative reproduction, see 575.4*

> *See Manual at 571.8 vs. 573.6, 575.6*

.7   Circulation, food storage, excretion

Standard subdivisions are added for circulation, food storage, excretion together; for circulation alone

Class transpiration in 575.8

> *For a specific circulatory tissue, see the tissue, e.g., xylem 575.4*

.8   Transpiration

.9   Animal-like physiological processes

Including predation by carnivorous plants, movement, sensitivity

Class here behavior of plants

Class comprehensive works on carnivorous plants in 583

> *For movement that is a direct result of growth, see 571.8*

> ## 576–578   General and external biological phenomena

Class general and external biological phenomena of specific kinds of organisms in 579–590; class comprehensive works in 578

576   Genetics and evolution

.5   Genetics

Including variation, population genetics

Class here heredity, experimental works on genetics of specific organisms, interdisciplinary works on genetics

> *For biochemical, molecular, physiological genetics; cytogenetics, see 572.8; for genetics of microorganisms, fungi, algae, see 579; for genetics of plants, see 581.3; for genetics of animals, see 591.3. For a specific aspect of genetics, see the aspect, e.g., medical genetics 616*

> *See Manual at 576.5 vs. 572.8*

.8   **Evolution**

Including astrobiology, extraterrestrial life, origin of life; natural selection, theories of evolution; evolution of sexes

Class creationism in 231.7; class sexual selection in 591.56

> *For evolution of microorganisms, fungi, algae, see 579; for evolution of plants, see 581.3; for evolution of animals, see 591.3. For evolution of a specific internal biological process or structure, see the process or structure, e.g., evolution of circulatory system 573.1*

> *See also 571.0919 for space biology*

> *See Manual at 231.7 vs. 213, 500, 576.8; also at 576.8 vs. 560*

.801   Philosophy and theory

Do not use for theories; class in 576.8

577   Ecology

Including biological productivity, food chains

Class here ecosystems, terrestrial ecology

Unless other instructions are given, class a subject with aspects in two or more subdivisions of 577 in the number coming last, e.g., grassland swamps 577.68 (*not* 577.4)

> *For paleoecology, see 560; for ecology of microorganisms, fungi, algae, see 579; for ecology of plants, see 581.7; for ecology of animals, see 591.7*

> *See Manual at 333.7–333.9 vs. 363.1, 363.73, 577; also at 577 vs. 578.7*

[.091 4–.091 9]   Treatment by areas, regions, places in general other than polar, temperate, tropical regions

Do not use; class in 577.3–577.7

.2   **Specific factors affecting ecology**

Including autecology, bioclimatology, fire ecology

> *See Manual at 577.2 vs. 579–590*

[.201–.209]   Standard subdivisions

Do not use; class in 577.01–577.09

.27   Effects of humans on ecology

Including nuclear winter

Class here effects of pollution on ecology

Class comprehensive works on ecotoxicology, environmental toxicology in 571.9

For soil pollution, see 577.5; for water pollution, see 577.6

See also 577.5 for ecology of environments made by humans

See Manual at 363.73 vs. 571.9, 577.27

> 577.3–577.7 **Ecology of specific environments**

Except for modifications shown under specific entries, add to each subdivision identified by * as follows:
01–08   Standard subdivisions
09   Historical, geographic, persons treatment
[0914–0919]   Treatment by areas, regions, areas in general other than polar, temperate, tropical regions
                     Do not use; class in base number without use of standard subdivisions

Class terrestrial ecology, comprehensive works on ecology in 577; class comprehensive works on biology of specific environments in 578.7

.3   *Forest ecology

.309 13   Torrid zone (Tropics)

Class tropical rain forests in 577.34

.34   *Rain forest ecology

Class here ecology of jungles, tropical rain forests

[.340 913]   Torrid zone (Tropics)

Do not use; class in 577.34

.4   *Grassland ecology

Including ecology of prairies, savannas

Class here ecology of rangelands

[.409 12–.409 13]   Temperate and torrid zones

Do not use; class in 577.4

---

*Add as instructed under 577.3–577.7

.5 **Ecology of miscellaneous environments**

Limited to topics named here and below

Including coastal, island, mountain, soil ecology; ecology of environments made by humans; ecology of hostile land environments, e.g., caves, sand dunes, tundra

For ecology of coastal and mountain forests, exploited forests, see 577.3; for ecology of coastal and mountain grasslands, rangelands, see 577.4

[.501–.509] Standard subdivisions

Do not use; class in 577.01–577.09

.54 *Desert ecology

Class here ecology in arid lands, in semiarid lands

Class sand dune ecology in 577.5

.6 ***Aquatic ecology   Freshwater ecology**

Including river and stream ecology, floodplain ecology

Class here biological limnology

Class interdisciplinary works on limnology in 551.48

For marine ecology, see 577.7

.63 *Lake and pond ecology

Standard subdivisions are added for lake and pond ecology together, for lake ecology alone

Class here ecology of freshwater lagoons, reservoirs

Class comprehensive works on ecology of lakes, ponds, rivers, streams in 577.6

.68 *Wetland ecology

Class here marsh, swamp ecology

For saltwater wetland ecology, see 577.69

.69 *Saltwater wetland and seashore ecology

Standard subdivisions are added for saltwater wetland and seashore ecology together, for saltwater wetland ecology alone

Class here ecology of coastal wetlands, salt and tide marshes

For sand dune ecology, see 577.5

*Add as instructed under 577.3–577.7

.7 ***Marine ecology**

Including reef ecology, nearshore ecology

Class here saltwater ecology

For salt lake ecology, see 577.63; for saltwater wetland and seashore ecology, see 577.69

.8 **Synecology and population biology**

Standard subdivisions are added for synecology and population biology together, for synecology alone

Including parasitism, symbiosis

Class here ecological aspects of sociobiology

Class pathology of parasitism, comprehensive works on parasitism in 571.9; class parasites in 578.6; class predation, behavioral aspects of sociobiology in 591.5; class interdisciplinary works on sociobiology in 304.5

When classifying parasitism of specific kinds of organisms in 579–590, prefer the number for the parasite. Emphasis on the host organism usually indicates that the work should be classed as a disease in 571.9

See also 576.5 for population genetics

578 **Natural history of organisms and related subjects**

Standard subdivisions are added for natural history of organisms and related subjects, for natural history of organisms alone

Class here descriptive biology, specific nontaxonomic kinds of organisms, comprehensive works on general and external biological phenomena

For genetics and evolution, see 576; for ecology, see 577; for natural history of microorganisms, fungi, algae, see 579; for natural history of plants, see 580; for natural history of animals, see 590

See Manual at 578 vs. 304.2, 508, 910

.01 Philosophy and theory

Including taxonomic classification

.02 Miscellany

.028 Auxiliary techniques and procedures, apparatus, equipment, materials; microscopy

.07 Education, research, related topics

.073 Collections and exhibits of living organisms

.074 Museums, collections, exhibits

Do not use for collections and exhibits of living organisms; class in 578.073

*Add as instructed under 577.3–577.7

.09   Historical, geographic, persons treatment

[.091 4–.091 9]   Treatment by areas, regions, places in general other than polar, temperate, tropical regions

> Do not use; class in 578.73–578.77

.099 9   Extraterrestrial worlds

> Class extraterrestrial life in 576.8

.4   Adaptation

Including acclimatization, camouflage, reproductive and seasonal adaptations

Class here organisms illustrating specific kinds of adaptations

Class reproductive physiology in 571.8; class adaptation of miscellaneous nontaxonomic kinds of organisms in 578.6

.6   Miscellaneous nontaxonomic kinds of organisms

Not provided for elsewhere

Including beneficial and harmful organisms, e.g., parasites

Class here economic biology

.68   Rare and endangered species

> Standard subdivisions are added for either or both topics in heading

> Including recently extinct species

.7   Organisms characteristic of specific kinds of environments

Class here biology of specific kinds of environments

Class specific kinds of adaptation characteristic of specific kinds of environments in 578.4; class miscellaneous nontaxonomic kinds of organisms characteristic of specific kinds of environments in 578.6

For ecology of specific kinds of environments, see 577

See Manual at 577 vs. 578.7

[.701–.709]   Standard subdivisions

> Do not use; class in 578.01–578.09

.73–.77   Specific kinds of environments

Add to base number 578.7 the numbers following 577 in 577.3–577.7, e.g., marine biology 578.77

Class comprehensive works on terrestrial organisms in 578

For space biology, see 571.0919; for extraterrestrial life, see 576.8

See Manual at 578.76–578.77 vs. 551.46

> ## 579–590 Natural history of specific kinds of organisms

Class here comprehensive works on biology of specific kinds of organisms

Except for modifications shown under specific entries, add to each subdivision identified by * as follows:

01–08   Standard subdivisions
                    Notation from Table 1 as modified under 578.01–578.08, e.g., collections of living organisms 073
09   Historical, geographic, persons treatment
[0914–0919]   Treatment by areas, regions, places in general other than polar, temperate, tropical regions
                    Do not use; class in base number without use of notation from Table 1

Class comprehensive works on biology in 570; class comprehensive works on natural history of organisms in 578

See Manual at 579–590; also at 577.2 vs. 579–590; also at 630 vs. 579–590, 641.3

579   *Microorganisms, fungi, algae

Standard subdivisions are added for microorganisms, fungi, algae together; for microorganisms alone

Including marine botany

Class here thallophytes [*formerly* 589], microbiology; natural history and descriptive biology of microorganisms, fungi, algae; interdisciplinary works on microorganisms, fungi, algae

For internal biological processes of microorganisms, fungi, algae, see 571.2. For a specific aspect of microorganisms, fungi, algae, see the aspect, e.g., cooking mushrooms 641.6

.2   *Viruses and subviral organisms

Standard subdivisions are added for viruses and subviral organisms together, for viruses alone

Class here animal viruses, vertebrate viruses, virology

.3   *Prokaryotes (Bacteria) [*formerly* 589.9]

Including blue-green algae, rickettsias

Class here bacteriology, comprehensive works on bacteria and viruses

For viruses, see 579.2

---

*Add standard subdivisions as instructed under 579–590

.4 ***Protozoa [*formerly* 593.1]**

Including amoebas

> *For a group of organisms that may be regarded as either protozoa or algae, see 579.8*

.5 ***Fungi**

Including molds, yeast

Class here mycology

> *For Agaricales, comprehensive works on mushrooms, see 579.6; for lichens, see 579.7*

.6 ***Mushrooms**

Class here Agaricales, toadstools

> *For mushrooms of a specific order other than Agaricales, see 579.5*

.7 ***Lichens**

.8 ***Algae**

Including diatoms, kelp, seaweeds

Class here phycology

> *For blue-green algae, see 579.3; for lichens, see 579.7*

> # 580–590 Plants and animals

Internal biological processes and structures relocated to 571–575

Class comprehensive works on biology of plants and animals in 570; class comprehensive works on natural history of plants and animals in 578

580 Plants

Class here botany; embryophytes, vascular plants, spermatophytes (seed plants), angiosperms (flowering plants); natural history and descriptive biology of plants; interdisciplinary works on plants

Class interdisciplinary works on food from plants in 641.3

> *For paleobotany, see 561; for internal biological processes and structures of plants, see 571.2; for fungi, see 579.5; for algae, see 579.8. For a specific aspect of plants, see the aspect, e.g., e.g., plant cultivation 631.5*
>
> *See Manual at 560–590; also at 577.2 vs. 579–590; also at 579–590; also at 580 vs. 582.13; also at 630 vs. 579–590, 641.3*

---

*Add standard subdivisions as instructed under 579–590

SUMMARY

580.1–.9	**Standard subdivisions**
581	**Specific topics in natural history of plants**
582	**Plants noted for specific vegetative characteristics and flowers**
583	**Dicotyledons**
584	**Monocotyledons**
585	**Gymnosperms** **Conifers**
586	**Seedless plants**
587	**Vascular seedless plants**
588	**Bryophytes**

.28   Microscopy [*formerly* 578], auxiliary techniques and procedures; apparatus, equipment, materials

.7   **Education, research, related topics**

.73   Collections and exhibits of living plants [*formerly* 580.74]

                Class here botanical gardens

.74   Museums, collections, exhibits

                Collections and exhibits of living plants relocated to 580.73

                Class here herbariums

.75   Museum activities and services   Collecting

                Class here collection and preservation of botanical specimens [*formerly* 579]

.9   **Historical, geographic, persons treatment**

[.914–.919]   Treatment by areas, regions, places in general other than polar, temperate, tropical regions

                Do not use; class in 581.7

.93–.99   Treatment of botany as a discipline by specific continents, countries, localities

                Class treatment of plants by specific continents, countries, localities in 581.9

581 Specific topics in natural history of plants

This schedule is extensively revised, 581.3–581.4 in particular having been prepared with little reference to earlier editions

A comparative table giving both old and new numbers for a substantial list of topics and equivalence tables showing the numbers in the old and new schedules are available in a separate booklet

Class here genetics and evolution, adaptation and parts other than flowers, miscellaneous kinds of plants noted for vegetative characteristics [*all formerly* 582.1]; specific nontaxonomic kinds of plants

Unless other instructions are given, observe the following table of preference, e.g., beneficial aquatic plants 581.6 (*not* 581.7):

Miscellaneous nontaxonomic kinds of plants	581.6
Adaptation	581.4
Genetics and evolution	581.3
Plants characteristic of specific environments, plant ecology	581.7
Treatment of plants by specific continents, countries, localities	581.9

Use of this number for comprehensive works on botany, on plants discontinued; class in 580

Class a specific topic in natural history of plants with respect to a specific taxonomic group with the group in 583–588, e.g., beneficial monocotyledons 584

For plants noted for specific vegetative characteristics and flowers, see 582

[.01–.09] Standard subdivisions

Do not use; class in 580.1–580.9

.3 *Genetics and evolution

Class experimental works on plant genetics, comprehensive works on genetics in 576.5

For biochemical genetics, see 572.8

.4 *Adaptation

Including acclimatization, seasonal adaptation; reproductive adaptation; fruits, leaves, seeds, stems

Class here plants illustrating specific kinds of adaptation

For physiology of specific parts of plants, see 575

*Add standard subdivisions as instructed under 579–590

.6 ***Miscellaneous nontaxonomic kinds of plants**

Not provided for elsewhere

Including beneficial and harmful plants

Class here economic botany

Class carnivorous plants in 583

.68 ***Rare and endangered plants**

Standard subdivisions are added for either or both topics in heading

Including recently extinct plants

.7 ***Plants characteristic of specific environments, plant ecology**

Standard subdivisions are added for either or both topics in heading

Class here autecology

Class marine botany in 579; class plants characteristic of specific environments noted for specific vegetative characteristics and flowers, ecology of such plants in 582

[.709 14–.709 19] Treatment by areas, regions, places in general other than polar, temperate, tropical regions

Do not use; class in 581.7

.9 **Treatment of plants by specific continents, countries, localities**

Add to base number 581.9 notation 3–9 from Table 2, e.g., plants in Argentina 581.982

582 Plants notable for specific vegetative characteristics and flowers

Use of this number for comprehensive works on spermatophytes (seed plants) discontinued; class in 580

For a specific taxonomic group of plants noted for either specific vegetative characteristics or flowers, see the group in 583–588, e.g., lilies noted for their flowers 584

[.01–.09] Standard subdivisions

Do not use; class in 580.1–580.9

.1 **Herbaceous and woody plants, plants noted for their flowers**

Including annuals, biennials, herbs, vines

Genetics and evolution, adaptation and parts other than flowers, miscellaneous kinds of plants noted for vegetative characteristics relocated to 581

See Manual at 635.9 vs. 582.1

---

*Add standard subdivisions as instructed under 579–590

[.101–.109]   Standard subdivisions

> Do not use; class in 580.1–580.9

.13   *Plants noted for their flowers

> Class here wild flowers, interdisciplinary works on flowers
>
> Use of this number for comprehensive works on flowering plants (angiosperms) discontinued; class in 580
>
> Class vines noted for their flowers in 582.1; class woody plants noted for their flowers in 582.16
>
> *For physiology of flowers, see 575.6. For a specific aspect of flowers, see the aspect, e.g., flower gardening 635.9, flower arrangement 745.92*
>
> *See Manual at 580 vs. 582.13*

.16   Trees

> Class here dendrology; comprehensive works on perennials, on woody plants
>
> Class forest ecology in 577.3; class herbaceous perennials, woody vines in 582.1
>
> *For shrubs, see 582.17*
>
> *See Manual at 577.2 vs. 579–590*

[.160 01–.160 08]   Standard subdivisions

> Relocated to 582.1601–582.1608

[.160 09]   Historical, geographic, persons treatment of dendrology

> Relocated to 582.1609

.160 1–.160 8   Standard subdivisions [*formerly* 582.16001–582.16008]

> Notation from Table 1 as modified under 580.1–580.9, e.g., trees in botanical gardens 582.16073

.160 9   Historical, geographic, persons treatment of dendrology [*formerly* 582.16009]

> Class here geographic treatment of trees

[.160 909–.160 92]   Treatment by areas, regions, places in general

> Numbers discontinued; class in 582.16

.17   *Shrubs

> ## 583–588 Specific taxonomic groups of plants
>
> Class comprehensive works in 580

---

*Add standard subdivisions as instructed under 579–590

583 *Dicotyledons

Including cacti, elms, grapes, ivies, laurels, legumes, maples, oaks, roses; carnivorous plants

See Manual at 583–585

584 *Monocotyledons

Including grasses, lilies, orchids, palms

See Manual at 583–585

585 *Gymnosperms   Conifers

Including cypresses, pines

See Manual at 583–585

586 Seedless plants

For fungi, see 579.5; for algae, see 579.8; for vascular seedless plants, see 587; for bryophytes, see 588

[.001–.008]   Standard subdivisions

> Relocated to 586.01–586.08

[.009]   Historical, geographic, persons treatment of the study of seedless plants

> Relocated to 586.09

.01–.08   Standard subdivisions [*formerly* 586.001–586.008]

> Notation from Table 1 as modified under 580.1–580.8, e.g., seedless plants in botanical gardens 586.073

.09   Historical, geographic, persons treatment of the study of seedless plants [*formerly* 586.009]

> Class here geographic treatment of seedless plants

[.090 9–.092]   Treatment by areas, regions, places in general

> Numbers discontinued; class in 586

587 *Vascular seedless plants

Including ferns, club mosses, horsetails, quillworts

588 *Bryophytes

Including mosses, hornworts, liverworts

See also 587 for club mosses

---

*Add standard subdivisions as instructed under 579–590

[589] **Thallophytes**

Relocated to 579

[.9] **Prokaryotes (Bacteria)**

Relocated to 579.3

590 Animals

This schedule is extensively revised, 591, 597, 599, and subdivisions built on zeros in particular having been prepared with little reference to earlier editions

A comparative table giving both old and new numbers for a substantial list of topics and equivalence tables showing the numbers in the old and new schedules are available in a separate booklet

Class here natural history and descriptive biology of animals, zoology, interdisciplinary works on animals

Class interdisciplinary works on food from animals in 641.3

> *For paleozoology, see 560; for comprehensive works on internal biological processes and structures in animals, see 571.1. For a specific aspect of animals, see the aspect, e.g., animal husbandry 636*

> *See Manual at 560–590; also at 577.2 vs. 579–590; also at 579–590; also at 630 vs. 579–590, 641.3; also at 800 vs. 398.24, 590, 636*

SUMMARY

590.1–.9	Standard subdivisions
591	Specific topics in natural history of animals
592	Invertebrates
593	Miscellaneous marine and seashore invertebrates
594	Mollusks and mollusk-like animals
595	Arthropods
596	Chordates
597	Cold-blooded vertebrates Fishes
598	Birds
599	Mammals

.28 Microscopy [*formerly* 578]; auxiliary techniques and procedures; apparatus, equipment, materials

.7 **Education, research, related topics**

.73 Collections and exhibits of living animals

Class here general zoos; zoos limited to vertebrates in general, to land vertebrates in general, to mammals in general

.74 Museums, collections, exhibits

Do not use for collections and exhibits of living organisms; class in 590.73

.75	Museum activities and services Collecting

Including taxidermy

Class here collection and preservation of zoological specimens [*formerly* 579]

.9   Historical, geographic, persons treatment

[.914–.919]   Treatment by areas, regions, places in general other than polar, temperate, tropical regions

Do not use; class in 591.73–591.77

.93–.99   Treatment of zoology as a discipline by specific continents, countries, localities

Class treatment of animals by specific continents, countries, localities in 591.9

591   Specific topics in natural history of animals

Class here specific nontaxonomic kinds of animals

Unless other instructions are given, observe the following table of preference, e.g., social behavior of beneficial animals 591.56 (*not* 591.6):

Behavior	591.5
Miscellaneous nontaxonomic kinds of animals	591.6
Physical adaptation	591.4
Genetics, evolution, young of animals	591.3
Animals characteristic of specific environments, animal ecology	591.7
Treatment by specific continents, countries, localities	591.9

Class a specific topic in natural history of animals with respect to a specific taxonomic group of animals with the group of animals, e.g., beneficial mammals 599.16

[.01–.09]   Standard subdivisions

Do not use; class in 590.1–590.9

.3   *Genetics, evolution, young of animals

Class experimental works on animal genetics, comprehensive works on genetics in 576.5

For biochemical genetics, see 572.8

.4   *Physical adaptation

Including acclimatization, seasonal adaptation; reproductive adaptation, sexual characteristics; eggs

Class here animals noted for specific kinds of physical adaptation, comprehensive works on animal adaptation

For physiology of eggs, see 573.6; for behavioral adaptation, see 591.5

*Add standard subdivisions as instructed under 579–590

.47 *Protective and locomotor adaptations

Standard subdivisions are added for protective and locomotor adaptations together, for protective adaptation alone

Including animal weapons, e.g., horns, tusks; camouflage, exoskeletons, shells; legs, wings, tracks

Class here animal defenses

For protective behavior, see 591.56

.5 ***Behavior [*formerly also* 574.5]**

Including predation, predatory animals

Class here animal psychology, behavioral adaptation, ethology

Class comparative psychology of humans and animals in 156; class physiology of nervous system in 573.8; class comprehensive works on animal adaptation in 591.4

.56 *Behavior relating to life cycle

Including courtship, hibernation, mating, migration, nesting, territoriality

Class here reproductive, social behavior

Class reproductive physiology in 573.6; class physical reproductive adaptation in 591.4; class interdisciplinary works on sociobiology in 304.5

For communication, see 591.59

.59 *Communication

Including animal language

For physiology of communication, see 573.9

.6 ***Miscellaneous nontaxonomic kinds of animals**

Not provided for elsewhere

Including beneficial and harmful animals

Class here economic zoology

.68 Rare and endangered animals

Standard subdivisions are added for either or both topics in heading

Including recently extinct animals

.7 **†Animals characteristic of specific environments, animal ecology**

Standard subdivisions are added for either or both topics in heading

Including animal communities

Class here autecology

*Add standard subdivisions as instructed under 579–590

†Add standard subdivisions as instructed under 579–590; however, class specific environments in 591.73–591.77

.73–.77 Specific kinds of environments

> Class here zoology of specific environments
>
> Add to base number 591.7 the numbers following 577 in 577.3–577.7, e.g., aquatic animals 591.76

.9 **Treatment of animals by continents, countries, localities**

> Add to base number 591.9 notation 3–9 from Table 2, e.g., animals in Brazil 591.981

> ## 592–599 Specific taxonomic groups of animals
>
> Class comprehensive works in 590

592 †Invertebrates

Including leeches, oncopods, worms; helminthology

For protozoa, see 579.4; for miscellaneous marine and seashore invertebrates, see 593; for mollusks and mollusk-like animals, see 594; for arthropods, see 595

.1 **General topics in natural history of invertebrates**

> Add to base number 592.1 the numbers following 591 in 591.3–591.7, e.g., invertebrates of specific environments 592.17

593 Miscellaneous marine and seashore invertebrates

Limited to groups of animals named below

See also 592 for marine and seashore worms, 594 for mollusks and mollusk-like animals, 595.3 for crustaceans

[.01–.09] Standard subdivisions

> Do not use; class in 592.01–592.09

[.1] **Protozoa**

> Relocated to 579.4

.4 ***Sponges**

.5 ***Coelenterates**

> Including jellyfish, Hydrozoa, Scyphozoa
>
> *For Anthozoa, see 593.6*

.6 ***Anthozoa**

> Class here corals

---

*Add standard subdivisions as instructed under 579–590

†Add standard subdivisions as instructed under 579–590; however, class specific environments in
  592.17

.8   *Comb jellies

.9   *Echinoderms and hemichordates

Standard subdivisions are added for echinoderms and hemichordates together, for echinoderms alone

Including starfish, sand dollars

594   †Mollusks and mollusk-like animals

Standard subdivisions are added for mollusks and mollusk-like animals together, for mollusks alone

Including clams, octopuses, oysters, snails

Class here comprehensive works on shellfish

For crustaceans, see 595.3

.1   General topics in natural history of mollusks and mollusk-like animals

Add to base number 594.1 the numbers following 591 in 591.3–591.7, e.g., mollusk shells 594.147, freshwater mollusks 594.176, mollusks of specific oceans and seas 594.177

595   *Arthropods

.3   *Crustaceans

Including barnacles, crabs, lobsters, shrimps

See also 595.4 for horseshoe crabs

.4   *Chelicerates   Arachnids

Including horseshoe crabs, mites, scorpions, spiders, ticks

.6   *Myriapods

Including centipedes, millipedes

.7   ‡Insects

Including cockroaches, crickets, dragonflies, grasshoppers, lice, locusts, termites

Class here entomology, Uniramia

For myriapods, see 595.6

---

*Add standard subdivisions as instructed under 579–590

†Add standard subdivisions as instructed under 579–590; however, class specific environments in 594.17

‡Add standard subdivisions as instructed under 579–590; however, class specific environments in 595.717

.71   General topics in natural history of insects

> Add to base number 595.7 the numbers following 591 in 591.3–591.7, e.g., insect behavior 595.715, insects of specific environments 595.717

.76   *Beetles

> Including fireflies, glowworms, weevils

.77   *Flies (Diptera) and fleas

> Standard subdivisions are added for flies and fleas together, for flies alone
>
> Including gnats, midges, mosquitoes

.78   *Moths and butterflies

> Standard subdivisions are added for moths and butterflies together, for moths alone
>
> Including caterpillars

.79   *Hymenoptera

> Including ants, bees
>
> Class here wasps, social insects

596   †Chordates

> Class here vertebrates, land vertebrates
>
> *For cold-blooded vertebrates, see 597; for birds, see 598; for mammals, see 599*

.1   General topics in natural history of chordates

> Add to base number 596.1 the numbers following 591 in 591.3–591.7, e.g., vertebrates of specific environments 596.17

597   ‡Cold-blooded vertebrates   Fishes

> Class here ichthyology

.1   General topics in natural history of cold-blooded vertebrates

> Add to base number 597.1 the numbers following 591 in 591.3–591.7, e.g., freshwater fishes 597.176, marine fishes 597.177

.3   *Selachii

> Including rays
>
> Class here sharks

---

*Add standard subdivisions as instructed under 579–590

†Add standard subdivisions as instructed under 579–590; however, class collections and exhibits of living vertebrates in 590.73, class specific environments in 596.17

‡Add standard subdivisions as instructed under 579–590; however, class specific environments in 597.17

.5   **Salmonids**

> Including chars, salmon, trout
>
> Class Australian salmon in 597

[.501–.509]   Standard subdivisions

> Do not use; class in 597.5

.8   *****Amphibians**

> Including salamanders, tadpoles
>
> Class here Anura (frogs and toads together)
>
> Class herpetology, comprehensive works on amphibians and reptiles in 597.9

.9   *****Reptiles**

> Class here herpetology, comprehensive works on amphibians and reptiles
>
> *For amphibians, see 597.8*

.92   *Turtles

.95   *Lizards

> Including chameleons, Gila monsters
>
> Class comprehensive works on lizards and snakes in 597.9

.96   *Snakes

.98   *Crocodiles

> Including alligators

598   †Birds

> Class here land birds, ornithology
>
> Interdisciplinary works on species of domestic birds relocated to 636.5
>
> Class comprehensive works on warm-blooded vertebrates in 599

.1   **General topics in natural history of birds**

> Add to base number 598.1 the numbers following 591 in 591.3–591.7, e.g., game birds, wildfowl 598.16; birds of specific environments 598.17, water birds 598.176
>
> Class lowland game birds, water fowl in 598.4; class upland game birds in 598.6

---

*Add standard subdivisions as instructed under 579–590

†Add standard subdivisions as instructed under 579–590, except use 598.07 also for birdbanding
   and bird watching; however, class specific environments in 598.17

> ### 598.3–598.4 Water birds

>> Class comprehensive works in 598.176

.3   ### *Gruiformes, Charadriiformes, Ciconiiformes, flamingos

>> Including cranes, gulls, herons, murres, sandpipers, storks; shore birds

>> Class here wading birds

.4   ### Miscellaneous orders of water birds

>> Limited to Anseriformes, Pelecaniformes, Procellariiformes; grebes, loons

>> Including albatrosses, ducks, geese, pelicans, swans; waterfowl, comprehensive works on lowland game birds

>> Class comprehensive works on waterbirds in 598.176

>>> *For a specific kind of lowland game bird not provided for here, see the kind, e.g., murres 598.3*

[.401–.409]   Standard subdivisions

>> Do not use; class in 598.17601–598.17609

.47   *Penguins

> ### 598.5–598.9 Land birds

>> Class comprehensive works in 598

.5   ### *Palaeognathae

>> Including kiwis, ostriches

>> Class here ratites

.6   ### *Galliformes and Columbiformes

>> Standard subdivisions are added for Galliformes and Columbiformes together, for Galliformes alone

>> Including doves, partridges, peafowl, pheasants, pigeons, quails, turkeys

>> Class here poultry, upland game birds

>> Class interdisciplinary works on domestic poultry in 636.5

>>> *For a specific kind of upland game bird, see the kind, e.g., crows 598.8*

*Add standard subdivisions as instructed under 579–590

.7 **Miscellaneous orders of land birds**

Limited to Apodiformes, Coliiformes, Coraciiformes, Cuculiformes, Piciformes, Psittaciformes, Trogoniformes

Including cuckoos, hornbills, hummingbirds, kingfishers, parakeets, parrots, swifts, woodpeckers

[.701–.709] Standard subdivisions

Do not use; class in 598.01–598.09

.8 ***Perching birds (Passeriformes)***

Including canaries, cardinals, crows, finches, larks, robins, sparrows, thrushes

Class here songbirds

.9 ***Falconiformes, Caprimulgiformes, owls***

Standard subdivisions are added for Falconiformes, Caprimulgiformes, owls together; for Falconiformes alone

Including condors, eagles, falcons, hawks, vultures, whippoorwill

Class here birds of prey, raptors

599 †Mammals

Class here placental mammals, warm-blooded vertebrates

Interdisciplinary works on species of domestic mammals relocated to 636

For birds, see 598

SUMMARY

599.1	**General topics in natural history of mammals**
.2	**Marsupials and monotremes**
.3	**Miscellaneous orders of placental mammals**
.4	**Bats**
.5	**Cetaceans and sea cows**
.6	**Ungulates**
.7	**Carnivores** **Land carnivores**
.8	**Primates**
.9	**Hominids** **Humans**

.1 **General topics in natural history of mammals**

Add to base number 599.1 the numbers following 591 in 591.3–591.7, e.g., mammals of specific environments 599.17; however, for marine mammals, see 599.5

---

*Add standard subdivisions as instructed under 579–590

†Add standard subdivisions as instructed under 579–590; however, class collections and exhibits of living vertebrates in 590.73, class specific environments in 599.17

.2   ***Marsupials and monotremes**

> Standard subdivisions are added for marsupials and monotremes together, for marsupials alone

> Including echidnas, kangaroos, koala, opossums, possums, platypus

.3   **Miscellaneous orders of placental mammals**

> Limited to Edentata, Pholidota, aardvark; and orders provided for below

> Including anteaters, armadillos

[.301–.309]   Standard subdivisions

> Do not use; class in 599.01–599.09

.32   ***Lagomorphs**

> Including hares, pikas

> Class here rabbits

> Class interdisciplinary works on domestic rabbits in 636.932

.33   ***Insectivora and related orders**

> Standard subdivisions are added for Insectivora and related orders together, for Insectivora alone

> Including elephant and tree shrews, hedgehogs, moles

.35   ***Rodents**

> Including chinchillas, gerbils, guinea pigs, hamsters, muskrats, pocket gophers, porcupines, voles

> Class here mice, rats

> Class results of experimental studies in internal biological processes using laboratory rats and mice in 571–573; class interdisciplinary works on domestic species of rodents, e.g., gerbils, in 636.935

>> *For squirrel family, see 599.36; for beavers, see 599.37*

>> *See also 599.36 for gopher of squirrel family*

.36   ***Squirrel family**

> Including chipmunks, gopher, prairie dogs

> Class here squirrels

>> *See also 599.35 for pocket gophers*

.37   ***Beavers**

.4   ***Bats**

---

*Add standard subdivisions as instructed under 579–590

.5 ***Cetaceans and sea cows**

   Standard subdivisions are added for cetaceans and sea cows together, for cetaceans alone

   Class here marine mammals, whales, baleen whales, great whales, toothed whales

    For marine carnivores, e.g., seals, see 599.79

.53 ***Dolphins and porpoises**

   Standard subdivisions are added for dolphins and porpoises together, for dolphins alone

   Including killer whales, pilot whale

.55 ***Sea cows**

   Class here manatees

.6 ***Ungulates**

   Including hyraxes

   Class here hoofed mammals, comprehensive works on big game

   Class sea cows in 599.55; class big game hunting in 799.2

    For a specific kind of nonungulate game animal, see the kind, e.g., bears 599.78

.63 ***Even-toed ungulates**

   Including camels, hippopotamuses, mouse deer, pigs, pronghorn

   Class here ruminants

   Class comprehensive works on even-toed and odd-toed ungulates in 599.6; class interdisciplinary works on camels in 636.2; class interdisciplinary works on domestic swine in 636.4

    For bovids, see 599.64; for deer, see 599.65

.638 ***Giraffe and okapi**

   Standard subdivisions are added for giraffe and okapi together, for giraffe alone

.64 ***Bovids**

   Including bison, buffalo, gazelles, goats, wild cattle

   Class here antelopes

   Class interdisciplinary works on domestic cattle in 636.2; class interdisciplinary works on domestic goats in 636.3

    See also 599.63 for pronghorn antelope

---

*Add standard subdivisions as instructed under 579–590

.649	*Sheep

Including bighorn sheep

Class interdisciplinary works on domestic sheep in 636.3

.65	*Deer

Including caribou (reindeer), elks, moose

See also 599.63 for mouse deer

.66	*Odd-toed ungulates

Including rhinoceroses, tapirs

.665	*Horse family

Including asses, mustang, zebras

Class interdisciplinary works on horses and asses in 636.1

.67	*Elephants

.7	***Carnivores Land carnivores**

Class here comprehensive works on fur-bearing animals

For a specific kind of noncarnivorous fur-bearing animal, see the kind, e.g., beavers 599.37

> 599.74–599.78   Land carnivores

Class comprehensive works in 599.7

.74	*Feloidea

Including hyena, mongooses

For cat family, see 599.75

.75	*Cat family

Including cheetah, leopards, mountain lion, lynx, ocelot

Class interdisciplinary works on domestic cats in 636.8

.756	*Tiger
.757	*Lion

*Add standard subdivisions as instructed under 579–590

.76   *Canoidea

Including badgers, ferrets, minks, raccoons, red (lesser) panda, skunks, weasels

Class interdisciplinary works on domestic ferrets in 636.976

For dog family, see 599.77; for bears, see 599.78

See also 599.789 for giant panda

.769   *Otters

.77   *Dog family

Including coyote

Class interdisciplinary works on dogs in 636.7

.773   *Gray (Timber) wolf and red wolf

Standard subdivisions are added for either or both topics in heading

Class here comprehensive works on wolves

Class a specific wolf other than gray or red wolf, e.g., maned wolf, in 599.77

.775   *Foxes

Class here red fox, foxes of genus Vulpes

For foxes of genera other than Vulpes, see 599.776

.776   *Foxes of genera other than Vulpes

Including Arctic, fennec, gray foxes

.78   *Bears

.784   *Grizzly bear

.786   *Polar bear

.789   *Giant panda

See also 599.76 for lesser (red) panda

.79   *Marine carnivores

Including eared seals, sea lions, walrus

Class here earless seals (hair seals, true seals); seals

.8   *Primates

Including baboons, lemurs

Class here monkeys

---

*Add standard subdivisions as instructed under 579–590

.88 *Apes

> Including gibbons, orangutan
>
> Class here great apes, comprehensive works on hominoids
>
> *For hominids, see 599.9*

.884 *Gorilla

.885 *Chimpanzees

.9 Hominids   Humans

> Including anthropometry, human biological ecology, variation
>
> Class here physical anthropology [*formerly* 573]
>
> Class social anthropology, comprehensive works on social and physical anthropology in 306; class interdisciplinary works on human ecology in 304.2
>
> *For prehistoric humans, see 569.9; for medicine, see 610*

.93 Genetics, sex and age characteristics, evolution

> Including heredity
>
> *For biochemical genetics, see 612*

.97 Human races [*formerly* 572]

> Including causes of physical differences
>
> Class here physical ethnology
>
> *For specific races, see 599.98*

.98 Specific races [*formerly* 572]

> Class extinct races in 569.9

Add standard subdivisions as instructed under 579–590

600

---

600 Technology (Applied sciences)

See also 303.48 for technology as a cause of cultural change, 306.4 for sociology of technology, 338.1–338.4 for economic aspects of industries based on specific technologies; 338.9 for appropriate technology and technology transfer

See Manual at 300 vs. 600; also at 500 vs. 600

SUMMARY

601 Philosophy and theory

602 Miscellany

Do not use for patents; class in 608

Including comprehensive works on trademarks generally used for products rather than services

Class interdisciplinary works on trademarks and service marks in 929.9

.2 Illustrations

Do not use for drafting illustrations; class in 604.2

.9 Commercial miscellany

Class commercial miscellany of products and services used in individual and family living in 640.29; class commercial miscellany of manufactured products in 670.29; class interdisciplinary commercial miscellany in 380.1029

603 Dictionaries, encyclopedias, concordances

604 Technical drawing, hazardous materials technology, history and description with respect to kinds of persons

.2   Technical drawing

Class here engineering graphics, drafting illustrations

> *For architectural drawing, see 720.28. For drafting illustrations in a specific subject, see the subject, plus notation 022 from Table 1, e.g., map drawing 526.022, drafting in electronics 621.381022*

.7   Hazardous materials technology

Methods of extracting, manufacturing, processing, utilizing, handling, transporting, storing solids, liquids, gases of corrosive, explosive, flammable, infectious, radioactive, toxic nature

Class interdisciplinary works on hazardous materials in 363.17. Class technology of a specific hazardous material with the technology, e.g., explosives 662; class safety techniques for a specific application of hazardous materials with the application outside 300, plus notation 028 from Table 1, e.g., safety techniques in working with hazardous paving materials 625.8028 (*not* 363.17)

> *See Manual at 363.17 vs. 604.7; also at 604.7 vs. 660*

.8   History and description with respect to kinds of persons

Add to base number 604.8 the numbers following —08 in notation 081–089 from Table 1, e.g., women 604.82

605   Serial publications

606   Organizations

[.8]   Management

Do not use; class in 658

607   Education, research, related topics

Including fairs and exhibitions, industrial and products research

Class commercial aspects of fairs and exhibitions in 381; class management of product research in 658.5; class interdisciplinary works on fairs and exhibitions in 907.4

[.4–.6]   Museums, collections, exhibits, and related activities; review and exercise

Do not use; class in 607

[.8–.9]   Use of apparatus and equipment in study and teaching; competitions, festivals, awards, financial support

Numbers discontinued; class in 607

608 Inventions and patents

Do not use for history and description of technology with respect to kinds of persons; class in 604.8

See Manual at 608 vs. 609

[.09] Historical, geographic, persons treatment

Do not use; class in 608.7

.7 Historical, geographic, persons treatment of patents and inventions

Add to base number 608.7 notation 1–9 from Table 2, e.g., patents from Brazil 608.781

For history of inventions, see 609

609 Historical, geographic, persons treatment

Class here history of inventions, technological aspects of industrial archaeology

Class historical and geographic treatment of production and economic aspects of industrial archaeology in 338.09; class historical aspects of industrial archaeology in 900

See Manual at 608 vs. 609

610 Medical sciences   Medicine

Class home care of persons with illnesses and disabilities in 649.8

For veterinary sciences, see 636.089

See Manual at 362.1–362.4 vs. 610; also at 571–573 vs. 610; also at 610 vs. 362.1; also at 610 vs. 616

SUMMARY

610.1–.9	[Standard subdivisions, medical personnel, nursing]
611	Human anatomy, cytology (cell biology), histology (tissue biology)
612	Human physiology
613	Promotion of health
614	Forensic medicine, incidence of disease, public preventive medicine
615	Pharmacology and therapeutics
616	Diseases
617	Miscellaneous branches of medicine Surgery
618	Other branches of medicine Gynecology and obstetrics
619	Experimental medicine

[.23] Medicine as a profession, occupation, hobby

Do not use; class in 610.69

.28 Auxiliary techniques and procedures; apparatus, equipment, materials

Class here comprehensive works on biomedical engineering

For biological aspects of biomedical engineering, see 570.28

.6 **Organizations, management, professions**

Including group practice

Class economics of group practice in 338.7–338.8

.69 Medical personnel

Including physicians, medical technicians and assistants, medical missionaries; medical relationships

Class medical secretaries in 651.3; class medical records librarians in 651.5. Class nature of duties, characteristics of profession, relationships of medical personnel (other than nurses) of a specific specialty with the specialty, e.g., obstetricians 618.2; class critical appraisal and description of work, individual and collected biographies with the specialty, e.g., biography of coroners 614, of psychiatrists 616.890092

For nursing personnel, see 610.7306

.7 **Education, research, nursing, related topics**

Class experimental medicine in 619

.73 Nursing and services of medical technicians and assistants

Including specialized nursing, e.g., psychiatric nursing

Class here general medical nursing

Class services of medical technicians and assistants as a profession, occupation, hobby in 610.69; class patient education by nurses in 615.5071

See Manual at 610.73

.730 1 Philosophy and theory of nursing

.730 2 Miscellany of nursing

[.730 23] Nursing as a profession, occupation, hobby

Do not use; class in 610.7306

.730 3–.730 5 Standard subdivisions of nursing

.730 6 Nursing organizations and personnel

Do not use for management of services of nurses; class in 362.1

Including professional and practical nurses, aides, attendants, orderlies, volunteers

.730 7–.730 9 Standard subdivisions of nursing

.9 **Historical, geographic, persons treatment**

See Manual at 610.9

611　Human anatomy, cytology (cell biology), histology (tissue biology)

Standard subdivisions are added for human anatomy, cytology (cell biology), histology together; for human anatomy alone

For pathological anatomy, see 616.07

See Manual at 612 vs. 611

.001–.009　　　Standard subdivisions

612　Human physiology

Including biophysics, biochemistry, control processes, tissue and organ culture; physiology of work and sports; regional physiology, e.g., physiology of back

Class here comprehensive works on human anatomy and physiology

Class physiological psychology in 152. Class biophysics, biochemistry, control processes, tissue and organ culture in a specific body system; physiology of work and sports in a specific body system; a specific system or organ of a region with the system or organ in 612.1–612.8, e.g., biophysics of circulation 612.1

For human anatomy, cytology (cell biology), histology (tissue biology), see 611; for pathological physiology, see 616.07

See Manual at 612 vs. 611; also at 616 vs. 612

.001–.009　　　Standard subdivisions

.1　　　**Blood and circulation**

Class bone marrow, spleen in 612.4

For lymph and lymphatics, see 612.4. For circulation in a specific system or organ, see the system or organ, e.g., brain 612.8

.2　　　**Respiration**

Including comprehensive works on physiology of the nose

Class physiology of the nose as an olfactory organ in 612.8

.3　　　**Digestion**

Including defecation, metabolism, comprehensive works on physiology of tongue

Class here nutrition

Class biosynthesis in 612; class dietetics and applied nutrition in 613.2

For physiology of tongue as a gustatory organ, see 612.8; for metabolism of drugs, see 615; for metabolism of toxic substances, see 615.9. For metabolism within a specific function, system, or organ, see the function, system, or organ, e.g., metabolism of plasma 612.1

.4   **Secretion, excretion, related functions**

> Including lymphatic, urinary system; hormones

> Class here endocrine system

>> *For defecation, see 612.3. For glands and glandular activity in a specific system or organ, see the system or organ, e.g., salivary glands 612.3, mammary glands and lactation 612.6*

.400 1–.400 9   Standard subdivisions

.6   **Reproduction, development, maturation**

> Including mammary glands and lactation; puberty, menopause, aging; comprehensive works on embryology

> Class here comprehensive medical works on sex

> Class comprehensive works on pregnancy and childbirth in 618.2; class interdisciplinary works on sex in 306.7

>> *For anatomic embryology, see 611. For a specific aspect of sex, see the aspect, e.g., sexual disorders 616.6; for postnatal development of a specific system, organ, region, see the system, organ, region, e.g., postnatal development of teeth 612.3*

>> *See also 616.07 for death*

.600 1–.600 9   Standard subdivisions

.7   **Musculoskeletal system, integument**

> Including bones, connective tissues, joints, muscles; exercise, rest; neurolinguistics, speech, voice; hair, nails, skin

> Class the total physiology of physical movements (including muscle contractions, breathing, blood flow, digestion during exercise) in 612; class bone marrow in 612.4. Class muscles of a specific system or organ with the system or organ, e.g., eye muscles 612.8

>> *For mastoid processes, ossicles, see 612.8*

.8   **Nervous functions   Sensory functions**

> Including brain, nerves; ears, eyes; hearing, smell, taste, touch, vision; sleep

> Class here neurophysiology, psychophysiology

>> *For innervation and neural activity in a specific system or organ, see the system or organ, e.g., heart innervation 612.1*

>> *See Manual at 612.8 vs. 152; also at 612.8 vs. 154.6*

613 Promotion of health

Including environmental factors, health resorts, inherited diseases as a factor, personal cleanliness

Class here measures to promote health and prevent disease taken by individuals and their medical advisers, comprehensive medical works on personal and public measures to promote health and prevent disease

Class personal grooming in 646.7

For public measures to promote health and prevent disease, see 614; for personal preventive measures applied to specific diseases or groups of diseases, see 616–618

See Manual at 613 vs. 615.8

[.081–.084] Persons of specific sex and age groups

Do not use; class in 613

.2 Dietetics

Including high-fiber, low-fiber, macrobiotic, vegetarian diets; weight-gaining and weight-losing programs; nutritional and general health aspects of breast feeding for both mother and infant, comprehensive medical works on breast feeding; specific nutritive elements, e.g., calories, carbohydrates, fats, minerals, proteins, vitamins, water

Class here applied nutrition [*formerly also* 641.1], comprehensive works on nutritive values of beverages [*formerly* 641.2], beverages, guides to nutritional aspects of food, comprehensive works on personal health aspects of food

Class human nutritional requirements considered in relation to physiological processes and the role of nutrients in the body in 612.3; class personal aspects of preventing alcohol abuse in 613.81; class diet therapy in 615.8; class nutritive values of specific beverages in 641.2; class nutritive values of specific foods in 641.3; class comprehensive works on diet and physical fitness in 613.7; class interdisciplinary works on food safety in 363.19; class interdisciplinary works on breast feeding in 649. Class diets to prevent a specific disease with the disease, e.g., diets to prevent hypertension 616.1

For a specific medical aspect of breast feeding not provided for here, see the aspect, e.g., physiology of human lactation 612.6

See also 616.3 for conditions resulting from nutritional deficiencies, 641.5 for cooking for preventive and therapeutic diets

See Manual at 363.8 vs. 613.2, 641.3; also at 649 vs. 613.2

.208 2 Women

Class dietetics for nursing women in 613.2; class dietetics for pregnant women in 618.2

.208 3   Young people

Class breast feeding in 613.2; class home economics and child-rearing aspects of feeding children, interdisciplinary works on feeding children in 649

.208 5   Relatives   Parents

Class dietetics for nursing mothers in 613.2

.6   Special topics of health and safety

Including military, occupational, travel health; self-defense; techniques of survival in accidents, disasters, other unfavorable circumstances

Class here personal safety

For personal safety in a specific field, see the field, plus notation 028 from Table 1, e.g., personal safety in recreational boating 797.1028

See Manual at 363.11 vs. 613.6

.7   Physical fitness

Including exercise, e.g., aerobic dancing, calisthenics, exercises from martial arts traditions, weight lifting for fitness; promotion of health of athletes; physical yoga; posture, rest, sleep; comprehensive works on exercise and sports activities for fitness and for improvement in the shape of the body

Class here comprehensive works on diet and physical fitness

Class breathing in 613; class exercises to aid childbirth in 618.2; class parental supervision of children's exercise and sports activities in 649

For diet, see 613.2; for exercise and sports activities to improve the shape of the body, see 646.7

See also 796.815 for jujitso and related martial arts as sports

See Manual at 613.7 vs. 646.7, 796

[.708 1–.708 4]   Persons of specific sex and age groups

Do not use; class in 613.7

.8   Substance abuse (Drug abuse)

Limited to personal preventive aspects

Including abuse of cocaine, hallucinogens, marijuana, narcotics, psychedelics, stimulants, tranquilizers

Class here appeals to the individual to avoid substance abuse for health reasons

Class comprehensive medical works on addictive and disorienting drugs in 615; class comprehensive medical works on substance abuse as a disease in 616.86; class interdisciplinary works on substance abuse in 362.29

.81   Alcohol

.85   Tobacco

.9 **Birth control, reproductive technology, sex hygiene**

Including artificial insemination, family planning, manuals of sexual technique, sexual abstinence as a method of birth control and disease prevention

Class the pharmacodynamics of chemical contraceptives in 615; class comprehensive works on surgical methods of birth control for males in 617.4; class comprehensive works on surgical methods of birth control for females in 618.1; class interdisciplinary works on birth control and family planning in 363.9

.907 1 Education

Class sex education of children in the home in 649

614 Forensic medicine, incidence of disease, public preventive medicine

Including disposal of the dead

Class social provision for public health services other than those concerned with incidence and prevention of disease in 362.1; class public safety programs and social provision for prevention of injuries in 363.1; class social aspects and services associated with the disposal of the dead, environmental problems and services in 363.7

.4 **Incidence of and public measures to prevent disease**

Including disease carriers and their control, disinfection, immunization, quarantine; health surveys, medical geography

Class here epidemiology

For incidence of and public measures to prevent specific diseases and kinds of diseases, see 614.5

See also 353.5 for registration and certification of births and deaths

See Manual at 614.4; also at 614.4–614.5 vs. 362.1–362.4

.409 Historical, geographic, persons treatment of epidemiology

Do not use for geographic treatment of incidence and distribution of diseases, for history of epidemics; class in 614.4

.5 **Incidence of and public measures to prevent specific diseases and kinds of diseases**

Class incidence of and public measures to prevent mental and emotional illnesses and disturbances in 362.2

See Manual at 614.4–614.5 vs. 362.1–362.4

615   Pharmacology and therapeutics

Including drugs (materia medica), pharmaceutical chemistry (manufacture, preparation, analysis of drugs), practical pharmacy (preparing prescriptions and dispensing drugs), pharmacodynamics (physiological and therapeutic action of drugs); methods of medication, e.g., oral

Class personal aspects of preventing drug addiction in 613.8; class drug therapy in 615.5

See Manual at 616–618 vs. 615

.5   Therapeutics

Including drug therapy, chemotherapy; pediatric and geriatric therapeutics; general therapeutic systems, e.g., chiropractic, osteopathy

Class here comprehensive works on iatrogenic diseases, patient compliance, placebo effect

Class general therapeutics of a specific drug or group of drugs, methods of medication in 615; class therapies applied to specific diseases or groups of diseases in 616–618; class comprehensive works on osteopathy as a medical science in 610

> *For specific therapies and kinds of therapies, see 615.8; for emergency care, first aid, intensive care, see 616.02. For a specific occurrence of iatrogenic diseases, patient compliance, placebo effect, see the occurrence, e.g., surgical shock 617.2; for a specific aspect of pediatric or geriatric therapeutics, see the aspect, e.g., acupuncture 615.8*
>
> *See Manual at 615.5*

.507 1   Education

> Class here comprehensive works on patient education
>
> > *For patient education on a specific topic, see the topic, plus notation 071 from Table 1, e.g., patient education about diseases of cardiovascular system 616.10071*

.8   Specific therapies and kinds of therapies

Including acupuncture, hypnotherapy, music, occupational therapy; physical therapies, e.g., electrotherapy, radiotherapy, therapeutic manipulations and exercises; faith, spiritual healing; folk medicine, patent medicines; quackery; interdisciplinary works on massage

Class comprehensive works in 615.5

> *For drug therapy, see 615.5; for surgery, see 617; for reducing and slenderizing massage, see 646.7*
>
> *See Manual at 615.8; also at 398, 398.27 vs. 615.8; also at 613 vs. 615.8; also at 615.8 vs. 234, 291.3*

.9   **Toxicology**

Including prevention, diagnosis, treatment of poisoning; environmental, industrial toxicology; specific kinds of poisons, e.g., food poisons, lead

Class here poisons and poisoning

Class forensic toxicology in 614; class toxic reactions and interactions of drugs in 615; class effects of poisons on specific systems and organs in 616–618

.900 1   Philosophy and theory

.900 2   Miscellany

.900 28   Auxiliary techniques and procedures; apparatus, equipment, materials

Do not use for testing and measurement; class in 615.9

.900 3–.900 9   Standard subdivisions

616   **Diseases**

Including chronic, congenital, genetic diseases; medical microbiology; symptoms as problems in their own right, e.g., pain; terminal care

Class here internal medicine

Class prenatal procedures to diagnose genetic diseases (e.g., by amniocentesis and chorionic villus biopsy) in 618.3; class comprehensive works on rehabilitation in 617. Class chronic, congenital, genetic diseases; medical microbiology; preventive measures by the individual and by medical personnel; symptoms as problems in their own right; terminal care in relation to a particular kind of disease or branch of medicine with the kind of disease or branch of medicine in 616–618 without use of notation 01–09 from Table 1, e.g., measures taken to prevent respiratory diseases 616.2

For incidence of and public measures to prevent diseases, see 614.4; for therapeutics, see 615.5; for wounds and injuries, surgical treatment of diseases, diseases by body region, diseases of teeth, eyes, ears, see 617; for gynecological, obstetrical, pediatric, geriatric diseases, see 618

See Manual at 610 vs. 616; also at 616–618 vs. 615; also at 616 vs. 612; also at 616 vs. 616.07; also at 616 vs. 617.4; also at 616 vs. 618.92; also at 616.9 vs. 616; also at 617 vs. 616

SUMMARY

616.001–.009	**Standard subdivisions**
.02–.08	**[Domestic medicine, medical emergencies, intensive (critical) care, pathology, psychosomatic medicine]**
.1	**Diseases of cardiovascular system**
.2	**Diseases of respiratory system**
.3	**Diseases of digestive system**
.4	**Diseases of blood-forming, lymphatic, glandular systems Diseases of endocrine system**
.5	**Diseases of integument, hair, nails**
.6	**Diseases of urogenital system Diseases of urinary system**
.7	**Diseases of musculoskeletal system**
.8	**Diseases of nervous system and mental disorders**
.9	**Other diseases**

>   616.001–616.009   Standard subdivisions

Class here standard subdivisions of comprehensive works on other diseases [*formerly also* 616.901–616.909]

Class comprehensive works in 616

.001   Philosophy and theory

.002   Miscellany

[.002 3]   Work with diseases as a profession, occupation, hobby

            Do not use; class in 610.69

.002 8   Auxiliary techniques and procedures; apparatus, equipment, materials

            Do not use for testing and measurement; class in 616.07

.003–.006   Standard subdivisions

.007   Education, research, related topics

            Do not use for experimental research; class in 619

.008   History and description with respect to kinds of persons

.008 3   Young people

            For diseases of infants and children up to puberty, comprehensive works on child and adolescent medicine, see 618.92

.008 4   Persons in specific stages of adulthood

            Do not use for diseases of persons in late adulthood; class in 618.97

.009   Historical, geographic, persons treatment

.009 2   Persons

            Class life with a physical disease in 362.1. Class life with a mental disorder with the disorder in 616.85–616.89, e.g., life with manic-depressive disorder 616.89

.02   Domestic medicine, medical emergencies, intensive (critical) care

> Domestic medicine: diagnosis and treatment of ailments without direction of physician

> Including advice on when to go to a doctor, first aid, comprehensive works on emergency therapy

>> *For a specific kind of emergency or intensive care therapy, see the therapy in 615, e.g., oxygen therapy 615.8*

[.020 1–.020 9]   Standard subdivisions

> Do not use; class in 616.02

.07   Pathology

> Including causes, effects, diagnosis, prognosis; death, immunity, comprehensive works on medical radiology

> Class social factors contributing to spread of disease in 362.1; class immunological drugs in 615; class genetic diseases, genetic aspects of diseases with complex causation, medical microbiology, symptoms as problems in their own right in 616; class nonprofessional diagnosis in 616.02; class diseases of immune system in 616.97; class interdisciplinary works on human death in 306.9

>> *For cytopathology and histopathology, see 611; for forensic pathology, see 614; for radiotherapy, see 615.8*

>> *See Manual at 616 vs. 616.07; also at 616.07 vs. 571.9*

.08   Psychosomatic medicine

> This number is largely limited to psychosomatic aspects of diseases defined in 616.1–616.7, 616.9

> Class psychosomatic symptoms considered as problems in their own right in 616; class neuroses, disorders of personality, intellect, impulse control and their somatic manifestation in 616.85; class mental disorders and their somatic manifestations in 616.89; class diseases caused by stress in 616.9; class comprehensive works on psychological and psychosomatic aspects of disease in 616.001

> ### 616.1–616.9 Specific diseases

Except for modifications shown under specific entries, use the following modified standard subdivisions:

001	Philosophy and theory
002	Miscellany
[0023]	The specialty as a profession, occupation, hobby
	Do not use; class in the number for the disease without adding 0023
0028	Auxiliary techniques and procedures; apparatus, equipment, materials
	Do not use for testing and measurement; class in the number for the disease without adding 0028
003–006	Standard subdivisions
007	Education, research, related topics
	Do not use for experimental research; class in the number for the disease without adding 007
008	History and description with respect to kinds of persons
0083	Young people
	For diseases of infants and children up to puberty, comprehensive works on child and adolescent medicine, see 618.92
0084	Persons in specific stages of adulthood
	Do not use for persons in late adulthood; class in 618.97
009	Historical, geographic, persons treatment
0092	Persons
	Class life with a physical disease in 362.1. Class life with a mental disorder with the disorder in 616.85–616.89, e.g., life with manic-depressive disorder 616.89

Class social factors contributing to the spread of a disease in 362.1; class public measures for preventing a specific disease in 614.5; class comprehensive works on measures to prevent disease in 613; class comprehensive works on therapy in 615.5; class comprehensive works on specific diseases in 616; class comprehensive works on rehabilitation in 617. Class a specific type of genetic disease that has an indirect etiology with the system showing the most visible manifestations, e.g., mental retardation caused by hereditary metabolic disorders 616.85

> ### 616.1–616.8 Diseases of specific systems and organs

Class comprehensive works in 616

For tuberculosis of specific systems and organs, see 616.9; for diseases of the immune system, see 616.97; for tumors of specific systems and organs, see 616.99

See Manual at 616.1–616.8; also at 616.1–616.8 vs. 616.9

.1   **Diseases of cardiovascular system**

Including cardiology, cardiopulmonary resuscitation (CPR), hematology

Class here cardiopulmonary diseases

Class diseases of blood-forming system in 616.4; class implantation and functioning of heart pacers in 617.4. Class diseases of blood vessels in a specific system or organ with the system or organ, e.g., cerebrovascular diseases 616.8

> *For pulmonary diseases, see 616.2; for bacterial blood diseases, see 616.9*

.100 1–.100 9   Standard subdivisions

As modified under 616.1–616.9

.2   **Diseases of respiratory system**

Including common cold, emphysema, hay fever, influenza, pneumonia; comprehensive works on asthma

Class here dyspnea

Class cystic fibrosis in 616.3; class pulmonary tuberculosis in 616.9; class otorhinolaryngology, comprehensive works on diseases of eyes, ears, nose, throat in 617.5

> *For cardiac asthma, see 616.1*

.200 1–.200 9   Standard subdivisions

As modified under 616.1–616.9

.3   **Diseases of digestive system**

Including gastroenterology; nutritional and metabolic diseases, e.g., obesity

Food addiction relocated to 616.85

Class diabetes in 616.4; class appetite and eating disorders as neuroses in 616.85; class allergies of digestive system in 616.97; class oral region (a broader concept than mouth as a digestive organ) in 617.5; class diseases of teeth and gums in 617.6. Class nutritional and metabolic diseases of a specific system or organ with the system or organ, e.g., metabolic bone diseases 616.7

> *For laryngology, see 616.2; for endocrinology, see 616.4; for Reye's syndrome, see 616.8; for cholera, dysenteries, typhoid fever, see 616.9; for hernias, see 617.5*

.300 1–.300 9   Standard subdivisions

As modified under 616.1–616.9

.4   **Diseases of blood-forming, lymphatic, glandular systems**   **Diseases of endocrine system**

Including diabetes; diseases of bone marrow, male breast, spleen

Class here endocrinology

Class endocrinal obesity in 616.3; class filiarial elephantiasis in 616.9; class Hodgkin's disease in 616.99; class comprehensive works on diseases of breast in 618.1. Class diseases of glands in a specific system or organ with the system or organ, e.g., diseases of female sex glands 618.1

For anemia, see 616.1; for myxedema, see 616.85

.400 1–.400 9   Standard subdivisions

As modified under 616.1–616.9

.5   **Diseases of integument, hair, nails**

Standard subdivisions are added for diseases of integument, hair, nails together; for diseases of integument alone

Including diseases of sebaceous and sweat glands; herpes simplex type 1 (cold sores, fever blisters); pigmentary nevi, comprehensive works on nevi

Class here dermatology

Class porphyria in 616.3; class herpes simplex type 2 (genital herpes) in 616.95; class comprehensive works on herpesvirus diseases in 616.9

For allergies of skin, dermatological manifestations of drug, food, or physical allergies, see 616.97; for capillary nevi, see 616.99

.500 1–.500 9   Standard subdivisions

As modified under 616.1–616.9

.6   **Diseases of urogenital system**   **Diseases of urinary system**

Including nephrology; comprehensive works on diseases of genital system, on human reproductive technology, on sexual disorders, e.g., male and female infertility, impotence

Class here urology

Class renal hypertension in 616.1; class kidney dialysis in 617.4; class comprehensive works on climacteric disorders in 618.1. Class urinary manifestations of a specific disease or of a disease in a specific organ with the disease or organ, e.g., enuresis as a manifestation of neurological or mental disorders 616.8

For sexual personality disorders, impotence as a psychological disorder, see 616.85; for diseases of female genital system, female sexual disorders, female infertility, human reproductive technology applied to female infertility, see 618.1

.600 1–.600 9   Standard subdivisions

As modified under 616.1–616.9

.7 **Diseases of musculoskeletal system**

Including neuromuscular diseases; rheumatology, comprehensive works on rheumatism

Class here nonsurgical aspects of and comprehensive works on orthopedics [*both formerly* 617.3]

Class pituitary gigantism, pituitary dwarfism in 616.4; class carpal tunnel syndrome, neuromuscular diseases resulting from disorders of the central nervous system in 616.8. Class diseases of muscles in a specific system or organ with the system or organ, e.g., diseases of heart 616.1

> *For rickets, gout, see 616.3; for fractures, see 617.1; for orthopedic surgery of musculoskeletal system, see 617.4; for orthopedic regional surgery, see 617.5. For a specific rheumatic disease, see the disease, e.g., rheumatic fever 616.9*

.700 1–.700 9 Standard subdivisions

As modified under 616.1–616.9

.8 **Diseases of nervous system and mental disorders**

Including cerebral palsy, epilepsy, locomotor ataxia, poliomyelitis; cerebrovascular diseases, e.g., stroke; diseases of nerves needed to make a specific region function properly, e.g., diseases of peripheral nerves needed to make the hand function properly; headaches, migraine; neurological aspects of paraplegia; sleep disturbances, e.g., insomnia

Class here neurology, neuropsychiatry

Class phenylketonuria in 616.3; class general paresis in 616.89; class comprehensive works on syphilis in 616.95; class comprehensive works on neurological and surgical aspects of paraplegia in 617.5. Class diseases of nerves needed to make a specific system or organ function properly with the system or organ, e.g., neuromuscular diseases 616.7

> *For shingles, see 616.5*

.800 1–.800 9 Standard subdivisions

.801–.809 Standard subdivisions of neurology, of brain diseases

As modified under 616.1–616.9

.85   Neuroses; speech and language disorders; disorders of personality, intellect, impulse control

Including food addiction [*formerly also* 616.3], other eating disorders, e.g., anorexia nervosa; amnesia, combat fatigue, depression, hypochondria, hysteria, multiple personality, phobias; dyslexia, stammering, stuttering; adult victims of child abuse; kleptomania, sadism, suicidal compulsions; hyperactivity, learning disabilities, mental retardation; homosexuality treated as a medical disorder

Class chronic fatigue syndrome in 616; class substance abuse in 616.86; class postpartum depression in 618.7; class abused children in 618.92; class comprehensive works on impotence in 616.6; class interdisciplinary works on homosexuality in 306.76. Class neurotic aspects of a specific disease with the disease, e.g., neurotic aspects of asthma 616.2; class a specific problem of adult victims of child abuse not provided for here with the problem, e.g., alcoholism 616.86

For manic-depressive psychoses, see 616.89

See Manual at 616.85

[.850 1–.850 9]   Standard subdivisions

Do not use; class in 616.85

.86   Substance abuse (Drug abuse)

Including abuse of a specific kind of substance, e.g., alcohol, cocaine, narcotics, tobacco; adult children of substance abusers, effect on persons close to substance abusers

Class here addiction, dependence, habituation, intoxication

Class personal measures to prevent substance abuse in 613.8; class food addiction in 616.85; class minor children of substance abusers in 618.92; class comprehensive medical works on addictive and disorienting drugs in 615; class interdisciplinary works on substance abuse in 362.29. Class a specific problem of adult victims of and persons close to substance abusers with the problem, e.g., depression 616.85

See Manual at 616.86 vs. 158.1, 248.8, 291.4, 362.29

.860 01–.860 09   Standard subdivisions

As modified under 616.1–616.9

.89   Mental disorders

Including autism, general paresis (neurosyphilis), manic-depressive psychoses, paranoia, schizophrenia, senile dementia; psychotherapy, e.g., behavior therapy, group and family psychotherapy, psychoanalysis

Class here abnormal and clinical psychologies, comparative abnormal behavior of animals, psychiatry

Class puerperal mental disorders in 618.7; class Alzheimer's disease, locomotor ataxia, manifestations of mental disorders when considered as symptoms so serious that they become problems in their own right, comprehensive works on dementia in 616.8; class comprehensive works on depression in 616.85; class comprehensive works on syphilis in 616.95. Class a specific organic psychosis not provided for here with the psychosis, e.g., psychosis due to brain tumors 616.99; class physical manifestations of mental disorders involving a specific system with the system, e.g., psychosomatic ulcers 616.3

For neuroses, disorders of personality, intellect, impulse control, see 616.85; for psychosurgery, see 617.4

.890 01–.890 09   Standard subdivisions

As modified under 616.1–616.9

.9   Other diseases

Including malaria, rabies, rheumatic fever, smallpox, tetanus, tuberculosis; bacterial, parasitic, rickettsial, viral diseases; zoonoses

Including noncommunicable diseases; environmental medicine; specialized medical services, e.g., aerospace, industrial medicine

Class here communicable diseases

Class a specific noncommunicable or environmentally linked disease or type of disease provided for elsewhere with the disease or type of disease, e.g., mental disorders 616.89

For parasitic skin diseases, see 616.5; for sports medicine; surgical aspects of radiation sickness, of radiation injuries, see 617.1. For a specific communicable disease not provided for here, see the disease, e.g., mumps 616.3, shingles 616.5

See Manual at 616.1–616.8 vs. 616.9; also at 616.9 vs. 616

.901–.909   Standard subdivisions of communicable diseases

As modified under 616.1–616.9

Standard subdivisions for comprehensive works on other diseases relocated to 616.001–616.009

.95   Sexually transmitted diseases

Former heading: Venereal diseases

For acquired immune deficiency syndrome (AIDS), see 616.97

[.950 1–.950 9]   Standard subdivisions

Do not use; class in 616.95

.97   Diseases of immune system

Including autoimmune diseases, autoimmunity; immune deficiency diseases, e.g., AIDS; contact, drug, food allergies; hypersensitivity to physical agents, e.g., heat, sunlight, humidity

Class here failures of immunity, comprehensive works on allergies

For a specific autoimmune disease, see the disease, e.g., systemic lupus erythematosus 616.7; for a specific allergy not provided for here, see the allergy, e.g., hay fever 616.2

.970 01–.970 09   Standard subdivisions

As modified under 616.1–616.9

.99   Tumors

Medical and surgical treatment

Including cancers, e.g., leukemia

Class here oncology

[.990 1–.990 9]   Standard subdivisions

Do not use; class in 616.99

617   Miscellaneous branches of medicine   Surgery

Only those branches named below

Including operative surgery; orthopedic appliances, self-help devices for persons with disabilities, rehabilitation

Except where contrary instructions are given, all notes under 616.02–616.08 are applicable here

Except for modifications shown under specific entries, use the following modified standard subdivisions:

001–007	Standard subdivisions	
	As modified under 616.1–616.9	
008	History and description with respect to kinds of persons	
0083	Young people	
	Class dentistry for infants and children in 617.6; class comprehensive works on surgery for infants and children up to puberty in 617.9; class regional medicine, ophthalmology, otology, audiology for infants and children up to puberty, comprehensive works on pediatrics in 618.92	
0084	Persons in specific stages of adulthood	
	Class comprehensive works on geriatric surgery in 617.9; class comprehensive works on geriatrics in 618.97	
0088	Occupational and religious groups	
	Class military surgery in 617.9	
[009]	Historical, geographic, persons treatment	
	Do not use; class in 09	
09	Historical, geographic, persons treatment	
	Add to 09 notation 1–9 from Table 2, e.g., the subject in India 0954	

Class comprehensive works on geriatric, pediatric, military, plastic surgery in 617.9. Class operative surgery of a specific system, organ, region with the system, organ, region in 617, e.g., operative heart surgery 617.4; class rehabilitation from a specific disease or injury with the disease or injury, e.g., rehabilitation from stroke 616.8, from back injury 617.5

> *See Manual at 616–618 vs. 615; also at 617 vs. 616; also at 618.92 vs. 617; also at 618.97 vs. 617*

> 617.001–617.5 Surgery

Class comprehensive works, operative surgery in 617

For surgical treatment of tumors, see 616.99; for geriatric, pediatric, military, plastic surgery; transplantation of tissue and organs, implantation of artificial organs, anesthesiology, see 617.9

.001   Philosophy and theory of surgery

.002   Miscellany of surgery

| [.002 3] | Surgery as a profession, occupation, hobby |

Do not use; class in 617

| [.002 8] | Auxiliary techniques and procedures; apparatus, equipment, materials |

Do not use; class in 617. Do not use for geriatric, pediatric, military, plastic surgery, transplantation of tissue and organs, implantation of artificial organs, anesthesiology; class in 617.9

| .003–.007 | Standard subdivisions of surgery |

| .008 | History and description of surgery with respect to kinds of persons |

| .008 3 | Young people |

Do not use for surgery for infants and children up to puberty; class in 617.9

| .008 4 | Persons in specific stages of adulthood |

Do not use for persons in late adulthood; class in 617.9

| .008 8 | Occupational and religious groups |

Do not use for military personnel; class in 617.9

| [.009] | Historical, geographic, persons treatment of surgery |

Do not use; class in 617.09

| .09 | Historical, geographic, persons treatment of surgery |

Add to base number 617.09 notation 1–9 from Table 2, e.g., collective biographies of surgeons 617.0922

.1 Injuries and wounds

Standard subdivisions are added for injuries and wounds together, for injuries alone

Including burns, dislocations, fractures, sprains; sports medicine

Class here traumatology

Class results of injuries in 617.2. Class a specific branch of sports medicine with the branch, e.g., promotion of health of athletes 613.7

For injuries and wounds of specific systems, regions, organs, see 617.4–617.5

| .100 1–.100 9 | Standard subdivisions |

.2 Results of injuries

Including shock

For results of injuries of specific systems, regions, organs, see 617.4–617.5

See also 617.1 for rehabilitation, rehabilitative therapy

[.3]   **Orthopedics**

Use of this number for orthopedic appliances discontinued; class in 617

Nonsurgical aspects of orthopedics and comprehensive works on orthopedics relocated to 616.7, orthopedic surgery of musculoskeletal system relocated to 617.4, orthopedic regional medicine and orthopedic regional surgery relocated to 617.5

> **617.4–617.5 Surgery by systems and regions**

Class here injuries and wounds of specific systems, regions, organs; surgery of specific organs

Class comprehensive works in 617

.4   **Surgery by systems**

Including orthopedic surgery of musculoskeletal system [*formerly* 617.3]; cardiovascular, digestive, endocrine, lymphatic, musculoskeletal, nervous, urogenital systems; circumcision, psychosurgery

Class chronic diseases of skeletal system in 616.7; class orthopedics of specific regions in 617.5; class ophthalmological surgery in 617.7; class otological surgery in 617.8. Class surgery of nerves of a specific system or organ with the system or organ, e.g., neurosurgery of the stomach 617.5

For dislocations, fractures, sprains, strains, see 617.1; for amputations, jaws, joints of extremities, respiratory system, skull, surgery of specific organs of digestive system, see 617.5; for gynecological and obstetrical surgery, see 618. For surgery of a specific gland, see the gland, e.g., thyroid gland 617.5

See Manual at 616 vs. 617.4

.5   **Regional medicine   Regional surgery**

Including appendectomies, oral surgery, otorhinolaryngology, podiatry, respiratory system; comprehensive works on diseases of eyes, ears, nose, throat

Class here orthopedic regional medicine, orthopedic regional surgery [*both formerly* 617.3]

Class nonsurgical medicine of specific systems or organs in specific regions in 616; except for spleen, respiratory system, specific organs of digestive system, class surgery of a specific system in a specific region in 617.4

For eyes, see 617.7; for ears, see 617.8

See Manual at 617.5; also at 617.6 vs. 617.5

.6   **Dentistry**

Including cavities, dental diseases, oral surgery, orthodontics, pedodontics; dentures, bridges

See Manual at 617.6 vs. 617.5

.600 1–.600 7   Standard subdivisions

As modified under 617

.600 8   History and description with respect to kinds of persons

[.600 83]   Young people

Number discontinued; class in 617.6

.600 9   Historical, geographic, persons treatment

.7   Ophthalmology

Treatment of ocular diseases; correction of errors of refraction, e.g., astigmatism

Including color blindness, cataracts, glaucoma; optometry; use of eyeglasses, contact lenses

For tuberculosis of eyes, see 616.9; for tumors of eyes, see 616.99

.700 1–.700 8   Standard subdivisions

As modified under 617

[.700 9]   Historical, geographic, persons treatment

Do not use; class in 617.709

.709   Historical, geographic, persons treatment

Add to base number 617.709 notation 1–9 from Table 2, e.g., collective biographies of ophthalmologists 617.70922

.8   Otology and audiology

Standard subdivisions are added for either or both topics in heading

Including pathology, medical and surgical treatment of diseases of ears; correction of impaired hearing through fitting and adjusting hearing devices

Class here loss and impairment of function (deafness and hearing impairment)

For tuberculosis of ears, see 616.9; for tumors of ears, see 616.99

.800 1–.800 8   Standard subdivisions

As modified under 617

[.800 9]   Historical, geographic, persons treatment

Do not use; class in 617.809

.809   Historical, geographic, persons treatment

Add to base number 617.809 notation 1–9 from Table 2, e.g., collective biographies of audiologists 617.80922

.9 **Geriatric, pediatric, military, plastic surgery; transplantation of tissue and organs, implantation of artificial organs; anesthesiology**

Class acupuncture as an anesthetic in 615.8. Class geriatric, pediatric, military surgery of a specific organ, system, disorder with the organ, system, disorder, e.g., fractures 617.1

For plastic surgery and transplantation of tissue of specific systems, regions, organs, see 617.4–617.5; for transplantation of a specific organ and implantation of artificial substitutes for a specific organ, see 617.4. For plastic surgery and transplantation of tissue and organs, implantation of artificial organs in gynecological and obstetrical surgery, see the tissue or organ in 618, e.g., breast implants 618.1

See also 362.1 for tissue and organ banks

[.901–.909] Standard subdivisions

Do not use; class in 617.9

618 Other branches of medicine   Gynecology and obstetrics

See Manual at 616–618 vs. 615

.01 Philosophy and theory of gynecology and obstetrics

.02 Miscellany of gynecology and obstetrics

.028 Auxiliary techniques and procedures; apparatus, equipment, materials

Do not use for testing and measurement; class in 618

.03–.07 Standard subdivisions of gynecology and obstetrics

.08 History and description of gynecology and obstetrics with respect to kinds of persons

.083 Young people

Do not use for gynecology for girls up to puberty; class in 618.92

.084 Persons in specific stages of adulthood

Do not use for persons in late adulthood; class in 618.97

.09 Historical, geographic, persons treatment of gynecology and obstetrics

Class life with a disease in 362.1

> **618.1–618.8 Gynecology and obstetrics**

Medical and surgical

Except where contrary instructions are given, all notes under 616.02–616.08 are applicable here

Class comprehensive works in 618

.1   Gynecology

Including artificial insemination, infertility, human reproductive technology applied to female infertility; comprehensive works on climacteric disorders, on diseases and surgery of male and female breast

Class involutional psychoses in 616.89; class tumors of genital system in 616.99; class comprehensive works on male and female infertility, on human reproductive technology in 616.6

> *For diseases of male breast, see 616.4; for male climacteric disorders, see 616.6; for tumors of breast, see 616.99; for surgery of male breast, see 617.5; for diseases of lactation, puerperal diseases, see 618.7; for pediatric gynecology, see 618.92*

.100 1–.100 9   Standard subdivisions

As modified under 616.1–616.9

.2   Obstetrics

Including prenatal care, multiple pregnancy

Class here midwifery, comprehensive works on pregnancy and childbirth

> *For physiology of pregnancy and childbirth, see 612.6; for diseases, disorders, management of pregnancy, parturition, puerperium, see 618.3–618.8*

.200 1–.200 9   Standard subdivisions

As modified under 616.1–616.9

\>   **618.3–618.8 Diseases, disorders, management of pregnancy, parturition, puerperium**

Class comprehensive works in 618.2

.3   Diseases and complications of pregnancy

Including fetal disorders, miscarriage, perinatal medicine

Class neonatal medicine in 618.92

> *For childbirth, see 618.4*

> *See Manual at 616 vs. 618.92*

.300 1–.300 9   Standard subdivisions

As modified under 616.1–616.9

.4   Childbirth (Parturition)   Labor

Class a specific aspect not provided for here with the aspect, e.g., obstetrical surgery in 618.8

.5   Complicated labor (Dystocia)

.6   Normal puerperium

Postpartum management and care

.7   Puerperal diseases

Including diseases of lactation

.700 1–.700 9   Standard subdivisions

As modified under 616.1–616.9

.8   Obstetrical surgery

Including cesarean section

Class embryo transplant in 618.1

.9   Pediatrics and geriatrics

.92   Pediatrics

Diseases of infants and children up to puberty

Class pediatric sports medicine in 617.1; class perinatal medicine in 618.3; class medicine for young people who have reached puberty in 616.00835

> *For pediatric preventive measures, see 613; for pediatric therapeutics, see 615.5; for pediatric aspects of wounds and injuries, see 617.10083; for pediatric aspects of results of injuries, see 617.2083; for pediatric dental disease, pedodontics, see 617.6; for pediatric surgery, see 617.9*
>
> *See Manual at 616 vs. 618.92; also at 618.92 vs. 617*

.920 001–.920 009   Standard subdivisions

As modified under 616.1–616.9

.97   Geriatrics

Diseases of persons in late adulthood

> *For geriatric preventive measures, see 613; for geriatric therapeutics, see 615.5; for geriatric aspects of wounds and injuries, see 617.10084; for geriatric aspects of results of injuries, see 617.2084; for geriatric surgery, see 617.9*
>
> *See Manual at 618.97 vs. 617*

.970 01–.970 09   Standard subdivisions

As modified under 616.1–616.9

619   Experimental medicine

Class here experimental research on diseases

Class animal experimentation with respect to anatomy and physiology in 571–573; class human experimentation with respect to anatomy in 611; class human experimentation with respect to physiology in 612; class experimental medicine with respect to pharmacology and therapeutics in 615; class experimental medicine with respect to specific diseases in 616–618

620 Engineering and allied operations

Standard subdivisions are added for engineering and allied operations together, for engineering alone

Including computer-aided design (CAD), engineering for specific kinds of geographic environments, fine particle and remote control technology, nanotechnology, surface engineering, interdisciplinary works on maintenance and repair

Class here manufacturing of products of various branches of engineering

Class comprehensive works on manufacturing in 670; class comprehensive works on computer-aided design/computer-aided manufacturing (CAD/CAM) in 670.285. Class a specific application of engineering for specific kinds of geographic environments with the application, plus notation 091 from Table 1 when the technology is not inherent in the subject, e.g., work environment engineering for deserts 620.80915, nautical engineering 623.8; class a specific application of nanotechnology with the technology, e.g., nanotechnology used in manufacturing thin-film circuits 621.3815

> For chemical engineering, see 660. For maintenance and repair in a specific subject, see the subject, plus notation 028 from Table 1, e.g., repair of electronic equipment 621.381028

SUMMARY

620.001–.009	Standard subdivisions
.1–.8	[Engineering mechanics and materials, sound and related vibrations, mechanical vibration, human factors and safety engineering]
621	Applied physics
622	Mining and related operations
623	Military and nautical engineering
624	Civil engineering
625	Engineering of railroads, roads, highways
627	Hydraulic engineering
628	Sanitary and municipal engineering Environmental protection engineering
629	Other branches of engineering

.001 Philosophy and theory

Do not use for mechanical principles in engineering; class in 620.1. Do not use for principles of sound and related vibrations in engineering; class in 620.2. Do not use for other physical principles in engineering; class in 621

Including systems engineering

Class design of engineering systems in 620; class manufacturing systems in 670.1; class interdisciplinary works covering systems in agriculture, home economics, and management in addition to engineering in 601; class interdisciplinary works on systems in 003

.002 Miscellany

.002 8	Auxiliary techniques and procedures; apparatus, equipment, materials

Do not use for maintenance and repair, testing and measurement; class in 620. Do not use for safety measures; class in 620.8

.003–.008	Standard subdivisions
.009	Historical, geographic, persons treatment
.009 1	Treatment by areas, regions, places in general

Class engineering to overcome problems of specific kinds of geographical environments in 620

.009 2	Persons

Class persons treatment of engineers known primarily as entrepreneurs in 338.7

[.009 99]	Engineering in extraterrestrial worlds

Do not use; class in 620

.1   **Engineering mechanics and materials**

Standard subdivisions are added for engineering mechanics and materials together, for engineering mechanics alone

Including applied dynamics, applied statics; applied mechanics of solids, liquids, gases; corrosion, failure, fatigue, resistance; strength of materials; comprehensive works on fluid-power technology

Class fine particle technology in 620; class hydraulic engineering in 627; class comprehensive works on materials, manufacture of materials in 670. Class manufacturing and chemical properties of a specific kind of material with the material, e.g., wood 674

For mechanical vibration, see 620.3; for steam engineering, see 621.1; for hydraulic-power technology, see 621.2; for pneumatic and vacuum technology, see 621.5; for hydraulic engineering, see 627; for aeromechanics of flight, see 629.132; for air-conditioning engineering, see 697.9

See also 531 for mechanics as a subject in physics, 621.8 for physical principles of machinery

See Manual at 530 vs. 621

.100 1–.100 9	Standard subdivisions

.2 **Sound and related vibrations**

Standard subdivisions are added for sound and related vibrations together, for sound alone

Including noise and countermeasures, subsonics, ultrasonics

Class here applied acoustics (acoustical engineering)

Class electroacoustical communications in 621.382; class engineering works on architectural acoustics in 690; class interdisciplinary works on architectural acoustics in 729

> *See also 534 for physics of sound*

> *See Manual at 530 vs. 621*

.3 **Mechanical vibration**

Class effects of vibrations on materials in 620.1

> *For sound and related vibrations, see 620.2*

.8 **Human factors and safety engineering**

Variant names for human factors engineering: biotechnology, design anthropometry, ergonomics

Class here work environment engineering

Class a specific application with the application, e.g., engineering of the home kitchen work environment 643

> *For safety engineering of a specific technology, see the technology, plus notation 028 from Table 1, e.g., safety in machine engineering 621.8028*

> *See also 628 for environmental protection engineering*

> *See Manual at 363.1 vs. 620.8*

621 Applied physics

Class here mechanical engineering

Class a specific application of applied physics with the application, e.g., military engineering 623

> *For engineering (applied) mechanics, see 620.1; for applied acoustics, see 620.2*

> *See Manual at 530 vs. 621*

SUMMARY

.04   Special topics

.042   Energy engineering

> Class here engineering of alternative and renewable energy sources

> Class interdisciplinary works on energy in 333.79

.044   Plasma engineering

> Class interdisciplinary works on plasma in 530.4

> **621.1–621.2 Fluid-power technologies**

> Class comprehensive works in 620.1

.1   **Steam engineering**

> Including engines, boilers, cogeneration of electric power and heat

> Class interdisciplinary works on cogeneration of electricity and heat in 333.793

> *For marine steam engines, see 623.8; for steam locomotives, see 625.2; for*
> *steam tractors and rollers, see 629.22*

.2   **Hydraulic-power technology**

> Including hydraulic pumps, water mills

> Class hydraulic control in 629.8; class comprehensive works on pumps in
> 621.6

.3   **Electrical engineering; lighting; superconductivity; magnetic**
            engineering; applied optics; paraphotic technology; electronics;
            communications engineering; computers

> Standard subdivisions are added for electromagnetic engineering, for combined
> electric and electronic engineering, for electrical engineering alone

> *See also 537 for physics of electricity and electromagnetism*

SUMMARY

.302 8   Auxiliary techniques and procedures; apparatus, equipment, materials

> Do not use for electrical equipment; class in 621.31. Do not use for electrical testing and measurement; class in 621.37

.31   Generation, modification, storage, transmission of electric power

> Including electrical machinery and equipment; batteries, fuel cells, solar cells; power electronics; direct nuclear generation

> Class here alternating current

> Class engineering of dams for hydroelectric power in 627; class comprehensive works on electrochemical engineering in 660. Class a specific application of electric machinery with the application, e.g., refrigerators 621.5

>> *For electric motors, see 621.46; for nuclear steam-powered generation of electricity, see 621.48*

.319   Transmission

> Including circuits, interior wiring, power failure

> Class here electrification

> Class interdisciplinary works on electrification, on power failure in 333.793

>> *For electric power transmission for railroads, see 621.33*

.319 01   Philosophy and theory

> Do not use for systems; class in 621.319

.32   Lighting

> Including candles, gas lighting

> Class here electric lighting

>> *For public lighting, see 628.9; for lighting of airports, see 629.136*

.33   Electric power transmission for railroads

.34   **Magnetic engineering**

Class here artificial magnets, electromagnets

Class electromagnets as parts of generators in 621.31; class electromagnets as parts of electric motors in 621.46; class comprehensive works on electromagnetic technology in 621.3

See also 538 for physics of magnetism, natural magnets

.36   **Applied optics and paraphotic technology**

Standard subdivisions are added for either or both topics in heading

Including spectroscopy; fiber optics; infrared and ultraviolet technology; integrated optics; lasers; technological photography and photo-optics, e.g., holography, optical data processing, remote sensing technology

Class manufacture of optical instruments in 681; class interdisciplinary works on photography in 770

For photogrammetry, see 526.9; for lighting, see 621.32; for photoelectric and photoelectronic devices, see 621.3815; for laser and optical communications, see 621.382

See also 535 for optics and light as subjects in physics, 621.381 for optoelectronics

See Manual at 006.3 vs. 006.4, 621.36, 621.39; also at 778.3 vs. 621.36

.37   **Testing and measurement of electrical quantities**

Instruments and their use

For testing and measurement of a specific apparatus, part, or function, see the apparatus, part, or function, plus notation 028 from Table 1, e.g., testing electromagnets 621.34028

.38   **Electronics, communications engineering**

.381   **Electronics**

Including microwave electronics, optoelectronics

Class here microelectronics

Class signal processing, electronic noise and interference in 621.382. Class a specific application of electronics with the application, e.g., laser technology 621.36, radio engineering 621.384

See also 537.5 for physics of electronics

.381 5   Components and circuits

Standard subdivisions are added for either or both topics in heading

Including photoelectric devices, e.g., electric eyes; photoelectronic devices; printed circuits; semiconductors, e.g., transistors

Class here analog, digital, integrated, microelectronic, semiconductor, superconductor, thin-film circuits; circuits and components common to electronics and communications engineering

Class microwave components and circuits in 621.381; class components and circuits of a specific branch of communications engineering in 621.383–621.389; class very large scale integration in 621.39

.381 502 8   Auxiliary techniques and procedures; apparatus, equipment, materials

Do not use for testing and measurement; class in 621.3815

.382   Communications engineering

(621.382)

Including acoustical, electroacoustical, optical communications; communications networks; satellite relay; facsimile transmission; information theory, signal processing; antennas; recording devices of two or more communication systems, e.g., discs, tapes

Class here analog, digital, electronic communications; telecommunications; comprehensive works on digital data and telecommunications engineering

Class a component or circuit common to electronics and communications engineering, e.g., amplifiers, switching circuits, in 621.3815; class video recorders in 621.388; class audio systems limited to recording and reproduction of sound in 621.389; class interdisciplinary works on information theory in 003

For specific communications systems, see 621.383–621.389; for data communications engineering, see 621.39. For communications networks based upon a specific technology, see the technology, e.g., telephone networks 621.385

See Manual at 004.6 vs. 621.382, 621.39

>   621.383–621.389   Specific communications systems

Class comprehensive works in 621.382

.383   Telegraphy

For radiotelegraphy, see 621.384

.384   Radio and radar

Standard subdivisions are added for radio and radar together, for radio alone

Including loran, radio control, radiotelegraphy

Class here broadcasting stations, comprehensive engineering works on radio and television

Class interdisciplinary works on radio and television in 384.5; class interdisciplinary works on broadcasting stations in 384.54

For television, see 621.388

.384 028   Auxiliary techniques and procedures; apparatus, equipment, materials

Class maintenance and repair of receiving sets in 621.384

.384 1   Amateur (Ham) radio

See Manual at 621.3841 vs. 621.3845

[.384 101–.384 109]   Standard subdivisions

Do not use; class in 621.3841

.384 5   Radiotelephony

Including cellular telephone systems, citizens band radio, portable radios, walkie-talkies

Class here mobile radio stations, comprehensive works on radio transmission in telephony

For radio relays, see 621.387

See Manual at 621.3841 vs. 621.3845

.384 8   Radar

.385   Telephony

Class here telephone systems based on wires, cables, lasers, optical fibers

Class cellular telephone systems in 621.3845; class data communications engineering in 621.39

For radiotelephony, see 621.3845; for telephone equipment and transmission, see 621.386–621.387

>   621.386–621.387   Telephone equipment and transmission

Class comprehensive works in 621.385

.386   Telephone terminal equipment

Dialing, transmitting, receiving equipment

.387 Telephone transmission and nonterminal equipment

Including radio relays, switches

Class comprehensive works on radio transmission in telephony in 621.3845

.388 Television

Including cameras, video recorders

.388 001 Philosophy and theory

.388 002 Miscellany

.388 002 8 Auxiliary techniques and procedures; apparatus, equipment, materials

Do not use for maintenance and repair of receiving sets; class in 621.388

Including maintenance and repair covering broadcast and transmission equipment as well as receiving sets

.388 003–.388 009 Standard subdivisions

.389 Security, sound recording, related systems

Including alarm systems, audiovisual engineering, electronic eavesdropping devices, public address systems, sonar, language translators

Class telephone message recording in 621.386; class comprehensive works on acoustical communications, on audio systems covering transmission as well as recording and reproduction in 621.382

.39 Computer engineering

Including analog computers; data communications engineering; interfacing and communications devices, e.g., modems; peripherals, e.g., terminals; memory, storage

Class here electronic digital computers, central processing units, computer reliability, general computer performance evaluation

Class selection and use of computer hardware, works treating both hardware and either programming or programs in 004; class storage of pictorial data in optical storage devices in 621.36; class programmable calculators in 681. Class a specific application of computers with the application, e.g., use of computers to regulate processes automatically 629.8

See Manual at 004–006 vs. 621.39; also at 004.6; also at 004.6 vs. 621.382, 621.39; also at 006.3 vs. 006.4, 621.36, 621.39

.390 28 Auxiliary techniques and procedures, apparatus, equipment, materials

Do not use for testing and measurement; class in 621.39

.4   **Heat engineering and prime movers**

Including windmills

Class here engines, power plants, propulsion systems

For steam engineering, see 621.1; for hydraulic-power technology, see 621.2

.400 1–.400 9   Standard subdivisions

.402   Heat engineering

Including combustion, electric heating, equipment

Class pollution by-products of combustion in 628.5. Class a kind of heat engineering with the kind, e.g., geothermal engineering 621.44, heating buildings 697

For low-temperature technology, see 621.5

See also 536 for physics of heat

.406   Turbines

Class here turbomachines

.43   Internal-combustion engines

Including diesel, jet, rocket, spark-ignition engines; gas turbines

Class generation of electricity by internal-combustion engines in 621.31

See Manual at 629.04 vs. 621.43

.44   Geothermal engineering

Including prospecting for sources of geothermal energy, utilization of differences in ocean temperature

.46   Electric and related motors

Standard subdivisions are added for electric and related motors together, for electric motors alone

Including ion, plasma motors

.47   Solar-energy engineering

Including solar engines

Class engineering of a secondary source of solar energy with the secondary source, e.g., generation of electricity from solar radiation 621.31, wind energy 621.4

.48 Nuclear engineering

Fission and fusion technology

Including nuclear reactors and power plants, nuclear propulsion, treatment and disposal of radioactive waste, comprehensive works on radioisotope technology

Class direct nuclear generation of electricity in 621.31

For a specific application of radioisotopes, see the application, e.g., radioactive isotope therapy 615.8

See also 539.7 for nuclear physics

.5 **Pneumatic, vacuum, low-temperature technologies**

Including air compression technology, cryogenic technology, ice manufacture, refrigeration, sandblasting

For blowers, fans, pumps, see 621.6; for pneumatic control, see 629.8

See also 533 for vacuum physics, 536 for physics of low temperatures

.6 **Blowers, fans, pumps**

For hydraulic pumps, see 621.2

.8 **Machine engineering**

Including fasteners, e.g., bolts, nails; friction, lubrication; machine parts, e.g., bearings, gears; materials-handling equipment, e.g., elevators, power shovels; conveying equipment, e.g., escalators, pipes and pipelines, people movers; hoisting equipment, e.g., cranes, derricks; power transmission

Class coal pipelines in 662.6; class petroleum pipelines in 665.5; class industrial gases pipelines in 665.7. Class a specific kind of machinery not provided for here with the kind, e.g., hydraulic machinery 621.2; class a specific use of machinery with the use, e.g., gears in clocks 681.1; class manufacturing pipes of a specific material with the material, e.g., metal pipes 671.8

See also 621.9 for fastening equipment

.801 Philosophy and theory

Do not use for physical principles of machinery; class in 621.8

.802 Miscellany

.802 8 Auxiliary techniques and procedures; apparatus, equipment, materials

Do not use for maintenance and repair; class in 621.8

Including strength tests of mechanisms

.9   **Tools**

Including drilling tools, grindstones, hammers, knives, lathes, molds, planes, saws, vises, wrenches

Class here fabricating equipment

Class a specific use with the use, e.g., lathes in woodworking 684

.900 1–.900 9   Standard subdivisions

622   Mining and related operations

Standard subdivisions are added for mining and related operations together, for mining alone

Including in-situ processing, ore dressing, prospecting, treasure hunting; mine safety

Class archaeological methods and equipment in 930.1028; class interdisciplinary works on mine safety in 363.11

For prospecting for water, water extraction, see 628.1

See Manual at 622 vs. 662, 669

.028   **Auxiliary techniques and procedures; apparatus, equipment, materials**

Do not use for safety measures; class in 622

623   Military and nautical engineering

Standard subdivisions are added for military and nautical engineering together, for military engineering alone

Including ballistics, camouflage, demolition, forts, gunnery, mine laying and clearance; military communications, intelligence, sanitation, transportation technology

Class manufacture of mines in 623.4; class artistic aspects of forts in 725

See Manual at 355 vs. 623

.4   **Ordnance**

Including artillery, biological and nuclear weapons; mines; missiles, rocket weapons; small arms; weaponry of prefirearm origin, e.g., armor, bows and arrows, swords

Class mine laying and clearance in 623; class vehicle-mounted small arms in 623.7; class combat ships in 623.8; class artistic aspects of arms and armor in 739.7; class comprehensive works on rocketry in 621.43

For combat vehicles, see 623.7

.7 **Vehicles**

Support vehicles, combat vehicles and their ordnance

Including airplanes, jeeps, spacecraft, tanks

Class railroad rolling stock in 623

For charge-containing devices, see 623.4; for nautical craft, see 623.8

See Manual at 629.04 vs. 388

[.701–.709] Standard subdivisions

Do not use; class in 623.7

.8 **Nautical engineering and seamanship**

Nautical engineering: engineering of ships and boats and their component parts

Standard subdivisions are added for nautical engineering and seamanship together, for nautical engineering alone

Including cargo-handling equipment, naval ordnance, shipyards

Class here naval engineering, comprehensive works on military water transportation

Class naval facilities in 623; class harbors, ports, roadsteads, on-shore cargo handling equipment in 627; class overwater hovercraft in 629.3

For naval artillery and charge-containing devices, see 623.4

See Manual at 629.04 vs. 388

.88 Seamanship

Including marine safety technology, rescue operations, wreckage studies, interdisciplinary works on knotting and splicing

Class safety equipment in 623.8

For navigation, see 623.89. For a specific application of knotting and splicing, see the application, e.g., knotting in camping 796.54

See Manual at 363.1 vs. 620.8

.880 28 Auxiliary techniques and procedures; apparatus, equipment, materials

Do not use for safety measures; class in 623.88

.89 Navigation

Selection and determination of course

Including piloting and pilot guides; aids to navigation, e.g., lighthouses

Class navigation procedures to prevent collision and grounding in 623.88; class construction of lighthouses, beacons, buoys, daymarks in 627; class construction of lightships in 628; class interdisciplinary works on lighthouses in 387.1

624 Civil engineering

Including bridges

Class here construction engineering

For military construction engineering, see 623. For a specific branch of civil engineering not provided for here, see the branch, e.g., construction of buildings 690

See Manual at 624 vs. 624.1; also at 624 vs. 690

.029 Commercial miscellany

Including estimates of labor, time, materials [*formerly* 624.1]

Class interdisciplinary works on quantity surveying in 692

.1 Structural engineering and underground construction

Standard subdivisions are added for structural engineering and underground construction together, for structural engineering alone

Including earthquake engineering, engineering geology, excavation, foundations, soil mechanics, soil surveys, tunnels; interdisciplinary works on structural analysis, design, theory

Estimates of labor, time, materials for civil engineering relocated to 624.029

Class subsurface mining in 622; class general soil surveys not focusing on engineering problems in 631.4. Class a specific application of structural engineering with the application, e.g., structural engineering of dams 627

For construction of underground waste disposal facilities, see 628.4. For specific application of structural analysis, design, theory, see the application, e.g., structural analysis of aircraft 629.134

See Manual at 624 vs. 624.1

.101 Philosophy and theory

Class structural analysis and design in 624.1

.102 9 Commercial miscellany

Including estimates of labor, time, materials

625 Engineering of railroads, roads, highways

Class bridge engineering in 624; class tunnel engineering in 624.1

For military transportation engineering, see 623

.1   Railroads

Including model railroads and trains; monorail railroads, comprehensive works on special-purpose railroads; railroad yards

Class electrification of railroads in 621.33; class play with model railroads and trains in 790.1; class interdisciplinary works on railroads in 385

> *For railroad rolling stock, see 625.2; for special-purpose railroads, see 625.3–625.6*

.100 1   Philosophy and theory

.100 2   Miscellany

.100 22   Illustrations

Do not use for models and miniatures; class in 625.1

.100 3–.100 9   Standard subdivisions

.2   Railroad rolling stock

Including freight, passenger-train cars

Class here comprehensive works on specific types of cars, on rolling stock for roads with two running rails

> *For rolling stock for special-purpose railways, see 625.3–625.6*

> *See Manual at 629.04 vs. 388*

.202 2   Illustrations

Do not use for models and miniatures; class in 625.1

.26   Locomotives

.260 22   Illustrations

Do not use for models and miniatures; class in 625.1

> **625.3–625.6 Special-purpose railroads**

Class here roadbeds, tracks and accessories, rolling stock

Class comprehensive works in 625.1

> *For mine railroads, see 622*

.3   Inclined, mountain, ship railroads

.4   Rapid transit systems

Including subways

> *For surface systems, see 625.6*

.5   Cable and aerial railways

> *For funicular railroads, see 625.3*

.6   **Surface rail and trolley systems**

Standard subdivisions are added for either or both topics in heading

Light interurban and local

.7   **Roads**

Including roadside barriers, roadside areas, traffic signs

Class here highways, streets

Class grade crossing (road crossings of railroads) in 625.1; class curbs in 625.8; class interdisciplinary works on roads and highways in 388.1; class interdisciplinary works on urban roads and streets in 388.4

For artificial road surfaces, see 625.8; for public lighting for roads, see 628.9; for forest roads, see 634.9

.702 8   Auxiliary techniques and procedures; apparatus, equipment, materials

Do not use for maintenance and repair; class in 625.7

.8   **Artificial road surfaces**

Including driveways, sidewalks

Class here comprehensive works on paving

For a paving surface not provided for here, see the surface, e.g., airport runways 629.136

.802 8   Auxiliary techniques and procedures; apparatus, equipment, materials

Do not use for maintenance and repair; class in 625.7

627   Hydraulic engineering

The branch of engineering dealing with utilization and control of natural waters of the earth

Including dams and reservoirs; flood control; harbors, ports, roadsteads; inland waterways, e.g., canals, rivers, streams; navigation aids, e.g., lighthouses; offshore structures, drilling platforms; reclamation, irrigation; underwater operations, e.g., dredging; comprehensive technological works on erosion and its control; interdisciplinary works on diving

Class here hydraulic structures, water resources engineering

Class use of navigation aids in 623.89; class bridges carrying canals in 624; class tunnels carrying canals in 624.1; class architectural aspects of port facilities in 725; class comprehensive works on ocean engineering in 620; class comprehensive works on cargo-handling equipment in 623.88; class interdisciplinary works on land reclamation in 333.73; class interdisciplinary works on canals in 386; class interdisciplinary works on harbors, ports, roadsteads in 387.1; class interdisciplinary works on erosion in 551.3; class interdisciplinary works on rivers and streams in 551.48. Class flood control for and wreckage studies of a specific type of structure with the structure, e.g., wreckage studies of bridges 624; class a specific use of dams and reservoirs with the use, e.g., water storage and conservation 628.1; class a specific use of offshore structures with the use, e.g., use of drilling platforms in petroleum extraction 622

> *For water supply engineering, see 628.1; for erosion of agricultural soils and its control, see 631.4; for on-farm irrigation, see 631.5; for reclamation of agricultural soils, revegetation and surface mine reclamation, see 631.6; for diving sports, see 797.2*

628   Sanitary and municipal engineering   Environmental protection engineering

Standard subdivisions are added for any or all topics in heading

Including rural sanitation, sewers

Class here environmental health engineering, public sanitation technology

Class interdisciplinary works on environmental protection in 363.7

> *For military sanitary engineering, see 623; for plumbing, see 696. For a specific aspect of municipal engineering not provided for here, see the aspect, e.g., road engineering 625.7, laying gas pipelines 665.7*

.091 73   Socioeconomic regions by concentration of population

Do not use for rural regions; class in 628

.1 **Water supply**

Including pollution countermeasures; reservoirs and their protection; sources, e.g., wells; testing; treatment, e.g., desalinization, fluoridation

Class here comprehensive works on engineering of water supply, sewers, sewage treatment and disposal

Class economic and social evaluation of adequacy, development requirements, conservation of sources in 333.91; class hydraulic engineering for water supply in 627; class sewers, water supply for rural and sparsely populated areas in 628; class interdisciplinary works on water supply in 363.6; class interdisciplinary works on water pollution and countermeasures in 363.73; class interdisciplinary works on sources, evaluation of sources in 553.7

> *For construction of dams and reservoirs, see 627; for sewage treatment and disposal, see 628.3. For pollution countermeasures in a specific technology outside sanitary engineering, see the technology, plus notation 028 from Table 1, e.g., pollution control in metallurgy plants 669.028*

> *See Manual at 363.6*

.102 8 Auxiliary techniques and procedures; apparatus, equipment, materials

Do not use for testing; class in 628.1

.3 **Sewage treatment and disposal**

Standard subdivisions are added for sewage treatment and disposal together, for sewage treatment alone

Including sanitary landfills

Class unsewered sewage disposal in 628

> *For sewage effluent treatment for reuse as water supply, see 628.1. For a specific use of sewage sludge, see the use, e.g., use as fertilizer 631.8; for sewage treatment and disposal in a specific technology, see the technology, plus notation 028 from Table 1, e.g., treatment of sewage from beverage plants by beverage makers 663.028*

> *See Manual at 363.6*

.4　Waste technology, public toilets, street cleaning

Standard subdivisions are added for waste technology, public toilets, street cleaning together; for waste technology alone

Including hazardous wastes, liquid wastes, solid wastes; recycling technology; sanitary landfills

Class here industrial waste treatment and disposal

Class waste technology for rural and sparsely populated area in 628; class pollution from wastes in 628.5; class interdisciplinary works on wastes in 363.72

> *For liquid wastes released into bodies of water, see 628.1; for sewage treatment and disposal, see 628.3; for gaseous wastes, see 628.5. For control and utilization of wastes in a specific technology, see the technology, plus notation 028 from Table 1, e.g., waste technology in petroleum industry 665.5028; for a specific recycling technology, see the technology, e.g., conversion of garbage into fertilizer 668*

.5　Pollution control technology and industrial sanitation engineering

Standard subdivisions are added for pollution control technology and industrial sanitation engineering together, for pollution control technology alone

Including plant sanitation; specific kinds of pollutants, e.g., pesticides

Class here industrial pollution

Class specific kinds of pollutants in water in 628.1; class interdisciplinary works on pollution in 363.73

> *For noise control, see 620.2; for water pollution control, see 628.1. For pollution control technology in a specific technology, see the technology, plus notation 028 from Table 1, e.g., engineering to control pollution in petroleum technology 665.5028*

.9　Other branches of sanitary and municipal engineering

Including fire fighting and fire safety technology, e.g., fireproofing, flammability testing, use of equipment and supplies and comprehensive works on their manufacture; general disaster and rescue technology; public lighting; comprehensive works on pest control technology

Class lighting of airports in 629.136; class interdisciplinary works on fire hazards and their control in 363.37; class interdisciplinary works on pest control in 363.7

> *For shipboard fire fighting technology, see 623.88; for firefighting technology in airports, see 629.136; for control of agricultural pests, see 632; for forest fire technology, see 634.9. For a specific disaster and rescue technology, see the technology, e.g., first aid 616.02; for fireproofing a specific product, see the product, e.g., textiles 677, buildings 693.8; for manufacture of a specific kind of fire fighting equipment and supplies, see the kind, e.g., fire engines 629.225, fire resistant clothing 687, fire stations 690*

629 Other branches of engineering

SUMMARY

629.04	**Transportation engineering**
.1	**Aerospace engineering**
.2	**Motor land vehicles, and cycles**
.3	**Air-cushion vehicles (Ground-effect machines, Hovercraft)**
.4	**Astronautics**
.8	**Automatic control engineering**

.04   Transportation engineering

Including technology of vehicles and other transportation equipment, of trafficways and other stationary transportation facilities; navigation; comprehensive works on water transportation engineering, on land transportation engineering

Class military transportation engineering in 623; class operation of transportation equipment for recreational purposes in 796–797; class interdisciplinary works on transportation in 338; class interdisciplinary works on remote-control models in 796.15. Class technical problems peculiar to transportation of a specific commodity with the commodity, e.g., slurry transportation of coal 662.6

> *For celestial navigation, see 527; for pipes and pipelines, see 621.8; for nautical engineering and seamanship, see 623.8; for railroads, roads, highways, see 625; for inland waterways, harbors, ports, roadsteads, see 627; for aerospace engineering, see 629.1; for motor land vehicles, cycles, see 629.2; for air-cushion vehicles, see 629.3; for nonmotor land vehicles, see 688.6; for transportation buildings, see 690*

> *See Manual at 629.04 vs. 388; also at 629.04 vs. 621.43; also at 796.15 vs. 629.04*

.1   **Aerospace engineering**

Including portable flight vehicles, e.g., hang gliders

Class military aerospace engineering in 623; class hang gliding as a sport in 797.5

> *For air-cushion vehicles, see 629.3; for astronautics, see 629.4*

.13   Aeronautics

> *See Manual at 629.04 vs. 388*

.130 01–.130 09   Standard subdivisions

.130 1   Philosophy and theory of flight

Do not use for aeromechanics of flight, aviation meteorology; class in 629.132

.130 2–.130 8   Standard subdivisions of flight

.130 9   Historical, geographic, persons treatment of flight

                          Do not use for flight guides; class in 629.132

                          Record of flying activities in all types of aircraft

.130 91   Transoceanic flight

                          Do not use for other regional treatment; class in 629.1309

.130 92   Fliers

                          Class here pilots

.132   **Mechanics of flight, flying and related topics**

                          Including automatic control, aviation meteorology, flight guides, navigation, piloting, wreckage studies

                          Class pilots in 629.13092; class flying model airplanes, kites in 796.15; class air sports in 797.5

                          See also 629.135 for automatic pilots

                          See Manual at 363.1 vs. 620.8

[.132 01–.132 09]   Standard subdivisions

                          Do not use; class in 629.1301–629.1309

.133   Aircraft types

                          Including airplanes, airships (dirigibles), balloons, gliders, helicopters, kites and their models and miniatures

                          Class hang gliders in 629.1; class models and miniatures of a specific aircraft component with the component in 629.134–629.135; class components and general techniques of specific aircraft types in 629.134; class flying kites and model aircraft, interdisciplinary works on building and flying model aircraft in 796.15

                          See Manual at 796.15 vs. 629.04

.133 022   Illustrations

                          Do not use for models and miniatures; class in 629.133

.133 028   Auxiliary techniques and procedures; apparatus, equipment, materials

                          Do not use for for maintenance and repair, safety equipment, testing and measurement; class in 629.134

.134   **Aircraft components and general techniques**

                          Including comfort and safety equipment; parachutes

                          For aircraft instrumentation, see 629.135

.134 028	Auxiliary techniques and procedures; apparatus, equipment, materials

> Do not use for maintenance and repair, testing and measurement; class in 629.134

.135	Aircraft instrumentation (Avionics)
.136	Airports

> Including air traffic control systems, heliports

> Class here commercial land airports

> *See Manual at 629.136 vs. 387.7*

.2   Motor land vehicles, and cycles

> Including nonsurface motor land vehicles, e.g., ocean floor vehicles; vehicles for extraterrestrial surfaces, e.g., moon cars; comprehensive works on motor land vehicle and highway safety engineering

> Class military motor land vehicles in 623.7

> *For highway safety engineering, see 625.7; for air-cushion vehicles, see 629.3*

> *See Manual at 629.04 vs. 388*

.202 2	Illustrations

> Do not use for models and miniatures; class in 629.22

.202 8	Auxiliary techniques and procedures; apparatus, equipment

> Do not use for materials; class in 629.2. Do not use for maintenance and repair, testing and measurement; class in 629.28

> Class safety engineering of motor land vehicles in 629.2

.22   Types of vehicles

> Including electric-powered and and steam-powered vehicles; off-road vehicles, e.g., all-terrain vehicles, snowmobiles; models of all types of vehicles

> Class nonsurface motor land vehicles, vehicles for extraterrestrial surfaces, and design, materials, construction, parts other than engines of specific vehicles in 629.2; class engines in 629.25; class driving a specific type of vehicle in 629.28

.220 22	Illustrations

> Do not use for models and miniatures; class in 629.22

.220 28	Auxiliary techniques and procedures; apparatus, equipment, materials

> Do not use for maintenance and repair, testing and measurement; class in 629.28

.222   *Passenger automobiles

Including buses, dune buggies, minivans, sports cars, station wagons, taxicabs

Class racing cars in 629.228

See also 629.223 for vans

.223   *Light trucks

Including pickup trucks, vans

See also 629.222 for minivans

.224   *Trucks (Lorries)

Class here tractor trailers

For light trucks, see 629.223

.225   *Work vehicles

Including bulldozers, fire engines, tractors

Class steam tractors in 629.22

For automotive materials-handling equipment, see 621.8; for trucks, see 629.224

.226   *Campers, motor homes, trailers (caravans)

Standard subdivisions are added for any or all topics in heading

Class here comprehensive works on recreational vehicles (RVs)

Class construction of towed mobile homes in 690

For a specific kind of recreational vehicle not provided for here, see the vehicle, e.g., dune buggies 629.222

See also 629.224 for tractor trailers

See Manual at 643, 690, 728.7 vs. 629.226

.227   *Cycles

Including bicycles, motorcycles

.228   *Racing cars

Conventional and converted

Including hot rods, karts

.25   Engines

Including spark-ignition engines; auxiliary systems, e.g., batteries

Class here pollution control

---

*Do not use notation 022 from Table 1 for models and miniatures; class in 629.22. Do not use notation 028 from Table 1 for testing and measurement, maintenance and repair; class in 629.28

.250 01–.250 09   Standard subdivisions

.28   Tests, driving, maintenance, repairs

Including garages, service stations

Class maintenance and repair, testing and measurement of specific parts of vehicles other than engines in 629.2; class testing and measurement, maintenance and repair of engines, works on car tune-ups limited to maintenance and repair of engines in 629.250028

.3   **Air-cushion vehicles (Ground-effect machines, Hovercraft)**

Class military air-cushion vehicles in 623.7

.4   **Astronautics**

Class military astronautics in 623; class interdisciplinary works on space policy in 333.9

See Manual at 629.04 vs. 388

.401   Philosophy and theory

Do not use for astromechanics; class in 629.4

.409 2   Astronautical engineers

Class astronauts in 629.450092

.43   Unmanned space flight

Including flight of artificial satellites

Class satellite flight for a specific purpose with the purpose, e.g., weather satellites 551.63

See Manual at 629.43, 629.45 vs. 919.904

.44   Auxiliary spacecraft

Including space laboratories, shuttles, stations

.45   Manned space flight

Including selection and training of astronauts

Projected accounts relocated to 919.904

Class auxiliary spacecraft in 629.44

See Manual at 629.43, 629.45 vs. 919.904

.450 01–.450 09   Standard subdivisions

.46   Engineering of unmanned spacecraft

Class here artificial satellites

.47   Astronautical engineering

Including launch complexes, space suits

Class here comprehensive works on spacecraft

For auxiliary spacecraft, see 629.44; for engineering of unmanned spacecraft, see 629.46

.8   Automatic control engineering

Including robots, servomechanisms, vending machines

Class here automatons that are not computer controlled

Class a specific application with the application, e.g., numerical control of machine tools 621.9

.801   Philosophy and theory

Do not use for control theory; class in 629.8

630   Agriculture and related technologies

Standard subdivisions are added for agriculture and related technologies together, for agriculture alone

Class here farming, farms, comprehensive works on plant crops

Class agricultural sociology in 306.3; class agricultural economics in 338.1

See also 307.72 for rural sociology, 333.76 for agricultural land economics, 909 for general works on rural conditions and civilization, 930–990 for rural conditions and civilization is specific areas

See Manual at 571–575 vs. 630; also at 630 vs. 579–590, 641.3

SUMMARY

630.1–.9	**Standard subdivisions**
631	**Specific techniques; apparatus, equipment, materials**
632	**Plant injuries, diseases, pests**
633	**Field and plantation crops**
634	**Orchards, fruits, forestry**
635	**Garden crops (Horticulture) Vegetables**
636	**Animal husbandry**
637	**Processing dairy and related products**
638	**Insect culture**
639	**Hunting, fishing, conservation, related technologies**

.1   Philosophy and theory

Do not use for scientific principles; class in 630.2

.2   Miscellany and scientific principles

For agricultural genetics, see 631.5

[.22–.29]   Specific miscellany

> Do not use for specific miscellany other than apparatus, equipment, materials; class in 630.2. Do not use for apparatus, equipment, materials; class in 631

631   Specific techniques; apparatus, equipment, materials

> Topics common to plant and animal husbandry or limited to plant culture

> Class comprehensive works on apparatus, equipment, materials used in a specific auxiliary techniques or procedure, e.g., computers, in 630.2

> *For plant injuries, diseases, pests, see 632; for specific techniques, apparatus, equipment, materials of specific plant crops, see 633–635; for specific techniques, apparatus, equipment, materials of animal husbandry, see 636*

.2   Agricultural structures

> Including barns, dams, fences; roads, bridges

> Class construction of bridges in 624; class construction of farm roads in 625.7; class construction of dams in 627; class construction of farm buildings and other structures in 690

> *For housing of domestic animals, see 636.08*

.3   Tools, machinery, apparatus, equipment

> Including workshops

> Class manufacture of tools, machinery, apparatus, equipment in 681. Class manufacture of a specific article with the article, e.g., manufacture of tractors 629.225

> *For equipment for a specific purpose, see the purpose, e.g., greenhouses 631.5*

> *See also 631.2 for agricultural structures*

.4   Soil science

> Including soil erosion, soil surveys, comprehensive agricultural works on soil and water conservation

> Class here interdisciplinary works on soils

> Class use of fertilizers and soil conditioners in 631.8; class comprehensive technological works on soil erosion in 627; class interdisciplinary works on soil conservation in 333.73; class interdisciplinary works on soil erosion in 551.3; class interdisciplinary works on soil mechanics in 624.1

> *For clearing, drainage, revegetation, see 631.6; for water conservation, see 631.7. For a specific aspect of soils, see the aspect, e.g., soil formation 551.3, engineering use of soils 624.1*

.401   Philosophy and theory

> Do not use for classification of soils, scientific principles; class in 631.4

[.409]　　　　　　　Historical, geographic, persons treatment

　　　　　　　　　Do not use; class in 631.4

.5　　　**Cultivation and harvesting**

Including agricultural genetics, nurseries, plant propagation, seeds and seed catalogs, varieties, yields; operations subsequent to harvesting, e.g., grading, storing; special methods of cultivation, e.g., crop rotation, dry farming, greenhouse agriculture, irrigation, organic farming, soilless agriculture (hydroponics)

Use this number for irrigation only for works describing what is done on the farm, e.g., installation and use of sprinkler systems

Class special methods of cultivation as topics in land economics in 333.76; class special methods of cultivation as topics in agricultural economics in 338.1; class biology of agricultural plants in 580; class digging wells in 628.1; class interdisciplinary works on irrigation in 333.91; class interdisciplinary works on technological aspects of irrigation, works on obtaining irrigation waters from off-farm sources in 627

> *For sewage irrigation, see 628.3; for conservation tillage, crop rotation to control erosion, see 631.4; for greenhouse, organic gardening, see 635. For a specific aspect of organic farming, see the aspect, e.g., compost 631.8*

> *See Manual at 338.1 vs. 631.5*

.6　　　**Clearing, drainage, revegetation**

Including surface mine reclamation

Class reforestation in 634.9; class off-farm drainage projects, interdisciplinary works on technological aspects of drainage and reclamation in 627

.7　　　**Water conservation**

> *For tillage for water conservation, see 631.5*

.8　　　**Fertilizers, soil conditioners, growth regulators**

Standard subdivisions are added for fertilizers, soil conditioners, growth regulators together; for fertilizers alone

Class here interdisciplinary works on agricultural chemicals

Class comprehensive works on soil fertility in 631.4

> *For pesticides, see 632; for manufacture of agricultural chemicals, see 668*

632   Plant injuries, diseases, pests

Standard subdivisions are added for plant injuries, diseases, pests together; for plant injuries alone

Including control methods, e.g., fumigation, pesticides; weeds

Class here pathology of agricultural plants; comprehensive works on plant and animal injuries, diseases, pests

Class use of agricultural plants in studies of basic pathological processes in 571.9; class interdisciplinary works on pests, works on pest control services in 363.7; class interdisciplinary works on environmental effects of pesticides in 363.738; class interdisciplinary works on physiology and pathology of agricultural plants in 571.2; class interdisciplinary works on pest control technology in 628.9

> *For injuries, diseases, pests of specific crops, see 633–635; for predator control in animal husbandry, see 636.08; for veterinary medicine, see 636.089*

> ## 633–635   Specific plant crops

Class comprehensive works in 630

See Manual at 633–635

633   Field and plantation crops

Large-scale production of crops intended for agricultural purposes or industrial processing other than preservation

Class truck farming in 635

> *For a specific field or plantation crop not provided for here, see the crop, e.g., plantation fruit crops 634*

[.001]	Philosophy and theory
	Relocated to 633.01
[.002]	Miscellany
	Relocated to 633.02
[.003–.009]	Standard subdivisions
	Relocated to 633.03–633.09
.01	Philosophy and theory [*formerly* 633.001]
.02	Miscellany [*formerly* 633.002]
[.028]	Auxiliary techniques and procedures; apparatus, equipment, materials

Do not use for auxiliary techniques and procedures; class in in 630.2. Do not use for apparatus, equipment, materials; class in 631

.03–.09   Standard subdivisions [*formerly* 633.03–633.09]

.1   Cereals

Including barley, buckwheat, corn, oats, rice, rye, wheat

For cereal crops grown for forage, see 633.2; for popcorn, see 635

.2   Forage crops

Including pastures and their grasses, cereal grasses

Class here forage grasses

Class pasture use of forests in 634.9; class comprehensive works on ranches and farms devoted to livestock in 636

For forage crops other than grasses, see 633.3

.200 1–.200 9   Standard subdivisions

.3   Legumes, forage crops other than grasses and legumes

Standard subdivisions are added for legumes and forage crops other than grasses and legumes together, for legumes alone

Including alfalfa, beans, clover, peanuts, peas

Class here comprehensive works on legumes [*formerly* 635], grain legumes, forage legumes

Class interdisciplinary works on legumes as food in 641.3

For leguminous fruits, see 634; for garden legumes, see 635

.5   Fiber crops

Including cotton, flax, jute; basketwork plants

Class fiber plants grown for paper pulp in 633.8

.6   Sugar, syrup, starch crops

Standard subdivisions are added for sugar, syrup, starch crops together; for sugar crops alone; for syrup crops alone

Including sugar beets, sugar cane, sugar maples, sweet sorghums; cassava, taro

Class a crop grown for starch and another product with the other product, e.g., potatoes 635

.7   Alkaloidal crops

Including cacao, coffee, marijuana, tea, tobacco

.8   Other crops grown for industrial processing

Including oilseed plants; spices; plants grown for dyes, flavors, medicine, perfume, rubber

For coconuts, olives, see 634; for onions and other alliaceous plants, aromatic and sweet herbs, see 635. For a crop producing medicine as a secondary product, see the primary product, e.g., poppy 633.7

634 Orchards, fruits, forestry

Fruits: reproductive bodies of seed plants having edible more or less sweet pulp associated with the seed

Standard subdivisions are added for orchards, fruits, forestry together; for orchards alone; for fruits alone

Including berries, nuts, olives

Class here comprehensive works on tree crops

> *For trees grown for plantation crops, see 633; for melons, see 635; for ornamental trees, see 635.9*

> *See Manual at 633–635*

.8 Grapes

Class here viticulture

.9 Forestry

Including agroforestry; forest fire technology; silviculture, e.g., afforestation, reforestation; forest products, e.g., pulpwood; logging, comprehensive works on lumbering

Class nonwoody plants grown for paper pulp in 633.8; class lumber in 674; class interdisciplinary works on afforestation and reforestation in 333.75. Class trees cultivated for a product other than lumber or pulp with the product, e.g., rubber trees 633.8, pecan trees 634

> *For sawmill operations, see 674*

.906 8 Management

Do not use for management of production; class in 634.9

635 Garden crops (Horticulture) Vegetables

Vegetables: crops grown primarily for human consumption without intermediate processing other than cooking and preservation

Including beans, cabbage, herbs, melons, mushrooms, onions, peas, potatoes, salad greens, sweet corn, tomatoes; greenhouse and organic gardening

Class here home gardening, truck farming

Comprehensive works on legumes relocated to 633.3

Class orchards in 634

> *For cassava, taro, see 633.6*

> *See Manual at 633–635*

.9 **Flowers and ornamental plants**

Standard subdivisions are added for either or both topics in heading

Including bonsai, hedges, houseplants, lawns, trees

Class here floriculture

Class hedges used as fences in 631.2; class landscape architecture of flower gardens in 712; class flower arrangement in 745.92

For planting and cultivation of roadside vegetation, see 625.7

See Manual at 635.9 vs. 582.1

.902 8 Auxiliary techniques and procedures

Do not use for apparatus, equipment, materials; class in 635.9

636 Animal husbandry

Including farms, ranches, young of animals

Class here interdisciplinary works on species of domestic animals [*formerly* 599]

Class farms and ranches for, young of specific kinds of animals in 636.1–636.9

For culture of nondomesticated animals, see 639

See Manual at 800 vs. 398.24, 590, 636

SUMMARY

636.001–.009	**Standard subdivisions**
.08	**Specific topics in animal husbandry**
.1	**Equines Horses**
.2	**Ruminants and camel family Bovines Cattle**
.3	**Smaller ruminants Sheep**
.4	**Swine**
.5	**Poultry Chickens**
.6	**Birds other than poultry**
.7	**Dogs**
.8	**Cats**
.9	**Other mammals**

.001 Philosophy and theory

Do not use for genetics; class in 636.08

.002 Miscellany

Do not use for ownership marks; class in 636.08

.003–.006 Standard subdivisions

.007 Education, research, related topics

.007 9 Competitions, festivals, awards, financial support

Animal shows and related awards relocated to 636.08

.008–.009	Standard subdivisions

.08   Specific topics in animal husbandry

Including animal shows and related awards [*formerly also* 636.0079]; animal welfare, e.g., animal hospitals; branding; breeding, genetics, germ plasm; feeding, nutrition, range management; grooming; housing, e.g., barns; predator control

Class growing forage crops in 633.2; class farms, ranches, young of animals in 636; class specific topics relating to animals raised for a specific purpose in 636.088; class construction of housing for domestic animals in 690; class interdisciplinary works on genetic resources in 333.95

For pasture use of forests, see 634.9; for predator control in wildlife conservation, see 639.9

See also 179 for ethical aspects of animal care

[.080 1–.080 9]   Standard subdivisions

Do not use; class in 636.001–636.009

.088   Animals for specific purposes

Including animals raised for food, hides, sport, work; laboratory animals; pets

Animals raised for fur (fur farming) relocated to 636.97

Class veterinary sciences of animals for specific purposes in 636.089; class milk and egg processing in 637; class reminiscences about and true accounts of pets in 808.88. Class reminiscences about and true accounts of pets in a specific literature with the literature in 800, plus notation 8 from Table 3 under the appropriate language, e.g., reminiscences in English about pets 828; class literary treatment of pets other than reminiscences with the appropriate literary form in 800, e.g., an English novel about pets 823

See Manual at 800 vs. 398.24, 590, 636

.089   Veterinary sciences   Veterinary medicine

Including anatomy and physiology of domestic animals

Class animal hospitals, animal welfare in 636.08

.1   Equines   Horses

Including donkeys, mules, ponies, zebras

Class training of riders and drivers, comprehensive works on training horses and their riders and drivers in 798

.100 1–.100 9   Standard subdivisions

.2   **Ruminants and camel family**   **Bovines**   **Cattle**

> Including bison, deer, llamas; dairy farming, raising cattle for beef
>
> Class milking and milk processing in 637
>
> *For smaller ruminants, see 636.3*

.200 1–.200 9   Standard subdivisions of ruminants and camel family

.3   **Smaller ruminants**   **Sheep**

> Including goats
>
> Class mouse deer in 636.963

.300 1–.300 9   Standard subdivisions

.4   **Swine**

.400 1–.400 9   Standard subdivisions

.5   **Poultry**   **Chickens**

> Including ducks, geese, peafowl, pheasants, turkeys
>
> Class here interdisciplinary works on species of domestic birds [*formerly* 598], comprehensive works on raising birds
>
> *For birds other than poultry, see 636.6*

.500 1–.500 9   Standard subdivisions

.6   **Birds other than poultry**

> Including game, ornamental, song birds
>
> Class comprehensive works on birds in 636.5
>
> *For peafowl, see 636.5*

.600 1–.600 9   Standard subdivisions

.7   **Dogs**

.700 1–.700 9   Standard subdivisions

>   636.72–636.75   Specific breeds and groups of dogs
>
> Class comprehensive works in 636.7
>
> *For toy dogs of any breed, see 636.76*
>
> *See Manual at 636.72–636.75*

.72   Nonsporting dogs

Including Boston terrier, bulldog, Chinese Shar-Pei, chow chow, Dalmatian, Finnish spitz, poodles, Tibetan spaniel, Tibetan terrier

Class here utility breeds (United Kingdom)

Class comprehensive works on terriers in 636.755

.73   Working and herding dogs

Standard subdivisions are added for working and herding dogs together, for working dogs alone

Including sled dogs, watchdogs (guard dogs); boxer, bullmastiff, Doberman pinscher, Eskimo dogs, Great Dane, mastiffs, Newfoundland, Rottweiler, Saint Bernard, Schnauzers (standard and giant), Siberian husky

Class Finnish spitz in 636.72; class Norwegian elkhound in 636.753; class miniature Schnauzer in 636.755

.737   Herding dogs

Including puli, Welsh corgis; sheep dogs, e.g., collies, German shepherd dog

.75   Sporting dogs, hounds, terriers

Class here hunting dogs, sporting dogs (United Kingdom)

.752   Sporting dogs

Including pointers, retrievers, setters, spaniels, Weimaraner

Class here bird dogs, gundogs (United Kingdom)

.753   Hounds

Including beagle, dachshund, greyhound, whippet

Class Italian greyhound, miniature dachshund in 636.76; class greyhound racing in 798.8

.755   Terriers

Including miniature Schnauzer

For Boston and Tibetan terriers, see 636.72; for toy terriers, see 636.76

.76   Toy dogs

Including Chihuahua, Italian greyhound, Japanese chin, Maltese, Mexican hairless, miniature dachshund, miniature pinscher, Pekingese, Pomeranian, pug, silky terrier, Yorkshire terrier

Class miniature poodle in 636.72; class miniature Schnauzer in 636.755

.8   Cats

Including nondomestic cats, e.g., ocelots

.800 1–.800 9   Standard subdivisions

.9   Other mammals

> Add to base number 636.9 the numbers following 599 in 599.2–599.8, e.g.,
> fur-bearing animals (fur farming) 636.97 [*formerly* 636.088], rodents 636.935;
> however, for equines, see 636.1; for camel family, ruminants other than mouse
> deer, see 636.2; for cat family, see 636.8

637   Processing dairy and related products

> Including milk, butter, cheese; eggs; frozen desserts, e.g., ice cream

> Class raising poultry for eggs in 636.5; class comprehensive works on dairy
> farming in 636.2

638   Insect culture

> Including bee keeping (apiculture), honey processing; butterfly gardening; raising
> silkworms

639   Hunting, fishing, conservation, related technologies

> Including culture and harvest of invertebrates, e.g., crustaceans, mollusks

> Comprehensive works on commercial and sports hunting relocated to 799.2

> *For insect culture, see 638; for sports hunting and fishing, see 799*

> *See also 636.97 for fur farming*

.091 6   Treatment in air and water

> Class aquaculture in 639.8

.2   Commercial fishing, whaling, sealing

> Standard subdivisions are added for commercial fishing, whaling, sealing
> together; for commercial fishing alone

> Class here works on fisheries encompassing culture as well as capture, on
> fisheries encompassing invertebrates as well as fishes

> Class fisheries for invertebrates in 639; class comprehensive works on
> aquaculture in 639.8

> *For culture of fishes, see 639.3*

.3   Culture of cold-blooded vertebrates   Of fishes

> Including fish hatcheries, frog farming, reptile farming

.34   Fish culture in aquariums

> Including marine aquariums

> Class here freshwater aquariums, home aquariums

> Class interdisciplinary works on aquariums in 597.073

.8 **Aquaculture**

Including aquaculture of plants

Class here mariculture

Class hydroponics in 631.5. Class aquaculture of a specific animal with the animal, e.g., aquaculture of fishes 639.3

.9 **Conservation of biological resources**

Including conservation of plants; control of diseases, pests, predators; habitat improvement, reserves and refuges

Class here conservation of animals, game animals, mammals, vertebrates, wildlife; game protection

Class comprehensive works on pest control in agriculture in 632; class comprehensive works on predator control in agriculture in 636.08; class interdisciplinary works on conservation of biological resources in 333.95

See also 636.088 for raising warm-blooded game animals

See Manual at 333.95 vs. 639.9

.97 Specific kinds of mammals

Class comprehensive works on conservation of mammals in 639.9

[.970 1–.970 9] Standard subdivisions

Do not use; class in 639.901–639.909

640 Home economics and family living

Including management of household employees, of money, of time

Class here management of home and personal life, domestic arts and sciences

Class personal health in 613

See Manual at 332.024 vs. 640

SUMMARY

640.1–.9	**Standard subdivisions**
641	**Food and drink**
642	**Meals and table service**
643	**Housing and household equipment**
644	**Household utilities**
645	**Household furnishings**
646	**Sewing, clothing, management of personal and family living**
647	**Management of public households (Institutional housekeeping)**
648	**Housekeeping**
649	**Child rearing; home care of persons with illnesses and disabilities**

.28 Auxiliary techniques and procedures; apparatus, equipment, materials

Do not use for maintenance and repair; class in 643

.29   Commercial miscellany

> Do not use for evaluation and purchasing manuals; class in 640.73

[.68]   Household management

> Do not use; class in 640

.7   **Education, research, related topics; evaluation and purchasing guides**

.73   Evaluation and purchasing guides

> Class here consumer education for home and personal needs

> Class comprehensive works on managing household money in 640; class interdisciplinary evaluation and purchasing guides and works on consumer education in 381.3. Class evaluation and purchasing guides for a specific product or service with the product or service, plus notation 029 from Table 1, e.g., a manual on evaluating automobiles 629.222029

641   Food and drink

> *For meals and table service, see 642*

.01   Philosophy and theory

> Including gastronomy, pleasures of eating

[.1]   **Applied nutrition**

> Relocated to 613.2

.2   **Beverages (Drinks)**

> Class here interdisciplinary works on beverages

> Comprehensive works on nutritive values of beverages relocated to 613.2

> > *For specific nonalcoholic beverages and kinds of beverages, see 641.3. For a specific aspect of beverages, see the aspect, e.g., manufacture (commercial preparation) 663*

.3   **Food**

> Class here interdisciplinary works on food

> Class interdisciplinary works on composite dishes in 641.8

> > *For a specific aspect of food, see the aspect, e.g., manufacture (commercial preparation) 664*

> > *See Manual at 363.8 vs. 613.2, 641.3; also at 630 vs. 579–590, 641.3*

.300 1   Philosophy and theory

.300 2   Miscellany

.300 29   Commercial miscellany

> Do not use for evaluation and purchasing manuals; class in 641.3

.300 3–.300 9   Standard subdivisions

>   **641.4–641.8   Food preservation, storage, cooking**

Class comprehensive works in 641.3

.4   **Food preservation and storage**

Including canning, cold storage, drying, pickling, smoking

Class interdisciplinary works on food preservation in 664

.5   **Cooking**

Preparation of food with and without use of heat

Including cooking leftovers

Class menus and meal planning in 642

For cooking specific materials, see 641.6; for specific cooking processes and techniques, see 641.7; for cooking specific kinds of composite dishes, see 641.8

.502   Miscellany

Do not use for persons in specific occupations; class in 641.5

.508   History and description with respect to kind of persons

[.508 3–.508 4]   Persons of specific ages

Do not use; class in 641.5

.508 7   Persons with disabilities, gifted persons

Do not use for cooking for persons with illnesses; class in 641.5

.508 8   Cooking with respect to occupational and religious groups

Do not use for cooking with respect to religious groups; class in 641.5

[.508 9]   Cooking with respect to racial, ethnic, national groups

Do not use; class in 641.59

.509   Historical, geographic, persons treatment

Do not use for cooking characteristic of specific geographic environments; class in 641.59

Class here collections of recipes from specific restaurants

.59　　　　　Cooking characteristic of specific geographic environments, ethnic cooking

> Including international cooking

> Class Jewish cooking in 641.5; class a specific kind of cooking characteristic of specific geographic environments, e.g., French gourmet cooking, in 641.5; class historical and geographic treatment of general cooking in 641.509

> *See also 641.509 for collections of recipes from specific restaurants*

.593–.599　　Cooking characteristic of specific continents, countries, localities

> Add to base number 641.59 notation 3–9 from Table 2, e.g., Mexican cooking 641.5972

> Class ethnic cooking of nondominant aggregates in 641.59

.6　　**Cooking specific materials**

> Including vegetables

> Class vegetarian cooking in 641.5; class specific kinds of composite dishes featuring specific materials, home preparation of beverages in 641.8

.7　　**Specific cooking processes and techniques**

> Including baking, barbecuing, broiling, frying, roasting; preparation of cold dishes

> Class specific processes applied to specific materials in 641.6; class specific processes applied to specific kinds of composite dishes in 641.8

.8　　**Cooking specific kinds of composite dishes**

> Including appetizers, beverages, breads, casseroles, desserts, salads, sandwiches, stews; bartenders' manuals, punch, comprehensive works on mixed drinks

> Class here interdisciplinary works on composite dishes

> Class interdisciplinary works on beverages in 641.2

> *For bottled and canned mixed drinks, see 663; for food technology of composite dishes, see 664*

642　　Meals and table service

> Including catering, menus, picnics, table furnishings and decorations

> Class operation of public eating places, catering which includes restaurant operation in 647.95

643 Housing and household equipment

Works for owner-occupants or renters covering activities of members of household

Including selecting, renting, buying, burglarproofing homes; renovation, improvement, remodeling; specific areas and their equipment, e.g., kitchens; appliances and installations; special kinds of housing, e.g., vacation homes

Class table furnishings in 642; class household utilities in 644; class household furnishings in 645; class home construction of articles made of fabric in 646.2; class moving in 648; class manufacture of household appliances in 683; class home workshops in 684. Class appliances and installations for a specific purpose with the purpose, e.g., sewing machines 646.2

> *See also 333.33 for economics of house acquisition, 346.04 for law of real property, 690 for construction of houses, 728 for interdisciplinary works on design and construction of houses*

> *See Manual at 363.5 vs. 643; also at 643, 690, 728.7 vs. 629.226; also at 690 vs. 643*

.028   Auxiliary techniques and procedures; apparatus, equipment, materials

Do not use for maintenance and repair; class in 643

644 Household utilities

Works for owner-occupants or renters covering activities by members of household

Including heating, lighting, water supply

Class here home energy conservation

Class lighting fixtures as furnishings in 645

645 Household furnishings

Works for owner-occupants or renters covering activities by members of household

Including draperies, floor covering, furniture, lighting fixtures

Class here comprehensive works on household furnishings and interior decoration of residential buildings

Class artistic aspects of furniture and accessories in 749

> *For home construction of fabric furnishings, see 646.2*

> *See also 684 for construction in wood and metal*

.029   Commercial miscellany

Do not use for evaluation and purchasing manuals; class in 645

646 Sewing, clothing, management of personal and family living

Including comprehensive works on fabrics in the home

Class interdisciplinary works on clothing and accessories in 391

> *For laundering and related operations, see 648. For fabrics for a specific use, see the use, e.g., use in furnishings 645*

> *See Manual at 391 vs. 646, 746.9*

.2 Sewing and related operations

Standard subdivisions are added for sewing and related operations together, for sewing alone

Including construction of home furnishings, e.g., slipcovers; reweaving; sewing machines

Class here mending, sewing for the home

Class mending of clothing in 646; class clothing construction in 646.4; class artistic and decorative aspects of construction of interior furnishings in 746.9

> *For knitting, crocheting, tatting, see 746.43; for embroidery, see 746.44*

.202 8   Auxiliary techniques and procedures

> Do not use for equipment other than sewing machines, apparatus, materials; class in 646. Do not use for sewing machines; class in 646.2

.4 Clothing and accessories construction

Standard subdivisions are added for clothing and accessories construction together, for clothing construction alone

Class here casual clothes, sports clothes

Class boots and shoes in 685; class commercial manufacture of clothing in 687; class handcrafted costume jewelry in 745.594

> *For construction of headgear, see 646.5*

.400 1–.400 7   Standard subdivisions

[.400 8]   Clothing with respect to kinds of persons

> Do not use; class in 646.4

.400 9   Historical, geographic, persons treatment

.5 Construction of headgear

Including millinery

.500 1–.500 7   Standard subdivisions

[.500 8]   Construction of headgear with respect to kinds of persons

> Do not use; class in 646.5

.500 9	Historical, geographic, persons treatment

.7 Management of personal and family living Grooming

Including care of hair, face, skin; charm, dating, mate selection; reducing and massage for appearance; retirement guides; wigs

Class here interdisciplinary works on success, successful living

Class clothing selection and dressing with style in 646; class interdisciplinary works on success in business and other public situations in 650.1

> *For parapsychological and occult means for achieving well-being, happiness, success, see 131; for psychological techniques for achieving personal well-being, happiness, success, see 158; for etiquette (manners), see 395; for child rearing, see 649*

> *See also 362.82 for social services to families, 613.2 for reducing for health, 613.7 for physical fitness*

> *See Manual at 613.7 vs. 646.7, 796*

.700 1–.700 7	Standard subdivisions of personal and family living
.700 8	Personal and family living with respect to kinds of persons
.700 84	Persons in specific stages of adulthood

Do not use for persons in late adulthood; class in 646.7

.700 9	Historical, geographic, persons treatment of personal and family living
.701–.707	Standard subdivisions of grooming
[.708]	Grooming with respect to specific kinds of persons

Do not use; class in 646.7

.709	Historical, geographic, persons treatment of grooming

647 Management of public households (Institutional housekeeping)

Including apartment houses, public housing, hospitals; employees

Class comprehensive works on household employees in 640. Class a specific aspect of public households and institutions with the aspect, e.g., laundering 648

.068	Management

Do not use for personnel management; class in 647

.9 Multiple dwellings for transient residents, eating and drinking places

> *See Manual at 913–919: Add table: 04*

[.901–.909]	Standard subdivisions

Do not use; class in 647.9

.94	Multiple dwellings for transient residents

.940 25   Directories of persons and organizations

> Do not use for directories of specific continents, countries, localities; class in 647.943–647.949

[.940 93–.940 99]   Treatment by specific continents, countries, localities

> Do not use; class in 647.943–647.949

.943–.949   Treatment by specific continents, countries, localities

> Class here directories; specific kinds of multiple dwellings, e.g., bed and breakfasts, hotels, trailer camps

> Add to base number 647.94 notation 3–9 from Table 2, e.g., hotels in Canada 647.9471; however, do not add notation 01–09 from Table 1 for specific kinds of facilities

.95   Eating and drinking places

> Standard subdivisions are added for either or both topics in heading

.950 25   Directories of persons and organizations

> Do not use for directories of specific continents, countries, localities; class in 647.953–647.959

[.950 93–.950 99]   Treatment by specific continents, countries, localities

> Do not use; class in 647.953–647.959

.953–.959   Treatment by specific continents, countries, localities

> Add to base number 647.95 notation 3–9 from Table 2, e.g., restaurants in Hawaii 647.95969

648   Housekeeping

> Including laundering and related operations, e.g., dyeing; moving, storage; pest control

> Class here household sanitation

> Class works about "housekeeping" in the sense of running the home, e.g., preparing meals and doing routine repairs as well as cleaning, in 640; class dry cleaning in 667

649   Child rearing; home care of persons with illnesses and disabilities

> Including breast feeding, creative activities, training

> Home schools and schooling relocated to 371.04; techniques of study for parents relocated to 371.3028; reading instruction in home schools at elementary level relocated to 372.4

> Class religious training of children in the home in 291.4; class Christian religious training of children in the home in 248.8; class nutritional aspects of breast feeding in 613.2

> *See Manual at 649 vs. 613.2*

.8 **Home care of persons with illnesses and disabilities**

Class services to persons with illnesses and disabilities in 362.1–362.4; class nursing aspects in 610.73

650 Management and auxiliary services

This division is concerned with the art and science of conducting organized enterprises and with auxiliary skills and operations. The auxiliary skills and operations consist chiefly of communication and record keeping fundamental to management

Class here business

See Manual at 330 vs. 650

SUMMARY

650.01–.09	**Standard subdivisions**
.1	**Personal success in business**
651	**Office services**
652	**Processes of written communication**
653	**Shorthand**
657	**Accounting**
658	**General management**
659	**Advertising and public relations**

.01 Philosophy and theory

Including business arithmetic

.02–.09 Standard subdivisions

.1 **Personal success in business**

Including financial success, personal efficiency, success in business relationships

Class here interdisciplinary works on success in business and other public situations

Class interdisciplinary works on success in general, on management of personal and family living in 646.7

For success as an executive, see 658.4. For a specific aspect of success in public situations, see the aspect, e.g., techniques of study for success as a student 371.3028

.14 Success in obtaining jobs and promotions

Standard subdivisions are added for either or both topics in heading

---

> **651–657 Auxiliary services**

Class comprehensive works in 650

For advertising and public relations, see 659

651   Office services

Including description, use, maintenance of office equipment and supplies; problems in security and confidentiality

Class procurement of office equipment and supplies in 658.7. Class a specific aspect of security and confidentiality in office services with the aspect, e.g., security and confidentiality in records management 651.5

For processes of written communication, see 652; for accounting, see 657. For a specific type of equipment, see the use of the equipment, e.g., typewriters 652.3

.028   Auxiliary techniques and procedures

Do not use for apparatus and equipment; class in 651

Use of this number for materials discontinued; class in 651

[.028 5]   Data processing   Computer applications

Do not use; class in 651.8

.3   Office management

Including activities of clerks, filers, messengers, receptionists, secretaries, stenographers, switchboard operators, typists

.5   Records management

Including retention, maintenance, final disposition of records; filing systems; computerization, microreproduction, storage of files

Class clerical services associated with records management in 651.3

For creation and transmission of records, see 651.7

.7   Communication   Creation and transmission of records

Including correspondence, minutes, reports; dictation and use of dictating equipment; mail handling

Class communication as a technique of management in 658.4; class interdisciplinary works on communication in 302.2

For processes of written communication, see 652

See Manual at 658.4 vs. 651.7, 808

.8   Data processing   Computer applications

Use in carrying out office functions

Class interdisciplinary works on data processing in 004

For computer applications for a specific office activity, see the activity, e.g., computerization of files 651.5, word processing 652.5

652 Processes of written communication

Including penmanship; duplication of records and duplicating methods, e.g., xerography; interdisciplinary works on cryptography

Class interdisciplinary works on photoduplication in 686.4

> *For shorthand, see 653. For cryptographic techniques used for a specific purpose, see the purpose, e.g., cryptographic techniques used for security in computer systems 005.8*
>
> *See also 745.6 for calligraphy*

.3 Typing

Including typing for specific uses, e.g., medical typing

Class here keyboarding

.300 1–.300 9 Standard subdivisions

.5 Word processing

Class here text editors

653 Shorthand

Including handwritten and machine systems; shorthand for specific uses, e.g., for court reporting

657 Accounting

Including auditing, bookkeeping

> *See Manual at 657 vs. 658.15*

658   General management

The science and art of conducting organized enterprises, projects, activities

Including management of big enterprises, of enterprises of specific forms of ownership organization (e.g., partnerships, corporations, international enterprises)

Class here management of technology; management of services rendered by nonpublic organizations, whether or not for profit; management of public corporations; management of public agencies that themselves provide direct services (in contrast to public agencies that regulate, support, or control services provided by other organizations)

Class sociology of management in 302.3; class control, decision making, information management, internal organization, planning, policy making in 658.4; class comprehensive works on management and economics in 330. Class a specific aspect of management of big enterprises, of enterprises of specific forms of ownership organization (e.g., partnerships, corporations, international enterprises) with the aspect in 658.1–658.8, e.g., financial management of corporations 658.15

> *For public administration, see 351. For management of enterprises engaged in a specific field of activity, see the field, plus notation 068 from Table 1, e.g., management of airlines 387.7068*
>
> *See also 306.3 for industrial sociology*
>
> *See Manual at 658 and T1—068; also at 658 vs. 658.1, 658.4; also at T1—068 vs. 353–354*

(Option: Including management of enterprises engaged in specific fields of activity; prefer specific subject, with use of notation 068 from Table 1, e.g., management of mines 622.068)

SUMMARY

658.001–.009	**Standard subdivisions**
.02	**Small enterprises**
.1	**Organization and finance**
.2	**Plant management**
.3	**Personnel management (Human resource management)**
.4	**Executive management**
.5	**Management of production**
.7	**Management of materials**
.8	**Management of distribution (Marketing)**

.001   Philosophy and theory

Do not use for systems theory and analysis; class in 658.4

.002   Miscellany

[.002 85]   Data processing   Computer applications

Do not use; class in 658

.003–.009   Standard subdivisions

.02 Small enterprises

Including minority enterprises

Class management of small enterprises of a specific form of ownership organization in 658

[.020 1–.020 9]   Standard subdivisions

Do not use; class in 658.02

.1   Organization and finance

Standard subdivisions are added for organization and finance together, for organization alone

Including initiation of business enterprises, e.g., initiation of specific forms of ownership organization such as partnerships, corporations; reorganization, e.g., mergers; organization of international enterprises and activities

Class general management of specific forms of ownership organization in 658

For internal organization, see 658.4

See Manual at 658 vs. 658.1, 658.4

.15   Financial management

Procurement and use of funds to establish and operate enterprises

Including budgeting, managerial accounting, valuation of businesses, ways that management can deal with taxes, what insurance is needed for the organization, comprehensive works on capital and its management

Class here financial decision making, financial planning

Class legal aspects of business taxes in 343.06; class accounting in 657; class interdisciplinary works on and economic aspects of business taxes in 336.2; class interdisciplinary works on insurance in 368

For wage and salary administration, see 658.3; for customer credit management, see 658.8

See Manual at 332 vs. 338, 658.15; also at 368 vs. 658.15; also at 657 vs. 658.15

.2   Plant management

Management of buildings, equipment, facilities, grounds

Including location of plants and warehouses, layout

Class here comprehensive business works on energy management

Class location of businesses in 658.1; class procurement of plants (land, buildings, heavy equipment) in 658.15; class procurement of office equipment in 658.7

For office equipment, see 651. For a specific aspect of energy management, see the aspect, e.g., energy management to promote efficiency in production 658.5

.200 1–.200 9   Standard subdivisions

.3   Personnel management (Human resource management)

Including days and hours of work, leaves of absence; collective bargaining, employee representation in management, labor unions and other employee organizations; employee dismissal; health, safety, welfare of employees; training; wage and salary administration

Class industrial democracy in 331.01; class worker control of industry in 338.6; class clerical techniques involved in maintaining payroll records in 651.3; class payroll accounting procedures in 657; class comprehensive works on safety management in 658.4; class industrial relations, interdisciplinary works on labor in 331; class interdisciplinary works on industrial safety in 363.11

For management of office personnel, see 651.3068; for management of executive personnel, see 658.4

See Manual at 331 vs. 658.3

.300 1–.300 7   Standard subdivisions

.300 8   History and description with respect to kinds of persons

Class here affirmative action, discrimination in employment, equal employment opportunity

.300 9   Historical, geographic, persons treatment

.4   Executive management

Limited to those activities named below

Including business intelligence and security, conflict and crisis management, decision making, information management, internal organization, management of executive personnel, management by objectives, managerial success, negotiation, planning and policy making, project management, quality management, social responsibility of executive management, comprehensive works on safety management

Class here role, function, powers, position of top and middle management

Class general success in business in 650.1; class mechanics of communication in 651.7; class management of small business in 658.02; class insurance in 658.15; class supervision in 658.3; class comprehensive management works on organization, on reorganization in 658.1; class interdisciplinary works on safety in 363.1. Class a specific executive managerial activity not provided for here with the activity in management, e.g., personnel management 658.3; class application of a specific activity named here in another branch of management with the branch, e.g., quality management in production 658.5

For allocation of personnel to specific responsibilities, see 658.3. For a specific aspect of safety management, see the aspect, e.g., safety of plant and equipment 658.2, product safety 658.5

See Manual at 658 vs. 658.1, 658.4; also at 658.4 and T1—068; also at 658.4 vs. 651.7, 808

.400 1–.400 9   Standard subdivisions

.5   Management of production

Including automation, modernization; labeling; product control, e.g., inspection, quality control, recall, safety; product planning; research and development (R and D); sequencing, e.g., assembly-line processes, scheduling; waste control and utilization; work, time and motion studies; comprehensive works on product development; interdisciplinary works on packaging

Class here production management in manufacturing enterprises, production management in service industries, comprehensive works on logistics

Class marketing, market research on new products, use of packaging in sales promotion in 658.8; class comprehensive works on energy management in 658.2; class comprehensive works on safety management in 658.4

For internal transportation (materials handling), physical distribution, packaging for shipment and for storage, see 658.7; for use of packaging in sales promotion, see 658.8; for factory operations engineering, see 670.42; for packaging technology, see 688.8. For production management in enterprises engaged in a specific kind of activity other than manufacturing, see the activity, plus notation 068 from Table 1, e.g., management of agricultural production 630.68

.500 1–.500 9   Standard subdivisions

.7   Management of materials

Including procurement, contracts and their negotiation, vendor selection; internal transportation (materials handling), storage (warehouse management), inventory control (stock control), physical distribution (shipment)

Class here management of supplies

Class financial control of inventories in 658.15; class location of warehouses and comprehensive works on energy management in 658.2; class comprehensive works on logistics and interdisciplinary works on packaging in 658.5

For management of office supplies, see 651; for procurement of land, buildings, heavy equipment, see 658.15

.8   Management of distribution (Marketing)

Of goods and services

Including auctions, direct-mail marketing, direct selling, franchises, garage sales, markets, telemarketing (telephone selling); consumer research, market research and analysis; credit management; customer relations, sales management and promotion; use of brand names, packaging, trademarks in sales promotion; wholesale and retail marketing

Class results of market research in 380–382; class management of sales personnel in 658.3; class product design, comprehensive works on logistics, interdisciplinary works on packaging in 658.5

> *For physical distribution, see 658.7; for advertising, see 659.1*

> *See Manual at 380.1 vs. 658.8; also at 658.8, T1—068 vs. 659*

.800 1   Philosophy and theory

Do not use for systems, for consumer psychology; class in 658.8

.800 2–.800 6   Standard subdivisions

.800 7   Education, research, related topics

Class market research in 658.8

.800 8–.800 9   Standard subdivisions

.85   Personal selling (Salesmanship)

Including retail salesmanship

659   Advertising and public relations

Class here publicity

> *See Manual at 658.8, T1—068 vs. 659*

.1   Advertising

Including demonstrations, exhibitions; counter and window displays; planning, control, managerial organization of advertising; general kinds of advertising, e.g., retail advertising; advertising campaigns; advertising specific kinds of organizations, products, services

Class planning, control, managerial organization of advertising, general kinds of advertising, advertising campaigns, advertising specific kinds of organizations, products, services, all in relation to advertising in printed or related media (e.g., outdoor advertising) or broadcast media in 659.13–659.14

.13   Advertising in printed and related media

Including directory advertising; direct advertising, e.g., mail-order catalogs; outdoor advertising, e.g., billboards, electric signs

Class direct-mail marketing in 658.8

[.130 1–.130 9]   Standard subdivisions

Do not use; class in 659.13

.14 Advertising by broadcast media

> Class television selling as a channel of distribution, television selling organizations in 658.8

.2 **Public relations**

> Planned and sustained effort to establish and maintain mutual understanding between an organization and its public

> Including public relations in specific kinds of organizations, in organizations producing specific kinds of products and services

> Public relations for religion relocated to 200; public relations for government relocated to 352.7; public relations for armed forces relocated to 355.3

> *For public relations in libraries, see 021.7*

660 Chemical engineering and related technologies

> Standard subdivisions are added for chemical engineering and related technologies together, for chemical engineering alone

> Class military applications in 623

> *For pharmaceutical chemistry, see 615; for pulp and paper technology, see 676; for elastomers and elastomer products, see 678*

> *See Manual at 604.7 vs. 660*

SUMMARY

660.01–.09	**Standard subdivisions**
.6	**Biotechnology**
661	**Technology of industrial chemicals**
662	**Technology of explosives, fuels, related products**
663	**Beverage technology**
664	**Food technology**
665	**Technology of industrial oils, fats, waxes, gases**
666	**Ceramic and allied technologies**
667	**Cleaning, color, coating, related technologies**
668	**Technology of other organic products**
669	**Metallurgy**

.01 Philosophy and theory

> Do not use for process control; class in 660

.02 Miscellany

.028 Auxiliary techniques and procedures

> Do not use for apparatus, equipment, materials, safety measures; class in 660

.03–.09 Standard subdivisions

.6   **Biotechnology**

Application of living organisms or their biological systems or processes to the manufacture of useful products

Including genetic engineering, industrial microbiology

661   Technology of industrial chemicals

Production of chemicals used as raw materials or reagents in manufacture of other products

Including ammonia, cellulose, coal tar; special-purpose chemicals, e.g., photographic chemicals

For carbon, see 662; for industrial gases, see 665.7; for gaseous elements, see 665.8; for plaster of paris, see 666; for glycerin, see 668

.001–.009   Standard subdivisions

662   Technology of explosives, fuels, related products

Including carbon black, charcoal, coke, fireworks, graphite, matches, synthetic petroleum; wood as a fuel; wastes as fuels, e.g., biomass as fuel

Class nuclear explosives in 621.48; class industrial oils, fats, waxes, gases as fuels in 665; class interdisciplinary works on energy from waste materials in 333.793; class interdisciplinary works on biomass as fuel in 333.95

See Manual at 622 vs. 662, 669

.6   **Coal**

Including treatment, e.g., desulfurization; storage, transportation, distribution; uses as a fuel, as a raw material

Class coke in 662. Class a specific use of coal with the use, e.g., metallurgical use 669

[.601–.609]   Standard subdivisions

Do not use; class in 662.6

663   Beverage technology

Commercial preparation, preservation, packaging

Including bottled water

Class household preparation of beverages in 641.8; class interdisciplinary works on beverages in 641.2

For milk, see 637

664 Food technology

Commercial preparation, preservation, packaging

Including fats and oils; flavoring aids, e.g., spices; food salts; special-purpose foods and aids, e.g., baby foods, baking powder; interdisciplinary works on food preservation

Class here comprehensive works on commercial food and beverage technology

Class home storage and cookery in 641.4–641.8; class interdisciplinary works on food in 641.3; class interdisciplinary works on animal fats and oils in 665

> *For commercial processing of dairy and related products, see 637; for honey, see 638; for home preservation of foods, see 641.4; for commercial beverage technology, see 663*

.001 Philosophy and theory

Do not use for process control; class in 664

.002 Miscellany

.002 8 Auxiliary techniques and procedures; apparatus, equipment

Do not use for materials, testing, measurement; class in 664

.003–.009 Standard subdivisions

665 Technology of industrial oils, fats, waxes, gases

Including interdisciplinary works on animal and vegetable fats and oils

Class here nonvolatile, lubricating, saponifying oils, fats, waxes

Class turpentine oils in 661; class polishing waxes in 667

> *For beeswax, see 638; for animal or vegetable fats and oils used in food and food preparation, see 664*

.5 Petroleum

Including asphalt, gasoline, kerosene; refining, storage, transportation, distribution, uses

Class here comprehensive works on technology of petroleum and natural gas

Class synthetic petroleum in 662; class asphalt concrete in 666. Class a specific use with the use, e.g., automobile engine lubricants 629.25

> *For technology of extraction of petroleum and natural gas, see 622; for petrochemicals other than fuels, lubricants, refinery residues (bottoms), see 661; for comprehensive works on technology of natural gas, see 665.7*

.7   **Natural gas and manufactured gases**

Standard subdivisions are added for natural gas and manufactured gases together; for natural gas alone

Including processing, storage, transportation, distribution, uses of natural gas and gases manufactured from coal, coke, petroleum, biological wastes

Class here comprehensive works on technology of industrial gases

Class a specific use with the use, e.g., heating buildings 697

> *For technology of extraction of natural gas, see 622; for technology of industrial gases not provided for here, see 665.8*

.8   **Other industrial gases**

Including hydrogen, nitrogen, oxygen

> *For ammonia, see 661*

666   Ceramic and allied technologies

Standard subdivisions are added for ceramic and allied technologies together, for ceramic technologies alone

Including asbestos, bricks, concrete, enamels, fiber glass, glass, synthetic and artificial gems and minerals; masonry adhesives, e.g., cement, plaster of paris; pottery, e.g., earthenware, stoneware

667   Cleaning, color, coating, related technologies

Including bleaching; dyeing and printing; inks, japans, lacquers, paints, polishes, varnishes; coatings, comprehensive works on materials and methods for producing protective and decorative coatings

Class household bleaching, cleaning, laundry in 648. Class coatings applied to a specific thing and methods of applying the coatings with the thing to which the coating is applied, e.g., coatings for metal 671.7, metal coatings for polymers 668.9, painting a building 698, varnishing a violin 787.2; class a coating made of a specific material with the material, e.g., enamel coatings 666, thermoset plastic coatings 668.4; class dyeing and printing of a specific material not provided for here with the material, e.g., dyeing leather 675

> *For carbon black, see 662; for detergents, soaps, see 668*

668   Technology of other organic products

Including adhesives, cosmetics, detergents, fertilizers, glue, gums, perfumes, pesticides, resins, soaps, soil conditioners

> *For masonry adhesives, see 666*

.4   **Plastics**

Class plastic fibers and fabrics in 677

[.402 8]   Auxiliary techniques and procedures; apparatus, equipment, materials

Do not use; class in 668.4

.9 **Polymers and polymerization**

Standard subdivisions are added for polymers and polymerization together; for polymers alone

Class here synthetic polymers

Class a specific application with the application, e.g., manufacture of nylon hosiery 687; class a specific polymer with the polymer, e.g., plastics 668.4

669 Metallurgy

Including physical and chemical analysis of metals

Class here alloys, extractive metallurgy, process metallurgy, interdisciplinary works on metals

For a specific aspect of metals, see the aspect, e.g., mineralogy 549, metalworking and primary metal products 671

See Manual at 622 vs. 662, 669

.028 **Specific kinds of techniques and procedures; apparatus, equipment**

Do not use for materials; class in 669

Including electrometallurgy

670 Manufacturing

Including planning and design for manufactured products

Class here manufactured products

Class military applications in 623; class planning and design of specific kinds of products in 671–679; class the arts in 700. Class comprehensive works on products made by a specific process with the process, e.g., seasoned wood 674

For manufacture of products based on specific branches of engineering, see 620; for manufacture of products based on chemical technologies, see 660; for manufacture of final products for specific uses not provided elsewhere, see 680

See Manual at 338 vs. 060, 382, 670.29, 910, T1—025, T1—029

SUMMARY

670.1–.9	Standard subdivisions and special topics
671	Metalworking processes and primary metal products
672	Iron, steel, other iron alloys
673	Nonferrous metals
674	Lumber processing, wood products, cork
675	Leather and fur processing
676	Pulp and paper technology
677	Textiles
678	Elastomers and elastomer products
679	Other products of specific kinds of materials

.285   Data processing   Computer applications

Class here computer-aided design/computer-aided manufacture (CAD/CAM), computer integrated manufacturing systems (CIM), comprehensive works on computer use in the management of manufacturing and computer-aided design or computer-aided manufacture

Class computer-aided design (CAD) in 620, class computer use in the management of manufacturing in 658

For computer-aided manufacture (CAM), see 670.42

See Manual at 670.42 vs. 670.285

.4   Special topics

.42   Factory operations engineering

Including inspection technology, machine-shop practice; mechanization and automation of factory operations, e.g., computer-aided manufacture (CAM), robots

Class here shop and assembly-line technology

Class computer-aided design (CAD) in 620; class computer-aided design/computer-aided manufacture (CAD/CAM), computer integrated manufacturing systems (CIM) in 670.285; class comprehensive works on computer control in 629.8

For tools and fabricating equipment, see 621.9; for packaging technology, see 688.8

See Manual at 670.42 vs. 670.285

.420 68   Management

Do not use for management of factory operations; class in 658.5

.68   Management

Do not use for management of production; class in 658.5

>   **671–679 Manufacture of products from specific materials**

Class here manufacture of primary products

Class comprehensive works in 670

For manufacture of ceramic products, see 666; for manufacture of plastic products, see 668.4

See Manual at 671–679 vs. 680

671   Metalworking processes and primary metal products

Standard subdivisions are added for metalworking processes and primary metal products together, for metalworking processes alone

Class metallurgy and interdisciplinary works on metals in 669

For metalworking processes and primary metal products with iron, steel, other iron alloys as the main metal, see 672; for metalworking processes and primary metal products with nonferrous metals as the main metal, see 673

> ### 671.2–671.7   Specific metal-working processes

Class specific processes applied to specific primary products in 671.8; class comprehensive works in 671

.2   Founding (Casting)

Including patternmaking, moldmaking

See also 671.3 for hot-working operations

.3   Mechanical working and related processes

Standard subdivisions are added for mechanical working and related processes together, for mechanical working alone

Including forging, machining, powder metallurgy, pressing, rolling, stamping

Class here cold-working and hot-working operations

.4   Electroforming of metals

.5   Joining and cutting of metals

Standard subdivisions are added for joining and cutting together, for joining alone

Including riveting, soldering, welding

Class ceramic-to-metal bonding in 666; class cutting as a machining process in 671.3

.7   Finishing and surface treatment of metals; metal coating of nonmetals

Including deburring, electroplating, polishing

Class enameling in 666; class comprehensive works on coating in 667. Class metal coating of a specific material with the material, e.g., metal coating of plastics 668.4, metal coating of ferrous metals 672.7

.8   Primary products

Including cables, pipes, sheets, wires

Class here comprehensive works on technology of metal products

For a specific metal product not provided for here, see the product, e.g., metal furniture 684.1

672   Iron, steel, other iron alloys

Metalworking processes and primary products

Add to base number 672 the numbers following 671 in 671.2–671.8, e.g., welding 672.5
> Subdivisions are added for any or all topics in heading

For small forge work, see 682

673   Nonferrous metals

Metalworking processes and primary products

Class here alloys of nonferrous metals

Class metalworking processes and primary products in which nonferrous metals are not the main metal of the final product with the process or the main metal, e.g., nickel plating of various metals 671.7, zinc coating of steel 672.7

674   Lumber processing, wood products, cork

Including barrels, crates, pallets, spools, toothpicks; particle board, plywood, veneers, wood laminates; products from wood waste and residues; comprehensive works on wood-using technologies

> *For a specific product or wood-using technology not provided for here, see the product or technology, e.g., wood as a fuel 662, pulp and paper technology 676, wooden furniture 684.1, carpentry 694*

.001–.009   Standard subdivisions

.01   Philosophy and theory of lumber technology

.02   Miscellany of lumber technology

> Do not use for specifications; class in 674

.028   Auxiliary techniques and procedures; apparatus, equipment, materials

> Do not use for grading lumber, waste technology; class in 674

.03–.09   Standard subdivisions of lumber technology

675   Leather and fur processing

Including manufacture of imitation leathers and furs

For leather and fur goods, see 685

676   Pulp and paper technology

Standard subdivisions are added for pulp and paper technology together, for paper technology alone

Including paper containers, e.g., paper bags; paperboard; products molded from pulp, e.g., fiberboards, pulpboards

.028   Auxiliary techniques and procedures; apparatus, equipment, materials

> Do not use for waste technology; class in 676

677 Textiles

Production of fibers, fabrics, cordage

Including chemistry of man-made fibers; blankets, carpets, rugs, tapestries; laces, ropes, string

Class here comprehensive works on manufacture of textiles and clothing

> *For dyeing and printing of textiles, see 667; for manufacture of clothing, see 687*

.001   Philosophy and theory

.002   Miscellany

.002 8   Auxiliary techniques and procedures

> Do not use for apparatus, equipment, materials, testing and measurement; class in 677

.003–.009   Standard subdivisions

678 Elastomers and elastomer products

Standard subdivisions are added for elastomers and elastomer products together, for elastomers alone

Including natural and synthetic rubber and latexes

679 Other products of specific kinds of materials

Including brooms, brushes, mops; cigars, cigarettes; feather and ivory products

680 Manufacture of products for specific uses

Not provided for elsewhere

Class here interdisciplinary works on handicrafts

Class repairs of household equipment by members of household in 643. Class manufacture of products based on specific branches of engineering with engineering in 620, e.g., military engineering 623, manufacture of motor vehicles 629.2; except for products provided for in 681–688, class manufacture of products of a specific material with the material in 671–679, e.g., manufacture of steel products 672, but manufacture of steel furniture 684.1

> *For artistic handicraft work, see 745.5*
>
> *See Manual at 671–679 vs. 680; also at 680 vs. 745.5*

681 Precision instruments and other devices

Standard subdivisions are added for precision instruments and other devices together, for precision instruments alone

Including medical equipment, e.g., artificial legs, crutches [*both formerly* 685]; calculators; cameras, eyeglasses, lenses, telescopes; printing, writing, duplicating machines and equipment; musical instruments; technological machines, e.g., agricultural machinery; testing, measuring, sensing instruments, e.g., electrical instruments for measuring nonelectrical quantities, measuring tools

Class facsimile recorders in 621.382; class film and other photographic supplies in 661; class wood-cased pencils in 674; class instruments for measuring time in 681.1; class hand construction of specific musical instruments or groups of instruments in 786–788; class comprehensive works on hand construction of musical instruments in 784.192; class interdisciplinary works on office equipment in 651. Class testing, measuring, sensing instruments for a specific technological application with the manufacturing number, e.g., aircraft instrumentation 629.135

> *For instruments for measuring electrical quantities, see 621.37; for instruments for testing and measuring electronic signals, see 621.3815; for computers, see 621.39*

.1 Instruments for measuring time

Including clocks, watches, sundials, hourglasses

> *For clocks and watches considered as works of art, see 739.3*

[.101–.109] Standard subdivisions

Do not use; class in 681.1

682 Small forge work (Blacksmithing)

Including horseshoeing, production of hand-forged tools and ironwork

683 Hardware and household appliances

Standard subdivisions are added for hardware and household appliances together, for hardware alone

Including locksmithing, kitchen utensils

Class here comprehensive works on manufacture of hardware and building supplies

> *For refrigerators and freezers, see 621.5; for heating, ventilating, air-conditioning equipment, see 697. For a specific hardware or building supply product not provided for here, see the product, e.g., tools 621.9, paints 667; for nonmetallic household utensils and appliances, see the material from which they are made, e.g., wood 674*

.4 Small firearms

Including pistols, revolvers, rifles, shotguns

Class here interdisciplinary works on small firearms, on gunsmithing

> *For military small arms, see 623.4*

.400 1   Philosophy and theory

.400 2   Miscellany

.400 28   Auxiliary techniques and procedures; apparatus, equipment, materials

         Do not use for maintenance and repair; class in 683.4

.400 3–.400 9   Standard subdivisions

684 Furnishings and home workshops

Including metalworking, woodworking; fabric furnishings, e.g., draperies, slipcovers

> *For carpets and rugs, see 677*

.001–.009   Standard subdivisions for furnishings and home workshops, for furnishings alone

.1 Furniture

Class camping furniture in 685

.100 1–.100 9   Standard subdivisions

685　Leather and fur goods, and related products

Standard subdivisions are added for leather and fur goods and related products together, for leather goods alone

Including leather and fur clothing; footwear and related products, e.g., skates, skis, snowshoes; gloves, mittens; harness making, saddlery; handbags, luggage; camping equipment, e.g., sleeping bags, tents

Artificial legs, crutches relocated to 681

Class manufacture of equipment connected with snow skiing in 688.7

> *For overshoes, see 678; for hosiery, see 687*

686　Printing and related activities

Class here design and manufacture of publications, book arts

Class interdisciplinary works on the book in 002

> *For book illustration, see 741.6*

> *See also 681 for manufacture of printing equipment*

.2　Printing

Including photocomposition; photomechanical printing; typefounding, typesetting; nonimpact techniques, e.g., electrophotographic printing, laser printing; works on desktop publishing that emphasize typography

Class comprehensive works on printing and publishing in 070.5; class interdisciplinary works on print media in 302.23

> *See also 070.5 for self publishing, 686.4 for electrophotographic processes in photocopying*

.209　Historical, geographic, persons treatment

Class invention of printing in 686

.3　Bookbinding

.300 1–.300 9　　Standard subdivisions

.4　Photocopying (Photoduplication)

Including blueprinting, microphotography, xerography

Class here interdisciplinary works on photocopying

Class telefax in 621.382

> *See also 681 for manufacture of photocopying equipment*

687 Clothing and accessories

Standard subdivisions are added for clothing and accessories together, for clothing alone

Including patternmaking, dressmaking, tailoring; items auxiliary to clothing construction (notions), e.g., buttons, needles, thread; comprehensive works on manufacture of sewing equipment and supplies

Class here casual clothes, sports clothes

Class interdisciplinary works on clothing and accessories in 391; class interdisciplinary works on sewing equipment and supplies in 646; class interdisciplinary works on clothing construction in 646.4; class interdisciplinary works on making costume jewelry in 688; class interdisciplinary works on making jewelry in 739.27

> *For manufacture of sewing machinery and equipment, see 681; for leather and fur clothing, footwear, gloves and mittens, see 685. For manufacture of a specific kind of sewing supply, see the kind, e.g., thread 677*

688 Other final products, and packaging technology

Including costume jewelry; smokers' supplies, e.g., pipes; accessories for personal grooming, e.g., combs, razors; interdisciplinary works on models and miniatures

Class handcrafted costume jewelry in 745.594; class interdisciplinary works on costume jewelry in 391.7; class interdisciplinary works on making jewelry in 739.27; class interdisciplinary works on handcrafted models and miniatures in 745.5928

> *For cosmetics, see 668; for brushes, see 679. For models and miniatures of a specific object, see the object, e.g., model airplanes 629.133*

> *See Manual at 745.5928*

.6 Nonmotor land vehicles

Including carriages, carts, wagons, wheelbarrows

> *For cycles, see 629.2*

> *See also 685 for skateboards*

> *See Manual at 629.04 vs. 388*

.7 Recreational equipment

Including equipment, not provided for elsewhere, for games and sports, e.g., tennis rackets, artificial flies; interdisciplinary works on mass-produced and handcrafted toys

> *For small firearms, see 683.4; for camping equipment, skateboards, skates, skis, see 685; for handcrafted toys, see 745.592*

.8 **Packaging technology**

Materials, equipment, techniques

Class artistic aspects of containers in 700, e.g., earthenware vases 738.3; class interdisciplinary works on packaging in 658.5. Class manufacture and use of containers made of a specific material with the material, e.g., paper containers 676

690 Buildings

Including planning, analysis, engineering design, construction, destruction of habitable structures and their utilities; specific types of buildings, e.g., air terminals, cathedrals, townhouses; specific structural elements, e.g., roofs

Class interdisciplinary works on design and construction of buildings in 721

> *For construction of buildings for defense against military action (e.g., forts), naval and military air facilities, see 623; for docks and port buildings, see 627; for home repairs by members of household, see 643; for chimneys and fireplaces, see 697*

> *See Manual at 624 vs. 690; also at 643, 690, 728.7 vs. 629.226; also at 690 vs. 643; also at 721 vs. 690*

.01 Philosophy and theory

.02 Miscellany

Do not use for specifications; class in 692

.022 Illustrations

Do not use for maps, plans, diagrams; class in 692

.028 Auxiliary techniques and procedures; apparatus, equipment

Do not use for maintenance and repair, safety measures; class in 690. Do not use for materials; class in 691

.029 Commercial miscellany

Do not use for estimates of labor, time, materials; class in 692

.03–.09 Standard subdivisions

691 Building materials

Including bricks, concrete, plastics, steel, wood; insulating materials

Class construction in a specific type of material in 693

692 Auxiliary construction practices

Including plans, drawings, specifications; estimates of labor, time, materials; contracting; interdisciplinary works on quantity surveying

Class application of a specific auxiliary practice to a specific subject with the subject, e.g., estimates for air conditioning 697.9

693   **Construction in specific types of materials and for specific purposes**

Including construction in masonry, metals, prefabricated materials; sandwich panels; plastering

Class comprehensive works on construction in all types of materials in 690

For selection, preservation, construction properties of building materials, see 691; for wood construction, see 694; for roofing materials, see 695

[.01–.09]   Standard subdivisions

Do not use; class in 690.01–690.09

.8   **Construction for specific purposes**

Including fireproofing, insulation, soundproofing; shock-resistant, moistureproof, waterproof construction

694   **Wood construction   Carpentry**

695   **Roof covering**

Class wooden roofs in 694; class comprehensive works on roofs as structural elements in 690

696   **Utilities**

Including pipe fitting, plumbing

Class here comprehensive works on energy and environmental engineering of buildings

Class interior electric wiring in 621.319; class interdisciplinary works on energy use in buildings in 333.79

For heating, ventilating, air-conditioning engineering, see 697. For a specific aspect of energy and environmental engineering, see the aspect, e.g., thermal insulation 693.8

697   **Heating, ventilating, air-conditioning engineering**

Including fireplaces, furnaces, stoves

.000 1–.000 9   Standard subdivisions

.001   Philosophy and theory of heating

.002   Miscellany of heating

.002 8   Auxiliary techniques and procedures; materials

Do not use for heating equipment; class in 697

Use of this number for heating apparatus discontinued; class in 697

.003–.009   Standard subdivisions of heating

.9   **Ventilation and air conditioning**

Class heating in 697

698   Detail finishing

Including finishing woodwork, painting, paperhanging; floor coverings, e.g., carpets

Class roof covering in 695; class comprehensive works on floors in 690

For lathing, plastering, stuccowork, see 693; for wooden moldings, paneling, inlays, see 694

700

700   The arts   Fine and decorative arts

Description, critical appraisal, techniques, procedures, apparatus, equipment, materials of the fine, decorative, literary, performing, recreational arts

Class here conceptual art

For book arts, see 686; for literature, see 800

See Manual at 700

SUMMARY

700.1–.9	**Standard subdivisions of the arts**
701–709	**Standard subdivisions of fine and decorative arts and iconography**
710	**Civic and landscape art**
720	**Architecture**
730	**Plastic arts Sculpture**
740	**Drawing and decorative arts**
750	**Painting and paintings**
760	**Graphic arts Printmaking and prints**
770	**Photography and photographs**
780	**Music**
790	**Recreational and performing arts**

> **700.1–700.9   Standard subdivisions of the arts**

Use this standard subdivision span for material that includes two or more of the fine and decorative arts and one or more of the other arts, e.g., a work about a painter who is also a sculptor and a poet 700.92. If only one fine or decorative art and one of the other arts is involved, class in the number coming first in the schedule, e.g., a United States painter and poet 759.13

Class comprehensive works in 700

See Manual at 700

.1–.8   Standard subdivisions of the arts

.9   Historical, geographic, persons treatment of the arts

.92   Persons

Class here the works themselves and critical appraisal and description of works of an artist or artists

See Manual at 700.92

> ### 701–770 Fine and decorative arts

Class comprehensive works in 700

> ### 701–708 Standard subdivisions of fine and decorative arts

Other than historical, geographic, persons treatment

Class standard subdivisions of specific schools, styles, periods of development in 709.01–709.05; class comprehensive works in 700

701   Philosophy and theory of fine and decorative arts

Including appreciative aspects, e.g., aesthetics, criticism and appreciation, psychology; inherent features, e.g., color, composition, light, perspective, style, time

Class works of critical appraisal in 709; class interdisciplinary works on aesthetics in 111

702   Miscellany of fine and decorative arts

.8   Technique, procedures, apparatus, equipment, materials

Including conservation, preservation, restoration; expertizing; mixed-media and composites, e.g., video art; forgeries, reproductions

Class finished works of mixed-media and composite art in 709; class two-dimensional mixed-media art or composites in 760

.81   Collage

Class decoupage in 745.54

[.810 1–.810 9]   Standard subdivisions

Do not use; class in 702.81

.9   Commercial miscellany

Class auction and sales catalogs in which an exhibition is involved in 707.4

703   Dictionaries, encyclopedias, concordances of fine and decorative arts

704   Special topics in fine and decorative arts

Including kinds of persons occupied with art, e.g., patrons

Class description, critical appraisal, works, biography of individual artists in 709.2

For art dealers, see 380.1; for the fine and decorative arts of nonliterate peoples, see 709.01

| .03 | History and description with respect to racial, ethnic, national groups |

Class history and description with respect to groups of miscellaneous specific kinds of persons of a specific racial, ethnic, national group in 704; class the fine and decorative arts of nonliterate peoples in 709.01; class history and description with respect to racial, ethnic, national groups in places where they predominate in 709.1–709.9

| .9 | **Iconography** |

Including architectural subjects, cityscapes; erotica, human figures, portraits; nature, e.g., animals, landscapes, marine scenes, plants; still life; mythology and legend, religion and religious symbolism, symbolism and allegory

Class significance and purpose of art in religion in 291.3; class significance and purpose of art in Christianity in 246; class significance and purpose of art in non-Christian religions in 292–299

See Manual at 704.9

705–706 Standard subdivisions of fine and decorative arts

707 Education, research, related topics of fine and decorative arts

| .4 | **Temporary and traveling collections and exhibits** |

Do not use for museums and permanent collections and exhibits; class in 708

Class here permanent collections on tour, temporary exhibits of a private collection, auction and sales catalogs in which an exhibition is involved

For temporary in-house exhibits selected from a museum's or gallery's permanent collection, see 708

708 Galleries, museums, private collections of fine and decorative arts

Do not use for history and description of fine and decorative arts with respect to kinds of persons; class in 704

General art collections

For temporary and traveling collections and exhibits, see 707.4

| .001–.008 | Standard subdivisions |
| .009 | Historical and persons treatment |

Do not use for geographic treatment; class in 708.1–708.9

| > | **708.1–708.9 Geographic treatment** |

Class here guidebooks and catalogs of specific galleries, museums, private collections

Class comprehensive works in 708

.1   **North America**

> *For galleries, museums, private collections in Middle America, see 708.972*

.11   Canada

.13–.19   United States

> Add to base number 708.1 the numbers following — 7 in notation 73–79 from Table 2, e.g., galleries, museums, private collections in Pennsylvania 708.148
>
> *For galleries, museums, private collections in Hawaii, see 708.9969*

\>   **708.2–708.8 Europe**

> Class comprehensive works in 708.94
>
> *For galleries, museums, private collections not provided for here, see 708.949, e.g., galleries, museums, private collections in Belgium 708.9493*

.2   **British Isles   England**

> Including Scotland, Ireland, Wales

.3–.8   **Miscellaneous parts of Europe**

> Add to base number 708 the numbers following — 4 in notation 43–48 from Table 2, e.g., galleries, museums, private collections in France 708.4

.9   **Other geographic areas**

> Add to base number 708.9 notation 1–9 from Table 2, e.g., comprehensive works on galleries, museums, private collections in Islamic areas 708.917, in European countries 708.94
>
> Class parts of Europe in notation 41–48 from Table 2 in 708.2–708.8

709   Historical, geographic, persons treatment of fine and decorative arts

> Development, description, critical appraisal, works
>
> Class here finished works of experimental and mixed-media art that do not fit easily into a recognized medium
>
> Class two-dimensional experimental and mixed-media art in 760

> 709.01–709.05 Periods of development, and arts of nonliterate peoples

Class here schools and styles not limited by country or locality, European art limited by period, school, or style

Add to each subdivision identified by * notation 01–08 from Table 1, e.g., exhibits of medieval art 709.02074

Class comprehensive works in 709

> *For European art limited to a specific location, see the location in 709.4, e.g., art of Germany 709.43*

> *See Manual at 709.01–709.05 vs. 709.3–709.9*

.01 Arts of nonliterate peoples, and earliest times to 499

Arts of nonliterate peoples regardless of place or time, but limited to nonliterate peoples of the past and nonliterate peoples clearly not a part of contemporary society

Including Paleolithic and rock art

.02 *6th-15th centuries, 500–1499

Including Byzantine, early Christian, Gothic, Renaissance, Romanesque art

Class here medieval art

> *For Byzantine, early Christian, Gothic, Renaissance art of any other period, see the specific period, e.g., early Christian art before 500 709.01*

.03 *Modern period, 1500–

Including art nouveau, baroque art, classical revival, impressionism, kitsch (trash), naturalism, realism, rococo art, romanticism

> *For 20th century, 1900–1999, see 709.04; for 21st century, 2000–2099, see 709.05. For art nouveau, baroque art, classical revival, kitsch, naturalism, realism, romanticism of any other period, see the specific period, e.g., realism of 20th century 709.04*

.04 20th century, 1900–1999

Including abstractionism, art deco, cubism, expressionism, op art, pop art, surrealism

Class here modern art

> *For 19th century, 1800–1899, see 709.03; for 21st century, 2000–2099, see 709.05*

.040 01–.040 08 Standard subdivisions

.05 *21st century, 2000–2099

*Add as instructed under 709.01–709.05

.1 **Treatment by areas, regions, places in general**

Class history and description of fine and decorative arts with respect to kinds of persons in 704; class art of nonliterate peoples regardless of place in 709.01

.2 **Persons**

Class here description, critical appraisal, biography, works of artists not limited to or chiefly identified with a specific form, e.g., painting, or group of forms, e.g., graphic arts

Class works of more than one artist in the same geographic area not limited by continent, country, locality in 709.1; class works of more than one artist in the same geographic area in the same continent, country, locality in 709.3–709.9

See Manual at 709.2 vs. 380.1

.3–.9 **Treatment by specific continents, countries, localities**

Class here art of specific periods, e.g., art of 1800–1899 in Germany 709.43

Class history and description of fine and decorative arts with respect to kinds of persons in 704; class art of nonliterate peoples regardless of place in 709.01. Class comprehensive works on European art of specific periods with the period in 709.01–709.05 (*not* 709.4), e.g., art of 1800–1899 in Europe 709.03 (*not* 709.4)

See Manual at 709.01–709.05 vs. 709.3–709.9

710 Civic and landscape art

711 Area planning (Civic art)

Design of physical environment for public welfare, convenience, pleasure

Including urban renewal

Class comprehensive works on area planning and architecture in 720; class interdisciplinary works on area planning in 307.1; class interdisciplinary works on urban renewal in 307.3

For landscape architecture, see 712

712 Landscape architecture (Landscape design)

Including landscaping of public, private, semiprivate parks and grounds; institutional grounds

Class engineering aspects of landscape architecture in 624

For trafficways, see 713; for specific elements in landscape design, see 714–717; for cemeteries, see 718; for natural landscapes, see 719

.01 Philosophy and theory

Class aesthetics, style, composition in 712

713   Landscape architecture of trafficways

> **714–717   Specific elements in landscape architecture**

> Class comprehensive works in 712

714   Water features in landscape architecture

Including fountains, pools

Class comprehensive works on fountains in 731

715   Woody plants in landscape architecture

Cultivated for flowers or for other attributes

Including topiary work; specific kinds of plants, e.g., shrubs, trees, vines

Class here comprehensive works on plants in landscape architecture

Class comprehensive works on plants cultivated for their flowers in landscape architecture in 716

See also 635.9 for planting and cultivation of woody plants

716   Herbaceous plants in landscape architecture

Cultivated for flowers or for other attributes

Including ground cover

Class here comprehensive works on plants cultivated for their flowers in landscape architecture

For woody plants cultivated for their flowers, see 715

See also 635.9 for planting and cultivation of herbaceous plants

717   Structures in landscape architecture

Relationship of buildings, terraces, fences, gates, steps, ornamental accessories to other elements of landscape architecture

718   Landscape architecture of cemeteries

719   Natural landscapes

Including forest and wildlife reserves

Class natural water features in 714

720   Architecture

Class here comprehensive works on architecture and civic and landscape art

For civic and landscape art, see 710

SUMMARY

.22 Illustrations, models, miniatures

Do not use for drafting illustrations; class in 720.28

Including architectural drawings

Class architectural drawings for one structure or a specific type of structure with the structure in 725–728, plus notation 022 from Table 1, e.g., architectural drawings of residential buildings 728.022

.28 Auxiliary techniques and procedures; apparatus, equipment, materials

Including architectural drawing, remodeling

Class architectural drawings in 720.22; class interdisciplinary works on conservation, preservation, restoration in 363.6

See Manual at 930–990: Historic preservation

.9 Historical, geographic, persons treatment

Class here architectural aspects of historic buildings, schools and styles limited to a specific country or locality

Class architectural drawings in 720.22; class comprehensive works on specific schools and styles not limited to a specific country or locality in 722–724

See Manual at 913–919: Historic sites and buildings; also at 930–990: Historic preservation

[.93] Ancient world

Do not use; class in 722

721 Architectural structure

Including structural elements, e.g., foundations, walls, roofs, floors, doors, windows, stairs

Class here interdisciplinary works on design and construction

Class architectural structure of specific types of structures in 725–728; class decoration of structural elements in specific mediums in 729

For structural engineering, see 624.1; for engineering design and construction, see 690; for design and decoration, see 729

See Manual at 721 vs. 690

> ## 722–724 Architectural schools and styles

Class architects of specific schools and styles not limited to a specific type of structure in 720.92; class details of construction of specific schools and styles in 721; class specific types of structures regardless of school or style in 725–728; class design and decoration of structures of specific schools and styles in 729; class comprehensive works, schools and styles from ca. 300 limited to a specific country or locality in 720.9

722   Architecture from earliest times to ca. 300

Including Greek and Roman architecture

723   Architecture from ca. 300 to 1399

Including Byzantine, Gothic, Moorish, Romanesque architectures

Class here medieval architecture

[.09]   Historical, geographic, persons treatment

> Do not use for architecture limited to a specific country or locality; class in 720.9. Do not use for persons treatment; class in 720.92

724   Architecture from 1400

Including baroque, classical revival, neoclassical, Renaissance, rococo architectures

Class here modern architecture

[.09]   Historical, geographic, persons treatment

> Do not use for architecture limited to a specific country or locality; class in 720.9. Do not use for persons treatment; class in 720.92

> ## 725–728 Specific types of structures

Class here development of architectural schools and styles, comprehensive works on specific structures and their interior design and decorations, interdisciplinary works on design and construction of specific types of structures

Class comprehensive works in 720. Class structures rehabilitated to a single new use with the new use, e.g., warehouses converted into apartments 728; class structures rehabilitated to multiple new uses with the old use, e.g., warehouses converted into retail stores and apartments 725

For structural engineering, see 624.1; for engineering design and construction of specific types of habitable structures, see 690; for interior decoration, see 747

725　Public structures

Not used primarily for religious, educational, research, residential purposes

Including concert halls, civic centers, factories, hospitals, monuments, office buildings, opera houses, railroad stations, restaurants, shopping malls, stores, theaters; bridges, towers; comprehensive works on public and domestic saunas and swimming pools

Class engineering of forts and fortresses, military air facilities in 623; class engineering of naval facilities in 623.8; class engineering of bridges in 624; class engineering of harbors, ports, roadsteads in 627; class comprehensive works on castles in 728.8. Class memorial buildings for a specific purpose with the purpose, e.g., memorial library buildings 727

For domestic saunas and swimming pools, see 728

726　Buildings for religious and related purposes

Including mosques, shrines, synagogues, temples; monasteries, tombs

.5　Church buildings

Class comprehensive works on buildings associated with Christianity in 726

For cathedrals, see 726.6

.6　Cathedrals

For details and parts of cathedrals, see 726.5

727　Buildings for educational and research purposes

Standard subdivisions are added for buildings for educational and research purposes together, for buildings for educational purposes alone

Including college and university buildings, laboratories, library buildings, museums and art galleries

Class here school buildings

728　Residential and related buildings

Standard subdivisions are added for residential and related buildings together, for residential buildings alone

Including houses, apartments, cottages, farmhouses, hotels; saunas, swimming pools; farm buildings other than human residence, e.g., barns

Class here domestic architecture, conventional housing

Class comprehensive works on saunas, swimming pools in 725

For official residences, see 725; for episcopal palaces, parsonages, see 726; for residential educational buildings, see 727

.7　Vacation houses, cabins, hunting lodges, houseboats, mobile homes

See Manual at 643, 690, 728.7 vs. 629.226

.8   **Large and elaborate private dwellings**

Including palaces, comprehensive works on architecture of castles

Class here chateaux, villas

> *For castles as military structures, palaces of rulers, see 725*

> *See also 725 for palaces of rulers, 726 for episcopal palaces*

729   **Design and decoration of structures and accessories**

Including acoustics, lighting, modular design; decoration in specific mediums

Class here interior design (the art or practice of planning and supervising the design and execution of architectural interiors and their furnishings)

Class design and decoration of structural elements, other than those in specific mediums, in 721; class design and decoration of structures and accessories of specific types of buildings in 725–728. Class decoration in a specific medium not in an architectural context with the medium, e.g., sculpture 730

> *For interior decoration, see 747*

> *See Manual at 729*

730   **Plastic arts   Sculpture**

SUMMARY

730.01–.09   Standard subdivisions of plastic arts
 .1–.9   Standard subdivisions of sculpture
731   Processes, forms, subjects of sculpture
732   Sculpture from earliest times to ca. 500, sculpture of nonliterate peoples
733   Greek, Etruscan, Roman sculpture
734   Sculpture from ca. 500 to 1399
735   Sculpture from 1400
736   Carving and carvings
737   Numismatics and sigillography
738   Ceramic arts
739   Art metalwork

.01   Philosophy and theory of plastic arts

.02   Miscellany of plastic arts

.028   Techniques, procedures, apparatus, equipment, materials of plastic arts

Class here techniques of two or more of the plastic arts, e.g., molding of clays in sculpture and ceramics

.03–.09   Standard subdivisions of plastic arts

\>   **730.1–730.9 Standard subdivisions of sculpture**

Class comprehensive works in 730

.1   **Philosophy and theory of sculpture**

Including criticism and appreciation

Class works of critical appraisal in 730.9

.2   **Miscellany of sculpture**

[.28]   Auxiliary techniques and procedures; apparatus, equipment, materials

Do not use for apparatus, equipment, materials; class in 731. Do not use for auxiliary techniques and procedures; class in 731.028

.3–.8   **Standard subdivisions of sculpture**

.9   **Historical, geographic, persons treatment of sculpture**

Class here schools and styles limited to a specific country or locality

Class sculpture of nonliterate peoples regardless of time or place in 732; class comprehensive works on specific schools and styles not limited to country or locality in 732–735

.92   Persons treatment

Including works of sculptors from several geographic areas

Class here description, critical appraisal, biography of sculptors and their works regardless of process, representation, style or school, period, place

Class sculptors who also work in the other plastic arts in 730.092; class works of more than one sculptor in the same geographic area, region, place in general (*not* limited by continent, country, locality) in 730.91; class works of more than one sculptor in modern world in 730.94–730.99; class works of more than one sculptor in ancient world in 732–733

[.93]   Ancient world

Do not use; class in 732–733

>   **731–735   Sculpture**

Class comprehensive works in 730

See Manual at 731–735 vs. 736–739

731   **Processes, forms, subjects of sculpture**

Including apparatus, equipment, materials; sculpture in relief; sculpture in the round, e.g., busts; mobiles and stabiles; iconography

Class specific processes, forms, subjects of sculpture associated with individual sculptors in 730.92; class processes, forms, subjects of sculpture of specific periods and by specific schools in 732–735

For monumental brasses, see 739.5

.028 Auxiliary techniques and procedures [*formerly* 731.4]

> Do not use for apparatus, equipment, materials; class in 731. Do not use for maintenance and repair; class in 731.4
>
> Comprehensive works on techniques, procedures, apparatus, equipment, materials together relocated to 731.4
>
> Class comprehensive works on basic and auxiliary techniques and procedures in 731.4

.092 Persons treatment

> Do not use for individual sculptors; class in 730.92

.4 Techniques and procedures

> Including carving, casting, modeling, molding, welding; conservation, preservation, restoration
>
> Class here comprehensive works on techniques, procedures, apparatus, equipment, materials together [*formerly* 731.028]
>
> Class forms and subjects employing specific techniques and procedures in 731
>
> Auxiliary techniques and procedures relocated to 731.028, e.g., data processing 731.0285

> **732–735 Schools and styles of sculpture**

> Class comprehensive works in 730.9

732 Sculpture from earliest times to ca. 500, sculpture of nonliterate peoples

> Class here ancient sculpture
>
> Class persons treatment of a specific school or style in 730.92
>
> *For Greek, Etruscan, Roman sculpture, see 733*

[.09] Historical, geographic, persons treatment

> Do not use for persons treatment; class in 730.92. Do not use for historical and geographic treatment; class in 732

733 Greek, Etruscan, Roman sculpture

> Class persons treatment of a specific school or style in 730.92

[.092] Persons treatment

> Do not use; class in 730.92

734   Sculpture from ca. 500 to 1399

Including Byzantine, Gothic, Romanesque sculpture

Class here medieval sculpture

Class a specific school or style limited to a specific country or locality in 730.9; class persons treatment of a specific school or style in 730.92

[.09]   Historical, geographic, persons treatment

Do not use for geographic treatment; class in 730.9. Do not use for persons treatment; class in 730.92. Do not use for historical treatment; class in 734

735   Sculpture from 1400

Including baroque, Renaissance sculpture

Class here modern sculpture

Class a specific school or style limited to a specific country or locality in 730.9; class persons treatment of a specific school or style in 730.92

[.09]   Historical, geographic, persons treatment

Do not use for geographic treatment; class in 730.9. Do not use for persons treatment; class in 730.92. Do not use for historical treatment; class in 735

> **736–739   Other plastic arts**

Processes and products

Class comprehensive works in 730. Class a plastic art not provided for here with the art in 745–749, e.g., textile arts 746

See also 731–735 for sculpture

See Manual at 731–735 vs. 736–739

736   Carving and carvings

Standard subdivisions are added for either or both topics in heading

Including glyptics, e.g., lapidary work; cameos; lettering of stone, origami, whittling

Class engraved seals, stamps, signets in 737; class setting of precious and semiprecious stones in 739.27

See also 731–735 for stone, wood sculpture; 745.51 for wood handicrafts

737 Numismatics and sigillography

Standard subdivisions are added for numismatics and sigillography together, for numismatics alone

Including buttons, medals, talismans, tokens; engraved seals, stamps, signets

Class interdisciplinary works on sigillography in 929.9

For paper money, see 769.5

.4 Coins

Class here counterfeit coins

.409 3–.409 9 Specific continents and localities

Do not use for specific countries; class in 737.49

.49 Coins of specific countries

By place of origin

Add to base number 737.49 notation 3–9 from Table 2, e.g., Roman coins minted in Egypt 737.4932

738 Ceramic arts

Class here pottery

Works about "pottery" in the sense of porcelain and earthenware or stoneware are classed here, in the sense of only porcelain are classed in 738.2

Class ceramic sculpture in 731–735

For glass, see 748

.028 Auxiliary techniques and procedures [*formerly* 738.1]

Do not use for apparatus, equipment, materials, maintenance and repair; class in 738.1

.092 Persons treatment

Class here ceramic artists; description, critical appraisal, biography of potters regardless of material or product

For enamelers, see 738.4092; for mosaicists, see 738.5092

.1 Techniques, procedures, apparatus, equipment, materials

Auxiliary techniques and procedures relocated to 738.028, e.g., data processing 738.0285

Class techniques of making specialized products in 738.4–738.8

> **738.2–738.8 Products**

Development, description, critical appraisal, collections of works

Class comprehensive works in 738

.2   **Porcelain**

Class comprehensive works on porcelain, earthenware, stoneware in 738

[.202 8]   Auxiliary techniques and procedures; apparatus, equipment, materials

Do not use for auxiliary techniques and procedures; class in 738.028.
Do not use for apparatus, equipment, materials; class in 738.1

[.209 2]   Persons treatment

Do not use; class in 738.092

.3   **Earthenware and stoneware**

Standard subdivisions are added for either or both topics in heading

Including delftware, faience, majolica

[.302 8]   Auxiliary techniques and procedures; apparatus, equipment, materials

Do not use for auxiliary techniques and procedures; class in 738.028.
Do not use for apparatus, equipment, materials; class in 738.1

[.309 2]   Persons treatment

Do not use; class in 738.092

> **738.4–738.8 Specialized products and techniques of making them**

Class comprehensive works in 738

.4   **Enamels**

For nielloing, see 739; for jewelry, see 739.27; for enameling glass, see 748.6

.5   **Mosaics**

Including mosaics used with architecture, e.g., pavements; mosaics applied to portable objects, e.g., mosaic jewelry

Class here mosaic painting, comprehensive works on mosaics in all materials

Class mosaics of a specific material not provided for here with the material, e.g., mosaic glass 748.5

.6   **Ornamental bricks and tiles**

Standard subdivisions are added for either or both topics in heading

.8 **Other products**

Including dolls, figurines, lamps, stoves

Class comprehensive works on handicrafting dolls in 745.592

739 Art metalwork

For numismatics, see 737

[.028] Auxiliary techniques and procedures; apparatus, equipment, materials

Do not use; class in 739

.2 **Work in precious metals**

Including goldsmithing, silversmithing

Class clocks and watches in precious metals in 739.3

.27 Jewelry

Design of settings, mounting gems, repair work

Class here interdisciplinary works on making fine and costume jewelry

Class interdisciplinary works on jewelry in 391.7; class interdisciplinary works on making costume jewelry in 688

For carving precious and semiprecious stones, see 736; for making handcrafted costume jewelry, see 745.594. For jewelry made in a material other than metal, see the material in 700–770, e.g., mosaic jewelry 738.5

[.270 28] Auxiliary techniques and procedures; apparatus, equipment, materials

Do not use; class in 739.27

.3 **Clocks and watches**

Standard subdivisions are added for either or both topics in heading

Class here clockcases regardless of material

Class clocks as furniture in 749; class interdisciplinary works on clocks and watches in 681.1

[.302 8] Auxiliary techniques and procedures; apparatus, equipment, materials

Do not use; class in 739.3

[.309] Historical, geographic, persons treatment

Do not use; class in 739.3

> **739.4–739.5 Work in base metals**

Class clocks and watches in base metals in 739.3; class comprehensive works in 739

For arms and armor, see 739.7

.4   Ironwork

Class here wrought iron, cast iron, stainless steel

[.402 8]   Auxiliary techniques and procedures; apparatus, equipment, materials

Do not use; class in 739.4

[.409]   Historical, geographic, persons treatment

Do not use; class in 739.4

.5   Work in metals other than iron

Including monumental brasses

.7   Arms and armor

Standard subdivisions are added for arms and armor together, for arms alone

Class interdisciplinary works in 623.4

740   Drawing and decorative arts

SUMMARY

741	**Drawing and drawings**
742	**Perspective in drawing**
743	**Drawing and drawings by subject**
745	**Decorative arts**
746	**Textile arts**
747	**Interior decoration**
748	**Glass**
749	**Furniture and accessories**

741   Drawing and drawings

Class comprehensive works on drawing and painting in 750; class comprehensive works on two-dimensional art in 760

For drawing and drawings by subject, see 743

.01   Philosophy and theory

Including criticism and appreciation

Class works of critical appraisal in 741.09; class perspective in 742

.02   Miscellany

.028   Auxiliary techniques and procedures [*formerly* 741.2]

> Class comprehensive works on basic and auxiliary techniques and procedures in 741.2

.07   Education, research, related topics

.074   Museums and exhibits

> Do not use for collections of drawings; class in 741.9

.09   Historical, geographic, persons treatment

> *For collections of drawings from specific periods and places, see 741.9*

.092   Persons treatment

> Class here description, critical appraisal, biography of artists regardless of medium, process, subject, period, place

> Class artists working in special applications in 741.5–741.7; class collections of drawings in 741.9

.2   Techniques, procedures, apparatus, equipment, materials

Including airbrush, chalk, charcoal, crayon, ink, pencil, scratchboard, silverpoint drawing

Auxiliary technique and procedures relocated to 741.028, e.g., data processing 741.0285

Class techniques, procedures, apparatus, equipment, materials used by individual artists in 741.092; class techniques, procedures, apparatus, equipment, materials used in special applications in 741.5–741.7; class techniques, procedures, apparatus, equipment, materials used in drawing specific subjects in 743

> *For perspective, see 742*

> *See also 751.42 for watercolor*

>   **741.5–741.7   Special applications**

Class here works that began with drawing but use other techniques such as painting, printing, photography to create the final product

Class comprehensive works in 741.6

.5   Cartoons, caricatures, comics

Including animated cartoons

Class here cartoon fiction, graphic novels (visual novels)

Class photographic techniques of animated cartoons in 778.5; class comprehensive works on cartoon films in 791.43. Class cartoons or caricatures whose purpose is to inform or persuade with the subject of the cartoon or caricature, e.g., political cartoons 320

.507 4	Museums and exhibits

Do not use for collections; class in 741.5

.509 2	Persons treatment

Class collections by individual artists in 741.5

.6 **Graphic design, illustration and commercial art**

Including advertisements, books and book jackets, calendars, covers for sheet music and recordings, greeting cards, magazines, match covers, newspapers, postcards; fashion drawing; comprehensive works on posters

Class here comprehensive works on special applications of drawing

Class illumination of manuscripts and books in 745.6; class fashion design in 746.9; class government-issued postcards without illustrations in 769.56; class graphic arts, comprehensive works on two-dimensional art in 760. Class a specific type of illustration, a specific form of graphic design, a specific form of commercial art not provided for here with the subject, e.g., original oil paintings for book jackets 759

> *For art posters (posters as a specific form of prints), see 769.5*

> *See Manual at 741.6 vs. 800*

.7 **Silhouettes**

Class cut-out silhouettes in 736

.9 **Collections of drawings**

Regardless of medium or process

Class here exhibition catalogs

Preliminary drawings are classed with the finished work unless they are treated as works of art in their own right

Class collections by artists devoted to special applications in 741.5–741.7; class collections of drawings by subject not from a specific period or place in 743

.93–.99	Specific continents, countries, localities

Add to base number 741.9 notation 3–9 from Table 2, e.g., collections of drawings from London 741.9421

Collections by individual artists are classed at country level only. Notation 074 from Table 1 for collections is not added. For example, a collection of an individual artist from London is classed in 741.942 (*not* 741.9421, 741.942074)

742 **Perspective in drawing**

Theory, principles, methods

Class perspective in special applications in 741.5–741.7; class perspective in drawing specific subjects in 743; class comprehensive works on perspective in the arts in 701

743   *Drawing and drawings by subject

Standard subdivisions are added for drawing and drawings by subject together, for drawing alone

Class collections of drawings by subject from a specific period or place in 741.9

[.028]   Techniques, procedures, apparatus, equipment, materials

Do not use; class in 743

.4   *Drawing human figures

Class here nudes

For drawing draped figures, see 743.5

.5   *Drawing draped figures

For fashion drawing, see 741.6

[.501–.509]   Standard subdivisions

Do not use; class in 743.5

.6   *Drawing animals

745   Decorative arts

Class here folk art

For a decorative art not provided for here, see the art in 736–739, 746–749, e.g., interior decoration 747

.1   Antiques

For a specific kind of antique, see the kind, e.g., brasses 739.5, passenger automobiles 629.222

See Manual at 745.1

.2   Industrial art and design

Creative design of mass-produced commodities

Standard subdivisions are added for either or both topics in heading

For design of a specific commodity, see the commodity, e.g., automobiles 629.2

.4   Pure and applied design and decoration

Standard subdivisions are added for any or all topics in heading

For industrial design, see 745.2. For design in a specific art form, see the form, e.g., design in architecture 729

[.409]   Historical, geographic, persons treatment

Do not use; class in 745.4

*Do not use notation 092 from Table 1 for artists; class in 741.092

.5 **Handicrafts**

Creative work done by hand with aid of simple tools or machines

Class home (amateur) workshops in 684; class interdisciplinary works on handicrafts in 680

For decorative coloring, see 745.7; for floral arts, see 745.92

See Manual at 680 vs. 745.5

> 745.51–745.58 Specific materials

Class specific objects made from specific materials in 745.59; class comprehensive works in 745.5

For textile handicrafts, see 746; for glass handicrafts, see 748

.51 Woods

Including inlaying, marquetry, ornamental woodwork, scrollwork; bamboo

Class treen (woodenware) in 674; class woodworking in 684; class cabinetmaking (wooden furniture making) in 684.1; class artistic aspects of furniture in 749

For ornamental woodwork in furniture, see 749

.53 Leathers and furs

Class construction of clothing in 646.4

.54 Papers

Including papier mâché, tissue papers, wallpapers; decoupage, gift wrapping

Class papier mâché used in sculpture in 731; class paper cutting and folding in 736

.55 Shells

.56 Metals

Class art metalwork in 739

.57 Rubber and plastics

.58 Beads, found and other objects

Class specific objects made from other objects in 745.59

For bead embroidery, see 746.5

.59 Making specific objects

Class here handicrafts in composite materials

.592   Toys, models, miniatures, related objects

Standard subdivisions are added for toys, models, miniatures, related objects together; for toys alone

Including dolls, stuffed animals, paper airplanes

Class porcelain dolls in 738.8; class interdisciplinary works on mass-produced and handcrafted toys in 688.7

.592 8   Models and miniatures

Standard subdivisions are added for either or both topics in heading

Including ships in bottles, toy soldiers

Class here interdisciplinary works on handcrafted models and miniatures

Class models and miniatures produced by assembly-line or mechanized manufacturing, interdisciplinary works on models and miniatures in 688. Class miniature and model educational exhibits, models for technical and professional use with the subject illustrated, e.g., handcrafted miniature physical anthropology exhibits 599.9074

See Manual at 745.5928

.593   Useful objects

Including candles, decoys, lampshades

Class carved birds not used for hunting in 730

For toys, models, miniatures, related objects, see 745.592

.594   Decorative objects

Including artificial flowers, Christmas decorations, costume jewelry, Easter eggs, greeting cards

Class interdisciplinary works on costume jewelry in 391.7; class interdisciplinary on making costume jewelry in 688; class interdisciplinary on making jewelry in 739.27; class arrangement of artificial flowers in 745.92

.6   **Calligraphy, heraldic design, illumination**

Including artistic, decorative lettering

Class development, description, critical appraisal of manuscripts in 091; class development, description, critical appraisal of illustrated books in 096; class penmanship in 652; class typography in 686.2

See also 741.6 for book illustration

.7   Decorative coloring

> Including gilding, japanning, lacquering, painting, stenciling
>
> Class gilding as an aspect of bookbinding in 686.3; class gilding as an aspect of illumination of manuscripts and books in 745.6; class printing, painting, dyeing textiles in 746.6

[.8]   Cycloramas, dioramas, panoramas

> Number discontinued; class in 745

.9   Other decorative arts

.92   Floral arts

> Flower arrangement: selection and arrangement of plant materials and appropriate accessories
>
> Class here arrangement of artificial flowers
>
> Class making artificial flowers in 745.594; class potted plants as interior decorations in 747

746   Textile arts

> Including string art
>
> Class here textile handicrafts
>
> Class domestic sewing and related operations in 646.2. Class a specific textile product not provided for here with the product, e.g., stuffed animals 745.592

> **746.1–746.9 Products and processes**
>
> Unless other instructions are given, observe the following table of preference, e.g., embroidered rugs 746.7 (*not* 746.44):
>
> | | |
> |---|---|
> | Laces and related fabrics | 746.2 |
> | Rugs | 746.7 |
> | Yarn preparation and weaving | 746.1 |
> | Needlework and handwork | 746.4 |
> | Bead embroidery | 746.5 |
> | Printing, painting, dyeing | 746.6 |
> | Pictures, hangings, tapestries | 746.3 |
> | Other textile products | 746.9 |
>
> Class home sewing and clothing in 646; class textile manufacturing in 677; class comprehensive works in 746

.1   Yarn preparation and weaving

> Including dyeing, spinning
>
> *For weaving unaltered vegetable fibers, see 746.41; for nonloom weaving, see 746.42*

.2   **Laces and related fabrics**

> Including passementerie
>
> *For tatting, see 746.43*

.3   **Pictures, hangings, tapestries**

> Standard subdivisions are added for any or all topics in heading
>
> Pictures, hangings, tapestries made by a specific process relocated to the process, e.g., needlepoint pictures 746.44

[.309]   Historical, geographic, persons treatment

> Do not use; class in 746.39

.39   Historical, geographic, persons treatment

> Add to base number 746.39 notation 1–9 from Table 2, e.g., artists 746.392

.4   **Needlework and handwork**

> Standard subdivisions are added for either or both topics in heading

.41   Weaving, braiding, matting unaltered vegetable fibers

> Including basketry, raffia work, rushwork

.42   Nonloom weaving and related techniques

> Including braiding, knotting, macramé, sprang, twining
>
> Class nonloom weaving of unaltered vegetable fibers in 746.41
>
> *For card weaving, see 746.1*

.43   Knitting, crocheting, tatting

.44   Embroidery

> Including appliqué, bargello, canvas embroidery, couching, crewelwork, cross-stitch, cutwork, drawn work, hardanger, needlepoint, smocking

.46   Patchwork and quilting

> Standard subdivisions are added for either or both topics in heading
>
> Class here quilts

.5   **Bead embroidery**

.6   **Printing, painting, dyeing**

> Including batik, silk-screen printing, tie-dyeing

.7   **Rugs**

> Class here carpets

[.709]   Historical, geographic, persons treatment

> Do not use; class in 746.79

.79 Historical, geographic, persons treatment

> Add to base number 746.79 notation 1–9 from Table 2, e.g., carpetmakers 746.792

.9 **Other textile products**

> Including costume, fashion design; interior furnishings, e.g., bedspreads, draperies, slipcovers, table linens, towels

> Other textile products made by a specific process relocated to the process, e.g., crocheted sweaters 746.43

> Class interdisciplinary works on clothing in 391; class interdisciplinary works on clothing construction in 646.4

> *For afghans, see 746.43; for quilts, see 746.46*

> *See Manual at 391 vs. 646, 746.9*

747 Interior decoration

> Design and decorative treatment with interior furnishings

> Including carpets, decorative lighting, draperies, rugs, upholstery, wallpapers; decorating with houseplants

> Class here interior decoration of residential buildings

> Class interior design in 729; class textile arts and handicrafts in 746

> *For furniture and accessories, see 749*

[.09] Historical, geographic, persons treatment

> Do not use; class in 747.2

.2 **Historical, geographic, persons treatment**

> Class here artists

> Add to base number 747.2 the numbers following 708 in 708.1–708.9, e.g., interior decoration and artists in France 747.24

> Individual artists are classed in notation at country level only

.7 **Decoration of specific rooms of residential buildings**

> Class specific decorations regardless of room in 747

748 Glass

.092 Persons treatment

> Class here glassmakers

> Class works about "glassmakers" when referring only to makers of glassware in 748.29

.2 **Glassware**

Class here blown, cast, decorated, fashioned, molded, pressed glassware

Class stained glass in 748.5

For methods of decoration, see 748.6; for specific articles, see 748.8

.202 8 Techniques, procedures, apparatus, equipment, materials

Including bottle cutting, glassblowing

[.209] Historical, geographic, persons treatment

Do not use; class in 748.29

.29 Historical, geographic, persons treatment

Class here glassware makers

Add to base number 748.29 the numbers following 708 in 708.1–708.9, e.g., glassware and glassmakers of Pennsylvania 748.29148

Individual glassmakers are classed in notation at country level only

.5 **Stained, painted, leaded, mosaic glass**

Standard subdivisions are added for stained, painted, leaded, mosaic glass together; for stained glass alone; for painted glass alone; for leaded glass alone

Class comprehensive works on mosaics in 738.5

For specific articles, see 748.8

[.509] Historical, geographic, persons treatment

Do not use; class in 748.59

.59 Historical, geographic, persons treatment

Class here artists

Add to base number 748.59 the numbers following 708 in 708.1–708.9, e.g., stained glass and artists of France 748.594

Individual artists are classed in notation at country level only

.6 **Methods of decoration**

Including engraving, etching

Class methods of decoration of specific articles in 748.8

For painted glass, see 748.5

[.609 2] Persons treatment

Do not use; class in 748.29

.8 **Specific articles**

Including bottles of artistic interest regardless of use, drinking glasses, mirrors, paperweights

Class manufacture of glass bottles in 666; class mirrors as furniture, glass lamps and lighting fixtures in 749

749 Furniture and accessories

Standard subdivisions are added for furniture and accessories together, for furniture alone

Including built-in furniture, fireplaces, lamps, picture frames

Class built-in church furniture in architectural design in 726

For upholstery, see 747

[.09] Historical, geographic, persons treatment

Do not use; class in 749.2

.2 **Historical, geographic, persons treatment**

Class here antiques and reproductions, furniture makers

Add to base number 749.2 the numbers following 708 in 708.1–708.9, e.g., English furniture and furniture makers in 749.22

Individual furniture makers are classed in notation at country level only

750 Painting and paintings

Class here comprehensive works on painting and drawing

Unless other instructions are given, observe the following table of preference, e.g., an individual Canadian painter of portraits 759.11 (*not* 757.0971), portrait painting in Canada 757.0971 (*not* 759.11):

Individual painters and their work	759.1–759.9
Techniques, procedures, apparatus, equipment, materials	751.2–751.6
Iconography	753–758
Specific forms	751.7
Geographic treatment	759.1–759.9
Periods of development	759.01–759.07
Color	752

Class comprehensive works on graphic arts, two-dimensional art in 760. Class painting in a specific decorative art with the art, e.g., illumination of manuscripts and books 745.6

For drawing and drawings, see 741

SUMMARY

.1   Philosophy and theory

Including criticism and appreciation

Class color in 752; class works of critical appraisal in 759

.2   Miscellany

.28   Auxiliary techniques and procedures [*formerly* 751.4]

Do not use for materials; class in 751.2. Do not use for apparatus and equipment; class in 751.3

> *For comprehensive works on basic and auxiliary techniques and procedures, see 751.4*

[.9]   Historical, geographic, persons treatment

Do not use; class in 759

751   *Techniques, procedures, apparatus, equipment, materials, forms

.2   *Materials

Class use of materials in specific techniques in 751.4

.3   *Apparatus, equipment, artists' models

Class use of apparatus and equipment in specific techniques in 751.4

.4   *Techniques and procedures

Including airbrush, ink painting; collage (with painting as the basic technique)

Class here comprehensive works on basic and auxiliary techniques and procedures

Auxiliary techniques and procedures relocated to 750.28, e.g., data processing 750.285

> *For mosaic painting, see 738.5; for techniques of reproduction, see 751.5; for maintenance and repair, see 751.6*

.42   *Watercolor painting

---

*Do not use notation 092 from Table 1 for individual painters; class in 759.1–759.9

[.420 1–.420 9]   Standard subdivisions

                      Do not use; class in 751.42

.45   *Oil painting

.5   ***Techniques of reproduction**

             Execution, identification, determination of authenticity of reproduction, copies, forgeries, alterations

             For printmaking and prints, see 760

.6   ***Maintenance and repair**

             Including expertizing

             Class identification of reproductions, copies, forgeries, alterations in 751.5

.7   ***Specific forms**

             Including frescoes, murals, scene paintings, miniatures

             Class miniatures done as illuminations in manuscripts and books in 745.6

752   ***Color**

             Class technology of color in 667; class comprehensive works on color in the fine and decorative arts in 701

>   **753–758 Iconography**

             Class here development, description, critical appraisal, works regardless of form

             Class comprehensive works in 750

             See Manual at 753–758

753   ***Symbolism, allegory, mythology, legend**

             For religious symbolism, see 755

754   ***Genre paintings**

755   ***Religion**

             Class here religious symbolism

757   ***Human figures**

             Not provided for in 753–755, 758

             Class here portraits

*Do not use notation 092 from Table 1 for individual painters; class in 759.1–759.9

758 Other subjects

Including animals, cityscapes, landscapes, marine scenes, plants, still life

Class individual painters in 759.1–759.9. Class hunting scenes in which animals are not the center of interest with the subject, e.g., hunters 757

759 Historical, geographic, persons treatment

Class here development, description, critical appraisal, works

Class exhibitions of paintings not limited by place, period, or subject in 750.74

> 759.01–759.07 Periods of development

Class here schools and styles not limited by country or locality, works on one or two periods of European painting

Class works on three or more periods of European painting in 759.94; class comprehensive works in 759. Class schools associated with a specific locality with the locality in 759.1–759.9, e.g., Florentine school of Italian painting 759.5

When classifying works of more than one painter, notation 074 and —075 from Table 1 for Museums, collections, exhibits and Museum activities, respectively, take preference over notation 092 Persons

.01 *Nonliterate peoples, and earliest times to 499

Including paintings of nonliterate peoples regardless of time or place

Class paintings of both literate and nonliterate cultures in 759.1–759.9

.02 *500–1399

Including Byzantine, early Christian, Gothic, Romanesque painting and paintings

Class here medieval painting and paintings

For Byzantine, early Christian, Gothic painting and paintings of any other period, see the specific period, e.g., early Christian painting before 500 759.01

See Manual at 753–758

.03 *1400–1599

Class here Renaissance painting and paintings

For Renaissance painting and paintings before 1400, see 759.02

.04 *1600–1799

Including baroque and rococo painting and paintings

---

*Do not use notation 092 from Table 1 for individual painters; class in 759.1–759.9

.05   *1800–1899

>   Including impressionism, kitsch, naturalism, pointillism, realism, romanticism

             For kitsch, naturalism, realism, romanticism of any other period, see the specific period, e.g., realism of 1900–1990 759.06

.06   *1900–1999

             Including abstractionism, cubism, expressionism, op art, pop art, surrealism

             Class here modern painting

             For 1800–1899, see 759.05; for 2000–2099, see 759.07

.07   *2000–2099

>   **759.1–759.9 Geographic treatment**

             Individual painters are classed in notation at country level only. Standard subdivisions —074, —075, and — 092 from Table 1 are not added for individual painters, e.g., an exhibition of the work of a Canadian painter, collecting the person's works, and a biography of the painter 759.11 (*not* 759.11074, 759.11075, or 759.11092, respectively)

             Class painting and paintings of nonliterate peoples in 759.01; class western painting of one or two specific periods in 759.02–759.07; class comprehensive works in 759

.1   **North America**

             For painting and paintings of Middle America, see 759.972

.11   Canada

.13   United States

             Class painting and paintings of specific states in 759.14–759.19

.14–.19   Specific states of United States

             Add to base number 759.1 the numbers following —7 in notation 74–79 from Table 2, e.g., painting and paintings of California 759.194

             Class individual painters in 759.13

             For painting and paintings of Hawaii, see 759.9969

>   **759.2–759.8 Europe**

             Class comprehensive works in 759.94

             For countries and localities not provided for here, see the country or locality in 759.949, e.g., painting and paintings of Belgium 759.9493

---

*Do not use notation 092 from Table 1 for individual painters; class in 759.1–759.9

.2   **British Isles**

.3–.8   **Miscellaneous parts of Europe**

Add to base number 759 the numbers following —4 in notation 43–48 from Table 2, e.g., painting and paintings of France 759.4; however, individual painters from countries of former Soviet Central Asia relocated from 759.7 to 759.9584–759.9587

.9   **Other geographic areas**

.91   Areas, regions, places in general

Add to base number 759.91 the numbers following —1 in notation 11–19 from Table 2, e.g., Western Hemisphere 759.9181

Individual painters are classed in the notation for their respective countries, e.g., painters from Canada 759.11

.93–.99   Continents, countries, localities

Class here painting and paintings of specific periods, e.g., painting and paintings of 1800–1899 in South America 759.98

Add to base number 759.9 notation 3–9 from Table 2, e.g., individual painters from countries of former Soviet Central Asia 759.9584–759.9587 [*formerly* 759.7], comprehensive works on painting and paintings of Europe 759.94, Etruscan painting and paintings 759.937; however, for individual Hawaiian painters, see 759.13; for individual Siberian painters, see 759.7

Class works on one or two periods of European painting in 759.02–759.07, e.g., painting and paintings of 1800–1899 in Europe 759.05 (*not* 759.94); class painting and paintings from parts of Europe in notation 41–48 from Table 2 in 759.2–759.8

760   Graphic arts   Printmaking and prints

Graphic arts: any and all nonplastic representation on flat surfaces, including painting, drawing, prints, and photographs

Including rubbings, two-dimensional mixed-media art and composites

Class here two-dimensional art; prints and at least one other of the graphic arts

Class comprehensive works on graphic and plastic arts in 701–709. Class rubbings used for study and research in a specific field with the field, e.g., rubbings used for study of monumental brasses 739.5

For printing, see 686.2; for drawing and drawings, see 741; for painting and paintings, see 750; for photography and photographs, see 770

.01–.09   Standard subdivisions of graphic arts

.1   **Philosophy and theory of printmaking and prints**

Including criticism and appreciation

Class works of critical appraisal in 769.9

.2	**Miscellany of printmaking and prints**
.28	Techniques, procedures, apparatus, equipment, materials

> Class techniques, procedures, apparatus, equipment, materials for making specific kinds of prints in 761–767

.3–.6	**Standard subdivisions of printmaking and prints**
.7	**Education, research, related topics of printmaking and prints**
.75	Museum activities and services

> Do not use for collecting; class in 769

.8	**History and description of printmaking and prints with respect to kinds of persons**
[.9]	**Historical, geographic, persons treatment of printmaking and prints**

> Do not use; class in 769.9

> ## 761–769   Printmaking and prints

Class comprehensive works in 760

> ## 761–767   Printmaking

Fine art of executing a printing block or plate representing a picture or design conceived by the printmaker or copied from another artist's painting or drawing or from a photograph

Techniques, procedures, equipment, materials

Class techniques, procedures, apparatus, equipment, materials used in reproduction, preservation, routine care in 769; class maintenance and repair in 769.028; class techniques, procedures, equipment, materials employed by individual printmakers in 769.92; class comprehensive works in 760.28

761   Relief processes (Block printing)

Printing from raised surfaces, e.g., wood, metal, linoleum blocks

763   Lithographic (Planographic) processes

Printing from flat surfaces, e.g., stone, aluminum, zinc

For chromolithography, see 764

764   Chromolithography and serigraphy

Including silk-screen printing

> **765–767 Intaglio processes**

Class comprehensive works in 765

765 Metal engraving

Class here comprehensive works on metal relief and metal intaglio processes, on intaglio processes

For metal relief processes, see 761; for mezzotinting and aquatinting, see 766; for etching and drypoint, see 767

766 Mezzotinting, aquatinting, related processes

767 Etching and drypoint

769 Prints

Works produced using a printing block, screen, or plate

Class here description, critical appraisal, collections regardless of process

.075 Museum activities and services

Do not use for collecting; class in 769

[.09] Historical, geographic, persons treatment

Do not use; class in 769.9

.5 **Forms of prints**

Including art posters, paper dolls, paper money; Christmas seals, savings stamps

Class prints other than postage stamps on a specific subject regardless of form in 769; class prints made by an individual printmaker regardless of form in 769.92; class comprehensive works on posters in 741.6

.56 Postage stamps and related devices

Standard subdivisions are added for postage stamps and related devices together, for postage stamps alone

Including cachets, cancellations, covers, postmarks; postal stationery, e.g., postcards

Class here philately (study and collecting of stamps)

Class illustrated postcards in 741.6; class stamps other than for prepayment of postage in 769.5

[.560 9] Historical, geographic, persons treatment

Do not use; class in 769.569

.569   Historical, geographic, persons treatment

> Add to base number 769.569 notation 1–9 from Table 2, e.g., postage stamps from San Marino 769.569454; however, for individual printmakers, see 769.92

.9   **Historical, geographic, persons treatment of printmaking and prints**

> Add to base number 769.9 notation 1–9 from Table 2, e.g., printmaking in England 769.942

> Class the history of a specific process with the process, e.g., history of lithography 763.09

.92   Persons

> Number built according to instructions under 769.9

> Class here engravers, printmakers

> *See Manual at 769.92*

770   Photography and photographs

> Standard subdivisions are added for photography and photographs together, for photography alone

> Class technological photography in 621.36

.2   **Miscellany**

.28   Auxiliary techniques and procedures [*formerly* 771]

> *For comprehensive works on basic and auxiliary techniques and procedures, see 771*

.9   **Historical, geographic, persons treatment**

.92   Persons treatment

> Class here photographers regardless of type of photography

> Class photographs in 779

> *For motion picture photographers, see 778.5; for television and video photographers, see 778.59092*

771 *Techniques, procedures, apparatus, equipment, materials

Including darkrooms, studios; comprehensive works on basic and auxiliary techniques and procedures

Class here interdisciplinary works on description, use, manufacture of apparatus, equipment, materials

Auxiliary techniques and procedures relocated to 770.28, e.g., data processing 770.285

Class techniques, procedures, apparatus, equipment, materials used in special processes in 772–774; class techniques, procedures, apparatus, equipment, materials used in specific fields and special kinds of photography in 778

For manufacture of a specific kind of apparatus, equipment, material, see the apparatus, equipment, or material, e.g., cameras 681

.3 Cameras and accessories

Standard subdivisions are added for cameras and accessories together; for cameras alone

Including tripods

> ### 772–774 Special processes

Techniques, procedures, apparatus, equipment, materials

Class processing techniques in specific fields and special kinds of photography in 778; class comprehensive works in 771

For photomechanical printing techniques, see 686.2

772 *Metallic salt processes

773 *Pigment processes of printing

Class xerography in 686.4

774 *Holography

778 Specific fields and special kinds of photography; cinematography and video production; related activities

Class here interdisciplinary works on use and manufacture of apparatus, equipment, materials used in specific fields and special kinds of photography

For manufacture of a specific kind of apparatus, equipment, materials, see the apparatus, equipment, or material, e.g., cameras 681

---

*Do not use notation 092 from Table 1 for photographers; class in 770.92

.2 ***Photographic projection**

Including filmstrips, slides

For stereoscopic projection, see 778.4; for motion picture projection, see 778.5

.3 ***Special kinds of photography**

Not provided for elsewhere

Including photomacrography, photomicrography, telephotography; aerial, close-up, high-speed, infrared, space photography

Class a special kind of photography in relation to cinematography and video production in 778.5. Class a specific application of photography with the application, e.g., use of photography in astronomy 522

For technological photography and photo-optics, see 621.36

See Manual at 778.3 vs. 621.36

.4 ***Stereoscopic photography and projection**

For stereoscopic motion picture photography and projection, see 778.5

.5 **Cinematography, video production, related activities**

Including animated cartoons, motion picture projection, preservation and storage of motion picture films

Class comprehensive works on motion picture production and cinematography in 791.43

See Manual at 791.43, 791.45 vs. 778.5

.59 Video production (Television photography)

Including interdisciplinary works on video recording formats and recorders

Class here home video systems

Class comprehensive works on television production in 791.45; class interdisciplinary works on television in 384.55. Class a specific application of video production with the application, e.g., use of video production in diagnosis of diseases 616.07

For manufacture of video recording formats and recorders, see 621.388

> **778.6–778.8 Specific topics in photography**

Class specific topics in relation to cinematography and video production in 778.5; class comprehensive works in 770

---

*Do not use notation 092 from Table 1 for photographers; class in 770.92

.6 ***Color photography**

Class here photography of colors

Class color photomicrography in 778.3

.602 8 Auxiliary techniques and procedures; apparatus, equipment, materials

Class processing techniques, procedures, apparatus, equipment, materials in color photography in 778.6

.7 ***Photography under specific conditions**

Including flashbulb, outdoor, underwater photography; photography by artificial light

Class short-duration flash in high-speed photography in 778.3

For infrared photography, see 778.3

.8 ***Special effects and trick photography**

Standard subdivisions are added for either or both topics in heading

Including tabletop photography

.9 **Photography of specific subjects**

Class here comprehensive works on techniques of photographing, photographs of, and photographers of a specific subject

Class photographers in 770.92; class photography by specific methods regardless of subject in 778.3–778.8

779 Photographs

Class biographies and critical appraisals, which may also contain some photographs, in 770.92

*Do not use notation 092 from Table 1 for photographers; class in 770.92

780   Music

After general topics (780 and 781) the basic arrangement of the schedule is based on the voice, instrument, or ensemble making the music. Vocal music is classed in 782–783; instrumental music in 784–788

Unless other instructions are given, class a subject with aspects in two or more subdivisions of 780 in the number coming last, e.g., sacred vocal music 782.2 (*not* 781.7)

This schedule does not distinguish scores, texts, or recordings
> (Option: To distinguish scores, texts, recordings, use one of the following:
> (Option A: Prefix a letter or other symbol to the number for treatises, e.g., music for violin M787.2 or &787.2, violin recordings R787.2 or MR787.2; use a special prefix to distinguish miniature scores from other scores, MM787.2
> (Option B: Add 026 to the number for treatises, e.g., scores for music for violin 787.2026
> (Option C: Class recordings in 789, e.g., recordings of folk music 789.2, recordings of violin folk music 789.2072)

SUMMARY

780.1–.9	**Standard subdivisions and treatises on music scores, recordings, texts**
781	**General principles and musical forms**
782	**Vocal music**
783	**Music for single voices The voice**
784	**Instruments and instrumental ensembles and their music**
785	**Ensembles with only one instrument per part**
786	**Keyboard, mechanical, electrophonic, percussion instruments**
787	**Stringed instruments (Chordophones) Bowed stringed instruments**
788	**Wind instruments (Aerophones)**

.1   Philosophy and theory

For general principles, theory of music, see 781

.15   Analytical guides and program notes

(.16)   Bibliographies, catalogs, indexes

> (Optional number; prefer 016.78)

(.162)   *Bibliographies and catalogs of music literature

(.164)   *Bibliographies and catalogs of scores and parts

(.166)   *Discographies

> Bibliographies and catalogs of music recorded on phonorecords (cylinders, discs, wires, tapes, films)

*(Optional number; prefer 016.78)

.2   **Miscellany**

Including thematic catalogs

For thematic catalogs of individual composers, see 780.92

.26   Treatises on music scores, recordings, texts

Standard subdivisions are added for a combination of two or more topics in heading, for scores alone

Including librettos, lyrics, plots

To be classed here, the words of the texts must be discussed in a musical context. If the words are presented as literature, folklore, or religious text, class the work in 800, 398, or 200, respectively

Use this subdivision for texts only for building other numbers, e.g., lyrics of songs 782.42026; never use it by itself

In schedules other than 780, indicate scores, recordings, texts, and treatises about them by adding 026 from 780.26, e.g., bibliography of music scores 016.78026, discography of violin music 016.7872026

See also 070.5 for music publishing, 686.2 for music printing, 781.49 for recording of music

See Manual at 780.26

(Option: To distinguish scores and recordings within 780, add to the number for treatises notation 026 from 780.26, e.g., scores of music for violin 787.2026. Other options are described at 780)

(Option: Class here law of music; prefer appropriate subdivisions of 340)

.28   Auxiliary techniques and procedures; apparatus, equipment, materials

For instruments, see 784

See also 780.26 for scores and recordings, 781.4 for techniques of music

.7   **Education, research, performances, related topics**

Including use of apparatus and equipment in study and teaching

For techniques for acquiring musical skills and learning a repertoire, see 781.4

.76   Review, exercises, examinations, works for self-instruction

.78   Performances (Concerts and recitals)

Do not use for use of apparatus and equipment in study and teaching; class in 780.7

See also 781.4 for performance techniques

.79   Competitions, festivals, awards, financial support

Class performances at festivals and competitions in 780.78

.8   **History and description of music with respect to kinds of persons**

.89   Music with respect to racial, ethnic, national groups

> *For folk music, see 781.62*
>
> *See Manual at 781.62 vs. 780.89*

.9   **Historical, geographic, persons treatment**

No distinction is made between the music of a place and music in a place, e.g., Austrian music and music played in Austria are both classed in 780.9436

Class critical appraisal in analytical guides and program notes in 780.15

.92   Persons associated with music

Class here composers, performers, critics; thematic catalogs of individual composers

Class general thematic catalogs in 780.2

> *See Manual at 780.92; also at 791.092*

(Option: Class individual composers in 789)

.94   Europe   Western Europe

Use only for works that stress that they are discussing the European origin and character of the music in contrast to music from other sources

---

> **781–788 Principles, forms, ensembles, voices, instruments**

Class here music of all traditions
  (Option: 781–788 may be used for only one tradition of music; in that case, class all other traditions in 789. For example, if it is desired to emphasize western art music, class it here, and class all other traditions of music in 789, e.g., jazz 789.5; or, if it is desired to emphasize jazz, class it here, and class all other traditions of music in 789, e.g., western art music 789.8)

Unless other instructions are given, class a subject with aspects in two or more subdivisions of 781–788 in the number coming last, e.g., rehearsing vocal music 782.044 (*not* 781.44), Johann Sebastian Bach's cello sonatas 787.4 (*not* 784.18)

Class comprehensive works in 780

781   ***General principles and musical forms**

Class here music theory

Use the subdivisions of 781 only when the subject is not limited to voice, instrument, or ensemble. If voice, instrument, or ensemble is specified, class with voice, instrument, or ensemble; and then add as instructed. For example, rehearsal of music 781.44, rehearsal of opera (a form for the voice) 782.1

---

*Use notation from Table 1 as modified under 780.1–780.9

SUMMARY

781.1	Aesthetics, appreciation, taste	
.2	Elements of music	
.3	Composition	
.4	Techniques of music	
.5	Kinds of music	
.6	Traditions of music	
.7	Sacred music	
.8	Musical forms	

.1   **Aesthetics, appreciation, taste**

[.101–.109]   Standard subdivisions

> Do not use; class in 781.1

.2   ***Elements of music**

> Including meter, rhythm; musical sound, e.g., pitch, tone color; melody; harmony; tonal systems, e.g., atonality, twelve-tone system; counterpoint

> Class here scientific principles

> Class comprehensive works on serialism in 781.3

> *For playing time, see 781.4*

.3   ***Composition**

> Including arrangement, improvisation, orchestration, serialism

> *For atonality, see 781.2*

.302 85   Data processing   Computer applications

> Do not use for computer composition; class in 781.3

.4   ***Techniques of music**

> Including score reading

> *For improvisation, techniques of composition, see 781.3*

> *See also 784.193 for techniques for playing instruments*

.44   *Rehearsal and practice

> Standard subdivisions are added for either or both topics in heading

.45   *Conducting

.46   *Interpretation

.47   *Accompaniment

---

*Use notation from Table 1 as modified under 780.1–780.9

.48   *Breathing and resonance

            Standard subdivisions are added for either or both topics in heading

            Class breathing and resonance associated with instrumental performance in
            784.193

.49   *Recording of music

            *See also 621.389 for sound recording and reproducing equipment,
            780.26 for treatises on music recordings*

.5   ***Kinds of music**

            Including music for specific times, e.g., harvest; music in specific settings, e.g.,
            street music; music for specific media (limited to background or mood music),
            e.g., television music; music accompanying public entertainments, e.g., ballet
            music; program music (music depicting nonmusical concepts, e.g., music
            depicting the sea); music accompanying activities, e.g., inaugurations; music
            accompanying stages of the life cycle, e.g., weddings; music reflecting other
            themes and subjects, e.g., military, patriotic, protest music

            Class dramatic vocal music in 782.1; class musical forms depicting nonmusical
            concepts, e.g., nocturnes, in 784.18

            *See also 778.5 for sound synchronization of motion pictures, 778.59 for
            sound synchronization of television programs*

.6   ***Traditions of music**

            Works emphasizing a specific tradition

            See Manual at 781.6

            (Option: If 781–788 is used for only one tradition of music, class all other
            traditions in 789)

.62   Folk music

            Music indigenous to the cultural group in which it occurs, usually evolved
            through aural transmission

            See also 780.9 for music of and performed in a specific location

            See Manual at 781.62 vs. 780.89; also at 781.62 vs. 781.62009

.620 01–.620 07   Standard subdivisions

            Notation from Table 1 as modified under 780.1–780.9, e.g.,
            performances of folk music 781.620078

.620 08   History and description of folk music with respect to kinds of persons

[.620 089]   Treatment with respect to specific racial, ethnic, national groups

            Do not use; class in 781.62

*Use notation from Table 1 as modified under 780.1–780.9

.620 09	Historical, geographic, persons treatment

> Class geographic treatment of folk music of specific racial, ethnic, national groups in 781.62

> *See Manual at 781.62 vs. 781.62009*

.63	*Popular music

> *For western popular music, see 781.64*

.64	*Western popular music

> Class country and western music in 781.642

> Most works on western popular music are predominantly about popular songs and are classed in 782.42164

> *For jazz, see 781.65; for rock, see 781.66*

.642	*Country music

> Class here bluegrass music

.643	*Blues

> Class here rhythm and blues

.644	*Soul
.646	*Reggae
.65	*Jazz

> Including swing

.66	*Rock (Rock 'n' roll)
.7	**Sacred music**

> Class sacred music accompanying stages of life cycle in 781.5; class works about "church music" in the sense of Christian church music in 781.71; class sacred vocal music in 782.2

.700 1–.700 9	Standard subdivisions

> Notation from Table 1 as modified under 780.1–780.9, e.g., performances of sacred music 781.70078

.71	Christian sacred music

> *For music of Christian church year, see 781.72*

.710 01–.710 09	Standard subdivisions

> Notation from Table 1 as modified under 780.1–780.9, e.g., performances of Christian sacred music 781.70078

.72	*Music of Christian church year

---

*Use notation from Table 1 as modified under 780.1–780.9

.723 *Christmas day

> Class here Christmas season
>
> Class Epiphany in 781.72

.727 *Easter Sunday

> Class here Eastertide (Easter season)
>
> Class Ascensiontide in 781.72

.76 *Judaic sacred music

.8 *Musical forms

> Including da capo form; chaconnes, rondos, theme and variations
>
> Class here formal analysis; works that do not specify voice, instrument, or ensemble
>
> Class works for specific voice, instrument, or ensemble with the voice, instrument, or ensemble, e.g., Brahm's Variations on a theme by Schumann (for solo piano) 786.2
>
> *For vocal forms, see 782.1–782.4; for instrumental forms, see 784.18*

782 Vocal music

> Class orchestral music with vocal parts in 784.2
>
> *For music for single voices, see 783*
>
> *See Manual at 782*

.001–.009 Standard subdivisions

> Notation from Table 1 as modified under 780.1–780.9, e.g., performances of vocal music 782.0078

.01–.07 General principles of vocal music

> Add to base number 782.0 the numbers following 781 in 781.1–781.7, e.g., rehearsing vocal music 782.044

.08 Musical forms

> *For vocal forms, see 782.1–782.4*

> **782.1–782.4 Vocal forms**

> Class here treatises about and recordings of vocal forms for specific voices and ensembles
>
> Class comprehensive works in 782

*Use notation from Table 1 as modified under 780.1–780.9

.1   ***Dramatic vocal forms   Operas**

Regardless of type of voice or vocal group

Including musicals, operettas, revues

Class here concert versions

See Manual at 782.1 vs. 792.5

.109 2   Persons associated with dramatic vocal forms, with operas

Class here biographies of singers known equally well as opera and recital singers, of conductors known primarily as opera conductors

Class biographies of singers known primarily as recital singers in 782.42168092; class biographies of conductors known equally well for conducting operas and orchestral music in 784.2092

.109 4   European opera

Use this number only for works that stress that they are discussing European opera in contrast to operas from all other sources

.2   ***Nondramatic vocal forms**

Including chants, plainsong, sacred vocal music; comprehensive works on cantatas

Class oratorios in 782.23; class sacred songs in 782.25; class Anglican, Gregorian chant in 782.32

For services, see 782.3; for secular forms, secular cantatas, see 782.4

.23   ***Oratorios**

Including passions

.25   ***Sacred songs**

Including gospel music, spirituals

Class here small-scale sacred vocal forms

If the songs are called hymns, class them in 782.27; if called carols, class them in 782.28; otherwise, class them here

Class motets in 782.2

.27   ***Hymns**

For hymns without music, see 264; for carols, see 782.28

.28   ***Carols**

*Use notation from Table 1 as modified under 780.1–780.9

.3   *Services (Liturgy and ritual)

> Musical settings of prescribed texts of specific religions
>
> Including services of specific religions other than Christianity
>
> Class texts used by a specific religion with the religion, e.g., liturgy and ritual of a Christian church 264

.32   *Christian services

> Including mass (communion service); morning, evening prayer

.4   *Secular forms

> Including ballads, madrigals, secular cantatas, song cycles

.42   *Songs

> Class here comprehensive works on songs
>
> *For sacred songs, see 782.25*

.421   General principles of songs

.421 6   Songs of specific traditions of music

.421 62   Folk songs

.421 620 01–.421 620 07   Standard subdivisions

> Notation from Table 1 as modified under 780.1–780.9, e.g., performances of folk songs 782.421620078

.421 620 08   History and description of folk music with respect to kinds of persons

[.421 620 089]   Treatment with respect to specific racial, ethnic, national groups

> Do not use; class in 782.42162

.421 620 09   Historical, geographic, persons treatment

> Class geographic treatment of folk music of specific racial, ethnic, national groups in 782.42162

.421 64   *Western popular songs

> *For jazz songs, see 782.42165; for rock songs, see 782.42166*

.421 642   *Country songs

.421 643   *Blues songs

.421 644   *Soul songs

.421 646   *Reggae songs

.421 649   *Rap

*Use notation from Table 1 as modified under 780.1–780.9

.421 65	*Jazz songs
.421 66	*Rock (Rock 'n' roll) songs
.421 68	*Art songs
	Including lieder
.421 680 92	Persons associated with art songs

> Class here biographies of singers known primarily as recital singers
>
> Class biographies of singers known equally well as opera and recital singers in 782.1092

> ### 782.5–782.9   Vocal executants

Use 782.5–782.9 for scores and parts of vocal forms for specific vocal ensembles, e.g., scores of pop songs arranged for all male choir 782.8. Use 782.1–782.4 for treatises about and recordings of vocal forms for specific vocal ensembles, e.g., recordings of pop songs by an all male choir 782.42164. Class performance techniques for a specific ensemble or form with the ensemble or form, e.g., conducting choral music 782.5, opera 782.1

Class dramatic vocal forms in 782.1; class comprehensive works in 782

.5   ***Mixed voices**

Class here choral music, music intended equally for choral or part-song performance, choral music with solo parts, unison voices

For part songs, see 783.1

> ### 782.6–782.9   Types of voices

Class comprehensive works in 782

.6   ***Women's voices**

Class here music intended equally for women's or children's voices

Class music for children's voices in 782.7

.7   ***Children's voices**

Class music intended equally for women's or children's voices in 782.6

.8   ***Men's voices**

.9   ***Other types of voices**

Including sprechgesang

---

*Use notation from Table 1 as modified under 780.1–780.9

783   Music for single voices   The voice

Use 783 for scores and parts of vocal forms for specific kinds or ensembles of single voice, e.g., scores of rock songs for soprano voice 783.6. Use 782.1–782.4 for treatises about and recordings of vocal forms for specific kinds or ensembles of single voice, e.g., recordings of rock songs sung by a soprano 782.42166. Class performance techniques for a specific kind or ensemble of single voice or for a specific form with the kind, ensemble, or form, e.g., conducting part songs 783.1, opera 782.1

Class dramatic vocal forms in 782.1

> *See Manual at 782*

.001–.009   Standard subdivisions

> Notation from Table 1 as modified under 780.1–780.9, e.g., performances of music for single voice 783.0078

.1   *Single voices in combination

> Class here part songs

> Class music intended equally for choral or part-song performance in 782.5

> ### 783.2–783.9 Solo voices

> Class comprehensive works in 783.2

.2   *Solo voice

> Class here comprehensive works on types of single voices

> *For specific types of single voices, see 783.3–783.9*

> ### 783.3–783.9 Specific types of single voices

> Class single voices in ensembles in 783.1; class comprehensive works in 783.2

.3   *High voice

> Class woman's soprano voice in 783.6; class child's soprano voice in 783.7; class man's treble, alto, tenor voices in 783.8

.4   *Middle voice

> Class woman's mezzo-soprano voice in 783.6; class child's mezzo-soprano voice in 783.7; class baritone voice in 783.8

.5   *Low voice

> Class woman's contralto voice in 783.6; class child's contralto voice in 783.7; class bass voice in 783.8

*Use notation from Table 1 as modified under 780.1–780.9

>   **783.6–783.9 Types of voices**

Class comprehensive works in 783

.6   ***Women's voices**

Class here music intended equally for women's or children's voices

Class music for children's voices in 783.7

.7   ***Children's voices**

Class music intended equally for women's or children's voices in 783.6

.8   ***Men's voices**

.9   ***Other types of voice**

Including sprechgesang; voice instruments, e.g., kazoo

>   **784–788 Instruments and their music**

Class comprehensive works in 784

See Manual at 784–788

784   Instruments and instrumental ensembles and their music

For ensembles with only one instrument per part, see 785; for specific instruments and their music, see 786–788

See also 787 for music for unspecified melody instrument

See Manual at 784–788

.01–.09   Standard subdivisions

Notation from Table 1 as modified under 780.1–780.9, e.g., performances 784.078

.1   **General principles, musical forms, instruments**

.11–.17   General principles

Add to base number 784.1 the numbers following 781 in 781.1–781.7, e.g., performance techniques 784.14

For techniques for playing instruments, see 784.193

---

*Use notation from Table 1 as modified under 780.1–780.9

.18   *Musical forms

         Including concertos, fugues, marches, overtures, sonatas, suites, symphonies; dance forms, e.g., minuets, waltzes

         Class comprehensive works on concertos in 784.2. Class a specific musical form in relation to an instrument or instrumental ensemble with the instrument or ensemble, e.g., Camille Saint-Saëns' Symphony No. 3 (for full orchestra including an organ) 784.2, Charles Marie Widor's Symphony No. 5 (for solo organ) 786.5

.19   Instruments

         For specific instruments, see 786–788

.190 28   Auxiliary techniques and procedures

         Do not use for testing, measurement, maintenance, repair; class in 784.192

[.190 94–.190 99]   Treatment by specific continents, countries, localities in modern world

         Do not use; class in 784.194–784.199

.192   Specific techniques and procedures

         Including description, design, construction, testing, measurement, maintenance, tuning, repair

         For construction by machine, see 681

         See also 784.193 for techniques for playing instruments

.193   *Techniques for playing instruments

         Including bowing, fingering

         Class comprehensive works on techniques of music in 784.14

.194–.199   Treatment by specific continents, countries, localities in modern world

         Add to base number 784.19 notation 4–9 from Table 2, e.g., instruments of Germany 784.1943

.2   ***Full (Symphony) orchestra**

         Including comprehensive works on concertos

         Class here comprehensive works on orchestral combinations, music intended equally for orchestral or chamber performance

         For concerto form, see 784.18; for other orchestral combinations, see 784.3–784.9; for chamber music, see 785

---

*Use notation from Table 1 as modified under 780.1–780.9

.209 2   Persons associated with full (symphony) orchestras

Class here biographies of conductors known equally well for conducting operas and orchestral music

Class biographies of conductors known primarily as opera conductors in 782.1092

> **784.3–784.9 Other orchestral combinations and band**

Class comprehensive works on orchestral combinations and band, on band in 784; class comprehensive works on orchestral combinations in 784.2

.3   ***Chamber orchestra**

For chamber music, see 785

.4   ***Light orchestra**

Including big bands; dance, school orchestras

Class here salon orchestra

.6   ***Keyboard, mechanical, electronic, percussion bands**

Including rhythm band

.7   ***String orchestra**

.8   ***Wind band**

Band consisting of woodwind instruments, brass instruments, or both

Including marching, military band

For brass band, see 784.9

.9   ***Brass band**

785   Ensembles with only one instrument per part

Class here chamber music

Class works for solo melody instrument with keyboard or other accompaniment in 786–788

See Manual at 784–788

.001–.009   Standard subdivisions

Notation from Table 1 as modified under 780.1–780.9, e.g., performances of chamber music 785.0078

---

*Use notation from Table 1 as modified under 780.1–780.9

.01–.07	General principles of ensembles with only one instrument per part

> Add to base number 785.0 the numbers following 781 in 781.1–781.7, e.g., performance techniques 785.04

> *For techniques for playing instruments, see 785.093*

.08	†Musical forms
.09	‡Instruments

> Add to base number 785.09 the numbers following 784.19 in 784.192–784.199, e.g., bowing techniques 785.093

> ## 786–788   Specific instruments and their music

Class here music for solo instrument, music for solo instruments accompanied by one other instrument when accompanying instrument clearly has a subsidiary role

Unless the forerunner of a modern instrument is listed in the schedule, class it with the modern instrument. For example, the shawm, a forerunner of the oboe and an instrument not listed, is classed with the oboe in 788.5; however, the vihuela, the forerunner of the guitar and an instrument listed at 787.8, is classed at 787.8, *not* with the guitar in 787.87

Class chamber music in 785; class comprehensive works in 784

> *For voice instruments, see 783.9*

786   *Keyboard, mechanical, electrophonic, percussion instruments

Class here comprehensive works on keyboard instruments, on keyboard stringed instruments; music for unspecified keyboard instrument

> *See Manual at 784–788*

> ### 786.2–786.5   Keyboard instruments

Class music for more than one performer on one keyboard instrument as an ensemble in 785; class mechanical keyboard instruments in 786.6; class keyboard idiophones in 786.8; class comprehensive works in 786

> ### 786.2–786.4   Keyboard stringed instruments

Class comprehensive works in 786

---

*Use notation from Table 1 as modified under 780.1–780.9 for the instrument and its music together, for its music alone

†Use notation from Table 1 as modified under 780.1–780.9

‡Use notation from Table 1 as modified under 784.19

.2 ***Pianos**

.3 ***Clavichords**

.4 ***Harpsichords**

.5 ***Keyboard wind instruments   Organs**

> Including comprehensive works on keyboard electrophones
>
> Class accordion, concertina in 788.8. Class a keyboard instrument whose sound is generated by conventional means, even though amplified or modified electronically, with the instrument, e.g., electric piano 786.2
>
> *See also 786.7 for synthesizers*

.6 ***Mechanical and aeolian instruments**

> Aeolian instruments: instruments activated by the blowing of the wind
>
> Standard subdivisions are added for mechanical and aeolian instruments together, for mechanical instruments alone
>
> Including carillons, music boxes, player pianos

.7 ***Electrophones   Electronic instruments**

> Including computers, tapes, synthesizers; electronic music
>
> Class here music made from electrically produced or manipulated sounds
>
> Class keyboard electrophones in 786.5. Class a specific electrically amplified or modified standard instrument other than keyboard instruments with the instrument, e.g., electric guitars 787.87
>
> *See also 781.3 for using computers to compose music*

.8 ***Percussion instruments**

> Including bells, chimes, cymbals, gongs, triangles, West Indian steel drums, xylophones; idiophones (vibrating sonorous solids)
>
> *For mechanical idiophones, see 786.6; for drums, see 786.9; for struck stringed instruments, see 787.7*

.9 ***Drums and devices used for percussion effects**

> Standard subdivisions are added for drums and devices used for percussion effects together, for drums alone
>
> Including bongos, tambourines, timpani

---

*Use notation from Table 1 as modified under 780.1–780.9 for the instrument and its music together, for its music alone

787 *Stringed instruments (Chordophones)   Bowed stringed instruments

Class here music for unspecified melody instrument

Class keyboard stringed instruments in 786; class mechanical stringed instruments in 786.6

See Manual at 784–788

.2 *Violins

Class here comprehensive works on violin family

For violas, see 787.3; for cellos, see 787.4; for double basses, see 787.5

.3 *Violas

.4 *Cellos

.5 *Double basses

.6 *Other bowed stringed instruments   Viols

For double basses, see 787.5

.7 *Plectral instruments

Including dulcimers, lyres

Class here zithers, comprehensive works on struck stringed instruments

For plectral lute family, see 787.8; for harps and musical bows, see 787.9

.8 *Plectral lute family

Including banjos, lutes, mandolins, vihuelas

.87 *Guitars

.9 *Harps and musical bows

Standard subdivisions are added for harps and musical bows together, for harps alone

788 *Wind instruments (Aerophones)

Class keyboard wind instruments in 786.5; class mechanical wind instruments in 786.6

See Manual at 784–788

---

*Use notation from Table 1 as modified under 780.1–780.9 for the instrument and its music together, for its music alone

.2   ***Woodwind instruments and free aerophones**

Free aerophones: aerophones in which the airstream is not directed into or through a cavity or tube but directly into the outer air, or the air remains static and the instrument when moved vibrates through friction with the air, e.g., bull-roarers

Standard subdivisions are added for woodwind instruments and free aerophones together, for woodwind instruments alone

For specific woodwind instruments, see 788.3–788.8

>   **788.3–788.8 Specific woodwind instruments**

Class comprehensive works in 788.2

.3   ***Flute family**

Including flutes, piccolos, recorders

.4   ***Reed instruments**

Including bagpipes

For double-reed instruments, see 788.5; for single-reed instruments, see 788.6; for free reeds, see 788.8

.5   ***Double-reed instruments**

Including bassoons, English horns, oboes

For bagpipes, see 788.4

.6   ***Single-reed instruments**

Including clarinets

For bagpipes, see 788.4; for saxophones, see 788.7

.7   ***Saxophones**

.8   ***Free reeds**

Including accordions, harmonicas

.9   ***Brass instruments (Lip-reed instruments)**

Including bugles, cornets, French horns (horns), trombones, trumpets, tubas

---

*Use notation from Table 1 as modified under 780.1–780.9 for the instrument and its music together, for its music alone

(789) Composers and traditions of music

(Optional number and subdivisions; prefer 780–788)

(Option A: Arrange treatises about all composers at 789 plus an alphabeting mark; then to the result add notation following 78 in 780–788

(Option B: Use 789 and its subdivisions for traditions of music

(Option C: Use 789 and its subdivisions for recordings of music

(If option A is used with either options B or C, class comprehensive works on traditions of music in 789.1)

Unless other instructions are given, class a subject with aspects in two or more subdivisions of 789 in the number coming last, e.g., rehearsing folk songs 789.20242 (*not* 789.20144)

(.1) †General principles of traditions of music

Add to base number 789.1 the numbers following 781 in 781.1–781.5, e.g., orchestration in various traditions 789.13

(If Option A is used with either Option B or C, class here comprehensive works on traditions of music)

(.2) †Folk music

Music indigenous to the cultural group in which it occurs, usually evolved through aural transmission

(.200 1–.200 7)　†Standard subdivisions

Notation from Table 1 as modified under 780.1–780.9, e.g., performances of folk music 789.20078

(.200 8)　†History and description of folk music with respect to kinds of persons

[.200 89]　Treatment with respect to specific racial, ethnic, national groups

Do not use; class in 789.2

(.200 9)　†Historical, geographic, persons treatment

Class geographic treatment of folk music of specific racial, ethnic, national groups in 789.2

(.201)　†General principles, stylistic influences of other traditions, musical forms

(.201 1–.201 5)　†General principles

Add to base number 789.201 the numbers following 781 in 781.1–781.5, e.g., rehearsing folk music 789.20144

(.201 6)　†Stylistic influences of other traditions of music

†(Optional number; prefer 781–788)

(.202–.208)   †Voices, instruments, ensembles

> Add to base number 789.20 the numbers following 78 in 782–788, e.g., folk songs 789.20242

>   **(789.3–789.9)   Other traditions of music**

> Add to each subdivision identified by * as follows:
> 001–009   Standard subdivisions
>> Notation from Table 1 as modified under 780.1–780.9, e.g., performance 0078
>
> 01   General principles, stylistic influences of other traditions of music, musical forms
> 011–015   General principles
>> Add to 01 the numbers following 781 in 781.1–781.5, e.g., melody 012
>
> 016   Stylistic influences of other traditions of music
> 1   Voices, instruments, ensembles
>> Add to 1 the numbers following 78 in 782–788, e.g., guitar music 1787

> Class comprehensive works in 789

(.3)   **†*Popular music**

> *For western popular music, see 789.4*

(.4)   **†*Western popular music**

> Class country and western music in 789.42

> *For jazz, see 789.5; for rock, see 789.6*

(.42)   **†*Country music**

> Class here bluegrass music

(.43)   **†*Blues**

> Class here rhythm and blues

(.44)   **†*Soul**

(.46)   **†*Reggae**

(.5)   **†*Jazz**

> Including swing

(.6)   **†*Rock (Rock 'n' roll)**

(.7)   **†Sacred music**

*Add as instructed under 789.3–789.9
†(Optional number; prefer 781–788)

(.700 1–.700 9) †Standard subdivisions

>Notation from Table 1 as modified under 780.1–780.9, e.g., performances of sacred music 789.70078

(.71) †*Christian sacred music

>*For music of Christian church year, see 789.72*

(.72) †*Music of Christian church year

(.723) †*Christmas music

(.76) †Judaic sacred music

(.760 01–.760 09) †Standard subdivisions

>Notation from Table 1 as modified under 780.1–780.9, e.g., performances of Judaic sacred music 789.760078

(.8) †*Western art (Classical) music

>Class here comprehensive works on art music

>*For nonwestern art music, see 789.9*

(.9) †*Nonwestern art music

790 Recreational and performing arts

Class here interdisciplinary works on recreation

For sociology of recreation, see 306.4; for music, see 780

SUMMARY

790.01–.09	**Recreation centers and standard subdivisions of recreation**
.1–.2	**[Recreational activities and the performing arts in general]**
791	**Public performances**
792	**Stage presentations**
793	**Indoor games and amusements**
794	**Indoor games of skill**
795	**Games of chance**
796	**Athletic and outdoor sports and games**
797	**Aquatic and air sports**
798	**Equestrian sports and animal racing**
799	**Fishing, hunting, shooting**

.01 Philosophy and theory of recreation

>Including influence, effective use of leisure

.02–.05 Standard subdivisions of recreation

.06 Organizations dealing with and management of recreation

>Including recreation centers

---

*Add as instructed under 789.3–789.9
†(Optional number; prefer 781–788)

[.068]   Management

> Do not use; class in 790.06

.07   Education, research, related topics of recreation

.08   History and description of recreation with respect to groups of persons

> Do not use for activities and programs for specific classes of people; class in 790.1

.09   Historical, geographic, persons treatment of recreation

.1   Recreational activities

> Including collecting, hobbies; play with toys, e.g., electric trains

> Class collecting a specific kind of object with the object, plus notation 075 from Table 1, e.g., coin collecting 737.4075, sports cards 796.075

> *For a specific activity, see the activity, e.g., paper cutting and folding 736, piano playing 786.2, outdoor sports 796; for play with a specific toy provided for elsewhere, see the toy, e.g., flying model airplanes 796.15*

> *See Manual at 796.15 vs. 629.04*

[.101–.109]   Standard subdivisions

> Do not use; class in 790.01–790.09

.2   The performing arts in general

> Works that treat only public performances, e.g., stage, radio, television, music, are classed in 791. Works that also include athletic and outdoor sports and games are classed here

> *For a specific art, see the art, e.g., symphony orchestra performance 784.2078, motion pictures 791.43*

791   Public performances

> Other than musical, sport, game performances

> Including traveling shows, e.g., medicine, minstrel shows

> *For stage presentations, see 792; for magic, see 793.8*

> *See also 780 for musical performances, 793–796 for sport and game performances*

.06   Organizations and management

> Including amusement parks

[.068]   Management

> Do not use; class in 791.06

.092   Persons

                See Manual at 791.092

.3   **Circuses**

.4   **Motion pictures, radio, television**

                Class texts of plays in 800. Class subject-oriented films and recorded programs themselves with the subject, e.g., flower gardening 635.9

                See also 302.23 for social aspects of motion pictures, radio, and television as mass media

                See Manual at 363.3 vs. 303.3, 791.4; also at 384 vs. 791.4

.43   Motion pictures

                Including actors, directors

                Class here dramatic films

                Class animation of films in 741.5; class photographic aspects of motion pictures in 778.5; class made-for-TV movies, videotapes of motion pictures in 791.45

                See also 384 for communication aspects of motion pictures, e.g., programming (scheduling)

                See Manual at 791.092; also at 791.43 and 791.44, 791.45, 792.9; also at 791.43, 791.45 vs. 778.5

.430 1   Philosophy, theory, aesthetics

                Including theory, technique, history of criticism and appreciation

[.430 2]   Miscellany

                Do not use; class in 791.43

.430 9   Historical, geographic, persons treatment

                Class here description, critical appraisal of specific companies and studios

                Class description, critical appraisal of specific films in 791.43

.430 92   Persons

                Do not use for persons associated with only one aspect of motion pictures, e.g., actors, directors; class in 791.43

.44   Radio

                Including actors, directors

                Class here dramatic programs

                See also 384.54 for communication aspects of radio, e.g., programming (scheduling)

                See Manual at 791.092; also at 791.43 and 791.44, 791.45, 792.9

.440 1 Philosophy, theory, aesthetics

Including theory, technique, history of criticism and appreciation

[.440 2] Miscellany

Do not use; class in 791.44

.440 9 Historical, geographic, persons treatment

Class here description, critical appraisal of specific companies and stations

Class description, critical appraisal of specific programs in 791.44

.440 92 Persons

Do not use for persons associated with only one aspect of radio, e.g., actors, directors; class in 791.44

.45 Television

Including actors, directors

Class here dramatic and audience programs, use of videotapes

Class use of videotapes not provided for here with the use, e.g., video recordings of rock music 781.66

See also 384.55 for communication aspects of television, e.g., programming (scheduling)

See Manual at 791.092; also at 791.43 and 791.44, 791.45, 792.9; also at 791.43, 791.45 vs. 778.5

.450 1 Philosophy, theory, aesthetics

Including theory, technique, history of criticism and appreciation

[.450 2] Miscellany

Do not use; class in 791.45

.450 9 Historical, geographic, persons treatment

Class here description, critical appraisal of specific companies, stations, networks

Class description, critical appraisal of specific programs in 791.45

.450 92 Persons

Do not use for persons associated with only one aspect of television, e.g., actors, directors; class in 791.45

.5 Puppetry and toy theaters

Class puppet films in 791.43; class texts of plays in 800

.6 **Pageantry**

Including cheerleading; festivals, pageants, parades, floats for parades

For circus parades, see 791.3; for water pageantry, see 797.2

See Manual at 394 vs. 791.6

.8 **Animal performances**

Including bullfighting, rodeos

For circus animal performances, see 791.3; for equestrian sports and animal racing, see 798

792 Stage presentations

Including actors, directors

Class here theater, dramatic presentation

Class texts of plays in 800

For motion pictures, radio, television, see 791.4; for puppetry and toy theaters, see 791.5

See Manual at 791.092

.01 Philosophy, theory, aesthetics

Including theory, technique, history of criticism and appreciation

[.02] Miscellany

Do not use; class in 792

.09 Historical, geographic, persons treatment

Class here description, critical appraisal of specific theaters and companies

For specific productions in specific theaters or by specific companies, see 792.9

.092 Persons

Do not use for persons associated with only one aspect of stage presentations, e.g., actors, directors; class in 792

.1 ***Tragedy and serious drama**

Including historical drama; religious, passion, miracle, mystery, morality plays

.2 ***Comedy and melodrama**

Including modern mystery (suspense) drama

.3 ***Pantomime**

---

*Use notation from Table 1 as modified under 792.01–792.09

.5   ***Dramatic vocal forms   Opera**

> Class interdisciplinary works on dramatic vocal forms, on opera in 782.1
>
> *For musical plays, see 792.6; for variety shows, see 792.7*
>
> *See Manual at 782.1 vs. 792.5*

.509   Historical, geographic, persons treatment

> Class here description, critical appraisal of specific theaters and companies
>
> Class specific productions in specific theaters or by specific companies in 792.5

.6   ***Musical plays**

> Class interdisciplinary works on musical plays in 782.1
>
> *See Manual at 782.1 vs. 792.5*

.609   Historical, geographic, persons treatment

> Class here description, critical appraisal of specific theaters and companies
>
> Class specific productions in specific theaters or by specific companies in 792.6

.7   ***Theatrical dancing [*formerly* 792.8] and variety shows**

> Standard subdivisions are added for theatrical dancing and variety shows together, for variety shows alone
>
> Including tap dancing
>
> Class here burlesque, cabaret, vaudeville, music hall and nightclub presentations
>
> Class stage productions in 792.9
>
> *For dancing in musical plays, see 792.6*
>
> *See also 791 for minstrel shows and skits*
>
> *See Manual at 792.7 vs. 792.8, 793.3*

*Use notation from Table 1 as modified under 792.01–792.09

.8   ***Ballet and modern dance**

> Standard subdivisions are added for either or both topics in heading
>
> Including choreography, dancers
>
> Class here comprehensive works on dancing
>
> Theatrical dancing relocated to 792.7
>
>> *For dancing in musical plays, see 792.6; for tap dancing, see 792.7; for social, folk, national dancing, see 793.3*
>>
>> *See Manual at 791.092; also at 792.7 vs. 792.8, 793.3*

.809   Historical, geographic, persons treatment

> Class here description, critical appraisal of specific theaters and companies
>
> Class specific productions in specific theaters or by specific companies in 792.8

.809 2   Persons

> Do not use for persons associated with only one aspect of ballet or modern dance, e.g., dancers, choreographers; class in 792.8

.9   **Stage productions**

> Class here production scripts and stage guides; description, critical appraisal of specific productions of specific theaters and companies
>
> Class description, critical appraisal, production scripts of operas in 792.5; class description, critical appraisal, production scripts of musical plays in 792.6; class description, critical appraisal, production scripts of ballets in 792.8
>
>> *See Manual at 791.43 and 791.44, 791.45, 792.9*

793   Indoor games and amusements

> *For indoor games of skill, see 794; for games of chance, see 795*

.2   **Parties and entertainments**

> Including charades, tableaux

.3   **Social, folk, national dancing**

> Including ballroom and square dancing
>
>> *See Manual at 792.7 vs. 792.8, 793.3*

.4   **Games of action**

.5   **Forfeit and trick games**

*Use notation from Table 1 as modified under 792.01–792.09

.7 Games not characterized by action

Including mathematical games and recreations

For charades and tableaux, see 793.2

.73 Puzzles and puzzle games

Including acrostics, crossword puzzles, quizzes; jigsaw puzzles

Class mathematical games and recreations in 793.7. Class puzzles as formal instructional devices for the teaching of a specific subject with the subject, plus notation 07 from Table 1, e.g., puzzles teaching the use of the Bible 220.07

.734 Word games

Including anagrams

.735 Riddles

Class riddles as folk literature, interdisciplinary works on riddles in 398.6

.8 Magic and related activities

Including card tricks [*formerly* 795.4], juggling, scientific recreations, ventriloquism

Class here conjuring

.9 Other indoor diversions

Including war games (battle games)

See also 355.4 for military use of war games, 796.1 for outdoor war games

.93 Adventure games   Fantasy games

Including Dungeons and Dragons®, RuneQuest®

Class here mystery games, role-playing games

See also 793.9 for war games (battle games)

See Manual at 793.93 vs. 794.8

[.930 285]   Data processing   Computer applications

Do not use; class in 793.93

794 Indoor games of skill

Class here board games

Class war games in 793.9; class adventure, fantasy, mystery games in 793.93; class games combining skill and chance in 795

For backgammon, see 795.1

.1   **Chess**

[.102 85]   Data processing   Computer applications

           Do not use; class in 794.1

.2   **Checkers (Draughts)**

.3   **Darts**

.6   **Bowling**

         See also 796.31 for lawn bowling

.7   **Ball games**

         Including billiards, pool, pinball games

         Class athletic ball games in 796.3

         For bowling, see 794.6

.8   **Electronic games**   **Computer games**

         Including arcade games

         Class here video games

         Class computerized war games (battle games) in 793.9; class computerized adventure, fantasy, mystery games in 793.93. Class computerized forms of a specific indoor game or amusement with the game or amusement in 793–795, plus notation 0285 from Table 1, e.g., computerized checkers 794.20285

         See Manual at 793.93 vs. 794.8

[.802 85]   Data processing   Computer applications

           Do not use; class in 794.8

795   **Games of chance**

         Class here gambling

         Class gambling on a specific activity with the activity, e.g., on horse racing 798.401

         See also 364.1 for gambling as a crime, 616.85 for compulsive gambling

.01   Philosophy and theory

         Including betting systems, probabilities of winning

         See Manual at 795.01 vs. 519.2

.1   **Games with dice**

         Including backgammon, craps

.2   **Wheel and top games**

         Including roulette, slot machines

.3 **Games dependent on drawing numbers or counters**

Including bingo, dominoes, lotteries, mah jong

.4 **Card games**

Including solitaire, twenty-one (blackjack)

Card tricks relocated to 793.8

.41 Games in which skill is a major element

Including bridge, cribbage, pinochle, poker; rummy and its variants, e.g., canasta

796 Athletic and outdoor sports and games

Class computerized athletic and outdoor sports and games in 794.8

For aquatic and air sports, see 797; for equestrian sports and animal racing, see 798; for fishing, hunting, shooting, see 799

See Manual at 613.7 vs. 646.7, 796

SUMMARY

796.01–.09	**Standard subdivisions and general kinds of sports and games**
.1	**Miscellaneous games**
.2	**Activities and games requiring equipment**
.3	**Ball games**
.4	**Weight lifting, track and field, gymnastics**
.5	**Outdoor life**
.6	**Cycling and related activities**
.7	**Driving motor vehicles**
.8	**Combat sports**
.9	**Ice and snow sports**

.01 Philosophy and theory

Activities and programs for specific classes of persons relocated to 796.08

.04 General kinds of sports and games

Including intramural sports [*formerly* 371.8]; amateur, college, professional sports; wheelchair sports

See Manual at 796.08 vs. 796.04

.06 Organizations, facilities, management

Including astrodomes, field houses, playgrounds, stadiums

[.068] Management

Do not use; class in 796.06

.07 Education, research, related topics

Including coaching

.08 History and description of sports and games with respect to kinds of persons

> Class here activities and programs for specific classes of persons [*formerly* 796.01]
>
> Class general kinds of sports and games for specific kinds of persons in 796.04
>
> *See Manual at 796.08 vs. 796.04*

.087 Persons with disabilities and illnesses, gifted persons

> Class sports and games modified for participation of persons with physical disabilities in 796.04

.1 **Miscellaneous games**

> Not provided for elsewhere
>
> *For activities and games requiring equipment, see 796.2*

.15 Play with remote-control models, kites, similar devices

> Standard subdivisions are added for play with remote-control models, kites, similar devices together; for play with remote-control models alone
>
> Class here play with control line models
>
> Class comprehensive works on play with mechanical and scientific toys in 790.1
>
> *For play with remote-control trains, see 790.1*
>
> *See Manual at 796.15 vs. 629.04*

.2 **Activities and games requiring equipment**

> Not provided for elsewhere
>
> Including flying discs (Frisbees®), horseshoes, Yo-Yos®

.21 Roller skating

> Class here in-line skating (rollerblading)

.22 Skateboarding

.3 **Ball games**

.31 Ball thrown or hit by hand

> Including handball, lawn bowling
>
> *See also 794.6 for indoor bowling*

.32 Inflated ball thrown or hit by hand

.323 Basketball

.323 01–.323 09		Standard subdivisions

Notation from Table 1 as modified under 796.33202–796.33207, e.g., coaching 796.32307

.324   Netball

.325   Volleyball

.33   Inflated ball driven by foot

Including Australian-rules football, pushball

.332   American football

.332 02   Miscellany

Including official rules, spectators' guides

.332 06   Organizations, facilities, management

Including clubs, leagues; grounds and their layout

[.332 068]   Management

Do not use; class in 796.33206

.332 07   Education, research, related topics

Including coaching

.333   Rugby   Rugby Union

.333 01–.333 09   Standard subdivisions

Notation from Table 1 as modified under 796.33202–796.33207, e.g., coaching 796.33307

.334   Soccer (Association football)

.334 01–.334 09   Standard subdivisions

Notation from Table 1 as modified under 796.33202–796.33207, e.g., coaching 796.33407

.335   Canadian football

.335 01–.335 09   Standard subdivisions

Notation from Table 1 as modified under 796.33202–796.33207, e.g., coaching 796.33507

.34   Racket games

Including court, paddle, table tennis; lacrosse

.342   Tennis (Lawn tennis)

.342 01–.342 09   Standard subdivisions

Notation from Table 1 as modified under 796.33202–796.33207, e.g., coaching 796.34207

.343	Squash

Class here rackets, racquetball

.345	Badminton

.35	Ball driven by club, mallet, bat

Including croquet, polo

.352	Golf

.352 01–.352 09	Standard subdivisions

Notation from Table 1 as modified under 796.33202–796.33207, e.g., official rules 796.35202

.355	Field hockey

Including indoor hockey

See also 796.962 for ice hockey

.357	Baseball

Including softball

.357 01–.357 09	Standard subdivisions

Notation from Table 1 as modified under 796.33202–796.33207, e.g., baseball leagues 796.35706

.358	Cricket

.358 01–.358 09	Standard subdivisions

Notation from Table 1 as modified under 796.33202–796.33207, e.g., coaching 796.35807

.4	**Weight lifting, track and field, gymnastics**

.406	Organizations, facilities, management

Including gymnasiums

[.406 8]	Management

Do not use; class in 796.406

.407	Education, research, related topics

Including coaching

.41	Weight lifting

See also 613.7 for weight training for fitness

See Manual at 613.7 vs. 646.7, 796

.42	Track and field

Including triathlon

Class here running

For field events, see 796.43; for orienteering, see 796.58

See also 613.7 for running as an exercise

.420 6	Organizations, facilities, management

Including athletic fields

[.420 68]	Management

Do not use; class in 796.4206

.43	Jumping, vaulting, throwing

Including pole vaulting, shot-putting

Class here field events

See also 796.2 for throwing games, 796.44 for gymnastic vaulting

.44	Sports gymnastics

Including rhythmic gymnastics, use of horizontal and parallel bars, vaulting

For trapeze work, rope climbing, tightrope walking, see 796.46; for acrobatics, tumbling, trampolining, contortion, see 796.47

See also 613.7 for gymnastic exercises

.46	Trapeze work, rope climbing, tightrope walking

See also 791.3 for trapeze work and tightrope walking as circus acts

.47	Acrobatics, tumbling, trampolining, contortion

Including floor exercise

See also 791.3 for acrobatics as circus acts

.48	Olympic games

Arrange specific games chronologically

Class Paralympics in 796.04; class Special Olympics in 796.087. Class a specific activity with the activity, e.g., basketball 796.323, swimming 797.2

For winter Olympic games, see 796.98

.480 93–.480 99	Geographic treatment

Do not use for specific games; class in 796.48

.5	**Outdoor life**

Including beach activities

Class a specific activity of outdoor life not provided for here with the activity, e.g., fishing 799.1

.51   Walking

Class here backpacking, hiking

> *For walking by kind of terrain, see 796.52*

> *See Manual at 913–919 vs. 796.51*

.52   Walking and exploring by kind of terrain

Including mountaineering, spelunking

.54   Camping

Including woodcraft

Class beach activities in 796.5

.56   Dude ranching and farming

.58   Orienteering

Class orientation in 912

.6   Cycling and related activities

Use of wheeled vehicles not driven by motor or animal power

Including bicycle touring, land sailing, soap box racing

Class triathlon in 796.42

> *For roller skating, see 796.21; for skateboarding, see 796.22*

.7   Driving motor vehicles

Including driving for pleasure, travel for pleasure by mobile home

> *For snowmobiling, see 796.94*

.72   Automobile racing

> *See also 796.15 for toy car racing*

.720 6   Organizations, facilities, management

Including racetracks and speedways

[.720 68]   Management

Do not use; class in 796.7206

.8   Combat sports

Class here martial arts

Class combat with animals in 791.8

.81   Unarmed combat

> *For boxing, see 796.83*

.812   Wrestling

| .815 | Jujitsu and related martial arts forms |
| | Including judo, karate |

> *See also 613.7 for related therapeutic exercises*

.83	Boxing
.86	Fencing
	Class here sword fighting

.9 Ice and snow sports

Including iceboating, snowboarding, snowshoeing, tobogganing; sledding, e.g., bobsledding

> *For sled dog racing, see 798.8; for ice fishing, see 799.1*

> *See also 796.54 for snow camping, 798 for horse-drawn sleighing*

.91	Ice skating
	Including figure, speed skating
.93	Skiing
	Including jumping
.94	Snowmobiling
.96	Ice games
.962	Ice hockey

> *See also 796.355 for field hockey*

| .962 01–.962 09 | Standard subdivisions |

Notation from Table 1 as modified under 796.33202–796.33207, e.g., coaching 796.96207

| .964 | Curling |
| .98 | Winter Olympic games |

Arrange specific games chronologically

Class a specific activity with the activity, e.g., skating 796.91

| .980 93–.980 99 | Geographic treatment |

Do not use for specific games; class in 796.98

797 Aquatic and air sports

Class computerized aquatic and air sports in 794.8

> **797.1–797.3 Aquatic sports**

Class comprehensive works in 797

For fishing, see 799.1

.1 Boating

Including canoeing, rowboating, sailboating, motorboating, yachting, boat racing and regattas

See also 643 for yachts permanently docked as dwellings

.2 Swimming and diving

Standard subdivisions are added for swimming and diving together, for diving alone

Including scuba, skin diving, snorkeling; springboard and platform diving; water pageantry; water polo

Class triathlon in 796.42

.200 1–.200 9   Standard subdivisions

.3 Other aquatic sports

Including jet skiing, surfing (surf riding), water skiing, windsurfing (boardsailing, sailboarding)

.5 Air sports

Including aircraft racing, balloon flying, flying for pleasure, hang gliding, skydiving, stunt flying

798 Equestrian sports and animal racing

Including driving, coaching

Class computerized equestrian sports and animal racing in 794.8; class hunting with aid of horses in 799.2

For polo, see 796.35

.2 Horsemanship

Including riding, jumping

For horse racing, see 798.4

.4 Horse racing   Flat racing

Including harness racing, steeplechasing

.400 1–.400 5   Standard subdivisions

.400 6   Organization, facilities, management

Including racetracks

[.400 68]	Management

> Do not use; class in 798.4006

.400 7–.400 9   Standard subdivisions

.401   Betting

> Including pari-mutuel

.8   **Dog racing**

> Including sled dog racing

799   Fishing, hunting, shooting

Class computerized fishing, hunting, shooting games in 794.8

See also 688.7 for the manufacture of both mass-produced and handcrafted equipment

.1   **Fishing**

Class shellfishing in 799.2; class interdisciplinary works on fishing in 639.2

.2   **Hunting**

Big and small game

Including falconry

Class here comprehensive works on commercial and sports hunting [*formerly* 639], sports trapping, comprehensive works on hunting and shooting sports

For commercial, subsistence hunting, see 639; for shooting other than game, see 799.3

.202   Miscellany

.202 8   Techniques, procedures, apparatus, equipment, materials

Including guns, bows and arrows

[.202 85]   Data processing   Computer applications

> Do not use; class in 799.2

[.209]   Historical, geographic, persons treatment

> Do not use; class in 799.29

.29   Historical, geographic, persons treatment

Add to base number 799.29 notation 1–9 from Table 2, e.g., hunting in Germany 799.2943

.3   **Shooting other than game**

Including archery, skeet shooting, trapshooting

For ballistic devices, see 799.2028

---

800 Literature (Belles-lettres) and rhetoric

Class here works of literature, works about literature

After general topics (800–809) the basic arrangement is literature by language, then literature of each language by form. More detailed instructions are given at the beginning of Table 3

Unless other instructions are given, observe the following table of preference, e.g., collections of drama written in poetry from more than two literatures 808.82 (*not* 808.81):

> Drama
> Poetry
>> Class epigrams in verse with miscellaneous writings
> Fiction
> Essays
> Speeches
> Letters
> Miscellaneous writings
> Humor and satire

Class folk literature in 398.2; class librettos, poems, words written to be sung or recited with music in 780.26; class interdisciplinary works on language and literature in 400; class interdisciplinary works on the arts in 700

> *See Manual at 800; also at 080 vs. 800; also at 400 vs. 800; also at 741.6 vs. 800; also at 800 vs. 398.2; also at 800 vs. 398.24, 590, 636*

SUMMARY

801–809	Standard subdivisions; rhetoric; collections; history, description, critical appraisal of more than two literatures
810	American literature in English
820	English and Old English (Anglo-Saxon) literatures
830	Literatures of Germanic (Teutonic) languages German literature
840	Literatures of Romance languages French literature
850	Literatures of Italian, Sardinian, Dalmatian, Romanian, Rhaeto-Romanic languages Italian literature
860	Literatures of Spanish and Portuguese languages Spanish literature
870	Literatures of Italic languages Latin literature
880	Literatures of Hellenic languages Classical Greek literature
890	Literatures of other specific languages and language families

801 Philosophy and theory

Including aesthetics; theory, technique, history of literary criticism

Class works of critical appraisal in 809

See Manual at 800: Literary criticism

802–803 Standard subdivisions

805 Serial publications

Class collections of literary texts in serial form in 808.80005; class history, description, critical appraisal in serial form in 809.005

806–807 Standard subdivisions

808 Rhetoric and collections of literary texts from more than two literatures

Rhetoric: effective use of language

Do not use for history and description of rhetoric with respect to kind of persons; class in 808.008. Do not use for collections of literary texts from more than two literatures with respect to kinds of persons; class in 808.8

Including literary plagiarism; professional, technical, expository literature on specific subjects

Style manuals, authorship and editorial techniques, e.g., preparation of manuscripts, writing for publication; rhetoric in specific languages are classed in 808, without use of 808.001–808.009; style manuals, authorship and editorial techniques, rhetoric in specific languages for specific literary forms are classed with the form in 808.1–808.7

Class here composition

Class general treatment of standard usage of language (prescriptive linguistics) in 418; class theory, technique, history of literary criticism in 801. Class a specific aspect of literary plagiarism with the aspect, e.g., plagiarism in the work of an American fiction writer 813; class treatment of standard usage in a specific language with the specific language, plus notation 8 from Table 4, e.g., English usage 428

For submission of manuscripts to agents and publishers, see 070.5

See also 001.4 for research

See Manual at 658.4 vs. 651.7, 808; also at 808; also at 808.001–808.7 vs. 070.5

.001–.009	Standard subdivisions of rhetoric
.06	Writing children's literature
[.060 1–.060 9]	Standard subdivisions

Do not use; class in 808.06

> **808.1–808.7   Rhetoric in specific literary forms**

Class here aesthetics, appreciation, character and nature, composition, theory, technique, history of literary criticism of specific literary forms

Observe table of preference under 800

Class specific forms for children in 808.06; class works of critical appraisal of specific literary forms in 809.1–809.7; class theory, technique, history of textual criticism of specific literary forms; comprehensive works on theory, technique, history of literary criticism in 801; class comprehensive works on rhetoric in specific literary forms in 808

See Manual at 800: Literary criticism

.1   **Rhetoric of poetry**

Class here prosody

.2   **Rhetoric of drama**

.3   **Rhetoric of fiction**

Including rhetoric of short stories

Class here rhetoric of novelettes and novels

.4   **Rhetoric of essays**

.5   **Rhetoric of speech**

Art or technique of oral expression

Including choral speaking; public speaking (oratory), e.g., after-dinner, platform, television speaking; recitation, e.g., reading aloud, storytelling

Class here voice, expression, gesture

For preaching, see 251

.53   Debating and public discussion

.56   Conversation

.6   **Rhetoric of letters**

.7   **Rhetoric of humor and satire**

Class here rhetoric of parody

.8   **Collections of literary texts from more than two literatures**

Texts by more than one author in more than two languages not from the same language family

Collections of works not limited to a specific literary form but either limited to a specific period or displaying specific features (displaying specific qualities of style, mood, perspective; displaying specific elements, e.g., stream of consciousness; treating specific themes; emphasizing subjects; or written for and by specific kinds of persons) are classed in 808.8, without use of 808.80001–808.80007; these topics limited to a specific literary form and either limited to a specific period or displaying specific features are classed with the form in 808.81–808.88, without adding further from the table under 808.81–808.87

Collections of texts from literatures of two languages relocated to 810–890

Class works that are limited to a specific topic found in subdivisions of 808.8 and consist equally of literary texts and history, description, critical appraisal of literature with the topic in 808.8, e.g., texts and criticism of drama 808.82; class collections of texts from more than two literatures in the same language with the literature of that language, e.g., collections of works from English, American, and Australian literatures in English (more than one literary form) 820.8; class collections of texts from literatures in more than two languages from the same family with the literature of that family, e.g., French, Italian, and Spanish literatures 840

.800 01–.800 07	Standard subdivisions
[.800 08]	History and description with respect to kinds of persons
	Do not use; class in 808.8
[.800 09]	Historical, geographic, persons treatment
	Do not use; class in 809

>   808.81–808.88   Collections in specific forms

Observe table of preference under 800

Class comprehensive works in 808.8

.81–.87   **Collections in specific forms**

Add to base number 808.8 the numbers following 808 in 808.1–808.7, e.g., collections of essays 808.84, of debates 808.853; then add further as follows:

001–008	Standard subdivisions
009	Geographic treatment
	Do not use for historical treatment; class with the specific form, without adding notation from Table 1
[0092]	Persons treatment
	Do not use; class with the specific form, without adding notation from Table 1

.88 Collections of miscellaneous writings

Including anecdotes, diaries, epigrams, graffiti, jokes, journals, quotations, reminiscences, riddles that are jokes, prose literature in more than one form, works without identifiable form

Class a specific identifiable form of literature with the form, e.g., essays 808.84

[.880 1–.880 9] Standard subdivisions

Do not use; class in 808.88

809 History, description, critical appraisal of more than two literatures

History, description, critical appraisal of works by more than one author in more than two languages not from the same language family

History, description, critical appraisal of works from specific periods are classed in 809, without use of 809.001–809.007; history, description, critical appraisal of works in a specific form from specific periods are classed with the form in 809.1–809.7, without adding further from the table under 808.81–808.87

Class here collected biography

History, description, critical appraisal of literatures of two languages relocated to 810–890

Class theory, technique, history of literary criticism in 801. Class history, description, critical appraisal of more than two literatures in the same language with the literature of that language, e.g., history of English, American, and Australian literatures in English (more than one literary form) 820.9; class history, description, critical appraisal of literatures in more than two languages from the same family with the literature of that family, e.g., French, Italian, and Spanish literatures 840

.001–.007 Standard subdivisions

[.008–.009] History and description with respect to kinds of persons; historical, geographic, persons treatment

Do not use; class in 809

.1–.7 **Literature in specific forms**

Add to base number 809 the numbers following 808 in 808.1–808.7, e.g., history, description, critical appraisal of poetry 809.1

Class theory, technique, history of literary criticism of specific literary forms in 808.1–808.7

> ## 810–890 Literatures of specific languages

Literature is classed by the language in which originally written
. (Option: Class translations into a language requiring local emphasis with the literature of that language)

Class here collections of texts from literatures of two languages [*formerly also* 808.8]; history, description, critical appraisal of literatures of two languages [*all formerly also* 809]

Unless there is a specific provision for a dialect, literature in a dialect is classed with the literature of the basic language

Literature in a pidgin or creole is classed with the source language from which more of its vocabulary comes than from its other source language(s)

The numbers used in this schedule for literatures of individual languages do not necessarily correspond exactly with those in 420–490

Unless other instructions are given, class a work containing or discussing literatures of two languages in 810–890 in the number coming first, e.g., a collection of English and French texts 820.8 (*not* 840.8), but a collection of classical Greek and Latin texts 880

Class texts by more than one author in more than two languages not from the same language family in 808.8; class history, description, critical appraisal of works by more than one author in more than two languages not from the same language family in 809; class comprehensive works in 800

810 American literature in English

English-language literature of North America, South America, Hawaii, and associated islands

Add to base number 81 as instructed at beginning of Table 3, e.g., a collection of American poetry in English 811.008

Class comprehensive works on American literature in English and English literature in 820

(Option: Distinguish literatures of specific countries by initial letters, e.g., literature of Canada C810, of United States U810; or class literatures not requiring local emphasis in 819)

811–818 Specific forms of American literature in English

Numbers built according to instructions at beginning of Table 3

(819) American literatures in English not requiring local emphasis

(Optional number; prefer 810–818 for all American literatures in English)

Class here English-language literatures of specific American countries other than the country requiring local emphasis, e.g., libraries emphasizing United States literature may class here Canadian literature, and libraries emphasizing Canadian literature may class here United States literature

820   English and Old English (Anglo-Saxon) literatures

For American literature in English, see 810

> ### 820.1–828   Subdivisions of English literature

Add to base number 82 as instructed at beginning of Table 3, e.g., a collection of English poetry 821.008

A special number for Shakespeare appears below at 822.3

Class comprehensive works in 820

(Option: Distinguish English-language literatures of specific countries by initial letters, e.g., literature of England E820, of Ireland Ir820 [or, of all British Isles B820], of Australia A820, of India In820; or class literatures not requiring local emphasis in 828.99)

821   English poetry

Number built according to instructions at beginning of Table 3

822   English drama

Number built according to instructions at beginning of Table 3

.3   William Shakespeare

823–827 Other specific forms of English literature

Numbers built according to instructions at beginning of Table 3

828   English miscellaneous writings

Number built according to instructions at beginning of Table 3

(.99)   English-language literatures not requiring local emphasis

(Optional number; prefer 820–828 for all non-American English-language literatures)

Class here English-language literatures of specific non-American countries other than the country requiring local emphasis, e.g., libraries emphasizing British literature may class here Australian, Indian, other literatures, and libraries emphasizing Indian literature may class here British literature

829   Old English (Anglo-Saxon) literature

[.08–.09]   History and description with respect to kinds of persons; historical, geographic, persons treatment

Do not use; class in 829

830   Literatures of Germanic (Teutonic) languages German literature

For English and Old English (Anglo-Saxon) literatures, see 820

.01–.09   Standard subdivisions of literatures of Germanic (Teutonic) languages

---

> **830.1–838 Subdivisions of German literature**

Add to base number 83 as instructed at beginning of Table 3, e.g., a collection of German poetry 831.008

Class comprehensive works in 830

.1–.9   Standard subdivisions; collections; history, description, critical appraisal of German literature

Numbers built according to instructions at beginning of Table 3

831–838 Specific forms of German literature

Numbers built according to instructions at beginning of Table 3

839   Other Germanic (Teutonic) literatures

Including Yiddish literature; low German literature; Scandinavian literatures, e.g., Icelandic literature, Old Norse literature

Class Swedish literature in 839.7; class Danish and Norwegian literatures in 839.8

.3   Netherlandish literatures

Including Afrikaans literature

.31   Dutch literature

Class here Flemish literature

[.310 8–.310 9]   History and description with respect to kinds of persons; historical, geographic, persons treatment

Do not use; class in 839.31

.7   Swedish literature

Add to base number 839.7 as instructed at beginning of Table 3, e.g., a collection of Swedish poetry 839.71008

.8   Danish and Norwegian literatures

Including New Norse (Landsmål) literature

.81   Danish literature

Class Dano-Norwegian literature in 839.82

[.810 8–.810 9]   History and description with respect to kinds of persons; historical, geographic, persons treatment

Do not use; class in 839.81

.82   Norwegian (Bokmål, Riksmål) literature

Class here Dano-Norwegian literature, comprehensive works on Norwegian literature

Class New Norwegian literature in 839.8

[.820 8–.820 9]   History and description with respect to kinds of persons; historical, geographic, persons treatment

Do not use; class in 839.82

840   Literatures of Romance languages   French literature

Class comprehensive works on literatures of Italic languages in 870

For literatures of Italian, Sardinian, Dalmatian, Romanian, Rhaeto-Romanic languages, see 850; for literatures of Spanish and Portuguese languages, see 860

.01–.09   Standard subdivisions of literatures of Romance languages

---

> **840.1–848   Subdivisions of French literature**

Add to base number 84 as instructed at beginning of Table 3, e.g., a collection of French poetry 841.008

Class comprehensive works in 840

See also 849 for Provençal literature

(Option: Distinguish French-language literatures of specific countries by initial letters, e.g., literature of Canada C840, of France F840)

.1–.9   **Standard subdivisions; collections; history, description, critical appraisal of French literature**

Numbers built according to instructions at beginning of Table 3

841–848 Specific forms of French literature

Numbers built according to instructions at beginning of Table 3

849   Provençal (Langue d'oc), Franco-Provençal, Catalan literatures

850   Literatures of Italian, Sardinian, Dalmatian, Romanian, Rhaeto-Romanic languages   Italian literature

Class comprehensive works on literatures of Romance languages in 840; class comprehensive works on literatures of Italic languages in 870

> **850.1–858   Subdivisions of Italian literature**

> Add to base number 85 as instructed at beginning of Table 3, e.g., a collection of Italian poetry 851.008

> Class comprehensive works in 850

.1–.9   Standard subdivisions; collections; history, description, critical appraisal of Italian literature

Numbers built according to instructions at beginning of Table 3

851–858 Specific forms of Italian literature

Numbers built according to instructions at beginning of Table 3

859   Romanian and Rhaeto-Romanic literatures

860   Literatures of Spanish and Portuguese languages   Spanish literature

**.01–.09   ** Standard subdivisions of literatures of Spanish and Portuguese languages

> **860.1–868   Subdivisions of Spanish literature**

> Class here Judeo-Spanish (Ladino), Papiamento literatures

> Add to base number 86 as instructed at beginning of Table 3, e.g., a collection of Spanish poetry 861.008

> Class comprehensive works in 860

> (Option: Distinguish Spanish-language literatures of specific countries by initial letters, e.g., literature of Chile Ch860, of Colombia Co860, of Mexico M860 [or, of all American countries A860], of Spain S860)

.1–.9   Standard subdivisions; collections; history, description, critical appraisal of Spanish literature

Numbers built according to instructions at beginning of Table 3

861–868 Specific forms of Spanish literature

Numbers built according to instructions at beginning of Table 3

869   Portuguese literature

Class here Galician literature

Add to base number 869 as instructed at beginning of Table 3, e.g., a collection of Portuguese poetry 869.1008

870   Literatures of Italic languages   Latin literature

Class comprehensive works of or on literatures of classical (Greek and Latin) languages in 880

For literatures of Romance languages, see 840

.01–.09   Standard subdivisions of literatures of Italic languages

---

> ### 870.1–878 Subdivisions of Latin literature

Add to base number 87 as instructed at beginning of Table 3, e.g., a collection of Latin poetry 871.008; however, observe the special interpretations of and exceptions to notation from Table 3 that appear below at 871–874

Class comprehensive works in 870

.1–.9   **Standard subdivisions; collections; history, description, critical appraisal of Latin literature**

Numbers built according to instructions at beginning of Table 3

871   Latin poetry

For dramatic poetry, see 872; for epic poetry, see 873; for lyric poetry, see 874

872   Latin dramatic poetry and drama

873   Latin epic poetry and fiction

874   Latin lyric poetry

875–878 Other specific forms of Latin literature

Numbers built according to instructions at beginning of Table 3

879   Literatures of other Italic languages

Including Osco-Umbrian literatures

880   Literatures of Hellenic languages   Classical Greek literature

Class here comprehensive works of or on literatures of classical (Greek and Latin) languages

For Latin literature, see 870

.01–.09   Standard subdivisions of classical (Greek and Latin) literatures

> **880.1–888 Subdivisions of classical Greek literature**

> Add to base number 88 as instructed at beginning of Table 3, e.g., a collection of classical Greek poetry 881.008; however, observe the special interpretations of and exceptions to notation from Table 3 that appear below at 881–884

> Class comprehensive works in 880

.1–.9 Standard subdivisions; collections; history, description, critical appraisal of classical Greek literature

Numbers built according to instructions at beginning of Table 3

881   Classical Greek poetry

For dramatic poetry, see 882; for epic poetry, see 883; for lyric poetry, see 884

882   Classical Greek dramatic poetry and drama

883   Classical Greek epic poetry and fiction

884   Classical Greek lyric poetry

885–888 Other specific forms of classical Greek literature

Numbers built according to instructions at beginning of Table 3

889   Modern Greek literature

Class here Katharevusa and Demotic literature

[.08–.09]   History and description with respect to kinds of persons; historical, geographic, persons treatment

Do not use; class in 889

890   Literatures of other specific languages and language families

Class texts by more than one author in more than two languages not from the same language family in 808.8; class history, description, critical appraisal of works by more than one author in more than two languages not from the same language family in 809

891   East Indo-European and Celtic literatures

Including Albanian, Armenian; Baltic literatures, e.g., Latvian, Lithuanian; Iranian literatures, e.g., Persian (Farsi); Sanskrit literature; comprehensive works on Indic literatures, on Prakrit literatures

Class modern Indic, modern Prakrit literatures in 891.4

.4 **Modern Indic literatures**

> Including Bengali, Hindi, Romany, Sinhalese, Urdu literatures
>
> Class here modern Prakrit literatures
>
> Class comprehensive works on Indic literatures, on Prakrit literatures in 891

.6 **Celtic literatures**

> Including Breton, Cornish, Irish and Scottish Gaelic, Welsh literatures

.7 **East Slavic literatures**   **Russian**

> Including Belarusian, Ukrainian literatures
>
> Class comprehensive works on Slavic literatures in 891.8

.700 1–.700 9   Standard subdivisions of East Slavic literatures

.701–.78   Subdivisions of Russian

> Add to base number 891.7 as instructed at beginning of Table 3, e.g., a collection of Russian poetry 891.71008

.8 **Slavic (Slavonic) literatures**

> Including Bulgarian, Czech, Polish, Serbo-Croatian, Slovak, Slovenian literatures
>
> Class here comprehensive works on literatures of Balto-Slavic languages
>
> Class Baltic literatures in 891
>
> *For East Slavic literatures, see 891.7*

892   Afro-Asiatic (Hamito-Semitic) literatures   Semitic literatures

> Including Ethiopian literatures
>
> *For non-Semitic Afro-Asiatic literatures, see 893*

.4 **Hebrew literature**

[.408–.409]   History and description with respect to kinds of persons; historical, geographic, persons treatment

> Do not use; class in 892.4

.7 **Literatures of Arabic and Maltese languages**   **Arabic literature**

> Class here classical Arabic literature, Judeo-Arabic literature

[.708–.709]   History and description with respect to kinds of persons; historical, geographic, persons treatment

> Do not use; class in 892.7

893   Non-Semitic Afro-Asiatic literatures

> Including Berber, Chadic, Coptic, Cushitic literatures

894 Altaic, Uralic, Hyperborean, Dravidian literatures

Including Estonian, Finnish, Hungarian, Sami literatures; Mongolian, Turkish literatures

.8 Dravidian literatures

Including Kannada, Malayalam, Tamil, Telugu literatures

895 Literatures of East and Southeast Asia   Sino-Tibetan literatures

Including Burmese, Tibetan literatures

Here are classed literatures of South Asian languages closely related to languages of East and Southeast Asia

> *For literature of Austronesian languages of East and Southeast Asia, see 899*

> *See also 891.4 for Nepali literature*

.1 Chinese literature

[.108–.109]   History and description with respect to kinds of persons; historical, geographic, persons treatment

Do not use; class in 895.1

.6 Japanese literature

[.608–.609]   History and description with respect to kinds of persons; historical, geographic, persons treatment

Do not use; class in 895.6

.7 Korean literature

[.708–.709]   History and description with respect to kinds of persons; historical, geographic, persons treatment

Do not use; class in 895.7

.9 Literatures of miscellaneous languages of Southeast Asia; Munda literatures

Limited to literatures of language families named here

Including literatures in Austroasiatic languages, e.g., Khmer (Cambodian), Vietnamese; Hmong-Mien languages, e.g., Hmong (Miao); Tai languages, e.g., Lao, Thai (Siamese)

> *For literatures in Austronesian languages, see 899*

896   African literatures

Including Fulani, Ibo, Yoruba literatures; literatures in Bantu languages, e.g., Swahili, Zulu literatures

Class Afrikaans literature in 839.3; class Malagasy literature in 899. Class literature in an African creole having a non-African primary source language with the source language, e.g., Krio literature 820

For Ethiopian literatures, see 892; for non-Semitic Afro-Asian literatures, see 893

897   Literatures of North American native languages

Including Inuit (Inuktitut), Maya, Nahuatl (Aztec) literatures

Class here comprehensive works on literatures of North and South American native languages

For literatures of South American native languages, see 898

898   Literatures of South American native languages

Including Guaraní, Quechua literatures

899   Literatures of non-Austronesian languages of Oceania, of Austronesian languages, of miscellaneous languages

Miscellaneous languages are limited to Basque, Sumerian; Caucasian languages, e.g., Georgian; artificial languages, e.g., Esperanto

Including literatures of Australian languages; of Malay-Polynesian literatures, e.g., Bahasa Indonesia, Bahasa Malaysia, Javanese, Malagasy, Maori, Tagalog (Filipino); of Papuan languages

900 Geography, history, and auxiliary disciplines

Class here social situations and conditions; general political history; military, diplomatic, political, economic, social, welfare aspects of specific wars

Class interdisciplinary works on ancient world, on specific continents, countries, localities in 930–990. Class historical and geographic treatment of a specific discipline or subject with the discipline or subject, plus notation 09 from Table 1, e.g., historical and geographic treatment of natural sciences 509, of economic situations and conditions 330.9, of purely political situations and conditions 320.9, history of military science 355.009

See also 303.49 for projected events (future history)

See Manual at 900

SUMMARY

900.1–.9	**Standard subdivisions of geography and history**
901–909	**Standard subdivisions of history, collected accounts of events, and world history**
910	**Geography and travel**
920	**Biography, genealogy, insignia**
930	**History of ancient world to ca. 499**
940	**General history of Europe Western Europe**
950	**General history of Asia Orient Far East**
960	**General history of Africa**
970	**General history of North America**
980	**General history of South America**
990	**General history of other parts of world, of extraterrestrial worlds Pacific Ocean islands**

.1–.9 Standard subdivisions of geography and history

901 Philosophy and theory of history

902 Miscellany of history

Including chronologies

903 Dictionaries, encyclopedias, concordances of history

904 Collected accounts of events

Class here adventure

Class collections limited to a specific area or region (but not limited by continent, country, locality) or to a specific period in 909; class travel in 910; class collections limited to a specific continent, country, locality in 930–990. Class history of a specific kind of event with the event, e.g., geological history of California earthquakes 551.2209794

See Manual at 900: Historical events vs. nonhistorical events

905–907 Standard subdivisions of history

908 History with respect to kinds of persons

[.9] Racial, ethnic, national groups

Do not use; class in 909

909 World history

Civilization and events not limited geographically

Including history with respect to racial, ethnic, national groups not limited by continent, country, locality, e.g., world history of Jews; history of areas, regions, places not limited by continent, country, locality, e.g., history of tropical regions; interdisciplinary works on areas, regions, places in general (other than landforms, oceans, seas)

Class collected accounts of events not limited by period, area, region, subject in 904; class history of ancient world to ca. 499 in 930; class history of specific continents, countries, localities in modern world in 940–990; class interdisciplinary works on land forms, oceans, seas in 551.4

For geography of and travel in areas, regions, places in general, see 910

See Manual at 305 vs. 306, 909, 930–990; also at 909, 930–990 vs. 320; also at 909, 930–990 vs. 320.4, 321, 321.09; also at 909, 930–990 vs. 910

[.001–.008] Standard subdivisions

Do not use; class in 901–908

[.009] Historical treatment

Do not use; class in 900

> 909.07–909.08 General historical periods

Class here general histories covering three or more continents (or three or more countries if not on the same continent)

Class comprehensive works in 909

For ancient history, see 930

.07	**Ca. 500–1450/1500**

Including Crusades

Class here Middle Ages

Class specific historical periods in 909

> *See also 940.1 for history of Europe during the Crusades and Middle Ages*

.08	Modern history, 1450/1500–

Class specific historical periods to 1700 in 909; class specific historical periods since 1700 in 909.7–909.8

> **909.7–909.8 Specific historical periods since 1700**

Class comprehensive works in 909

> *See also 930 for historical periods to 499, 909 for historical periods between 500 and 1699*

.7	**18th century, 1700–1799**
.8	**1800–**
.81	19th century, 1800–1899

Class here industrial revolution

.82	20th century, 1900–1999

> *For World War I, see 940.3; for World War II, see 940.53*

.83	21st century, 2000–2099

> *See also 303.49 for futurology*

910 Geography and travel

Including physical geography

Class general works on civilization, other than accounts of travel in 909; class physical geography of specific continents, countries, localities in 913–919; class works on civilization, other than accounts of travel, in ancient world and specific places in modern world in 930–990. Class physical geography of a specific feature with the feature in 550, e.g., glaciers 551.31; class geographic treatment of a specific discipline or subject with the discipline or subject, e.g., geographic treatment of religion 200.9, of geomorphology 551.4109

> *See Manual at 338 vs. 060, 381, 382, 670.29, 910, T1—025, T1—029; also at 550 vs. 910; also at 578 vs. 304.2, 508, 910; also at 909, 930–990 vs. 910*

(.1)   **Topical geography**

(Optional number; prefer specific subject, e.g., economic geography 330.9)

Do not use for philosophy and theory of geography and travel; class in 910

Add to base number 910.1 notation 001–899, e.g., economic geography 910.133; then add 0* and to the result add notation 1–9 from Table 2, e.g., economic geography of British Isles 910.133041

.2   **Miscellany**

Including world travel guides

Class guides to areas, regions, places in general in 910.91; class guides to specific continents, countries, localities in 913–919, plus notation 04 from table under 913–919

.22   Illustrations, models, miniatures

Do not use for maps and plans; class in 912

.25   Directories of persons and organizations

Class here city directories, telephone books

Class city directories, telephone books of a specific place in 913–919, plus notation 0025 from table under 913–919

.3   **Dictionaries, encyclopedias, concordances, gazetteers**

Class here works on place names systematically arranged for ready reference

Class discourses on place names in 910; class historical material associated with place names in general in 909; class historical material associated with place names of specific places in 930–990

.4   **Accounts of travel**

Not geographically limited

Including trips around the world, ocean travel, seafaring life, shipwrecks; pirates' expeditions

Class travel accounts that emphasize civilization of places visited in 909; class travel in specific oceans in 910.9163–910.9167

For discovery and exploration, see 910.9

See also 508 for scientific exploration and travel, 910.2 for world travel guides

.5–.8   **Standard subdivisions**

.9   **Historical, geographic, persons treatment**

Class here discovery, exploration, growth of geographic knowledge

*Add 00 for standard subdivisions; see instructions at beginning of Table 1

.91   Geography of and travel in areas, regions, places in general

> Class physical geography of areas, regions, places in general in 910; class interdisciplinary works on landforms, oceans, seas in 551.4

.92   Geographers, travelers, explorers regardless of country of origin

.93–.99   Discovery and exploration by specific countries

> Do not use for geography of and travel in specific continents, countries, localities; extraterrestrial worlds; class in 913–919

> Add to base number 910.9 notation 3–9 from Table 2 for the country responsible, e.g., explorations by Great Britain 910.941

> Class discovery and exploration by a specific country in areas, regions, places in general in 910.91; class discovery and exploration by a specific country in specific continents, countries, localities, extraterrestrial worlds in 913–919; class periods of discovery and exploration in history in 930–990

911   Historical geography

> Growth and changes in political divisions

> Class here historical atlases

.09   Historical treatment

> Do not use for geographic and persons treatment; class in 911

912   Graphic representations of surface of earth and of extraterrestrial worlds

> Including map reading

> Class here atlases, maps, charts, plans

> Class map drawing in 526.022

> *For graphic representation of a specific subject other than geography and travel, see the subject, plus notation 022 from Table 1, e.g., railroad atlases 385.022*

> *See Manual at 912 vs. T1—022*

.09   Historical and persons treatment of maps and map making

> Class maps of specific areas, regions, places in general in 912; class maps of specific continents, countries, localities, extraterrestrial worlds in 912.3–912.9

.3–.9   **Specific continents, countries, localities, extraterrestrial worlds**

> Add to base number 912 notation 3–9 from Table 2, e.g., maps of Illinois 912.773

913–919 Geography of and travel in ancient world and specific continents, countries, localities in modern world; extraterrestrial worlds

Add to base number 91 notation 3–9 from Table 2, e.g., geography of England 914.2; then add further as follows:

001	Philosophy and theory
002	Miscellany
0022	Illustrations, models, miniatures
	Do not use for atlases, maps, diagrams; class in 912
003	Dictionaries, encyclopedias, concordances, gazetteers
	Class here works on place names systematically arranged for ready reference
	Class discourses on place names in 913–919 without adding from this table; class historical material associated with place names in 930–990
005–007	Standard subdivisions
008	Geography and travel with respect to kinds of persons
[009]	Historical, geographic, persons treatment
	Do not use; class in 913–919 without adding from this table
04	Travel
	Class here discovery, exploration; guidebooks
	Class world travel guides in 910.2; class travel accounts that emphasize the civilization of country visited in 930–990
	See Manual at 913–919: Add table: 04; also at 913–919 vs. 796.51

Class comprehensive works, geography of and travel in more than one continent in 910; class historical geography in 911; class graphic representations in 912; class interdisciplinary works on geography and history of ancient world, of specific continents, countries, localities in 930–990; class archaeology in 930.1; class area studies in 940–990

See Manual at 913–919; also at 333.7–333.9 vs. 508, 913–919, 930–990

919 Travel in other parts of world and on extraterrestrial worlds Travel in Pacific Ocean islands

Number built according to instructions under 913–919

See Manual at 520 vs. 500.5, 523.1, 530.1, 919.9

.904   Travel on extraterrestrial worlds

       Number built according to instructions under 913–919

       Class here projected accounts [*formerly* 629.45]

       See Manual at 629.43, 629.45 vs. 919.904

920   Biography, genealogy, insignia

Class here autobiographies, diaries, reminiscences, correspondence

Class biography of persons associated with a specific discipline or subject with the discipline or subject, plus notation 092 from Table 1, e.g., biography of chemists 540.92
> (Option: Class individual biography in 92 or B, collected biography in 92 or 920 undivided)

See Manual at T1—092

.001–.007	Standard subdivisions of biography
.008	History and description of biography with respect to kinds of persons
[.008 1–.008 2]	Men and women

> Do not use; class in 920.7

[.008 8]	Occupational and religious groups

> Do not use; class with the specific group, plus notation 092 from Table 1, e.g., biography of Lutherans 284.1092
> > (Option: Class in in 920.1–928)

[.008 9]	Racial, ethnic, national groups

> Do not use; class in 920.0092

.009	General collections of biography by period, region, group

> Class collections by specific continents, countries, localities in 920.03–920.09

.009 1	Areas, regions, places in general

> Add to base number 920.0091 the numbers following —1 in notation 11–19 from Table 2, e.g., biographies of suburbanites 920.009173

.009 2	Racial, ethnic, national groups
.02	General collections of biography

> Not limited by period, place, group and not associated with a specific subject

.03–.09	General collections of biography by specific continents, countries, localities

> Not associated with a specific subject

> Add to base number 920.0 notation 3–9 from Table 2, e.g., collections of biographies of persons resident in England 920.042

> Class collections by sex regardless of continent, country, locality in 920.7

> **920.1–928 Biography of specific classes of persons**

Class comprehensive works in 920.02

(Option A: Use subdivisions identified by *

(Option B: Class individual biography in 92 or B, collected biography in 92 or 920 undivided

(Option C: Class individual biography of men in 920.71, of women in 920.72

(Prefer specific discipline or subject, plus notation 092 from Table 1, e.g., collected biography of scientists 509.2)

(.1) ***Bibliographers**

(.2) ***Librarians and book collectors**

(.3) ***Encyclopedists**

Class lexicographers in 924

(.4) ***Publishers and booksellers**

(.5) ***Journalists and news commentators**

.7 **Persons by sex**

Class here individual biography of persons not associated with a specific discipline or subject, collected biography of persons by sex

(Option: Class here all individual biography; prefer specific discipline or subject, plus notation 092 from Table 1)

.71 Men

.72 Women

(.9) ***Persons associated with other subjects**

Not provided for in 920.1–920.5, 921–928

(921) ***Philosophers and psychologists**

(922) ***Religious leaders, thinkers, workers**

(923) ***Persons in social sciences**

(924) ***Philologists and lexicographers**

(925) ***Scientists**

(926) ***Persons in technology**

(927) ***Persons in the arts and recreation**

For persons in literature, see 928

*(Optional number; prefer specific subject or discipline, as described under 920.1–928)

(928) ***Persons in literature, history, biography, genealogy**

> Including historians, writers and critics of literature

> *See also 923 for explorers, geographers, pioneers*

929 **Genealogy, names, insignia**

> Including family histories; cemetery records, e.g., epitaphs; genealogical sources, e.g., census records, court records, tax lists, wills

> Use only for genealogical sources published by a genealogical organization or compiled by a genealogist. Sources published or compiled by other agencies are normally classed with the subject of the publication, e.g., United States population census records 304.60973; however, if the source has been enhanced or rearranged to emphasize the genealogical content, e.g., United States population census records with name indexes added, the source is classed here

> Class family histories emphasizing the contributions of the members of the family to a specific occupation with the occupation, e.g., the Rothschilds as a family of bankers 332.1092; class family histories of a prominent person that emphasize the person's life with the biography number for the person, e.g., forebears, family, and life of Winston Churchill 941.082092

.4 **Personal names**

> *See also 929.9 for names of houses, pets, ships*

.6 **Heraldry**

> Including crests

> Class here armorial bearings, comprehensive works on coats of arms [*both formerly 929.8*]

> *For royal houses, peerage, gentry, orders of knighthood, see 929.7*

.7 **Royal houses, peerage, gentry, orders of knighthood**

> Class here rank, precedence, titles of honor; history and genealogy of royal families

> Class Christian orders of knighthood in 255; class Christian orders of knighthood in church history in 271; class histories of a royal family that include general events or biographies of members of the royal family in 930–990

[.709 41–.709 49]   Specific countries of Europe

> Do not use; class in 929.7

---

*(Optional number; prefer specific subject or discipline, as described under 920.1–928)

.8   Awards, orders, decorations, autographs

Armorial bearings, comprehensive works on coats of arms relocated to 929.6; seals relocated to 929.9

Class awards, orders, decorations associated with a specific subject with the subject, plus notation 079 from Table 1, e.g., American football awards 796.332079

.9   Forms of insignia and identification

Including seals [*formerly* 929.8], ownership and service marks; trademarks; national, state, provincial, ship, ownership flags; names of houses, pets, ships

Class military use of flags and banners in 355.1; class etymology of names in 412. Class forms of insignia and identification not provided for here with the form, e.g., coats of arms 929.6; class identification marks in a specific subject with the subject, e.g., airline insignia 387.7

For place names, see 910; for personal names, see 929.4

> ## 930–990   History of ancient world; of specific continents, countries, localities; of extraterrestrial worlds

Civilization and events

Class here interdisciplinary works on geography and history of ancient world, of specific continents, countries, localities

Add to base number 9 notation 3–9 from Table 2, e.g., general history of Europe 940, of England 942; then add further as follows:

001–007	Standard subdivisions
008	History with respect to kinds of persons
[0089]	Racial, ethnic, national groups
	Do not use; class in 930–990 without adding from this table
009	Persons
	Description, critical appraisal, biography of persons associated with the history of the continent, country, locality but limited to no specific period
	Class historians and historiographers in 930–990 without adding from this table
	Persons of a specific period which is set forth in the 930–990 schedules are classed in 01–09, plus notation 092 from Table 1; persons of other periods are classed in 930–990 without adding from this table
	See Manual at 930–990: Biography
01–09	Historical periods
	Use historical period notation only when it is specifically set forth in the 930–990 schedules, e.g., World War II 940.53, England during Tudor period 942.05
	Class here indigenous groups in the prehistoric period, e.g., Australian native peoples before European settlement 994.01
	Class areas, regions, places in general and racial, ethnic, national groups in a specific period in 930–990 without adding from this table
	See Manual at 930–990: Biography; also at 930–990: Add table: 01–09

The schedules that follow do not enumerate all the countries and localities that appear in Table 2; however, the foregoing instructions apply to history of any place in notation 3–9 from Table 2, e.g., London during Tudor period 942.1 (*not* 942.105)

Class sociology of war in 303.6; class sociology of military institutions in 306.2; class social factors affecting war, social causes of war in 355.02; class historical geography in 911; class geography of ancient world, of specific continents, countries, localities in 913–919; class comprehensive works in 909

See Manual at 930–990; also at 305 vs. 306, 909, 930–990; also at 333.7–333.9 vs. 508, 913–919, 930–990; also at 909, 930–990 vs. 320; also at 909, 930–990 vs. 320.4, 321, 321.09; also at 909, 930–990 vs. 910; also at 930–990 vs. 355.009

930   History of ancient world to ca. 499

.01–.09   Standard subdivisions

> As modified under 930–990; however, for archaeology, see 930.1

.1   Archaeology

Study of past civilizations through discovery, collection, interpretation of material remains

Including specific archaeological ages, e.g., Paleolithic (Old Stone) Age

Class here prehistoric archaeology; interdisciplinary works on archaeology

> *For industrial archaeology, see 609; for archaeology of specific oceans and seas, see 909; for archaeology of continents, countries, localities provided for in notation 3 from Table 2, see 931–939; for archaeology of modern period, ancient and prehistoric archaeology of continents, countries, localities not provided for in notation 3 from Table 2, see 940–990*

> *See also 700 for artistic aspects of archaeological objects*

>   **931–939   Specific places**

Class archaeology and history of specific oceans and seas in 909; class archaeology and history of modern period, ancient and prehistoric archaeology of continents, countries, localities not provided for in notation 3 from Table 2 in 940–990; class comprehensive works in 930

931   *China to 420

932   *Egypt to 640

933   *Palestine to 70

> *See also 220.9 for Biblical archaeology, history of Biblical events*

934   *India to 647

935   *Mesopotamia and Iranian Plateau to 637

> *For Persian Wars, see 938*

936   *Europe north and west of Italian peninsula to ca. 499

Class here comprehensive works on ancient Europe

> *For a specific part of ancient Europe not provided for here, see the part, e.g., Italy 937, Russia 947*

937   *Italian Peninsula and adjacent territories to 476

938   *Greece to 323

939   *Other parts of ancient world to ca. 640

*Add as instructed under 930–990

> ## 940–990   General history of modern world, of extraterrestrial worlds

Class here area studies; comprehensive works on ancient and modern history of specific continents, countries, localities

Class comprehensive works in 909

For general history of ancient world, see 930

940   General history of Europe   Western Europe

SUMMARY

940.01–.09	**Standard subdivisions**
.1–.5	**[Historical periods]**
941	**British Isles**
942	**England and Wales**
943	**Central Europe** **Germany**
944	**France and Monaco**
945	**Italian Peninsula and adjacent islands** **Italy**
946	**Iberian Peninsula and adjacent islands** **Spain**
947	**Eastern Europe** **Russia**
948	**Scandinavia**
949	**Other parts of Europe**

.01–.09   Standard subdivisions

As modified under 930–990

.1   **Early history to 1453**

Class here Middle Ages, 476–1453

Class comprehensive works on Crusades in 909.07

For ancient history to ca. 499, see 936

.2   **1453–**

Including Renaissance period, 1453–1517, Reformation period, 1517–1789; Thirty Years' War, 1618–1648; War of the League of Augsburg, 1688–1697; War of the Spanish Succession, 1701–1714; War of the Austrian Succession, 1740–1748; Seven Years' War, 1756–1763; Napoleonic Wars

For World War I, see 940.3; for 1918 to present, see 940.5; for North American aspects of War of the League of Augsburg, War of the Spanish Succession, War of the Austrian Succession, Seven Years' War, see 973.2

See also 945 for Renaissance period in Italy

.3   **World War I, 1914–1918**

Class results in and effects on a specific country with the history of the country, e.g., effects on Germany 943.085

For military history, see 940.4

.4   **Military history of World War I**

Including commemorations, medical services, social services

.400 1–.400 8   Standard subdivisions

.400 9   Historical, geographic, persons treatment

Do not use for military participation of specific countries, military campaigns, personal narratives; class in 940.4

.5   **1918–**

.53   World War II, 1939–1945

Including Holocaust, 1933–1945

Class results in and effects on a specific country with the history of the country, e.g., effects on Norway 948.104

For military history, see 940.54

.54   Military history of World War II

Including commemorations, medical services, social services

.540 01–.540 08   Standard subdivisions

.540 09   Historical, geographic, persons treatment

Do not use for military participation of specific countries, military campaigns, personal narratives; class in 940.54

.55   1945–1999

.56   2000–

941   *British Isles

Class here Great Britain, United Kingdom

See Manual at 941

.01   Early history to 1066

For ancient history to 410, see 936.1

.02–.05   Norman period through House of Tudor period, 1066–1603

Add to base number 941.0 the numbers following 942.0 in 942.02–942.05, e.g., period of House of Tudor 941.05

*Add as instructed under 930–990

.06   House of Stuart and Commonwealth periods, 1603–1714

   Class Civil War in 942.06

.07   Period of House of Hanover, 1714–1837

   Including formation of United Kingdom

.08   Period of Victoria and House of Windsor, 1837–

.081   Reign of Victoria, 1837–1901

   Class here 19th century

   For 1800–1837, see 941.07

.082   1901–1999

   For reign of George V, see 941.083; for 1936–1945, see 941.084; for 1945–1999, see 941.085

.083   Reign of George V, 1910–1936

.084   1936–1945

   Class here reigns of Edward VIII, 1936, and George VI, 1936–1952; period of World War II, 1939–1945

   For reign of George VI during 1945–1952, see 941.085

.085   1945–1999

   Class here reign of Elizabeth II, 1952 to present

   For 2000 and beyond, see 941.086

.086   2000–

.1   ***Scotland**

   For northeastern Scotland, see 941.2; for southeastern Scotland, see 941.3; for southwestern Scotland, see 941.4

.101   Early history to 1057

   For ancient history to 410, see 936.1

.102   1057–1314

   Including Battle of Bannockburn, 1314

.103   1314–1424

.104   Reigns of James I through James V, 1424–1542

.105   Reformation period, 1542–1603

   Class here 16th century

   For 1500–1542, see 941.104

*Add as instructed under 930–990

.106–.108   Personal union with England to present time, 1603–

> Add to base number 941.10 the numbers following 941.0 in 941.06–941.08, e.g., reign of George V 941.1083

.5   ***Ireland**

.501   Early history to 1086

> *For ancient history to 410, see 936.1*

.502   1086–1171

.503   Period under House of Plantagenet, 1171–1399

.504   Period under Houses of Lancaster and York, 1399–1485

.505   Period under House of Tudor, 1485–1603

.506   Period under House of Stuart, 1603–1691

.507   1691–1799

.508   1800–

.508 1   1800–1899

.508 2   1900–

.508 24   1970–

.6   ***Ulster**   **Northern Ireland**

.601–.607   Early history to 1800

> Add to base number 941.60 the numbers following 941.50 in 941.501–941.507, e.g., period under House of Tudor 941.605

.608   1800–

.608 1   1800–1899

.608 2   1900–

.608 24   1969–

.7   ***Republic of Ireland**

> *For Leinster, see 941.8; for Munster, see 941.9*

.701–.707   Early history to 1800

> Add to base number 941.70 the numbers following 941.50 in 941.501–941.507, e.g., period under House of Tudor 941.705

.708   1800–

.708 1   1800–1899

*Add as instructed under 930–990

.708 2	1900–

Including period as Irish Free State, 1922–1937; as Eire, 1937–1949

.708 24	1970–

942   *England and Wales

Subdivisions are added for England and Wales together, for England alone

See Manual at 941

>   942.01–942.08   Historical periods for England and Wales together, for England alone

Class comprehensive works in 942

.01   Early history to 1066

For ancient history to 410, see 936.2

.02   Norman period, 1066–1154

Including Battle of Hastings, 1066

Class here 12th century

For 1154–1199, see 942.03

.03   Period of House of Plantagenet, 1154–1399

Class here medieval period

For 1066–1154, see 942.02; for 1399–1485, see 942.04

.04   Period of Houses of Lancaster and York, 1399–1485

Class here Wars of the Roses, 1455–1485

.05   Period of House of Tudor, 1485–1603

.06–.08   House of Stuart and Commonwealth periods to present time, 1603–

Add to base number 942.0 the numbers following 941.0 in 941.06–941.08, e.g., reign of Victoria 942.081

.9   *Wales

.901–.908   Historical periods

Add to base number 942.90 the numbers following 942.0 in 942.01–942.08, e.g., Wales during Wars of the Roses 942.904

*Add as instructed under 930–990

943   Central Europe   Germany

Including East Germany, 1945–1990; German Democratic Republic, 1949–1990

Class here Holy Roman Empire

For ancient history of Germany, see 936.3

.000 1–.000 9   Standard subdivisions of central Europe

As modified under 930–990

.001–.009   Standard subdivisions of Germany

As modified under 930–990

.08   Germany since 1866

.085   Period of Weimar Republic, 1918–1933

.086   Period of Third Reich, 1933–1945

Class Holocaust in 940.53

.087   1945–1999

Class here 20th century; Federal Republic, 1949 to present, comprehensive works on Federal and Democratic Republics

Class German Democratic Republic in 943; class 1900–1918 in 943.08

For period of Weimar Republic, 1918–1933, see 943.085; for period of Third Reich, 1933–1945, see 943.086; for 2000 and beyond, see 943.088

.088   2000–

[.1]   **Northeastern Germany**

Number discontinued; class in 943

.6   ***Austria and Liechtenstein**

Subdivisions are added for Austria and Liechtenstein together, for Austria alone

For ancient history to 481, see 936.3

.605   Austria since 1919

.7   ***Czech Republic and Slovakia**

.703   1918–1992

Class here Czechoslovakia

For 1945–1992, see 943.704

.704   1945–1992

---

*Add as instructed under 930–990

.705	1993–
	Period of two sovereign nations
.71	*Czech Republic
	For Moravia, see 943.72
.710 5	1993–
.72	*Moravia
[.720 5]	1993–
	Number discontinued; class in 943.72
.73	*Slovakia
.730 5	1993–
.8	***Poland**
.805	1939–
.9	***Hungary**
	For ancient history to ca. 640, see 939
.905	1918–

944   *France and Monaco

Including Hundred Years' War, 1337–1453

Subdivisions are added for France and Monaco together, for France alone

For ancient history to 486, see 936.4

>	944.04–944.08 France since 1789
	Class comprehensive works in 944
.04	Revolutionary period, 1789–1804
.05	Period of First Empire, 1804–1815
	Class here reign of Napoleon I, 1804–1814
	Class Napoleonic Wars in 940.2
.06	Period of Restoration, 1815–1848
	Class here 19th century
	For a specific part of 19th century not provided for here, see the part, e.g., Second Empire 944.07

*Add as instructed under 930–990

.07   Period of Second Republic and Second Empire (period of Napoleon
                 III), 1848–1870

.08   1870–

.081   Period of Third Republic, 1870–1945

                        Class here 20th century

                            For 1945–1958, see 944.082; for 1958–1999, see 944.083

.082   Period of Fourth Republic, 1945–1958

.083   Period of Fifth Republic, 1958–

                            For 2000 and beyond, see 944.084

.084   2000–

945   *Italian Peninsula and adjacent islands   Italy

                    For ancient history to 476, see 937

.09   Italy since 1900

.091   Reign of Victor Emmanuel III, 1900–1946

                        Class here 20th century, Fascist period

                            For 1946–1999, see 945.092

.092   Period of Republic, 1946–

                            For 2000 and beyond, see 945.093

.093   2000–

946   Iberian Peninsula and adjacent islands   Spain

                    For ancient history to 415, see 936.6

.000 1–.000 9   Standard subdivisions of Iberian Peninsula and adjacent islands

                        As modified under 930–990

.001–.009   Standard subdivisions of Spain

                        As modified under 930–990

.08   Spain since 1931

                    Class here 20th century

                    Class 1900–1931 in 946

.081   Period of Second Republic, 1931–1939

                        Class here Civil War, 1936–1939

*Add as instructed under 930–990

.082	Period of Francisco Franco, 1939–1975
.083	Reign of Juan Carlos I, 1975–
.9	***Portugal**
.904	1910–

947 Eastern Europe   Russia

.000 1–.000 9	Standard subdivisions of eastern Europe
	As modified under 930–990
.001–.009	Standard subdivisions of Russia
	As modified under 930–990
.08	Russia since 1855
.084	1917–1991

Class here 20th century; Communist period; comprehensive works on Union of Soviet Socialist Republics, 1923–1991

Class 1900–1917 in 947.08

For 1953–1991, see 947.085

.085	1953–1991
.086	1991–

Class here comprehensive works on Commonwealth of Independent States, 1991–

For a specific part of Commonwealth of Independent States, see the part, e.g., Ukraine 947.708

.5	***Caucasus**
.54	*Azerbaijan
.540 8	1991–
[.540 801–.540 809]	Standard subdivisions
	Do not use; class in 947.5408
.56	*Armenia
.560 8	1991–
[.560 801–.560 809]	Standard subdivisions
	Do not use; class in 947.5608
.58	*Georgia

*Add as instructed under 930–990

.580 8   1991–

[.580 801–.580 809]   Standard subdivisions

>   Do not use; class in 947.5808

.6   *Moldova

.608   1991–

[.608 01–.608 09]   Standard subdivisions

>   Do not use; class in 947.608

.7   *Ukraine

.708   1991–

[.708 01–.708 09]   Standard subdivisions

>   Do not use; class in 947.708

.8   *Belarus

.808   1991–

[.808 01–.808 09]   Standard subdivisions

>   Do not use; class in 947.808

.9   *Lithuania, Latvia, Estonia

>   Class here Baltic States

.908   1991–

[.908 01–.908 09]   Standard subdivisions

>   Do not use; class in 947.908

.93   *Lithuania

.930 8   1991–

[.930 801–.930 809]   Standard subdivisions

>   Do not use; class in 947.9308

.96   *Latvia

.960 8   1991–

[.960 801–.960 809]   Standard subdivisions

>   Do not use; class in 947.9608

.98   *Estonia

.980 8   1991–

*Add as instructed under 930–990

[.980 801–.980 809]   Standard subdivisions

           Do not use; class in 947.9808

948   *Scandinavia

     Class here northern Europe

      For ancient history to 481, see 936.3

.08   1905–1999

.09   2000–

.1   *Norway

      For ancient history to 481, see 936.3; for southeastern Norway, see 948.2; for southwestern Norway, see 948.3; for central and northern Norway, see 948.4

.104   1905–1999

.105   2000–

.5   *Sweden

      For ancient history to 481, see 936.3; for southern Sweden, see 948.6; for central Sweden, see 948.7; for northern Sweden, see 948.8

.505   1905–1999

.506   2000–

.9   Denmark and Finland

      For ancient history of Denmark to 481, see 936.3

.900 1–.900 9   Standard subdivisions of Denmark

           As modified under 930–990

\>   948.905–948.906   Denmark since 1906

          Class comprehensive works in 948.9

.905   1906–1999

.906   2000–

.97   *Finland

.970 3   1917–

949   Other parts of Europe

.1   *Northwestern islands

*Add as instructed under 930–990

.12   *Iceland

.120 5   1940–

                              Class here 20th century; period of Republic, 1944–

                              Class 1900–1940 in 949.12

.2   **Netherlands (Holland)**

                      For ancient history to 481, see 936.3

.207   1901–

.3   **Southern Low Countries   Belgium**

                      For ancient history of Belgium to 486, see 936.4

[.300 01–.300 09]   Standard subdivisions of southern Low Countries

                              Relocated to 949.3001–949.3009

.300 1–.300 9   Standard subdivisions of southern Low Countries [*formerly*
                      949.30001–949.30009], of Belgium

                              As modified under 930–990

.304   1909–

.35   *Luxembourg

                      For ancient history to 486, see 936.4

.350 4   1890–

.4   ***Switzerland**

                      For ancient history to 486, see 936.4

.407   1945–

.5   ***Greece**

                      Including Aegean Islands, Crete [*both formerly* 949.9]; Byzantine Empire

                      *For ancient history of Greece to 323, see 938; for ancient history of Aegean
                      Islands and Crete to 323, see 939*

.507   1830–

.6   ***Balkan Peninsula**

                      Including Balkan Wars, 1912–1913

.65   *Albania

                      For ancient history to 323, see 939

.650 3   1946–1992

                              Class here period of People's Republic, 1946–1991

*Add as instructed under 930–990

.650 4	1992–

.7　　　　***Yugoslavia, Croatia, Slovenia, Bosnia and Hercegovina, Macedonia**

　　　　　　　For ancient history to ca. 640, see 939

.702　　　　　Yugoslavia, 1918–1991

.703　　　　　Period of five sovereign nations, 1991–

　　　　　　　　See also 949.7103 for Yugoslavia (1991–　)

.71　　　　　*Serbia

.710 3　　　　　1991–

　　　　　　　　Class here Yugoslavia (1991–　)

　　　　　　　　See also 949.702 for Yugoslavia (1918–1991)

.72　　　　　*Croatia

.720 3　　　　　1991–

.73　　　　　*Slovenia

.730 3　　　　　1991–

.74　　　　　*Bosnia and Hercegovina, Montenegro

.742　　　　　　*Bosnia and Hercegovina

.742 03　　　　　1991–

.76　　　　　*Macedonia

.760 3　　　　　1991–

[.77]　　　　Bulgaria

　　　　　　　Relocated to 949.9

.8　　　　***Romania**

　　　　　　　For ancient history to ca. 640, see 939

.803　　　　　1947–

.9　　　　***Bulgaria [*formerly* 949.7]**

　　　　　　　Aegean Islands and Crete relocated to 949.5

　　　　　　　For ancient history to ca. 640, see 939

.903　　　　　1946–

950　　General history of Asia　　　Orient　　　Far East

*Add as instructed under 930–990

SUMMARY

950.01–.09	**Standard subdivisions**
.4	1905–
951	**China and adjacent areas**
952	**Japan**
953	**Arabian Peninsula and adjacent areas**
954	**South Asia India**
955	**Iran**
956	**Middle East (Near East)**
957	**Siberia (Asiatic Russia)**
958	**Central Asia**
959	**Southeast Asia**

.01–.09   Standard subdivisions

As modified under 930–990

.4   **1905–**

951   China and adjacent areas

For ancient history to 420, see 931

[.000 1–.000 9]   Standard subdivisions of China and adjacent areas

Relocated to 951.001–951.009

.001–.009   Standard subdivisions of China and adjacent areas [*formerly* 951.0001–951.0009], of China alone

As modified under 930–990

.04   Period of Republic, 1912–1949

.05   Period of People's Republic, 1949–

Class here 20th century

Class 1900–1912 in 951

For 1912–1949, see 951.04; for 2000 and beyond, see 951.06

.06   2000–

.2   **Hong Kong, Macao**

[.201–.209]   Standard subdivisions

Do not use; class in 951.2

.25   *Hong Kong

.250 5   1945–

.9   ***Korea**

*Add as instructed under 930–990

.904 1945–

.93 *North Korea (People's Democratic Republic of Korea)

.930 4 1945–

.95 *South Korea (Republic of Korea)

.950 4 1945–

952 *Japan

.03 1868–1945

  Including 20th century

  For 1945–1999, see 952.04

.04 1945–1999

.05 2000–

953 *Arabian Peninsula and adjacent areas

  For ancient history to 622, see 939

.05 1926–

.3 *Yemen

  For ancient history to 622, see 939

.305 1918–

  Including period as Republic of Yemen, 1990 to present

.32 *Northern Yemen

  For ancient history to 622, see 939

.320 5 1918–

  Including Yemen Arab Republic, 1962–1990; period as part of Republic of Yemen, 1990 to present

.35 *Southern Yemen

  For ancient history to 622, see 939

.350 5 1967–

  Including People's Democratic Republic of Yemen, 1970–1990; period as part of Republic of Yemen, 1990 to present

.6 *Persian Gulf States

*Add as instructed under 930–990

.67   *Kuwait

             Class Gulf Crisis and War, 1990–1991, in 956.7044

             For ancient history to 622, see 939

.8   *Saudi Arabia

             For ancient history to 622, see 939

.805   1926–

             Class military operations in Saudi Arabia during Gulf Crisis and War, 1990–1991, in 956.7044

954   *South Asia   India

             For ancient history of India to 647, see 934

.02   647–1785

.03   Period of British rule, 1785–1947

             For governorships of Lord Clive, Warren Hastings, see 954.02

.04   1947–1971

             For prime ministership of Indira Gandhi during 1971–1977, see 954.05

.05   1971–

.9   Other jurisdictions

             Class here Pakistan (West and East, 1947–1971)

.900 1–.900 9   Standard subdivisions of Pakistan (West and East, 1947–1971)

             As modified under 930–990

>   954.902–954.905   Historical periods of Pakistan (West and East, 1947–1971)

             Class comprehensive works in 954.9

             For ancient history to 647, see 934

.902   647–1785

.903   Period of British rule, 1785–1947

.904   1947–1971

.905   1971–

.91   *Pakistan

.910 2   647–1785

*Add as instructed under 930–990

.910 3	Period of British rule, 1785–1947
.910 4	Period of union of West and East Pakistan, 1947–1971
.910 5	1971–
.92	*Bangladesh
.920 2	647–1785
.920 3	Period of British rule, 1785–1947
.920 4	Period of union of West and East Pakistan, 1947–1971
.920 5	1971–
.93	*Sri Lanka
.930 3	1948–

955 *Iran

For ancient history to 637, see 935

.05　　　1906–

Including Iraqi-Iranian Conflict, 1980–1988

956 *Middle East (Near East)

For ancient history to ca. 640, see 939

.04　　　1945–1980

Including Israel-Arab War, 1948–1949; Sinai Campaign, 1956; Israel-Arab War, 1967 (Six Days' War); Israel-Arab War, 1973 (Yom Kippur War)

Class here 20th century

Class 1900–1945 in 956

.05　　　1980–

Including Israel-Lebanon-Syria Conflict, 1982–1985

.1　　*Turkey

For Turkey in Europe, see 949.61; for divisions of Turkey, see 956.2–956.6

.103　　　1950–1999

.104　　　2000–

.4　　*South central Turkey

For ancient history to ca. 640, see 939

[.45]　　Cyprus

Relocated to 956.93

*Add as instructed under 930–990

.7   ***Iraq**

                For ancient history to 637, see 935

.704   1920–

.704 4   Administration of Saddam Hussein, 1979–

                  Including Gulf Crisis and War, 1990–1991

                  Class Iraqi-Iranian Conflict, 1980–1988, in 955.05

.9   ***Syria, Lebanon, Cyprus, Israel, Jordan**

.91   *Syria

                For ancient history to ca. 640, see 939

.910 4   1920–

                  Class Israel-Arab wars of 1948–1949, 1967, and 1973, in 956.04; class Israel-Lebanon-Syria Conflict, 1982–1985, in 956.05

.92   *Lebanon

                For ancient history to ca. 640, see 939

.920 4   1926–

                  Class Israel-Arab War, 1948–1949, in 956.04; class Israel-Lebanon-Syria Conflict, 1982–1985, in 956.05

.93   *Cyprus [*formerly* 956.45]

                For ancient history to ca. 640, see 939

.930 4   1960–

.94   *Palestine   Israel

                For early history to 70, ancient Judah, Judaea, see 933; for ancient Edom to 70, see 939

                See also 320.54095694 for Zionism, 909 for world history of Jews

.940 5   1948–

                  Class here 20th century

                  Class Israel-Arab wars of 1948–1949, 1967, and 1973, Sinai Campaign, 1956, in 956.04; class Israel-Lebanon-Syria Conflict, 1982–1985, in 956.05; class 1900–1948 in 956.94

.95   *West Bank and Jordan

             Subdivisions are added for West Bank and Jordan together, for Jordan alone

                For early history to 70, see 933; for ancient Moab, Petra to 70, see 939

*Add as instructed under 930–990

.950 4 1923–

Class Israel-Arab wars of 1948–1949 and 1967 in 956.04

957 *Siberia (Asiatic Russia)

.08 1855–

958 *Central Asia

For early history to ca. 640, see 939

.1 *Afghanistan

For early history to ca. 640, see 939

.104 1919–

.4 *Turkestan

For Turkmenistan, see 958.5; for Tajikistan, see 958.6; for Uzbekistan, see 958.7

.408 1991–

[.408 01–.408 09] Standard subdivisions

Do not use; class in 958.408

.5 *Turkmenistan

.508 1991–

[.508 01–.508 09] Standard subdivisions

Do not use; class in 958.508

.6 *Tajikistan

.608 1991–

[.608 01–.608 09] Standard subdivisions

Do not use; class in 958.608

.7 *Uzbekistan

.708 1991–

[.708 01–.708 09] Standard subdivisions

Do not use; class in 958.708

959 *Southeast Asia

.05 1900–

.1 *Myanmar (Burma)

*Add as instructed under 930–990

.105   1948–

.3   *Thailand

.304   1910–

.4   *Laos

.404   1949–

> Class here 20th century

> Class 1900–1949 in 959.4; class military operations in Laos during Vietnamese War in 959.704

.5   *Commonwealth of Nations territories   Malaysia

.505   Period of federation, 1963–

> Class here 20th century

> Class 1900–1963 in 959.5

.55   *Brunei

.550 5   1984–

> Use of this number for 1946–1983 discontinued; class in 959.55

.57   *Singapore

.570 5   Periods of federation with Malaysia, 1963–1965, and separate nationhood, 1965–

> Class here 20th century

> Class 1900–1963 in 959.57

.6   *Cambodia (Khmer Republic, Kampuchea)

.604   1949–

> Class here 20th century

> Class 1900–1949 in 959.6; class military operations in Cambodia during Vietnamese War in 959.704

.7   *Vietnam

.704   1949–

> Including Vietnamese War, 1961–1975

.8   *Indonesia

*Add as instructed under 930–990

.803   Period of Republic, 1945–

Class here 20th century

Class 1900–1945 in 959.8

For 2000 and beyond, see 959.804

.804   2000–

.9   *Philippines

.904   Period of Republic, 1946–

960   General history of Africa

SUMMARY

960.01–.09	**Standard subdivisions**
.3	**1885–**
961	**Tunisia and Libya**
962	**Egypt and Sudan**
963	**Ethiopia and Eritrea**
964	**Northwest African coast and offshore islands Morocco**
965	**Algeria**
966	**West Africa and offshore islands**
967	**Central Africa and offshore islands**
968	**Southern Africa Republic of South Africa**
969	**South Indian Ocean islands**

.01–.09   Standard subdivisions

As modified under 930–990

.3   1885–

961   *Tunisia and Libya

For early history to ca. 640, see 939

.04   1950–1999

.05   2000–

.1   *Tunisia

For early history to 647, see 939

.105   1956–

.2   *Libya

For early history to 644, see 939

.204   1952–

*Add as instructed under 930–990

962   Egypt and Sudan

For early history to 640, see 932

.000 1–.000 9   Standard subdivisions of Egypt and Sudan

As modified under 930–990

.001–.009   Standard subdivisions of Egypt

As modified under 930–990

.05   Egypt since 1922

Class Israel-Arab wars of 1948–1949, 1967, and 1973, Sinai Campaign, 1956, in 956.04

.4   *Sudan

For parts of Sudan, see 962.5–962.9

.404   1956–

963   *Ethiopia and Eritrea

Subdivisions are added for Ethiopia and Eritrea together, for Ethiopia alone

See also 939 for ancient Ethiopia (a part of what is now modern Sudan, not modern Ethiopia)

.07   1974–

.5   *Eritrea

.507   1974–

964   Northwest African coast and offshore islands   Morocco

For early history of Morocco to 647, see 939

[.000 1–.000 9]   Standard subdivisions of northwest African coast and offshore islands

Relocated to 964.001–964.009

.001–.009   Standard subdivisions of northwest African coast and offshore islands [*formerly* 964.0001–964.0009], of Morocco

As modified under 930–990

.05   Morocco since 1956

965   *Algeria

For early history to 647, see 939

.05   1962–

---

*Add as instructed under 930–990

966   *West Africa and offshore islands

.03   1885–

.1   *Mauritania

.105   1960–

.2   *Mali, Burkina Faso, Niger

.203   1960–

.23   *Mali

.230 5   1960–

.25   *Burkina Faso

.250 5   1960–

.26   *Niger

.260 5   1960–

.3   *Senegal

.305   1960–

> Including Confederation of Senegambia, 1982 to present
>
> *For Gambian part of Senegambia, see 966.5103*

.4   *Sierra Leone

.404   1961–

.5   *Gambia, Guinea, Guinea-Bissau, Cape Verde

.51   *Gambia

.510 3   1965–

> Including period as a part of Senegambia, 1982 to present
>
> Class comprehensive works on Senegambia in 966.305

.52   *Guinea

.520 5   1958–

.57   *Guinea-Bissau

.570 3   1974–

.58   *Cape Verde

.580 3   1975–

.6   Liberia and Côte d'Ivoire

---

*Add as instructed under 930–990

.62	*Liberia
.620 3	1945–
.68	*Côte d'Ivoire (Ivory Coast)
.680 5	1960–
.7	***Ghana**

See also 966.1 for Ghana Empire

.705	1957–
.8	**Togo and Benin**
.81	*Togo
.810 4	1960–
.83	*Benin

See also 966.9 for kingdom of Benin

.830 5	1960–
.9	***Nigeria**
.905	1960–

967 *Central Africa and offshore islands

.03	1885–
.1	***Cameroon, Sao Tome and Principe, Equatorial Guinea**
.11	*Cameroon
.110 4	1960–
.15	*Sao Tome and Principe
.150 2	Period of Republic, 1975–
.18	*Equatorial Guinea
.180 3	1968–
.2	***Gabon and Republic of the Congo**
.205	1959–
.21	*Gabon
.210 4	1960–
.24	*Republic of the Congo
.240 5	1960–

*Add as instructed under 930–990

.3	***Angola**
.304	1975–
.4	***Central African Republic and Chad**
.41	*Central African Republic
.410 5	1960–
.43	*Chad
.430 4	1960–
.5	**Zaire, Rwanda, Burundi**
.51	*Zaire
.510 3	1960–
.57	*Rwanda and Burundi
	Class here former Ruanda-Urundi
.570 4	1962–
.571	*Rwanda
.571 04	1962–
.572	*Burundi
.572 04	1962–
.6	***Uganda and Kenya**
.604	1961–
.61	*Uganda
.610 4	1962–
.62	*Kenya
.620 4	1963–
.7	***Djibouti and Somalia**
	Class here Somaliland
.71	*Djibouti
.710 4	1977–
.73	*Somalia
.730 5	1960–
.8	***Tanzania**

*Add as instructed under 930–990

.804	Period as United Republic, 1964–
.9	***Mozambique**
.905	1975–

968   *Southern Africa   Republic of South Africa

.000 1–.000 9   Standard subdivisions of southern Africa [*formerly* 968.001–968.009]

> As modified under 930–990

.001–.009   Standard subdivisions of Republic of South Africa

> As modified under 930–990
>
> Standard subdivisions of southern Africa relocated to 968.0001–968.0009

> 968.02–968.06   Historical periods of Republic of South Africa

> Class comprehensive works in 968

.02	Early history to 1488
.03	Period of European exploration and settlement, 1488–1814
.04	1814–1910
.05	Period of Union, 1910–1961
.06	Period as Republic, 1961–
.8	***Namibia, Botswana, Lesotho, Swaziland**
.803	1885–
.81	*Namibia
.810 3	South African period, 1915–1990
.810 4	1990–
.83	*Botswana
.830 3	1966–
.85	*Lesotho
.850 3	1966–
.87	*Swaziland
.870 3	1968–
.9	***Zimbabwe, Zambia, Malawi**

*Add as instructed under 930–990

.904	1964–
.91	*Zimbabwe
.910 5	Period as Republic of Zimbabwe, 1980–
.94	*Zambia
.940 4	Period as Republic of Zambia, 1964–
.97	*Malawi
.970 4	1964–

969   *South Indian Ocean islands

.1   *Madagascar

.105   1960–

970   General history of North America

SUMMARY

970.001–.009	**Standard subdivisions**
.01–.05	**Historical periods**
971	**Canada**
972	**Middle America Mexico**
973	**United States**
974–979	**Specific states of United States**

.001–.003   Standard subdivisions

.004   North American native peoples

> Class history and civilization of North American native peoples in a specific place with the place, e.g., the Hopi in Arizona 979.1004
>
> *See Manual at 970.004*
>
> (Option: Class North American native peoples in North America in 970.1; class specific native peoples in 970.3)

[.004 01–.004 09]   Standard subdivisions

> Do not use; class in 970.004

.005–.007   Standard subdivisions

.008   History with respect to kinds of persons

[.008 9]   Racial, ethnic, national groups

> Do not use for racial, ethnic, national groups other than North American native peoples; class in 970. Do not use for North American native peoples; class in 970.004

*Add as instructed under 930–990

.009   Persons

> Description, critical appraisal, biography of persons associated with the history of North America but limited to no specific period
>
> Class historians and historiographers in 970; class persons of a specific period in 970.01–970.05, plus notation 092 from Table 1

>   970.01–970.05   Historical periods
>
> Class comprehensive works in 970

.01   Early history to 1599

.02   1600–1699

.03   1700–1799

.04   1800–1899

.05   1900–

.051   1900–1918

> Class here period of World War I, 1914–1918

.052   1918–1945

> Class here period of World War II, 1939–1945

.053   1945–1999

> Class here 20th century
>
> *For 1900–1918, see 970.051; for 1918–1945, see 970.052*

.054   2000–

(.1)   **North American native peoples**   **Indians of North America**

> (Optional number; prefer 970.004)
>
> Class special topics in 970.3–970.5

(.3)   **Specific native peoples**

> (Optional number; prefer 971–979, plus notation 004 from table under 971–979, e.g., the Hopi in Arizona 979.1004)
>
> Class government relations with specific native peoples in 970.5

(.4) **Native peoples in specific places in North America**

(Optional number; prefer 971–979, plus notation 004 from table under 971–979, e.g., native peoples in United States 973.04, in Arizona 979.1004)

Add to base number 970.4 the numbers following —7 in notation 71–79 from Table 2, e.g., Indians in Arizona 970.491

Class specific native peoples in specific places in 970.3; class government relations in specific places in 970.5

(.5) **Government relations with North American native peoples**

(Optional number; prefer 323.1 for comprehensive works; a specific subject with the subject, e.g., Black Hawk War 973.5)

History and policy

> ## 971–979   Countries and localities

Add to base number 97 the numbers following —7 in notation 71–79 from
Table 2, e.g., general history of Canada 971, of Quebec 971.4; then add further
as follows:

001–003	Standard subdivisions
004	North American native peoples
	(Option: Class specific native peoples in 970.3, native peoples in specific places in North America in 970.4)
[00401–00409]	Standard subdivisions
	Do not use; class in 004
005–007	Standard subdivisions
008	History with respect to kinds of persons
[0089]	Racial, ethnic, national groups
	Do not use for North American native peoples; class in 004. Do not use for racial, ethnic, national groups other than North American native peoples; class in 971–979 without adding from this table
009	Persons
	Description, critical appraisal, biography of persons associated with the history of the continent, country, locality but limited to no specific period
	Class historians and historiographers in 971–979 without adding from this table
	Persons of a specific period which is set forth in the 971–979 schedules are classed in 01–09, plus notation 092 from Table 1; persons of other periods are classed in 971–979 without adding from this table
01–09	Historical periods
	Use historical period notation only when it is specifically set forth in the 971–979 schedules, e.g., period of 1791–1841 in Canadian history 971.03
	Class here indigenous groups in the prehistoric period, e.g., Canadian native peoples before European settlement 971.01
	Class North American native peoples in a specific period in 004; class areas, regions, places in general and racial, ethnic, national groups other than North American native peoples in a specific period in 971–979 without adding from this table
	See Manual at 930–990: Biography; also at 930–990: Add table: 01–09

Class comprehensive works in 970

*See Manual at 930–990; also at 305 vs. 306, 909, 930–990; also at
333.7–333.9 vs. 508, 913–919, 930–990; also at 909, 930–990 vs. 320; also
at 909, 930–990 vs. 320.4, 321, 321.09; also at 909, 930–990 vs. 910; also
at 930–990 vs. 355.009*

971   †Canada

†Add as instructed under 971–979

.01   Early history to 1763

Class North American aspects of War of the League of Augsburg, War of
the Spanish Succession, War of the Austrian Succession, Seven Years' War
in 973.2; class comprehensive works on War of the League of Augsburg,
War of the Spanish Succession, War of the Austrian Succession, Seven
Years' War in 940.2

(Option: Class here North American aspects of War of the League of
Augsburg, War of the Spanish Succession, War of the Austrian Succession,
Seven Years' War; prefer 973.2)

.02   Period of early British rule, 1763–1791

.03   Period of Upper and Lower Canada, 1791–1841

Class here 19th century

For 1841–1867, see 971.04; for 1867–1899, see 971.05

(Option: Class here War of 1812; prefer 973.5)

.04   Period of Province of Canada, 1841–1867

.05   Period of Dominion of Canada, 1867–

For 1911 to present, see 971.06

.06   1911–

.061   1911–1921

.062   1921–1935

.063   1935–1957

.064   1957–

972   Middle America   Mexico

.000 1–.000 9   Standard subdivisions of Middle America

As modified under 971–979

.001–.009   Standard subdivisions of Mexico

As modified under 971–979

.08   Mexico since 1867

\>   **972.8–972.9 Other parts of Middle America**

Class comprehensive works in 972

.8   †Central America

†Add as instructed under 971–979

.805	1900–
.81	†Guatemala
.810 5	1871–
.82	†Belize
.820 5	1964–
.83	†Honduras
.830 5	1838–
.84	†El Salvador
.840 5	1859–
.85	†Nicaragua
.850 5	1893–
.86	†Costa Rica
.860 5	1948–

> Class here 20th century
>
> Class 1900–1948 in 972.86

.87	†Panama
.870 5	1903–

.9 †West Indies (Antilles) and Bermuda

Class here Caribbean Area

For a part of Caribbean Area not provided for here, see the part, e.g., Venezuela 987

.905	1902–
.91	†Cuba
.910 6	1899–

> Class here period of Republic, 1902 to present

.92	†Jamaica and Cayman Islands

Subdivisions are added for Jamaica and Cayman Islands together, for Jamaica alone

.920 6	Jamaica since 1962
.93	†Dominican Republic
.930 5	1902–

†Add as instructed under 971–979

.94	†Haiti
.940 7	1957–
.95	†Puerto Rico
.950 5	1900–
.98	†Windward and other southern islands
.983	†Trinidad and Tobago
.983 04	1962–

973   United States

For specific states, see 974–979

.01–.09   Standard subdivisions

As modified under 971–979

.1   Early history to 1607

.2   Colonial period, 1607–1775

Including King William's War (North American aspects of War of the League of Augsburg), 1688–1697; Queen Anne's War (North American aspects of War of the Spanish Succession), 1701–1714; King George's War (North American aspects of War of the Austrian Succession), 1740–1748; French and Indian War (North American aspects of Seven Years' War), 1756–1763

(Option: Class North American aspects of War of the League of Augsburg, War of the Spanish Succession, War of the Austrian Succession, Seven Years' War in 971.01)

Class events of 1763–1775 as causes of American Revolution in 973.3; class comprehensive works on War of the League of Augsburg, War of the Spanish Succession, War of the Austrian Succession, Seven Years' War in 940.2

.3   Periods of Revolution and Confederation, 1775–1789

.4   Constitutional period, 1789–1809

Including Tripolitan War, 1801–1805

.5   1809–1845

Including War of 1812; War with Algiers, 1815
(Option: Class War of 1812 in 971.03)

Class here 19th century

Class events of 1809–1845 as causes of Civil War in 973.7

For a specific part of 19th century not provided for here, see the part, e.g., Civil War 973.7

†Add as instructed under 971–979

.6   1845–1861

Including Mexican War, 1845–1848

Class events of 1845–1861 as causes of Civil War in 973.7

.7   Administration of Abraham Lincoln, 1861–1865   Civil War

.709 2   Persons

Do not use for personal narratives; class in 973.7

.8   Reconstruction period, 1865–1901

Including Spanish-American War, 1898

.9   1901–

.91   1901–1953

Class here 20th century

For 1900–1901, see 973.8; for 1953–1999, see 973.92

.917   Administration of Franklin Delano Roosevelt, 1933–1945

.918   Administration of Harry S Truman, 1945–1953

.92   1953–

.921   Administration of Dwight David Eisenhower, 1953–1961

.922   Administration of John Fitzgerald Kennedy, 1961–1963

.923   Administration of Lyndon Baines Johnson, 1963–1969

.924   Administration of Richard Milhous Nixon, 1969–1974

.925   Administration of Gerald Rudolph Ford, 1974–1977

.926   Administration of Jimmy (James Earl) Carter, 1977–1981

.927   Administration of Ronald Reagan, 1981–1989

.928   Administration of George Bush, 1989–1993

.929   Administration of Bill Clinton, 1993–

974–979 Specific states of United States

Add to base number 97 the numbers following —7 in notation 74–79 from Table 2, e.g., Arizona 979.1; then add further as instructed under 971–979, e.g., Indians of Arizona 979.1004

Class comprehensive works in 973

For Hawaii, see 996.9

980   General history of South America

Class here Latin America

For Middle America, see 972

.001–.009   Standard subdivisions

As modified under 930–990

.03   1830–1999

.04   2000–

981   *Brazil

.06   Period of Second Republic, 1930–

Class here 20th century

Class 1901–1930 in 981

982   *Argentina

.06   1910–

983   *Chile

.06   1861–

Including War of the Pacific, 1879–1883

984   *Bolivia

For War of the Pacific, see 983.06

.05   1899–

985   *Peru

.06   1867–

For War of the Pacific, see 983.06

986   *Colombia and Ecuador

.1   *Colombia

.106   1863–

.6   *Ecuador

.607   1896–

987   *Venezuela

.06   Period of Republic, 1830–

---

*Add as instructed under 930–990

988 *Guiana

.03   1945–

> Class here 20th century
>
> Class 1901–1945 in 988

.1   *Guyana

.103   1945–

> Class here 20th century
>
> Class 1901–1945 in 988.1

.3   *Surinam (Suriname)

.303   1945–

> Class here 20th century
>
> Class 1901–1945 in 988.3

989   Paraguay and Uruguay

.2   *Paraguay

.207   1902–

.5   *Uruguay

.506   1886–

990   General history of other parts of world, of extraterrestrial worlds   Pacific Ocean islands

.01–.09   Standard subdivisions of Pacific Ocean islands

> As modified under 930–990

993   *New Zealand

.01   Early history to 1840

> Including history of Maoris before European settlement, of European settlers

.02   Colonial period, 1840–1908

.03   Dominion period, 1908–

[.1]   Specific islands

> Number discontinued; class in 993

---

*Add as instructed under 930–990

994   *Australia

.01   Early history to 1788

.02   Period of settlement and growth, 1788–1851

.03   Period of development of self government, 1851–1901

.04   Period of Commonwealth, 1901–

Class here 20th century

> For 1945–1966, see 994.05; for 1966–1999, see 994.06; for 2000 and beyond, see 994.07

.05   1945–1966

.06   1966–1999

.07   2000–

995   *Melanesia   New Guinea

Class here Oceania

Class Polynesia in 996

.3   *Papua New Guinea   New Guinea region

> For Papuan region, see 995.4; for Highlands region, see 995.6; for Momase region, see 995.7; for Bismarck Archipelago, see 995.8; for North Solomons Province, see 995.92

.305   Period of independence, 1975–

996   Other parts of Pacific   Polynesia

.001–.009   Standard subdivisions of Polynesia

As modified under 930–990

.9   North central Pacific islands   Hawaii

.900 01–.900 09   Standard subdivisions of north central Pacific islands

As modified under 930–990

.900 1–.900 9   Standard subdivisions of Hawaii

As modified under 930–990

997   *Atlantic Ocean islands

> For each specific island or group of islands not provided for here, see the island or group of islands, e.g., Azores 946.9

998   *Arctic islands and Antarctica

*Add as instructed under 930–990

999   Extraterrestrial worlds

Class here extraterrestrial civilization

Do not add from table under 930–990

Relative Index

Use of the Relative Index

Full instructions on the use of the Relative Index are found in section 11 of the Introduction to the Dewey Decimal Classification.

Alphabetizing is word by word. A hyphenated word is filed as two words. Initialisms and acronyms are entered without punctuation and are filed as if spelled as one word.

The first class number displayed in an index entry (the unindented term) is the number for interdisciplinary works. If the term also appears in a table, the table number is listed next, followed by subentries arranged in alphabetical order. See-also references or see-Manual references come at the end of the alphabet of subentries or under the subentry to which the reference applies. See-Manual references follow see-also references under the same term.

Digits are printed in groups of three for ease in reading and copying. The spaces are not part of the numbers, and the groups are not related to the segmentation shown in DDC numbers on Library of Congress cataloging records.

The abbreviations used in this index are:

T1	Table 1	Standard Subdivisions	T3	Table 3	Subdivisions for Individual Literatures, for Specific Literary Forms
T2	Table 2	Geographic Areas, and Persons			
			T4	Table 4	Subdivisions of Individual Languages

B.C.	Before Christ	N.Y.	New York
Colo.	Colorado	N.Z.	New Zealand
D.C.	District of Columbia	Nfld.	Newfoundland
Inc.	Incorporated	Ont.	Ontario
Md.	Maryland	Qld.	Queensland
Mich.	Michigan	S. Aust.	South Australia
N.S.W.	New South Wales	U.S.	United States of America
N.W.T.	Northwest Territories	Va.	Virginia

A

Aardvark	599.3
Abandoned children	305.9
	T1—086
social services	362.73
Abbreviations	411
specific languages	T4—1
Ability grouping in education	371.2
Ability testing	153.9
Abkhaz language	499
Abnormal psychology	616.89
see also Mental illness	
Abolition of slavery	326
Abominable snowman	001.944
Aborigines	306.08
Abortion	363.46
demographic effect	304.6
ethics	179.7
religion	291.5
Christianity	241
Judaism	296.3
law	342
social problem	363.46
law	344
social theology	291.1
Christianity	261.8
Judaism	296.3
surgery	618.8
Abrasives	
mineral resources	553.6
Absentee ownership	
land economics	333
Absenteeism	331.25
personnel management	658.3
Abstinence	178
Abstract algebra	512
Abstract thought	153.2
Abstracting techniques	025.402 8
information science	025.402 8
rhetoric	808
Abstractionism	709.04
painting	759.06
Abused children	305.9
	T1—086
pediatrics	618.92
social welfare	362.76
see also Child abuse	
Abyssinia	T2—63
Academic costume	378.2
Academic degrees	378.2
Academic freedom	371.1
higher education	378.1

Academic high schools	373.24
Academic libraries	027.7
Academic placement	371.26
Academic prognosis	371.26
Academic year	371.2
Access control (Computers)	005.8
Accessories (Clothing)	391.4
customs	391.4
home sewing	646.4
see also Clothing	
Accident insurance	368.38
industrial casualty	368.7
Accident investigation	363.1
see Manual at 363.1 vs. 620.8	
Accidents	363.1
personal safety	613.6
psychology	155.9
social services	363.1
public administration	353.9
tort law	346.03
see also Safety	
Acclimatization	
animals	591.4
biology	578.4
plants	581.4
Accompaniment	
musical technique	781.47
Accordions	788.8
Accountability	
public administration	352.3
public education	379.1
teachers	371.14
Accountants	657.092
Accounting	657
see Manual at 657 vs. 658.15	
Accreditation	352.8
education	379.1
Accreditation of prior learning	371.26
Acculturation	303.48
Achievement tests	371.26
Acid rain	363.738
meteorology	551.57
weather forecasting	551.64
see also Pollution	
Acids	546
chemical engineering	661
Acne	
medicine	616.5
Acoustical communications	
engineering	621.382
Acoustical engineering	620.2
Acoustical engineers	620.209 2

Acoustics	534
architectural design	729
engineering	620.2
Acquired immune deficiency	
syndrome	362.1
incidence	614.5
medicine	616.97
social services	362.1
Acquisition of territory	325
Acquisitions (Libraries)	025.2
Acrobatics	796.47
circuses	791.3
sports	796.47
Acronyms	411
specific languages	T4—1
Acrostics	793.73
Acting	792
motion pictures	791.43
radio	791.44
stage	792
television	791.45
Actors	792
motion pictures	791.43
radio	791.44
stage	792
television	791.45
see Manual at 791.092	
Acts of the Apostles	226.6
Acupressure	
therapeutics	615.8
Acupuncture	
therapeutics	615.8
Adaptability	
psychology	155.2
children	155.4
late adulthood	155.67
situational influences	155.9
Adaptation (Biology)	578.4
animals	591.4
plants	581.4
Addiction	362.29
customs	394.1
pastoral theology	291.6
Christianity	259
social welfare	362.29
see also Substance abuse	
Addicts	T1—087
Addition	512.9
algebra	512.9
arithmetic	513.2
Addresses	080
Adhesives	668
Adjudication	347
international law	341.5

Adjustment (Psychology)	155.2
children	155.4
late adulthood	155.67
Adlerian psychology	150.19
Administration	658
	T1—068
see Manual at 658 and	
T1—068	
Administration of estates	346.05
Administration of justice	347
Administrative agencies	351
see also Executive	
departments	
see Manual at 352–354	
Administrative law	342
Administrative regulations	
(Compilations)	348
Administrative reports	T1—06
Admiralty law	343.09
Admission to schools	371.2
Adobe	
building construction	693
Adolescence	305.235
human physiology	612.6
psychology	155.5
social aspects	305.235
Adolescent development	305.235
psychology	155.5
Adolescent medicine	616.008 35
Adolescent psychiatry	616.890 083 5
Adolescent psychology	155.5
Adolescents	305.235
	T1—083 5
etiquette	395.1
labor economics	331.3
libraries for	027.62
physiology	612.6
psychology	155.5
reading	
library science	028.5
religion	200.835
Christianity	270.083 5
guides to life	248.8
pastoral care of	259
religious education	268
social theology	261.8
Judaism	296.083 5
guides to life	296.708 35
religious education	296.6
social welfare	362.708 3
public administration	353.536
Adopted children	306.874
psychology	155.44

Africa, Southern	968
	T2—68
Africa, Sub-Saharan	967
	T2—67
Africa, West	966
	T2—66
African Americans	973
social group	305.896
African independent churches	289.9
African languages	496
African literature	808.8
history and criticism	809
in African languages	896
African religions	299
Africans	960
social group	305.896
Afrikaans language	439.3
Afrikaners	
social group	305.83
Afro-Americans	973
social group	305.896
Afro-Asiatic languages	492
non-Semitic	493
Afro-Asiatic peoples	
social group	305.89
After-dinner speeches	
literature	808.85
history and criticism	809.5
specific literatures	T3—5
rhetoric	808.5
Agaricales	579.6
Age characteristics	
physical anthropology	599.93
Age discrimination in	
employment	331.3
Age groups	305.2
Aged persons	305.26
	T1—084
see also Older persons	
Agency law	346.02
Aggadah	296.1
Aggression	302.5
law of war	341.6
psychology	155.2
drives	153.8
emotions	152.4
personality trait	155.2
social psychology	302.5
Aging	571.8
biology	571.8
human physiology	612.6
psychology of late adulthood	155.67
Agnosticism	211
philosophy	149

Agnosticism (continued)	
philosophy of religion	211
Agoraphobia	
medicine	616.85
Agricultural banks	332.3
Agricultural chemicals	631.8
Agricultural commodities	338.1
public administration	354.5
Agricultural cooperatives	334
Agricultural credit	332.7
Agricultural ecology	577.5
Agricultural economics	338.1
Agricultural enterprises	338.7
Agricultural equipment	631.3
manufacturing technology	681
Agricultural genetics	631.5
Agricultural industries	338.1
Agricultural lands	333.76
Agricultural machinery	631.3
manufacturing technology	681
Agricultural marketing	
public administration	354.5
Agricultural pests	632
Agricultural products	338.1
Agricultural structures	631.2
Agricultural workers	630.92
economics	331.7
Agriculture	630
economics	338.1
law	343
public administration	354.5
Agriculture and state	338.1
Agroforestry	634.9
Aid to families with dependent	
children	362.71
AIDS (Disease)	362.1
incidence	614.5
medicine	616.97
social services	362.1
Air bases	358.4
Air compression technology	621.5
Air conditioning	
buildings	697.9
Air-cushion vehicles	
engineering	629.3
see also Automotive vehicles	
Air forces	358.4
Air pilots	629.130 92
Air pollution	363.739
ecology	577.27
social welfare	363.739
technology	628.5
Air raid shelters	363.3
military engineering	623

Aliens (continued)
legal status	346.01
constitutional law	342
private law	346.01
Alimony	346.01
Aliphatic compounds	547
Alkaloidal plants	581.6
agriculture	633.7
Alkaloids	572
chemistry	547
All-age schools	371
All-terrain vehicles	388.3
engineering	629.22
All-volunteer army	355.2
Allah	297.2
Allegory	
paintings	753
Allergies (Human)	
medicine	616.97
Alliances	327.1
Allied health personnel	610.73
medicine	610.73
role and function	610.69
Alligators	597.98
Allosaurus	567.912
Alloys	669
materials science	620.1
metallurgy	669
Almanacs	030
Almanacs (Ephemerides)	528
Almsgiving	291.4
Christianity	248.4
Islam	297.5
Alphabets	411
decorative arts	745.6
specific languages	T4—1
Alpine plants	581.7
floriculture	635.9
Alps	T2—494
Altaic languages	494
Altered states of consciousness	154.4
Alternating current	621.31
Alternative energy resources	333.79
economics	333.79
engineering	621.042
Alternative medicine	610
health	613
therapeutics	615.5
Alternative schools	371.04
Altitude sickness	
medicine	616.9
Altruism	
ethical systems	171
personality trait	155.2

Aluminum	669
chemistry	546
metallurgy	669
metalworking	673
Alzheimer's disease	362.1
geriatrics	618.97
medicine	616.8
social services	362.1
Amateur radio	384.54
communications services	384.54
engineering	621.384 1
see Manual at 621.3841 vs. 621.3845	
Amateur sports	796.04
see Manual at 796.08 vs. 796.04	
Amazon River	T2—81
Amber	553.8
Ambition	
social psychology	302.5
Ambulance services	362.18
American English dialects (U.S.)	427
American Federation of Labor and Congress of Industrial Organizations	331.880 973
American football	796.332
American Indian languages	497
South America	498
American Indians	970.004
see also Native American peoples	
American Legion	369
American literature (English)	810
American native languages	497
South America	498
American native peoples	970.004
see also Native American peoples	
American Reformed Church	285.7
American Revolution, 1775–1783	973.3
American Sign Language	419
American Veterans of World War II, Korea, and Vietnam	369
Americans (U.S.)	973
social group	305.813
Amhara (African people)	
social group	305.892
Amharic language	492
Amino acids	572
Amish churches	289.7
Ammonia	546
chemical engineering	661

Animal diseases	571.9
veterinary medicine	636.089
Animal ecology	591.7
Animal experimentation	571.107
medicine	619
Animal feeds	636.08
animal husbandry	636.08
commercial processing	664
Animal hormones	573.4
Animal hospitals	636.08
Animal husbandry	636
Animal industry	338.1
Animal intelligence	591.5
Animal language	591.59
Animal migration	591.56
Animal pest control	363.7
Animal pests	591.6
Animal physiology	571.1
see Manual at 571–575	
Animal populations	591.7
Animal psychology	591.5
comparative psychology	156
Animal resources	333.95
see Manual at 338.3 vs.	
333.95	
Animal rights	
ethics	179
Animal sounds	591.59
Animal viruses	579.2
Animal weapons	591.47
Animal welfare	636.08
Animals	590
agricultural pests	632
agriculture	636
art representation	704.9
conservation	333.95
conservation technology	639.9
see Manual at 333.95 vs.	
639.9	
drawing	743.6
folklore	398.24
food source	
agriculture	636.088
growth	571.8
painting	758
physiology	571.1
see Manual at 571–575	
resource economics	333.95
see Manual at 333.95 vs.	
639.9	
treatment of	
ethics	179

Animals (continued)	
zoology	590
see Manual at 800 vs. 398.24,	
590, 636	
Animated cartoons	
cinematography	778.5
drawing	741.5
motion pictures	791.43
Ankylosauria	567.915
Anniversaries	394.2
Annuals (Plants)	582.1
floriculture	635.9
Annuals (Publications)	050
	T1—05
almanacs	030
encyclopedia yearbooks	030
Annuities	
insurance	368.3
personal finance	332.024
Anonymous works	
bibliographies	014
Anorexia nervosa	362.2
medicine	616.85
social welfare	362.2
Anseriformes	598.4
Answers	
study and teaching	T1—076
Antarctic regions	T2—98
Antarctic waters	T2—167
Antarctica	T2—98
Anteaters	599.3
Antelopes	599.64
Antennas	621.382
Anthologies	080
literature	808.8
specific literatures	T3—08
see Manual at 080 vs. 800;	
also at 081–089	
Anthozoa	593.6
paleontology	563
Anthropology	301
philosophical	128
physical	599.9
theological	291.2
Christianity	233
philosophy of religion	218
Anthropometry	599.9
Anthroposophy	299
Anti-Semitism	305.892
political aspects	323.1
Anti-Trinitarianism	289.1
Antibiotics	615
Antichrist	236

Aptitude tests	153.9
education	371.26
see Manual at 153.9	
Aptitudes	
psychology	153.9
'Aqā'id (Islam)	297.2
Aquaculture	639.8
economics	338.3
Aquariums	597.073
fish culture	639.34
Aquatic animals	591.76
Aquatic biological resources	354.5
Aquatic biology	578.76
see Manual at 578.76–578.77	
vs. 551.46	
Aquatic birds	598.176
Aquatic ecology	577.6
Aquatic gardens	635.9
botany	581.7
Aquatic plants	581.7
Aquatic resources	333.91
Aquatic sports	797
Aquatinting	766
Aquifers	553.7
hydrology	551.49
Arab countries	T2—17
Arab League	341.24
Arabia	953
	T2—53
ancient	939
	T2—39
Arabia Deserta	T2—39
Arabian Peninsula	953
	T2—53
Arabic language	492.7
Arabic literature	892.7
Arabs	
civilization	909
social group	305.892
Arachnids	595.4
Arafura Sea	T2—164
Aramaic languages	492
Arbitration	
international law	341.5
labor economics	331.89
law	347
personnel management	658.3
Arcade games	794.8
see Manual at 793.93 vs.	
794.8	
Archaeocyatha	563
Archaeologists	930.109 2
Archaeology	930.1
ancient places	931–939

Archaeology (continued)	
Bible	220.9
modern places	940–990
Archery	799.3
Architects	720.92
Architectural decoration	729
see Manual at 729	
Architectural design	729
see Manual at 729	
Architectural drawing	720.28
Architectural drawings	720.22
Architectural schools and styles	720.9
ancient	722
construction details	721
Architecture	720
religious significance	291.3
Christianity	246
Archives	027
see also Libraries	
Archosaurs	567.9
Arctic fox	599.776
Arctic islands	T2—98
Arctic Ocean	T2—163
Area planning	307.1
arts	711
community sociology	307.1
Area studies	940–990
Argentina	982
	T2—82
Argentine literature	860
Argentine Republic	T2—82
Argentines	982
Argument (Logic)	168
Arianism	273
Arid lands	551.41
	T2—15
biology	578.754
ecology	577.54
economics	333.73
geomorphology	551.41
Aristocracy	305.5
political system	321.5
Aristotelian philosophy	185
modern	149
Arithmetic	513
elementary education	372.7
Arizona	T2—791
Arkansas	T2—767
Armadillos	599.3
Armed services	355
law	343
life insurance	368.36
relation to state	322

Arts (continued)	
sociology	306.4
see Manual at 700	
Arts and crafts	745
Aruba	T2—729 8
Asbestos	553.6
technology	666
Ascension of Jesus Christ	232.9
Asceticism	291.4
Christianity	248.4
Asexual reproduction	571.8
plants	575.4
Asia	950
	T2—5
Asia, Central	958
	T2—58
Asia, Southeastern	959
	T2—59
Asia Minor	956.1
	T2—561
ancient	939
	T2—39
Asian Americans	
social group	305.895
Asian languages	490
Asians	950
social group	305.895
Asiatic cholera	
medicine	616.9
Asphalt	553.2
economic geology	553.2
petroleum product	665.5
Assamese language	491.4
Assault and battery	364.15
law	345
Assaying	
metallurgy	669
Assemblers (Computer	
programs)	005.4
Assemblies of God	289.9
Assembly languages	005.13
Assembly-line processes	670.42
production management	658.5
technology	670.42
Assertiveness training	
applied psychology	158.2
Asses	636.1
animal husbandry	636.1
zoology	599.665
Assimilation (Sociology)	303.48
Assisted suicide	
ethics	179.7
Association	302.3
Association football	796.334

Association of ideas	
psychology	153.2
Associations	060
fraternal organizations	366
see also Organizations	
Associative learning	
psychology	153.1
Assyria	935
	T2—35
Asteroids	523.44
Asthma	
medicine	616.2
Astigmatism	
optometry	617.7
Astral projection	133.9
Astrobiology	576.8
Astrodomes	796.06
Astrology	133.5
Astromechanics	
engineering	629.4
Astronautical engineering	629.47
Astronautical engineers	629.409 2
Astronautics	629.4
Astronauts	629.450 092
Astronomers	520.92
Astronomical almanacs	528
Astronomical geography	525
Astronomy	520
see Manual at 520 vs. 523.1,	
523.8	
Astrophysics	523.01
Asylum	323.6
international law	341.4
law	342
Atheism	211
Atherosclerosis	
medicine	616.1
Athletes	796.092
health	613.7
Athletic fields	796.420 6
Athletic games	796
Athletic sports	796
Atlantic Coastal Plain	T2—75
Atlantic Islands	997
	T2—97
Atlantic Ocean	T2—163
see Manual at T2—163,	
T2—164, T2—165 vs.	
T2—182	
Atlantic Provinces	T2—715
Atlantic Region	T2—182
Atlantis	001.94
folklore	398.23

Atlases	912
	T1—022
see Manual at 912 vs.	
T1—022	
Atmosphere	551.5
	T2—161
Atmospheric electricity	551.56
Atmospheric optics	551.56
Atmospheric pressure	551.5
Atmospheric radiation	
meteorology	551.5
Atolls	551.42
Atomic bomb	355.8
see also Nuclear weapons	
Atomic energy	333.792
law	343.09
physics	539.7
Atomic physics	539.7
Atomic structure	539
chemistry	541.2
Atomic weight	541.2
Atoms	539.7
Atonality	781.2
Atonement	291.2
Atonement of Jesus Christ	232
Attack (Military science)	355.4
Attention	
psychology	
learning	153.1
perception	153.7
Attention deficit disorder	
medicine	616.85
pediatrics	618.92
Attitudes	152.4
psychology	152.4
sociology	303.3
Attributes of God	212
Christianity	231
comparative religion	291.2
philosophy of religion	212
Auction catalogs	T1—029
Auctions	381
management	658.8
Audiologists	617.809 2
Audiology	617.8
Audiovisual engineering	621.389
Audiovisual materials	
bibliographies	011
cataloging	025.3
instructional use	371.33
library treatment	025.17
reviews	028.1
Auditing	657
Auditory memory	153.1

Augsburg, War of the League of,	
1688–1697	940.2
North American history	973.2
Aura	
parapsychology	133.8
Auroras (Geomagnetism)	538
Australasia	T2—9
Australia	994
	T2—94
Australian aboriginal languages	499
Australian aborigines	
social group	305.89
Australian Capital	
Territory	T2—947
Australian literature (English)	820
Australians	994
social group	305.82
Austria	943.6
	T2—436
Austrian Succession, War of the,	
1740–1748	940.2
North American history	973.2
Austrians	943.6
social group	305.83
Austroasiatic languages	495.9
Austronesian languages	499
Autecology	577.2
animals	591.7
plants	581.7
see Manual at 577.2 vs.	
579–590	
Author catalogs	025.3
bibliography	018
Authoritarian government	321.9
Authoritarianism	320.53
Authority	303.3
religion	291.6
Christianity	262
social control	303.3
Authority control (Cataloging)	025.3
Authority files (Cataloging)	025.3
name and title	025.3
subject	025.4
Authors	
relations with publishers	070.5
see Manual at	
808.001–808.7 vs.	
070.5	
Authors (Literature)	809
collected biography	809
specific literatures	T3—09
Authorship of Bible	220.6
Authorship techniques	808

Autism
medicine 616.89
pediatrics 618.92
special education 371.94
Autobiography 920
　T1—092
Autographs 929.8
Autoimmune diseases (Human)
medicine 616.97
Autoimmunity 571.9
medicine 616.97
Automata 511.3
artificial intelligence 006.3
Automated information systems 025.04
Automatic control engineering 629.8
Automatic data collection
systems 006
Automatic data processing 004
　T1—028 5
Automatic piloting
aircraft 629.132
Automatic pilots
aircraft 629.132
Automatic speech recognition 006.4
Automation
control engineering 629.8
economics 338
manufacturing technology 670.42
production management 658.5
social effects 303.48
Automation engineers 629.809 2
Automatons 629.8
Automobile accidents 363.12
Automobile driving 629.28
Automobile engineers 629.209 2
Automobile industry 338.4
Automobile insurance 368
liability 368.5
Automobile racing 796.72
Automobile rallies 796.7
Automobile transportation 388.3
engineering 629.2
public administration 354.76
transportation services 388.3
Automobiles 388.3
engineering 629.222
law 343.09
military engineering 623.7
repair 629.28
sports 796.7
transportation services 388.3
see Manual at 629.04 vs. 388
Automotive vehicles 388.3
engineering 629.2

Automotive vehicles (continued)
law 343.09
military engineering 623.7
repair 629.28
see Manual at 629.04 vs. 388
Autumn 508.2
Auxiliary party organizations 324
Auxiliary procedures T1—028
Auxiliary storage
computer science 004.5
Auxiliary techniques T1—028
Aves 598
see also Birds
Avestan language 491
Aviation 387.7
see also Air transportation
Aviation fuel 665.5
Aviation law 343.09
Aviation medicine 616.9
Aviation meteorology 629.132
Avionics 629.135
Avon (England) T2—423
Awards 929.8
　T1—079
Axiology 121
Ayatollahs 297.092
biography 297.092
specific sects 297.8
role and function 297.6
Aymara Indians
social group 305.898
Aymara language 498
Azerbaijan 947.54
　T2—475 4
Azerbaijan (Region) T2—55
Azerbaijan T2—475 4
Iran T2—55
Azerbaijani language 494
Azores T2—469
Aztec language 497
Aztecs
civilization 972

B

Babies 305.232
　T1—083
see also Infants
Babism 297.9
Baboons 599.8
Baby animals 591.3
domestic animals 636

Baptism (continued)	
theology	234
Baptism in the Holy Spirit	234
Baptists	286
biography	286.092
Bar coding	006.4
Bar mitzvah	296.4
customs	392.1
etiquette	395.2
Barbados	972.981
	T2—729 81
Barbary States	T2—61
Barbecuing	641.7
indoor cooking	641.7
outdoor cooking	641.5
Barbering	646.7
customs	391.5
Barbuda	T2—729 74
Bargello	746.44
Bark	581.4
descriptive botany	581.4
physiology	575.4
Barley	641.3
cereal crop	633.1
food	641.3
Barnacles	595.3
Barns	631.2
animal welfare	636.08
architecture	728
Barometric pressure	551.5
Baroque architecture	724
Baroque art	709.03
Baroque painting	759.04
Baroque sculpture	735
Barracks	355.7
Barrels	688.8
wooden	674
Bars (Drinking places)	647.95
Bartenders' manuals	641.8
Baseball	796.357
Baseball cards	796.357 075
Baseband local-area networks	004.6
Bases (Chemicals)	546
chemical engineering	661
Bases (Military installations)	355.7
Bashfulness	155.2
Basic Christian communities	250
see Manual at 260 vs.	
251–254, 259	
Basic education	370
adults	374
Basic English	428
Basic training (Military)	355.5
Basketball	796.323

Basketry	
handicrafts	746.41
Basketwork plants	
agriculture	633.5
Basque language	499
Basques	
civilization	946
social group	305.89
Basses (Stringed instruments)	787.5
Bassoons	788.5
Bastille Day	394.263 5
Basutoland	T2—688 5
Bat mitzvah	296.4
customs	392.1
etiquette	395.2
Bathing	613
health	613
personal care	646.7
Bathrooms	643
Batik	746.6
Bats	599.4
Batteries (Electric)	621.31
automotive	629.25
Battles	355.4
Beach activities	
recreation	796.5
Beaches	551.45
	T2—14
geography	910.914
geomorphology	551.45
recreational resources	333.78
resource economics	333.91
Bead embroidery	746.5
Beads	
handicrafts	745.58
Beagle	636.753
Beams (Light)	535.5
Beans	641.3
cooking	641.6
field crop	633.3
food	641.3
garden crop	635
Beard	646.7
customs	391.5
Bearings	621.8
Bears	599.78
Beatitudes	226.9
Beauty	111
Beauty shops	646.7
Beavers	599.37
Bechuanaland	T2—688 3
Bed and breakfasts	647.94
Bedfordshire (England)	T2—425

Betting	306.4	Bihari language	491.4
Betting systems	795.01	Bilingual dictionaries	T4—3
Beverages	641.2	*see Manual at* T4—3	
commercial processing	663	Bilingual education	370.117
cooking with	641.6	Bilingual instruction	
customs	394.1	elementary education	372.65
health	613.2	Bilingualism	306.44
home economics	641.2	linguistics	400
home preparation	641.8	sociology	306.44
product safety	363.19	Billboards	659.13
Bhutan	954.98	Billiards	794.7
	T2—549 8	Binary numbers	513.5
Bhutia (Asian people)		Bingo	795.3
social group	305.895	Binoculars	
Bible	220	manufacturing technology	681
use in public worship	264	Binomial equations	512.9
see Manual at 220; *also at*		Bioastronautics	571.4
220.9		humans	612
Bible as literature	809	Biobibliographies	012
Bible colleges	230.071	Biochemical genetics	572.8
Bible meditations	242	*see Manual at* 576.5 vs. 572.8	
Bible stories	220.9	Biochemicals	572
Biblical characters		organic chemistry	547
art representation	704.9	Biochemistry	572
Biblical Greek language	487	humans	612
Biblical theology		Bioclimatology	577.2
Christianity	230	Biodiversity	333.95
Judaism	296.3	biology	578.7
see Manual at 220		ecology	577
Bibliographic analysis	025.3	resource economics	333.95
Bibliographic control	025.3	*see Manual at* 333.7–333.9 vs.	
Bibliographic instruction	025.5	363.1, 363.73, 577	
Bibliographies	011	Bioelectricity	572
Bibliography	010	electric organs	573.9
Biculturalism		Bioethics	174
sociolinguistics	306.44	Biofeedback	152.1
Bicycle paths	388.1	Biogas	
engineering	625.7	technology	665.7
transportation services	388.1	Biogeography	578.09
urban	388.4	Biography	920
Bicycle racing	796.6		T1—092
Bicycle touring	796.6	literary form	809
Bicycles	388.3	specific literatures	T3—09
engineering	629.227	*see Manual at* T1—092; *also*	
Biennials (Plants)	582.1	*at* 913–919: Add table:	
floriculture	635.9	04: Biography; *also at*	
Big bands	784.4	930–990: Biography	
Big bang theory (Cosmogony)	523.1	Biological communities	577.8
Big business	338.6	Biological control of pests	
management	658	agriculture	632
Big game	599.6	Biological control systems	571.7
Big game hunting	799.2		
Bigfoot	001.944		
Bighorn sheep	599.649		

Boys	305.23	Breast (continued)	
	T1—083	women's physiology	612.6
education	371.823	Breast cancer	
psychology	155.43	medicine	616.99
see also Children		Breast feeding	649
Boys' societies	369.42	child rearing	649
Brahmanism	294.5	health	613.2
Brahmans		*see Manual at* 649 vs. 613.2	
biography	294.509 2	Breast implants	618.1
Brahmaputra River	T2—549 2	Breathing	573.2
Brahui language	494.8	biology	573.2
Braiding textiles	677	human physiology	612.2
arts	746.42	musical technique	781.48
Braille	411	Breeding	
printing	686.2	animal husbandry	636.08
specific languages	T4—1	Breton language	491.6
Braille publications		Breviaries	264
bibliographies	011.63	Bricks	666
Brain	573.8	building construction	693
biology	573.8	building materials	691
human diseases		ceramic arts	738.6
medicine	616.8	Bridge (Game)	795.41
human physiology	612.8	Bridges	388
surgery	617.4	architecture	725
Brain-damaged persons	305.9	construction	624
	T1—087	military engineering	623
education	371.91	transportation services	388
social welfare	362.3	Bridges (Dentistry)	617.6
Brain drain	331.12	Briquettes	662
Brainwashing	153.8	Britain	941
Braising	641.7		T2—41
Branch libraries		ancient	936.1
public librarianship	027.4		T2—361
Branches of government	320.4	*see Manual at* 941	
Brand name products		Britain, Northern	941.1
sales promotion	658.8		T2—411
Branding animals	636.08	ancient	936.1
Brass	669		T2—361
metallurgy	669	Britain, Southern	942
metalworking	673		T2—42
Brass bands	784.9	ancient	936.2
Brass instruments	788.9		T2—362
Brazil	981	British Columbia	T2—711
	T2—81	British Empire	T2—171
Brazilian literature	869	British Guiana	T2—881
Brazilians	981	British Honduras	T2—728 2
social group	305.86	British Isles	941
Bread	641.8		T2—41
Breakfast	642	ancient	936.1
cooking	641.5		T2—361
Breast		*see Manual at* 941	
medicine	618.1	British North America Act, 1867	971.04
men	616.4	British Solomon Islands	T2—959 3
women	618.1		

Burial of dead (continued)
technology 614
Burkina Faso 966.25
T2—662 5
Burlesque shows 792.7
Burma 959.1
T2—591
Burmese 959.1
Burmese language 495
Burnout (Psychology) 158.7
Burns
medicine 617.1
Burundi 967.572
T2—675 72
Bus drivers 388.3
Buses 388.3
engineering 629.222
Bush, George
United States history 973.928
Business 650
see Manual at 330 vs. 650
Business arithmetic 650.01
Business cycles 338.5
Business districts 307.3
area planning 711
Business enterprises 338.7
economics 338.7
initiation 338.7
management 658.1
international law 341.7
law 346
location 338.09
management 658
relations with government 322
social welfare 361.7
valuation 658.15
see Manual at 380; *also at* 658
vs. 658.1, 658.4
Business ethics 174
Business etiquette 395.5
Business forecasting 338.5
Business income tax 336.24
Business insurance 368
Business intelligence
management use 658.4
Business law 346.07
Business liability insurance 368.8
Business libraries 027.6
Business management 658
T1—068
see Manual at 658 and
T1—068
Business organizations 338.7
see also Business enterprises

Business security
management 658.4
Business success 650.1
Business tax 336.2
law 343.06
Business writing 808
see Manual at 658.4 vs. 651.7,
808
Businessmen 338.092
see Manual at 338.092
Busing (School desegregation) 379.2
Busing students (Transportation) 371.8
Busts (Sculpture) 731
Butter 641.3
cooking 641.6
food 641.3
processing 637
Butterflies 595.78
Butterfly gardening 638
Buttons 391.4
commercial technology 687
customs 391.4
home sewing 646
numismatics 737
Buyers' guides 381.3
T1—029
Byelarus 947.8
T2—478
Bypass surgery (Coronary) 617.4
Byzantine architecture 723
Byzantine art 709.02
Byzantine Empire 949.5
Byzantine Greek language 487
Byzantine painting 759.02
Byzantine sculpture 734

C

Cabala 296.1
Jewish mysticism
experience 296.7
movement 296.8
Jewish religious sources 296.1
occultism 135
Cabaret shows 792.7
Cabbages 641.3
cooking 641.6
food 641.3
garden crop 635
Cabinetmakers 684.1
Cabinetmaking 684.1
Cabinets (Government councils) 321.8
public administration 352.24

Cancer (Human)	362.1
medicine	616.99
social services	362.1
Candidiasis	
medicine	616.9
Candles	621.32
handicrafts	745.593
Candy	641.8
commercial processing	664
Canidae	599.77
Cannabis abuse	362.29
Canning foods	664
commercial preservation	664
home preservation	641.4
Cannons	355.8
engineering	623.4
military equipment	355.8
Canoeing	
sports	797.1
Canoidea	599.76
Canon law	262.9
Canon of Bible	220.1
Canonization of saints	235
Cantatas	782.2
Canticle of Canticles	223
Canvas embroidery	746.44
Canyons	551.44
Cape of Good Hope (South Africa)	T2—687
Cape Verde	966.58
	T2—665 8
Cape Verde Islands	T2—665 8
Capillarity	541.3
physics	530.4
Capital	332
Capital gains tax	336.24
Capital management	658.15
Capital movements	332
Capital punishment	364.66
ethics	179.7
law	345
penology	364.66
Capitalism	330.12
Caprimulgiformes	598.9
Caravans (Vehicles)	388.3
engineering	629.226
Carbohydrates	572
applied nutrition	613.2
biochemistry	572
chemistry	547
Carbon	
chemical engineering	661
chemistry	546
organic chemistry	547
Carbon black	662
Carbonaceous materials	553.2
Carboniferous period	551.7
Card catalogs	025.3
Card games	795.4
Card tricks	793.8
Cardinals (Birds)	598.8
Cardiology	616.1
Cardiopulmonary diseases	
medicine	616.1
Cardiopulmonary resuscitation	
medicine	616.1
Cardiovascular system	573.1
biology	573.1
human anatomy	611
human diseases	362.1
medicine	616.1
social services	362.1
human physiology	612.1
surgery	617.4
Cards	
divination	133.3
Cards (Games)	795.4
CARE (Firm)	361.7
Career development	370.11
business	650.1
industrial psychology	158.7
see also Vocational education	
Career education	370.11
	T1—071
see also Vocational education	
Career opportunities	331.7
	T1—023
see also Vocational guidance	
Cargo-handling equipment	623.8
Caribbean Area	972.9
	T2—729
Caribbean Islands	972.9
	T2—729
Caribbean Sea	T2—163
Caribbees	T2—729
Caribou	599.65
Caricatures	741.5
Carillons	786.6
Caring	
ethics	177
Carlow (Ireland : County)	T2—418
Carnivals	791
customs	394.25
performing arts	791
Carnivores	599.7
Carnivorous dinosaurs	567.912
Carnivorous plants	583
physiology	575.9

Caucasus	947.5
	T2—475
ancient	T2—39
Caucus nomination	324.5
Cauliflower	641.3
cooking	641.6
food	641.3
Causation	
philosophy	122
Causes of war	355.02
Cavalry forces	357
Cavan (Ireland : County)	T2—416 9
Cave dwellers	569.9
Caves	551.44
	T2—14
biology	578.75
ecology	577.5
exploring	796.52
geography	910.914
geomorphology	551.44
Cavitation	532
Cavities (Teeth)	
dentistry	617.6
Cayman Islands	T2—729 2
CB radio	384.5
communications services	384.5
engineering	621.384 5
CBR warfare	358
CD-ROMs	
computer memory	004.5
CDs (Compact discs)	384
see also Sound recordings	
Celebrations	394.2
Celestial bodies	520
folklore	398.26
Celestial mechanics	521
engineering	629.4
Celestial navigation	527
Celibacy	306.73
customs	392.6
ethics	176
psychology	155.3
religious practice	291.4
Christianity	248.4
clergy	253
sociology	306.73
Cell biology	571.6
Cell chemistry	572
Cell physiology	571.6
Cell reproduction	571.8
Cellists	787.409 2
Cellos	787.4
Cells (Biology)	571.6
humans	611

Cellular telephones	384.5
engineering	621.384 5
Cellulose derivatives	
chemical engineering	661
Celtic languages	491.6
Celtic regions	944
	T2—44
ancient	936.4
	T2—364
Celts	
ancient civilization	936
social group	305.891
Cement	666
materials science	620.1
Cemeteries	363.7
landscape architecture	718
Cemetery records	
genealogy	929
Cenozoic era	551.7
Censored books	098
Censorship	363.3
law	344
libraries	025.2
social control	303.3
see Manual at 363.3 vs. 303.3,	
791.4	
Census	
public administration	352.7
statistical reports	310
Census records	
genealogy	929
Centaurs	
folklore	398.21
Centipedes	595.6
Central Africa	967
	T2—67
Central African Empire	T2—674 1
Central African Republic	967.41
	T2—674 1
Central America	972.8
	T2—728
Central American native	
languages	497
Central Americans	972.8
social group	305.868
Central Asia	958
	T2—58
ancient	939
	T2—39
Central Australia	T2—942
Central banks	332.1
Central Europe	943
	T2—43
Central Pacific islands	T2—96

Chelicerates	595.4
Chemical analysis	543
Chemical bonds	541.2
Chemical compounds	546
engineering	660
Chemical elements	546
Chemical engineering	660
Chemical engineers	660.092
Chemical industries	338.4
technology	660
Chemical instruments	542
Chemical laboratories	542
Chemical pollution	363.738
Chemical reactions	541.3
Chemical technology	660
Chemical warfare	358
Chemical weapons	358
engineering	623.4
military equipment	358
Chemicals	540
Chemiluminescence	541.3
Chemistry	540
applied	660
see Manual at 530 vs. 540	
Chemists	540.92
Chemotherapy	
medicine	615.5
Cheques	332.7
Cherokee Indians	
social group	305.897
Chesapeake Bay (Md. and	
Va.)	T2—163
Cheshire (England)	T2—427
Chess	794.1
Chest	
human physiology	612
regional medicine	617.5
Chicago school of economics	330.15
Chicanos	
social group	305.868
Chichewa language	496
Chicken (Meat)	641.3
cooking	641.6
food	641.3
Chicken pox	
medicine	616.9
Chickens	636.5
Chief executives	
executive management	658.4
public administration	352.23
Chihuahua (Dog)	636.76
Child abuse	362.76
criminology	364.15
criminal law	345

Child abuse (continued)	
medicine	616.85
social welfare	362.76
Child care	649
Child development	305.231
physiology	612.6
psychology	155.4
sociology	305.231
Child labor	331.3
law	344.01
Child molesting	364.15
law	345
medicine	616.85
Child-parent relations	306.874
see also Parent-child relations	
Child prostitution	306.74
Child psychology	155.4
Child rearing	649
customs	392.1
personal religion	291.4
Christianity	248.8
Judaism	296.7
Child study	305.23
physiology	612.6
psychology	155.4
sociology	305.23
Child support	346.01
Childbirth	618.4
human physiology	612.6
obstetrics	618.4
preparation	
obstetrics	618.2
Childhood	305.23
psychology	155.4
Childlessness	306.87
Children	305.23
	T1—083
cooking for	641.5
etiquette	395.1
health	613
home care	649
labor economics	331.3
psychology	155.4
publications for	
bibliographies	011.62
reading	
library science	028.5
religion	200.83
Christianity	270.083
guides to Christian life	248.8
pastoral care of	259
religious education	268
social theology	261.8
guides to life	291.4

Christian sacred music	781.71
public worship	782.32
music	782.32
religion	264
Christian schools (General education)	371.071
Christian Science	289.5
Christian Scientists	
biography	289.509 2
Christian socialism	335
Christianity	230
art representation	704.9
religious significance	246
Christianity and culture	261
Christianity and other religions	261.2
Christianity and politics	261.7
Christianity in public schools	379.2
Christians	270.092
see Manual at 230–280	
Christmas	263
customs	394.266 3
devotional literature	242
Christmas carols	782.28
Christmas cooking	641.5
Christmas decorations	394.266 3
customs	394.266 3
handicrafts	745.594
Christmas music	781.723
Christmas seals (Prints)	769.5
Christmas story	232.92
Christology	232
Chromolithography	764
Chromosomes	572.8
Chronic diseases	
medicine	616
Chronic fatigue syndrome	
medicine	616
Chronicles	900
see also History	
Chronicles (Biblical books)	222
Chronologies	902
Chronology	529
Church	260
history	270
local	250
Church and state	322
social theology	291.1
Christianity	261.7
see also Politics and religion	
see Manual at 322 vs. 261.7, 291.1	
Church authority	262
Church buildings	
architecture	726.5

Church buildings (continued)	
management	254
religious significance	246
Church fathers	270
biography	270.092
Church furniture	247
Church government	262
Church history	270
specific denominations	280
Church holidays	263
customs	394.266
Church in public education	379.2
Church law	262.9
Church libraries	027.6
Church membership	
local church	254
Church music	781.71
Church of Christ, Scientist	289.5
Church of England	283
Church of God in Christ, Mennonites	289.7
Church of Jesus Christ of Latter-Day Saints	289.3
Church of North India	287.9
Church of Scotland	285
Church of South India	287.9
Church of the Nazarene	287.9
Church of the New Jerusalem	289
Church organization	262
Church-related colleges and universities	378
Church renewal	262.001
Church schools (General education)	371.071
Church services	264
music	782.32
Church year	263
devotional literature	242
music	781.72
Church youth groups	259
Churches of Christ	286.6
Churches of God	289.9
Chuvash language	494
Ciconiiformes	598.3
Cigarettes	679
Cigars	679
CIM (Manufacturing)	670.285
Cinematography	778.5
see Manual at 791.43, 791.45 vs. 778.5	
Ciphers (Cryptography)	652
Circle-squaring	516.2
Circuits	621.319
electronics	621.381 5

Circulation (Biology)	573.1
animals	573.1
human physiology	612.1
plants	575.7
Circulation (Meteorology)	551.51
Circulation services	
library science	025.6
Circulatory system	573.1
animals	573.1
plants	575.7
see also Cardiovascular	
system	
Circumcision	392.1
customs	392.1
Jewish rites	296.4
male	
surgery	617.4
Circuses	791.3
Cirrhosis	
medicine	616.3
Cities	307.76
	T2—173
government	320.8
psychological influence	155.9
public administration	352.16
see Manual at 351.3–351.9	
vs. 352.13–352.19	
public administrative support	352.7
sociology	307.76
Citizen participation	323
election campaigns	324.7
Citizens band radio	384.5
communications services	384.5
engineering	621.384 5
see Manual at 621.3841 vs.	
621.3845	
Citizenship	323.6
elementary education	372.83
ethics	172
international law	341.4
law	342
political science	323.6
City core	
community development	307.3
City directories	910.25
City planning	307.1
civic art	711
law	346.04
public administration	354.3
City-states	321
Cityscapes	
fine arts	704.9
painting	758
Civic art	711

Civic centers	307.3
architecture	725
community sociology	307.3
Civics	320.4
elementary education	372.83
Civil commotion insurance	368.1
Civil defense	363.3
public administration	353.9
Civil disobedience	303.6
political action	322.4
social conflict	303.6
Civil disorder	303.6
Civil engineering	624
see Manual at 624 vs. 624.1;	
also at 624 vs. 690	
Civil engineers	624.092
Civil law (Legal system)	340.5
see Manual at 340.5 vs.	
342–347	
Civil liberties	323
see also Civil rights	
Civil-military relations	322
Civil procedure	347
Civil rights	323
government programs	353.4
international law	341.4
law	342
political science	323
social theology	291.1
Christianity	261.7
Islam	297.2
Judaism	296.3
Civil service (Merit system)	352.6
law	342
Civil service (Nonmilitary	
government agencies)	351
Civil service examinations	351.076
	T1—076
Civil war	355.02
social conflict	303.6
Civil War (England), 1642–1649	942.06
Civil War (Spain), 1936–1939	946.081
Civil War (United States),	
1861–1865	973.7
Civilization	909
elementary education	372.89
history	909
specific places	930–990
sociology	306
see Manual at 305 vs. 306,	
909, 930–990; *also at*	
909, 930–990 vs. 910	
Claims (Insurance)	368
Clairvoyance	133.8

Collage	702.81
Collage painting	751.4
Collectibles	T1—075
see Manual at 745.1	
Collecting	069
	T1—075
museology	069
recreation	790.1
Collection analysis	
library science	025.2
Collection development	
library science	025.2
Collection management	
library operations	025.8
Collections	069
description	T1—074
museology	069
of texts	080
see Manual at 080 vs. 800;	
also at 081–089	
preparation	T1—075
Collective bargaining	331.89
economics	331.89
law	344.01
personnel management	658.3
public administration	354.9
see Manual at 331.2 vs.	
331.89	
Collective security	327.1
Collectivism	335
economics	335
political ideology	320.53
see Manual at 335 vs. 306.3,	
320.53	
College buildings	378.1
architecture	727
College education	378
College entrance examinations	378.1
College libraries	027.7
College readers (Reading	
comprehension textbooks)	
applied linguistics	418
specific languages	T4—86
College readers (Rhetoric	
textbooks)	808
College sports	796.04
see Manual at 796.08 vs.	
796.04	
College students	
pastoral care	259
Colleges	378.1
Collies	636.737
Colloids	541.3

Colloquial language	418
specific languages	T4—8
Colombia	986.1
	T2—861
Colombian literature	860
Colombians	986.1
Colonialism	325
Colonies (Territories)	321
international law	341.2
public administration	353.1
Colonization	325
Color	535.6
animal physiology	573.5
animals	591.47
arts	701
painting	752
physics	535.6
technology	667
Color blindness	
ophthalmology	617.7
Color perception	
psychology	152.14
Color photography	778.6
Color printing	686.2
Colorado	T2—788
Colorado River	
(Colo.-Mexico)	T2—791
Colors (Flags)	929.9
armed forces	355.1
Colossians (Biblical book)	227
Colostomy	617.5
Columbiformes	598.6
Comb jellies	593.8
Combat aircraft	358.4
engineering	623.7
military equipment	358.4
Combat fatigue	
medicine	616.85
Combat readiness	355
Combat sports	796.8
Combat vehicles	355.8
engineering	623.7
military equipment	355.8
Combinations (Enterprises)	338.8
management	658
Combinatorial analysis	511
Combinatorial topology	514
Combs	646.7
manufacturing technology	688
Combustion	541.3
chemical engineering	660
chemistry	541.3
heat engineering	621.402

Communications (continued)
public administration 354.75
see Manual at 380
Communications engineering 621.382
military 623
Communications engineers 621.382 092
Communications media 302.23
see also Mass media
Communications network
architecture
communications engineering 621.382
computer science 004.6
engineering 621.39
Communications protocols
computer science 004.6
Communion service 264
music 782.32
Communism 335.4
political ideology 320.53
Communist bloc T2—171
Communist government 321.9
Communist International 324.1
Communist parties 324.2
Communists 335.409 2
Marxist-Leninist 335.430 92
Communities 307
psychological influence 155.9
see Manual at 307
Community action (Social
welfare) 361.8
see Manual at 361.6 vs. 361.7,
361.8
Community antenna television
systems 384.55
Community development 307.1
public administration 354.2
Community information services
libraries 021.2
Community planning 307.1
Community-school relations 306.43
education 371.19
sociology 306.43
Community schools 371.03
Comoros 969.4
T2—694
Compact discs 384
engineering 621.389
music 780
see also Sound recordings
Companies 338.7
see also Business enterprises
Companies (Military units) 355.3
Company unions 331.88
Comparable worth 331.2

Comparative advantage
economics 338.6
Comparative anatomy 571.3
Comparative education 370.9
Comparative government 320.3
Comparative law 340
Comparative librarianship 020.9
Comparative linguistics 410
see Manual at 410
Comparative literature 809
Comparative physiology 571.1
Comparative psychology 156
Comparative religion 291
see Manual at 291
Comparison shopping 381.3
T1—029
consumer products 640.73
Compatibility
computer science 004
hardware 004
software 005
Compensation 331.2
economics 331.2
legislators 328.3
Compensatory education 370.11
Competition 338.6
Competition (Social) 302
Competitions T1—079
Compilers (Computer programs) 005.4
Complexes (Psychology) 154.2
Composers 780.92
see Manual at 780.92
Composite foods 641.8
commercial processing 664
cooking 641.8
Composites (Art) 702.8
two-dimensional 760
Composition (Arts) 701
Composition (Music) 781.3
Composition (Printing) 686.2
Composition (Writing) 808
applied linguistics 418
specific languages T4—8
elementary education 372.62
rhetoric 808
see Manual at 808.001–808.7
vs. 070.5
Composition of atmosphere 551.51
Compounds (Chemicals) 546
chemical engineering 660
Comprehensive high schools 373.2
Compressed air 621.5
Compressed work week 331.25

Computers	004
access control	005.8
elementary education	372.3
engineering	621.39
instructional use	371.33
law	343.09
music	780.285
composition	781.3
musical instrument	786.7
social effects	303.48
Concentration	
psychology of learning	153.1
Concentration camps	365
Concepts	
psychology	153.2
Conceptual art	700
Concert halls	
architecture	725
Concertos	784.2
musical form	784.18
Concerts	780.78
Conciliation	
labor economics	331.89
Concordances	T1—03
Concrete	666
building construction	693
building materials	691
materials science	620.1
Condensation	536
Conditions of employment	331.2
economics	331.2
personnel management	658.3
armed forces	355.1
public administration	354.9
see Manual at 331.2 vs.	
331.89	
Condominiums	643
law	346.04
Condors	598.9
Conduct of life	
ethics	170
religion	291.5
Christianity	241
Islam	297.5
Judaism	296.3
etiquette	395
parapsychology	131
personal religion	291.4
Christianity	248.4
Islam	297.5
Judaism	296.7
psychology	158.1
Conducting	781.45

Confederate States of America	973.7
	T2—75
Confederations	321.02
Conferences	060
Confessions of faith	291.2
Christianity	238
Confidentiality	
office services	651
Confirmation (Religious rite)	291.3
Christianity	234
public worship	265
theology	234
Conflict	303.6
social groups	305
subconscious psychology	154.2
Conflict management	303.6
business relationships	650.1
executive management	658.4
Conflict of interest	
public administration	353.4
Conflict of laws	340.9
domestic	342
Conflict resolution	303.6
Conformity	303.3
psychology	153.8
Confraternities	267
Confucianism	181
philosophy	181
religion	299
Congenital diseases (Human)	
medicine	616
Congestive heart failure	
medicine	616.1
Conglomerates (Enterprises)	338.8
Congo (Brazzaville)	967.24
	T2—672 4
Congo (Democratic	
Republic)	T2—675 1
Congo River	T2—675 1
Congregationalism	285.8
Congregationalists	
biography	285.809 2
Congregations	
Christianity	
local church	250
Congresses	060
Congresses (Legislative bodies)	328
Conifers	585
Conjuring	
magic	133.4
recreation	793.8
Connacht (Ireland)	T2—417
Connecticut	T2—746
Connecticut River	T2—74

Continents	551.41
	T2—14
geography	910.914
geomorphology	551.41
Continuing education	374
	T1—071
Continuum mechanics	531
see Manual at 530.12 vs. 531	
Continuum physics	530
theory	530.14
Contraception	363.9
see also Birth control	
Contract labor	331.5
Contracting	346.02
see also Contracts	
Contraction (Effect of heat)	536
Contractors (Builders)	690.092
Contracts	346.02
armed forces	355.6
construction	692
materials management	658.7
public administration	352.5
Contracts (Labor agreements)	331.89
Contradictions	
logic	165
Contrastive linguistics	410
see Manual at 410	
Control	
public administration	352.8
external control	352.8
internal control	352.3
social process	303.3
Control line models	796.15
Control mechanisms (Biology)	571.7
human physiology	612
Control of usage	
natural resources	333.7
Control theory	003
automation engineering	629.8
Controversial knowledge	001.9
see Manual at 001.9 and 130	
Convalescent homes	362.1
Convenience foods	
home serving	642
Conventions	060
labor unions	331.87
political nominations	324.5
Conversation	
ethics	177
etiquette	395.5
literature	808.856
history and criticism	809.56
specific literatures	T3—5
rhetoric	808.56

Conversation (continued)	
social psychology	302.3
Conversational language study	418
specific languages	T4—83
Conversion (Religious experience)	291.4
Christianity	248.2
Islam	297.5
Judaism	296.7
Converts	291.4
missions for	291.7
Conveyancing	346.04
Conveying equipment	621.8
Convict labor	365
economics	331.5
Cook Islands	T2—962
Cookies	641.8
Cooking	641.5
customs	392.3
Cooks	641.509 2
Cooperation	303.3
social process	303.3
social psychology	302
Cooperative cataloging	025.3
Cooperative education	371.2
higher education	378.3
secondary level	373.2
Cooperative marketing	658.8
Cooperatives	334
Coordination (Social process)	303.3
Coordination chemistry	541.2
Coordination of movement	
psychology	152.3
Copper	669
chemistry	546
metallurgy	669
metalworking	673
Coptic Church	281
Coptic language	493
Copyright	346.04
international law	341.7
law	346.04
Coraciiformes	598.7
Corals	593.6
paleozoology	563
Core of earth	551.1
Corinthians (Biblical books)	227
Cork	674
Cork (Ireland : County)	T2—419
Corn	641.3
cereal crop	633.1
food	641.3
garden crop	635
Cornetists	788.9

Counterfeit coins	
numismatics	737.4
Counterfeiting	364.1
law	345
Counterintelligence	327.12
see also Espionage	
Counterpoint	781.2
Counties	320.8
government	320.8
public administration	352.15
see Manual at 351.3–351.9	
vs. 352.13–352.19	
Counting	513.2
Counting-out rhymes	398.8
Country music	781.642
songs	782.421 642
Coups d'état	321.09
see Manual at 909, 930–990	
vs. 320.4, 321, 321.09	
Courage	
ethics	179
Court costs	347
Court decisions	
texts	348
Court records	347
genealogy	929
Courtesy	
ethics	177
etiquette	395
Courts (Law)	347
international law	341.5
Courts-martial	343
Courtship	306.73
customs	392.4
ethics	177
personal living	646.7
sociology	306.73
Courtship (Animal behavior)	591.56
Covenant relationship with God	
Christianity	231.7
Covered bridges	
construction	624
Covers (Philately)	769.56
Cowardice	
ethics	179
Cowboys	636.2
Cows	636.2
Coyote	599.77
CPR (Resuscitation)	
medicine	616.1
CPU (Central processor)	004
engineering	621.39
Crabs	595.3
cooking	641.6

Crabs (continued)	
fishing	639
food	641.3
paleozoology	565
zoology	595.3
Craft unions	331.88
Crafts	680
arts	745
see Manual at 680 vs. 745.5	
Cranes (Birds)	598.3
Cranes (Hoisting machinery)	621.8
Craps	795.1
Craters (Depressions)	551.21
Crates	
wooden	674
Crayon drawing	741.2
Creation	
philosophy	113
religion	291.2
Christianity	231.7
Islam	297.2
Judaism	296.3
philosophy of religion	213
Creation science	231.7
see Manual at 231.7 vs. 213,	
500, 576.8	
Creationism	231.7
public education	379.2
see Manual at 231.7 vs. 213,	
500, 576.8	
Creative ability	153.3
see also Creativity	
Creative activities	
child care	649
education	371.3
Creative arts	700
elementary education	372.5
Creative thinking	153.4
see also Creativity	
Creative writing	
elementary education	372.62
Creativity	153.3
arts	701
educational objective	370.11
educational psychology	370.15
Creativity (Literary)	801
Credit	332.7
law	346.07
public administration	354.8
see Manual at 332.7 vs. 332.1	
Credit cards	332.7
banking services	332.1
see Manual at 332.7 vs. 332.1	
Credit institutions	332.3

Crucifixes	
religious significance	246
Cruelty	
ethics	179
Crusades	909.07
church history	270.4
European history	940.1
Crust of earth	551.1
Crustaceans	595.3
fishing	639
paleozoology	565
Crutches	
manufacturing technology	681
Cryogenic engineering	621.5
Cryogenics	536
Cryosurgery	617
Cryptography	652
computer science	005.8
recreation	793.73
Crystal gazing	133.3
Crystallography	548
see Manual at 549 vs. 548	
Crystals	548
occultism	133
Ctenophora	593.8
paleozoology	563
Cub Scouts	369.43
Cuba	972.91
	T2—729 1
Cuban literature	860
Cubans	972.91
Cube-doubling	516.2
Cubism	709.04
painting	759.06
Cuckoos	598.7
Cuculiformes	598.7
Cucumbers	641.3
cooking	641.6
food	641.3
Cultivation (Tillage)	631.5
Cults	291.9
see Manual at 291	
Cultural anthropology	306
Cultural ethnology	305.8
Cultural exchanges	303.48
Cultural influence	
psychology	155.9
Cultural programs	
libraries	021.2
Culture	306
public administrative support	353.7
see Manual at 305 vs. 306,	
909, 930–990	
Cumbria (England)	T2—427

Curaçao	T2—729 8
Curling (Sport)	796.964
Currency	332.4
see also Money	
Current awareness programs	025.5
Curricula	375
	T1—071
Christian education	268
elementary education	372.19
public control	379.1
secondary education	373.19
Curriculum libraries	027.7
Cushitic languages	493
Customer relations	
marketing management	658.8
Customized vans	388.3
engineering	629.223
Customs (Social)	390
Customs (Tariff)	382
international law	341.7
law	343.05
public finance	336.2
Customs unions	382
Cutlery	642
manufacturing technology	683
table setting	642
Cutting metals	671.5
Cutwork	
arts	746.44
Cybernetics	003
Cycles (Vehicles)	388.3
engineering	629.227
repair	629.28
riding	629.28
sports	796.6
transportation services	388.3
Cyclic compounds	547
Cycling	
sports	796.6
Cyclones	551.55
Cycloramas	745
Cyclotrons	539.7
Cymbals	786.8
Cypresses	585
Cypriots	956.93
social group	305.88
Cyprus	956.93
	T2—569 3
ancient	T2—39
Cystic fibrosis	
medicine	616.3
Cystitis	
medicine	616.6
Cytochemistry	572

Deacons (continued)

pastoral theology	253
personal religion	248.8

Dead

disposal	363.7
see also Undertaking	
(Mortuary)	

Dead animal disposal	363.7

Dead Sea (Israel and

Jordan)	T2—569 4
Dead Sea Scrolls	296.1
Deaf persons	305.9
	T1—087
education	371.91
social welfare	362.4
see also Disabled persons	

Deafness

medicine	617.8
social welfare	362.4
Deans of students	371.4
Death	306.9
biology	571.9
customs	393
demography	304.6
ethics	179.7
family sociology	306.88
folklore	398.27
medicine	616.07
philosophy	113
humans	128
psychology	155.9
religion	291.2
Christianity	236
Islam	297.2
Judaism	296.3
philosophy of religion	218
religious rites	291.3
Christianity	265
Islam	297.3
Judaism	296.4
social services	363.7
see also Undertaking	
(Mortuary)	
sociology	306.9

Death certificates

public administration	353.5
Death penalty	364.66
Debaters	809.53

Debates

literature	808.853
history and criticism	809.53
specific literatures	T3—5
rhetoric	808.53
Debating	808.53

Debit cards	332.7
banking services	332.1

Debt limits

public finance	336.3
Debt management (Personal)	332.024

Debtors

law	346.07
Debugging (Computer science)	004.2
programs	005.1
Deburring metals	671.7
Decimal numbers	513.5

Decision making

executive management	658.4
political science	320.01
psychology	153.8
public administration	352.3
social psychology	302.3
Decision theory	003
Decision theory (Mathematics)	519.5

Declaration of Independence,

1776	973.3

Decoding skills (Reading)

elementary education	372.46

Deconstruction

philosophy	149
Decoration	745.4
architecture	729
Decorations (Awards)	929.8
armed forces	355.1
Decorative arts	745
Decorative coloring	745.7
Decorative lettering	745.6
Decoupage	745.54

Decoys

handicrafts	745.593
Deductive reasoning	162
logic	162
psychology	153.4
Deep-sea surveys	551.46
Deer	599.65
animal husbandry	636.2
conservation technology	639.97
zoology	599.65

Defecation

human physiology	612.3
Defense (Legal)	347
criminal law	345
Defense (Military operation)	355.4
engineering	623
Defense (National security)	355
international law	341.7
law	343
Defense contracts	355.6
Defense departments	355.6

Defense industries 338.4
Defense mechanisms
  (Psychology) 155.2
Deflation (Economic) 332.4
Deformation 531
  geology 551.8
Deformities
  biology 571.9
Dehydrating foods 664
Deism 211
Deities 291.2
Delaware T2—751
Delegate counts 324.5
Delftware 738.3
Delicts 346.03
  see Manual at 345 vs. 346.03
Delinquency in schools 371.7
Delinquent students 371.93
Deltas 551.45
Delusions 001.9
Demand
  forecasts 338
  microeconomics 338.5
  natural resources 333.7
Dementia
  medicine 616.8
Democracy 321.8
Democratic centralism 335.43
Democratic Party (U.S.) 324.273 6
Democratic Republic of the
  Congo T2—675 1
Democratic-Republican Party
  (U.S.) 324.273 6
Democratic socialism 335.5
  economics 335.5
  political ideology 320.53
Demography 304.6
Demolition (Military) 623
Demolition operations (Military) 358
  underwater 359.9
Demoniac possession 133.4
Demonology 133.4
Demonstrations (Advertising) 659.1
Demotic language (Modern
  Greek) 489
Demythologizing (Bible) 220.6
Dendrology 582.16
Denmark 948.9
  T2—489
Denominations 291.9
  Christianity 280
  Judaism 296.8
  see Manual at 291

Dental diseases
  dentistry 617.6
Dental surgery 617.6
  see Manual at 617.6 vs. 617.5
Dentistry 617.6
Dentists 617.600 92
Dentures
  dentistry 617.6
Deoxyribonucleic acid 572.8
Department stores 381
  management 658.8
Departments
  public administration 351
    see also Executive
      departments
Departments of agriculture 354.5
Departments of commerce 354.73
Departments of defense 355.6
Departments of education 353.8
Departments of energy 354.4
Departments of foreign affairs 353.1
Departments of health 353.6
Departments of interior 353.3
Departments of justice 353.4
Departments of labor 354.9
Departments of natural resources 354.3
Departments of treasury 352.4
Dependence
  personality trait 155.2
Deposits (Bank) 332.1
Depression (Mental state) 362.2
  medicine 616.85
  social welfare 362.2
Depressions (Economic)
  economic cycles 338.5
  personal finance 332.024
Depressions (Physiography) 551.44
Deputy chief executives
  public administration 352.23
Derbyshire (England) T2—425
Derivatives (Speculation) 332.64
  multiple forms of investment 332.64
  securities 332.63
Dermatology 616.5
Derricks 621.8
Desalinization 628.1
Descriptive biology 578
  see Manual at 578 vs. 304.2,
    508, 910
Descriptive cataloging 025.3
Descriptive geometry 516
Descriptive linguistics 410
  see Manual at 410
Descriptive research 001.4

Dice games	795.1
Dicotyledons	583
Dictation (Office practice)	651.7
shorthand	653
Dictatorship	321.9
Dictionaries	413
specific languages	T4—3
see Manual at T4—3 vs.	
T4—81	
specific subject	T1—03
see Manual at T1—01 vs.	
T1—03	
Dictionary catalogs	025.3
bibliography	019
Die casting	671.2
Diesel engines	621.43
Diet	
elementary education	372.3
health	613.2
Diet cooking	641.5
Diet therapy	
medicine	615.8
see Manual at 615.8	
Dietary laws	
Judaism	296.7
Dietetics	613.2
see Manual at 363.8 vs. 613.2,	
641.3	
Differential calculus	515
Differential equations	515
Differential geometry	516.3
Differential psychology	155
Differential topology	514
Differentiated teacher staffing	371.14
Diffusion	530.4
Digestion	573.3
human physiology	612.3
Digestive system	573.3
biology	573.3
human anatomy	611
human diseases	362.1
medicine	616.3
social services	362.1
human physiology	612.3
surgery	617.4
Digests of laws	348
Digital circuits	621.381 5
Digital codes (Computer)	005.7
Digital communications	384
communications services	384
engineering	621.382
see Manual at 004.6 vs.	
621.382, 621.39	
Digital computers	004

Digital microcomputers	004.16
Dinner	642
cooking	641.5
Dinosaurs	567.9
Dioramas	745
Diphtheria	
medicine	616.9
Diplodocus	567.913
Diplomacy	327.2
international law	341.3
Diplomatic customs	399
Diplomatic history	327.09
Diptera	595.77
Direct-mail advertising	659.13
Direct-mail marketing	381
management	658.8
Direct nuclear generation of	
electricity	621.31
Direct selling	381
management	658.8
Directories	T1—025
see Manual at 338 vs. 060,	
381, 382, 670.29, 910,	
T1—025, T1—029	
Directors (Drama)	792
motion pictures	791.43
radio	791.44
stage	792
television	791.45
see Manual at 791.092	
Directory advertising	659.13
Dirigibles	387.7
engineering	629.133
Disability	
psychological influence	155.9
social welfare	362.4
Disability income insurance	368.38
Disabled children	305.9
	T1—087
home care	649
psychology	155.45
Disabled persons	305.9
	T1—087
architecture for	720.87
education	371.9
home care	649.8
libraries for	027.6
publications for	
bibliographies	011.63
self-help devices	617
social group	305.9

Donegal (Ireland : County)	T2—416 9
Donkeys	636.1
Doors	721
architecture	721
construction	690
Dorset (England)	T2—423
Double basses	787.5
Double-reed instruments	788.5
Double taxation	336.2
international law	341.4
Doubling the cube	516.2
Doubt	
epistemology	121
Doves	598.6
Down's syndrome	
medicine	616.85
Downsizing of organizations	
personnel management	658.3
Downtown	307.3
Dowsing	133.3
Draft (Conscription)	355.2
law	343
Draft animals	636.088
Drafting (Drawing)	604.2
	T1—022
Draftsmen	604.209 2
Dragonflies	595.7
Dragons	398.24
folklore	398.24
mysteries	001.944
Drainage	
agriculture	631.6
engineering	627
Drama (Literature)	808.82
criticism	809.2
theory	808.2
history	809.2
rhetoric	808.2
specific literatures	T3—2
see Manual at T3—2 vs.	
T3—1	
Drama (Theater)	792
Dramatic monologues (Poetry)	808.81
see Manual at T3—2 vs.	
T3—1	
Dramatic poetry	808.81
see Manual at T3—2 vs.	
T3—1	
Dramatic vocal forms	782.1
see Manual at 782.1 vs. 792.5	
Dramatists	809.2
collected biography	809.2
specific literatures	T3—200 9
individual biography	T3—2

Draped figures	704.9
drawing	743.5
Draperies	645
arts	746.9
commercial technology	684
home sewing	646.2
household management	645
interior decoration	747
Draughts	794.2
Dravidian languages	494.8
Dravidians	954
social group	305.89
Drawers (Artists)	741.092
Drawing (Delineating)	741
arts	741
elementary education	372.5
technology	604.2
Drawings	T1—022
arts	741
Drawn work	
arts	746.44
Dream books	135
Dreams	154.6
human physiology	612.8
parapsychology	135
Dredging	627
Dress accessories	391.4
Dressmakers	646.400 92
Dressmaking	646.4
commercial technology	687
Dried foods	
cooking	641.6
home preservation	641.4
Drill (Military training)	355.5
Drilling platforms	627
Drilling tools	621.9
Drinking	
customs	394.1
Drinking glasses	
decorative arts	748.8
Drinks	641.2
home preparation	641.8
see also Beverages	
Drives (Psychology)	153.8
physiological drives	152.5
Driveways	625.8
Driving horses (Recreation)	798
Dropouts (Education)	371.2
Droughts	
meteorology	551.57
see also Disasters	
Drug abuse	362.29
see also Substance abuse	

Ears	573.8
animal physiology	573.8
descriptive zoology	591.4
human diseases	
medicine	617.8
human physiology	612.8
Earth	550
astronomy	525
extraterrestrial influences	001.94
geologic history	551.7
internal structure	551.1
Earth sciences	550
see Manual at 550 vs. 910	
Earthenware	666
arts	738.3
technology	666
Earthquake engineering	624.1
Earthquakes	551.22
see also Disasters	
Earthwork	624.1
Earthy materials	553.6
Easements	346.04
East	950
	T2—5
East Africa	967.6
	T2—676
East Anglia (England)	T2—426
East Asia	T2—5
East Bengal (Pakistan)	T2—549 2
East China Sea	T2—164
East Germany (Democratic	
Republic)	943
	T2—43
East Indo-European languages	491
East Pakistan (Pakistan)	954.920 4
	T2—549 2
East Slavic languages	491.7
East Sussex (England)	T2—422
Easter	263
customs	394.266 7
devotional literature	242
Easter eggs	394.266 7
customs	394.266 7
handicrafts	745.594
Easter Island	T2—961
Easter music	781.727
Eastern Canada	T2—713
Eastern Canadian Inuktitut	
language	497
Eastern Europe	947
	T2—47
Eastern Hemisphere	T2—181
Eastern Orthodox Christians	
biography	281.909 2

Eastern Orthodox Church	281.9
Eastern rite churches	281
Eating	
animal physiology	573.3
child training	649
customs	394.1
descriptive zoology	591.5
gastronomy	641.01
Eating disorders	
medicine	616.85
Eating places	647.95
household management	647.95
meal service	642
Ecclesiastes	223
Ecclesiastical law	262.9
Ecclesiology	
Christianity	262
Echidnas	599.2
Echinoderms	593.9
paleozoology	563
Echoes	
physics	534
Eclecticism	
philosophy	148
Eclipses	523.9
moon	523.3
sun	523.7
Ecology	577
animals	591.7
elementary education	372.3
ethics	179
plants	581.7
social theology	291.1
sociology	304.2
specific environments	577
see Manual at 577 vs. 578.7	
see Manual at 333.7–333.9 vs.	
363.1, 363.73, 577; also	
at 577.2 vs. 579–590	
Econometrics	330.01
Economic anthropology	306.3
Economic assistance	338.9
international politics	327.1
law	343
production economics	338.9
public administration	352.73
Economic biology	578.6
Economic botany	581.6
Economic concentration	338.8
Economic conditions	330.9
Economic cooperation	
international economics	337.1
see Manual at 337.3–337.9	
vs. 337.1	

Edward VIII, King of Great
  Britain
  British history — 941.084
Efficiency
  economics — 338
  promotion of
    personnel management — 658.3
    production management — 658.5
Efik language — 496
Eggs — 591.4
  animal husbandry — 636.5
  cooking — 641.6
  descriptive zoology — 591.4
  food — 641.3
  physiology — 573.6
  processing — 637
Ego (Psychology) — 154.2
Egypt — 962
  T2—62
  ancient — 932
  T2—32
Egyptian language — 493
Egyptian literature
  Arabic — 892.7
  Egyptian — 893
Egyptians (Ancient) — 932
  religion — 299
  social group — 305.89
Egyptians (Modern) — 962
  social group — 305.892
Eire — 941.7
  T2—417
Eire (1937–1949) — 941.708 2
Eisenhower, Dwight D. (Dwight
  David)
  United States history — 973.921
EKG (Medicine) — 616.1
El Salvador — 972.84
  T2—728 4
Elamite language — 499
Elasticity — 531
  materials science — 620.1
Elastomers — 678
Elder abuse — 362.6
  criminology — 364.15
    criminal law — 345
  social welfare — 362.6
Elderly persons — 305.26
  T1—084
  see also Older persons
Election campaigns — 324.9
  elections — 324.9
  nominations — 324.5
  techniques — 324.7

Election fraud — 324.6
Election law — 342
Election procedures — 324.6
Election returns — 324.9
Electioneering — 324.7
Elections — 324
  labor unions — 331.87
Electoral systems — 324.6
Electric automobiles
  engineering — 629.22
  see also Automotive vehicles
Electric circuits — 621.319
Electric currents
  physics — 537.6
Electric eyes — 621.381 5
Electric heating — 621.402
Electric lighting — 621.32
  see also Lighting
Electric motors — 621.46
Electric organs (Animals) — 573.9
Electric power — 333.793
  economics — 333.793
  engineering — 621.31
  law — 343.09
  see also Public utilities
Electric power generation — 621.31
Electric railroads — 385
  electrification — 621.33
  engineering — 625.1
  transportation services — 385
Electric signs
  advertising — 659.13
Electric utilities — 333.793
  see Manual at 333.7–333.9 vs.
    363.6
Electric welding — 671.5
Electrical appliances — 643
  manufacturing technology — 683
Electrical engineering — 621.3
Electrical engineers — 621.309 2
Electrical machinery — 621.31
Electricians (Interior wiring) — 621.319
Electricity — 333.793
  economics — 333.793
  meteorology — 551.56
  physics — 537
Electrification — 333.793
  technology — 621.319
Electroacoustical
  communications
  engineering — 621.382
Electrocardiography
  medicine — 616.1

Employee benefits	331.25
Employee dismissal	
personnel management	658.3
Employee morale	
personnel management	658.3
Employee organizations	331.88
personnel management	658.3
Employee participation in	
management	331.01
personnel management	658.3
Employee representation in	
management	331.01
personnel management	658.3
Employees	331.11
Employment	331.12
see Manual at 331.1 vs.	
331.11, 331.12	
Employment agencies	331.12
Employment rights	331.01
Employment security	331.25
Employment services	331.12
public administration	354.9
Enactment of laws	328.3
Enameling	
ceramic arts	738.4
Enamels	666
Encyclicals	262.9
Encyclopedia yearbooks	030
Encyclopedias	030
	T1—03
End of the world	
controversial knowledge	001.9
religion	291.2
Christianity	236
Endangered animals	591.68
Endangered birds	598.168
Endangered plants	581.68
Endangered species	578.68
resource economics	333.95
Endocrine system	573.4
biology	573.4
human diseases	362.1
medicine	616.4
social services	362.1
human physiology	612.4
surgery	617.4
see Manual at 573.4 vs. 571.7	
Endocrinology	573.4
medicine	616.4
Endodontics	617.6
Endometriosis	
gynecology	618.1
Endoscopy	
medicine	616.07

Energy	333.79
classical physics	531
philosophy	118
physics	530
public administration	354.4
resource economics	333.79
see Manual at 333.7–333.9 vs.	
363.6	
Energy conservation	333.791
home economics	644
Energy consumption	333.79
Energy development	333.79
Energy engineering	621.042
buildings	696
Energy management	333.79
business	658.2
	T1—068
Energy policy	333.79
Energy resources	333.79
economic geology	553.2
extraction	622
economics	338.2
public administration	354.4
Engagement (Betrothal)	392.4
customs	392.4
etiquette	395.2
Engineering	620
Engineering drawing	604.2
Engineering geology	624.1
Engineering graphics	604.2
Engineering materials	620.1
Engineering mechanics	620.1
Engineering optics	621.36
Engineering services (Armed	
forces)	358
air forces	358.4
navy	359.9
Engineers	620.009 2
Engines	621.4
automotive	629.25
England	942
	T2—42
ancient	936.2
	T2—362
see Manual at 941	
England, Northern	T2—427
English (People)	942
social group	305.82
English as a second language	
elementary education	372.652
English Channel	T2—163
English creole languages	427
English horns	788.5

Episcopal Church	283
Epistemology	121
Epistles (Bible)	227
Epitaphs	
genealogy	929
Equal economic opportunity	
government programs	354.08
Equal education opportunity	379.2
Equal employment opportunity	331.13
economics	331.13
labor unions	331.87
government programs	354.908
personnel management	658.300 8
government employees	352.608
Equal opportunity	
government programs	353.53
Equal pay for equal work	331.2
Equal protection of the law	323.42
Equality	305
civil right	323.42
political theory	320.01
Equations	511.3
algebra	512.9
calculus	515
Equatorial Guinea	967.18
	T2—671 8
Equatorial Islands	T2—964
Equestrian sports	798
Equidae	599.66
animal husbandry	636.1
Equilibrium	
macroeconomic policy	339.5
Equipment	T1—028
armed forces	355.8
educational use	T1—078
local Christian parishes	254
Ergonomics	620.8
Erie, Lake	T2—771
Eritrea	963.5
	T2—635
Eritreans	963.5
social group	305.892
Erogeneity	155.3
Erosion	551.3
agriculture	631.4
engineering	627
geology	551.3
Erotica	
fine arts	704.9
Error-correcting codes	005.7
Errors	001.9
logic	165
psychology of perception	153.7
Escalators	621.8

Eschatology	291.2
Christianity	236
Islam	297.2
Judaism	296.3
philosophy of religion	218
Eskimo	
social group	305.897
Eskimo dogs	636.73
Eskimo languages	497
Esoteric societies	366
ESP (Extrasensory perception)	133.8
Esperanto language	499
Espionage	327.12
armed forces	355.3
ethics	172
international politics	327.12
public administration	353.1
Essayists (Literature)	809.4
collected biography	809.4
specific literatures	T3—400 9
individual biography	T3—4
Essays	080
see Manual at 080 vs. 800	
Essays (Literature)	808.84
criticism	809.4
theory	808.4
history	809.4
rhetoric	808.4
specific literatures	T3—4
Essence (Philosophy)	111
Essex (England)	T2—426
Estate planning	332.024
law	346.05
Estate tax	336.2
law	343.05
Esther (Biblical book)	222
Estimates	T1—029
building construction	692
Estonia	947.98
	T2—479 8
Estonian language	494
Estonians	947.98
social group	305.89
Estuaries	551.46
see Manual at T2—162	
Etching	
graphic arts	767
Etching glass	
arts	748.6
Eternity	
philosophy	115
Ethical education	370.11
Ethical systems	171

Evangelism	269
Evangelistic writings	243
Evaporation	536
meteorology	551.57
Even-toed ungulates	599.63
Evening prayer	
music	782.32
Everyday life	
art representation	704.9
Eviction	346.04
Evidence	
epistemology	121
Evidence (Law)	347
criminal law	345
Evil (Concept)	111
ethics	170
religion	291.5
religion	291.2
Christianity	230
freedom of choice	233
philosophy of religion	214
Evil eye	133.4
Evil spirits	133.4
Evolution	576.8
animals	591.3
biology	576.8
ethical systems	171
humans	599.93
philosophy	116
plants	581.3
see Manual at 576.8 vs. 560	
Evolution versus creation	291.2
Christianity	231.7
see Manual at 231.7 vs.	
213, 500, 576.8	
Judaism	296.3
philosophy of religion	213
Evolutional psychology	155.7
Evolutionism	
philosophy	146
Ewe language	496
Ex-convicts	364.8
labor economics	331.5
Examinations (Educational tests)	371.26
	T1—076
teacher-prepared tests	371.27
Excavation	624.1
Excelsior	674
Exceptional children	
psychology	155.45
Exceptional students	371.9
Excise tax	336.2
law	343.05

Excretion	573.4
animals	573.4
human physiology	612.4
plants	575.7
Excretory system	573.4
Executive agencies	351
Executive branch of government	351
law	342
Executive councils	
public administration	352.24
Executive departments	351
description and duties	351
law	342
organization and structure	352.2
see Manual at 352–354	
Executive management	658.4
	T1—068
military administration	355.6
public administration	352.3
see Manual at 658.4 and	
T1—068	
Executive messages	
public administration	352.23
Executives	
personnel management	658.4
public administration	352.3
Exegesis	
sacred books	291.8
Bible	220.6
Talmud	296.1
Exercise	613.7
human physiology	612.7
physical fitness	613.7
therapeutics	615.8
see Manual at 613.7 vs. 646.7,	
796	
Exercise therapy	
medicine	615.8
Exercises (Education)	T1—076
Exhibitions	907.4
	T1—074
advertising	659.1
civilization	907.4
commerce	381
public administrative support	352.7
technology	607
Exhibits	
museology	069
preparation	T1—075
Existence	111
Existence of God	212
Existential psychology	150.19
Existentialism	142
Exodus (Bible)	222

Facsimile transmission	384.1
engineering	621.382
Fact books	030
Fact finding	001.4
public administration	352.7
Factor analysis	519.5
Factories	
architecture	725
manufacturing industries	338.4
manufacturing technology	670
organization of production	338.6
Factors of production	338
income distribution	339.2
microeconomics	338.5
Factory operations engineering	670.42
Faculty	371.1
Faeroes	T2—491 5
Faeroese dialect	439
Faience	738.3
Failure (Materials science)	620.1
Fairies	398.21
Fairs	
customs	394
distribution channels	381
see also Exhibitions	
Fairy tales	398.2
Faith	121
epistemology	121
religion	291.2
Christianity	234
knowledge of God	231
Islam	297.2
Judaism	296.3
Faith and reason	210
Christianity	231
philosophy of religion	210
Faith healing	
medicine	615.8
see Manual at 615.8 vs. 234,	
291.3	
Falangism	335.6
Falconiformes	598.9
Falconry	799.2
Falcons	598.9
Falkland Islands	T2—97
Fall	508.2
Fall of humankind	233
Fallacies	001.9
logic	165
False arrest	346.03
Families	306.85
applied psychology	158.2
histories	929

Families (continued)	
psychological influence	155.9
religion	
guides to life	291.4
Christianity	248.4
pastoral theology	291.6
Christianity	259
worship	291.4
Christianity	249
Judaism	296.4
social welfare	362.82
public administration	353.53
sociology	306.85
Families of clergymen	
pastoral theology	253
Family	306.85
see also Families	
Family abuse	362.82
psychiatry	616.85
social welfare	362.82
sociology	306.87
Family budgets	
macroeconomics	339.4
Family counseling	362.82
Christian pastoral counseling	259
Family dissolution	306.88
Family ethics	173
Family histories	929
Family law	346.01
Family life	306.85
applied psychology	158.2
customs	392.3
elementary education	372.82
religion	291.4
Christianity	248.4
Family living	646.7
elementary education	372.82
Family medicine	610
Family names	929.4
Family planning	363.9
see also Birth control	
Family psychotherapy	
psychiatry	616.89
Family relationships	306.87
Family size	
demography	304.6
Family violence	362.82
psychiatry	616.85
social welfare	362.82
sociology	306.87
Famine	363.8
Fans (Machinery)	621.6
Fantasy	154.3
Fantasy fiction	808.83

Females (Human)	305.4
	T1—082
see also Women	
Femininity	155.3
Feminism	305.42
Fencers	796.860 92
Fences	631.2
Fencing (Swordplay)	796.86
Fennec fox	599.776
Fens, The (England)	T2—426
Fermentation	547
chemical engineering	660
Ferns	587
Ferrous metals	669
decorative arts	739.4
metallurgy	669
metalworking	672
Ferry transportation	386
Fertilization in vitro	
ethics	176
medicine	618.1
Fertilizers	631.8
chemical engineering	668
Festivals	394.26
	T1—079
customs	394.26
performing arts	791.6
Fetal disorders	
medicine	618.3
Fetishism	
religion	291.2
Feudal law	340.5
Fever	
symptomatology	616
Fever blisters	
medicine	616.5
Few-bodies problem	530.14
Fiber crops	633.5
Fiber glass	666
Fiber optics	621.36
Fiberboards	676
Fibers	
textile materials	677
Fiction	808.83
criticism	809.3
theory	808.3
folklore	398.2
history	809.3
rhetoric	808.3
specific literatures	T3—3
Fiction writers	809.3
collected biography	809.3
specific literatures	T3—300 9
individual biography	T3—3

Fictions	
logic	165
Fiduciary trusts	346.05
Field athletics	796.43
Field crops	633
see Manual at 633–635	
Field hockey	796.355
Field houses	796.06
Field theory (Physics)	530.14
Field trips	371.3
Fields (Mathematics)	512
Fife (Scotland)	T2—412
Fighters (Aircraft)	358.4
engineering	623.7
military equipment	358.4
Figure skating	796.91
Figurines	666
ceramic arts	738.8
Fiji	996.11
	T2—961 1
File formats	
computer science	005.74
File management systems	
computer science	
data file programs	005.74
systems programs	005.4
see Manual at 005.74 vs.	
005.4	
File organization	
computer science	
data files	005.74
systems programs	005.4
see Manual at 005.74 vs.	
005.4	
File processing	
databases	005.74
File structure	
computer science	
data files	005.74
see Manual at 005.74 vs.	
005.4	
File system management	
computer science	005.4
see Manual at 005.74 vs.	
005.4	
Filers (Clerks)	651.3
Files (Data)	
computer science	005.74
Filing	
records management	651.5
Filipino language	499
Filipinos	959.9
social group	305.89
Film music	781.5

Fluid-power technology	620.1
Flukes (Worms)	592
Fluoridation	
water supply engineering	628.1
Fluorine	553
chemistry	546
economic geology	553
Flutes	788.3
Flutists	788.3
Flying (Aeronautics)	629.132
sports	797.5
Flying (Animals)	
behavior	591.5
physiology	573.7
Flying discs (Game)	796.2
Flying reptiles	567.918
Flying saucers	001.942
Foams	541.3
Fogs	541.3
colloid chemistry	541.3
meteorology	551.57
Folds (Geology)	551.8
Folk arts	745
Folk beliefs	
folklore	398
Folk dancing	793.3
see Manual at 792.7 vs. 792.8,	
793.3	
Folk high schools	374
Folk literature	398.2
see also Literature	
see Manual at 398.2; *also at*	
398.2 vs. 291.1; *also at*	
398.2 vs. 398; *also at* 800	
vs. 398.2	
Folk medicine	398.27
folklore	398.27
therapeutics	615.8
see Manual at 398, 398.27 vs.	
615.8; *also at* 615.8	
Folk music	781.62
see Manual at 781.62 vs.	
780.89; *also at* 781.62 vs.	
781.62009	
Folk musicians	781.620 092
Folk singers	782.421 620 92
Folk songs	782.421 62
Folklore	398
history and criticism	398.09
Folklorists	398.092
Folkways	306
sociology	390
Food	641.3
agricultural economics	338.1

Food (continued)	
commercial processing	
economics	338.4
technology	664
cooking	641.5
customs	394.1
elementary education	372.3
folklore	398.27
health	613.2
home economics	641.3
home preservation	641.4
preservation techniques	664
product safety	363.19
see Manual at 363.8 vs. 613.2,	
641.3; *also at* 630 vs.	
579–590, 641.3	
Food addiction	
medicine	616.85
Food additives	641.3
commercial technology	664
food	641.3
home preservation	641.4
product safety	363.19
Food allergies	
medicine	616.97
Food chains (Ecology)	577
Food poisons	
human toxicology	615.9
Food processing industry	338.4
Food safety	363.19
Food services	
schools	371.7
Food services industry	338.4
Food stamp programs	363.8
Food storage (Plant physiology)	575.7
Food supply	363.8
economics	338.1
social welfare	363.8
see Manual at 363.5, 363.6,	
363.8 vs. 338; *also at*	
363.8 vs. 338.1; *also at*	
363.8 vs. 613.2, 641.3	
Food technology	664
Foot forces (Military)	356
Football	796.33
Footwear	391.4
commercial technology	685
customs	391.4
see also Clothing	
Forage crops	633.2
Force (Energy)	
philosophy	118
Ford, Gerald R.	
United States history	973.925

Forecasting	003	Forests	333.75
	T1—01		T2—15
business	338.5	Forfeit games	793.5
investments	332.67	Forgeries	
management decision making	658.4	arts	702.8
marketing management	658.8	books	098
occultism	133.3	paintings	751.5
social change	303.49	Forgetting	153.1
weather	551.63	Forging	671.3
Forecasts	003	blacksmithing	682
	T1—01	decorative arts	739
Foreign aid	338.91	Forgiveness (Christian doctrine)	234
economics	338.91	Form (Concept)	
international law	341.7	philosophy	117
international relations	327.1	Form letters	
Foreign economic relations	337	office use	651.7
Foreign exchange	332.4	Formal languages	511.3
international law	341.7	Former Yugoslav Republic of	
Foreign investment	332.67	Macedonia	949.76
Foreign languages			T2—497 6
elementary education	372.65	Formosa	951.24
Foreign legions	355.3		T2—512 4
Foreign policy	327.1	Forms of address	
Foreign relations	327	etiquette	395.4
see also International relations		Forms of music	781.8
Foreign students	371.826	instrumental	784.18
Foreign study	370.116	vocal	782
Foreign trade	382	Formula plans	
public administration	354.74	investments	332.67
see also Commerce		Fort Smith (N.W.T.)	T2—719
Foreign words	412	Fortification	
specific languages	T4—2	military engineering	623
Forensic medicine	614	Forts	
Forensic science	363.25	military engineering	623
Forest fires	363.37	military installations	355.7
forestry	634.9	Fortune-telling	133.3
social services	363.37	Fossil fuels	553.2
Forest lands	333.75	resource economics	333.8
biology	578.73	*see also* Energy resources	
ecology	577.3	Fossils	560
economics	333.75	Foster children	306.874
landscape architecture	719	psychology	155.44
recreational resources	333.78	social welfare	362.73
see Manual at 338.1 vs.		Foster homes	362.73
333.75		Foster parents	306.874
Forest products	634.9		T1—085
economics	338.1	social welfare	362.73
Forest reserves	333.75	Foucault's pendulum	525
see also Conservation of		Found objects	
natural resources		handicrafts	745.58
Foresters	634.909 2	Foundations (Building elements)	721
Forestry	634.9	architecture	721
public administration	354.5	structural engineering	624.1

Freshwater lagoons (continued)	
ecology	577.63
Freshwater plants	581.7
Freudian psychology	150.19
Friction	531
machine engineering	621.8
Friendly Islands	T2—961 2
Friends (Religious society)	289.6
biography	289.609 2
Friends of the library	
organizations	021.7
Friendship	177
applied psychology	158.2
ethics	177
psychological influence	155.9
social psychology	302.3
Frigid zones	T2—11
biology	578.091 1
Fringe benefits	331.25
personnel management	658.3
executives	658.4
Frisbees®	796.2
Frisian language	439
Frogs	597.8
farming	639.3
Front-end systems	025.04
Frontier troops	355.3
Frost	551.3
cold spell	551.5
geologic agent	551.3
hydrometeorology	551.57
Frozen desserts	641.8
commercial processing	637
home preparation	641.8
Frozen dinners	
home serving	642
Frozen foods	
cooking	641.6
Fruits	581.4
commercial processing	664
cooking	641.6
descriptive botany	581.4
food	641.3
home preservation	641.4
orchard crop	634
physiology	575.6
product safety	363.19
Frustration	152.4
Frying	641.7
Fuel alcohols	662
Fuel cells	621.31
Fuel oils	665.5
Fuels	662
chemical engineering	662

Fuels (continued)	
heat engineering	621.402
public administration	354.4
resource economics	333.8
Fuelwood	333.95
Fugues	784.18
Fulani language	496
Full employment policies	331.12
macroeconomics	339.5
see Manual at 331.12 vs.	
331.13	
Full-text databases	
computer science	005.75
Fumaroles	551.2
Fumigation	
agricultural pest control	632
public health	614.4
Function theory	515
Functional analysis	515
Functionalism	
psychology	150.19
Functions (Mathematics)	511.3
calculus	515
Fund raising	658.15
	T1—068
local Christian church	254
social welfare	361.706 8
study and teaching	T1—079
Fundamental education	370.11
adult level	374
Fundamental interactions	
(Nuclear physics)	539.7
Fundamental theology	
(Christianity)	230.01
Fundamentalism	
Christianity	270.8
independent denominations	289.9
Protestantism	280
Islam	297.09
see Manual at 320.5 vs.	
297.09, 322	
Fundamentalist theology	230
Funerals	393
Christian rites	265
customs	393
etiquette	395.2
Islamic rites	297.3
Jewish rites	296.4
religious rites	291.3
Fungi	579.5
Fungicides	668
agricultural use	632
chemical engineering	668
Funnies	741.5

Garage sales	381
management	658.8
Garages	
automotive engineering	629.28
Garbage collection	
technology	628.4
Garbage disposal	363.72
see also Waste control	
Garden crops	635
see Manual at 633–635	
Gardeners	635.092
Gardening	635
Gardens	635
landscape architecture	712
Garment workers	687.092
Garments	391
see also Clothing	
Gas engineering	665.7
Gas lighting	621.32
Gas mechanics	533
engineering	620.1
Gas-turbine engines	621.43
Gaseous-state physics	530.4
Gaseous wastes	363.72
social services	363.72
technology	628.5
see also Waste control	
Gases (Fuels)	665.7
public utilities	363.6
Gasohol	662
Gasoline	665.5
Gasoline engines	621.43
Gastroenterology	616.3
Gastronomy	641.01
Gateways	
landscape architecture	717
GATT (Commerce)	382
Gaul	936.4
	T2—364
Gautama Buddha	294.3
Gay men	305.38
Gay women	305.48
Gay workers	331.5
Gays	305.9
	T1—086
female	305.48
labor economics	331.5
male	305.38
Gaza Strip	T2—53
Gazelles	599.64
Gazetteers	910.3
	T1—03
Gazettes (Official publications)	351.05
Gears	621.8

Geese	598.4
animal husbandry	636.5
Geez language	492
Gels	541.3
Gems	553.8
carving	736
economic geology	553.8
mining	622
synthetic	666
Gender identity	305.3
Gene therapy	
medicine	616
Genealogists	929
Genealogy	929
General Agreement on Tariffs	
and Trade (1947)	382
General paresis	
medicine	616.89
General services agencies	352.5
Generating machinery	
electrical engineering	621.31
Generation gap	305.2
family relationships	306.874
Generative grammar	415
specific languages	T4—5
Generative organs	573.6
see also Genital system	
Genes	572.8
Genesis (Bible)	222
Genetic disorders (Human)	
medicine	616
Genetic engineering	660.6
agriculture	631.5
ethics	174
Genetic psychology	155.7
Genetics	576.5
animal husbandry	636.08
animals	591.3
humans	599.93
plants	581.3
sociology	304.5
see Manual at 576.5 vs. 572.8	
Geneva Conventions	341.6
Genital herpes	
medicine	616.95
Genital system	573.6
animals	573.6
gynecology	618.1
human anatomy	611
human diseases	362.1
medicine	616.6
social services	362.1
human physiology	612.6

Gestures
  psychology (continued)
    nonverbal communication   153.6
Geysers   551.2
Ghana   966.7
    T2—667
Ghanaians   966.7
Ghettos   307.3
Ghosts   133.1
  folklore   398.25
  occultism   133.1
Giant panda   599.789
Giant schnauzer   636.73
Gibbons   599.88
Gibraltar   946.8
    T2—468
Gift tax   336.2
  law   343.05
Gift wrappings   745.54
Gifted children
  psychology   155.45
Gifted persons   305.9
    T1—087
  special education   371.95
Gigantism (Pituitary)
  medicine   616.4
Gila monsters   597.95
Gilding
  decorative arts   745.7
Gilles de la Tourette syndrome
  medicine   616.8
Giraffe   599.638
Girl Guides Association   369.463
Girl Scouts   369.463
Girls   305.23
    T1—083
  education   371.823
  psychology   155.43
  see also Children
Girls' societies   369.46
Glaciers   551.31
Glaciology   551.31
Glands   571.7
  biology   571.7
    endocrine system   573.4
  human physiology   612.4
  medicine   616.4
Glass   666
  building construction   693
  building materials   691
  decorative arts   748
  materials science   620.1
  technology   666
Glass insurance   368.6

Glassblowing
  decorative arts   748.202 8
Glassware
  decorative arts   748.2
  table setting   642
Glaucoma
  ophthalmology   617.7
Gliders (Aircraft)
  engineering   629.133
Gliding
  sports   797.5
Global analysis   514
Global warming   363.738
Glossolalia   234
Gloucestershire (England)   T2—424
Gloves   391.4
  commercial technology   685
  customs   391.4
Glowworms   595.76
Glue   668
Gluttony   178
Glyptics   736
Gnats   595.77
Gnosticism   299
  Christian heresy   273
GNP (Macroeconomics)   339.3
Goats   636.3
  animal husbandry   636.3
  zoology   599.64
Gobi Desert (Mongolia and
  China)   T2—517
God   211
  Christianity   231
  comparative religion   291.2
  Islam   297.2
  Judaism   296.3
  philosophy of religion   211
Goddesses   291.2
Gods   291.2
Gods and goddesses   291.2
  African   299
  Buddhist   294.3
  Celtic   299
  classical   292.2
  Egyptian   299
  folklore   398.21
  Germanic   293
  Greek   292.2
  Hindu   294.5
  Native American   299
  Norse   293
  Roman   292.2
Gold   669
  chemistry   546

Grammar	415
applied linguistics	418
specific languages	T4—8
elementary education	372.61
linguistics	415
specific languages	T4—5
Grammar schools (United Kingdom)	373.24
Grammar schools (United States)	372
Grammarians	415.092
Grampian (Scotland)	T2—412
Grand Army of the Republic	369
Grand jury	345
Grandchildren	306.874
Grandparents	306.874
	T1—085
Granite	553.5
Grants	
education	379.1
	T1—079
public policy	379.1
student aid	371.2
higher education	378.3
public administration	352.73
research	001.4
	T1—079
Grants-in-aid (Government)	336.1
public administration	352.73
Grapes	641.3
botany	583
cooking	641.6
food	641.3
viticulture	634.8
Graph theory	511
Graphic artists	760.092
Graphic arts	760
Graphic design	
arts	741.6
Graphic novels	741.5
Graphical user interfaces	
systems programs	005.4
Graphics	
computer science	006.6
Graphite	553
chemical engineering	662
economic geology	553
Graphology	155.2
divination	137
Grasses	584
forage crops	633.2
Grasshoppers	595.7
Grasslands	333.74
	T2—15

Grasslands (continued)	
biology	578.74
ecology	577.4
economics	333.74
geomorphology	551.45
Gravel	553.6
Graves registration service (Armed forces)	355.6
Gravity	531
celestial mechanics	521
Gray fox	599.776
Gray wolf	599.773
Grazing lands	333.74
Great apes	599.88
Great Barrier Reef (Qld.)	T2—943
Great Basin	T2—79
Great Britain	941
	T2—41
ancient	936.1
	T2—361
see Manual at 941	
Great Dane	636.73
Great Lakes	T2—77
Canada	T2—713
United States	T2—77
Great Northern War, 1700–1721	947
Great Plains	T2—78
Great Rift Valley	T2—676
Great whales	599.5
Greater Antilles	T2—729
Greater Manchester (England)	T2—427
Grebes	598.4
Greece	949.5
	T2—495
ancient	938
	T2—38
Greed	178
Greek architecture	722
Greek language	480
Greek language (Modern)	489
Greek-letter societies	371.8
	T1—06
Greek literature	880
Greek philosophy	180
modern	199
Greek religion	292.08
Greek sculpture	733
Greeks	949.5
ancient	938
modern	949.5
social group	305.88
Greenhouse effect	363.738
pollution aspects	363.738

Gulf Coast (U.S.)	T2—76
Gulf of Mexico	T2—163
Gulf Stream	551.47
Gulf War, 1980–1988	955.05
Gulf War, 1991	956.704 4
Gulls	598.3
Gums	572
Gums (Substances)	
commercial processing	668
Gun control	363.3
civil rights issue	323.4
law	344
public safety	363.3
Gundogs	636.752
Gunnery	623
Guns (Artillery)	355.8
engineering	623.4
military equipment	355.8
Guns (Small arms)	683.4
art metalwork	739.7
manufacturing technology	683.4
military engineering	623.4
military equipment	355.8
shooting game	799.2
sports	799.202 8
target shooting	799.3
Gunsmithing	683.4
Gunsmiths	683.400 92
Gurus	200.92
Buddhist	294.309 2
Hindu	294.509 2
role and function	291.6
Sikh	294.609 2
Guyana	988.1
	T2—881
Guyane	988.2
	T2—882
Gymnasiums (Secondary schools)	373.24
Gymnasiums (Sports)	796.406
Gymnastic exercises	613.7
Gymnastics	796.44
Gymnasts	796.440 92
Gymnosperms	585
Gynecologists	618.100 92
Gynecology	618.1
Gypsies	
social group	305.891
Gypsum	553.6
Gypsy language	491.4

H

Habakkuk (Biblical book)	224

Habeas corpus	347
criminal law	345
Habit breaking	152.3
Habitat improvement (Wildlife)	
technology	639.9
Habits	
customs	390
psychology	152.3
Hadith	297.1
Haggadah (Passover)	296.4
Haggai (Biblical book)	224
Hail	551.57
Hailstorms	551.55
Hair	599.147
animal physiology	573.5
descriptive zoology	599.147
human diseases	
medicine	616.5
human physiology	612.7
personal care	646.7
Hair styles	646.7
customs	391.5
Hairdressing	646.7
customs	391.5
Haiti	972.94
	T2—729 4
Haitian literature	840
Haitians	972.94
social group	305.896
Hajj	297.3
Halakhah	296.1
Halfway houses	365
corrections	365
maladjusted young people	362.74
Halley's Comet	523.6
Halloween	394.264 6
Hallucinations	
psychology	154.4
Hallucinogen abuse	362.29
Ham radio	
engineering	621.384 1
see Manual at 621.3841 vs. 621.3845	
Hamito-Semitic languages	492
Hammers	621.9
Hampshire (England)	T2—422
Hamsters	636.935
animal husbandry	636.935
zoology	599.35
Hand tools	621.9
Handbags	391.4
customs	391.4
manufacturing technology	685
Handball	796.31

Hiking	796.51
Hill climbing	796.52
Hills	551.43
Himalaya Mountains	T2—549 6
Hindi language	491.4
Hindis	
civilization	954
social group	305.891
Hindu philosophy	181
Hinduism	294.5
Hindus	
biography	294.509 2
Hippies	305.5
Hippopotamuses	599.63
Hiring halls	331.88
Hispanic Americans	
social group	305.868
Hispaniola	T2—729 3
Histochemistry	572
Histology	571.5
humans	611
Histopathology	571.9
Historians	907
Historic buildings	
preservation	363.6
see Manual at 913–919:	
Historic sites and	
buildings	
Historic preservation	363.6
see Manual at 930–990:	
Historic preservation	
Historical atlases	911
Historical bibliography	002
Historical books (Old	
Testament)	222
Historical chronology	902
Historical drama	792.1
literature	808.82
stage presentation	792.1
Historical events	900
art representation	704.9
see also History	
see Manual at 900	
Historical fiction	808.83
Historical geography	911
Historical geology	551.7
see Manual at 551.7 vs. 560	
Historical linguistics	417
specific languages	T4—7
see Manual at 410	
Historical materialism	
Marxian theory	335.4
Historical research	001.4

Historical themes	
folklore	398.27
History	900
	T1—09
Biblical events	220.9
elementary education	372.89
specific places	930–990
see Manual at 930–990 vs.	
355.009	
world	909
see Manual at 305 vs. 306,	
909, 930–990; *also at*	
909, 930–990 vs. 320	
Hittite language	491
HMO (Social welfare)	362.1
Hmong (Asian people)	
social group	305.895
Hmong language	495.9
Hmong-Mien languages	495.9
Hoaxes	001.9
books	098
Hobbies	T1—023
recreation	790.1
Hobgoblins	133.1
folklore	398.25
occultism	133.1
Hoboes	305.5
Hockey (Field sports)	796.355
Hockey (Ice sports)	796.962
Hockey players (Ice sports)	796.962 092
Hogs	636.4
animal husbandry	636.4
zoology	599.63
Hoisting equipment	621.8
Holding companies	338.8
Holidays	394.26
cooking	641.5
customs	394.26
religion	291.3
Christianity	263
see also Holy days	
Holiness	291.2
Christian doctrine	234
Holistic medicine	610
health	613
therapeutics	615.5
Holland	949.2
	T2—492
ancient	936.4
	T2—364
Holocaust, 1933–1945	940.53
Holography	774
arts	774
engineering	621.36

Holy Communion	234	Homemakers	640.92
public worship	264		T1—088
theology	234	Homemaking	640
Holy days	291.3	Homeopathy	
Christianity	263	therapeutic system	615.5
customs	394.265	Homes	640
see Manual at 263, 291.3		customs	392.3
vs. 394.265		home economics	640
Islam	297.3	Homework	371.302 8
Judaism	296.4	Homicide	364.15
Holy Family	232.92	ethics	179.7
Holy Roman Empire	943	law	345
	T2—43	Homiletics	
church history	270	Christianity	251
Holy Spirit	231	Hominids	599.9
Holy war (Islam)	297.7	paleozoology	569.9
Holy Week	263	Hominoids	599.88
devotional literature	242	Homosexuality	306.76
Home affairs departments	353.3	ethics	176
Home aquariums	639.34	*see also* Sexual relations—	
Home-based enterprises		ethics	
management	658	medicine	616.85
Home buying	643	*see Manual at* 616.85	
Home care services	362.1	social problem	363.4
Home computers	004.16	Homosexuals	305.9
see also Microcomputers			T1—086
Home Counties	T2—422	female	305.48
Home departments	353.3	male	305.38
Home economics	640	Honduran literature	860
customs	392.3	Hondurans	972.83
elementary education	372.82	Honduras	972.83
Home finance	332.7		T2—728 3
Home gardens	635	Honesty	179
Home guards	355.3	Honey	641.3
Home improvement	690	cooking	641.6
home economics	643	food	641.3
see Manual at 690 vs. 643		processing	638
Home instruction	371.39	Hong Kong	951.25
Home loan associations	332.3		T2—512 5
Home medicine	616.02	Honor societies	
Home remedies		education	371.8
therapeutics	615.8	Honorary degrees	378.2
Home rental	643	Honorary titles	T1—079
Home repairs	690	Honors	
see Manual at 690 vs. 643		awards	929.8
Home safety	363.13	Honors work	371.39
Home schools	371.04	Hoofed mammals	599.6
Home selection	643	Hope	
Home video systems	778.59	Christianity	234
engineering	621.388	psychology	152.4
video production	778.59	Hopi Indians	
Home workshops	684	social group	305.897
Homeless persons	305.5	Hormones	571.7
social welfare	362.5	animal physiology	573.4

Hormones (continued)	
biochemistry	571.7
human physiology	612.4
see Manual at 573.4 vs. 571.7	
Horn of Africa	T2—63
Horn players	788.9
Hornbills	598.7
Horned dinosaurs	567.915
Horns	788.9
English	788.5
French	788.9
Horns (Animals)	591.47
descriptive zoology	591.47
physiology	573.5
Hornworts (Bryophytes)	588
Horology	529
Horoscopes	133.5
Horror	
psychology	152.4
Horror fiction	808.83
Horse cavalry	357
Horse racing	798.4
Horsemanship	
sports	798.2
Horses	636.1
animal husbandry	636.1
zoology	599.665
Horseshoeing	682
Horseshoes (Game)	796.2
Horsetails (Plants)	587
Horticulture	635
Horticulturists	635.092
Hosea (Biblical book)	224
Hosiery	391.4
see also Clothing	
Hospices (Inns)	647.94
Hospices (Terminal care	
facilities)	362.1
Hospital chaplaincy	259
Hospital insurance	368.38
Hospital libraries	027.6
Hospitality	
ethics	177
etiquette	395.3
Hospitals	362.1
architecture	725
institutional housekeeping	647
social welfare	362.1
Hostels	647.94
Hostile environments	
biology	578.75
ecology	577.5
Hot rods	796.72
engineering	629.228

Hot rods (continued)	
sports	796.72
Hot springs	551.2
Hot-water supply	
buildings	696
Hot-working operations	
metals	671.3
Hotel industry	338.4
Hotels	647.94
architecture	728
Hounds	636.753
Hourglasses	
technology	681.1
Hours of work	331.25
House organs	T1—05
House painting	698
House selling	333.33
Houseboats	643
architecture	728.7
Housecleaning	648
Household appliances	643
manufacturing technology	683
product safety	363.19
Household budgets	
home economics	640
macroeconomics	339.4
Household employees	640
Household equipment	643
Household finances	640
see Manual at 332.024 vs. 640	
Household furnishings	645
customs	392.3
household management	645
manufacturing technology	684
Household income	
macroeconomics	339.2
Household management	640
public households	647
Household pests	
control technology	628.9
Household sanitation	648
Household security	643
Household utilities	644
Housekeeping	648
Houseplants	635.9
interior decoration	747
Houses	643
architecture	728
construction	690
home economics	643
see Manual at 363.5 vs. 643	
Housewives	640.92
	T1—088
social group	305.43

Humor (continued)	
specific subjects	T1—02
see Manual at T1—02 vs.	
T3—7, T3—8	
Humorists	809.7
collected biography	809.7
specific literatures	T3—700 9
Humorous fiction	808.83
Humorous poetry	808.81
Hundred Years' War,	
1337–1453	944
Hungarian language	494
Hungarians	943.9
social group	305.89
Hungary	943.9
	T2—439
Hunger	
psychology	152.1
social welfare	363.8
Hunters	
commercial	639
sports	799.292
Hunting	799.2
commercial	639
production economics	338.3
public administration	354.3
ethics	179
game laws	346.04
public administration	354.3
sports	799.2
Hunting dogs	636.75
Hunting lodges	
architecture	728.7
Huron, Lake (Mich. and	
Ont.)	T2—774
Hurrian languages	499
Hurricanes	551.55
weather forecasting	551.64
see also Disasters	
Husband and wife	306.872
law	346.01
Husbands	306.872
Huskies	636.73
Hussein, Saddam	
Iraqi history	956.704 4
Hussites	284
Hutterian Brethren	289.7
HVAC (Building systems)	697
Hydraulic engineering	627
Hydraulic engineers	627.092
Hydraulic machinery	621.2
Hydraulic-power engineering	621.2
Hydraulic pumps	621.2
Hydraulic structures	627
Hydraulics	532
Hydrocarbons	547
chemical engineering	661
Hydrodynamics	532
Hydroelectric power	333.91
Hydroelectric power plants	621.31
Hydrogen	553
chemistry	546
economic geology	553
gas technology	665.8
Hydrography	551.46
Hydrological cycle	551.48
Hydrology (Fresh waters)	551.48
Hydromechanics	532
Hydrometeorology	551.57
Hydroponics	631.5
Hydrosphere	551.46
Hydrostatics	532
Hydrotherapy	
medicine	615.8
Hydrozoa	593.5
Hyenas	599.74
Hygiene	613
customs	391.6
elementary education	372.3
personal	613
Hygienists	613.092
Hymenoptera	595.79
Hymns	782.27
religion	291.3
Christianity	264
Judaism	296.4
Hyperactive students	371.93
Hyperactivity	
medicine	616.85
pediatrics	618.92
Hyperborean languages	494
Hypersensitivity	
medicine	616.97
Hypertension	
medicine	616.1
Hypertext databases	
computer science	005.75
Hypnotherapy	
medicine	615.8
Hypnotism	154.7
parapsychology	133.8
Hypochondria	
medicine	616.85
Hypoglycemia	
medicine	616.4
Hypotheses	
logic	167
Hypothesis testing (Statistics)	519.5

Hyraxes	599.6
Hysterectomies	
surgery	618.1
Hysteria	
medicine	616.85

I

Iatrogenic diseases	
medicine	615.5
Iberia (Kingdom)	T2—39
Iberian Peninsula	T2—46
ancient	T2—366
Ibo language	496
Ice	551.31
economic geology	553.7
geology	551.31
manufacturing technology	621.5
Ice age	551.7
paleontology	560
Ice cream	641.8
commercial processing	637
Ice games	796.96
Ice hockey	796.962
Ice hockey players	796.962 092
Ice skates	
manufacturing technology	685
Ice skating	796.91
Ice sports	796.9
Icebergs	551.34
Iceboating	796.9
Iceland	949.12
	T2—491 2
Icelanders	949.12
social group	305.83
Icelandic language	439
Ichthyology	597
Iconography	
fine arts	704.9
see Manual at 704.9	
painting	753–758
Icons	
religious significance	291.3
Christianity	246
Id (Psychology)	154.2
Idaho	T2—796
Ideal states	321
Idealism	141
education	370.1
Ideas	
psychology	153.2
Identification marks	929.9
	T1—02

Identity (Human)	155.2
philosophy	126
Ideographs	411
specific languages	T4—1
Ideology	140
see Manual at 140	
Igneous rocks	552
Iguanodon	567.914
Illegitimacy	306.874
law	346.01
Illegitimate children	305.9
	T1—086
family relationships	306.874
social welfare	362.708 6
Illinois	T2—773
Illiteracy	302.2
see also Literacy	
Illness	362.1
medicine	616
see also Diseases (Human)	
Illumination (Decorative arts)	745.6
Illusions	001.9
psychology of perception	153.7
sensory perception	152.1
Illustration	
arts	741.6
see Manual at 741.6 vs. 800	
Illustrations	T1—022
notable books	096
Illustrators	741.609 2
Illyria	T2—39
Image processing	621.36
see Manual at 006.3 vs. 006.4, 621.36, 621.39	
Imagery (Psychology)	153.3
Images	
fine arts	704.9
Imagination	153.3
educational psychology	370.15
philosophy	128
Imams	297.092
biography	297.092
specific sects	297.8
role and function	297.6
Imitation furs	675
Imitation leathers	675
Immigrants	305.9
	T1—086
labor economics	331.6
Immigration	304.8
international law	341.4
law	342
political science	325
public administration	353.4

Immigration (continued)
sociology	304.8

Immortality
philosophy	129
religion	291.2
Christianity	236
Islam	297.2
Judaism	296.3
philosophy of religion	218

Immune deficiency diseases (Human)
medicine	616.97

Immune system
	571.9
human diseases	
medicine	616.97
humans	616.07

see Manual at 616.07 vs. 571.9

Immunity
	571.9
humans	616.07

see Manual at 616.07 vs. 571.9

Immunity of legislators	328.3

Immunization
disease control	614.4

Immunology
	571.9
humans	616.07

see Manual at 616.07 vs. 571.9

Impeachment	342
Imperial system (Measurement)	530.8
social aspects	389
Imperialism	325
international relations	327.1
Import quotas	382
Import tax	382
public finance	336.2
Import trade	382

see also Commerce

Impotence
medicine	616.6

Impressionism
fine arts	709.03
painting	759.05

Imprisonment	365
Improvisation (Music)	781.3

Impulse control disorders
medicine	616.85

In-laws	306.87
In-line skating	796.21
In-service training	331.25
	T1—071
libraries	023

In-service training (continued)
teachers	370.71

see also Vocational education

In-situ processing	622

see Manual at 622 vs. 662, 669

In vitro fertilization
ethics	176
medicine	618.1
Inaudible sound	534.5

Inaugural addresses
public administration	352.23

Inaugurations
customs	394

Inca
civilization	985
Incarnation of Jesus Christ	232
Incest	306.877
medicine	616.85
Inclined railroads	385
engineering	625.3

Income
increase	
personal finance	332.024
labor economics	331.2
macroeconomics	339.3

Income-consumption relations
macroeconomics	339.4

Income distribution
macroeconomics	339.2

Income policy
macroeconomics	339.5

Income redistribution
macroeconomic policy	339.5

Income tax	336.24
law	343.05
Incunabula	093
Independence Day (United States)	394.263 4
Independence days	394.26

Independent agencies
public administration	352.2

Independent Order of Odd Fellows | 366 |

Independent reading
elementary education	372.45
Independent study	371.39
Indexing	025.3
information science	025.3
subject	025.4
India	954
	T2—54
ancient	934
	T2—34

Industrial oils	665
Industrial pollution	363.73
social welfare	363.73
technology	628.5
Industrial productivity	338
Industrial property	346.04
Industrial psychology	158.7
Industrial railroads	385.5
Industrial relations	331
see Manual at 331 vs. 331.8	
Industrial research	
technology	607
Industrial resources	338.09
military science	355.2
Industrial revolution	909.81
economic history	330.9
Industrial safety	363.11
engineering	620.8
law	344
public administration	353.9
social services	363.11
Industrial sanitation	363.72
engineering	628.5
see also Waste control	
Industrial sociology	306.3
Industrial surveys	338.09
Industrial toxicology	
medicine	615.9
Industrial trusts	338.8
management	658
Industrial unions	331.88
Industrial wastes	363.72
pollution technology	628.5
social services	363.72
technology	628.4
see also Waste control	
Industrial workers	331.7
Industrial yellow pages	T1—029
see Manual at 338 vs. 060,	
381, 382, 670.29, 910,	
T1—025, T1—029	
Industrialization	338.9
Industry	338
economics	338
law	343
location	
economic rationale	338.6
public administration	354
relations with government	322
Industry-school relations	371.19
Inequality	305
Inerrancy (Bible)	220.1
Inertia	531

Infancy	305.232
see also Infants	
Infancy of Jesus Christ	232.92
Infant schools (United Kingdom)	372.24
Infantry	356
Infants	305.232
	T1—083
cooking for	641.5
home care	649
pediatrics	618.92
psychology	155.42
social aspects	305.232
Infectious diseases (Human)	362.1
incidence	614.5
medicine	616.9
see Manual at 616.1–616.8	
vs. 616.9; also at 616.9	
vs. 616	
social services	362.1
Inference	
psychology	153.4
statistical mathematics	519.5
Infertility	
gynecology	618.1
medicine	616.6
Infinite (Philosophy)	111
Inflammable materials	363.17
public safety	363.17
technology	604.7
see also Safety	
Inflammatory bowel disease	
medicine	616.3
Inflation (Economic)	332.4
personal finance	332.024
Inflection tables (Grammar)	
applied linguistics	418
specific languages	T4—82
Influence	
psychology	155.9
Influenza	
medicine	616.2
Informatics	
computer science	004
Information and referral services	025.5
Information centers	027
see also Libraries	
Information control	363.3
see also Censorship	
Information management	
executive management	658.4
office services	651
public administration	352.3

Information policy
 economics 338.9
  see Manual at 338.9 vs.
   352.7, 500
Information retrieval
 information sciences 025.5
Information science 020
 see Manual at 020
Information scientists 020.92
Information sources
 use 028.7
Information storage and retrieval
  systems 025.04
 computer science 005.74
Information technology
 computer science 004
 social effects 303.48
Information theory 003
 communications engineering 621.382
Infrared astronomy 522
Infrared photography 778.3
Infrared radiation 535.01
 engineering 621.36
Ingroups 302.4
Inheritance law 346.05
Inheritance tax 336.2
 law 343.05
Inherited diseases (Human)
 medicine 616
Initiation of business enterprises 338.7
 management 658.1
     T1—068
 see Manual at 658 vs. 658.1,
  658.4
Initiation rites
 customs 392.1
 etiquette 395.2
 religion 291.3
Initiative
 personality trait 155.2
Initiative (Legislation) 328.2
Injuries
 medicine 617.1
Injurious animals 591.6
Injurious organisms 578.6
Injurious plants 581.6
Ink drawing 741.2
Ink painting 751.4
Inks 667
Inland seas 551.46
     T2—16
Inland water transportation 386
 public administration 354.78

Inland waterways 386
 engineering 627
 land economics 333.91
Inlay trim
 wood handicrafts 745.51
Inmates (Prisoners) 365
Innocent passage 341.4
Inns 647.94
Inorganic chemistry 546
 applied 660
 see Manual at 541 vs. 546;
  also at 549 vs. 546
Inquisition (Church history) 272
Insanity 362.2
 see also Mental illness
Insect culture 638
Insecticides 668
 agricultural use 632
 chemical engineering 668
Insectivora 599.33
Insectivorous plants 583
Insects 595.7
 agricultural pests 632
 disease carriers
  medicine 614.4
 paleozoology 565
 zoology 595.7
Insignia 929.9
 armed forces 355.1
Insolvency
 credit economics 332.7
Insomnia
 medicine 616.8
Inspection
 production management 658.5
 public administration 352.8
Inspection technology 670.42
Inspectors general
 military administration 355.6
Inspiration
 Bible 220.1
Installations (Armed forces) 355.7
Installment sales
 consumer credit 332.7
 law 346.07
Instinctive movements
 psychology 152.3
Institutional housekeeping 647
Institutional investment 332.67
Institutionalized children
 psychology 155.44
Institutions (Sociology) 306
 see Manual at 302–307 vs.
  320

Instructional materials	371.33
elementary education	372.133
reading	372.41
public control	379.1
Instructional materials centers	027.7
college libraries	027.7
school libraries	027.8
Instrumental ensembles	784
Instrumental forms	784.18
Instrumentation	T1—028
Instruments	T1—028
Instruments (Musical)	784.19
see also Musical instruments	
Insulating materials	
building materials	691
materials science	620.1
Insulation	
building construction	693.8
Insurance	368
financial management	658.15
law	346
public administration	354.8
Insurance agents	368.009 2
Insurance companies	368.006
credit functions	332.3
Intaglio printing	765
Integral calculus	515
Integral equations	515
Integral geometry	516.3
Integrated circuits	621.381 5
Integrated optics	621.36
Integrated programs	005.3
Integration in education	379.2
Integument	573.5
animal physiology	573.5
descriptive zoology	591.47
human physiology	612.7
medicine	616.5
Intellect	153.9
see also Intelligence	
Intellectual freedom	323.44
library policies	025.2
Intellectual history	001.09
Intellectual life	001.1
Intellectual processes	153
children	155.4
Intellectual property	346.04
public administrative support	352.7
Intellectuals	305.5
Intelligence	153.9
evolutional psychology	155.7
psychology	153.9

Intelligence (Information)	327.12
armed forces	355.3
international relations	327.12
public administration	353.1
military technology	623
Intelligence tests	153.9
Intensive care	362.1
medicine	616.02
social welfare	362.1
Intentionality	
psychology	153.8
Interactive multimedia	006.7
Interactive processing	004
Interactive video	006.7
computer science	006.7
instructional use	371.33
	T1—078
Intercession of Jesus Christ	232
Intercultural communication	303.48
Intercultural education	370.117
Interest (Income)	332.8
Interest (Psychology)	
learning	153.1
Interest groups (Political	
science)	322.4
political process	324
relation to government	322.4
Interest rate futures	332.63
Interfacing (Computer)	004.6
engineering	621.39
programs and programming	005.7
Interfacing protocols	
computer science	004.6
Interfaith marriage	306.84
Intergovernmental fiscal	
relations	336
Intergovernmental revenues	
public finance	336.1
Intergovernmental tax relations	336.2
Interindustry accounts	
macroeconomics	339.2
Interior decoration	747
home economics	645
Interior decorators	747.2
Interior departments	353.3
Interior design	729
see Manual at 729	
Interior furnishings	
arts	747
customs	392.3
household management	645
textile arts	746.9
Interior wiring	621.319
Interlibrary loans	025.6

James (Biblical book)	227
Jams	641.8
Jan Mayen Island	T2—98
Jansenism	273
denominations	284
Japan	952
	T2—52
Japan, Sea of	T2—164
Japanese	952
social group	305.895
Japanese chin	636.76
Japanese language	495.6
Japanese literature	895.6
Japanning	
decorative arts	745.7
technology	667
Jargon	417
specific languages	T4—7
Java Sea	T2—164
Javanese language	499
Jazz	781.65
songs	782.421 65
Jazz bands	784.4
Jazz musicians	781.650 92
Jealousy	152.4
Jeeps	388.3
engineering	629.222
military engineering	623.7
transportation services	388.3
Jeffersonian Republicans	
(Political party)	324.273 2
Jehovah's Witnesses	289.9
Jellies	641.8
Jellyfish	593.5
Jeremiah (Biblical book)	224
Jesus Christ	232
art representation	704.9
biography	232.9
see Manual at 230–280	
see Manual at 232	
Jet (Precious stone)	553.8
Jet engines	621.43
see Manual at 629.04 vs.	
621.43	
Jet fuel	665.5
Jet skiing	797.3
Jet streams (Meteorology)	551.51
Jewelers	739.270 92
Jewelry	391.7
customs	391.7
making	739.27
costume jewelry	688
handicrafts	745.594
fine jewelry	739.27

Jewish cooking	641.5
Jewish day schools	371.076
Jewish holidays	296.4
customs	394.267
Jewish philosophy	181
Jewish sacred music	781.76
religion	296.4
Jews	
civilization	909
social group	305.892
Jews (Religious group)	305.6
biography	296.092
specific denominations	296.8
Jigsaw puzzles	793.73
Jihad	297.7
Jivaroa language	498
Job (Biblical book)	223
Job analysis	658.3
Job banks	331.12
Job burnout	158.7
Job control languages	005.4
Job creation	331.12
see Manual at 331.12 vs.	
331.13	
Job hunting	650.14
see also Résumé writing	
Job information	331.12
Job rights	331.01
Job satisfaction	
personnel management	658.3
psychology	158.7
Job security	331.25
personnel management	658.3
Job sharing	331.25
Job stress	158.7
Job vacancies	331.12
Joel (Biblical book)	224
Jogging	613.7
John (Biblical books)	226.5
epistles	227
gospel	226.5
Revelation	228
John, the Baptist, Saint	232.9
Johnson, Lyndon B. (Lyndon	
Baines)	
United States history	973.923
Joinery	
construction	694
Joining metals	671.5
Joints (Body parts)	573.7
animal physiology	573.7
diseases	
medicine	616.7
human physiology	612.7

Karts (Racing cars)	796.7
engineering	629.228
sports	796.7
Katharevusa language (Modern Greek)	489
Kazakh language	494
Kazakhstan	958.45
	T2—584 5
Kazoo	783.9
Keewatin (N.W.T.)	T2—719
Kelps	579.8
Kennedy, John F. (John Fitzgerald)	
United States history	973.922
Kent (England)	T2—422
Kentucky	T2—769
Kenya	967.62
	T2—676 2
Kenyans	967.62
Kerosene	665.5
Kerry (Ireland)	T2—419
Ketuvim	223
Keyboard electrophones	786.5
Keyboard instruments	786
Keyboard wind instruments	786.5
Keyboarding	652.3
Keyboards (Computer)	004.7
Keynesian economic school	330.15
Keys	683
Khalkha Mongolian language	494
Khmer	
social group	305.895
Khmer language	495.9
Khmer Republic	959.6
	T2—596
Khond language	494.8
Kibbutzim	307.77
Kidnapping	364.15
Kidneys	573.4
biology	573.4
human physiology	612.4
medicine	616.6
surgery	617.4
Kikuyu language	496
Kildare (Ireland : County)	T2—418
Kilkenny (Ireland : County)	T2—418
Killer whale	599.53
Kimbundu language	496
Kindergarten	372.21
Kindness	
ethics	177
King George's War, 1740–1748	940.2
North American history	973.2
King William's War, 1688–1697	940.2
North American history	973.2
Kingdom of God	231.7
eschatology	236
Kingfishers	598.7
Kings (Biblical books)	222
Kings (Rulers)	321
folklore	398.22
political science	321
public administration	352.23
Kingship of Jesus Christ	232
Kinship	306.83
genealogy	929
Kirghiz language	494
Kirghizia	958.43
	T2—584 3
Kiribati	996.81
	T2—968 1
Kitchen utensils	641.502 8
cooking	641.502 8
manufacturing technology	683
Kitchens	643
Kites	629.133
recreation	796.15
Kitikmeot (N.W.T.)	T2—719
Kitsch	709.03
painting	759.05
Kiwis (Birds)	598.5
Kleptomania	362.2
medicine	616.85
social welfare	362.2
Knees (Human)	612
human physiology	612
regional medicine	617.5
Knighthood	
genealogy	929.7
Knights of Pythias	366
Knitting	677
arts	746.43
manufacturing technology	677
Knives	621.9
Knotting (Seamanship)	623.88
Knotting textiles	677
arts	746.42
manufacturing technology	677
Knowledge	001
psychology	153.4
theory of	121
Knowledge-based systems	006.3
Knowledge of God	212
Christianity	231
comparative religion	291.2
philosophy of religion	212
Koala	599.2

Lagoons	551.46
	T2—16
Lahnda language	491.4
Laity (Church members)	262
biography	270.092
specific denominations	280
see Manual at 230–280	
church government	262
pastoral theology	253
social group	305.6
Lake District (England)	T2—427
Lake Erie	T2—771
Lake Huron (Mich. and	
Ont.)	T2—774
Lake Michigan	T2—774
Lake Ontario (N.Y. and	
Ont.)	T2—747
Lake States	T2—77
Lake Superior	T2—774
Lake transportation	386
Lakes	551.48
	T2—16
biology	578.763
ecology	577.63
hydrology	551.48
resource economics	333.91
Lamarckism	576.8
Lamentations (Bible)	224
Laminated wood	674
Lamps	621.32
ceramic arts	738.8
furniture arts	749
Lampshades	
handicrafts	745.593
LAN (Computer network)	004.6
Lancashire (England)	T2—427
Land	333
	T2—14
economics	333
see Manual at 333.7–333.9	
vs. 333; *also at*	
333.73–333.78 vs. 333,	
333.1–333.5	
investment economics	332.63
property law	346.04
public administration	354.3
Land-atmosphere interactions	551.5
Land banks	332.3
Land carnivores	599.7
Land forces (Military science)	355
Land gift	333.33
Land grants	
economics	333.1

Land reclamation	333.73
agriculture	631.6
economics	333.73
hydraulic engineering	627
Land reform	333.3
Land resources	333.73
see also Natural resources	
see Manual at 333.73–333.78	
vs. 333, 333.1–333.5	
Land sailing	796.6
Land sale	333.33
Land settlement	
economics	333.3
Land surveys	333
economics	333
technology	526.9
Land tenure	333.3
see Manual at 333.73–333.78	
vs. 333, 333.1–333.5	
Land transfer	333.33
Land transportation	388
engineering	629.04
Land use	333.73
agricultural surveys	631.4
community sociology	307.3
economics	333.73
see Manual at 333.73–333.78	
vs. 333, 333.1–333.5	
Land vertebrates	596
Landforms	551.41
	T2—14
Landlord and tenant	333.5
law	346.04
Landowners	333.009 2
Landscape architects	712.092
Landscape architecture	712
Landscape design	712
Landscapes	
art representation	704.9
painting	758
Landslides	551.3
Landsmål language	439.8
Language	400
	T1—01
philosophy	401
philosophical works	121
sociology	306.44
see Manual at 400 vs. 800	
Language acquisition	401
see Manual at 407.1, T1—071	
vs. 401, 410.71,	
418.0071, T4—80071	
Language arts	
elementary education	372.6

Lead	669
chemistry	546
human toxicology	615.9
metallurgy	669
metalworking	673
Leaded glass	
arts	748.5
Leadership	303.3
armed forces	355.3
executive management	658.4
public administration	352.3
political parties	324.2
psychology	158
social control	303.3
League of Arab States	341.24
League of Augsburg, War of the,	
1688–1697	940.2
North American history	973.2
League of Nations	341.22
public administration	352.11
Learning	153.1
educational psychology	370.15
psychology	153.1
children	155.4
see Manual at 153.1 vs.	
370.15; *also at*	
155.4–155.6 vs. 153.1	
Learning (Scholarship)	001.2
Learning ability	153.9
Learning curves	153.1
Learning disabilities	371.9
medicine	616.85
Leases	
law	346.04
real property	333.5
Leather	675
handicrafts	745.53
Leather clothing	391
commercial technology	685
Leather goods	
commercial technology	685
Leaves (Absences)	331.25
personnel management	658.3
Leaves (Plants)	581.4
descriptive zoology	581.4
physiology	575.5
Lebanese	956.92
social group	305.892
Lebanon	956.92
	T2—569 2
Lebanon Conflict, 1982–1985	956.05
Lecture method	371.39
Lectures	080
Leeches	592

Leeward Islands (West	
Indies)	T2—729 7
Left-handedness	
psychology	152.3
Leftovers (Cooking)	641.5
Legal aid	362.5
law	347
social service	362.5
Legal codes	348
Legal counsel	
management use	658.1
Legal ethics	174
Legal procedure	347
Legal profession	340.023
Legal responsibility	346.02
Legal services	347
Legal systems	340.5
Legendary animals	398.24
folklore	398.24
mysteries	001.944
Legendary beings	398.21
Legendary places	398.23
folklore	398.23
mysteries	001.94
Legends	
folklore	398.2
see Manual at 398.2 vs.	
291.1	
paintings	753
Legislation (Enactment and	
repeal)	328.3
Legislative bodies	328
see Manual at 909, 930–990	
vs. 320	
Legislative branch	328
Legislative immunity	328.3
Legislative powers	328.3
Legislative process	328
Legislative representation	328.3
Legislators	
biography	328.092
role and function	328.3
Legitimacy of government	320.01
Legs	591.47
animal physiology	573.7
descriptive zoology	591.47
regional medicine	617.5
Legumes	583
botany	583
cooking	641.6
food	641.3
forage crop	633.3
garden crop	635
Leicestershire (England)	T2—425

Library of Congress
  Classification 025.4
Library orientation 025.5
Library science 020
  see Manual at 020
Library trustees 021.8
Library use studies 025.5
Librettos 780
  treatises 780.26
Libya 961.2
  T2—612
Libyans 961.2
  social group 305.892
Lice 595.7
Licensing 352.8
Lichens 579.7
Liechtenstein 943.64
  T2—436 4
Lieder 782.421 68
Liens
  law 346.07
Life
  biological nature 570.1
  origin 576.8
  philosophy 113
  respect for
    ethics 179
Life after death
  occultism 133.9
  philosophy 129
  religion 291.2
    Christianity 236
    Islam 297.2
    Judaism 296.3
    philosophy of religion 218
  see Manual at 133.9 vs. 129
Life cycle 571.8
  animal behavior 591.56
  customs 392
  developmental biology 571.8
  etiquette 395.2
Life expectancy 304.6
Life insurance 368.32
Life sciences 570
  see Manual at 560–590
Lifelong education 374
Light 535
  arts 701
  engineering 621.36
  meteorology 551.56
  physics 535
Light trucks 388.3
  engineering 629.223

Lighthouses 387.1
  engineering 627
  navigation aid 623.89
  transportation services 387.1
Lighting 621.32
  architectural design 729
  engineering 621.32
  household management 644
  interior decoration 747
  public areas 628.9
Lighting fixtures
  household management 645
Lightning 551.56
Lilies 584
Lime 553.6
Limerick (Ireland :
  County) T2—419
Limericks 808.81
  see also Poetry
Limitation of rights 323.4
Limited companies 338.7
Limited government 320.51
Limited monarchy 321.8
Limited war 355.02
Limnology 551.48
  biology 577.6
Lincoln, Abraham
  United States history 973.7
Lincolnshire (England) T2—425
Line and staff organization 658.4
Line Islands T2—964
Linear algebras 512
Linear programming 519.7
Linear systems 003
Linen textiles 677
Lingala language 496
Linguistic change 417
Linguistic disorders
  special education 371.91
Linguistic philosophies 149
Linguistics 410
  see Manual at 410
Linguists
  language specialists 409.2
    specific languages T4—092
  linguistics specialists 410.92
    specific languages T4—092
  philologists 409.2
    specific languages T4—092
Linoleum-block printing 761
Linotype composition 686.2
Lion 599.757
Lions International 369.5
Lip-reed instruments 788.9

Location of business enterprises	338.09
Location of plants	
management	658.2
Loch Ness monster	001.944
Lockouts	331.89
Locksmithing	683
Locomotion	573.7
animal physiology	573.7
physical adaptation	591.47
psychology	152.3
Locomotives	385
engineering	625.26
Locomotor ataxia	
medicine	616.8
Locusts	595.7
Logarithms	512.9
algebra	512.9
arithmetic	513.2
Logging	634.9
Logic (Reasoning)	160
see Manual at 153.4 vs. 160	
Logistics	
management	658.5
military operations	355.4
London (England)	T2—421
Loneliness	155.9
applied psychology	158.2
Longevity	571.8
human physiology	612.6
Longford (Ireland :	
County)	T2—418
Longitude	526
Looking	
psychology	153.7
Loons	598.4
Loran	
radio engineering	621.384
Lord's Prayer	226.9
private devotions	242
Lord's Supper	234
public worship	264
theology	234
Lorries	388.3
engineering	629.224
Loss (Psychology)	155.9
Lothian (Scotland)	T2—413
Lotteries	795.3
occupational ethics	174
public finance	336.1
Louisiana	T2—763
Louth (Ireland : County)	T2—418
Love	
ethics	177
folklore	398.27

Love (continued)	
God's love	212
Christianity	231
comparative religion	291.2
philosophy of religion	212
philosophy	128
psychology	152.4
see also Virtues	
Love stories	808.83
see also Fiction	
Low-calorie cooking	641.5
Low-calorie diets	
health	613.2
Low-carbohydrate cooking	641.5
Low-carbohydrate diet	
health	613.2
Low-cholesterol cooking	641.5
Low-cholesterol diet	
health	613.2
Low Countries	T2—492
Low-fat cooking	641.5
Low-fat diet	
health	613.2
Low-fiber diet	
health	613.2
Low Germanic languages	439
Low-salt cooking	641.5
Low-salt diet	
health	613.2
Low-temperature technology	621.5
Lower classes	305.5
Lower criticism	
Bible	220.4
Lower Guinea	T2—671
Lowlands (Scotland)	T2—413
Lubricating oil	665
Lubrication	621.8
Luggage	
manufacturing technology	685
Luke (Gospel)	226.4
Lullabies	781.5
folk literature	398.8
music	781.5
Lumber	674
Lumber industry	338.4
Lumbering	634.9
Luminescence	535
Lunch	642
cooking	641.5
Lung cancer	
medicine	616.99
Lungs	573.2
biology	573.2
human physiology	612.2

Lungs (continued)
  medicine 616.2
  surgery 617.5
Lupus erythematosus
  medicine 616.7
Lutes 787.8
Lutheran church 284.1
Lutherans
  biography 284.109 2
Luxembourg 949.35
    T2—493 5
  ancient 936.4
    T2—364
Lycées (Secondary schools) 373.24
Lying
  ethics 177
Lyme disease
  medicine 616.9
Lymphatic system 573.1
  biology 573.1
  human diseases 362.1
    medicine 616.4
    social services 362.1
  human physiology 612.4
  surgery 617.4
Lymphocytes 571.9
  human immunology 616.07
Lynx 599.75
Lyres 787.7
Lyric poetry 808.81
Lyrics 780
  treatises 780.26

M

Macao 951.26
    T2—512 6
Macedonia (Region) T2—495
  ancient T2—38
  Greece T2—495
  Macedonia (Republic) T2—497 6
Macedonia (Republic) 949.76
    T2—497 6
Macedonian language 491.8
Macedonians
  social group 305.891
Machine engineering 621.8
Machine languages 005.13
Machine learning 006.3
Machine-Readable Cataloging
  format 025.3

Machine-readable materials
  bibliographies 011
    see Manual at 011 vs.
      005.3029
  cataloging 025.3
  library treatment 025.17
    see Manual at T1—0285
Machine-shop practice 670.42
Machine theory
  mathematics 511.3
Machine tools 621.9
Machine translating
  linguistics 418
  specific languages T4—8
Machinery 621.8
Machinery in industry 338
Machinery insurance 368.7
Machining metals 671.3
Macramé 746.42
Macro processors 005.4
Macrobiotic diet
  health 613.2
Macroeconomic policy 339.5
Macroeconomics 339
  see Manual at 332, 336 vs.
    339
Macromolecules 572
  biochemistry 572
  chemistry 547
Madagascar 969.1
    T2—691
Madeira Islands T2—469
Madonna and Child
  art representation 704.9
Madrigals 782.4
Mafia 364.106
Magazines 050
    T1—05
Magic 133.4
  folklore 398.2
  recreation 793.8
Magicians (Occultists) 133.4
  folklore 398.21
Magnet schools 373.24
Magnetic engineering 621.34
Magnetic resonance imaging
  medicine 616.07
Magnetic tapes
  engineering 621.382
  music 786.7
Magnetic tapes (Computer) 004.5
Magnetism 538
Magnetosphere 538
  meteorology 551.51

Magnets	538
artificial	621.34
Mah jong	795.3
Maiasaura	567.914
Mail	383
Mail handling	383
office services	651.7
Mail-order catalogs	T1—029
direct advertising	659.13
Mail-order houses	381
management	658.8
Maimonides, Moses	
Jewish legal writings	296.1
Main memory (Computer)	004.5
Maine	T2—741
Mainframe computers	004.1
programming	005.2
programs	005.3
Mainstreaming	
education	371.9
grouping of students	371.2
Maintenance	620
	T1—028
plant management	658.2
	T1—068
Majolica	738.3
Make-work arrangements	
economics	331.12
unions	331.88
Makeup	646.7
see also Cosmetics	
Malachi (Biblical book)	224
Maladjusted students	371.93
Maladjusted young people	
social welfare	362.74
Malagasy	969.1
social group	305.89
Malagasy language	499
Malagasy Republic	T2—691
Malaria	
medicine	616.9
Malawi	968.97
	T2—689 7
Malay Archipelago	T2—598
Malay language	499
Malay Peninsula	T2—595
Malayalam language	494.8
Malayo-Polynesian languages	499
Malayo-Polynesians	
social group	305.89
Malays (Asian people)	
social group	305.89
Malaysia	959.5
	T2—595

Malaysians	959.5
social group	305.89
Maldives	954.95
	T2—549 5
Male breast (Human)	
medicine	616.4
Males (Human)	305.31
	T1—081
see also Men	
Mali	966.23
	T2—662 3
Malians	966.23
Malls (Shopping)	381
Malnutrition	
medicine	616.3
Malpractice	346.03
Malpractice insurance	368.5
Malta	945.8
	T2—458
ancient	937
	T2—37
Maltese	945.8
social group	305.892
Maltese (Dog)	636.76
Maltese language	492.7
Malvinas Islands	T2—97
Mammals	599
agricultural pests	632
animal husbandry	636
art representation	704.9
commercial hunting	639
conservation technology	639.9
paleozoology	569
resource economics	333.95
sports hunting	799.2
zoology	599
Mammaplasty	618.1
Mammary glands	573.6
biology	573.6
human physiology	612.6
Man	301
see also Humans	
Man, Isle of (England)	T2—427
Man-made environments	
biology	578.75
ecology	577.5
Man-made fibers	
textiles	677
Management	658
	T1—068
see Manual at T1—068 vs.	
353–354; *also at* 330 vs.	
650; *also at* 658 and	
T1—068	

Measuring instruments	
electric measurement	621.37
manufacturing technology	681
Meat	641.3
commercial processing	
technology	664
cooking	641.6
food	641.3
home preservation	641.4
Meat processing industry	338.4
Meath (Ireland)	T2—418
Mechanical drawing	604.2
Mechanical engineering	621
Mechanical engineers	621.092
Mechanical musical instruments	786.6
Mechanics	530
classical physics	531
engineering	620.1
physics	530
quantum physics	530.12
see Manual at 530.12 vs. 531	
Mechanism (Philosophy)	146
Mechanisms	
engineering	621.8
Mechanization	
economics	338
factory operations engineering	670.42
Mechanized cavalry	357
Medals	
armed forces	355.1
numismatics	737
Media	302.23
see also Mass media	
Media centers	027
see also Libraries	
Media production	
elementary education	372.67
Median	519.5
Mediation	
labor economics	331.89
law	347
Medical bacteriology	616
Medical economics	338.4
Medical emergencies	362.18
medicine	616.02
social services	362.18
Medical ethics	174
Medical examinations	616.07
Medical genetics	616
Medical geography	614.4
Medical instruments	610.28
manufacturing technology	681
Medical insurance	368.38
Medical jurisprudence	614

Medical libraries	026
Medical machinery	
manufacturing technology	681
Medical malpractice	
torts	344
Medical microbiology	616
see Manual at 616.9 vs. 616	
Medical missionaries	
role and function	610.69
Medical missions	362.1
Christian	266
social welfare	362.1
Medical personnel	610.92
role and function	610.69
see Manual at 362.1–362.4 vs.	
610	
Medical radiology	616.07
Medical records management	651.5
Medical sciences	610
Medical services	362.1
armed forces	355.3
Medical social work	362.1
Medical technicians	610.73
role and function	610.69
Medication methods	615
Medicinal plants	615
agriculture	633.8
economic botany	581.6
pharmacognosy	615
Medicine	610
applied science	610
law	344
sociology	306.4
see Manual at 610 vs. 362.1;	
also at 610 vs. 616	
Medicines	615
Medieval architecture	723
Medieval art	709.02
Medieval law	340.5
Medieval painting	759.02
Medieval period	909.07
	T1—09
church history	270.3
English history	942.03
European history	940.1
Medieval philosophy	
Oriental	181
western	189
Medieval sculpture	734
Meditation	158.1
religion	291.4
Christianity	248.3
Islam	297.3
Judaism	296.7

Merchant seamen	387.509 2
technologists	623.880 92
Merchants	380.109 2
Mercury (Element)	669
Mercury (Planet)	523.41
Mergers	338.8
economics	338.8
management	658.1
Merging data	005.74
Merit (Christian doctrine)	234
Merit system (Civil service)	352.6
Mermaids	398.21
Merseyside (England)	T2—427
Mesopotamia	T2—567
ancient	T2—35
Mesozoic era	551.7
Messenger services	
office services	651.3
Messiahs	
Christianity	232
Judaism	296.6
Metabolism	572
human physiology	612.3
medicine	616.3
Metal engraving	765
Metal products	671
Metal relief engraving	761
Metallic salt processes	
photography	772
Metallography	669
Metallurgy	669
Metals	669
building construction	693
building materials	691
chemical engineering	661
chemistry	546
decorative arts	739
economic geology	553.4
handicrafts	745.56
materials science	620.1
metallurgy	669
mining	622
Metalworking	671
home workshops	684
technology	671
Metamorphic rocks	552
Metaphysics	110
Meteorite craters	551.3
Meteorites	523.5
Meteoroids	523.5
Meteorologists	551.509 2
Meteorology	551.5
aeronautics	629.132
see Manual at 551.5 vs. 551.6	

Meteors	523.5
Meter (Music)	781.2
Meter (Prosody)	808.1
Methodist Church	287
Methodists	
biography	287.092
Methodology (Principles)	T1—01
Metric system	530.8
social aspects	389
Metrology	
commerce	389
Metropolitan areas	307.76
Mexican Americans	
social group	305.868
Mexican hairless	636.76
Mexican literature	860
Mexican War, 1845–1848	973.6
Mexicans	972
Mexico	972
	T2—72
Mexico, Gulf of	T2—163
Mezzotinting	766
Miao (Asian people)	
social group	305.895
Miao language	495.9
Miao-Yao languages	495.9
Micah (Biblical book)	224
Mice (Computer)	004.7
Mice (Mus)	599.35
animal husbandry	636.935
Michigan	T2—774
Michigan, Lake	T2—774
Microbiology	579
applied	660.6
medicine	616
see Manual at 616.9 vs. 616	
Microcode	005.6
Microcomputer workstations	004.16
Microcomputers	004.16
engineering	621.39
operating systems	005.4
programming	005.26
programs	005.36
see Manual at 004.165	
Microeconomics	338.5
Microelectronic circuits	621.381 5
Microelectronics	621.381
Microforms	
bibliographies	011
production	
office records	651.5
Micrometeorology	551.6
Micronesia	T2—965
Micronesian languages	499

Military policy	355
Military reservations	355.7
Military resources	355.2
Military schools (Secondary education)	373.24
Military schools (Service academies)	355.007 1
see Manual at 378 vs. 355.0071	
Military science	355
Military service (Conditions of work)	355.1
Military service (Manpower procurement)	355.2
Military services	355
Military situation	355
Military sociology	306.2
Military supplies	355.8
Military surgery	617.9
Military training	355.5
Military transportation	358
engineering	623
land forces	358
naval forces	359.9
Military units	355.3
see Manual at 930–990: Wars: Military units	
Milk	641.3
cooking	641.6
food	641.3
processing	637
Milking	637
Milky Way	523.1
Millennium	
Christianity	236
Millinery	646.5
Milling tools	621.9
Millipedes	595.6
Mind	128
philosophy	128
psychology	150
Mind reading	133.8
Mine laying (Military)	623
Mine safety	363.11
social services	363.11
technology	622
Mined lands	333.76
Mineral fertilizers	631.8
economic geology	553.6
Mineral industries	338.2
enterprises	338.7
Mineral oils	
processing	665

Mineral resources	
land economics	333.8
law	346.04
public administration	354.3
Mineral rights	
law	346.04
public revenue	336.1
sale and rental	333.33
Mineral waters	553.7
commercial processing	663
economic geology	553.7
Mineralogy	549
see Manual at 549 vs. 546; *also at* 549 vs. 548; *also at* 552 vs. 549	
Minerals	553
applied nutrition	613.2
economic geology	553
economics	338.2
resources	333.8
see Manual at 553 vs. 333.8, 338.2	
folklore	398.26
mineralogy	549
synthetic	666
Miners	622.092
Mines (Excavations)	622
Mines (Weapons)	355.8
engineering	623.4
laying and clearing	623
military equipment	355.8
Miniature books	099
Miniature dachshund	636.76
Miniature paintings	751.7
Miniature pinscher	636.76
Miniature Schnauzer	636.755
Miniatures	688
	T1—022
handicrafts	745.592 8
see Manual at 745.5928	
manufacturing technology	688
Minicomputers	004.1
engineering	621.39
programming	005.2
programs	005.3
Minimum wage	331.2
Mining	622
production economics	338.2
Mining engineers	622.092
Mining industry	338.2
Ministates	321
Ministerial authority	262

Mobile homes (continued)
  recreation   796.7
  see Manual at 643, 690, 728.7
    vs. 629.226
Mobile libraries
  public library use   027.4
Mobile radio stations   621.384 5
Mobiles   731
Mobility-impaired persons   305.9
                                               T1—087
  education   371.91
Mobilization   355.2
Mobs   302.3
Mode   519.5
Model airplanes   629.133
  recreation   796.15
  see Manual at 796.15 vs.
    629.04
Model cars   629.22
  recreation   796.15
  see Manual at 796.15 vs.
    629.04
Model trains   625.1
  recreation   790.1
  see Manual at 796.15 vs.
    629.04
Modeling
  elementary education   372.5
  plastic arts   730.028
  sculpture   731.4
Modeling (Simulation)   003
Models (Fashion)   746.9
Models (Representations)   688
                                               T1—022
  handicrafts   745.592 8
    see Manual at 745.5928
  manufacturing technology   688
Models (Simulations)   003
Modems   004.6
  engineering   621.39
Modern algebra   512
Modern architecture   724
Modern art   709.04
Modern dance   792.8
Modern Greek language   489
Modern history   909.08
                                               T1—09
Modern Indic languages   491.4
Modern languages   410
Modern painting   759.06

Modern philosophy   190
  Oriental   181
  western   190
  see Manual at 190 vs. 100,
    109
Modern physics   539
Modern Prakrit languages   491.4
Modern sculpture   735
Modern world   T2—4–9
Modernism
  church history   273
Modernization
  executive management   658.4
  production management   658.5
Modesty   179
Modular design   729
Moesia   T2—39
Mogul Empire   954.02
                                               T2—54
Mohammed, Prophet   297.6
Mohawk Indians
  social group   305.897
Moisture
  meteorology   551.57
Moistureproof construction
  buildings   693.8
Moldavia   T2—498
  Moldova   T2—476
  Romania   T2—498
Moldavian language   459
Molding
  arts   730.028
  sculpture   731.4
Moldmaking
  metal casting   671.2
Moldova   947.6
                                               T2—476
Molds (Fungi)   579.5
Molds (Tools)   621.9
Molecular biology   572.8
Molecular genetics   572.8
Molecular physics   539
Molecular structure   541.2
Moles (Animals)   599.33
Mollusks   594
  fishing   639
  paleozoology   564
  zoology   594
Momentum   531
Mon-Khmer languages   495.9
Monaco   944.9
                                               T2—449
Monaghan (Ireland :
  County)   T2—416 9

Morale	
armed forces	355.1
personnel management	658.3
Morality	170
public control	363.4
see also Moral theology	
see Manual at 170	
Morality plays	
literature	808.82
see also Drama (Literature)	
stage presentation	792.1
Moravia (Czech Republic)	943.72
	T2—437 2
Moravian Church	284
Moravians (Religious group)	
biography	284
Mores	306
customs	390
sociology	306
Mormon Church	289.3
Mormons	
biography	289.309 2
Morning prayer	264
music	782.32
Moroccans	964
social group	305.892
Morocco	964
	T2—64
Morphing	
computer graphics	006.6
Morphology	571.3
Morphology (Grammar)	415
specific languages	T4—5
Morrison plan	371.39
Morse code telegraphy	384.1
Mortality	
demography	304.6
Mortgage banks	332.3
Mortgage bonds	332.63
Mortgage defaults	332.7
Mortgage insurance	368.8
Mortgages	332.7
investment economics	332.63
law	346.04
Mosaic glass	
arts	748.5
Mosaics	738.5
Mosques	297.3
architecture	726
Mosquitoes	595.77
Mosses	588
Motels	647.94
Mother and child	306.874
Motherhood	306.874

Mothers	306.874
	T1—085
psychology	155.6
Mother's Day	394.262
Moths	595.78
Motion	
celestial bodies	521
philosophy	116
physics	531
Motion picture photography	778.5
Motion picture plays	791.43
literature	808.82
see also Drama (Literature)	
Motion picture projection	778.5
Motion pictures	791.43
communications services	384
ethics	175
instructional use	371.33
journalism	070.1
performing arts	791.43
see Manual at 791.43,	
791.45 vs. 778.5	
sociology	302.23
see Manual at 384 vs. 791.4	
Motion sickness	
medicine	616.9
Motion studies	
production management	658.5
Motivation	153.8
elementary education	
reading	372.42
learning psychology	153.1
Motor functions	
psychology	152.3
Motor homes	388.3
engineering	629.226
see Manual at 643, 690, 728.7	
vs. 629.226	
Motor land vehicles	388.3
see also Automotive vehicles	
Motor learning	
psychology	152.3
Motor vehicle racing	796.7
Motor vehicles	388.3
see also Automotive vehicles	
Motorboating	
sports	797.1
Motorcycle accidents	363.12
Motorcycle racing	796.7
Motorcycle troops (Armed	
forces)	357
Motorcycles	388.3
engineering	629.227
sports	796.7

Musculoskeletal system	573.7
biology	573.7
human anatomy	611
human diseases	362.1
medicine	616.7
social services	362.1
human physiology	612.7
surgery	617.4
Museology	069
	T1—075
Museum catalogs	069
	T1—074
Museum libraries	027.6
Museum science	069
Museum services	069
	T1—075
Museums	069
	T1—074
architecture	727
public administrative support	352.7
Mushrooms	579.6
agriculture	635
cooking	641.6
food	641.3
Music	780
elementary education	372.87
ethics	175
publishing	070.5
religion	291.3
Christianity	246
public worship	264
Judaism	296.4
Music appreciation	781.1
Music boxes	786.6
Music hall presentations	792.7
Music libraries	026
Music theory	781
Music therapy	
medicine	615.8
Musical bows	787.9
Musical forms	781.8
instrumental	784.18
vocal	782
Musical instrument makers	784.190 92
see Manual at 784–788	
Musical instruments	784.19
construction	784.192
by hand	784.192
by machine	681
Musical traditions	781.6
Musicals	782.1
music	782.1
stage presentation	792.6
see Manual at 782.1 vs. 792.5	

Musicians	780.92
see Manual at 780.92; *also at* 781.6; *also at* 784–788; *also at* 791.092	
Muskrats	599.35
Muslims	297.092
biography	297.092
specific sects	297.8
Mustang	636.1
zoology	599.665
Mutation (Genetics)	576.5
Mutual funds	332.63
Myanmar	959.1
	T2—591
Mycology	579.5
Myopia	
optometry	617.7
Myriapods	595.6
Mysteries	
occultism	135
unexplained phenomena	001.94
Mystery games	793.93
see Manual at 793.93 vs. 794.8	
Mystery plays (Religious)	
stage presentation	792.1
Mystery plays (Suspense)	792.2
stage presentation	792.2
Mystery stories	808.83
see also Fiction	
Mysticism	291.4
Christianity	248.2
Islam	297.4
see Manual at 297.4	
Judaism	296.7
Mythical animals	398.24
Mythological interpretation	
Bible	220.6
Mythology	398.2
African religions	299
Buddhism	294.3
Celtic religion	299
classical religion	292.1
Egyptian religion	299
folklore	398.2
Germanic religion	293
Greek religion	292.1
Hinduism	294.5
Native American religions	299
Norse religion	293
paintings	753
religion	291.1
Roman religion	292.1

Mythology (continued)
  Scandinavian religion   293
  see Manual at 398.2 vs. 291.1
Myxedema
  medicine   616.85

N

Nahuatl language   497
Nahum (Biblical book)   224
Nails (Body parts)
  human diseases
    medicine   616.5
  human physiology   612.7
  personal care   646.7
Nails (Fasteners)   621.8
Names   929.9
  customs   392.1
  etymology   412
    specific languages   T4—2
  geographic   910
    gazetters   910.3
  personal   929.4
Namibia   968.81
         T2—688 1
Namibians   968.81
Nanotechnology   620
Napkin folding   642
Napoleon I, Emperor of the
  French
  French history   944.05
Napoleon III, Emperor of the
  French
  French history   944.07
Napoleonic Wars   940.2
Narcotics   362.29
  customs   394.1
  ethics   178
  see also Substance abuse
Narcotics abuse   362.29
Narcotics traffic   363.45
Narrow-gage railroads   385.5
Natal (South Africa)   T2—684
Nation of Islam   297.8
Nation-states   321
National bibliographies   015
National characteristics   305.8
  psychology   155.8
National dances   793.3
  see Manual at 792.7 vs. 792.8,
    793.3
National debt   336.3
  law   343

National debt (continued)
  macroeconomic policy   339.5
National forests   333.75
National groups   305.8
         T1—089
  see also Ethnic groups
National income   339.3
National libraries   027.5
National parks   363.6
  conservation of natural
    resources   333.7
  see Manual at 333.7–333.9 vs.
    508, 913–919, 930–990
National planning
  civic art   711
  economics   338.9
National product
  macroeconomics   339.3
National psychology   155.8
National resources
  conservation   339.4
National security   355
  law   343
    police powers   342
  public administration   353.1
National socialism   335.6
  political ideology   320.53
National unions   331.87
Nationalism   320.54
Nationalist China   T2—512 4
Nationality (Citizenship)   323.6
Nationality clubs   369
Nationalization of industry   338.9
Nationalization of property   333.1
Native American languages   497
  South America   498
Native American peoples   970.004
  North America   970.004
    social group   305.897
  religion   299
  social group   305.897
  South America   980
    social group   305.898
  see Manual at 970.004
Native peoples   306.08
Nativity of Jesus Christ   232.92
Natural childbirth
  obstetrics   618.4
Natural environments
  health   613
Natural foods   641.3
Natural gas   553.2
  economic geology   553.2
  extraction   622

Natural gas (continued)
  extractive economics — 338.2
  resource economics — 333.8
  technology — 665.7
    economics — 338.4
Natural history — 508
  animals — 590
  biology — 578
  plants — 580
  see also Nature
  see Manual at 578 vs. 304.2,
    508, 910
Natural landscapes
  landscape architecture — 719
Natural language processing
  computer science — 006.3
  see Manual at 410.285 vs.
    006.3
Natural law
  ethical systems — 171
  law — 340
Natural magnets — 538
Natural phenomena — 508
  see also Nature
Natural religion — 210
Natural resource management — 333.7
  see Manual at 333.7–333.9 vs.
    363.1, 363.73, 577
Natural resources — 333.7
  conservation — 333.7
    see also Conservation of
      natural resources
  economics — 333.7
    see Manual at 333.7–333.9
      vs. 333
  ethics — 178
  law — 346.04
  public administration — 354.3
  see Manual at 333.7–333.9 vs.
    363.1, 363.73, 577; *also*
    at 333.7–333.9 vs. 363.6
Natural sciences — 500
  see also Science
Natural selection — 576.8
Natural theology — 210
Naturalism — 146
  fine arts — 709.03
  painting — 759.05
Naturalists — 508.092
Naturalization — 323.6
  public administration — 353.4
Nature — 508
  art representation — 704.9

Nature (continued)
  folklore — 398.24
    nonliving — 398.26
  painting — 758
  philosophy — 113
  religious worship — 291.2
  respect for
    ethics — 179
Nature conservation — 333.7
  see also Conservation of
    natural resources
Nature study — 508.07
  elementary education — 372.3
Nature versus nurture
  psychology
    evolutional psychology — 155.7
    individual psychology — 155.2
Naturopathy
  therapeutic system — 615.5
Nauru — 996.85
    T2—968 5
Nautical almanacs — 528
Nautical engineering — 623.8
Nautical engineers — 623.809 2
Navajo Indians
  social group — 305.897
Naval administration — 359.6
Naval air forces — 359.9
Naval bases — 359.7
  military engineering — 623
Naval engineering — 623.8
Naval engineers — 623.809 2
Naval forces — 359
Naval operations — 359.4
Naval ordnance — 359.8
  engineering — 623.8
  naval equipment — 359.8
Naval warfare — 359
Navigation — 629.04
  air transportation — 629.132
  engineering — 629.04
  maritime transportation — 623.89
  space flight — 629.45
Navigation aids — 387.1
  hydraulic engineering — 627
Navigators — 629.04
Navy life — 359.1
Nazism — 335.6
  political ideology — 320.53
Neanderthal man — 569.9
Near-death experience
  occultism — 133.9
Near East — 956
    T2—56

New England	T2—74
New Guinea	995
	T2—95
New Guinea (Territory)	T2—953
New Hampshire	T2—742
New Hebrides	T2—959 5
New Jersey	T2—749
New left	320.53
New Mexico	T2—789
New Norse language	439.8
New religions	291
see Manual at 291	
New religious movements	291
see Manual at 291	
New South Wales	T2—944
New Southwest	T2—79
New Testament	225
New Thought	299
Christian	289.9
New Year	394.261 4
customs	394.261 4
Jewish	394.267
Jewish	296.4
New York (State)	T2—747
New Zealand	993
	T2—93
New Zealand literature	820
New Zealanders	993
social group	305.82
Newfoundland	T2—718
Newfoundland (Dog)	636.73
News agencies	
journalism	070.4
News gathering	070.4
News media	070.1
Newsletters	050
Newspaper advertising	659.13
Newspapers	070
	T1—05
bibliographies	011
journalism	070.1
publishing	070.5
sociology	302.23
Nicaragua	972.85
	T2—728 5
Nicaraguan literature	860
Nicaraguans	972.85
Nickel	669
chemistry	546
metallurgy	669
metalworking	673
Niger	966.26
	T2—662 6

Nigeria	966.9
	T2—669
Nigerians	966.9
Night schools	
adult education	374
Nightclub presentations	792.7
Nihilism	
philosophy	149
Nile River	T2—62
Nitrates	553.6
Nitrogen	553
chemistry	546
economic geology	553
gas technology	665.8
organic chemistry	547
Nixon, Richard M. (Richard Milhous)	
United States history	973.924
NMR imaging	
medicine	616.07
Nobility (Social class)	305.5
Noise	363.74
communications engineering	621.382
engineering	620.2
psychology	152.1
environmental psychology	155.9
social welfare	363.74
Nominalism	149
Nominating conventions (Political parties)	324.5
Nomination (Political parties)	324.5
Nomination hearings	352–354
see Manual at 300, 320 vs. 352–354	
Non-Austronesian languages of Oceania	499
Non-Euclidean geometry	516.9
Non-self-governing territories	
international law	341.2
public administration	353.1
Non-Trinitarian concepts	
Christianity	
God	231
Jesus	232.9
Nonbeing	111
Nonbook materials	
cataloging	025.3
library treatment	025.17
Noncombatants	
law of war	341.6
Noncommercial television	384.55
Noncommissioned officers	355.009 2
role and function	355.3

Novelettes	808.83
see also Fiction	
Novelists	809.3
collected biography	809.3
specific literatures	T3—300 9
individual biography	T3—3
Novels	808.83
see also Fiction	
NOW accounts	332.1
Nuclear accidents	363.17
Nuclear energy	333.792
economics	333.792
law	343.09
physics	539.7
Nuclear engineering	621.48
Nuclear engineers	621.480 92
Nuclear fission	539.7
Nuclear fuels	
resource economics	333.8
Nuclear fusion	539.7
Nuclear magnetic resonance	
imaging	
medicine	616.07
Nuclear medicine	616.07
Nuclear missiles	358.1
engineering	623.4
military equipment	358.1
Nuclear physicists	539.709 2
Nuclear physics	539.7
Nuclear power plants	621.48
Nuclear propulsion	621.48
Nuclear reactors	621.48
Nuclear warfare	355.02
operations	355.4
see also Disasters	
Nuclear weapons	355.8
control	327.1
international law	341.7
engineering	623.4
military equipment	355.8
Nuclear winter	577.27
Nucleic acids	572.8
Nudes	
art representation	704.9
drawing	743.4
painting	757
Number	
philosophy	119
Number theory	512
Numbers	513
fortune-telling	133.3
Numbers (Biblical book)	222
Numeration systems	513.5
Numerical analysis	515

Numerology	133.3
Numismatics	737
Nuns	291.6
Christian	255
biography	271
see Manual at 230–280	
guides to Christian life	248.8
Nurse and patient	610.730 6
Nurse practitioners	610.730 92
role and function	610.730 6
Nurseries (For plants)	631.5
horticulture	635
Nursery rhymes	398.8
Nursery schools	372.21
Nurses	610.730 92
health services	362.1
role and function	610.730 6
Nurses' aides	610.730 92
role and function	610.730 6
Nursing	
medicine	610.73
see Manual at 610.73	
Nursing (Breast feeding)	649
child rearing	649
health	613.2
Nursing homes	362.1
Nutrition	363.8
animal husbandry	636.08
biology	572
elementary education	372.3
health	613.2
human physiology	612.3
social welfare	363.8
see Manual at 363.8 vs. 613.2,	
641.3	
Nutritional diseases	
medicine	616.3
Nutritional services	
public administration	353.5
Nutritionists	613.209 2
Nuts	581.4
cooking	641.6
descriptive botany	581.4
food	641.3
orchard crop	634
physiology	575.6
Nyanja language	496
Nyasaland	T2—689 7
Nylons (Plastics)	668.4
textiles	677

O

Oaks	583

Oats	641.3	Occupied territory	355.4
cooking	641.6	Ocean basins	T2—182
food	641.3	*see Manual at* T2—163,	
food crop	633.1	T2—164, T2—165 vs.	
forage crop	633.2	T2—182	
Obadiah (Biblical book)	224	Ocean bottom	551.46
Obedience (Christian doctrine)	234	Ocean currents	551.47
Obesity		Ocean engineering	620
medicine	616.3	Ocean floor vehicles	
reducing diet	613.2	engineering	629.2
Object-oriented databases		Ocean transportation	387.5
computer science	005.75	public administration	354.78
Object-oriented programming	005.1	Ocean travel	910.4
Oboes	788.5	Oceania	995
Obscenity			T2—95
ethics	176	Oceanic languages	499
social problem	363.4	Oceanographers	551.460 092
Observatories		Oceanography	551.46
astronomy	522	Oceans	551.46
Obstetrical surgery	618.8		T2—162
Obstetricians	618.200 92	biology	578.77
Obstetrics	618.2	ecology	577.7
Occident	T2—182	geologic agent	551.3
Occultations	523.9	interactions with atmosphere	551.5
Occultism	133	international law	341.4
religious practice	291.3	physical geology	551.46
see Manual at 133 vs. 200		resource economics	333.91
Occupational aptitude tests	153.9	*see Manual at* T2—162	
Occupational diseases		Ocelot	599.75
medicine	616.9	animal husbandry	636.8
Occupational ethics	174	OCR (Computer science)	006.4
Occupational groups	305.9	Octopuses	594
	T1—088	Odd-toed ungulates	599.66
see Manual at 305.9 vs. 305.5		Off-road vehicles	388.3
Occupational guidance	331.7	engineering	629.22
Occupational health	613.6	Offaly (Ireland)	T2—418
see Manual at 363.11 vs.		Offenders	364.3
613.6			T1—086
Occupational health services		criminology	364.3
personnel management	658.3	law	345
Occupational mobility	305.9	pastoral care of	259
economics	331.12	punishment	364.6
Occupational safety	363.11	welfare services	364.6
see also Industrial safety		Offenses against property	364.16
Occupational stress	158.7	law	345
Occupational therapy		Offenses against the person	364.15
medicine	615.8	law	345
Occupational training	370.11	Office buildings	
see also Vocational education		architecture	725
Occupations	331.7	Office employees	651.309 2
	T1—023	Office equipment	
Occupied countries	355.4	office services	651
see Manual at 930–990: Wars:		procurement	658.7
Occupied countries		Office management	651.3

Office services	651
Office supplies	
office services	651
procurement	658.7
Office workers	651.309 2
personnel management	651.306 8
Officers (Armed forces)	355.009 2
role and function	355.3
Official gazettes	351.05
Offset printing	686.2
Offshore structures	627
Ohio	T2—771
Ohio River	T2—77
Ohio River Valley	T2—77
Oil (Petroleum)	553.2
economic geology	553.2
extraction	622
extractive economics	338.2
processing	665.5
economics	338.4
resource economics	333.8
Oil painting	751.45
Oil shale	553.2
see also Petroleum	
Oil spills	363.738
water pollution engineering	628.1
Oil wells	622
Oils	
industrial	665
Oils (Food)	
food technology	664
Oilseed plants	
agriculture	633.8
Okapi	599.638
Okhotsk, Sea of	T2—164
Oklahoma	T2—766
Oktoberfest	394.264 4
Old age	305.26
Old-age and survivors' insurance	368.3
government-sponsored	368.4
law	344
Old Bulgarian language	491.8
Old English language	429
Old Latin language	477
Old Norse language	439
Old Northwest	T2—77
Old Persian language	491
Old persons	305.26
	T1—084
see also Older persons	
Old Prussian language	491
Old Southwest	T2—76
Old Testament	221

Older persons	305.26
	T1—084
architecture for	720.84
geriatrics	618.97
government-sponsored	
insurance	368.4
home care	649.8
libraries for	027.6
physiology	612.6
psychology	155.67
religion	200.84
Christianity	270.084
guides to life	248.8
pastoral care of	259
social aspects	305.26
social welfare	362.6
public administration	353.537
Older workers	331.3
Oligarchy	321.5
Olives	641.3
agriculture	634
cooking	641.6
food	641.3
Olympic Games	796.48
summer	796.48
winter	796.98
Oman	953.53
	T2—535 3
Ombudsmen	352.8
law	342
legislative branch	328.3
public administration	352.8
Omens	133.3
Omotic languages	493
On-the-job training	331.25
	T1—071
see also Vocational education	
Oncology	616.99
Oncopods	592
One-act plays	
literature	808.82
see also Drama (Literature)	
Onions	641.3
cooking	641.6
food	641.3
garden crop	635
Online catalogs	025.3
Online help facilities	005.3
Online information systems	025.04
Online processing	004
Only child	306.874
psychology	155.44
Ontario	T2—713

Oregon	T2—795
Ores	553
Organ culture	571.5
humans	612
Organ transplants	362.1
social services	362.1
surgery	617.9
Organic chemistry	547
applied	661
Organic farming	631.5
Organic gardening	635
Organic geochemistry	553.2
Organists	786.509 2
Organization (Management)	658.1
	T1—068
executive	658.4
Organization of American States	341.24
public administration	352.11
Organizational behavior	302.3
Organizations	060
	T1—06
business enterprises	338.7
law	346
organizational behavior	302.3
social	366
Organized crime	364.106
Organs (Musical instruments)	786.5
Orient	950
	T2—5
Oriental architecture	720.95
Oriental arts	709.5
Oriental churches	281
Oriental languages	490
Oriental law	340.5
Oriental philosophy	181
Oriental sculpture	730.95
Orienteering	796.58
Origami	736
Origin of life	576.8
religion	291.2
Christianity	231.7
philosophy of religion	213
Original sin	233
Oriya language	491.4
Ornamental birds	636.6
Ornamental plants	635.9
see Manual at 583–585; *also*	
at 635.9 vs. 582.1	
Ornamental woodwork	
handicrafts	745.51
Ornaments	
handicrafts	745.594
Ornithischia	567.914
Ornithologists	598.092

Ornithology	598
Ornithopoda	567.914
Orogeny	551.8
Oromo (African people)	
social group	305.89
Oromo language	493
Orphans	305.9
	T1—086
social services	362.73
Orthodontics	617.6
Orthodox Eastern Church	281.9
Orthodox Judaism	296.8
Orthopedic surgery	617.4
Orthopedics	616.7
Osco-Umbrian languages	479
Osco-Umbrians	
social group	305.8
Oslo (Norway)	T2—482
Osteoarthritis	
medicine	616.7
Osteopathy	610
therapeutic system	615.5
Osteoporosis	
medicine	616.7
Østlandet (Norway)	T2—482
Ostriches	598.5
Otologists	617.809 2
Otology	617.8
Otorhinolaryngology	617.5
Otters	599.769
Ottoman Empire	956
	T2—56
Ouija board	133.9
Out-of-body experience	133.9
Outdoor advertising	659.13
Outdoor furniture	645
Outdoor games	796
Outdoor life	796.5
Outdoor photography	778.7
Outdoor sports	796
Outer Mongolia	951.7
	T2—517
Outer space	520
	T2—19
see Manual at 520 vs. 500.5,	
523.1, 530.1, 919.9	
Outlines	T1—02
Over-the-counter drugs	615
Over-the-counter market	332.64
Overpopulation	363.9
Oversight	658.4
public administration	352.3
Overtime pay	331.2
Overtime work	331.25

Palestinians	956.94	Papua New Guinea	995.3
social group	305.892		T2—953
Pali language	491	Papua New Guineans	995.3
Pallets		social group	305.89
wooden	674	Papuan languages	499
Palm reading	133.6	Parables in the Gospels	226.8
Palmistry	133.6	Parachutes	629.134
Palms	584	Parachuting	
Palmtop computers	004.16	sports	797.5
see also Microcomputers		Parades	394
Palmyra Atoll (Line		customs	394
Islands)	T2—969	performing arts	791.6
Pan-Africanism	320.54	*see Manual at* 394 vs. 791.6	
Pan movements	320.54	Paradoxes	
Panama	972.87	logic	165
	T2—728 7	Paraguay	989.2
Panama Canal (Panama)	T2—728 7		T2—892
Panamanian literature	860	Paraguayan literature	860
Panamanians	972.87	Paraguayans	989.2
Panic		Parakeets	598.7
social psychology	302	Parallel processing	004
Panic disorders		Parallel programming	005.2
psychiatry	616.85	Paralympics	796.04
Panics (Economics)	338.5	Paralysis	
Panjabi language	491.4	symptomatology	
Panoramas	745	neurological diseases	616.8
Pantheism	211	Paranoia	
philosophy	147	medicine	616.89
philosophy of religion	211	Paranormal phenomena	130
Pantomime	792.3	*see Manual at* 001.9 and 130	
Papal administration	262	Paraphotic phenomena	535.01
Paper	676	engineering	621.36
handicrafts	745.54	Paraplegia	
Paper airplanes	745.592	neurology	616.8
Paper bags	676	Parapsychology	133
Paper dolls	769.5	*see Manual at* 133 vs. 200	
Paper industry	338.4	Parasites	578.6
Paper money	332.4	Parasitic animals	591.6
arts	769.5	Parasitic diseases (Biology)	571.9
printing	686.2	Parasitic diseases (Human)	
Paperbacks	002	medicine	616.9
publishing	070.5	Parasitic plants	581.6
Paperboard	676	Parasitic skin diseases	
Paperhanging	698	medicine	616.5
interior decoration	747	Parasitism (Biology)	
Papermaking	676	animals	591.7
Paperweights		ecology	577.8
glass		pathology	571.9
decorative arts	748.8	plants	581.7
Papiamento dialect	467	Paratroops	356
Papiamento literature	860	Parazoa	593.4
Papier mâché		Pardon	364.6
handicrafts	745.54	law	345
Papua	T2—954	penology	364.6

Pastoral theology (continued)		Patristics (Christianity)	270	
Judaism	296.6	Patrol		
Pastors	270.092	police services	363.2	
biography	270.092	Pattern perception		
specific denominations	280	psychology	152.14	
see Manual at 230–280		Pattern recognition		
ecclesiology	262	computer science	006.4	
pastoral theology	253	Patternmaking		
personal religion	248.8	clothing		
Pastries	641.8	commercial technology	687	
commercial processing	664	metal casting	671.2	
home preparation	641.8	Pavements		
Pasture lands	333.74	road surfaces	625.8	
Pastures	633.2	Paving roads	625.8	
Patchwork		Pavlovian conditioning	153.1	
arts	746.46	Pay equity	331.2	
Patent medicines		Pay television	384.55	
therapeutics	615.8	Payroll administration	658.3	
Patents	346.04	public administration	352.4	
international law	341.7	Payroll tax	336.24	
law	346.04	PDA (Computer)	004.16	
Patents (Collections)	608	*see also* Microcomputers		
	T1—02	Peace	303.6	
Paternity	346.01	ethics	172	
Pathogenic microorganisms	579	international law	341.7	
medical microbiology	616	international politics	327.1	
Pathological psychology	616.89	social theology	291.1	
see also Mental illness		Christianity	261.8	
Pathology	571.9	Islam	297.2	
agricultural plants	632	Judaism	296.3	
humans	616.07	sociology	303.6	
see Manual at 616 vs.		Peace conferences	341.7	
616.07		Peace Corps (U.S.)	361.6	
see Manual at 571–575 vs.		Peace movements	327.1	
630		sociology	303.6	
Patience	179	Peace pipe	399	
Patient compliance		Peacekeeping forces	355.3	
medicine	615.5	international law	341.5	
Patient education	615.507 1	Peaches	641.3	
Patients' libraries	027.6	cooking	641.6	
Patio furniture	645	food	641.3	
Patios	721	Peafowl	598.6	
domestic	643	animal husbandry	636.5	
Patriarchs	200.92	Peanuts	641.3	
Biblical	222	cooking	641.6	
biography	200.92	field crop	633.3	
Christian	270.092	food	641.3	
biography	270.092	Peas	641.3	
specific denominations	280	cooking	641.6	
see Manual at 230–280		field crop	633.3	
Patriotic holidays	394.26	food	641.3	
Patriotic music	781.5	garden crop	635	
Patriotic societies	369	Peasants	305.5	
Patristic philosophy	189	Pedestrian paths	388.1	

Persian Gulf War, 1991	956.704 4
Persian language	491
Persian Wars, 500–479 B.C.	938
Persians	955
social group	305.891
Personal analysis	
applied psychology	158.1
Personal appearance	646.7
customs	391.6
ethics	177
Personal budgets	
home economics	640
Personal computers	004.16
see also Microcomputers	
Personal conduct	
public administrative control	353.3
Personal counseling	
education	371.4
Personal digital assistants	004.16
see also Microcomputers	
Personal efficiency	
business	650.1
executives	658.4
Personal finance	332.024
see Manual at 332.024 vs. 640	
Personal grooming accessories	
manufacturing technology	688
Personal health	613
Personal hygiene	613
Personal improvement	
applied psychology	158.1
Personal income tax	336.24
Personal living	646.7
Personal loans	332.7
Personal names	929.4
Personal property	
law	346.04
Personal property tax	336.2
Personal religion	291.4
Christianity	240
Islam	297.5
Sufi	297.4
Judaism	296.7
Personal safety	613.6
	T1—028
Personal selling	
management	658.85
Personal survival	
occultism	133.9
see Manual at 133.9 vs. 129	
Personalism	
philosophy	141
Personality	155.2
applied psychology	158.1

Personality (continued)	
children	155.4
late adulthood	155.67
philosophy	126
sex psychology	155.3
Personality assessment	155.2
Personality disorders	
medicine	616.85
Personality inventories	155.2
Personality tests	155.2
Personality types	155.2
Personnel management	658.3
	T1—068
armed forces	355.6
libraries	023
public administration	352.6
see Manual at 331 vs. 658.3	
Persons	T1—092
individuals	T1—092
see Manual at T1—092	
international law	341.4
kinds	T1—08
law	346.01
Perspective	
arts	701
Persuasion	303.3
logic	168
psychology	153.8
rhetoric	808
social psychology	303.3
Peru	985
	T2—85
Peruvian literature	860
Peruvians	985
Pesach	296.4
Pessimism	
philosophy	149
Pest control	363.7
agriculture	632
conservation technology	639.9
control technology	628.9
household sanitation	648
social welfare	363.7
Pesticides	668
agricultural use	632
chemical engineering	668
pollution	363.738
environmental engineering	628.5
Pests	591.6
agriculture	632
Peter (Biblical books)	227
Petrography	552
Petroleum	553.2
economic geology	553.2

Phrase books	418	Physiographic regions	T2—1
specific languages	T4—83	*see Manual at* T2—4–T2—9	
Phrenology	139	Physiological balance	571.7
Phycology	579.8	Physiological genetics	572.8
Physical anthropology	599.9	Physiology	571
Physical chemistry	541.3	animals	571.1
applied	660	domestic animals	636.089
see Manual at 541 vs. 546		humans	612
Physical constants	530.8	*see Manual at* 612 vs. 611;	
Physical diagnosis		*also at* 616 vs. 612	
medicine	616.07	microorganisms	571.2
Physical distribution of goods		plants	571.2
management	658.7	*see Manual at* 571–575; *also*	
Physical education	613.7	*at* 571–575 vs. 630	
elementary school	372.86	Pianists	786.209 2
health	613.7	Piano concertos	784.2
sports	796.07	Pianos	786.2
Physical environment		Piccolos	788.3
psychological influence	155.9	Piciformes	598.7
Physical ethnology	599.97	Picketing	331.892
Physical fitness	613.7	Pickling foods	664
Physical geography	910	commercial preservation	664
see Manual at 550 vs. 910;		home preservation	641.4
also at 909, 930–990 vs.		Pickup trucks	388.3
910		engineering	629.223
Physical geology	551	Picnics	642
Physical illness	362.1	Picture dictionaries	413
see also Diseases (Human)		specific languages	T4—3
Physical sciences	500.2	specific subject	T1—03
Physical therapy		Picture frames	684
medicine	615.8	furniture arts	749
Physical training		Pictures	T1—022
health	613.7	fine arts	760
Physical units	530.8	textile arts	746.3
Physical yoga		Pidgin English	427
health	613.7	Pidgins	417
Physically disabled persons	305.9	specific languages	T4—7
	T1—087	*see Manual at* T4—7	
education	371.91	Piedmont (U.S. : Region)	T2—75
social welfare	362.4	Piers (Port facilities)	387.1
Physician and patient	610.69	engineering	627
Physicians	610.92	Pies	641.8
biography	610.92	Pietism	273
law	344	Pigeons	598.6
role and function	610.69	Piggyback transportation	385
Physicists	530.092	Pigment processes	
Physics	530	photographic printing	773
engineering	621	Pigments	547
see Manual at 530 vs. 540;		chemistry	547
also at 530 vs. 621		paint technology	667
Physiognomy		Pigs	636.4
divination	138	animal husbandry	636.4
Physiographic features	T2—1	zoology	599.63
see Manual at T2—4–T2—9		Pikas (Conies)	599.32

Plants (continued)	
resource economics	333.95
Plants (Buildings and	
equipment)	
management	658.2
	T1—068
Plasma engineering	621.044
Plasma motors	621.46
Plasma physics	530.4
Plaster of paris	666
Plastering	693
Plastic arts	730
see Manual at 731–735 vs.	
736–739	
Plastic surgery	617.9
Plastics	668.4
building materials	691
construction materials	693
handicrafts	745.57
materials science	620.1
Plate tectonics	551.1
Plateaus	551.43
Platform diving	797.2
Platform speeches	
rhetoric	808.5
Platforms (Party programs)	324.2
Platonism	184
ancient	184
modern	141
Platypus	599.2
Play	790
psychology	155
recreation	790
sociology	306.4
Play groups	
agent of socialization	303.3
social psychology	302.3
Player pianos	786.6
Playgrounds	796.06
Plays	
literature	808.82
see also Drama (Literature)	
musical	782.1
music	782.1
stage presentation	792.6
theater	792
Playwrights	809.2
collected biography	809.2
specific literatures	T3—200 9
individual biography	T3—2
Playwriting	808.2
Pleasant Island	996.85
	T2—968 5

Pleasure	
psychology	152.4
Pleasures of eating	641.01
Plectral instruments	787.7
Plumbing	696
Pluralism	
philosophy	147
Pluto (Planet)	523.48
Plutocracy	321.5
Plywood	674
PMS (Syndrome)	
gynecology	618.1
Pneumatic engineering	621.5
Pneumatics	533
Pneumonia	
medicine	616.2
Pocket computers	004.16
see also Microcomputers	
Pocket gophers	599.35
Podiatry	617.5
Poems	808.81
see also Poetry	
Poetic books (Old Testament)	223
Poetry	808.81
criticism	809.1
theory	808.1
history	809.1
rhetoric	808.1
specific literatures	T3—1
Poets	809.1
collected biography	809.1
specific literatures	T3—100 9
individual biography	T3—1
Pointers (Dogs)	636.752
Pointillism	
painting	759.05
Poisoning	
human toxicology	615.9
Poisonous animals	591.6
Poisonous organisms	578.6
Poisonous plants	581.6
Poisons	363.17
human toxicology	615.9
public safety	363.17
see also Safety	
Poker (Game)	795.41
Polabian language	491.8
Poland	943.8
	T2—438
Polar bear	599.786
Polar regions	T2—11
Polarization of light	535.5
Pole vaulting	796.43

Polyglot dictionaries	413
specific subject	T1—03
Polymerization	547
chemical engineering	668.9
Polymers	547
chemical engineering	668.9
inorganic chemistry	541.2
organic chemistry	547
Polynesia	996
	T2—96
Polynesian languages	499
Polynesians	996
social group	305.89
Polytheism	211
comparative religion	291.1
philosophy of religion	211
Pomeranian (Dog)	636.76
Ponds	551.48
biology	578.763
ecology	577.63
hydrology	551.48
resource economics	333.91
Ponies	636.1
Pony express	383
Poodle	636.72
Poodle (Toy dog)	636.76
Pool (Game)	794.7
Pools (Water)	
landscape architecture	714
Poor people	305.5
	T1—086
social welfare	362.5
public administration	353.53
Pop art	709.04
painting	759.06
Popes	282.092
biography	282.092
ecclesiology	262
Popular culture	306
Popular music	781.63
Popular songs	
western	782.421 64
Population	304.6
social problems	363.9
see Manual at 363.9 vs.	
304.6	
sociology	304.6
Population biology	577.8
Population control	363.9
see also Birth control	
see Manual at 363.9 vs. 304.6	
Population genetics	576.5
Population geography	304.6
Population movement	304.8

Population transfer	325
Porcelain	666
arts	738.2
technology	666
Porcupines	599.35
Porifera	593.4
paleozoology	563
Pork	641.3
cooking	641.6
food	641.3
Pornography	363.4
criminology	364.1
criminal law	345
ethics	176
social problem	363.4
Porphyria	
medicine	616.3
Porpoises	599.53
Portability	
computer software	005
Portable radios	621.384 5
Portable telephones	384.5
communications services	384.5
engineering	621.384 5
Portfolio management	332.6
Portland cement	666
Portraits	
art representation	704.9
drawing	743.4
painting	757
Ports	387.1
engineering	627
inland waterway	386
transportation services	387.1
see Manual at 386 vs. 387.1	
Portugal	946.9
	T2—469
ancient	936.6
	T2—366
Portuguese (People)	946.9
social group	305.86
Portuguese Guinea	T2—665 7
Portuguese language	469
Portuguese literature	869
Portuguese man-of-war	593.5
Positional astronomy	522
Positivism	146
Possums	599.2
Post offices	383
Post-traumatic stress disorder	
medicine	616.85
Postage stamps	383
philately	769.56
postal service	383

Precalculus	510	Presbyterians	
see Manual at 510		biography	285.092
Precambrian era	551.7	Preschool children	305.233
Precious metals	669	home care	649
Precious stones	553.8	psychology	155.42
Precipitation (Meteorology)	551.57	social aspects	305.233
Precision instruments		Preschool education	372.21
technology	681	Prescription drugs	615
Preclassical Greek language	487	Prescriptive linguistics	418
Preclassical Latin language	477	specific languages	T4—8
Precognition	133.8	*see Manual at* 410	
Predation (Biology)	591.5	Preservation	620
plants	575.9		T1—028
Predator control		arts	702.8
animal husbandry	636.08	bibliographic materials	025.8
conservation technology	639.9	Preserved foods	
Predatory animals	591.5	home economics	641.4
Predelinquents		Preserves (Whole fruits)	
social welfare	362.74	home preparation	641.4
Predestination		Presidents	321
Christianity	234	democratic systems	321.8
Predictions	003	public administration	352.23
occultism	133.3	Press	070
Prefabricated materials		civil rights issues	323.44
building materials	691	Press control	363.3
construction	693	*see also* Censorship	
Preferential hiring		Press law	343.09
union security arrangements	331.88	Pressing metals	671.3
Pregnancy	573.6	Pressure groups	322.4
biology	573.6	political process	324
human physiology	612.6	Pretrial release	345
obstetrics	618.2	Preventive medicine	613
Pregnancy programs in schools	371.7	public	614.4
Prehistoric animals	560	*see Manual at* 614.4–614.5	
Prehistoric archaeology	930.1	vs. 362.1–362.4	
Prehistoric humans	569.9	Price control (Government)	338.5
Prejudice	303.3	public administration	352.8
ethics	177	Price determination	338.5
sociology	303.3	marketing management	658.8
Premarital counseling		Price fixing	
Christian pastoral counseling	259	criminology	364.16
Premarital sexual relations	306.73	criminal law	345
social problem	363.4	Price lists	T1—029
Premature infants		Price trends	T1—029
pediatrics	618.92	collectibles	T1—075
Premenstrual syndrome		Prices	338.5
gynecology	618.1	economics	338.5
Premium television	384.55	land economics	333.33
Prenatal care		regulation	
obstetrics	618.2	law	343
Preparatory schools	373.2	Priesthood of Jesus Christ	232
Prerelease guidance centers	365		
Presbyterian Church	285		

Procedural rights	323.42
Procellariiformes	598.4
Process	
philosophy of nature	116
Process control	003
production management	658.5
Process metallurgy	669
Process philosophy	146
Processing (Libraries)	025
Processions	394
customs	394
performing arts	791.6
see Manual at 394 vs. 791.6	
Processors	
computer hardware	004
engineering	621.39
Procurement	658.7
armed forces	355.6
public administration	352.5
Producers' cooperatives	334
Product development	
management	658.5
Product directories	T1—029
see Manual at 338 vs. 060,	
381, 382, 670.29, 910,	
T1—025, T1—029; *also*	
at 380.1 and 381, 382	
Product evaluation	381.3
	T1—029
Product liability	346.03
Product recall	363.19
production management	658.5
Product safety	363.19
law	344
production management	658.5
social services	363.19
Production	
sociology	306.3
Production economics	338
Production efficiency	338
Production management	658.5
	T1—068
Productivity	
agricultural industries	338.1
labor economics	331.11
mineral industries	338.2
secondary industries	338.4
Products	
agricultural industries	338.1
commerce	380.1
economics	338
mineral industries	338.2
secondary industries	338.4

Products research	
technology	607
Profanity	179
Professional education	378
	T1—071
Professional ethics	174
Professional relationships	T1—023
Professional services	338.4
Professional sports	796.04
see Manual at 796.08 vs.	
796.04	
Professional workers	331.7
Professional writing	808
Professionals	305.5
Professions	331.7
Profit sharing	
labor economics	331.2
personnel management	658.3
Profits	338.5
financial management	658.15
Prognosis	
medicine	616.07
Program compatibility	005
Program design	005.1
Program documentation	
preparation	005.1
text	005.3
Program languages	005.13
Program music	781.5
Program notes (Music)	780.15
Program portability	005
Program reliability	005
Programmable calculators	510.285
Programmed instruction	371.39
	T1—07
electronic	371.33
Programming (Mathematics)	519.7
see Manual at 005.1 vs. 510	
Programming computers	005.1
graphics	006.6
multimedia systems	006.7
see Manual at 005.1 vs. 510	
Programming languages	005.13
see Manual at 005.362	
Programs (Computer)	005.3
	T1—028 5
coding	005.13
graphics	006.6
multimedia systems	006.7
see Manual at T1—0285	
Programs (Party platforms)	324.2
Progress	303.44
Progressive Conservative Party	
of Canada	324.271 04

Provinces	320.8
public administration	352.14
see Manual at 351.3–351.9	
vs. 352.13–352.19; *also*	
at 352.13 vs. 352.15	
Provinces (Local government	
units)	320.8
public administration	352.15
Provinces (State-level units)	321.02
public administration	352.13
Psalms	223
Psalters	264
Pseudepigrapha	229
Pseudo gospels	229
Pseudonymous works	
bibliographies	014
Psi phenomena	133.8
Psittaciformes	598.7
Psychedelics abuse	362.29
Psychiatric hospitals	362.2
Psychiatric nursing	
medicine	610.73
Psychiatric social work	362.2
Psychiatry	616.89
see also Mental illness	
Psychic messages	133.9
Psychic phenomena	133.8
Psychoanalysis	150.19
psychiatry	616.89
psychology	150.19
see also Mental illness	
Psychokinesis	133.8
Psycholinguistics	401
Psychological principles	T1—01
Psychological systems	150.19
Psychological warfare	355.3
Psychologists	150.92
Psychology	150
	T1—01
see Manual at 302–307 vs.	
150, T1—01	
Psychology of religion	200.1
Psychopharmacology	615
Psychophysiology	
humans	612.8
Psychoses	362.2
medicine	616.89
social welfare	362.2
Psychosomatic medicine	616.08
Psychosurgery	617.4
Psychotherapy	
psychiatry	616.89
see also Mental illness	
Pteridophytes	587
Pterodactyls	567.918
Pterosauria	567.918
Puberty	612.6
Public address systems	
engineering	621.389
Public administration	351
ethics	172
subordinate jurisdictions	352.14
see Manual at 351.3–351.9	
vs. 352.13–352.19; *also*	
at 352.13 vs. 352.15	
see Manual at T1—068 vs.	
353–354; *also at* 320.9,	
320.4 vs. 351; *also at* 351;	
also at 363 vs. 340,	
353–354	
Public administrators	352.3
biography	351.092
executive management	352.3
Public borrowing	336.3
Public buildings	
architecture	725
Public contracts	352.5
Public debt	336.3
law	343
macroeconomic policy	339.5
see also Public finance	
Public defenders	345
Public discussion	
literature	808.853
rhetoric	808.53
Public education	370
government control	379.1
policy issues	379
public support	379.1
see Manual at 371 vs. 353.8,	
371.2, 379	
Public enterprise (Organization	
of production)	338.6
Public enterprises	338.7
public revenue source	336.1
Public expenditures	336.3
macroeconomic policy	339.5
Public finance	336
administration	352.4
economics	336
law	343
see Manual at 332, 336 vs.	
339; *also at* 336 vs. 352.4	
Public health	362.1
international law	341.7
law	344
medicine	614
public administration	353.6

Public health (continued)
  social welfare — 362.1
Public health nursing
  medicine — 610.73
Public hearings
  public administration — 351
    see Manual at T1—068 vs.
      353–354; *also at* 300,
      320 vs. 352–354
Public housing — 363.5
  household management — 647
  law — 344
  social services — 363.5
Public insolvency — 336.3
Public lands — 333.1
  administration — 352.5
Public law — 342
Public libraries — 027.4
  public administrative support — 353.7
Public lighting — 628.9
Public opinion — 303.3
Public policy — 320
  see Manual at 300, 320 vs.
    352–354
Public property
  law — 343
  public administration — 352.5
Public records — 352.3
  archival treatment — 025.17
Public relations — 659.2
  armed forces — 355.3
  libraries — 021.7
  local churches — 254
  public administration — 352.7
Public safety — 363.1
  public administration — 353.9
  social services — 363.1
Public sanitation — 363.72
  technology — 628
  see also Waste control
Public schools — 371.01
  see also Education
Public services
  libraries — 025.5
Public speaking — 808.5
  elementary education — 372.62
Public speeches
  literature — 808.85
    history and criticism — 809.5
    specific literatures — T3—5
Public television — 384.55
Public toilets — 363.72
  technology — 628.4

Public utilities — 363.6
  law — 343.09
  public administration — 354.72
    energy — 354.4
  social services — 363.6
  see Manual at 333.7–333 9 vs.
    363.6; *also at* 363.5,
    363.6, 363.8 vs. 338
Public welfare — 361.6
Public works — 363
  public administration — 352.7
  see Manual at 363
Public worship — 291.3
  Christianity — 264
  Islam — 297.3
  Judaism — 296.4
  music — 782.3
Publicity — 659
  see Manual at 658.8, T1—068
    vs. 659
Publishers — 070.509 2
  relations with authors — 070.5
Publishers' catalogs — 015
Publishing — 070.5
  see Manual at 808.001–808.7
    vs. 070.5
Pubs — 647.95
Puerperal diseases
  obstetrics — 618.7
Puerperium
  obstetrics — 618.6
Puerto Rican literature — 860
Puerto Ricans — 972.95
Puerto Rico — 972.95
  — T2—729 5
Pug (Dog) — 636.76
Puli — 636.737
Pulp — 676
Pulpboards — 676
Pulpwood
  forest products — 634.9
Pulsars — 523.8
Pumpkins — 641.3
  cooking — 641.6
  food — 641.3
Pumps — 621.6
Punch (Beverage) — 641.8
Punctuation — 411
  specific languages — T4—1
Punishment
  armed forces — 355.1
  law — 345
  penology — 364.6

Punjabis (South Asian people)
  social group — 305.891
Puppetry — 791.5
  elementary education — 372.67
Puppets — 791.5
  making — 688.7
    handicrafts — 745.592
    technology — 688.7
  performing arts — 791.5
Purchasing manuals — 381.3
      T1—029
Purchasing power
  macroeconomics — 339.4
  value of money — 332.4
  see Manual at 339.4 vs. 332.4
Purgatory — 291.2
  Christianity — 236
Puritanism — 285
Puritans
  biography — 285
Purses — 391.4
  customs — 391.4
  manufacturing technology — 685
Pursuit (Law enforcement) — 363.2
Pushball — 796.33
Put and call transactions — 332.64
  multiple forms of investment — 332.64
  stocks — 332.63
Putonghua (Standard Chinese
  language) — 495.1
Puzzles — 793.73
Pyramid power — 001.94
Pyramids (Buildings) — 909
  Aztec — 972
  Egyptian — 932
  Incan — 985
  Mayan — 972.81
    Guatemala — 972.81
    Mexico — 972
  Mexican — 972
Pyrenees (France and
  Spain) — T2—46
Pythagorean theorem — 516.22

Q

Qatar — 953.63
      T2—536 3
Qohelet — 223
Qoran — 297.1
Quackery
  medicine — 615.8
Quadratic equations — 512.9

Quadruplets — 306.875
Quails — 598.6
Quakers — 289.6
  biography — 289.609 2
Qualitative analysis — 544
  see Manual at 543 vs.
    544–545
Quality control
  management — 658.4
  production management — 658.5
  statistical mathematics — 519.8
Quality engineering — 620
Quality of life — 306
Quantitative analysis — 545
  see Manual at 543 vs.
    544–545
Quantity
  philosophy — 119
Quantity surveying — 692
Quantum chemistry — 541.2
Quantum electronics — 537.5
Quantum mechanics — 530.12
  see Manual at 530.12 vs. 531
Quantum physics — 539
Quantum statistics — 530.13
Quantum theory — 530.12
Quarantine
  disease control — 614.4
Quarks — 539.7
Quarrying — 622
Quasars — 523.1
Quasi-judicial agencies — 352.8
Quebec (Province) — T2—714
Quechua Indians
  social group — 305.898
Quechua language — 498
Queen Anne's War, 1701–1714 — 940.2
  North American history — 973.2
Queens
  folklore — 398.22
Queensland — T2—943
Question-answering systems — 006.3
Questions and answers
  study and teaching — T1—076
Queuing theory — 519.8
Quillworts — 587
Quilting
  arts — 746.46
Quilts — 643
  arts — 746.46
Quizzes
  recreation — 793.73
Qumran community — 296.8

Quotations	080
literature	808.88
specific literatures	T3—8
see Manual at 080 vs. 800;	
also at 081–089	

R

R and D (Research)	
production management	658.5
Rabbis	296.092
biography	296.092
specific denominations	296.8
role and function	296.6
training	296.071
Rabbits	599.32
animal husbandry	636.932
Rabies	
medicine	616.9
veterinary medicine	636.089
Raccoons	599.76
Race discrimination	305.8
law	342
Race relations	305.8
Racehorses	636.1
sports	798.4
Races (Ethnology)	305.8
physical ethnology	599.97
see also Ethnic groups	
Racetracks	
automobiles	796.720 6
horses	798.400 6
Racial characteristics	
physical ethnology	599.97
psychology	155.8
Racial conflict	305.8
Racial discrimination	305.8
Racial groups	305.8
	T1—089
see also Ethnic groups	
Racial minorities	305.8
see also Ethnic groups	
Racing	796
aircraft	797.5
animals	798
dogs	798.8
horses	798.4
automobiles	796.72
bicycles	796.6
boats	797.1
humans	796.42
motor vehicles	796.7
soapboxes	796.6

Racing cars	796.72
engineering	629.228
sports	796.72
Racism	305.8
political ideology	320.5
Racism in textbooks	
public control	379.1
Rackets (Game)	796.343
Racquetball	796.343
Radar	621.384 8
military engineering	623
weather reporting	551.63
Radiant energy	539.2
Radiation	539.2
human physiology	612
meteorology	551.5
physics	539.2
Radiation sickness (Human)	
medicine	616.9
Radiation warfare	358
Radicalism	
political ideology	320.53
Radicals (Chemicals)	541.2
Radio	384.5
communications services	384.5
engineering	621.384
instructional use	371.33
journalism	070.1
performing arts	791.44
see Manual at 384 vs. 791.4	
sociology	302.23
Radio advertising	659.14
Radio astronomy	522
Radio communication	384.5
see also Radio	
Radio control	
engineering	621.384
Radio engineers	621.384 092
Radio music	781.5
Radio news	070.1
Radio plays	791.44
literature	808.82
see also Drama (Literature)	
radio programs	791.44
see Manual at 791.43 and	
791.44, 791.45, 792.9	
Radio programs	384.54
broadcasting	384.54
performing arts	791.44
Radio relay	
telephone engineering	621.387
Radio waves	537.5
Radioactive materials	
public safety	363.17

Radioactive wastes	363.72
social services	363.72
technology	621.48
see also Waste control	
Radioactivity	539.7
Radiobroadcasting	384.54
see Manual at 384 vs. 791.4	
Radiochemistry	541.3
chemical engineering	660
Radiography	
engineering	621.36
Radioisotope scanning	
medicine	616.07
Radioisotopes	539.7
chemistry	541.3
physics	539.7
technology	621.48
therapeutics	615.8
Radiotelegraphy	384.5
communications services	384.5
engineering	621.384
Radiotelephony	384.5
communications services	384.5
engineering	621.384 5
Radiotherapy	
medicine	615.8
Raffia	
textile arts	746.41
Railroad accidents	363.12
Railroad atlases	385.022
specific areas	385.09
Railroad cars	385
engineering	625.2
Railroad engineers	625.100 92
Railroad stations	385.3
architecture	725
transportation services	385.3
local transit	388.4
Railroad transportation	385
engineering	625.1
law	343.09
transportation services	385
urban	388.4
Railroad workers	385.092
Railroad yards	385.3
engineering	625.1
Railroads	385
electrification	
technology	621.33
engineering	625.1
landscape architecture	713
transportation services	385
Rain	551.57
weather forecasting	551.64

Rain forests	333.75
biology	578.734
ecology	577.34
Rainbows	551.56
Rajasthani language	491.4
Rallies (Automobile sport)	796.7
RAM (Computer memory)	004.5
Ramadan	297.3
Ranchers	636
Ranches	636
Random-access memory	004.5
Random processes	519.2
Random walks	519.2
Range management	636.08
Rangelands	
biology	578.74
ecology	577.4
Rangers (Armed forces)	356
Rap (Music)	782.421 649
Rape (Crime)	364.15
law	345
Rape prevention	362.883
Rape victims	362.883
Rapid reading	418
specific languages	T4—84
Rapid transit	388.4
Rapid transit railroads	388.4
engineering	625.4
Raptors (Birds)	598.9
Rapture (Christian doctrine)	236
Rare animals	591.68
Rare birds	598.168
Rare books	090
bibliographies	011
Rare plants	581.68
Rare species	578.68
resource economics	333.95
Rates (United Kingdom)	336.22
law	343.05
see also Taxes	
Rationalism	149
philosophy	149
philosophy of religion	211
political ideology	320.51
Rationality	128
Rationing	333.7
public administration	352.8
see Manual at 333.7–333.9 vs. 363.6	
Ratites	598.5
Rats	599.35
animal husbandry	636.935
Raw materials	333.7
military resources	355.2

Ray tracing
  computer graphics   006.6
Rayon
  textiles   677
Rays (Fishes)   597.3
Razors
  manufacturing technology   688
Reaction-time studies   152.8
Reactors
  nuclear engineering   621.48
Readability
  rhetoric   808
Reader advisory services
  library operations   025.5
Readers (Textbooks)   418
  applied linguistics   418
    specific languages   T4—86
    see Manual at T1—01 vs.
      T4—86; *also at*
      T4—86
  rhetoric   808
  see Manual at 808
  see Manual at 420–490
Readers' theater
  elementary education   372.67
Reading   418
  child care   649
  elementary education   372.4
  library science   028
  recreation   790.1
  specific languages   T4—84
Reading aloud
  child care   649
  rhetoric   808.5
Reading comprehension
  elementary education   372.47
Reading disorders
  special education   371.91
Reading failure
  elementary education   372.43
Reading interests   028
Reading is Fundamental
    (Reading program)
  elementary education   372.42
Reading materials   418
  see also Readers (Textbooks)
Reading readiness   372.41
Reading-skill strategies
  elementary education   372.45
Reagan, Ronald
  United States history   973.927

Real estate   333.3
  investment economics   332.63
  see Manual at 333.73–333.78
    vs. 333, 333.1–333.5
Real estate business   333.33
  law   346.04
Real estate finance   332.7
Real estate market   333.33
Real property   333.3
  law   346.04
  public administration   354.3
  see Manual at 333.73–333.78
    vs. 333, 333.1–333.5
Real property tax   336.22
Real-time processing   004
  programs   005.3
Real-time programming   005.2
Realism
  education   370.1
  fine arts   709.03
  literature   808.8
    history and criticism   809
    specific literatures   T3—08
      history and criticism   T3—09
  painting   759.05
  philosophy   149
Reapportionment (Legislatures)   328.3
Reason   128
  epistemology   121
  ethical systems   171
  philosophical anthropology   128
Reason (Theology)
  Christianity   231
Reasoning   153.4
  logic   160
  psychology   153.4
  see Manual at 153.4 vs. 160
Recall (Elections)   324.6
Recall (Memory)   153.1
Recataloging
  library operations   025.3
Receivership
  credit economics   332.7
  law   346.07
Recently extinct species   578.68
Receptionists
  office services   651.3
Recessions (Economics)   338.5
Recipes
  cooking   641.5
Recitals
  music   780.78
Recitation
  rhetoric   808.5

Recitation (Education) 371.3
Recitations
  literature 808.85
    history and criticism 809.5
    specific literatures T3—5
Reclamation of land 333.73
  agriculture 631.6
  economics 333.73
  hydraulic engineering 627
Reclassification
  library operations 025.3
Recognition (International law) 341.26
Recognition (Psychology) 153.1
Recollection (Psychology) 153.1
Reconnaissance (Military
  operations) 355.4
Reconstruction (Aftermath of
  war) 355.02
  United States history 973.8
Recorders (Musical instruments) 788.3
Recording
  music 781.49
Recording devices
  communications engineering 621.382
Recordings (Sound) 384
  see also Sound recordings
Records management 651.5
Recovery from addiction
  pastoral theology 291.6
    Christianity 259
  therapy 616.86
  see Manual at 616.86 vs.
    158.1, 248.8, 291.4,
    362.29
Recreation · 790
  child care 649
  ethics 175
  folklore 398.27
  public administrative support 353.7
  sociology 306.4
Recreation centers 790.06
Recreation facilities 790.06
  social services 363.6
Recreation safety 363.14
Recreational arts 790
Recreational equipment
  manufacturing technology 688.7
Recreational lands 333.78
Recreational reading 790.1
  library science 028
Recreational vehicles 388.3
  engineering 629.226
Recruiting
  armed forces 355.2

Recruiting (continued)
  personnel management 658.3
    executives 658.4
Recurrent education 374
Recursion theory 511.3
Recycling technology 628.4
Recycling waste 363.72
  see also Waste control
Red Cross 361.7
Red fox 599.775
Red panda 599.76
Red Sea T2—165
Red wolf 599.773
Redemption 291.2
  Christian doctrine 234
  Judaism 296.3
Redevelopment
  community sociology 307.3
Reducing
  dietetics 613.2
  for appearance 646.7
Reduction (Chemical reaction) 541.3
Reductionism (Psychology) 150.19
Reed instruments 788.4
Reefs 551.42
  biology 578.77
  ecology 577.7
  geomorphology 551.42
Reference groups
  social psychology 302.5
Reference services 025.5
Reference works 028.7
  reviews 028.1
Referendum (Legislation) 328.2
Reflexes
  psychology 152.3
Reforestation 333.75
  resource economics 333.75
  silviculture 634.9
Reform Judaism 296.8
Reform movements
  relation to government 322.4
  social action 361.2
Reformation 270.6
  European history 940.2
Reformatories 365
Reformed Church 284
Reformed Church (American
  Reformed) 285.7
Reformed Episcopal Church 283
Refraction errors
  optometry 617.7
Refractory materials 553.6

Religious education	291.7
Christianity	268
see Manual at 268 vs.	
230.071	
Islam	297.7
Judaism	296.6
see Manual at 291.7 vs.	
200.71	
Religious experience	291.4
Christianity	248.2
Islam	297.5
Sufi	297.4
Judaism	296.7
Religious freedom	323.44
civil right	323.44
social theology	291.1
Christianity	261.7
Judaism	296.3
Religious groups	T1—088
legal status	346.01
constitutional law	342
private law	346.01
libraries for	027.6
sociology	305.6
see Manual at 322 vs. 261.7,	
291.1	
Religious holidays	291.3
customs	394.265
see Manual at 263, 291.3	
vs. 394.265	
Religious ideologies	320.5
Religious law	291.8
Christianity	262.9
Islam	297.1
Judaism	296.1
Religious leaders	200.92
Buddhist	294.309 2
Christian	270.092
biography	270.092
specific denominations	280
see Manual at 230–280	
ecclesiology	262
pastoral theology	253
personal religion	248.8
training	230.071
Hindu	294.509 2
Islamic	297.092
biography	297.092
specific sects	297.8
role and function	297.6
Jewish	296.092
biography	296.092
specific denominations	296.8
role and function	296.6

Religious leaders (continued)	
occupational ethics	174
role and function	291.6
Religious life	291.4
Christianity	248.4
Islam	297.5
Judaism	296.7
Religious mythology	291.1
Religious orders	291.6
Christianity	255
church history	271
Religious organizations	291.6
Christianity	260
associations for religious	
work	267
local church	250
religious orders	255
Judaism	296.6
welfare services	361.7
see Manual at 322 vs. 261.7,	
291.1	
Religious plays	
literature	808.82
see also Drama (Literature)	
stage presentation	792.1
Religious schools (General	
education)	371.07
libraries	027.8
Religious studies	200.71
see Manual at 291.7 vs.	
200.71	
Religious symbolism	291.3
Christianity	246
Islam	297.3
Judaism	296.4
painting	755
Religious therapy	
medicine	615.8
see Manual at 615.8 vs. 234,	
291.3	
Remarriage	306.84
see also Marriage	
Remedial education	
adult level	374
Remedial readers (Textbooks)	
applied linguistics	418
specific languages	T4—86
see Manual at T4—86	
Remedial reading	418
elementary education	372.43
specific languages	T4—84
Remedies (Legal actions)	347

Revelation of God (continued)		Ribonucleic acid	572.8
philosophy of religion	212	Rice	641.3
Revenue	336.02	cooking	641.6
law	343	food	641.3
public administration	352.4	food crop	633.1
public finance	336.02	Rich (Social class)	305.5
Revenue sharing	336.1	Rickettsial diseases (Human)	
public administration	352.73	medicine	616.9
Reveries	154.3	Rickettsias	579.3
Review		Riddles	398.6
study and teaching	T1—076	folk literature	398.6
Revival meetings	269	jokes	
Revolution	303.6	literature	808.88
ethics	172	specific literatures	T3—8
political science	321.09	recreation	793.735
social conflict	303.6	Riding horses (Recreation)	798.2
see Manual at 909, 930–990		Riel's Rebellion, 1869–1870	971.05
vs. 320.4, 321, 321.09		Riel's Rebellion, 1885	971.05
Revolutionary groups	322.4	Rifles	683.4
Revolutionary warfare	355.02	*see also* Guns (Small arms)	
Revolvers	683.4	Rift valleys	551.8
see also Guns (Small arms)		Right and wrong	170
Revues	782.1	*see also* Ethics	
music	782.1	Right-handedness	
stage presentation	792.6	psychology	152.3
Reweaving	646.2	Right of assembly	323.4
Reye's syndrome		Right of asylum	323.6
medicine	616.8	international law	341.4
Rhaeto-Romanic languages	459	Right of petition	323.4
Rhetoric	808	Right of privacy	323.44
see Manual at 808.001–808.7		Right to bear arms	323.4
vs. 070.5		Right to die	
Rheumatic fever		ethics	179.7
medicine	616.9	law	344
Rheumatic heart disease		Right to education	379.2
medicine	616.1	Right to hold office	323.5
Rheumatism		Right to information	323.44
medicine	616.7	Right to life	323.4
Rheumatoid arthritis		ethics	179.7
medicine	616.7	law	342
Rheumatology	616.7	Right to life (Prenatal)	
Rhinoceroses	599.66	ethics	179.7
conservation technology	639.97	law	342
Rhode Island	T2—745	Right to read	379.2
Rhodesia and Nyasaland	T2—689	Right to strike	331.892
Rhyme	808.1	Right to vote	324.6
Rhymes		Right to work	331.88
folk literature	398.8	government policy	331.89
Rhyming games	398.8	Rights of man	323
Rhythm (Musical element)	781.2	*see also* Civil rights	
Rhythm and blues	781.643	Riksmål language	439.8
Rhythm bands	784.6	Riksmål literature	839.82
Rhythm perception	153.7	Rings (Mathematics)	512
Rhythmic gymnastics	796.44	Rings (Planets)	523.9

Rio Grande	T2—764
Riot control	363.3
Riot insurance	368.1
Riots	303.6
political action	322.4
social conflict	303.6
see also Disasters	
Riparian biology	578.768
Riparian ecology	577.68
Risk	
economics	338.5
insurance	368
Risk assessment	
natural resources	333.7
see Manual at 333.7–333.9	
vs. 363.1, 363.73, 577	
Risk management	
financial management	658.15
insurance	368
see Manual at 368 vs. 658.15	
Rites	390
customs	390
religion	291.3
Christianity	264
Islam	297.3
Judaism	296.4
music	782.3
River basins	
land economics	333.73
River transportation	386
Rivers	551.48
	T2—16
ecology	577.6
geography	910.916
hydraulic engineering	627
hydrology	551.48
recreational resources	333.78
resource economics	333.91
Riveting	671.5
RNA (Genetics)	572.8
Road engineers	625.709 2
Road maps	912
Road transportation	388.3
law	343.09
urban	388.4
Roads	388.1
agricultural use	631.2
area planning	711
engineering	625.7
landscape architecture	713
military engineering	623
public administration	354.77
transportation services	388.1
urban	388.4

Roadside areas	625.7
Roadside barriers	625.7
Roadsteads	
hydraulic engineering	627
Roasting	
home cooking	641.7
Robbery	364.15
law	345
Robbery insurance	368.8
Robins (American)	598.8
Robotics	629.8
Robots	629.8
elementary education	372.3
factory operations engineering	670.42
Rock (Music)	781.66
songs	782.421 66
Rock art	709.01
Rock climbing	796.52
Rock gardens	635.9
Rock musicians	781.660 92
Rock 'n' roll	781.66
Rock singers	782.421 660 92
Rocket engines	621.43
spacecraft	629.47
see Manual at 629.04 vs.	
621.43	
Rocket fuels	662
Rocket weapons	358.1
engineering	623.4
military equipment	358.1
Rocketry	621.43
Rockets	621.43
see Manual at 629.04 vs.	
621.43	
Rocks	552
determinative mineralogy	549
Rocky Mountains	T2—78
Canada	T2—711
United States	T2—78
Rococo architecture	724
Rococo art	709.03
Rococo painting	759.04
Rodents	599.35
animal husbandry	636.935
Rodeos	791.8
Role-playing games	793.93
see Manual at 793.93 vs.	
794.8	
Role theory	302
Roller skates	
manufacturing technology	685
Roller skating	796.21
Rollerblading	796.21
Rolling metals	671.3

Rules of order	060.4
legislatures	328
Ruminants	599.63
animal husbandry	636.2
Rummy	795.41
Runaway children	305.9
	T1—086
social welfare	362.74
Rundi language	496
Runes	
divination	133.3
Running	
animal behavior	591.5
animal physiology	573.7
humans	
physical fitness	613.7
sports	796.42
Runoff (Hydrology)	551.48
Rural areas	T2—173
Rural communities	307.72
psychological influence	155.9
Rural development	307.1
public administration	354.2
Rural exodus	307.2
Rural government	320.8
public administration	352.17
public administrative support	352.7
Rural lands	333.76
Rural sanitation	363.720 917 3
technology	628
Rural sociology	307.72
Rural-urban migration	307.2
Rushwork	746.41
Russia	947
	T2—47
Asia	957
	T2—57
Russian language	491.7
Russian literature	891.7
Russian Soviet Federated	
Socialist Republic	947
	T2—47
Russians	947
social group	305.891
Russo-Finnish War, 1939–1940	948.970 3
Rust	
materials science	620.1
Ruth (Biblical book)	222
RV (Vehicle)	388.3
engineering	629.226
Rwanda	967.571
	T2—675 71
Rwanda language	496

Rye	641.3
cooking	641.6
food	641.3
food crop	633.1

S

Saba (Netherlands Antilles)	T2—729 7
Sabbath	296.4
Christianity	263
Judaism	296.4
Sabbatical leave	
education	
higher education	378.1
Sabotage	364.16
military science	355.3
Sacramentals	264
Sacraments	234
public worship	265
theology	234
Sacred books	291.8
Christianity	220
Judaism	296.1
Bible	221
see Manual at 133 vs. 200	
Sacred music	781.7
Sacred places	291.3
Christianity	263
Islam	297.3
Judaism	296.4
Sacred songs	782.25
Sacred vocal music	782.2
Sacrifices (Religion)	291.3
Saddlery	636.1
manufacturing technology	685
Sadism	
medicine	616.85
Safe-deposit services	332.1
Safes	683
Safety	363.1
international law	341.7
law	344
management	658.4
personal safety	613.6
	T1—028
personnel management	658.3
public administration	353.9
social services	363.1
see Manual at 363; *also at*	
363.1	
Safety engineering	620.8
	T1—028
roads	625.702 8

Salvation	291.2
Christianity	234
Judaism	296.3
Salvation Army	287.9
Samaria	933
	T2—33
Sami (European people)	
social group	305.89
Sami language	494
Samoa	T2—961
Samoan Islands	T2—961
Samoan language	499
Sampling techniques	001.4
Sampling theory	519.5
Samuel (Biblical books)	222
San Marino	945.4
	T2—454
Sanatoriums	362.1
Sanctification (Christian	
doctrine)	234
Sanctions (International politics)	327.1
international law	341.5
Sand	553.6
Sand dollars	593.9
Sand dunes	551.3
ecology	577.5
geomorphology	551.3
land economics	333.73
Sandblasting	621.5
Sandpipers	598.3
Sandwich panels	
construction materials	693
Sandwiches	641.8
Sango language	496
Sanitary engineering	628
military engineering	623
Sanitary engineers	628.092
Sanitary landfills	363.72
technology	628.4
sewage sludge	628.3
see also Waste control	
Sanitation	363.72
home economics	648
public administration	353.9
social services	363.72
see also Waste control	
Sanitation equipment	
plant management	658.2
Sanskrit language	491
Santeria	299
Sao Tome and Principe	967.15
	T2—671 5
Sardinia	T2—45
ancient	T2—37

Sardinian language	457
Sarmatia	T2—39
Saskatchewan	T2—712 4
Sasquatch	001.944
Sassanian Empire	935
	T2—35
SAT (Assessment test)	378.1
Satan	
Christianity	235
occultism	133.4
Satanism	133.4
religion	299
Satellite communication	384.5
communications services	384.5
engineering	621.382
Satellites (Moons)	523.9
Satire	808.87
literary criticism	809.7
theory	808.7
literary history	809.7
literature	808.87
specific literatures	T3—7
rhetoric	808.7
Satirists	809.7
collected biography	809.7
specific literatures	T3—700 9
Saturn (Planet)	523.46
Sauces	641.8
Saudi Arabia	953.8
	T2—538
Saudis	953.8
social group	305.892
Saunas	
architecture	725
domestic	728
public	725
Saurischia	567.912
Savannas	
biology	578.74
ecology	577.4
Savings	332
Savings accounts	332.1
Savings and loan associations	332.3
Savings banks	332.2
Savings-consumption	
relationship	339.4
Savings stamps	
prints	769.5
Savories	641.8
Sawmill operations	674
Saws	621.9
Saxony (Germany)	T2—43
Saxophones	788.7
Saxophonists	788.709 2

Science (continued)
 sociology 306.4
  see Manual at 303.48 vs.
   306.4
 see Manual at 500 vs. 001;
  also at 500 vs. 600
Science and religion 291.1
 Christianity 261.5
  see Manual at 261.5 vs.
   231–239
 Islam 297.2
 Judaism 296.3
 philosophy of religion 215
Science fair projects 507.8
Science fiction 808.83
Science laboratories 507
Science museums 507.4
Science policy
 economics 338.9
  see Manual at 338.9 vs.
   352.7, 500
Science projects in schools 507.8
Sciences (Knowledge) 001
Scientific method 001.4
Scientific principles 500
 T1—01
  see Manual at T1—01 vs.
   T1—02
Scientific recreations 793.8
Scientific travels 508
Scientific writing 808
Scientists 509.2
Scientology 299
Score reading 781.4
Scores (Music) 780
 treatises 780.26
  see Manual at 780.26; *also at*
   782
Scorpions 595.4
Scotland 941.1
 T2—411
 ancient 936.1
 T2—361
  see Manual at 941
Scots 941.1
 social group 305.891
Scottish Gaelic language 491.6
Scottish Highlands
 (Scotland) T2—411
Scottish literature
 English 820
 Gaelic 891.6
Scouts (Boy and girl) 369.409 2

Scrap metal 363.72
 metallurgy 669
 social services 363.72
Scratchboard drawing 741.2
Screenplays 791.43
 literature 808.82
  see also Drama (Literature)
 motion pictures 791.43
  see Manual at 791.43 and
   791.44, 791.45, 792.9
Scripture readings
 public worship
  Christianity 264
Scrollwork
 wood handicrafts 745.51
Scuba diving
 sports 797.2
Sculptural stone 553.5
Sculpture 730
 elementary education 372.5
  see Manual at 731–735 vs.
   736–739
Scyphozoa 593.5
SDI (Strategic Defense
 Initiative) 358.1
Sea basins T2—182
  see Manual at T2—163,
   T2—164, T2—165 vs.
   T2—182
Sea cows 599.55
Sea forces 359
Sea ice 551.34
Sea lions 599.79
Sea of Japan T2—164
Sea of Okhotsk T2—164
Sea warfare 359
Seafaring life 910.4
Seafood 641.3
 cooking 641.6
Sealing (Hunting) 639.2
Sealing devices 621.8
Seals (Animals) 599.79
Seals (Devices) 929.9
 insignia 929.9
 numismatics 737
Seamanship 623.88
Seamen 387.509 2
Seaports 387.1
 engineering 627
Search algorithms 005.74
Search strategy
 information science 025.5

Semiarid lands   551.41
    T2—15
    see also Arid lands
Semiconductor circuits   621.381 5
Semiconductors   621.381 5
    physics   537.6
Semimetals
    economic geology   553.4
Seminaries   200.71
    Christianity   230.071
    Judaism   296.071
Seminars   371.3
Seminole Indians
    social group   305.897
Semiotics   302.2
    linguistics   401
      specific languages   T4—01
    philosophy   121
    social aspects   302.2
Semisovereign states   321
    international law   341.27
Semites
    social group   305.892
Semitic languages   492
Senegal   966.3
    T2—663
Senegalese   966.3
Senegambia   966.305
    T2—663
Senile dementia
    medicine   616.89
Senior citizens   305.26
    T1—084
    see also Older persons
Senior high schools   373.238
Seniority
    labor economics   331.25
Sensation   152.1
Sensationalism (Philosophical
    school)   145
Sense organs   573.8
    animal physiology   573.8
    descriptive zoology   591.4
    human anatomy   611
    human physiology   612.8
Senses   573.8
    psychology   152.1
Sensitivity in plants   575.9
Sensitivity training
    applied psychology   158.2
Sensors
    manufacturing technology   681

Sensory functions   573.8
    human physiology   612.8
    see Manual at 612.8 vs. 152
Sensory perception   152.1
    see Manual at 153.7 vs. 152.1;
      also at 612.8 vs. 152
Sentences (Legal decisions)   345
Sentiments   152.4
Separation (Domestic relations)   306.89
    ethics   173
Separation from parents
    child psychology   155.44
Separation of powers   320.4
Sequences (Mathematics)   515
Sequencing
    production management   658.5
Sequential machines   511.3
Serbia   949.71
    T2—497 1
Serbian language   491.8
Serbians
    social group   305.891
Serbo-Croatian language   491.8
Serial publications   050
    T1—05
    journalism   070.1
Serialism
    music   781.3
Serials   050
    T1—05
    journalism   070.1
Series (Mathematics)   515
Series (Publications)
    bibliographies   011
Serigraphy   764
Sermon on the Mount   226.9
    Christian moral theology   241.5
Sermons   291.4
    Christian   252
    Islam   297.3
    Jewish   296.4
Serpents   597.96
Service clubs   369.5
Service directories   338.4
    see Manual at 338 vs. 060,
      381, 382, 670.29, 910,
      T1—025, T1—029
Service districts
    local public administration   352.19
Service industries   338.4
    public administration   354.6
Service marks   929.9
Service stations
    automotive engineering   629.28

Sheep	636.3
animal husbandry	636.3
zoology	599.649
Sheep dogs	636.737
Sheet metal	671.8
Shelflisting	
library science	025.4
Shellac	667
Shellfish	594
cooking	641.6
culture	
economics	338.3
fishing	639
fishing industry	338.3
food	641.3
zoology	594
Shells (Animals)	591.47
descriptive zoology	591.47
mollusks	594.147
handicrafts	745.55
physiology	573.7
Shelving	
library collection maintenance	025.8
library plant management	022
Shia Islam	297.8
Shintoism	299
Ship accidents	363.12
Ship railroads	385
engineering	625.3
Shipbuilding	623.8
Shipbuilding industry	338.4
Shipping	387.5
materials management	658.7
Ships	387.2
engineering	623.8
naval equipment	359.8
naval units	359.3
transportation services	387.2
see Manual at 629.04 vs. 388	
Ships in bottles	745.592 8
Shipwrecks	363.12
adventure	910.4
Shipyards	
technology	623.8
Shoah	940.53
Shock (Pathological)	
result of injury	617.2
Shock-resistant construction	624.1
buildings	693.8
Shoes	391.4
commercial technology	685
customs	391.4
Shona language	496

Shoots (Plants)	581.4
descriptive botany	581.4
physiology	575.4
Shop stewards	331.87
Shop technology	670.42
Shopping malls	381
architecture	725
management	658.8
Shops (Retail trade)	381
management	658.8
see also Commerce	
see Manual at 381 vs. 658.8	
Shore biology	578.769
Shore birds	598.3
Shore ecology	577.69
Shore protection	333.91
engineering	627
Shorelands	551.45
Short stories	808.83
see also Fiction	
Shortages	
agricultural industries	338.1
natural resources	333.7
secondary industries	338.4
Shorthand	653
Shot-putting	796.43
Shotguns	683.4
see also Guns (Small arms)	
Show animals	
animal husbandry	636.08
Show windows	
advertising	659.1
Shows	791
Shrews	599.33
Shrimps	595.3
cooking	641.6
fishing	639
food	641.3
zoology	595.3
Shrines	291.3
architecture	726
Christianity	263
Shropshire (England)	T2—424
Shrubs	582.17
floriculture	635.9
landscape architecture	715
see Manual at 635.9 vs. 582.1	
Shuar language	498
Shut-in persons	
home care	649.8
Shyness	155.2
Siam	T2—593
Siamese language	495.9

Sisters (Women religious)	255
biography	271
see Manual at 230–280	
guides to Christian life	248.8
Sisters and brothers	306.875
see also Siblings	
Sit-down strikes	331.892
Situation ethics	171
Situational influences	
psychology	155.9
Six Days' War, 1967	956.04
Size	530.8
Size standards	
production management	658.5
Skateboarding	796.22
Skating (Ice)	796.91
hockey	796.962
Skating (Roller)	796.21
Skeet shooting	799.3
Skeleton	573.7
see also Bones	
Skepticism	
philosophy	149
ancient	186
epistemology	121
philosophy of religion	211
Ski troops	356
Skiing	796.93
Skilled workers	331.7
Skin	573.5
animal physiology	573.5
descriptive zoology	591.47
human diseases	362.1
medicine	616.5
social services	362.1
human physiology	612.7
personal care	646.7
surgery	617.4
Skin diving	797.2
Skis	796.93
commercial technology	685
Skull	
surgery	617.5
Skunks	599.76
Skydiving	797.5
Slander	364.15
ethics	177
law	345
Slang	417
specific languages	T4—7
Slave trade	
commerce	380.1

Slavery	306.3
ethics	177
law	342
political science	326
Slaves	305.5
Slavic languages	491.8
Slavonic languages	491.8
Slavs	
civilization	947
social group	305.891
Sled dog racing	798.8
Sled dogs	636.73
Sledding	796.9
Sleep	154.6
human physiology	612.8
physical fitness	613.7
psychology	154.6
see Manual at 612.8 vs. 154.6	
Sleep disorders	
medicine	616.8
Sleeping bags	
manufacturing technology	685
Sleepwalking	
psychology	154.6
Slide preparation	502.8
biology	570.28
Slides (Photographs)	778.2
instructional use	371.33
Sligo (Ireland : County)	T2—417
Slipcovers	645
arts	746.9
commercial technology	684
home sewing	646.2
household management	645
Slopes	551.43
Slot machines	795.2
Slovak language	491.8
Slovakia	943.73
	T2—437 3
Slovaks	943.73
social group	305.891
Slovenes	949.73
social group	305.891
Slovenia	949.73
	T2—497 3
Slovenian language	491.8
Slow learners	371.92
Slums	307.3
Small business	338.6
economics	338.6
government programs	354.2
management	658.02
Small business loans	332.7

Social participation | 302
Social pathology | 361.1
  see Manual at 301–307 vs.
    361–365
Social planning | 361.2
Social prediction | 303.49
Social pressure | 303.3
Social problems | 361.1
  see Manual at 301–307 vs.
    361–365; *also at*
    361–365; *also at* 361–365
    vs. 353.5; *also at* 361 vs.
    362; *also at* 362–363 vs.
    364.1; *also at* 363 vs. 340,
    353–354
Social processes | 303
  see Manual at 302–307 vs.
    320
Social progress | 303.44
Social protest | 303.6
Social psychology | 302
  see Manual at 302–307 vs.
    150, T1—01; *also at*
    302–307 vs. 155.9, 158.2
Social reform | 303.48
Social relations | 302
  ethics | 177
Social responsibility
  educational objective | 370.11
  executive management | 658.4
Social role | 302
Social sciences | 300
  see Manual at 300 vs. 600
Social security | 362
  government-sponsored
    insurance | 368.4
    law | 344
    see Manual at 336.249 vs.
      368.4
  law | 344
  public administration | 353.5
  social welfare | 362
  United States | 368.4
  see Manual at 362 vs. 368.4
Social security tax | 336.249
  law | 343.05
  see Manual at 336.249 vs.
    368.4
Social services | 361
  see also Welfare services
Social skills
  personal living | 646.7
  social psychology | 302
Social stratification | 305

Social studies | 300
  elementary education | 372.83
Social theology | 291.1
  Christianity | 261
    see Manual at 241 vs. 261.8
  Islam | 297.2
  Judaism | 296.3
Social welfare | 361
  see also Welfare services
Social work | 361.3
Social workers | 361.309 2
Socialism | 335
  economics | 335
  political ideology | 320.53
  sociology | 306.3
  see Manual at 335 vs. 306.3,
    320.53
Socialist International | 324.1
Socialist parties | 324.2
Socialists | 335.009 2
Socialization | 303.3
Socially disadvantaged persons | 305.9
                          T1—086
  social welfare | 362
    public administration | 353.53
Societies | 060
  see also Organizations
Society | 301
Society of Friends | 289.6
Socinianism | 289.1
Sociobiology | 304.5
  animal behavior | 591.56
  biological ecology | 577.8
  human behavior | 304.5
Socioeconomic classes | 305.5
Socioeconomic problems | 361.1
  social theology | 291.1
    Christianity | 261.8
    Islam | 297.2
    Judaism | 296.3
Sociolinguistics | 306.44
Sociology | 301
  see Manual at 301–307 vs.
    361–365
Socratic philosophy | 183
Sodalities | 267
Sodas (Chemicals) | 546
  chemical engineering | 661
Sodium
  chemistry | 546
Softball | 796.357
Software | 005.3
  see Manual at 004 vs. 005

Software documentation	
preparation	005.1
text	005.3
Software engineering	005.1
Software maintenance	005.1
Software packages	005.3
Soil conditioners	631.8
chemical engineering	668
Soil conservation	333.73
agriculture	631.4
land economics	333.73
Soil erosion	551.3
agriculture	631.4
engineering	627
geology	551.3
Soil formation	551.3
Soil mechanics	624.1
Soil pollution	363.739
social welfare	363.739
technology	628.5
Soil science	631.4
Soil surveys	631.4
agriculture	631.4
engineering	624.1
Soilless culture	631.5
Soils	631.4
agriculture	631.4
biology	578.75
ecology	577.5
Solar cells	621.31
Solar energy	333.792
economics	333.792
engineering	621.47
Solar engineers	621.470 92
Solar engines	621.47
Solar heating	621.47
buildings	697
Solar radiation	523.7
meteorology	551.5
Solar system	523.2
	T2—99
Solar wind	523.5
Soldering	671.5
Soldiers	355.009 2
Sole bargaining rights	331.88
Solid geometry	516
Euclidean	516.23
Solid mechanics	531
engineering	620.1
Solid-state physics	530.4
Solid wastes	363.72
social services	363.72
technology	628.4
see also Waste control	

Solitaire	795.4
Solitude	
psychology	155.9
Solo instruments	786–788
Solo voices	783.2
Solomon Islands	995.93
	T2—959 3
Solubility	541.3
Solution chemistry	541.3
applied	660
Solvents	541.3
Somali language	493
Somalia	967.73
	T2—677 3
Somaliland	967.7
	T2—677
Somerset (England)	T2—423
Sonar	621.389
Sonatas	784.18
Song cycles	782.4
Song of Solomon	223
Song of Songs	223
Songbirds	598.8
animal husbandry	636.6
Songs	782.42
Sonography	
diagnosis	616.07
Sons	306.874
Sophistic philosophy	183
Sorghums	584
botany	584
syrup crop	633.6
Sørlandet (Norway)	T2—483
Sororities	366.008 2
education	371.8
Sorrow	152.4
Sort algorithms	005.74
Sorting data	005.74
Soteriology	291.2
Christianity	234
Sotho-Tswana languages	496
Soul	128
philosophy	128
religion	291.2
Christianity	233
Islam	297.2
Judaism	296.3
philosophy of religion	218
Soul music	781.644
songs	782.421 644
Sound	534
engineering	620.2
musical element	781.2
physics	534

Sound engineers	620.209 2	Southeastern Europe	949.6
Sound recording systems	621.389		T2—496
Sound recordings	384	Southeastern States	T2—75
communications services	384	Southern Africa	968
engineering	621.389		T2—68
instructional use	371.33	Southern Britain	942
music	780		T2—42
treatises	780.26	ancient	936.2
see Manual at 780.26			T2—362
Sound reproducing systems	621.389	Southern Europe	940
Sound synthesis			T2—4
computer science	006.5	ancient	938
Soundproofing	620.2		T2—38
buildings	693.8	Southern Hemisphere	T2—181
Soups	641.8	Southern Low Countries	T2—493
South Africa	968	Southern Rhodesia	T2—689 1
	T2—68	Southern Sotho language	496
South African Blacks		Southern States	T2—75
social group	305.896	Southern Yemen	953.35
South African War, 1899–1902	968.04		T2—533 5
South Africans (Afrikaners)	968	Southwest, New	T2—79
social group	305.83	Southwest, Old	T2—76
South Africans (British origin)	968	Sovereignty	320.1
social group	305.82	international law	341.26
South Africans (National group)	968	Sovereignty of God	212
social group	305.896	Christianity	231.7
South America	980	comparative religion	291.2
	T2—8	Judaism	296.3
South American native		philosophy of religion	212
languages	498	Soviet Central Asia	958.4
South American native peoples	980		T2—584
social group	305.898	Soviet communism	335.43
South Americans	980	Soviet Union	947.084
social group	305.868		T2—47
South Arabian languages	492	Asia	957
South Asia	954		T2—57
	T2—54	Space	T2—19
South Asians		astronomy	520
social group	305.891	international law	341.4
South Atlantic States	T2—75	philosophy	114
South Australia	T2—942 3	physics	530.1
South Carolina	T2—757	resource economics	333.9
South China Sea	T2—164	*see Manual at* T2—99 vs.	
South Dakota	T2—783	T2—19; *also at* 520 vs.	
South Island (N.Z.)	T2—93	500.5, 523.1, 530.1, 919.9	
South Korea	951.95	Space and time	530.11
	T2—519 5	Space biology	571.091 9
South-West Africa	T2—688 1	Space communications	
South Yorkshire (England)	T2—428	engineering	621.382
Southeast Asia	959	Space engineering	620
	T2—59	Space flight	387.8
Southeastern Asia	959	engineering	629.4
	T2—59	*see Manual at* 629.43, 629.45	
		vs. 919.904	

Speeches	080
literary criticism	809.5
theory	808.5
literary history	809.5
literature	808.85
specific literatures	T3—5
rhetoric	808.5
Speed reading	418
elementary education	372.45
specific languages	T4—84
Speed skating	796.91
Speedways	
automobile racing	796.720 6
Spellers	418
specific languages	T4—81
Spelling	411
applied linguistics	418
specific languages	T4—81
elementary education	372.63
linguistics	411
specific languages	T4—1
Spelling reform	418
specific languages	T4—81
Spells (Occultism)	133.4
Spelunking	796.52
Spermatophytes	580
see also Plants	
Spheres of influence	327.1
Spices	641.3
agriculture	633.8
cooking with	641.6
food	641.3
Spiders	595.4
Spina bifida	
medicine	616.8
Spinach	641.3
cooking	641.6
food	641.3
Spinal cord surgery	617.4
Spinning textiles	677
arts	746.1
manufacturing technology	677
Spirit photography	133.9
Spirit writings	133.9
Spirits (Discarnate beings)	133.9
apparitions	133.1
Spiritual beings	291.2
Christianity	235
Spiritual direction	291.6
Christianity	253.5
Spiritual gifts	
Christian doctrines	234
Spiritual healing	
medicine	615.8

Spiritual healing (continued)	
religion	291.3
Christianity	234
see Manual at 615.8 vs. 234,	
291.3	
Spiritual life	291.4
Christianity	248.4
Spiritual renewal	291.3
Christianity	269
Spiritualism	133.9
comparative religion	291.2
philosophy	141
Spirituality	291.4
Christianity	248
Judaism	296.7
Spirituals	782.25
Spitsbergen Island	
(Norway)	T2—98
Spleen	
human physiology	612.4
medicine	616.4
surgery	617.5
Splicing	
ropes and cables	623.88
Sponges	593.4
paleozoology	563
Spontaneous abortion	
obstetrics	618.3
Spools	
wooden	674
Sport animals	
animal husbandry	636.088
Sporting dogs (United Kingdom)	636.75
Sporting dogs (United States)	636.752
Sporting goods	
manufacturing technology	688.7
Sports	796
ethics	175
human physiology	612
law	344
physical fitness	613.7
public administration support	353.7
safety	363.14
social services	363.14
techniques	796.028
sociology	306.4
see Manual at 613.7 vs. 646.7,	
796	
Sports cards	796.075
Sports cars	388.3
driving	629.28
recreation	796.7
engineering	629.222
transportation services	388.3

States (Independent	
governments)	320.1
international law	341.26
States of matter	530.4
chemical engineering	660
Statics	531
engineering	620.1
Station wagons	
engineering	629.222
Stations of the cross	232.96
Statistical inference	519.5
Statistical mathematics	519.5
Statistical mechanics	530.13
Statistical methods	001.4
Statistics (Collections)	310
	T1—02
Statuary	731
Statutes	348
STD (Diseases)	
medicine	616.95
Steam engineering	621.1
Steam engines	621.1
Steam heating	621.1
buildings	697
Steam-powered automobiles	
engineering	629.22
see also Automotive vehicles	
Steam-powered electric	
generation	621.31
Steel	669
building construction	693
building material	691
metallurgy	669
metalworking	672
production economics	338.4
Steel drums	786.8
Steeplechase races	
horses	798.4
Stegosaurus	567.915
Stems (Plants)	581.4
descriptive botany	581.4
physiology	575.4
Stenciling	
decorative arts	745.7
Stenographers	651.3
Stenography	653
Stepchildren	306.874
Stepparents	306.874
	T1—085
Steppes	T2—14
see also Prairies	
Stereochemistry	547
inorganic chemistry	541.2

Stereophonic sound systems	
engineering	621.389
Stereoscopic photography	778.4
Stereotypes	
sociology	303.3
Sterility	
gynecology	618.1
medicine	616.6
Sterilization (Birth control)	
social services	363.9
see also Birth control	
Stews	641.8
Still life	
art representation	704.9
painting	758
Stimulant abuse	362.29
see also Substance abuse	
Stochastic processes	519.2
Stock breeding	636.08
Stock control	
materials management	658.7
Stock exchange	332.64
Stock options	332.63
Stock ownership plans	331.2
Stock purchase plans	331.2
Stockholm (Sweden)	T2—487
Stockmen	636.009 2
Stockpiles	
secondary industries	338.4
Stocks	332.63
Stoic ethics	171
Stoic philosophy	188
Stomach	573.3
biology	573.3
human physiology	612.3
medicine	616.3
Stone	553.5
building construction	693
building materials	691
economic geology	553.5
Stoneware	666
arts	738.3
technology	666
Storage	
coal technology	662.6
gas technology	665.7
home economics	648
petroleum technology	665.5
warehouse management	658.7
Storage (Computer)	004.5
engineering	621.39
Storage of office records	651.5
Stores (Retail trade)	381
architecture	725

Stores (Retail trade) (continued)
  management   658.8
  see also Commerce
  see Manual at 381 vs. 658.8
Storing crops   631.5
Storing electric power   621.31
Storks   598.3
Storms   551.55
  weather forecasting   551.64
  see also Disasters
Storytelling   808.5
  elementary education   372.67
  library services   027.62
  rhetoric   808.5
Stoves
  ceramic arts   738.8
  heating buildings   697
  household appliances   644
    manufacturing technology   683
  kitchen appliances   641.502 8
Strabismus
  ophthalmology   617.7
Strategic Defense Initiative   358.1
Strategic materials   355.2
  land economics   333.8
Strategic missile forces   358.1
Strategic weapons   355.8
  international law   341.7
Strategy   355.02
  military operations   355.4
  overall military objectives   355.02
  see Manual at 355.02 vs.
    355.4
Strathclyde (Scotland)   T2—414
Stratifications (Rock formations)   551.8
  specific areas   554–559
Stratigraphic geology   551.7
Stratigraphic paleontology   560
Stratosphere   551.51
    T2—161
Streaming (Education)   371.2
Streams   551.48
  see also Rivers
Street cleaning   363.72
  technology   628.4
Street cries   398.8
Street music   781.5
Street songs   398.8
Streetcars   388.4
  engineering   625.6
Streets   388.4
  engineering   625.7
  see also Roads

Strength
  materials science   620.1
Stress
  medicine   616.9
  psychiatry   616.89
  psychology   155.9
  psychology of late adulthood   155.67
Strike insurance   368.8
Strike requirements   331.89
Strikebreaking   331.89
Strikes (Work stoppages)   331.892
  labor law   344.01
  personnel management   658.3
String art   746
String orchestras   784.7
Stringed instruments   787
Strings   677
Stroke (Disorder)
  medicine   616.8
Structural analysis   624.1
  construction   690
Structural decoration   729
  see Manual at 729
Structural design   624.1
Structural elements
  architecture   721
  see Manual at 721 vs. 690
Structural engineering   624.1
  see Manual at 624 vs. 624.1
Structural engineers   624.109 2
Structural geology   551.8
Structural materials
  construction   691
Structural stone   553.5
Structuralism
  philosophy   149
Structured programming   005.1
Student activism   371.8
Student activities   371.8
Student aid   371.2
    T1—079
  higher education   378.3
Student competitions   371.8
Student discipline   371.5
Student employment   371.2
  higher education   378.3
Student exchanges   370.116
Student experiments   T1—078
Student expulsion   371.5
Student government   371.5
Student health programs   371.7
Student housing   371.8
Student journalism   371.8
Student life   371.8

Supply management	658.7
armed forces	355.6
Supply services (Armed forces)	
issuing units	355.3
Supply-side economics	330.15
Supreme courts	347
Surf riding	797.3
Surface chemistry	541.3
applied	660
Surface engineering	620
Surface-mined lands	333.76
reclamation technology	631.6
Surface physics	530.4
Surface rail transit systems	388.4
engineering	625.6
Surface tension	541.3
physics	530.4
Surface water	553.7
economic geology	553.7
hydrology	551.48
Surfing	797.3
Surgeons	617.092
Surgery	617
see Manual at 616 vs. 617.4;	
also at 617 vs. 616	
Surgical abortion	363.46
medicine	618.8
Surgical insurance	368.38
Surgical nursing	
medicine	610.73
Surinam	988.3
	T2—883
Suriname	988.3
	T2—883
Surpluses	
agricultural industries	338.1
natural resources	333.7
secondary industries	338.4
Surrealism	
fine arts	709.04
painting	759.06
Surrey (England)	T2—422
Surrogate motherhood	306.874
ethics	176
Surveillance	
law enforcement	363.2
Survey methodology	001.4
Surveying	526.9
Surveyors	526.909 2
Surveys	
public administration of	352.7
Survival after accidents,	
disasters	613.6
Survival skills	613.6

Survivors' insurance	368.3
Suspense drama	792.2
literature	808.82
stage presentation	792.2
Suspense stories	808.83
Suspension of rights	323.4
Svalbard (Norway)	T2—98
Svealand (Sweden)	T2—487
Swahili language	496
Swamps	551.41
see also Wetlands	
Swans	598.4
Swazi	968.87
social group	305.896
Swazi language	496
Swaziland	968.87
	T2—688 7
Sweat glands	573.5
medicine	616.5
Sweden	948.5
	T2—485
Swedenborgianism	289
Swedes	948.5
Swedish language	439.7
Swedish literature	839.7
Sweet corn	641.3
cooking	641.6
food	641.3
garden crop	635
Sweet potatoes	641.3
cooking	641.6
food	641.3
Sweet sorghums	633.6
Sweets	641.8
Swifts	598.7
Swimming	797.2
physical fitness	613.7
Swimming pools	
architecture	725
domestic	728
public	725
Swine	636.4
animal husbandry	636.4
zoology	599.63
Swing (Music)	781.65
Swiss	949.4
social group	305.83
Swiss literature	
French	840
German	830
Italian	850
Switchboard operators	
office services	651.3

Tableware	642
handicrafts	745.593
Taboos	390
Tabulated materials	T1—02
Tactics (Military science)	355.4
Tadpoles	597.8
Tadzhikistan	958.6
	T2—586
Tagalog language	499
Tahiti	T2—962
Tahitian language	499
Tai languages	495.9
Tailoring	646.4
commercial technology	687
home sewing	646.4
Tailors	646.400 92
Taiwan	951.24
	T2—512 4
Taiwanese	951.24
social group	305.895
Tajik language	491
Tajikistan	958.6
	T2—586
Talismans	133.4
numismatics	737
Talking books	
bibliographies	011
Talmud	296.1
Tamashek language	493
Tamazight language	493
Tambourines	786.9
Tamil	
social group	305.89
Tamil language	494.8
Tanakh	221
Tanganyika	T2—678
Tank warfare	358
Tanks (Vehicles)	358
engineering	623.7
military equipment	358
Tanning leather	675
Tanzania	967.8
	T2—678
Tanzanians	967.8
Taoism	
religion	299
Taoist philosophy	181
Tap dancing	792.7
Tape drives (Computer)	
computer science	004.5
Tapes (Adhesives)	668
Tapes (Recording devices)	621.382
Tapes (Sound)	384

Tapestries	677
manufacturing technology	677
textile arts	746.3
Tapirs	599.66
Target shooting	799.3
Tariff	382
see also Customs (Tariff)	
Taro	641.3
food	641.3
starch crop	633.6
Tarot	133.3
Tasmania	T2—946
Taste	573.8
animal physiology	573.8
human physiology	612.8
Taste perception	
psychology	152.1
Tatar Empire	950
	T2—5
Tatar language	494
Tatting	
arts	746.43
Tattooing	
customs	391.6
Tax assessment	336.2
Tax credits	336.2
income tax law	343.05
Tax deductions	336.2
Tax evasion	364.1
law	345
Tax law	343.04
see Manual at 343.04 vs.	
336.2, 352.4	
Tax loopholes	336.2
Tax planning	
law	343.04
income tax	343.05
Tax reform	336.2
Tax shelters	336.2
Taxation	336.2
see also Taxes	
Taxes	336.2
accounting	657
financial management	658.15
international law	341.4
law	343.04
macroeconomic policy	339.5
public administration	352.4
public finance	336.2
see Manual at 343.04 vs.	
336.2, 352.4	
Taxicab drivers	388.4
Taxicab service	388.4

Theatrical dancing	792.7
see Manual at 792.7 vs. 792.8,	
793.3	
Thecodontia	567.91
Theft	364.16
law	345
Theft insurance	368.8
Theism	211
Christianity	231
comparative religion	291.2
Judaism	296.3
philosophy of religion	211
Thematic catalogs	780.2
Theme and variations	781.8
Theocracy	321.5
political ideology	320.5
political system	321.5
Theodicy	291.2
Christianity	231
comparative religion	291.2
Judaism	296.3
philosophy of religion	214
Theologians	291.209 2
Christian	230.092
see Manual at 230–280	
Theological seminaries	
Christianity	230.071
Theology	291.2
Christianity	230
see Manual at 261.5 vs.	
231–239	
Islam	297.2
Judaism	296.3
Theoretical chemistry	541.2
see Manual at 541 vs. 546	
Theory	T1—01
Theosophy	299
Therapeutic manipulations	
medicine	615.8
Therapeutic systems	615.5
see Manual at 615.5	
Therapeutics	615.5
veterinary medicine	636.089
see Manual at 613 vs. 615.8;	
also at 615.8	
Therapists	615.509 2
Therapy	615.5
Thermal engineering	621.402
Thermal waters	333.8
economics	333.8
geophysics	551.2
Thermobiology	572
Thermochemistry	541.3

Thermodynamics	536
chemical engineering	660
engineering	621.402
meteorology	551.5
physics	536
Thermoelectricity	537.6
Thermonuclear reaction	539.7
Thesauri (Synonym dictionaries)	413
specific languages	T4—3
Theses (Academic)	378.2
bibliographies	011
Thessalonians (Biblical books)	227
Thin-film circuits	621.381 5
Thin films	530.4
Thinking	153.4
Third Reich	943.086
Third World (Unaligned	
blocs)	T2—171
Thirst	
psychology	152.1
Thirteen Articles of Faith	
(Judaism)	296.3
Thirty Years' War, 1618–1648	940.2
Thomist philosophy	189
modern	149
Thought	153.4
Thrace	T2—495
ancient	T2—39
Thrace, Eastern (Turkey)	T2—496 1
Thread	687
Threats	
international relations	327.1
Three-dimensional graphics	
computer graphics	006.6
Thrift industry	332.3
Thrift institutions	332.3
Throat	
medicine	616.3
Thrushes	598.8
Thunderstorms	551.55
Thuringia (Germany)	T2—43
Tibet (China)	951
	T2—51
Tibetan language	495
Tibetan spaniel	636.72
Tibetan terrier	636.72
Tibetans	951
social group	305.895
Ticks	595.4
Tidal waves	551.47
Tide marshes	
biology	578.769
ecology	577.69
Tidelands (Shorelands)	551.45

Toothed whales	599.5	Toys	
Toothpicks		making (continued)	
wooden	674	technology	688.7
Top games	795.2	product safety	363.19
Top management	658.4	recreation	790.1
Topiary work	715	use in child care	649
Topographic surveying	526.9	Toys (Dogs)	636.76
Topological algebras	512	TQM (Management)	658.4
Topological vector spaces	515	Track (Sports)	796.42
Topology	514	Track and field	796.42
Torah (Bible)	222	Tracks (Animals)	591.47
Tornadoes	551.55	Tractor trailers	388.3
see also Disasters		engineering	629.224
Torrid zone	T2—13	Tractors	629.225
Tortoises	597.92	Trade	380.1
Torts	346.03	see also Commerce	
see Manual at 345 vs. 346.03		Trade agreements	382
Total quality management	658.4	Trade barriers	382
Totalitarian government	321.9	Trade bibliographies	015
Totalitarianism	320.53	Trade catalogs	T1—029
Touch	573.8	see Manual at 338 vs. 060,	
animal physiology	573.8	381, 382, 670.29, 910,	
human physiology	612.8	T1—025, T1—029	
psychology	152.1	Trade shows	381
Tourette syndrome		advertising	659.1
medicine	616.8	Trade unions	331.88
Tourism	338.4	Trademarks	929.9
Tourist trade	338.4	international law	341.7
economics	338.4	law	346.04
international law	341.7	sales promotion	658.8
law	343	Traders	380.109 2
public administration	354.73	Traditionalism	
transportation services	388	philosophy	148
Towels	643	political ideology	320.52
arts	746.9	Traffic accidents	363.12
home economics	643	Traffic control	388
Towers (Structures)		air transportation	387.7
architecture	725	road transportation	388.3
Towns	307.76	police services	363.2
Toxic shock syndrome		public administration	354.77
medicine	616.9	urban	388.4
Toxic wastes	363.72	Traffic flow (Road)	388.3
technology	628.4	urban	388.4
see also Waste control		Traffic regulations	343.09
Toxicologists	615.900 92	Traffic safety	363.12
Toxicology	571.9	law	343.09
medicine	615.9	Traffic signs	388.3
Toy dogs	636.76	engineering	625.7
Toy soldiers		Trafficways	
handicrafts	745.592 8	engineering	629.04
Toy theaters	791.5	Tragedies (Drama)	792.1
Toys	790.1	literature	808.82
making	688.7	stage presentation	792.1
handicrafts	745.592	Trailer camps	647.94

Trailers (Freight)	388.3	Transportation (continued)	
engineering	629.224	military engineering	623
Trailers (Passenger)	388.3	mining	622
engineering	629.226	petroleum technology	665.5
recreation	796.7	public administration	354.76
transportation services	388.3	social effects	303.48
Train accidents	363.12	*see Manual at* 380	
Training		Transportation accidents	363.12
armed forces	355.5	Transportation engineering	629.04
child care	649	Transportation facilities	388
employee education	370.11	construction	690
see also Vocational		Transportation insurance	368.2
education		Transportation safety	363.12
Trains	385	law	343.09
engineering	625.2	Transvaal (South Africa) T2—682	
Traits		Transvestism	306.77
individual psychology	155.2	Trapeze work	
Trampolining	796.47	circuses	791.3
Tramps	305.5	sports	796.46
Tramways	388.4	Trapping	639
engineering	625.6	sports	799.2
Tranquilizer abuse	362.29	Trapshooting	799.3
Trans-Uranian planets	523.48	Trash (Art style)	709.03
Transactional analysis		Traumatology	
applied psychology	158.2	medicine	617.1
system	158	Travel	910
psychiatry	616.89	*see Manual at* 550 vs. 910;	
Transcaucasus	T2—475	*also at* 900; *also at* 909,	
Transcendental meditation	158.1	930–990 vs. 910; *also at*	
system	158	913–919: Add table: 04	
Transcendentalism		Travel guides	910.2
philosophy	141	Travel health	613.6
Transfer tax	336.2	Travelers	910.92
Transference (Psychology)	154.2	Traveling shows	791
Transistors	621.381 5	Treason	364.1
Transit insurance	368.2	law	345
Transits	523.9	Treasure hunting	622
Translating		Treasury bills	332.63
linguistics	418	Treasury departments (Public	
specific languages	T4—8	administration)	352.4
Translators	418	Treaties	341.3
specific languages	T4—8	texts	341
Translators (Computer science)		*see Manual at* 341.3	
programming languages	005.4	Tree crops	634
Transmission modes		Tree shrews	599.33
computer communications	004.6	Trees	582.16
Transmitting electricity	621.319	forestry	634.9
Transpiration	575.8	landscape architecture	715
Transport phenomena	530.4	ornamental agriculture	635.9
Transportation	388	*see Manual at* 635.9 vs. 582.1	
coal technology	662.6	Trial practice	347
gas technology	665.7	Trials (Law)	347
international law	341.7	criminal law	345
law	343.09	Triangles (Music)	786.8

Triangulation	526.3	Trumpeters (Musicians)	788.9
Triathlon	796.42	Trumpets	788.9
Tribal communities	307.77	Trust companies	332.2
Tribal groups	306.08	Trust services	332.1
Triceratops	567.915	Trust Territory of the	
Trick games	793.5	Pacific Islands	T2—965
Trick photography	778.8	Trusts (Fiduciary)	346.05
Trigonometry	516.24	Trusts (Organizations)	338.8
Trilobites	565	management	658
Trinidad	972.983	Truth	121
	T2—729 83	Truthfulness	
Trinidad and Tobago	972.983	ethics	177
	T2—729 83	Tsonga language	496
Trinity	231	Tswana language	496
Triplets	306.875	Tuamotu Islands	T2—963
Tripods (Cameras)	771.3	Tubas	788.9
Tripolitan War, 1801–1805	973.4	Tuberculosis	362.1
Trisecting an angle	516.2	medicine	616.9
Trogoniformes	598.7	social services	362.1
Trojan horses (Computer		Tuition	371.2
science)	005.8	higher education	378.1
Trolleys	388.4	Tumbling	796.47
engineering	625.6	Tumors (Human)	
Trolls	398.21	medicine	616.99
Trombones	788.9	Tundras	551.45
Trombonists	788.9	ecology	577.5
Trøndelag (Norway)	T2—484	Tuning	784.192
Tropical diseases		Tunisia	961.1
medicine	616.9		T2—611
Tropical forests		Tunisians	961.1
biology	578.730 913	social group	305.892
ecology	577.309 13	Tunnels	388
Tropical rain forests		construction	624.1
biology	578.734	transportation services	388
ecology	577.34	railroads	385.3
Tropics	T2—13	Tupí language	498
biology	578.091 3	Turbines	621.406
ecology	577.091 3	Turbomachines	621.406
Troposphere	551.51	Turkestan	958.4
	T2—161		T2—584
Trotskyism	335.43	Turkey	956.1
Trout	641.3		T2—561
food	641.3	Turkey in Europe	T2—496 1
zoology	597.5	Turkeys	636.5
Troy (Extinct city)	T2—39	zoology	598.6
Truancy	371.2	Turkic languages	494
Trucial States	T2—535 7	Turkish language	494
Truck accidents	363.12	Turkish Thrace	T2—496 1
Truck farming	635	Turkmen language	494
Truckers	388.3	Turkmenistan	958.5
Trucks	388.3		T2—585
engineering	629.224	Turks	956.1
Truman, Harry S.		social group	305.89
United States history	973.918		

Turnips	641.3
cooking	641.6
food	641.3
Turtles	597.92
Tusks	591.47
descriptive zoology	591.47
physiology	573.3
Tutoring	371.39
Tuvalu	996.82
	T2—968 2
Twelve step programs	
pastoral theology	291.6
Christianity	259
substance abuse	
medicine	616.86
see Manual at 616.86 vs.	
158.1, 248.8, 291.4,	
362.29	
Twelve-tone system	781.2
Twentieth century	909.82
Twenty-first century	909.83
Twenty-one (Game)	795.4
Twi language (Ghana)	496
Twilight	525
Twining	
arts	746.42
Twins	306.875
psychology	155.44
Tyne and Wear (England)	T2—428
Typefounding	686.2
Typesetting	686.2
Typewriters	652.3
manufacturing technology	681
office practice	652.3
Typewriting	652.3
Typhoid fever	
medicine	616.9
Typhoons	551.55
Typing	652.3
Typists	651.3
Typography	686.2
Typology	
Bible interpretation	220.6
Christian doctrines	232
Typology (Psychology)	155.2
Tyrannosaurus	567.912

U

Ubangi-Shari	T2—674 1
UFOs (Objects)	001.942
Uganda	967.61
	T2—676 1

Ugandans	967.61
Ugaritic language	492
Uighur language	494
Ukraine	947.7
	T2—477
Ukrainian language	491.7
Ukrainians	947.7
social group	305.891
Ulcers	
digestive system	
medicine	616.3
Ulster (Northern Ireland and	
Ireland)	941.6
	T2—416
Ultrasonic vibrations	534.5
engineering	620.2
Ultrasonography	
medicine	616.07
Ultraviolet radiation	535.01
engineering	621.36
Umbrellas	
customs	391.4
UN (United Nations)	341.23
Unarmed combat	796.81
Unconscious	
philosophy	127
Unconventional warfare	355.3
Underachievers (Students)	371.2
special education	371.9
Underdeveloped areas	T2—172
Underground construction	624.1
Underpopulation	363.9
Undertaking (Mortuary)	363.7
customs	393
social services	363.7
technology	614
Underwater engineering	627
Underwater photography	778.7
Underwriting	368
Unemployed persons	305.9
	T1—086
labor economics	331.13
social group	305.9
Unemployment	331.13
economics	331.13
sociology	306.3
see Manual at 331.1 vs.	
331.11, 331.12; *also at*	
331.12 vs. 331.13	
Unemployment compensation	331.25
Unemployment insurance	368.4
law	344
public administration	353.5

Unesco	001.06
law	341.7
public administration	353.7
Unfair economic competition	338.6
Ungulates	599.6
UNICEF (Children's Fund)	362.7
Unicorns	398.24
Unidentified flying objects	001.942
Unification Church	289.9
Unified field theory	530.14
Uniforms	391
armed forces	355.1
customs	391
Union catalogs	025.3
bibliography	017
Union dues checkoff	331.88
Union federations	331.87
Union of Soviet Socialist	
Republics	947.084
	T2—47
Union organizing	331.89
Union shop	331.88
Unions	331.88
Uniramia	595.7
Unison voices	782.5
Unitarian and Universalist	
churches	289.1
Unitarianism	289.1
Unitarians	
biography	289.109 2
United Arab Emirates	953.57
	T2—535 7
United Brethren in Christ	289.9
United charities	361.8
United Church of Canada	287.9
United Church of Christ	285.8
United Kingdom	941
	T2—41
see Manual at 941	
United Nations	341.23
finance	336
public administration	352.11
United Nations Children's Fund	362.7
United Nations Educational,	
Scientific, Cultural	
Organization	001.06
law	341.7
public administration	353.7
United Pentecostal Church	289.9
United Society of Believers in	
Christ's Second Appearing	289

United States	973
	T2—73
see Manual at T2—73 vs.	
T2—71	
United States customary	
measurements	530.8
United States people (National	
group)	973
social group	305.813
Uniting Church in Australia	287.9
Unitized cargo services	385
Unity	111
Christian church	262
Unity School of Christianity	289.9
Universal algebra	512
Universal history	909
Universal languages	401
Universalist churches	289.1
Universalists	
biography	289.109 2
Universe	
astronomy	523.1
philosophy	113
see Manual at 520 vs. 523.1,	
523.8	
Universities	378
University extension	378.1
University libraries	027.7
University presses	
publishing	070.5
Unmanned space flight	
engineering	629.43
see Manual at 629.43, 629.45	
vs. 919.904	
Unmanned spacecraft	
engineering	629.46
Unmarried mothers	306.874
	T1—086
social welfare	362.83
Unskilled workers	331.7
Untouchables	305.5
Unwed parenthood	306.85
ethics	173
Upholstery	645
home sewing	646.2
interior decoration	747
Upland game birds	598.6
Upper classes	305.5
Upper Guinea	T2—665
Upper Volta	966.25
	T2—662 5
Ural-Altaic languages	494
Uralic languages	494
Uranium	669

Vaporization	536	Venezuela	987
Variation (Biology)	576.5		T2—87
humans	599.9	Venezuelan literature	860
Variations (Musical forms)	781.8	Venezuelans	987
Varicose veins		Ventilation	
medicine	616.1	buildings	697.9
Varieties		household management	644
agriculture	631.5	plant management	658.2
Variety shows	792.7	Ventriloquism	793.8
Varnishing	667	Venus (Planet)	523.42
Vascular plants	580		T2—99
Vascular seedless plants	587	Verb tables	
Vasectomy (Birth control)		applied linguistics	418
health	613.9	specific languages	T4—82
surgery	617.4	Verbal communication	302.2
see also Birth control		psychology	153.6
Vatican City	945.6	Verdicts	347
	T2—456	criminal law	345
Vaudeville	792.7	Vermont	T2—743
VCR (Cassette recorders)	384.55	Versification	808.1
Vector algebra	512	Vertebrate viruses	579.2
Vedas	294.5	Vertebrates	596
Vedic language	491	conservation technology	639.9
Vegetable gardening	635	paleozoology	566
Vegetables	641.3	Vestlandet (Norway)	T2—483
commercial processing	664	Veterans	305.9
cooking	641.6		T1—086
food	641.3	education benefits	371.2
garden crop	635	college and university	378.3
home preservation	641.4	labor economics	331.5
Vegetarian cooking	641.5	law	343
Vegetarianism		social group	305.9
dietary regimen	613.2	social welfare	362.86
ethics	179	public administration	353.538
Vegetative reproduction	571.8	Veterinarians	636.089 092
plants	575.4	Veterinary hospitals	636.08
see Manual at 571.8 vs. 573.6,		Veterinary law	344
575.6		Veterinary medicine	636.089
Vehicles	388	Vibrations	620.3
engineering	629.04	engineering	620.3
military engineering	623.7	physics	531
military equipment	355.8	Vices	179
transportation services	388	religion	291.5
see Manual at 629.04 vs. 388		Christianity	241
Vehicular transportation		Islam	297.5
(Automotive)	388.3	Judaism	296.3
law	343.09	Victimology	362.88
Vending machines	629.8	Victims of crime	362.88
Vendor selection		school programs	371.7
materials management	658.7	social welfare	362.88
Veneers	674	public administration	353.53
Venereal diseases		Victims of oppression	
medicine	616.95	social welfare	362.87

Vocal music	782
see Manual at 782	
Vocalists	782.009 2
Vocation	
applied psychology	158.6
Vocational education	370.11
	T1—071
adult level	374
on the job	331.25
personnel management	658.3
	T1—068
executives	658.4
secondary level	373.246
Vocational guidance	331.7
	T1—023
education	371.4
psychology	158.6
Vocational interest tests	153.9
see Manual at 153.9	
Vocational interests	
applied psychology	158.6
Vocational schools	370.11
see also Vocational education	
Vocational training	370.11
	T1—071
see also Vocational education	
Voice	
human physiology	612.7
music	783
see Manual at 782	
rhetoric of speech	808.5
Voice instruments	783.9
Volcanic gases	551.2
Volcanic rocks	552
Volcanoes	551.21
Voles	599.35
Volition	153.8
Volleyball	796.325
Voluntarism	361.3
Voodooism	299
Vortex motion	532
Vote counting	324.6
Voter registration	324.6
Voting behavior	324.9
Voting qualifications	324.6
Voting rights	324.6
law	342
Voucher system (Education)	379.1
Vulgar Latin language	477
Vulpes	599.775
Vultures	598.9

W

Wading birds	598.3
Wage discrimination	331.2
Wage-price controls	332.4
Wage-price policy	331.2
Wages	331.2
economics	331.2
personnel management	658.3
executives	658.4
public administration	354.9
Wagons	388.3
manufacturing technology	688.6
Wakes	393
Waldensianism	273
denomination	284
Waldorf method of instruction	371.39
Wales	942.9
	T2—429
ancient	936.2
	T2—362
see Manual at 941	
Walkie-talkies	621.384 5
Walking	
physical fitness	613.7
sports	796.51
see Manual at 913–919 vs. 796.51	
Wallabies	599.2
Wallis and Futuna Islands	T2—961 6
Walloons	
social group	305.84
Wallpaper	676
handicrafts	745.54
household management	645
interior decoration	747
Walls (Building element)	721
architecture	721
construction	690
Walrus	599.79
Waltzes	793.3
music	784.18
War	355.02
ethics	172
religion	291.5
Christianity	241
Judaism	296.3
law	341.6
military science	355.02
social effects	303.48
social theology	291.1
Christianity	261.8
Islam	297.2

Water transportation	387	Weather modification	551.68
engineering	629.04	Weather satellites	
international law	341.7	use	551.63
law	343.09	Weathering	551.3
military engineering	623.8	Weaving	677
public administration	354.78	arts	746.1
safety	363.12	vegetable fibers	746.41
Water treatment	628.1	manufacturing technology	677
Water witching	133.3	Wedding music	781.5
Watercolor painting	751.42	Weddings	
Waterfalls		customs	392.5
hydrology	551.48	etiquette	395.2
Waterford (Ireland :		Weeding (Library collections)	025.2
County)	T2—419	Weeds	632
Waterfowl	598.4	control	363.7
Watermelons	641.3	agriculture	632
Waterpower	333.91	environmental engineering	628.9
Waterproof construction		social services	363.7
buildings	693.8	Weeks	529
Watersheds		Weevils	595.76
land economics	333.73	Weight-gaining diet	
Waterways (Inland		health	613.2
transportation)	386	Weight lifting	613.7
engineering	627	physical fitness	613.7
land economics	333.91	sports	796.41
Waterwheels	621.2	Weight-losing programs	
Wave mechanics	530.12	health	613.2
Wave theories	530.14	Weights and measures	530.8
Waves		physics	530.8
fluid mechanics	532	social use	389
mechanics	531	Weimar Republic	943.085
oceanography	551.47	Weimaraner (Dog)	636.752
Waxes	665	Welding	671.5
Way of the cross	232.96	decorative arts	739
Wealth	330.1	sculpture	731.4
economic theory	330.1	Welfare	361
ethics	178	*see also* Welfare services	
macroeconomics	339.3	Welfare reform	361.6
distribution	339.2	Welfare rights	361.6
Wealthy classes	305.5	Welfare services	361
Weapons	355.8	international law	341.7
engineering	623.4	law	344
military	355.8	personnel management	658.3
Weasels	599.76	prisoner services	365
Weather	551.6	public administration	353.5
aeronautics	629.132	specific groups	362
earth sciences	551.6	World War I	940.4
folklore	398.26	World War II	940.54
social effects	304.2	*see Manual at* 301–307 vs.	
see Manual at 551.5 vs. 551.6		361–365; *also at*	
Weather bureaus	354.3	361–365; *also at* 361–365	
Weather control	551.68	vs. 353.5; *also at* 361 vs.	
Weather forecasting	551.63	362	
Weather lore	551.63		

Wife abuse	362.82	Wings (Animals)	591.47
see also Family violence		descriptive zoology	591.47
Wife and husband	306.872	physiology	573.7
law	346.01	Winter	508.2
Wight, Isle of (England)	T2—422	Winter Olympic Games	796.98
Wigs	646.7	Winter sports	796.9
customs	391.5	Wire services	
manufacturing technology	679	journalism	070.4
personal care	646.7	Wires	
Wild flowers	582.13	metal	671.8
Wild horse	599.665	Wiretapping	
Wildcat strikes	331.892	electronic engineering	621.389
Wilderness areas		Wisconsin	T2—775
natural resources	333.78	Wisdom literature (Bible)	223
Wildlife	590	Wisdom of God	212
see also Animals		Christianity	231
Wildlife conservation	333.95	comparative religion	291.2
law	346.04	Judaism	296.3
resource economics	333.95	philosophy of religion	212
technology	639.9	Wit and humor	152.4
Wildlife management	333.95	Witchcraft	133.4
technology	639.9	religious practice	291.3
Wildlife reserves	333.95	African religions	299
conservation technology	639.9	modern revival of old	
economics	333.95	religions	299
landscape architecture	719	Native American religions	299
see also Conservation of		Witches (Occultists)	133.4
natural resources		folklore	398.21
Will	153.8	Withholding tax	336.24
philosophy	128	law	343.05
freedom of will	123	Witnesses	347
Wills	346.05	Wives	306.872
Wiltshire (England)	T2—423	Wives of clergymen	
Wind	551.51	biography	270.092
Wind bands	784.8	*see Manual at* 230–280	
Wind energy	333.9	Wizardry	133.4
Wind engines	621.4	Wizards (Occultists)	133.4
Wind erosion	551.3	folklore	398.21
Wind instruments	788	Wolof language	496
Windmills	621.4	Wolves	599.773
Window displays		Women	305.4
advertising	659.1		T1—082
Window managers (Systems		biography	920.72
programs)	005.4	civil rights	323.3
Windowing programs	005.4	education	371.822
Windows		legal status	346.01
buildings	721	constitutional law	342
Windsor, Edward, Duke of		private law	346.01
British history	941.084	psychology	155.6
Windsurfing	797.3	religion	200.82
Windward Islands	T2—729 84	Christianity	270.082
Wine	641.2	guides to Christian life	248.8
cooking with	641.6	social theology	261.8

Worker security | 331.25
Workers | 331.11
Workers' compensation
  insurance | 368.4
  law | 344
  public administration | 353.6
Workforce diversity
  personnel management | 658.300 8
Working classes | 305.5
Working dogs | 636.73
Workshops (Adult
  education) | T1—071
Workshops (Workrooms)
  agriculture | 631.3
World Bank | 332.1
  law | 341.7
World community
  international law | 341.2
World Community of al-Islam in
  the West | 297.8
World Court | 341.5
World government | 321
  law | 341.2
World history | 909
World Trade Organization | 382
World views | 140
  see Manual at 140
World War I, 1914–1918 | 940.3
World War II, 1939–1945 | 940.53
Worms | 592
  culture | 639
  paleozoology | 562
Worms (Computer science) | 005.8
Worry | 152.4
Worship | 291.4
  Christianity | 248.3
  Islam | 297.3
  Judaism | 296.4
Worth
  epistemology | 121
Wounds
  medicine | 617.1
Wreckage studies | 363.1
  aeronautics | 629.132
  seamanship | 623.88
  see Manual at 363.1 vs. 620.8
Wrecking buildings | 690
Wrenches | 621.9
Wrestlers | 796.812 092
Wrestling | 796.812
Writing instruments
  manufacturing technology | 681
Writing skills
  elementary education | 372.62

Writing systems (Linguistics) | 411
  specific languages | T4—1
Written communication | 302.2
  elementary education | 372.62
  office services | 651.7
  rhetoric | 808
  sociology | 302.2
WTO (World Trade
  Organization) | 382
Wyoming | T2—787

X

X-ray examination
  medicine | 616.07
X-ray therapy
  medicine | 615.8
X rays | 539.7
Xerography | 686.4
  see also Photocopying
Xhosa language | 496
Xylem | 575.4
Xylophones | 786.8

Y

Yachting | 797.1
Yakut language | 494
Yams (Dioscorea) | 641.3
  cooking | 641.6
  food | 641.3
Yarn | 677
Yearbooks | 050
  | T1—05
  encyclopedia | 030
Years | 529
Yeasts | 579.5
Yeasts (Common yeasts) | 579.5
  leaven | 664
Yellow-dog contracts | 331.89
Yellow fever
  medicine | 616.9
Yellow pages (Directories) | T1—029
  see Manual at 338 vs. 060,
    381, 382, 670.29, 910,
    T1—025, T1—029
Yemen | 953.3
  | T2—533
Yemen (People's Democratic
  Republic) | 953.350 5
  | T2—533 5
Yemen (Republic of Yemen) | 953.305
  | T2—533

Yemen Arab Republic	953.320 5
	T2—533 2
Yemenis	953.3
Yeshivot	296.071
Yeti	001.944
Yiddish language	439
Yields	
crop production	631.5
YMCA (Association)	267
Yo-Yos®	796.2
Yoga	181
comparative religion	291.4
health	613.7
Hinduism	294.5
philosophy	181
Yom Kippur	296.4
Yom Kippur War, 1973	956.04
Yorkshire terrier	636.76
Yoruba language	496
Young adult literature	808.8
history and criticism	809
specific literatures	T3—08
history and criticism	T3—09
Young adults	305.242
	T1—084
etiquette	395.1
labor economics	331.3
political organizations	324
psychology	155.6
religion	200.84
Christianity	270.084
guides to Christian life	248.8
pastoral care of	259
religious education	268
social theology	261.8
social theology	291.1
social aspects	305.242
social welfare	362
under eighteen	
social welfare	362.708 3
under twenty-one	305.235
	T1—083 5
see also Adolescents	
Young animals	591.3
domestic animals	636
Young men	305.242
	T1—084
psychology	155.6
social aspects	305.242
social welfare	362
under eighteen	
social welfare	362.708 3

Young men (continued)	
under twenty-one	305.235
	T1—083 5
psychology	155.5
social aspects	305.235
Young Men's Christian	
Associations	267
Young people	305.23
	T1—083
publications for	
bibliographies	011.62
reading	
library science	028.5
religion	200.83
Christianity	270.083
pastoral care of	259
social aspects	305.23
social welfare	362.7
public administration	353.536
Young people's books	
bibliographies	011.62
Young people's societies	369.4
Young women	305.242
	T1—084
psychology	155.6
social aspects	305.242
social welfare	362
under eighteen	
social welfare	362.708 3
under twenty-one	305.235
	T1—083 5
psychology	155.5
social aspects	305.235
Young Women's Christian	
Associations	267
Young workers	331.3
Youth	305.235
	T1—083 5
over twenty	305.242
	T1—084
see also Adolescents	
Yucatec Maya language	497
Yugoslavia	949.710 3
	T2—497 1
Yugoslavia (1918–1991)	949.702
	T2—497
Yugoslavs	949.710 3
social group	305.891
Yukon	T2—719
YWCA (Association)	267

Z

Zaire	967.51
	T2—675 1
Zaire River	T2—675 1
Zairians	967.51
Zakat	297.5
Zambia	968.94
	T2—689 4
Zambians	968.94
Zanzibar	T2—678
Zebras	599.665
animal husbandry	636.1
Zechariah (Biblical book)	224
Zen Buddhism	294.3
Zephaniah (Biblical book)	224
Zimbabwe	968.91
	T2—689 1
Zimbabwe Rhodesia	T2—689 1
Zimbabweans	968.91
Zinc	669
chemistry	546
metallurgy	669
metalworking	673
Zionism	320.540 956 94
see Manual at 322 vs. 296.3,	
320.54095694	
Zip code	383
Zithers	787.7
Zodiac	
astrology	133.5
astronomy	523
folklore	398.26
Zodiacal light	523.5
Zoning	333.73
area planning	711
land use	333.73
urban	333.77
law	346.04
public administration	354.3
Zoological gardens	590.73
Zoological specimens	
preservation	590.75
Zoologists	590.92
Zoology	590
Zoonoses (Human)	
medicine	616.9
Zoos	590.73
animal care	636.088
Zoroastrianism	295
Zoroastrians	
biography	295.092
Zulu language	496

Manual

Use of the Manual

Full instructions on the use of the Manual are found in section 10 of the Introduction to the Dewey Decimal Classification.

The Manual contains three kinds of notes:

(A) Notes on problems common to more than one number (the notes for numbers linked by "–" or "and," e.g., 583–585 or 380.1 and 381, 382).

(B) Notes on problems involving only one number (or a single number and its subdivisions).

(C) Notes on differentiating numbers (the notes linked by "vs.," e.g., 500 vs. 600).

The Manual is arranged in the numerical order of the tables and schedules. For classes with more than one note, the notes are usually arranged in the order listed above. Within each sequence, the broader span comes before the narrower span (e.g., the notes beginning with 571–575 precede the one beginning with 571–573); however, a note for a single number ending in 0 always comes first in the sequence. A "vs." note always appears last (e.g., 571–575 vs. 630 follows 571–575).

The numbers are accompanied by their corresponding captions from the tables and schedules. The captions are listed in boldface type on the line following the numbers. Additional terms are added in square brackets to provide context. If the note is narrower than the caption would suggest, a subheading is included (centered in bold-face type). Subheadings are also used to divide lengthy notes into sections. In several places, sections in notes are divided into subsections. The headings for sub-sections appear centered in italics.

There is a lengthy note explaining 560–590 Life sciences, a major revision introduced in this edition.

See-Manual references in the schedules, tables, and Relative Index refer the classifier to the entries in the Manual. In addition, there are several see-also refer-ences within the Manual.

The appendix to the Manual describes the policies and procedures of the Decimal Classification Division of the Library of Congress with respect to segmentation in centrally cataloged records, alternate DDC notation in LC bibliographic records, and the classification of children's books in the Decimal Classification Division.

Notes on Table Numbers

Table 1. Standard Subdivisions T1

Table 1. Standard Subdivisions

T1—01 vs. T1—02

Philosophy and theory vs. Miscellany

Scientific applications

Use the organization of the table of contents as a guide to distinguish between the scientific principles of a technology (e.g., mathematical principles of engineering) and the corresponding science written for technologists and engineers (e.g., mathematics for engineers). If the table of contents is developed in terms of concepts found in subdivisions of the science (or in the tables of contents of common treatises on the science), class with the science plus notation 02 from Table 1. Conversely, if the table of contents is developed in terms of concepts found in subdivisions of the technology (or in the tables of contents of common treatises on the technology), class with the technology plus notation 01 from Table 1. If in doubt between science and technology, prefer the technology number.

When not to use either subdivision

Do not use T1—01 and T1—02 for scientific principles and the subject for specific occupations in 500 and 600 when there is a direct relationship between a science and a corresponding technology, e.g., do not use 540.24 for chemistry for chemical engineers, or 660.01 for chemical principles in chemical engineering.

T1—01 vs. T1—03

Philosophy and theory vs. Dictionaries, encyclopedias, concordances

Dictionaries and terminology

Use T1—01 for discourses on terminology; T1—03 for works systematically arranged for ready reference, e.g., alphabetical and picture dictionaries, thesauri in classified order. However, use T1—01 for etymological dictionaries, and for lists of abbreviations and symbols. If in doubt, prefer T1—01.

T1—01 vs. T4—86

[Table 1 notation for] Philosophy and theory vs. [Table 4 notation for] Readers

Terminology and readers

Class in T4—86 readers for nonnative speakers intended to instill a knowledge of the special vocabulary of a specific subject or discipline, e.g., science readers (in a language other than Spanish) for Spanish-speaking people T4—86, German-language science readers for Spanish-speaking people 438.6. Class works on the terminology of a specific subject or discipline written without regard to the language status of the user with the subject or discipline, plus notation 01 from Table 1, e.g., science vocabulary 501. If in doubt, prefer T1—01.

T1—02

Miscellany

The subject for persons in specific occupations

Do not use T1—02 for works directed toward persons who would normally be expected to study the subject, e.g., engineering for engineers, students, beginners 620, not 620.002.

Also, use T1—02 with caution for works that effectively cover the subject for the general reader but simply draw examples from one broad discipline or for one kind of professional user. For example, a work on cardiopulmonary diseases for nurses is often just as suitable for patients, relatives, social workers as for nurses. Therefore prefer 616.1 over 616.1002 unless the work emphasizes special instructions for nurses that the general reader would not find useful.

T1—02 vs. T3—7, T3—8

Miscellany vs. Humor and satire vs. Miscellaneous writings

Humor

Jokes and humorous literary works without identifiable form are classed in T3—8. In T3—7 are classed *only* collections of humor or satire in more than one literary form, including both verse and prose. (Works in a particular form are classed with the form, e.g., drama T3—2; works in prose are classed as prose in T3—8.)

Any subject may be dealt with in a humorous or satirical manner. Works dealing with a subject in such a manner fall in one of the following categories:

    1. The humor involved is entirely incidental to the serious treatment of the subject, e.g., a joke injected in a lecture to provide a respite from a serious mood;

    2. The author's intent is serious—to inform, to persuade, to criticize—but humor or satire is the method, e.g., political satire grounded on genuine political criticism;

    3. The subject merely provides the occasion for humor, the author's primary concern being to amuse, e.g., a collection of jokes about cats.

Only works falling in the third category are classed in literature. Works in the second category are classed in the subject plus notation 02 from Table 1. Works in the first category are classed with the subject without T1—02. If in doubt between literature and the subject, prefer the subject. If in doubt whether to use T1—02, prefer the subject without it.

Table 1. Standard Subdivisions T1

T1—0285

Data processing   Computer applications

Machine-readable materials and programs

Do not use T1—0285 to indicate that a work is in machine-readable form, e.g., for census data stored on machine-readable tapes use 310 (*not* 310.285). T1—028 (Auxiliary techniques and procedures; apparatus, equipment, materials) is not used as a form subdivision. A program, however, may be regarded as a kind of apparatus, that is, a device to make a computer work properly or to accomplish a particular task, and works about programs typically discuss techniques and procedures. Hence T1—0285 should be used for programs themselves and for works about programs, regardless of form (e.g., for programs in machine-readable form, such as disk or tape, and printed program listings bound into books).

Do not use T1—0285 for items that include both programs and data files, unless the data files are clearly of minor importance, e.g., small files intended merely to help beginners learn to use the programs.

If in doubt, do not use T1—0285.

T1—068 vs. 353–354

[Table 1 notation for] Management vs. [Specific fields of public administration]

In the Dewey Decimal Classification "public administration" refers primarily to running government agencies that regulate and exercise control of various fields, while "management" refers to running organizations, public or private, that directly perform the work within their scope. In several fields traditionally dominated by public agencies, this operational management is called administration, as in library, hospital, or school administration.

The word "system" is often an indicator pointing to the use of a number outside public administration, because in normal usage it refers to an agency operating (rather than regulating) a number of units. In this sense, a system is usually analogous to a company operating a number of plants. Managing the company or system as well as the individual plants or units is normally classed in the subject of the operations plus notation 068 from Table 1, e.g., managing a prison system 365.068.

Other indicators pointing outside public administration are emphasis on subordinate decision makers; on internal policy formulation; on delegated activities; on routine financial, personnel, and property administration; or on how the reader should exercise control in person. For example, class a work on how to manage the nationalized railways of the United Kingdom in 385.068.

Public hearings are *not* an indicator of public administration. Class hearings on a subject like any other work on the subject. For example, hearings on the performance of a regulatory agency are classed in public administration, but hearings on public policy or on management of an agency delivering services are normally classed outside public administration. Nomination hearings, however, are classed in 352–354 regardless of how much public policy is discussed.

Foreign affairs are among the few major activities for which administration of an actual operation is classed in 353–354, since it is hard to think of "managing" foreign relations in the usual sense. Use 353.1, not 327.068 or related numbers in 327.4–.9. Similarly, foreign intelligence management is classed in 353.1, not 327.12. The administration of activities specific to government such as licensing, taxing, and gathering census information (that is, activities found in 352 that are not also found in 658) are likewise classed in 353–354 when applied to specific fields of public administration.

There is a small handful of large "bureaucratic" organizations based on either a nationwide monopoly or coercive laws for which the organization and management aspects of the national department or agency (sometimes called a "service") are classed in public administration. The two most common examples are agencies running government-sponsored insurance, e.g., the United States Social Security Administration (353.5), and agencies running postal or other communications services, e.g., the United States Post Office and the United States Postal Service (both 354.75). However, the management of specific activities of postal and communications services is classed in 383–384, e.g., management of radio broadcasting 384.54068. (*See also discussion at 380: Add table: 09 vs. 06.*)

Nevertheless, size is not a factor in differentiating between public administration and management. Running a one-person bureau licensing commercial establishments is classed in public administration (354.73), while running a transcontinental nationalized railroad is classed in railroad transportation plus notation 068 for management (385.068).

Often a field has both public administration and management aspects. For example, managing railroads is classed in 385.068, while running agencies that regulate railroads is found in 354.76; administering a public library system is classed in 025.1, while administering agencies that support public libraries is found in 353.7.

If in doubt, prefer the number outside public administration.

See also discussion at note in schedule under 353.3–.9.

T1—081 and T1—082

Men [and] Women

Subdivisions for men and women should be used only for works explicitly emphasizing the sex of people treated. For example, do not use 363.37081 for men as a group in respect to fire fighting unless the work makes clear that fire*men* are being contrasted to fire*women*.

Table 1. Standard Subdivisions   T1

T1—09

Historical, geographic, persons treatment

Be alert for distinctions occasionally made between the historical and geographic treatment of a subject and the historical and geographic treatment of the discipline within which the subject is studied. For example, 364.9 is provided for historical and geographic treatment of crime and its alleviation, while 364.09 is provided for comparable treatment of criminology. Use 364.9 for area treatment of offenses, offenders, causes, prevention, and treatment (when all are considered together). Use 364.09 for area treatment of the criminology and of the principles and methods used in analyzing causes and remedies of crime. Where the distinction is not made between the subject and the discipline, use T1—09 for either or both aspects.

T1—09 vs. T1—089

Historical, geographic, persons treatment vs. Racial, ethnic, national groups

Prefer T1—089 over T1—09 except for groups which predominate in an area, e.g., French people in Australia T1—089, but French people in France T1—0944; Arabs generally or Arabs in France T1—089, but Arabs in Egypt T1—0962. Notation 0917 (socioeconomic regions) is not used for groups of persons treatment since such use would practically duplicate the group treatment numbers. For example, Arabs living in all areas where Arabs predominate constitute the overwhelming majority of all Arabs; therefore, use T1—089 for treatment of Arabs as a group, and limit T1—0917 to works about the area where they live, and works about styles prevailing in areas where they live.

Use T1—09 to identify distinguishing characteristics of a subject in an area where a specific group of people lives rather than T1—089, e.g., Arab architecture 720.917, not 720.89; French agricultural practices 630.944, not 630.89.

If in doubt, prefer T1—09.

T1—092

Persons

These instructions apply also to notation 2 from Table 2 when numbers from Table 2 are added directly without the interposition of T1—09.

In the notes below, the word "biography" is used for stylistic convenience; however, the instructions apply fully to description and critical appraisal as well as other "persons" aspects.

T1—092 is not used for the actual works of a person except where so instructed at certain numbers in 700–770.

See also discussion at 930–990: Wars: Personal narratives.

Comprehensive biography

Class a comprehensive biography of a person with the subject of the person's most noted contribution. If the person made approximately equal contributions to a number of fields, class in the subject which provides the best common denominator, giving some extra consideration to the person's occupational commitment. For example, a physicist who became a science teacher, then head of a school of science, but went on to become a university president would be classed in the university's area number under 378. The biography of a person who made significant contributions in political science, in university education, and in the study of administrative and economic aspects of utility regulation will be classed in 300.92, since social science is the common denominator for the person's work. However, a famous woman doctor who also served as a feminist leader, wrote novels, and often served as a delegate to political conventions will normally be classed in 610.92 unless there is an obvious emphasis on her avocations. Give weight to designations listed first in biographical dictionaries, but make allowances for the tendency to list occupation first even when a career transcends occupation.

If in doubt between a number for a discipline and a number for a specific subject within the discipline, prefer the number for the discipline, e.g., a mechanical engineer who also did important work in transportation and construction engineering 620.0092 rather than 621.092.

Public figures

Biographies of public figures frequently present difficulties because the figures may have filled several positions which are given varying emphasis by different authors, or may have filled one position which had many facets. For persons who held such positions, prefer history numbers in 930–990 for comprehensive works. However, for biographies that emphasize one position or interest of a person's career, prefer a number reflecting that position or interest, e.g., a biography emphasizing Wayne Morse's promotion of the National Institutes of Health 362.1092, even though he was a U.S. senator. (*See also Partial biography, below.*)

There are a number of offices a public figure may hold that afford an opportunity to exert a wide-ranging impact upon the history of the jurisdiction served. For example, Daniel Webster is most famous as a U.S. senator, although he served twice as secretary of state. In both positions, as well as in his position as lawyer and orator, he influenced the history of his time; thus, the best number for his biography is 973.5092, not 328.73 for his senatorial service, 327.730092 for his foreign relations service, or 349.73092 for his legal activities.

For public figures who served in several capacities, give greatest weight to the highest office reached, normally the one in the highest category in the following table. When there is no clear reason to the contrary, use the following table of preference:

Table 1. Standard Subdivisions   T1

1. 930–990 for monarchs, presidents, other heads of state, prime ministers, vice presidents, and regents, using the number for the period during which they held office. Also class here public figures of any position or combination of positions who had a significant impact upon general history, including the king makers and the powers behind the throne, using the period numbers which best approximate their period of influence. Candidates of major political parties for the highest office of a country are also assigned history numbers, generally using the period for which they ran for office, e.g., 973.6 for Stephen Douglas, who ran against Lincoln in 1860.

2. The number for the field of service for cabinet members, e.g., a finance minister of France 336.44092.

3. 327.3–.9 for ambassadors and pre-World War II ministers plenipotentiary.

4. 328.4–.9 for legislators not warranting a specific subject number, e.g., a floor leader, party whip, or member noted for promoting legislative work. Consider, however, that biographers tend to concentrate upon legislators who left their mark on general history; therefore, always weigh the number in 900 for the area the legislature served before assigning another. Only occasionally will a work focus on a legislator's own constituency.

5. 327.3–.9 for diplomats below the level of ambassador; if associated with notable events, then with the events.

6. The number for field of service for public administrators not holding cabinet positions, if their contribution to the service was significant; otherwise 352–354.

Give comparable preference to public figures of state, provincial, and local jurisdictions. Normally national office takes precedence over other levels, but the weight of contributions must be considered. For example, DeWitt Clinton, the famous governor of New York, was briefly U.S. senator, and was a minor party candidate for president, but his comprehensive biography should be classed in 974.7 for the state history of his time.

Families and close associates of the famous

Class a history of the immediate or extended family of a famous person with the biography of that person if the work strongly emphasizes the famous person. The same rule applies to the biography of a single relative or close associate of a famous person. However, if the relative or associate is important in his or her own right, or if the famous person is not strongly featured, class the life of the relative in the subject warranted by his or her own work, e.g., a biography of evangelist Ruth Carter Stapleton, sister of President Jimmy Carter, that treats the president only incidentally in 269. If in doubt, do not use the number assigned to a famous person for a relative or close friend; prefer a number warranted by the biographee's own activities. Class a general family history in 929.

Partial biography

Each biography featuring a specific contribution of a person is classed with the contribution. However, a biography of the portions of a person's life that preceded the activity with which the person is chiefly associated is classed in the person's comprehensive biography number when there is no significant alternative subject emphasis. For example, Justice Byron White's life as an All-American football player 796.332092; but the childhood of Elizabeth II of Great Britain 941.085092, the number for the period of her reign as queen.

Table 2. Geographic Areas, and Persons

T2—162

Oceans and seas

Parts of oceans and non-inland seas limited by either country or locality are classed in T2—163–167, not in T2—3–9. For example, Chesapeake Bay, an arm of the Atlantic Ocean that is almost surrounded by Maryland and Virginia, is classed in T2—163, not in either T2—752 or T2—755. Be alert that estuaries are sometimes named rivers. Estuaries that are parts of oceans and non-inland seas are classed in T2—16. For example, the York River, an estuary of the Chesapeake Bay, is classed in T2—163 (*not* T2—755).

Comprehensive works on the coastal waters of a country are classed in T2—163–168 with the number that includes the majority of the waters, e.g., coastal waters of the Republic of South Africa T2—165 (*not* T2—163), of the United States T2—163 (*not* T2—164). If the areas are approximately equal in size, class in the number coming first, e.g, coastal waters of Panama T2—163 (*not* T2—164).

See also discussion at T2—163, T2—164, T2—165 vs. T2—182.

T2—163, T2—164, T2—165 vs. T2—182

Atlantic Ocean [and] Pacific Ocean [and] Indian Ocean vs. Ocean and sea basins

T2—163, T2—164, and T2—165 deal with the oceans and seas themselves, i.e., their waters. Specific lands are classed in T2—3–9, while the total lands around an ocean or sea or surrounded by an ocean or sea are classed in T2—182. Class works on both the land and water of an ocean basin in T2—182. If in doubt, class in T2—163, T2—164, or T2—165.

T2—3 vs. T2—4–9

The ancient world vs. The modern world; extraterrestrial worlds

Under T2—3 "The ancient world" are gathered those parts of the world more or less known to classical antiquity, and considered only during the period of

Table 2. Geographic Areas, and Persons   T2

"ancient history." The same areas in later times, as well as other areas such as America in both ancient and later times, are classed in T2—4–9. Examples include ancient China T2—31, later China T2—51; ancient Palestine T2—33, later Palestine T2—5694; ancient Gaul T2—364, France T2—44; Guatemala, both ancient and later, T2—7281. The approximate date of demarcation between "ancient" and "later" varies from place to place and may be determined by examination of the terminal dates in classes 931–939, e.g., 931 China to 420, 933 Palestine to 70.

T2—4–9

The modern world; extraterrestrial worlds

Physiographic regions and features

Class a specific feature or region not named in the area table and that is wholly or almost wholly contained within a political or administrative unit with the unit, e.g., the Everglades, Florida T2—759; Lake Tahoe, which is mainly in California, T2—794. Class a river with the unit where its mouth is located, e.g., Arkansas River T2—767. However, if the upper part of the stream is more important politically, economically, or culturally, class the river with that part, e.g., Rhine River T2—43 rather than T2—492.

Class general treatment of a specific kind of feature or region limited to a specific continent with the continent, country, or locality, e.g., rivers of Europe T2—4, rivers of England T2—41. Class treatment of a specific kind of feature or region not limited to a specific continent in T2—1, e.g., rivers T2—16.

T2—7 vs. T2—181

North America vs. Hemispheres

Use T2—181 for the Western Hemisphere, i.e., the portion of the world between 20° west longitude and 160° east longitude. The Western Hemisphere includes not only North and South America but also most of the North Atlantic Ocean (excluding the northeastern portion), Southwest Atlantic Ocean, Northeast Pacific Ocean, and most of the South Pacific Ocean (excluding the southwestern portion). Use T2—7 for the comprehensive works on North and South America, including neighboring islands. When the work includes not only the land portion but also the waters of the Western Hemisphere, use T2—181, e.g., weather patterns of the Americas and Atlantic and Pacific Oceans 551.65181. When the work deals primarily with only the land portion, use T2—7, e.g., reptiles of the Western Hemisphere 597.9097. (Most reptiles are land or freshwater animals.) If in doubt, prefer T2—7.

T2—73 vs. T2—71

United States vs. Canada

Books about the United States and Canada are usually predominately about the United States and are classed in T2—73. Books are classed in T2—71 when Canada receives fuller treatment or the United States and Canada are given equal treatment. Even though Canada and the United States are assigned most of the numbers of T2—7, i.e., T2—71 and T2—73–79, T2—7 is used only when the work also discusses areas in T2—72.

T2—99 vs. T2—19

Extraterrestrial worlds vs. Space

Class in T2—19 only space itself. The various bodies of the universe moving through space are classed in T2—99, e.g., moon rocks 552.0999. Limited use of T2—19 is anticipated.

Table 3. Subdivisions for Individual Literatures, for Specific Literary Forms

To determine the comprehensive number for collected works, critical evaluation, or biography of an author, follow the criteria given below on language and form.

Language

Class an author with the language in which the author writes.

For an author who continues to write in the same language, but who changes place of residence or national affiliation to a country with a different language, use the language in which the author writes. For example, class a novel in Russian by Solzhenifsyn in 891.73, even if the novel was written while he was living in the United States.

For an author who changes national affiliation to a country with the same language as that in which the author has been writing, use the literature number for the country of which the author is now a citizen. Thus T.S. Eliot is classed as a British author. All works of such an author, including individual works written before the change of citizenship, are classed with the same national literature.

For an author who changes place of residence, but not national affiliation, to another country with the same language as that in which the author has been writing, continue to use the literature number of the author's original country. Thus, a New Zealand author living in London, but still retaining New Zealand citizenship, is classed as a New Zealand author.

If information about an author's national affiliation is not readily available in the work being classed or in standard reference books, use the literature number of the author's country of origin, if known; or the literature number of the country in which the author's earlier works were published.

Class an author who writes in more than one language with the language that the author used last, e.g., Samuel Beckett 848. However, if another language is predominant, class with that language. (Individual works of such an author are classed with the language in which they were originally written.)

Table 3. Individual Literatures, Specific Forms T3

Literary form

Use the form with which an author is chiefly identified, e.g., Jane Austen 823. If the author is not chiefly identified with one form, use form T3—8 Miscellaneous writings. Thus, class a late-20th-century English author who is equally famous as a novelist, dramatist, and poet in 828. (An individual work of such an author, of course, is classed with the form exemplified by the work.)

Biography

Do not use notation 092 from Table 1 for biography. Class literary reminiscences in T3—8, e.g., Hemingway's *A Moveable Feast* 818.

Examples of number building

Here are examples of basic number building for works in an individual language by or about individual authors and by or about more than one author. The following elements are used to build the numbers: base number; form; notation 08 Collections or notation 09 Criticism (plus additional 0s in some cases).

Note: notation 08 and 09 are not used for works by or about single authors, e.g., a collection of poetry by Walt Whitman 811; nor are notation 08 and 09 used for works consisting equally of literary texts and history, description, critical appraisal, e.g., a collection of texts and criticism of literary works in German 830.

More than one form: works by or about more than one author

Base no. + notation 08 or 09

81 + 08 = 810.8 (an anthology of American literature)

83 + 09 = 830.9 (criticism of 18th-century German literature)

Forms T3—1–7

1. Works by or about an individual author or more than one author: restricted to a specific form and to a specific period

Base no. + form

82 + 1 = 821 (Spenser's *Faerie Queene*)

83 + 2 = 832 (criticism of German drama of the second half of the 20th century)

2. Works by or about more than one author: restricted to a specific form, but not limited to a specific period nor to a specific kind, scope, or medium

Base no. + form + notation 008 or 009

82 + 3 + 009 = 823.009 (criticism of English fiction)

3. Works by or about more than one author: restricted to a specific form and to a specific kind, scope, or medium

Base no. + form

84 + 3 = 843 (a collection of French short stories)

Form T3—8 Miscellaneous writings

Works by or about an individual author or more than one author: restricted to a specific form, period, and subform

Base no. + form

81 + 8 = 818 (a collection of epigrams of an individual American author of the later 19th century)

84 + 8 = 848 (a collection of jokes of several French authors of the later 20th century)

T3—2 vs. T3—1

Drama vs. Poetry

Dramatic poetry in T3—1 is poetry that employs dramatic form or some element of dramatic technique as a means of achieving poetic ends. Poetic plays intended for theatrical presentation, such as the plays of Shakespeare and Marlowe, are classed in T3—2. Poetic plays designed to be read rather than acted, such as Milton's *Samson Agonistes*, are also classed in T3—2.

The dramatic monologues classed in T3—1 are poems in which the speaker is a fictional or historical character speaking to an identifiable but silent listener at a dramatic moment in the speaker's life, for example, Robert Browning's "My Last Duchess." The monologues classed in T3—2 are typically intended for use in theatrical presentations featuring only one actor.

If in doubt, prefer T3—2.

T3—6

Letters

Class in T3—6 letters compiled from several authors to be read for their literary value. Class collections of the letters of an individual author that are biographical in the comprehensive works number for the author. Class the letters of an individual author in T3—6 only if they have been published for a literary purpose, e.g., to exhibit the style of the writer.

Table 3. Individual Literatures, Specific Forms T3

T3—8

Miscellaneous writings

Diaries

Class in T3—8 diaries of literary authors not identified with a specific form of literature, in which the life of the author or authors as such is of key interest. If the author or authors are identified with a specific form, class the diary or diaries with that form. However, class the diaries of literary authors that emphasize some other subject besides the general life of the author with the subject emphasized. For example, class the diary of an author compiled while in a prisoner-of-war camp during World War II in 940.54.

Table 4. Subdivisions of Individual Languages

T4—1–5, T4—8 vs. T4—7

Description and analysis of the standard form of the language [and] Standard usage of the language (Prescriptive linguistics)   Applied linguistics vs. Historical and geographic variations, modern nongeographic variations

Remember that a language may have multiple standard forms. A work on standard Australian English pronunciation, for example, is classed in 421, not 427. A work on Australian English pronunciation is classed in 427 only if it stresses the distinctive characteristics that make Australian pronunciation different from British or American pronunciation. If in doubt, prefer T4—1–5 and T4—8.

T4—3

Dictionaries of the standard form of the language

Bilingual dictionaries

The Decimal Classification Division classes a bilingual dictionary with entry words in both languages with the language coming later in the sequence 420–490.

T4—3 vs. T4—81

Dictionaries of the standard form of the language vs. [Standard usage of] Words

Works classed in T4—3 are intended for ready-reference use. While specialized dictionaries may be arranged in other ways besides alphabetically (e.g., picture dictionaries in subject order, thesauri in classified order), the order must be appropriate for ready reference.

Works classed in T4—81 are intended to be read or studied in full in order to learn vocabulary. They may be informal and entertaining, e.g., narratives for small children, or they may be formally organized into lessons with quizzes.

If in doubt, prefer T4—3.

T4—7

Historical and geographic variations, modern nongeographic variations

A specific pidgin or creole is classed as a variation of the source language from which more of its vocabulary comes than from its other source language(s), e.g., the Krio language of Sierra Leone 427, Haitian Creole 447.

T4—86

Readers

Readers for new literates

Works intended to serve as readers to help newly literate adults improve their reading skills are classed in T4—86, even if they focus on a specific subject or discipline. Readers for newly literate adults usually indicate the work's intended use somewhere in the prefatory material. The works may contain questions to check reading comprehension and glosses to help with difficult words. If in doubt, prefer T4—86 over subject or discipline.

Notes on Schedule Numbers

001.9 and 130

Controversial knowledge [and] Paranormal phenomena

001.9 and 130 both pertain to topics in the twilight realms of half-knowledge, topics that refuse either to be disproved or to be brought into the realm of certain and verifiable knowledge. Certain characteristics of a work are good indicators that it belongs in either 001.9 or 130:

1. A claim of access to secret or occult sources;

2. A rejection of established authority;

3. A pronounced reverence for iconoclasts, for laypersons-become-experts;

4. An uncritical acceptance of lay observation of striking phenomena;

5. A fixation on the unexplained, the enigmatic, the mysterious;

6. A confidence verging on certainty in the existence of conspiracies and the working of malevolent forces;

7. An acknowledgment of the powers of extraterrestrial beings or intelligences (other than religious beings).

Phenomena classed in 130 are closely linked to human beings—the human mind, human capabilities and powers, human happiness. Phenomena classed in 001.9 are not closely linked to humans. In case of doubt, and for interdisciplinary works, prefer 001.9.

003

Systems

Class works treating systems in related disciplines in the appropriate broad number for those disciplines, using notation 01 from Table 1, e.g., systems in medicine, engineering, management, and manufacturing 601. To be classed in 003 a work must be applicable to at least three main classes (e.g., 300, 500, 600).

Class use of systems analysis and operations research in management in 658.4. Be especially careful with works on operations research, because they often appear at first glance to be general, but in fact emphasize management applications.

Most works on forecasting and forecasts treat primarily social forecasting; such works are classed in 303.49. Works classed in 003 treat forecasting as applied in a variety of social and nonsocial disciplines. Such works typically focus on methods of forecasting.

See also discussion at 003 vs. 004.2.

003 vs. 004.2

Systems vs. Systems analysis and design, computer architecture, performance evaluation

In addition to the analysis and design of computer-based systems, class in 004.2 systems analysis of a user's problem in order to design a computer-based system to solve it. Class a work on systems analysis and design that is not concerned primarily with computer-based systems in 003 or with the specific system. If in doubt, prefer 003.

004–006

[Data processing   Computer science]

Here are key questions to guide in classifying works about computer science, with sample titles and references to relevant Manual notes.

004–006 vs. other disciplines

1. Is the work (A) computer science per se (004–006), or (B) an application of computers to another discipline (T1—0285)?

    A. Understanding computers 004

    B. Computer applications in accounting 657.0285
        657 Accounting + T1—0285 (Data processing   Computer applications)

See also discussion at T1—0285.

2. If the work gives broad coverage to computers, is it (A) predominantly about computer science (004), or (B) predominantly about the role of computers in society (300), e.g., computers and the right of privacy (323.44)? Works that are predominantly about computer science often have a chapter about the role of computers in society; such works should still be classed in 004.

    A. Introduction to computers 004

    B. Computers and social change 303.48

See also discussion at 303.48 vs. 306.4.

3. If the work covers hardware topics, is it about (A) computer engineering (621.39), or (B) use of computer hardware (004), or hardware and software combined (004)?

    A. Build your own PC clone and save a bundle 621.39
        Discusses hardware only; says nothing about software.

    B. Upgrade your PC: hardware and software to give your PC a new lease on life 004.165

See also discussion at 004–006 vs. 621.39.

4. If the work is highly mathematical, is it (A) mathematics (510), or (B) mathematics applied to computer science (004–006 + T1 — 01)?

 A. Introduction to symbolic logic 511.3

 B. The role of mathematical logic in computer science 004.01
  004 (Data processing   Computer science) + T1 — 01 (Philosophy and theory)

See also discussion at 005.1 vs. 510.

5. If the work is about databases or information systems, is it (A) computer science (005.74–.75) or (B) information science (025.04–.06)?

 A. Full-text database management systems: data structures and database design 005.75

 B. User's guide to searching full-text databases online 025.04

See also discussion at 005.74.

6. If the work is about computer communications, is it about (A) computer science aspects (004–005) or (B) economic and related aspects (384.3)?

 A. The Internet: what it is and how it works 004.67

 B. Directory of Internet access providers 384.3

See also discussion at 004.6 vs. 384.3; also at 004.67 vs. 025.04, 384.3.

Within 004–006

Once you have determined that the work belongs in 004–006 rather than in one of the alternative class numbers discussed above, you must decide whether the work is about a special computer method only (006); programming, programs, and data only (005); hardware only (004); or hardware plus programming, programs, data (004). For special computer methods, both software (programming, programs, data) and hardware aspects are classed in 006.

The best way to approach the computer science schedule is to start at the end (006.7) and work backward toward 004. At 004, 005, and 006 there are instructions to class complex subjects with aspects in two or more subdivisions in the subdivision coming last in the schedule. Many works in computer science treat complex subjects to which these preference notes apply. The questions are:

1. Is the work limited to a special computer method (006)?

 A. Yes: Class in the appropriate topical subdivisions.

  Macintosh animation software 006.6

 B. No: Go to question 2.

2. Does the work cover 005 concepts only (programming, programs, data)?

A. Yes: Go to Key question: 005.

B. No: Go to question 3.

3. Does the work cover both hardware (004) and computer programming, programs, data (005)?

A. Yes: Go to Key question: 004–005

B. No: Go to Key questions: 004.

Key questions: 004

These key questions apply only to works limited to 004 concepts.

1. Does the work cover more than one 004 concept?

A. Yes: Are all the 004 concepts aspects of a single complex subject?

i. Yes: Class with the last number for a covered topic (following third note at 004).

Microcomputer architecture 004.2 (*not* 004.165)

ii. No: Unless there are notes to the contrary, follow the first-of-two rule.

Computer storage and communications 004.5 (*not* 004.6)

B. No: Class in the appropriate subdivision of 004.

Computer tape cartridges: care and handling 004.5

See also discussion at 004.165.

Key question: 004–005

This key question applies only to works that cover concepts expressed in both 004 (computer hardware) and 005 (computer programming, programs, data).

1. What is the relationship between the 004 concept(s) and the 005 concept(s)?

A. The 004 and 005 concepts together constitute a single system. Class in 004 or a subdivision of 004.

Local area networking with Novell Netware 004.6 (*not* 005.4)
005.4, the number for operating systems for distributed computer systems, is not used because the work covers hardware aspects of local area networks as well as the networking software Novell Netware.

B. The information on the 004 concept is a brief supplement or background for the 005 concept. Class in 005 or a subdivision of 005.

> Using microcomputers: core concepts and applications 005.36 (*not* 004.16) 004.16 is not used because only a small portion of the work treats microcomputer hardware; the work focuses on how to use micro-computer software.

C. The 005 concept is applied to the 004 concept. Class in 005 or a subdivision of 005.

> Data security in client-server computer systems 005.8 (*not* 004)

D. The 004 concept is applied to the 005 concept. Class in 005 or a subdivision of 005. If the topic of the work approximates the whole of the class number, add T1—0285.

> The Clipper chip: a microprocessor for data encryption 005.8 (*not* 004.165)

See also discussion at 004 vs. 005; also at 004.6 vs. 005.7.

Key question: 005

This key question applies only to works limited to 005 concepts (computer programming, programs, data).

1. Are all the 005 concepts aspects of a single complex subject?

A. Yes: Class with the last number in the schedule for a covered aspect, following the second note at 005.

> Programming with Think Pascal on the Macintosh 005.265 (*not* 005.13) The number for programming for specific microcomputers (005.265) comes later in the schedule than the number for programming languages (005.13).

B. No: Unless there are notes to the contrary, follow the first-of-two rule.

> Operating systems and database management systems 005.4 (*not* 005.75)

See also discussion at 004 vs. 005; also at 004.6 vs. 005.7; also at 005: Examples from 005; also at 005.1–.2 vs. 005.4; also at 005.1 vs. 005.3; also at 005.3; also at 005.3 vs. 005.4; also at 005.362.

004–006 vs. 621.39

[Data processing   Computer science] vs. [Engineering of] Computers

Works classed in 004–006 treat (a) computer hardware from the user's view-point and/or (b) software. Works classed in 621.39 (a) treat computer hardware solely from the viewpoint of engineering or manufacturing and (b) do not treat software. Works limited to assembling the physical components of a computer system—the kind of activity that requires screwdrivers and a wrist grounding wire—are classed in 621.39. Comprehensive works on assembling the physical components and installing the software of a computer system are classed in 004. Comprehensive works on the computer science and computer engineering aspects of a computer topic are classed in 004–006. If in doubt, prefer 004–006.

004 vs. 005

Data processing   Computer science vs. Computer programming, programs, data

Class in 004 works on computer hardware and works treating both computer hardware and the "soft" aspects of computer systems—programs, programming, and data. Class works treating only these "soft" aspects in 005. Be alert to words that can refer to either hardware or software: architecture, processing, communication, interfacing, system analysis, system design. Like other "system" phrases, system development and system specification can refer to hardware or to hardware plus software; however, they usually refer to software. If in doubt, prefer 004.

See also discussion at 004.6 vs. 005.7.

004.165

Specific digital microcomputers

Do not class here or in any other number for specific microcomputers a work treating more than one microcomputer or microprocessor unless:

> 1. The work treats a single series of very closely related microcomputers or microprocessors (e.g., the Intel 80x86® microprocessors 004.165); or

> 2. The work treats primarily one specific computer or processor but adds that it is also applicable to other similar machines (e.g., a work about programming the IBM PC® that says it can also be used as a guide to programming "IBM-compatible" computers 005.265).

Note: A work that discusses a computer and its processor is in effect a work about the computer and should be treated as such (e.g., a work about the Macintosh® computer and the Motorola 68000 series of microprocessors 004.165).

In case of doubt, do not use a number for specific microcomputers.

004.6 vs. 005.7

Interfacing and communications vs. Data in computer systems

Class in 004.6 selection and use of computer interfacing and communications equipment—the "hard" aspects. Class in 005.7 comprehensive works on the "soft" aspects of computer interfacing and communications—programming, programs, and data in interfacing and communications. Class comprehensive works on both the "hard" and "soft" aspects of computer interfacing and communications in 004.6.

004.6 vs. 384.3

Interfacing and communications vs. Computer communication

Class economic and related aspects of providing computer communication services to the public in 384.3. Works focusing on services and service providers, on broad issues of public good in relation to computer communications are classed in 384.3. Class computer communication and its hardware in office and private use, computer science applied to the technological aspects of computer communication, and interdisciplinary works in 004.6. Practical works explaining how to use the hardware and software involved in computer communications are classed in 004.6. If in doubt, prefer 004.6.

004.6 vs. 621.382, 621.39

Interfacing and communications [in computer science] vs. Communications engineering vs. [Engineering of] Computers

Digital communications

Exercise caution in classifying works on digital communications. If they emphasize engineering, they may be either computer data communications (621.39), digital telecommunications (621.382), or digital aspects of both telecommunications and data communications (also 621.382). If in doubt between 621.382 or 621.39, prefer 621.382.

However, in works that do not emphasize engineering, "digital communications" is apt to refer to communications in computer science 004.6. This number is used for works dealing with telecommunications and data communications engineering plus interfacing and communications in computer science. For the other choices for works not emphasizing engineering, see 004.6 vs. 005.7; 384.3 vs. 004.6.

If in doubt between 004.6 and 621.382 or 621.39, prefer 004.6.

004.67 vs. 025.04, 384.3

Wide-area networks vs. Information storage and retrieval systems vs. Computer communication

Internet

Class interdisciplinary works about the Internet in 004.67 if they contain a substantial amount of computer science material and at least some information about computer hardware. If an interdisciplinary work about the Internet does not contain enough computer science material to be classified in 004.67, the first alternate number to consider is 025.04.

Class computer science works about the Internet that are wholly or predominantly about communications software in 005.7, e.g., works emphasizing software packages for connecting to the Internet or emphasizing the commands needed for electronic mail, FTP, and telnet.

Class in 025.04 interdisciplinary works about the Internet that do not contain enough computer science material to be classified in 004.67, but that do contain some information science material. Class in 025.04 information science works that emphasize search and retrieval, including use of front-end systems and interfaces such as Gopher and Netscape to facilitate search and retrieval on the Internet. Also class in 025.04 works that describe information resources available on the Internet.

Class in 384.3 works on Internet access providers and works on economic and public policy issues concerning the Internet.

If in doubt, prefer 004.67. If in doubt between 025.04 and 384.3, prefer 025.04.

005

Computer programming, programs, data

Text processing

Text processing as classed here is broader than word processing; it includes all computer processing of information coded as characters or sequences of characters (as contrasted with information coded as numbers), e.g., counting word frequency, making concordances, storing and retrieving text, sorting lists alphabetically. Class specific applications of text processing with the application, e.g., alphabetic sorting 005.74, word processing 652.5.

Examples from 005

Application programming for Windows 95® 005.26
  (Windows 95® is a specific operating system.)
Easy object programming for Windows® using Visual C++ 005.26
  (Windows® is a specific user interface)
Structured programming in Macintosh® assembly language 005.265
A guide to the hottest Mac software 005.365
Using microcomputer applications for DOS®: WordPerfect®, Lotus 1–2–3®,
  dBase IV® 005.368
Learning to use Windows® applications: Microsoft Word® for Windows®,
Microsoft Excel® for Windows®, Paradox® for Windows® 005.368
Mastering Quattro Pro® for Windows® 005.369
Developing utilities in Microsoft C® for the IBM PC® 005.4
Symantec learning tools for the Norton Utilities® 005.4
Hard disk management in DOS® 005.4
Intermediate user's guide to Microsoft Windows® 3.1 005.4
System 7.5® book: getting the most from your Macintosh operating system
  005.4
Paradox® for Windows®: self-instruction guide 005.75
Understanding HyperCard 005.75
How to back up your PC® 005.8

See also discussion at 004 vs. 005.

005.1–.2 vs. 005.4

[Programming] vs. Systems programming and programs

Class in 005.4 works about writing systems programs, e.g., writing operating systems, user interfaces. Class in 005.1–.2 works on writing application programs and comprehensive works about writing both application and systems programs. Class in 005.1–.2 works about writing application programs that run on specific operating systems or user interfaces, e.g., writing application programs that run on the microcomputer operating system MS-DOS, writing application programs that run on the microcomputer graphical user interface Microsoft Windows, both 005.26. The key distinction is, What kind of programs are being written, systems programs or application programs? If in doubt, prefer 005.1–.2.

See also discussion at 005.3 vs. 005.4 for the distinction between systems programs and application programs.

005.1 vs. 005.3

Programming vs. Programs

Class in 005.1 and other programming numbers works on writing programs, on software engineering, on modifying existing programs in ways that are typically done by computer programmers. Class in 005.3 and other numbers for programs works on using programs that have already been created by others, including works on writing macros of the kind that are typically written by end users of software packages.

Class in 005.1 and other programming numbers works on programming to achieve reliability, compatibility, portability, and other ideal qualities. Class in 005.3 and other numbers for programs works that discuss whether existing programs actually have these qualities.

Class in 005.1 and 005.102 standards for programs and program documentation that are aimed at programmers and documentation writers, to ensure that they produce good programs and documentation. Class in 005.302 and other numbers for programs works that discuss standards to help users in selecting from among existing programs and documentation.

Class in 005.1 testing and measurement as part of program development. Class in 005.3028 and other numbers for programs works that discuss ways for users to test or measure programs as an aid in selection.

Class a work devoted equally to programming and programs in 005.1 Programming or 005.2 Programming for specific types of computers.

005.1 vs. 510

[Computer] Programming vs. Mathematics

Certain terms may be used for both a computer science concept and a mathematics concept. *Algorithm*, for example, may be used for processes to solve mathematical problems—with or without the aid of a computer. General works on algorithms in this sense are classed in 511. *Algorithm* may also be used in the context of computer programming for processes to solve many different kinds of problems—information-retrieval and word-processing problems, for example, as well as mathematical problems. General works on algorithms in this sense are classed in 005.1.

Programming may refer to a branch of applied mathematics that has no necessary connection with computers, though computations necessary for this branch are commonly accomplished with the aid of a computer. Programming in this sense is classed in 519.7. *Programming* may also refer to writing instructions to direct the operation of a computer or its peripheral equipment. Programming in this sense is classed in 005.1.

005.3

Programs

Class a program or programs designed to run on two types of computers with the predominant type if there is one, e.g., a program that runs on five minicomputers and one microcomputer 005.3. If neither of two types is predominant, class with the smaller type, e.g., a program equally for minicomputers and microcomputers 005.369.

Class programs for a specific application in computer science with the application in 005–006, but never in 004. Among the numbers most frequently used for software besides 005.3 and its subdivisions are 005.4 for systems software and operating systems, 005.7 for interfacing and data communications programs, 005.74 for database management systems, and 006.6 for computer graphics programs.

Programs applied to a particular subject or discipline are classed with the subject or discipline, plus notation 0285 from Table 1, e.g., computer programs for manufacturing 670.285.

005.3 vs. 005.4

Programs vs. Systems programming and programs

Class in 005.4 systems programs and works about them. Systems programs are programs that enable computers to function properly; in effect, they provide life support and housekeeping for computers. Systems programs accomplish little that interests users except to make it possible for application programs to run. Examples of systems programs are operating systems, utilities packages, user interfaces, and programming language translators.

Class application programs and comprehensive works on application programs and systems programs in 005.3. Application programs are programs that do things users want done, for example, electronic spreadsheets, statistical packages, computer games, word processing programs, desktop publishing programs, educational programs, tax preparation programs, inventory control programs. A specific type of application program is classed with the type, e.g., computer games 794.8. General-purpose application programs and works on many types of applications programs are classed in 005.3.

Works about application programs that run on specific systems programs are classed in appropriate subdivisions of 005.3, e.g., application programs that run on a specific microcomputer operating system such as DOS, application programs that run on a specific microcomputer graphical user interface such as Microsoft Windows®, both 005.36. Works about the specific systems programs themselves, as distinct from works about the application programs that run on them, are of course classed in 005.4.

If in doubt, prefer 005.3 and its subdivisions.

See also discussion at 005.368 vs. 005.365.

005.362

Programs in specific programming languages

Class here programs and works about programs only if the material being classified emphasizes the programming language. For much off-the-shelf software, the user does not need to know in what programming language it was written; such software is classed in subdivisions of 005.3 not devoted to specific programming languages.

005.368 vs. 005.365

Programs for specific operating systems and for specific user interfaces vs. Programs for specific computers

Class in 005.365 application programs that run on specific microcomputers, and comprehensive works on application and systems programs that run on specific microcomputers. Class in 005.368 application programs that run on specific microcomputer operating systems or on specific user interfaces, and comprehensive works on application and systems programs that run on specific microcomputer operating systems or on specific user interfaces.

If both numbers are applicable to the same work, follow the preference note at 005 and class with number coming last in the schedule (with the exception specified below). For example, if a work treats application programs that run on a specific computer (IBM PC®), on a specific operating system (MS-DOS®), and on a specific add-on user interface (Microsoft Windows®), prefer 005.368. Exception: If a specific computer has only one operating system, so that all programs that run on that computer also run on the operating system, e.g., the Macintosh® and System 7®, class programs that run on that computer and operating system with the computer in 005.365. Earlier and later versions of the same operating system (e.g., Macintosh System 6 and Macintosh System 7) count as one operating system, even though the differences between the earliest and the latest versions may be great.

If in doubt, prefer 005.368.

See also discussion at 005.3 vs. 005.4.

005.369

Specific programs

Class here specific programs having interdisciplinary applications, such as electronic spreadsheets (which can be used in research, business, personal finance, indeed any time a matrix format is useful) and statistics packages that are used more widely than just in research and that have report formatting or other features beyond statistical capabilities. If a work discussing how to use such a program is a guide that would be helpful to users applying the program in many fields, class it in 005.369 even if most of the examples come from one field. If a work truly focuses on how to use such a program in a particular field, however, class it with that field plus notation 0285 from Table 1, e.g., use of a particular electronic spreadsheet in financial administration 658.150285. If in doubt, the work's table of contents may serve as a guide: if the table of contents is organized by functions and features of the computer program, prefer 005.369. If the table of contents is organized by topics in the field of application (e.g., topics found in DDC subdivisions in the field or in tables of contents of works in the field), class with the field of application. If in doubt, prefer 005.369.

005.7

Data in computer systems

Data communications programs

An example of a program for data communications is one that enables a user with a microcomputer and a modem to transmit and receive data and possibly also to store and manipulate data. The program may also prepare a computer to handle different forms of data, change transmission speeds to suit the hardware, store phone numbers and provide automatic routines so that the user need not repeat the connect process, etc.

005.74

Data files and databases

Although there are technical differences between data files and databases, they are treated as the same for classification.

Class in 005.74 computer science aspects of databases, that is, the narrowly technical issues of designing, programming, and installing databases and database management systems—the kinds of things that system designers and programmers need to know but that users generally do not need to know unless they are installing a database on their own computer. Class the subject content of databases (and works discussing that content) as if the databases were books, e.g., encyclopedic databases 030, bibliographic databases 010, nonbibliographic chemistry databases 540. Do not add notation 0285 from Table 1 except for works that focus on the computer science aspects of the databases rather than the subject content. Class in 025.04 the information science aspects of the automated storage and retrieval systems that make databases available—the kinds of things that users need to know about the systems in order to benefit fully from them. Class in 025.06 the information science aspects of the automated systems that make databases on specific subjects available to users. Class interdisciplinary works on databases in 025.04.

005.74 vs. 005.4

Data files and databases vs. Systems programming and programs

A file manager in the sense of software that manages data files provides the ability to create, enter, change, query and produce reports on a data file or data files; file managers of this type are classed in 005.74 or 005.75. A file manager in the sense of software used to manage files on a disk provides the ability to delete, copy, move, rename and view files as well as create and manage directories. A file manager in this sense may be part of an operating system or a separate utility program. File managers of this type are classed in 005.4.

File organization may refer to the structure of data within a single file that permits access to the data; file organization in this sense is classed in 005.74. File organization may refer to the way that multiple files are organized on a disk; file organization in that sense is classed in 005.4.

Class comprehensive works on both 005.4 and 005.74 in 005.4. If in doubt, prefer 005.74.

006.3 vs. 006.4, 621.36, 621.39

Artificial intelligence vs. Computer pattern recognition vs. Applied optics and paraphotic technology vs. Computer engineering

Optical data processing

Computer vision (006.3) and optical pattern recognition (006.4) both involve recognition of forms, shapes, or other optical patterns for the purpose of classification, grouping, or identification; but computer vision makes extensive use of artificial intelligence for the complex interpretation of visual information, whereas optical pattern recognition involves only simple interpretation.

Most works on computer vision and optical pattern recognition give substantial treatment to the computer programs needed to interpret optical patterns; such works are classed in 006.3 and 006.4, as are also works treating computer-vision and optical-pattern-recognition devices from the user's point of view. Class at 621.39 works on designing and manufacturing the hardware for computer vision and optical pattern recognition.

Class in 621.36 works on devices that record and process optical signals while doing virtually no interpreting (either because interpretation is not needed or because interpretation is left to others—computers or humans), e.g., devices for image enhancement.

At 621.39 *optical computer* refers to general-purpose computers in which the central data processing mechanism is based on light (e.g., lasers). Sometimes *optical computer* is used for special-purpose computers designed to process optical data, regardless of the type of central data processing mechanism. Works on such computers are classed in 006.3, 006.4, or 621.39.

011 vs. 005.3029

Bibliographies vs. Commercial miscellany [about computer programs]

Class general bibliographies of machine-readable works and general lists of software in 011. Class annotated lists of software in 011 if the annotations are relatively brief; but class lists with lengthy reviews as buyers' guides in 005.3029, e.g., a collection of reviews of microcomputer software 005.36029. If in doubt, prefer 011.

See also discussion at 005.74.

016 vs. 026, T1—07

Bibliographies and catalogs of works on specific subjects or in specific disciplines vs. Libraries, archives, information centers devoted to specific subjects and disciplines vs. [Table 1 notation for] Education, research, related topics

Notation 07 from Table 1 is used for comprehensive works on resources for education, research, and related topics. Many of the resources are encompassed by subdivisions of T1—07, e.g., schools, collections of objects (such as botanical collections), and financial support. Books, manuscripts, recordings, and the like are also resources, but works that describe such resources will normally be classed in 016 or 026 unless the work (a) also describes kinds or resources not found in 016 or 026 or (b) emphasizes how to use the library or archival resources for study and teaching. If in doubt, prefer 016 or 026.

To be classed in 016, a work about resources in a field must describe individual works, such as books and articles. A work about kinds of material not traditionally described in detail, however, is also classed in 016 if small units are described, e.g., five shelf feet of correspondence of a particular person on a particular subject. Inventories and calendars of archives are typically classed in 016. Works about resources in a field that give broad descriptions of whole collections held by libraries, archives, and other information organizations are classed in 026. Such works often include directory information about the institutions and organizations. If in doubt, prefer 016.

Notation 07 may be used in 016 if the resources being described treat education and research, e.g., a bibliography of material on education and research of mathematics 016.5107.

020

Library and information sciences

The preference order in the schedule for library and information science is complex. The following table shows preference among 022, 023, 025, 026, and 027:

025 Operations, such as technical services, e.g., acquisitions, cataloging; readers' services, e.g., reference, circulation
  Exceptions: (a) Prefer other operations over Administration (025.1) (see below). (b) Readers' services for special groups and organizations are classed with libraries for special groups and organizations in 027.6, not in 025.5. (c) Comprehensive works on operations in a specific kind of institution are classed with the kind of institution in 026–027, not in 025.

022, 023, 025.1 Administration

026 Institutions devoted to specific disciplines and subjects

027 General institutions

Examples follow:

Administration of cataloging 025.3068
Administration of school libraries 025.3
Book selection in public libraries 025.2
Reference services in prison libraries 027.6

080 vs. 800

General collections vs. Literature (Belles-lettres) and rhetoric

Class a collection of quotations in 800 if all or nearly all the quotations come from works of poetry, drama, or fiction. Otherwise, class a collection of essays or quotations in 800 only if the intent of the collection, as revealed in prefatory matter, is clearly literary, e.g., to exhibit literary style. Usually essays and quotations are collected for nonliterary purposes, e.g., quotations collected to answer reference questions about who said something familiar; such collections belong in 080. If in doubt, prefer 080.

081–089

General collections in specific languages and language families

Collections originally written in one language or language family are classed with that language or language family. Collections originally written in two or more languages or language families are classed with the preponderant language or language family if there is one. If no original language or language family is preponderant, but the work appears in one language as a result of translation, class it with the language in which it appears. Class in 080 collections in which the material appears in multiple languages with none preponderant, even if accompanied by translations into the language of the intended audience.

133 vs. 200

Parapsychology and occultism vs. Religion

If the author of a work about parapsychological or occult phenomena describes them as religious, or the believers and practitioners consider them to be religious, the work is classed in 200. If parapsychological and occult phenomena are not presented as religious, or if in doubt as to whether they have been so presented, prefer 133.

Class knowledge reputedly derived from secret and ancient religious texts but not applied for religious purposes in 133; however, class editions of the texts in 200, even if annotated from an occultist viewpoint, e.g., discussion of occult traditions derived from the Zohar, a cabalistic text, 135; but the text of the Zohar 296.1.

133.9 vs. 129

Spiritualism vs. Origin and destiny of individual souls

Life after death

Class in 133.9 accounts of life after death from personal sources or from within the occult tradition. Class in 129 philosophical discussions of personal survival and life after death. If in doubt, prefer 133.9.

140

Specific philosophical schools and viewpoints

Viewpoints or schools of philosophy are sets of attitudes or presuppositions that a given philosopher or group of philosophers brings to the study of various topics. Topics are the questions studied by philosophy, such as the self 126. Only general works that discuss how a viewpoint or school treats a wide variety of topics are classed in 140, e.g., existentialism 142, but existentialist views of the self 126.

140 vs. 180–190

Specific philosophical schools and viewpoints vs. Historical, geographic, persons treatment of philosophy

Unless other instructions are given, class in 140 specific modern western schools and viewpoints and comprehensive works on specific schools and viewpoints, but class in 180 ancient, medieval, and Oriental schools and viewpoints, e.g., modern western idealism, comprehensive works on ancient and modern idealism or on Indian and western idealism 141, but Indian idealism 181. Class in 190 historical and geographic treatment of modern western philosophy not limited to a specific viewpoint, but class a specific school or viewpoint with the school or viewpoint regardless of time or place, e.g., French philosophy 194, but existentialism in France 142.

Class collected works of an individual philosopher and criticism of the philosopher's work as a whole in 180–190, even if the philosopher's work falls entirely within one philosophical viewpoint or serves as the foundation of a school, e.g., the works of Immanuel Kant 193, but Kantianism as a viewpoint espoused by philosophers 142.

153 vs. 006.3

Conscious mental processes and intelligence vs. Artificial intelligence

Cognitive science

Class cognitive science (interdisciplinary study of the mind and computers as information processing systems) in 153 if the goal is to understand better how the human mind works. Class cognitive science in 006.3 if the goal is to produce computer systems with better artificial intelligence. If in doubt, prefer 153.

153 vs. 153.4

Conscious mental processes and intelligence vs. Thought, thinking, reasoning, intuition, value, judgment

The terminology in this field is used in a variety of overlapping senses. Many works that claim to be about thought and thinking or reasoning also cover such subjects as memory, communication, perception, motivation, and intelligence. These broader works are classed in 153, not 153.4. A book about "cognitive psychology" is more apt to belong at 153 than 153.4. Use 153.4 only for works that focus narrowly on thought and thinking, reasoning, intuition, value, judgment. If in doubt, prefer 153.

153.1 vs. 370.15

Memory and learning vs. Educational psychology

Be careful to distinguish between studies that use students as subjects for research into the fundamental processes of learning, which are classed in 153.1 and related numbers, and studies on the application of learning psychology to education, which are classed in 370.15 and related numbers. In case of doubt, prefer 153.1.

153.4 vs. 160

Thought, thinking, reasoning, intuition, value, judgment vs. Logic

Class the psychology of reasoning and problem solving in 153.4. Class the science of reasoning and problem solving, that is, the logical processes considered apart from internal mental operations, in 160. If in doubt, prefer 153.4.

153.7 vs. 152.1

Perceptual processes vs. Sensory perception

Class in 153.7 works treating both perceptual processes and sensory perception in general, and works that focus on the active, interpretative mental processes associated with perception in general. Also class in 153.7 types of perception that involve more than one sense, e.g., space perception that involves vision and touch. Class in 152.1 works that focus on the receptive aspects of sensory perception and comprehensive works on perception by a specific sense, e.g., visual perception 152.14. If in doubt, prefer 153.7.

153.9

Intelligence and aptitudes

Aptitude and vocational interest tests

When it is used to refer to aptitude or vocational interest tests, 153.9 has priority over other psychology numbers, as shown in the table of preference at 150. Class in 153.9 tests to determine aptitude in specific fields even if drawn from other branches of psychology, e.g., color matching tests for interior decorators 153.9 (*not* 152.14), personality tests for social workers 153.9 (*not* 155.2). Also class in 153.9 aptitude and vocational interest tests and testing limited to categories of persons defined in 155.3–.6, e.g., vocational interest tests for young people twelve to twenty 153.9 (*not* 155.5).

155.4–.6 vs. 153.1

Psychology of specific ages vs. Memory and learning

Class a work on the learning psychology of people of a specific age bracket in 155.4–.6 when age is actually the focus of the work. If the reference to age is vague or incidental, class the work in 153.1. If in doubt, prefer 155.4–.6.

158 vs. 155.2

Applied psychology vs. Individual psychology

Works of applied psychology that treat topics named at 155.2 in a loose or vaguely defined way are classed in 158 or subdivisions of 158, most commonly in 158.1 Personal improvement and analysis. Such topics include the self, character, identity, individuality, and personality (named at 155.2). Only analytical and explanatory works on these topics are classed in 155.2, e.g., how character develops. The above also holds true of vague topics not named, e.g., self-actualization, self-esteem.

In contrast, both works of applied psychology and analytical and explanatory works that treat specific, clearly defined topics of individual psychology are classed in subdivisions of 155.2. For example, works of applied psychology on specific character traits, such as perfectionism and aggressiveness, on typology, and on appraisals and tests are classed in 155.2.

If in doubt, prefer 158.

170

Ethics (Moral philosophy)

Ethics is an exception to the rule that the philosophy of a discipline or subject is classed with the discipline or subject. Class the ethics of a discipline or subject in 172–179. Class ethics within or based on a religious tradition with the religion in 200. For example, class philosophy and theory of international relations in 327.101; the ethics of relations between states in 172; the ethics of those relations treated as part of Christian moral theology in 241.

170 vs. 303.3

Ethics (Moral philosophy) vs. Coordination and control [in sociology]

Social ethics

Social ethics may be a subject either in moral philosophy or in methods of social control. Social ethics in 170 refers to the rightness or wrongness of conduct as it affects individuals or society. Social ethics in 303.3 refers to beliefs and system of beliefs influencing the way society and its institutions operate. 303.3 is descriptive, while 170 is prescriptive. If in doubt, prefer 170.

170.92 vs. 171

Persons [associated with ethics] vs. Ethical systems

Class collected works, biography, and critical appraisal of the work of an individual moral philosopher in 171 if the ethical system represented can be determined (e.g., critical appraisal of the ethics of Jeremy Bentham, who is associated with utilitarianism, 171). Otherwise, class such works in 170.92.

174

Occupational ethics

Occupational ethics of clergy

Class in 174 a discussion of occupational ethics for clergy from a secular or philosophical viewpoint. If the subject is treated as part of the moral theology or ethics of a particular religion, class it with the religion, e.g., a discussion of the occupational ethics of clergy as part of Christian morality 241.

180–190

Historical, geographic, persons treatment of philosophy

Class single works by individual philosophers with the topic in philosophy. If there is no focus on a specific topic, class a work expressing primarily the philosopher's own viewpoint with the collected works of the philosopher in 180–190. For example, a general work by Hegel, such as *Phenomenology of Spirit*, is classed in 193.

Class a work by an individual philosopher that is primarily a discussion of other philosophers' writings with the other philosophers' writings. For example, a work by a western philosopher that is mostly a criticism of contemporary philosophers is classed in 190.

Class a work by an individual that takes a broad look at many questions in philosophy and does not seek to argue for the individual's own viewpoint in 100.

190 vs. 100, 109

Modern western and other non-Oriental philosophy vs. Philosophy, paranormal phenomena, psychology [and] Historical and collected persons treatment of philosophy

190 is the comprehensive number for (a) Christian philosophy; (b) western philosophy from ancient Greece to the present; (c) modern philosophy, even when both modern western and modern Oriental philosophies are treated; and (d) European philosophy. For this reason, 190 is used more often than 100 or 109 for what appear to be general works on philosophy.

To be classed in 100 or 109, works must include (a) discussion of the discipline of philosophy itself or several of philosophy's major questions and branches, as is common in introductory works; or (b) discussion of philosophy broad enough to include non-western and ancient or medieval as well as modern western philosophy. If in doubt, prefer 190.

200 vs. 100

Religion vs. Philosophy, paranormal phenomena, psychology

Both philosophy and religion deal with the ultimate nature of existence and relationships, but religion treats them within the context of revelation, deity, worship. Philosophy of religion (210) does not involve revelation or worship but does examine questions within the context of deity.

Any work that emphasizes revelation, deity, or worship is classed in 200, even if it uses philosophical methods, e.g., a philosophical proof of the existence of God 212. Sometimes the thought of a religious tradition is used to examine the questions of philosophy without reference to deity or religious topics, e.g., Jewish philosophy 181, Christian philosophy 190. However, class ethics based on a religion in 200. If in doubt, prefer 200.

200.9 vs. 294, 299

Historical, geographic, persons treatment [of religion] vs. Religions of Indic origin [and] Other religions

Religions of Indic and Asian origin

294 and 299 refer to religions that originated in particular geographic areas. Most of these religions have spread beyond the area where they originated. The areas also have adherents of religions that originated elsewhere, e.g., Buddhism (which originated in India) is present in China. If a work covers various religious traditions in an area, not just the religions that originated there, class it in 200.9. For example, class the religions of India (including Christianity and Islam besides those listed under 294) in 200.954, of China (including Christianity and Buddhism) in 200.951.

220

Bible

Biblical theology

Biblical theology usually means using the Bible for the basis of Christian or Jewish doctrine and is classed as directed at 220. But if a book on Biblical theology does no more than interpret the text of the Bible, it is classed in 220.6 or with the specific part in 221–229. The key difference is whether the author adheres to the Biblical text and its meaning, or whether the author uses the Biblical text as a springboard to the interpretation of theological concepts.

220.9

Geography, history, chronology, persons of Bible lands in Bible times

Biblical biography

Class a comprehensive biography of a Biblical character with the book or books with which the character is most closely associated. In many cases this is the historical part of the Bible in which persons' lives are narrated, e.g., Solomon, King of Israel, in 1st Kings 222. Solomon's association with 223 Poetic books is weaker. However, some Biblical characters are more closely associated with nonhistorical books. For example, class Isaiah and Timothy with the books that bear their names. They appear briefly in historical narratives, but their lives are not narrated in full there. Class the apostles John, Peter, and Paul at 225.9 since each is associated with a number of books in the New Testament, but class the rest of the original Apostles, associated primarily with Gospels and Acts, in 226.

See also discussion at 230–280: Biography.

Christianity

Biography

Use the following table of preference for comprehensive biographies:

Jesus Christ, Mary, Joseph, Joachim, Anne, John the Baptist	232.9
Other persons in the Bible	220
Founders of denominations	280
Founders of religious orders	271
Higher clergy (e.g., popes, metropolitans, archbishops, bishops) prior to 1054	270.1–.3
Higher clergy subsequent to 1054	280
Theologians	230
Moral theologians	241
Missionaries	266
Evangelists	269
Persons noted for participation in associations for religious work	267
Martyrs	272
Heretics	273
Saints	270
Saints prior to 1054	270.1–.3
Saints subsequent to 1054	280
Mystics	248.2
Hymn writers	264
Religious educators	268
Members of religious orders	271
Clergy and members of the early church prior to 1054	270.1–.3
Clergy and members of denominations subsequent to 1054	280
Christian biography of persons who fall in none of the above categories	270

Class in 270 biographies of persons known not to be members of any church or for whom it has not been possible to determine whether there is church membership or not. Use the historical period that most closely matches the individual's life span or the time period of the individual's greatest prominence, e.g., biography of a twentieth century Christian 270.8. Class in 280 without subdivision church members whose affiliation is not known and members of nondenominational and interdenominational churches.

Except for religious mysticism, do not use 248.2 Religious experience for comprehensive biographies, e.g., a biography of Teresa of Avila's religious life 282.092, not 248.2092. However, biographical accounts written for devotional purposes, not as comprehensive accounts of a person's life, may be classed in 248.2, e.g., the story of one's conversion 248.2.

253, 255, and 262 are not used for biographies of the kinds of persons listed above in the table of preference.

Certain numbers in the range 220–269 other than those listed in the table of preference above may be used for comprehensive biographies of persons with specialized religious careers, but are more commonly used for books treating only one aspect of a person's life and work, e.g., 220.092 for a Biblical scholar.

Examples:

270.092	(Collected biography of saints)
225.9	(New Testament biography) Paul the Apostle
230	(Catholic theology) Saint Thomas Aquinas
232.9	(Family and life of Jesus) John the Baptist
266	(Catholic missions) Saint Francis Xavier
269	(Evangelism) Billy Graham
271	(Trappist order in church history) Thomas Merton
270.2092	(Church history, 325–787) Pope Gregory the Great
283.092	(Anglican churches) Thomas Cranmer
287.092	(Methodist churches) John Wesley

See also discussion at 220.9; also at 232

231.7 vs. 213, 500, 576.8

[God's] Relation to the world vs. Creation [in philosophy of religion] vs. Natural sciences and mathematics vs. Evolution

Evolution versus creation

Most works on creation science or creationism are classed in 231.7 because they are written by Christians who assume that the Bible provides a chronology of natural history and who rely upon religious premises in responding to theories from the natural sciences. On the other hand, works by creationist authors that attempt to refute evolution theory by examining the writings, hypotheses, and findings of scientists are classed in 500 with the branch of science criticized. Similarly, works that attempt to refute creation science are usually classed in 231.7, unless they take the writings of creationists as a starting point from which to demonstrate the case for evolution.

The difficulty stems from the fact that on the question of evolution the *pro* and *con* positions differ so radically that they normally belong in different disciplines, science and religion, respectively. However, when a religious author is trying to enlighten scientists on a specific scientific matter, class the work with science, while if a scientist is trying to enlighten the religious on a specific religious matter, class the work with religion. The place in the classification is determined by the intent of the author and the interest of the readers that the author is seeking to reach, not by the truth, falsity, or validity of interpretations and premises.

Class comprehensive works including both religion and science in 231.7.

Among the works that belong in 500, the most common focus of interest is on biological evolution. Class these works in 576.8. If the emphasis of a work is mainly on stellar evolution, class in 523.8; if on basic physical principles, in 530; if on historical geology, in 551.7; and if on paleontology, in 560. If there is no clear emphasis on a specific branch of science, then class in the broad number, 500.

Works that consider the relation between divine creation and evolution as a philosophical problem, without appealing to a particular religion or scripture, are classed in 213. If in doubt between 213 and 231.7, prefer 231.7.

232

Jesus Christ and his family   Christology

Class doctrine and theories about Jesus Christ in 232, events in the life of Jesus in 232.9, e.g., the doctrine of the resurrection 232, historicity and narration of events surrounding the resurrection 232.9.

Use notation 092 from Table 1 for criticism, biography of Christologists (232.092) and Mariologists (232.91092). Class biography of Jesus and his family, of John the Baptist in 232.9; of Mary in 232.91.

241 vs. 261.8

[Christian] Moral theology vs. Christianity and socioeconomic problems

Some topics are covered in both moral and social theology, e.g., family relationships. Works classed in 241 focus on what conduct is right or wrong. Works classed in 261.8 may discuss right and wrong, but they treat the topic in a broader context as a problem in society and discuss Christian attitudes toward and influence on the problem. Class in 241 works that emphasize what is right and wrong, or what the individual should do. Class in 261.8 works that stress what the church's stance should be, what response the church or Christian community should make to alleviate the problem, or the church's view on problems transcending individual conduct. If in doubt, prefer 241.

260 vs. 251–254, 259

Christian social and ecclesiastical theology vs. Local church [and] Pastoral care of specific kinds of persons

The local church is the group in which individual believers can meet regularly face to face for worship, fellowship, and church activities—for example, a congregation, a college church group.

Among the more recent forms of the local church are the small groups called basic Christian communities or basic ecclesial communities. These are smaller than parishes or congregations, but, like other forms of the local church, are organized for the general religious welfare of their members, not just for special projects or functions. They are classed in the same way as parishes, i.e., comprehensive works are classed in 250 (or in 262 when treated as part of ecclesiology) and specific aspects are classed with the aspect in the subdivisions of 250.

Activities undertaken by the church may be classed in 250 or 260, depending on the context. Most of the works in 250 are intended for the individual practitioner in the local setting. The local setting may be as small as a parish youth group or as large as a counseling program that serves a metropolitan area. Class the church's attitude to cultural and social problems, and its activities regarding them in 261 unless the context is limited to the local church, e.g., a practical work for the prison chaplain 259, but the church's attitude to the treatment of criminals 261.8. If in doubt, prefer 260.

Some activities that can be conducted by the local church are classed in 260, e.g., public worship (264–265), religious education (268), spiritual renewal and evangelism (269). The context of works on these subjects is often broader than that of the local church.

Class church organization in 262, unless the scope is limited to administration of the local church (254).

261.5

Christianity and secular disciplines

Class here personal Christian views and church teachings about secular disciplines as a whole, their value, how seriously a Christian should take them, how far the disciplines should affect faith. Class Christian philosophy of a secular discipline or Christian theories within a discipline with the discipline, e.g., a Christian philosophy of psychology 150.1. Be alert for specific uses of secular disciplines for religious purposes, e.g., use of drama 246. If in doubt, class with the secular discipline.

261.5 vs. 231–239

Christianity and secular disciplines vs. Christian doctrinal theology

Class in 261.5 works treating generally antagonism between and reconciliation of Christian belief and another discipline. Class antagonism between a specific Christian doctrine and another discipline with the doctrine in 231–239. For example, class the relation between Christian doctrines in general and science in 261.5; but class the relation between Christian doctrine on the soul and modern biology in 233.

263, 291.3 vs. 394.265

Days, times, places of [Christian] religious observance and Public worship and other practices [among religions] vs. Religious holidays

Religious holidays

Class in 263, 291.3, and related numbers in 292–299 the religious customs associated with religious holidays, e.g., sunrise Easter services 263. Class in 394.265 the secular customs associated with religious holidays, e.g., Easter egg hunts. If in doubt, prefer 263, 291.3, and related numbers in 292–299.

268 vs. 230.071

[Christian] Religious education vs. Education in Christianity, in Christian theology

Class education in and teaching of Christianity as an academic subject in 230.071, e.g., a course on Christianity in secular secondary schools 230.071. Class in 268 religious education as a ministry of the church for the purpose of confirming believers in Christian faith and life, and religious education programs sponsored by the local church, whether the students are children or adults. If in doubt, prefer 268.

Higher education in Christianity and Christian theology usually takes place in divinity schools, theological seminaries, and graduate departments of theology or ministry in universities. Students and scholars in such institutions may be preparing for the ordained ministry or they may be following a course of studies in the academic discipline of theology, or they may be doing both simultaneously. Such institutions are usually engaged both in religious education as a ministry of the church and in the academic study of Christianity and Christian theology. Class all such institutions with higher education in theology, i.e., in 230.071, rather than in 268. Education or training of the clergy for specialized work is classed with the specialty, e.g., courses in Biblical studies 220.071, programs in pastoral counseling 253.5071.

Study and teaching with regard to any specific topic in Christianity are classed as follows:

> For religious education of children of elementary-school age, class a work on teaching a specific topic with works on religious education of children in general in 268.

> For religious education of persons of secondary-school age and older, class a work on teaching a specific topic with the topic plus notation 071 from Table 1, e.g., study and teaching of church history 270.071.

See also discussion at 291.7 vs. 200.71.

281

Early church and Eastern churches

Early church

The early church is considered to be undivided by denominations until the schism of 1054. Therefore, the history of the Church prior to 1054 is classed in 270.1–.3, not here. The history of specific churches prior to 1054 is classed in 274–279.

The early history of the Eastern and Roman Catholic churches is also classed in 270. The history of these churches before 1054 is classed in 270.1–.3 or 274–279. Works on later history or works that cover both the early and later history are classed in 281, 281.9, or 282.

290

Comparative religion and religions other than Christianity

290 by itself will never be used, since 291 has been designated as the number for comprehensive works on the non-Christian religions, on Christian and non-Christian religions, and for works on comparative religion.

291

Comparative religion

A comparison of the topics in 291 with the subdivisions of Christianity can sometimes be helpful in determining what goes where. A comparative list follows:

Social theologies	291.1	261
Doctrinal theologies	291.2	230
Public worship	291.3	246–247, 263–265
Religious experience, life, practice	291.4	242, 248
Moral theology	291.5	241
Leaders and organizations	291.6	250, 262, 267
Pastoral theology and work	291.6	253
Missions, religious education	291.7	266, 268
Sources	291.8	220
Denominations, sects, reform movements	291.9	280

291.2 includes the topics listed at 231 (God) that are not limited to Christianity: ways of knowing God, general concepts of God, attributes, providence, love and wisdom, relation to human experience, justice, and goodness.

Denominations and sects

In some cases, there is disagreement as to whether a specific sect should be listed under a religion or whether it should be considered a separate religion. The majority or mainstream members of the religion may not consider it a part of their religion. The criterion used in the Classification is that a denomination or sect is listed in the schedule with the religion to which its members say it belongs.

Common terms

Some terms that have their origin in a particular religion have become commonly used in other religions. Such terms as "karma" and "yoga" originated in Hinduism or other religions of Indic origin. These terms appear in the schedule under 291, because they may be discussed from a point of view not limited to the religion of origin. However, a work on yoga from a Hindu point of view should be classed with Hinduism in 294.5 rather than in 291.4.

291.7 vs. 200.71

Missions and religious education vs. Education [in religion]

Class in 200.71 education in and teaching of comparative religion, the religions of the world, and religion as an academic subject. 291.7 is meant for discussion of how various religions educate their members (especially young members) to be good followers of their own religions. Such education stresses knowledge of the faith and living as a member of a religion. It is meant to instill the values of a particular religion, not to study it in a detached manner. This type of education is usually termed "religious education" in contrast to the study of religion or "religious studies." In case of doubt as to which type of education is being treated, prefer 291.7.

At the level of higher education, students may be studying their own religion as an academic subject or they may be studying in order to become members of the clergy or they may be doing both at the same time. Religious education at the level of higher education is classed in 200.71 rather than in 291.7. Works about the education of the clergy are also classed with higher education in 200.71.

With regard to any specific topic in comparative religion or the specific religions in 292–299, study and teaching are classed as follows:

> For religious education of children of elementary-school age, class a work on teaching a specific topic with works on religious education of children in general, e.g., Jewish religious education courses on the Tanakh (scriptures) for children 296.6.

> For religious education of persons of secondary-school age and older, class a work on teaching a specific topic with the topic plus notation 071 from Table 1, e.g., study of the Tanakh in Jewish colleges and universities 221.071.

See also discussion at 268 vs. 230.071.

297.4

Sufism (Islamic mysticism)

All works on Sufism, e.g., Sufi concepts of God, Sufi orders, are classed in 297.4. Comprehensive and non-Sufi works on Islam are classed in 297 and its subdivisions other than 297.4, e.g., comprehensive works on Sufi and non-Sufi Islamic views of God 297.2. If in doubt, prefer a number outside 297.4.

300, 320 vs. 352–354

Social sciences [and] Political science (Politics and government) vs. Specific topics of public administration

Public policy

Public policy in specific fields of social concern is normally classed with the field in the social sciences, regardless of whether the policy is formulated by legislation, administrative decision, or informal public consensus. For example, economic development and growth policies are classed in 338.9; welfare policies in 361.6. Public policy in matters outside the social sciences is normally classed in public administration, e.g., art policy 353.7, not 700. However, a policy with civil rights implications will be classed with civil rights in 323, e.g., religious policy 323.44, not 200 or 353.7. Be alert for exceptions given elsewhere in the schedules, e.g., public policy for libraries 021.8.

For policy formulation, there is a choice between the interdisciplinary number 320 and the public administration number 352.3. The former covers how society as a whole makes up its mind; the latter concerns details of how an executive decides upon policies and gets them carried out. Governments usually, but not always, make up the leading parties in policy formulation, e.g., presidents, governors, courts, and legislatures at various levels. Hence the distinction must be made between policy formulation led or mediated by agencies in two or more branches of government (320) and that conducted by executive agencies (352.3). Policy formulation in a specific field by "the government" or society is classed with the policy as explained above, but policy formulation by executive agencies in specific fields is classed in 352–354.

For example, class a work about what civil rights policies are or should be, and on how society as a whole decides what they should be, in 323; however, class a work on how to administer civil rights policies or a work on how a civil rights agency resolves policy issues in 353.4.

If in doubt about a work other than a nomination hearing, prefer the number outside public administration.

Nomination hearings

One exception to the rule on hearings on public policy is nomination hearings. Because it is difficult to determine whether emphasis is on matters like personal qualifications and administrative issues or on the policies that the agency should carry out, all nominations for executive officers are classed in 352–354. Class nominations for the head of an agency in the field that the agency administers.

See also discussion at T1—068 vs. 353–354.

300 vs. 600

Social sciences vs. Technology (Applied sciences)

Many topics can be discussed from either a technological or a social point of view. If a work discusses how to make, operate, maintain, or repair something, it is normally classed in technology. If, on the other hand, it discusses the social implications of a technological operation, it falls in the social sciences, e.g., the economics of agriculture 338.1, not 630 (where the technology of agriculture is found).

The following criteria will be useful in determining what material should be classed in 300 rather than 600:

1. When the emphasis is on the social use or effect of the topic rather than on operating or processing it, e.g., how the automobile has affected modern society 303.48, how to drive an automobile 629.28.

2. When the emphasis is on the overall perspective, e.g., the value of solar heating 333.792, not 621.47.

3. When the emphasis is on social control as opposed to the control exercised during the manufacturing process, e.g., standards of drug quality imposed by a government agency or a trade association 363.19, not 615.

4. When raw statistics are cited, e.g., crop production 338.1, not 630.

Interdisciplinary works

Generally speaking, the 300 number is the interdisciplinary number for a phenomenon of social significance; it is used as the place of last resort for general works on a subject lacking disciplinary focus, e.g., a work on the history of clothing that does not emphasize how the clothing was made 391, not 646.4 or 687. However, works that emphasize descriptions of products or structures, such as clocks, locomotives, windmills, are classed in technology.

Biography and company history

Works on artisans, engineers, and inventors are usually classed in technology. Works on artisans, engineers, and inventors who are more of interest as entrepreneurs are classed in 338.7. Descriptions of the products of a company, such as Ford trucks, are classed in technology (which includes the 700s when the products under examination are not found in the 600s). However, when the organization or history of the company receives significant attention, class the works in 338.7, e.g., Ford trucks 629.223, the Ford Motor Company 338.7.

Technical reports

Many technical and research reports actually emphasize procedural technicalities and may refer to economic, legal, administrative, or regulatory complexities. Such reports should be classed in the social sciences. In determining the classification of a report series, and of individual reports in a series, consider the purpose of the writer and the mission of the agency authorizing the reports. If the emphasis is on the exercise of social control over a process, the report is classed in 300, not with the process in technology which is being controlled. For example, water quality monitoring systems are more likely to be classed in 363.739 than 628.1.

Most of the social sciences are involved in technological processes, but are quite distinct from them. The classifier must go behind the technological vocabulary that often dominates title pages and tables of contents and analyze what is being described. If a book describes how railroads serve Argentina, it is classed in

385.0982 (*not* 625.100982); a report on fertilizer and rice studying production efficiency in developing countries is classed in 338.1 (*not* 633.1).

301–307 vs. 361–365

[Sociology and anthropology] vs. Social problems and services

Use 301–307 for social problems when they are discussed primarily as social phenomena, rather than as matters that society should take action to solve.

Consideration of social pathology apart from remedial measures is often found in 301–307, but is more likely to be considered in connection with actual and potential remedies found in the 361–365 span. The family as a social phenomenon is classed in 306.85. The dissolution of the family can be classed in either 306.88 or 362.82 depending on the focus of the work. A work discussing the effect of the changing social role of women in bringing about family dissolution is classed at 306.88. When the work discusses the actual and potential remedies for the topic, then the work is classed in 362.82, e.g., what can or should be done to prevent family dissolution 362.82. If in doubt, prefer 301–307.

Criminal anthropology (criminal sociology) is found in 364.2.

302–307 vs. 150, T1—01

Specific topics in sociology and anthropology vs. Psychology [and Table 1 notation for] Philosophy and theory

Psychology and social psychology

Class in 150 works that focus on the individual, including those that discuss the influence of group behavior on the individual. Class in 302–307 works that focus on group behavior, including those that discuss the role of the individual in group behavior. If in doubt, prefer 302–307.

While application of psychology to any subject is classed in with the subject plus notation 01 from Table 1, application of social psychology to a subject is classed in the social sciences (most often in 302–307) without adding notation 01. For example, class individual psychology of religion in 200.1, social psychology of religion in 306.6. If in doubt, prefer 302–307.

302–307 vs. 155.9, 158.2

Specific topics in sociology and anthropology vs. Environmental psychology vs. [Applied psychology of] Interpersonal relations

Class in 155.9 the influence of family, friends, and other people upon the individual. Class in 158.2 the art of getting along with people. Class in 302–307 social interaction regarded as group behavior. If in doubt, prefer 302–307.

When a work treats both the psychology of social influences (155.9) and social interaction (302–307), prefer 302–307, e.g., the influence of a rural community on individuals and interactions within a rural community 307.72 (*not* 155.9).

302–307 vs. 320

Specific topics in sociology and anthropology vs. Political science (Politics and government)

Some works on major social institutions, processes, and phenomena may have a decidedly political cast, but if they emphasize how the social topics are related to and manifested in political ones, they are classed in 302–307. For example, a work on the relation between the feminist movement and the enfranchisement of women is classed in 305.42, not 324.6. If in doubt, prefer 302–307.

303.48 vs. 306.4

Causes of change vs. Specific aspects of culture

Social effects of science and technology

Class in 303.48 the effects of scientific discoveries and technological innovations upon society, e.g., a work on the transformation of religious, economic, and leisure institutions stemming from the development of electronic media 303.48. Class in 306.4 the patterns of behavior of the individuals and groups engaged in scientific or technical endeavors, e.g., a description of the milieu which seems to be conducive to technological innovation 306.4. If in doubt, prefer 303.48.

305

Social groups

It is the policy of the Decimal Classification Division not to add notation 08 from Table 1 to numbers in 305 unless otherwise instructed.

305 vs. 306, 909, 930–990

Social groups vs. Culture and institutions vs. World history [and] History of ancient world, of specific continents, countries, localities; of extraterrestrial worlds

305 is the comprehensive number for social groups interacting more or less freely with the rest of society. The role of social groups in specific institutions of society, however, is classed with the institution in 306 plus notation 08 from Table 1, e.g., women as a social category 305.4, but women in the family 306.85082; improvement of the status of gays in society 305.9, but sexual institutions and orientation of gays 306.76. The role of social groups in history is classed in 909 and 930–990. The history of specific social groups, particularly that part of their history that is called their civilization, is more troublesome. Class in 909 and 930–990 only accounts of the major events shaping the history and civilization of a group. Normally, "history" is written only about racial, ethnic, and national groups, while "civilization" of all social groups tends to equate more with their culture (broadly conceived) than with the major events of their history. But be alert for exceptions: histories of major events, and

description of nonanthropological civilization can be written for any group. If in doubt between 305 and 909, 930–990, prefer 305; if in doubt between 305 and 306, prefer 306.

305.8 vs. 306.08

Racial, ethnic, national groups [as social groups] vs. [Culture and institutions of] Indigenous racial, ethnic, national groups

Use 305.8 as the comprehensive number for specific racial, ethnic, national groups which interact more or less freely (whether in a dominant, nondominant, or intermediate position) with the rest of society. Use 306.08 only for indigenous groups living in distinct communities or "tribal areas" not fully integrated into the economic and social life of the nation in which they are (often involuntarily) incorporated. Such groups are normally perceived as culturally autonomous societies with their own distinctive cultures and institutions. If in doubt, prefer 305.8.

305.81

North Americans

Use this number for (a) comprehensive works on all the peoples of North America, (b) the people of Canada (305.811) and the United States (305.813) as national groups, (c) North Americans of British origin, and (d) Canadians of French origin (305.811). Works on noncitizens of British origin in either Canada or the United States are classed in 305.82; on noncitizens of French origin in Canada, in 305.84. Works focusing on other national or ethnic groups in North America are also classed elsewhere in 305.8, e.g., people of French origin in the United States 305.84, Mexicans as a national group 305.868, the Inuit 305.897.

305.9 vs. 305.5

Occupational and miscellaneous groups vs. Social classes

Social classes take precedence over occupational and miscellaneous groups. Therefore, whenever a group found in 305.9 is considered in terms of its specific social status, 305.5 must be used. Use 305.9 for works on its component groups when there is little or no emphasis on class, the group is well represented in two or more distinct classes, or the group has an indefinite or transitional status. If in doubt, prefer 305.9.

306.7 vs. 155.3

Institutions pertaining to relations of the sexes vs. Sex psychology and psychology of the sexes

Most works on the psychology of sexual relations treat social psychological aspects—the interaction between the partners. Such works are classed in 306.7. Only an occasional work emphasizes the psychology of the individual and is therefore classed in 155.3, e.g., a work that focuses on the anxieties of the individual with regard to sexual relations. In case of doubt, prefer 306.7.

307

Communities

This section includes works on the community in a relatively restricted area as a social phenomenon and works on community planning, development, and redevelopment. These terms are used here in their ordinary meaning to imply the planning for and development of the community as a whole. When specific subjects of community interest are addressed, the work is classed elsewhere in 300, e.g., economic development of the community 338.93–.99, developing hospitals for the community 362.1, planning community housing 363.5, planning the city water supply 363.6, planning the education system 379.4–.9.

320

Political science (Politics and government)

The state and government

The concepts of "the state" and "government" are emphasized in varying proportions in the subdivisions in 320–323. The state refers to the politically organized body of people occupying a more or less definite territory, while government (in the sense relevant here) is the organization through which the state exercises its authority and functions. The state may be considered an abstraction, the government its concrete embodiment. Comprehensive works on the abstraction are classed in 320.1; specific kinds of states in 321; and the relation of the state to people (and *vice versa*) in 322–323, e.g., political rights 323.5.

In contrast to "the state," the concept of "government" is more central to political science, and the word is often used loosely as an approximate equivalent of political science; therefore, it has no separate number. However, specific aspects do have separate numbers, notably comparative government in 320.3, structure and functions of government in 320.4, and kinds of government in 321.3–.9.

320 vs. 306.2

Political science (Politics and government) vs. [Sociology of] Political institutions

Be alert for works that discuss not politics and government but the dynamics of political institutions. The basic thrust of 306.2 is to find out the social sources (e.g., race, class, family) and the social processes of political institutions, or the impact of these institutions and their activity on the social environment. In addition, it is used for works dealing with political institutions and processes as models for social institutions and processes. In contrast, the objective in 320 is the descriptive, comparative, historical, and theoretical study of political institutions and processes. In these political studies, the social environment is considered only as a background. If in doubt, prefer 320.

320.5 vs. 297.09, 322

Political ideologies vs. Historical, geographic, persons treatment [of Islam] vs. Relation of the state to organized groups and their members

Islamic fundamentalism

Class in 297.09 and other subdivisions of 297 only works that emphasize religious aspects of Islamic fundamentalism, such as concern to maintain and hand down a pure version of Islamic faith, a mindfulness to follow the strict letter of the Koran and Hadith, and an attempt to generate a religious awakening through preaching, teaching, and other forms of religious communication. Class in 297.2, the number for Islam and politics, only works that treat politics from a religious point of view.

Many works about Islamic fundamentalism, however, emphasize political aspects from a secular point of view; such works are classed in political science. Works emphasizing the religiously oriented political ideologies of Islamic fundamentalism are classed in 320.5. Works emphasizing the political role of Islamic fundamentalist organizations and groups in relation to the state are classed in 322.

If in doubt between a political science number and a subdivision of 297, prefer a political science number. If in doubt between 320.5 and 322, prefer 320.5.

320.9, 320.4 vs. 351

Political situation and conditions [and] Structure and functions of government vs. Public administration

The terms "government" and "public administration" can be easily confused and are sometimes used interchangeably. In the Dewey Decimal Classification, however, they are kept quite distinct. Government is limited to top-level considerations: the nature, role, goals, structure of states; their political direction and control; and the critical matter of forms by which central controls are exercised and balanced against each other. Public administration concentrates on executive agencies and the procedures used to carry out their goals, policies, and actions in various fields.

Of the several numbers in 320 concerning different aspects of government, 320.4 is the one most often confused with public administration. It includes works on the overall structure of governments, emphasizing their chief legislative, judicial, and executive organs. It may be used for works that discuss typical activities of the different branches, e.g., regulating safety as an illustration of the police function. It is also used for comprehensive works on government and public administration of specific areas. However, it should not be used for works emphasizing the work of carrying out goals and policies. Interdisciplinary works on government and public administration not limited to specific areas are classed in 320.

Some works that seem to cover the activities of government are simply discussing the habitual conduct and methods of people in high office, and should be classed in 320.9.

Most works that should be classed in 351 will clearly emphasize agencies of the executive branch, or the usual components of administration: planning, organizing, staffing, financing, and equipping agencies to do a job.

If in doubt, prefer 320.4 or 320.9 over 351, and 320.9 over 320.4.

322 vs. 261.7, 291.1

Relation of state to organized groups and their members vs. Christianity and political affairs [and] Religious mythology, social theology, interreligious relations and attitudes

Religion and the state

261.7, 291.1 and related numbers in 292–299 are in social theology, and are used for works on the position that religious people and organizations take or should take toward political affairs (including the state). 322 is used for works with a secular perspective, discussing the relationships between religious organizations or movements and states or governments. If in doubt, prefer 322.

322 vs. 296.3, 320.54095694

Relation of the state to organized groups and their members vs. [Jewish] Theology, ethics, view of social issues vs. [Nationalism in] Palestine   Israel

Judaism and politics

Class in 296.3 works concerning politics and the state from the point of view of the religion of Judaism, e.g., whether it is a religious duty to support civil rights, whether Judaism encourages political freedom. Class political ideologies which are inspired by Judaism with Zionism in 320.54095694. Class the relation of religious groups to the state from the secular viewpoint in 322, e.g., religion and state in Israel. If in doubt between 296.3 and a political science number, prefer a political science number. If in doubt between 320.54095694 and 322, prefer 322.

324 vs. 320.5, 320.9

The political process vs. Political ideologies vs. Political situation and conditions

Political movements

The word "movement" is used in various different senses in each of these numbers, and a given ideological movement may be treated in subdivisions of any one of them, depending upon the emphasis of the work. Use 320.5 for works concerning the thought and internal history or dynamics of such movements,

324 for their attempts to achieve power by nonviolent means and their ventures into electoral politics (even as splinter parties with scant chance of success), and 320.9 for the impact of the movements upon the political system and their interaction with other political forces. Class comprehensive works on specific ideological movements in 320.5, but if in doubt, give preference first to 324, then to 320.9. However, also consider history numbers for movements which come to power or directly affect the major events of history.

See also discussion at 909, 930–990 vs. 320.

324.2094–.2099 and 324.24–.29

Treatment [of political parties] by specific continents [and] Parties in specific countries in modern world

For political parties, the three kinds of areas that are usually treated in a single span (continents, countries, localities) are treated in three different ways. They are differentiated because the country (nation) is the main effective unit of political activity, and thus of party life and power. In most countries the local party is a branch of the national party, or, at most, a local organization of persons who regard themselves as members of a national party. Treatment by locality within a country is classed in the country number, with use of standard subdivision 009 (under country notation) or T1—09 (after party notation) at the appropriate point, e.g., the parties of Scotland 324.241009411, the Liberal party in London 324.2410609421. However, for Australia, Canada, and the United States, each of which has strong traditions of autonomy for state and provincial parties, the states and their parties are treated like "countries" rather than like "localities."

Treatment of parties in general by continent and by region larger than a specific country is classed in 324.209, while treatment of specific kinds of parties (e.g., socialist parties) in such regions is classed in 324.2 without further subdivision.

330 vs. 650

Economics vs. Management and auxiliary services

Works about business can be classed in several places. Most often the choice is between 330 and 650. Use 330 if the work presents general information, economic conditions, financial information (such as interest rates), and reports on what certain companies are doing. Use 650 when the work presents only practical managerial information that covers 651 Office services as well as 658 General management. If the work is limited to general management, use 658. Class comprehensive works on 330 and 650 in 330. If in doubt, prefer 330.

331 vs. 331.8

Labor economics vs. Labor unions (Trade unions), labor-management (collective) bargaining and disputes

Industrial relations in the broad sense of all relations between management and individual employees or employee groups are classed in 331. Industrial relations in the narrow sense of relations between management and labor unions are classed in 331.8. If in doubt, prefer 331.

331 vs. 658.3

Labor economics vs. Personnel management

Many of the topics in 658.3 are paralleled in 331. Class in 658.3 works written from the viewpoint of management, in 331 works written from the viewpoint of the employee (the worker). Also class in 331 works written from a neutral standpoint, simply describing the phenomena, and comprehensive works including both management and employee views. If in doubt, prefer 331.

331.1 vs. 331.11, 331.12

Labor force and market vs. Labor force vs. Labor market

Class comprehensive works on labor force and labor market in 331.1. Class works that discuss the labor force only in relation to the demand for labor in 331.12. Also class employment and the part of the labor force that is actively employed in 331.12. If in doubt, prefer 331.1.

Class comprehensive works on employment and unemployment in 331.1; however, class works that merely give the number and characteristics of employed and unemployed workers without discussing the labor market in 331.11. If in doubt, prefer 331.1.

331.12 vs. 331.13

Labor market vs. Maladjustments in labor market

Government labor policies and programs

Class in 331.12 government labor policies and programs discussed in terms of broader purposes than just combating unemployment, e.g., public service employment as a countercyclical measure to provide both jobs for the unemployed and assistance to distressed areas and state and local governments. Class in 331.13 works about government labor policies and programs that discuss them solely in terms of prevention and relief of unemployment. If in doubt, prefer 331.12.

331.2 vs. 331.89

Conditions of employment vs. Labor-management (Collective) bargaining and disputes

Class the process of collective bargaining on compensation and other conditions of employment in 331.89. Class the compensation and other conditions that result in 331.2. Class comprehensive works in 331.2.

332, 336 vs. 339

Financial economics [and] Public finance vs. Macroeconomics and related topics

Macroeconomics is the study of the economy as a whole, especially with reference to its general level of output and income and the interrelationships among sectors of the economy. Some topics appearing in 332 and 336 are considered in macroeconomics (339). These topics, however, will be classed in 339 only when they are clearly discussed in relation to the total economic picture of a country or region. For example, monetary policy, normally 332.4, is classed in 339.5 when undertaken primarily to carry out macroeconomic policy. If in doubt, prefer 332 and 336.

332 vs. 338, 658.15

Financial economics vs. Production vs. Financial management

The choice among 332, 338, and 658.15 depends upon the point of view from which the topics are treated. Class in 332 works treating financial topics from the viewpoint of people or organizations with money to invest and those who serve them—investors, bankers, stockbrokers, and the like. Class in 338 works that treat financial topics from the viewpoint of people concerned with the production of goods and services, people who are interested in capital because it is necessary for production. For example, class in 332.67 (investments by field of investment, kind of enterprise, kind of investor) a work discussing whether mining is a safe and profitable field of investment for the general public; but class in 338.2 (extraction of minerals) a work discussing whether the mining industry will attract enough investment to expand production. Class in 658.15 (or with the subject plus notation 068 from Table 1) works that treat financial topics from the viewpoint of an executive responsible for the financial management of an organization, works that focus narrowly on managerial concerns. If in doubt, prefer 332.

332.024 vs. 640

Personal finance vs. Home economics and family living

Class in 640 works that deal only with everyday household finance, e.g., how to control day-to-day expenditures, how to budget for rent and groceries. Class in 332.024 works that are broader in scope, e.g., how to plan for one's financial future, including such topics as insurance and IRAs (Individual Retirement Accounts). Class interdisciplinary works in 332.024.

332.7 vs. 332.1

Credit vs. Banks

At 332.7 credit is divided by the type of credit, e.g., agricultural credit, home finance, personal loans, credit cards. At 332.1 (including 332.2 and 332.3, which are logically subordinate to 332.1), credit is divided by the type of financial institution offering it as a service, e.g., commercial banks, savings and loan associations, consumer finance institutions, insurance companies. Comprehensive works on a particular type of credit are classed in 332.7, e.g., a work discussing home mortgages as issued by commercial banks, mutual savings banks, savings and loan associations, and insurance companies. Comprehensive works on the credit offered by a particular type of institution and works discussing only one type of credit offered by a particular type of institution are both classed with the institution in 332.1–.3. For example, a work discussing all the kinds of loans and debit cards available from savings and loan associations and a work discussing the home mortgages available from savings and loan associations are both classed in 332.3. Similarly, comprehensive works on credit cards offered by commercial banks, department stores, oil companies, and travel agencies are classed in 332.7, but works about credit cards issued by commercial banks are classed in 332.1. If in doubt, prefer 332.7.

333.7–.9 vs. 333

[Natural resources and energy] vs. Economics of land and energy

Use 333 for comprehensive works on natural resources only if the works contain substantial discussion of ownership. Use 333.7–.9 for comprehensive works on natural resources that treat predominantly nonownership aspects. If in doubt, prefer 333.7–.9.

It is more common for comprehensive works on land than for comprehensive works on other natural resources to be classed in 333 because it is more common for comprehensive works on land to contain substantial discussion of ownership.

See also discussion at 333.73–.78 vs. 333, 333.1–.5.

333.7–.9 vs. 363.1, 363.73, 577

[Natural resources and energy] vs. Public safety programs vs. Pollution vs. Ecology

Social aspects of ecology

Many works on ecology and specific natural environments are more about public policy and resource economics than biology. Terms that indicate a possible emphasis on economic and social problems are biodiversity, conservation, development, environmental impacts and monitoring, natural resource management, and risk assessment. Specific numbers to consider for these terms are:

1. For biodiversity: 333.95 (especially for works emphasizing its value or importance).

2. For conservation: 333.7 or the number for the specific resource, e.g., conservation of biodiversity 333.95.

3. For development: 333.7 or the number for the specific resource, e.g., hydroelectric power development 333.91.

4. For environmental impacts and monitoring:

A. The resource situation in general: 333.7 or the number for the specific resource, e.g., monitoring biodiversity 333.95;

B. Environmental impacts: 333.7 or the number for the specific resource, e.g., monitoring the impact of reclamation projects on wetlands 333.91;

C. Potential environmental impacts: Class with the development whose impact is being studied, e.g., the potential impact of an oil pipeline on tundra ecology 388.5;

D. Pollution levels: 363.73 or the number for the specific kind of pollutant or environment, e.g. monitoring oil pollution 363.73. (The *impact* of pollution, however, is classed in 333.7–.9 as instructed under 4.B above, e.g., monitoring the impact of oil pollution on wetlands 333.91.)

5. For natural resource management: 333.7 or the number for the specific resource, e.g., management of wetlands 333.91. (Resource management is considered to approximate the whole of 333.7 or of the numbers for specific resources.)

6. For risk assessment:

A. Generalized risks to the environment: Treat as an impact study and class in 333.7 or the number for the specific resource, e.g., contemporary risks to wetlands of America 333.91;

B. Risks of specific developments: Treat as a study of potential impacts, and class with the specific development, e.g., assessing the risk of tourism to biodiversity in East Africa 916.7604;

C. Safety risks: Use the subdivision for the specific threat in 363.1, e.g., assessing the risk to humans of pesticides in food 363.19.

If in doubt, prefer 333.7–.9, 363.1, and 363.73, in that order.

See also discussion at 363.73 vs. 571.9, 577.27.

333.7–.9 vs. 363.6

[Natural resources and energy] vs. Public utilities and related services

Use care in distinguishing between the resources and energy (333.7–.9) and the utilities delivering the resources to customers (363.6). For instance, class in 333.7–.9 comprehensive works on resources, projection of needs and supplies, development, conservation, protection of resources. Class in 363.6 problems and services related to distributing the resources to users. A useful device in distinguishing the two is to consider that "supply" as a noun is classed in 333.7–.9, while "supply" as a verb is classed in 363.6. If in doubt, class in 333.7–.9.

An exception is made for electrical power companies. Works about these utilities almost always emphasize the problems of developing the "supply" as a noun, saying little about the problems of distributing the electricity to customers, and seldom discuss prices without reference to production costs. A work about electrical power utilities focusing on distribution should be classed in 333.793 with the bulk of works about electrical power companies.

Class the rationing of natural resources still in their natural state at 333.7 and related numbers in 333.7–.9, but of final products in 363, e.g., wellhead allocation of natural gas for companies or jurisdictions 333.8, but rationing of natural gas among consumers or classes of consumers at the other end of the line 363.6. If in doubt, prefer 333.7–.9.

333.7–.9 vs. 508, 913–919, 930–990

[Natural resources and energy] vs. Natural history vs. Geography of and travel in ancient world and specific continents, countries, localities in modern world; extraterrestrial worlds vs. History of ancient world; of specific continents, countries, localities; of extraterrestrial worlds

National parks and monuments

Class general guidebooks to all the national parks of an area in 913–919 plus notation 04 from the add table at 913–919, e.g., a 1997 general guidebook to the national parks of South America 918.04.

Class general works about historical monuments with the events commemorated. For example, class a battlefield national park with the battle, e.g., Gettysburg National Military Park 973.7. Class a park associated with the life of an individual in the biography number for that individual, e.g., Lyndon B. Johnson National Historical Park 973.923092, George Washington Carver National Monument 630.92.

For works on national parks where the main attraction is nature, use 333.7–.9 if the emphasis is on conservation and protection of natural resources, e.g., forest parks 333.78, game reserves 333.95. If the emphasis is on description of and guides to natural phenomena, use 508 or related numbers in the 500s, e.g., a comprehensive guide to the natural history of Yellowstone National Park 508.787, a guide to the geology of Yellowstone 557.87.

If in doubt, prefer 333.7–.9 over 508 and related numbers or 900; prefer 508 and related numbers over 900; prefer 930–990 over 913–919.

See also discussion at 913–919; also at 930–990.

333.7 vs. 304.2, 363.7

Natural resources and energy vs. Human ecology vs. Environmental problems and services

"Environmentalism" refers to two different sets of issues. Use 363.7 when the issues are preserving and restoring the quality of the social living space, i.e., taking care of waste, pollution, noise, the dead, and pests. Use 333.7 for the broader concept of preserving and protecting the supply as well as the quality of natural resources. Works about the environmental movement that focus on the concerns it shares with the long established conservation movement are classed in 333.7. Use 304.2 for works that emphasize the effect upon society of overuse, misuse, or pollution of the environment. If in doubt between 333.7 and either 363.7 or 304.2, prefer 333.7. If in doubt between 304.2 and 363.7, prefer 304.2.

333.73–.78 vs. 333, 333.1–.5

[Land] vs. Economics of land and energy vs. Ownership of land

Land as property is classed in 333.1–.5, where the central issues are the right to possession and use, and the right to transfer possession and use. The only control of land that belongs in 333.1–.5 is the control that stems from ownership.

Land as a natural resource, as a source of economic goods (chiefly agricultural and mineral), is classed in 333.73–.78. The usage of the land and its resources is classed there, as distinct from the right to use that is classed in 333.1–.5. The controls of usage that hold regardless of who owns the land, e.g., price control and zoning, are classed in 333.73–.78. Comprehensive works on land policy are classed in 333.73.

Land inventories often focus on land as a resource and land usage; such inventories are classed in 333.73–.78.

Comprehensive works on both 333.1–.5 and 333.73–.78 concepts are classed in 333 only if they contain substantial discussion of ownership. If in doubt, prefer 333.73–.78.

See also discussion at 333.7–.9 vs. 333.

333.95 vs. 639.9

Biological resources vs. Conservation [technology] of biological resources

Conservation and management of specific kinds of animals

When determining whether works on specific kinds of animals should be classed in economics (333.95) or technology (639.9), one should bear in mind that conservation and resource management are primarily economic concepts. Discussion of public policy and programs; estimates or statistics of populations, abundance, harvest, catches, and kills; appeals for resource management; and calls to protect an animal or save it from extinction are all signs that a work belongs in economics.

A few terms used in conservation work are troublesome because they may refer to either economics or technology. Class works on rescue, reintroduction, management, and habitat improvement in technology only if they are focused on hands-on activities where the animals are living. Class the works in economics if they are focused on programs and the rationale behind the activities.

If in doubt, class in 333.95.

335 vs. 306.3, 320.53

Socialism and related systems [of economics] vs. [Sociology of] Economic systems vs. Collectivism and fascism [as political ideologies]

Socialism

Since socialism and related systems are based upon theories of how the economy does or should work, interdisciplinary works and works on their philosophic foundations are classed in 335. The number is also used for wide-ranging works that do not fit within normal disciplinary boundaries but are clearly about socialism and related systems. Other numbers are used only for works clearly limited to a specific discipline.

Use 320.53 for works that emphasize how political movements intend to introduce socialism and what political forces they expect to harness to attain and keep power, or that discuss political movements and forces without in-depth discussion of the economic dynamics or theory. Works on political ideology often discuss questions such as the class bias or motivation of political forces, the dependability of political allies of different economic background, and progress (or lack of it) toward economic goals, but do not usually get into economics *per se*.

In contrast to 306.3, both the other numbers may include material that is prescriptive, that says how society, the economy, or the political system ought to be organized. 306.3 is intended for sociological studies of how socialist economic systems work out in practice. It should be limited to such studies. Works discussing how another economic system should be reorganized into a socialist system must be classed in 335.

336 vs. 352.4

Public finance vs. Financial administration and budgets

Class in 352.4 works focusing on the practical aspects and details of financial management and accounting in the public sector. For example, class financial control, debt management, and government budgets in 352.4. Class in 336 works on the economics of public finance, e.g., economic analyses of government spending policy 336.3. Class works treating both public finance and public financial administration in 336.

336.249 vs. 368.4

Social security taxes [in public finance] vs. Government-sponsored insurance

Class broad economic, public finance, tax policy aspects of social security taxes in 336.249. Class actuarial and administrative aspects of finance, of rates and rate making for social security in 368.4. If in doubt, prefer 336.249.

337.3–.9 vs. 337.1

Foreign economic policies and relations of specific jurisdictions and groups of jurisdictions vs. Multilateral economic cooperation

Class cooperative relations among the states of multistate groups in 337.1, e.g., cooperation within the European Union in 337.1; but class relations between a cooperative group treated as a whole and other countries or groups in 337.3–.9, e.g., economic relations of the European Union with Japan 337.4052 (*not* 337.1), economic relations of the European Union with the rest of the world 337.4 (*not* 337.1). If in doubt, prefer 337.3–.9.

338 vs. 060, 381, 382, 670.29, 910, T1—025, T1—029

Production vs. General organizations and museology vs. Internal commerce (Domestic trade) vs. International commerce (Foreign trade) vs. Commercial miscellany [of manufacturers] vs. Geography and travel vs. [Table 1 notation for] Directories of persons and organizations vs. [Table 1 notation for] Commercial miscellany

1. Directories

Business directories should be classed in business numbers, usually 338 or 381–382, while nonbusiness directories should be classed in nonbusiness numbers in 001–999. There are many qualifications about what constitutes business directories; thus, the following guidelines need to be considered.

2. Directories of products and services

Product directories

Class comprehensive directories of manufacturers that emphasize the products for sale and give little information about the companies beyond address and phone number (the basic information needed to help the buyer obtain and use the product) in 670.29.

Directories listing services

Class directories that include a wide range of services as well as products in 338 or 338.4, depending upon coverage, even though they are aimed at end users and give little information about the companies beyond that needed to help buyers obtain goods and services.

Directories including economic or organizational information

Class in 338.7 directories of manufacturers and/or other enterprises that in addition to information about products and services give an approximately equal amount of economic and/or organizational information about individual enterprises (that is, information intended for people who might want to invest in the companies, go into joint ventures with them, hire them as subcontractors, or serve as sales representatives for them). Directories that give information about the ownership of companies, approximate worth of companies, names of companies' bankers, for example, as well as the product information, belong to this category.

Directories of importers and exporters

Class product directories of importers and exporters (which are usually aimed at establishing trade relationships between importers in one country and exporters in another) in 382.

Retail directories

Class retail directories (often called commercial directories or industrial buyers' guides) in 381.

3. Directories of persons and organizations

Class directories that give details of the internal organization of, or list the directors of, business enterprises in 338.7, 338.8, or 334, plus notation 025 from Table 1, regardless of the field of operation of the enterprises. However, class comprehensive directories on all types of organizations, comprehensive directories on nonbusiness organizations, and directories of specific general noncommercial organizations in 060. Class directories of *nonbusiness* organizations limited to a specific subject with the subject plus notation 025 from Table 1. Class a combined organizational handbook and membership directory with the subject plus notation 06 from Table 1, even if the membership part predominates. However, if the organizational part consists of only a few preliminary pages followed by an extensive directory of members, then the work may be more useful classed as a directory of the organization with the subject plus notation 025 from Table 1.

Class local telephone and city directories in 914–919 plus notation 0025 from table under 913–919; and international telephone directories not limited to one continent in 910.25. Class yellow pages published in connection with city or telephone directories with the city or telephone directory.

Class all other directories of persons with the subject in 001–999 plus notation 025 from Table 1.

See also discussion at 380.1 and 381, 382: Commercial miscellany.

338.092

[Business biography]

Class a biography of an entrepreneur or business leader associated with a specific business enterprise, e.g., the founder of a cosmetics manufacturing company, in 338.7. Class biographies of business leaders not limited to a specific enterprise but limited to a specific field in 338.1–.4, e.g., business leaders in the automotive manufacturing industry 338.4. Class biographies of people associated with the development and operation of specific types of enterprises but not confined to a specific industry or group of industries in 338.6–.8, e.g., small-business owners 338.6, persons associated with trusts 338.8. Class company directors on the boards of companies in several industries or groups of industries in 338.7092.

Class collected biography of entrepreneurs in many fields in 338. Class collected biography of businessmen in many fields in 338.092.

338.1 vs. 333.75

Agriculture vs. Forest lands

Timber as a product or resource

Several of the concepts provided at 333.75 by virtue of the scatter reference at 333.7 potentially conflict with concepts provided at 338.1, e.g., supply and demand. The general distinction is that works classed in 333.75 are primarily concerned with forest land and uncut timber as present and future resources, whereas works classed in 338.1 are primarily concerned with cut timber as a product to be sold. Class comprehensive works in 338.1.

338.1 vs. 631.5

[Economics of] Agriculture vs. Cultivation and harvesting

Crop yields

Usually works on crop yields are compilations giving the total production of an area, and are classed in 338.1. Works on yields per unit of area are classed in 338.1 if they are taken as indicators of production efficiency, either of agricultural systems using various methods (e.g., crop rotation) or of agricultural systems prevailing in various areas. If yield studies per unit of area are used in technical tests of varieties or specific production techniques, they are classed with the subject in agriculture, e.g., yield tests of fertilizer use 631.8028. Use of 631.5 is limited to works that have little or no economic or testing implications, e.g., lists of record yields of various crops. If in doubt, class in 338.1.

338.3 vs. 333.95

Other extractive industries vs. biological resources

Animals as products or resources

Several of the concepts provided at 333.95 by virtue of the scatter reference at 333.9 potentially conflict with concepts provided at 338.3, e.g., reserves (stock, supply), development. To distinguish between the two numbers, apply the same general criteria as explained at 338.1 vs. 333.75. For example, class the supply of uncaught animals in 333.95. Class the supply of caught animals in 338.3. Works classed in 333.95 may, however, use statistics of catches as an aid in estimating the population of uncaught animals. Class comprehensive works in 338.3.

Class measures to increase the supply of animals in nature as a long-term resource in 333.95, e.g., stocking mountain streams with fish. Class the culture of nondomesticated animals viewed as a way to produce crops that can be harvested and sold in 338.3. Do not use 338.3 for measures to increase the supply of animals.

If in doubt, prefer 338.3.

338.9 vs. 352.7, 500

Economic development and growth vs. Administration of general forms of assistance vs. Natural sciences and mathematics

Science policy

"Science policy" generally focuses on what society should do to promote the utilization of science and the growth of industries and activities based on science. Thus, it generally should be regarded as a policy or program to promote economic development and growth (338.9 and 338.93–.99). Class works on public administration of science policy in 352.7 and numbers for specific fields of public administration in 352–354. If there is an emphasis on administration of economic development use 354. In the absence of a focus on the social sciences, use 509 for natural science policy in an area. If in doubt, prefer 338.9.

339.4 vs. 332.4

Factors affecting national product, wealth, income vs. Money

Purchasing power

Class in 332.4 works on purchasing power that focus on the value of money as measured by the goods and services it can buy. Class in 339.4 works on purchasing power that focus on the ability of consumers to buy. If in doubt, prefer 339.4.

340

Law

Forms of legal literature

Three general forms of literature may be distinguished in this field:

1. the laws themselves as promulgated by a body officially authorized to do so;

2. decisions of the courts or other adjudicative bodies on matters of dispute that arise under these laws;

3. treatises written on various aspects of the laws.

The first two of these, laws and decisions, are considered to be original materials. Treatises are derivative in nature and are considered to be secondary. A special section (348) has been provided for original materials and guides to them when such materials are not confined to any specific branch or subject in law. Original materials that are confined to a specific branch or subject are classed with that branch or subject. Treatises have no special section; they are classed in 349 if dealing with the total law of a jurisdiction, or in the number for the specific branch or subject.

Law and aboriginal groups

Certain groups, such as the aborigines of Australia and the native peoples of the United States, had legal systems of their own prior to their incorporation into the national systems of other groups. Such laws are classed in 340.5. Class laws of such groups on a specific subject with the subject in 342–347, e.g., family law of North American native peoples 346.01.

Class in international law the relations between aboriginal groups and a nation established in their territory before their incorporation into the nation, e.g., treaties between the United States and native American peoples on territorial matters 341.4.

Relations between an aboriginal group and a nation established in its territory after its incorporation into the nation are classed in the regular numbers for the law of the jurisdiction, e.g., property law of Australia applied to land holdings of Australian aborigines 346.9404.

Terminology and notation used

To avoid cumbersome repetition, the phrase "the law of" is frequently omitted. Unless otherwise stated, law is understood. If, for example, the phrase "For public property, see 343" is used, it means that the law of public property is classed in 343. Similarly, in references to the law of specific subjects in 342–348 the number is given as it appears in the schedule, e.g., tax law 343.04. It is to be understood that in most instances, to use the same example, the number will actually be 343 plus notation from Table 2 plus 04.

340.02–.09 vs. 349

Standard subdivisions [of law] vs. Law of specific jurisdictions, areas, socioeconomic regions

Geographic treatment

The presence of a geographic concept does not automatically mean that the work must be classed in 349 instead of 340.02–.09. To be classed in 349, the book must emphasize that the law is limited to a specific jurisdiction. For example, even though the majority of the cases cited in *Black's Law Dictionary* are from the United States, it is classed in 340.03, general law dictionaries, instead of 349.7303, dictionaries of American law. A directory of Maryland lawyers may be classed either in 340.025 (for a directory of lawyers who can practice law not only in Maryland but in other parts of the United States but whose place of residence is in Maryland) or in 349.752025 (for a directory of lawyers who can practice in Maryland but whose place of residence need not be in Maryland). If in doubt, prefer 340.02–.09.

340.5 vs. 297.1

Legal systems vs. Sources of Islam

Islamic law

Class in 297.1 comprehensive works on Islamic law concerning religious matters, such as ritual purification, ritual prayer, fasting, zakat, the ḥajj, sacred places. Class Islamic law on a specific religious topic with the topic, e.g., fasting 297.5. Class Islamic law on religious topics in religion even if the laws are being enforced by the state rather than just by religious organizations.

Class in 340.5 comprehensive works on Islamic law concerning secular matters, such as contract law, criminal law, social welfare law, law of inheritance. Class Islamic law on a specific secular topic with the topic in 342–347, e.g., law of inheritance in Saudi Arabia 346.53805.

Class in 340.5 interdisciplinary works about Islamic law covering both religious and secular topics. If in doubt, prefer 340.5.

Some topics, such as family and marriage, have both religious and secular aspects. Works on the Islamic law of such topics are rarely limited to the religious aspects and thus rarely classed in religion. In particular, always class in 340 works about laws on such topics if the laws under discussion are enforced by the state. For example, class family law of Pakistan in 346.54901.

340.5 vs. 342–347

Legal systems vs. Branches of law

Civil law

Civil law has two meanings that must be distinguished. In one sense it is the name of a system of law derived from Roman law and in use to a greater or lesser extent in most countries in the modern world, e.g., Germany, France, Japan, Brazil, and even in some subordinate jurisdictions of countries that otherwise use another system, e.g., the province of Quebec in Canada and the state of Louisiana in the United States. It is frequently used in contrast to the other great systems of law, e.g., common law, though they are all classed in the same number 340.5. The more common meaning of the term is all law that is not international or criminal law, i.e., 342–344 and 346–347.

Common law

The phrase "common law" is used in several ways: (1) Law that is not the result of legislation but rather of custom and judicial decision; (2) The branch of English law that derives from the old English courts of common law as opposed to the branch of law known as equity that grew up in the Court of Chancery; (3) The system of law of England and other countries, such as the United States, whose law is derived from English law. Common law in the first sense is found in 340.5. Common law in the second and third senses gives form and structure to 342–347.

341 vs. 327

International law vs. International relations

Works on international relations will discuss what is actually transpiring (including the theory as to why things happen as they do), and the effects of what has happened. Works on international law will discuss those standards and principles that should govern international relations, and will also discuss concrete events from the standpoint of the problems that they pose to this system of order. Included in international law will also be works on treaties and the cases of international courts. If in doubt, prefer 341.

341.22–.24

International governmental organizations

Interdisciplinary works on international governmental organizations and works dealing with the structure and overall functions of such organizations are classed in 341.22–.24, even when no substantial discussion of the organic law establishing such organizations appears in the work under consideration, e.g., interdisciplinary works on the European Union 341.242. A specific aspect of one of these organizations is classed with the subject outside of law, e.g., the economic aspects of the European Union 337.1.

However, interdisciplinary works on a specialized international governmental organization are classed with the subject with which the organization deals plus notation 06 from Table 1, e.g., Interpol, an international police organization, 363.206. The legal aspects of the organization are classed with the subject with which it deals in 341.2–.7, e.g., Interpol 341.7.

341.3

Relations between states

Treaties

Class the approval of a treaty by a nation in international law. However, class legislation to enforce the provisions of a treaty within national boundaries with the law of that nation. For example, a work on a treaty between the United States and Canada with respect to fish and wildlife conservation is classed in 341.7, but a work on a fish and game law passed by the United States Congress to enforce the provisions of such a treaty on the citizens of the United States is classed in 346.7304.

342–349

Branches of law; laws (statutes), regulations, cases; law of specific jurisdictions, areas, socioeconomic regions

Law of countries with federal governments

In federally organized countries, e.g., the United States, Australia, Federal Republic of Germany, there are two sets of laws: those of the central jurisdiction (national laws) and those of subordinate jurisdictions (laws of the provinces or states). Laws of an individual state or province are classed using the area number for the jurisdiction in question, e.g., criminal law of Virginia 345.755, of New South Wales 345.944. However, laws of the states or provinces taken as a whole are classed in the same numbers as the laws of the federal jurisdiction, e.g., criminal laws of the states of the United States 345.73, of the states of Australia 345.94. Normally the discussion of state and provincial laws of a region are classed in the same manner, e.g., provincial criminal law of western Canada 345.712.

Use of area number for capital districts

Use notation 753 from Table 2 for laws of Washington, D.C., even though some of these laws are passed by the United States Congress. These are, in effect, local laws even though passed by the national legislature. The same situation may occur in other countries.

Jurisdiction in time

Laws of an area that was at some point not an independent jurisdiction are classed as follows:

1. If the law is still operative in the now-independent jurisdiction, class with the jurisdiction in question, e.g., class the Limitation Act of 1908 (which was enacted before Pakistan became independent but is the currently operating law for Pakistan) in 347.5491.

2. If the law is no longer operative in the now-independent jurisdiction, class with the laws of the jurisdiction that was previously dominant, e.g., a law of 1908 no longer operative in Pakistan is classed with the law of India plus notation 54 from Table 2.

343.04 vs. 336.2, 352.4

Tax law vs. Taxes and taxation vs. Financial administration and budgets

Most works on taxes, especially popular works, are classed in law, because they explain what the law allows and prohibits. For example, a work for taxpayers about U.S. income tax deductions is classed in 343.7305. Tax administration, which includes especially the administration of assessment and collection, is classed in 352.4. Works on the economics of taxes and interdisciplinary works on taxes are classed in 336.2, e.g., an economic and political analysis of U.S. tax policy 336.200973. If in doubt, class in 343.04.

345 vs. 346.03

Criminal law vs. Torts (Delicts)

Certain acts listed as criminal offenses here are also to be found in 346.03 as torts (a part of civil law). Works on these acts should be classed according to the point of view taken in the work or the type of legal action being brought. Thus libel and slander considered from the standpoint of criminal law are classed in 345, considered as a tort in 346.03. Whether a particular act is regarded as a crime or as a tort or as neither will often depend on the jurisdiction in which it is regarded. For example, adultery may be regarded as a crime for which the offender may be prosecuted, a tort for which the offender may be sued, or merely as a fact to be adduced in evidence in a divorce case. If in doubt, prefer 345.

351

Public administration

A new emphasis on subject over jurisdiction

The new *completely revised schedule* for public administration places the emphasis upon classifying by subject rather than by jurisdiction as was done in earlier editions. Two adjustments have been made, however, to recognize the importance of jurisdiction. First, for comprehensive works on public administration in a specific area, area notation 3–9 is added directly to 351, saving two digits when compared with the use of standard subdivision notation 09. For example, public administration in or of Germany is classed in 351.43.

The second adjustment is indirect, the result of a liberal use of class-here and standard-subdivisions-are-added notes. These notes are signals that differences among jurisdictions are considered more important than the differences among the particular topics named in the notes. When public administration topics are named in these two kinds of notes, standard subdivisions may be added freely.

For example, grants-in-aid to subordinate jurisdictions are combined with grants to private parties in the number for financial support (352.73), since the methods of dispensing public grants varies in unpredictable ways among jurisdictions, and varies in a single jurisdiction over time. Hence, administration of grants to either public bodies *or* to private individuals in Germany is classed in 352.73<u>0943</u>.

Similarly, price supports and price controls are distinct, if overlapping concepts. The supports naturally fall under financial assistance in 352.73, while the controls naturally fall under general forms of control in 352.8. However, it is hard to get into one activity without getting into the other, and any specific program might shift its emphasis over time, therefore both concepts are classed in 352.8.

351.3–.9 vs. 352.13–.19

Public administration in specific continents, countries, localities vs. Administration of subordinate jurisdictions

Administration in and of specific subordinate jurisdictions

A distinction is made between practical and theoretical works on subordinate jurisdictions. Practical works on individual jurisdictions are classed in 351.3–.9, while theoretical works on state and provincial or local administration are classed in 352.13–.19 plus notation 09 from Table 1. Use the latter only for general treatises on subordinate jurisdictions or on specific kinds of subordinate jurisdictions, e.g., provincial administration in Canada 352.130971, county administration in Illinois 352.1509773, rural administration in United Kingdom 352.170941. Use 351.3–.9 for administrative activity in any specific subordinate jurisdiction, e.g., administration of the government of Ontario 351.713, of Cook County (Illinois) 351.773, of Ross and Cromarty (Scotland) 351.411.

This distinction insures consistent classification of works on administration of specific subordinate jurisdictions, since a classifier does not need to decide to which category a specific government belongs, e.g., whether Cook County is urban, or Ross and Cromarty is rural. The answer would be easy in these two cases, but often it is not.

The distinction is carried over under specific topics of public administration. Area notation 093–099 from Table 1 brings together reports and practical works on the administration of a specific activity in a given region. In contrast, theoretical works on how state (provincial) and local administration of a subject has been or should be conducted is left in standing room in the base number for the topic, e.g., personnel management in Cook County 352.609773, but in county governments in Illinois 352.6.

If in doubt, prefer 351.3 .9.

352–354

Specific topics of public administration

Agencies and their divisions

No distinction is made between the administration of a function and the administration of an agency designated to perform that function. For example, public administration of agriculture in the United States and administration of the United States Department of Agriculture are both classed in 354.50973. Administrative reports of specific agencies are also classed in the same numbers as independent studies of the functions that the agencies perform. For example, the Annual Report of the United States Department of Agriculture and an independent journal on agricultural administration in the United States are both classed in 354.50973.

Nominal subordination of an agency to a nonexecutive branch of government does not affect classification. For example, the United States General Accounting Office is officially part of the legislative branch, but it performs a classical executive function of reviewing accounts and judging the effectiveness of expenditures throughout the government. It is, therefore, classed in 352.4.

A representative list of departments and agencies of the United States government is given below with the recommended public administration numbers in the middle column. The list provides a useful guide to classifying comparable agencies of any jurisdiction, since when notation for area (T1−0973) is given, it can easily be replaced by notation specifying any other area. (*The list includes a few agencies and institutions with administrative numbers outside 352–354 that are nevertheless listed in the "352–354 number" column.*)

The numbers in the rightmost column are the ones that are most likely to fit typical works on the fields that the agencies administer. This column serves as a reminder that many works that conspicuously identify a given agency may discuss either public policy or the situation and conditions in the field rather than public administration. The numbers are for guidance only; always classify according to the emphasis of the work in hand. (*When there is no single appropriate non-352–354 number, the 352–354 number is repeated in this column.*) (*See also discussion at 300, 320 vs. 353–354: Public policy.*)

Representative list of United States government agencies

Agency name	352–354 number	Non-352–354
ACTION	352.7	361.3
Agency for International Development	353.13	338.91
Bureau of Indian Affairs	353.534	305.897
Bureau of Mines	354.3	338.20973
Bureau of the Census	352.7	317.3
Central Intelligence Agency	353.1	327.1273
Council of Economic Advisors	354.2	330.973
Department of Agriculture	354.50973	338.10973
Department of Commerce	354.730973	380.10973
Department of Defense	355.60973	355.00973
Department of Education	353.80973	370.973
Department of Energy	354.40973	333.790973
Department of Health and Human Services	353.60973	362.10973
Department of Housing and Urban Development	353.5	363.50973
Department of Justice	353.40973	349.73
Department of Labor	354.90973	331.0973
Department of State	353.1	327.73
Department of the Air Force	358.4	358.400973
Department of the Army	355.60973	355.00973
Department of the Interior	354.30973	333.70973
Department of the Navy	359.60973	359.00973
Department of the Treasury	352.40973	336.73
Department of Transportation	354.760973	388.0973
Department of Veterans Affairs	353.5380973	362.860973
Environmental Protection Agency	354.3	363.70973
Equal Employment Opportunity Commission	354.908	331.13
Executive Office of the President	352.23	352.23
Federal Bureau of Investigation	363.25068	363.250973
Federal Communications Commission	354.75	384.0973
Federal Emergency Management Agency	353.9	363.340973
Federal Highway Administration	354.770973	388.10973
Federal Trade Commission	354.73	381.0973
Food and Drug Administration	353.9	363.19
General Accounting Office	352.4	352.4
General Services Administration	352.50973	352.50973
Government Printing Office	070.509753	070.509753
Information Service	353.13	327.1
Internal Revenue Service	352.4	336.240973
International Trade Commission	354.74	382.0973
Interstate Commerce Commission	354.76	388.0973

Library of Congress	025.1	027.573
Merit System Protection Board	352.6	352.6
National Aeronautics and Space Administration	354.79	629.40973
National Archives and Records Administration	025.1	026
National Foundation on the Arts and the Humanities	353.7	001.30973
National Labor Relations Board	354.9	331.80973
National Oceanic and Atmospheric Administration	354.3	333.91
National Park Service	353.7	363.6
National Security Council	353.1	355
National Transportation Safety Board	353.9	363.1200973
National Weather Service	354.3	551.6573
Nuclear Regulatory Commission	354.4	333.792
Occupational Safety and Health Administration	353.9	363.1100973
Office of Personnel Management	352.60973	352.60973
Office of the Comptroller of the Currency	354.8	332.10973
Post Office Department	354.75	383
Postal Service	354.75	383
Rural Electrification Administration	354.4	333.793
Securities and Exchange Commission	354.8	332.64
Small Business Administration	354.2	338.6
Social Security Administration	353.5	368.4
Veterans Administration	353.5380973	362.860973

See also discussion at T1—068 vs. 353–354 for the choice between management and public administration for agencies providing the actual services.

Terminology of administration and management

To avoid cumbersome repetition, the phrase "public administration" is used only in headings and notes referring to three-digit numbers, and the word "administration" is normally limited to headings and notes referring to four-digit numbers. Elsewhere the word "administration" is used only if needed to make a heading complete e.g., 352.14 Local administration.

An important feature of public administration is the application of principles and concepts of management to public agencies. Normally the phrases used in management (that is, in 658) are carried over to 352–354 without qualification, except that phrases ending in the word "management" end in the word "administration." For example, financial management in public administration is called financial administration. ("Executive management," however, remains executive management in 352.3.)

The interdisciplinary numbers for specific topics in management, as well as for management as a whole, are found in 658. The indexing of management terms reflects the fact that management in public administration is a part of management by listing the public administration numbers in subheadings under the management terms. For example:

Financial management	658.3
public administration	352.6

352.13 vs. 352.15

State and provincial administration vs. Intermediate units of local administration

Territorial subdivisions with an extent that places them distinctly above "local administration" go by a variety of names. Unfortunately, the names used for very large units in some countries are often used in other countries for very small units. The Decimal Classification Division of the Library of Congress considers the major territorial units of the countries in the list given below to constitute states or provinces in the meaning intended for 352.13. It considers comparably named units in other countries to belong in 352.15.

The degree of autonomy is not the deciding factor in classification, especially since it changes over time. The list includes some "regions" that have been superimposed over long established and still important districts, departments, or provinces. These regions may not have been given fully developed administrative functions. Similar units that may be created in the future will also be considered to belong in 352.13.

Argentina   (provinces)
Australia   (states)
Brazil   (federal units)
Canada   (provinces)
China   (provinces, autonomous regions)
(former) Czechoslovakia   (regions)
France   (regions)
Germany   (states)
India   (states)
Indonesia   (provinces)
Italy   (regions)
Japan   (regions)
Korea   (regions)
Mexico   (states)
Nigeria   (states)
Pakistan   (provinces)
Philippines   (regions)
Russia   (provinces, territories, autonomous republics)
South Africa   (provinces)
(former) Soviet Union   (union republics, autonomous republics)
Spain   (autonomous communities)
Sudan   (regions)
United States   (states)
(former) Yugoslavia   (republics, autonomous provinces)

Class "territories" in the sense of areas on the road to statehood in 352.13, but general treatment of special urban units coordinate with states and provinces in 352.16. For example, class historic treatment of administration in territories of the United States 352.130973, administration of nationally controlled municipalities in China 352.160951.

353.53 vs. 351.08

Programs directed to kinds of persons vs. History and description with respect to kinds of persons

Comprehensive works on administration of programs directed to kinds of persons are found in 353.53, e.g., programs for African Americans 353.534. 351.08 is limited to other relationships between the group and public administration, e.g., contributions of African Americans to public administration 351.089, the success of women in public administration 351.082. Neither provision should be used for works involving basic policy matters, which should be classed outside public administration, e.g., lobbying for government programs for African Americans 362.84 (*not* 353.534).

Elsewhere in public administration, the distinction is not made. Administration of specific kinds of services directed to kinds of persons is classed with the kind of service plus notation 08 from Table 1, e.g., veterans T1—086.

355 vs. 623

Military science vs. Military and nautical engineering

Use 623 for physical description, design, manufacture, operation, and repair of ordnance; use 355–359 for procurement and deployment, and also for the units and services that use ordnance. Histories of the development of weapons emphasizing the interplay of human and social factors are regarded as procurement history, and are classed in 355.8 or with specific services in 356–359. If in doubt, prefer 355–359.

355.02 vs. 355.4

War and warfare vs. Military operations

Strategy

Use 355.02 for works on strategy that consider the overall problems and objectives of national policy; use 355.4 for works on strategy that emphasize military operations. If in doubt, prefer 355.02.

361–365

Social problems and services

Problems and services in this section of the schedules are often linked terms, and, where one is spelled out, the other is implied. Thus, addiction at 362.29 implies services to the addicted, while public safety programs at 363.1 imply the problems that require such services.

See also discussion at 300 vs. 600.

Political, economic, and legal considerations

Many publications give considerable emphasis to the political and legal considerations related to social services. If the focus is on the problem or the service, class such publications here. For example, class a discussion of political obstacles to effective poverty programs in 362.5, a discussion of the political maneuvering behind the adoption of an act of the United States Congress spelling out a new housing program in 363.5.

361–365 vs. 353.5

Social problems and services vs. [Public] Administration of social welfare

Much of the material on social problems and services consists of government reports. Reports about welfare programs and institutions are classed in 361–365. Reports concentrating on the administrative activities of agencies supporting and regulating the programs and institutions are classed in 353.5. If in doubt, class in 361–365; however, prefer 353.5 for administrative annual reports of agencies not actually providing the services.

361 vs. 362

Social problems and social welfare in general vs. Social welfare problems and services

361 is used for two kinds of material: comprehensive works on the whole range of problems and services found in 362–363, and works on principles and methods of assessing and solving the problems. The second kind of material normally does not address specific problems but may refer to welfare problems, usually found in 362. Material on the principles and methods of welfare work in general is classed in 361. Application of the principles and methods to a specific problem is classed with the problem.

A helpful guide in deciding between 361 and 362 is the table of contents. If it reads like a summary of the subdivisions of 362, class in 362; if like a summary of the subdivisions of 361, class in 361. In the absence of a table of contents or summary, the arrangement of topics is a useful guide. If topics in both 361 and 362 are covered, class in 361. If in doubt, class in 361.

361.6 vs. 361.7, 361.8

Governmental action vs. Private action vs. Community action

Organizations are classed in 361.6, 361.7, and 361.8 depending upon who has financial control. For example, the Peace Corps, a governmentally funded organization of overseas volunteers, is classed in 361.6; Canadian University Service Overseas, a privately funded organization of overseas volunteers, is classed in 361.7.

362–363 vs. 364.1

Specific social problems and services vs. Criminal offenses

Some human activities can be considered either as social problems or as crimes. An activity as a social problem is classed in 362–363. The activity treated as a crime is classed in 364.1. For example, drug addiction as a social problem is classed in 362.29, but illegal use of drugs is classed in 364.1. Suicide as a social problem is classed in 362.28, but suicide treated as a crime is classed in 364.15. If in doubt, prefer 362–363.

362 vs. 368.4

Social welfare problems and services vs. Government-sponsored insurance

Social security

Social security as a government-sponsored insurance scheme is classed in 368.4, e.g., social security in the United States. Social security that is not insurance is classed in 362, e.g., social security in the United Kingdom 362.941. If in doubt, prefer 362.

362.1–.4 vs. 610

Problems of and services to persons with illnesses and disabilities vs. Medical sciences   Medicine

Class health services from the social viewpoint in 362.1–.4, from the technological viewpoint in 610. For example, class social measures for the provision of dental care through clinics in 362.1, but how dentists actually use their skill in 617.6. Class works treating both the medical sciences and the medical social services in 362.1–.4. If in doubt, prefer 362.1–.4.

Biographies

Class in 362.1–.4, plus notation 092 from Table 1, biographies and memoirs of the dying and persons with illnesses and disabilities that lack any other disciplinary focus. The rationale behind this rule is that these biographies illustrate the way society addresses itself to fundamental health problems and their solution. Be alert, however, for significant disciplinary emphasis, e.g., a work offering guidance in the Christian life with respect to health misfortunes is classed in 248.8, Christian meditations in 242. Class studies of individual cases designed for the use of researchers, practitioners, and students in the field in the number for the field, without adding notation 092 from Table 1. Class in 616–618 studies of patients describing their illnesses in medical terms rather than their lives in social terms, e.g., case studies of heart disease 616.1. If in doubt, prefer 362; however, prefer 616.89 and related numbers for psychiatric disorders, since the consideration of external circumstances is generally subordinated to the discussion of the state of mind of the patient.

While most personal and biographical treatment of medical personnel is classed in 610, works on public health doctors or nurses emphasizing their influences on public health services and awareness are classed in 362, e.g., a biography of a doctor noted chiefly for promoting nursing homes 362.1.

362.1 vs. 368.38

Physical illness vs. Health insurance, accident insurance, disability income insurance

Health insurance

Works on health insurance plans that focus on their insurance features, e.g., a work on prepaid health care rates, are classed in 368.38. Works that focus on the health services features of insurance plans, e.g., a work on the adequacy of managed care plans, are classed in 362.1. If in doubt, prefer 362.1.

363

Other social problems and services

Several subdivisions involve the control of technology, particularly under safety (363.1) and environment (363.7). Class in 363 works addressing what must be done, regulating how it is to be done, inspecting to see whether or not it has been done, and investigating when it was not done. Only works dealing with the technological procedures for carrying out a given operation are classed in technology. Finding out what broke is 600; finding out who let it break is 363. Machinery breakdown is 600; institutional breakdown is 363.

A useful clue in choosing the appropriate discipline is the perspective of the author or publishing agency. If the author is interested in social service and social need, the work is classed in 363; in economics, 333.7; in human ecology, 304.2; in how to make things, 620–690; in how organisms survive, 570–590; in how crops survive, 632–635; in physical techniques for controlling pollution, 628.5. In general, commercial publishers and environmental or safety advocacy groups tend to produce works that are classed in the social sciences, e.g., 304.2, 333.7, or 363.

To summarize: class comprehensive works and works oriented toward problems and their solution in 363, resource-oriented material in 333.7, works giving significant consideration to the social dynamics of the problem in 302–307, those emphasizing technology in 600.

See also discussion at 300 vs. 600; also at 301–307 vs. 361–365.

363 vs. 340, 353–354

Other social problems and services vs. Law vs. [Specific fields of public administration]

Class the work of agencies by which the government carries out the detailed intent of the law in matters of population, safety, the environment, and provision of basic necessities in 363. Class the internal administration of agencies concerned with these fields, including their administrative annual reports, in 353–354. The law itself, draft laws, and enforcement of the law in courts are classed in 341–346. Most of the discussion of policy and most detailed procedures for enforcing law, policy, or regulation are classed in 363. If in doubt, prefer 363.

Law enforcement

Law enforcement is not necessarily a police matter, although it may be. Any government agency may enforce the law. A department of education, for instance, is enforcing the law when it sees that the requirements of the law are being met by the schools. Enforcement of law in this sense is classed with the government agency outside of law. A work about the law enforcement activities of the department of education mentioned above would be classed in 353.8. Law enforcement by the police is classed in 363.2. It should be noted, however, that laws governing how such enforcement should be carried out are classed in law, e.g., the law governing what measures police may use in enforcing the law 344 (or 345 if it pertains to matters of criminal investigation). If in doubt, prefer 363.2.

Enforcement of the law through the courts is always classed in law, e.g., court procedure that promotes the enforcement of tax law 343.04.

363.1

Public safety programs

Safety regulations

Class safety regulations that spell out operating and construction techniques with the technology involved even if they are in the form of an officially promulgated regulation by a safety authority. On the other hand, manuals written by or for safety agencies may discuss, among other things, various technical details useful as background for regulation and inspection of various operations while still focusing primarily on safety services. These are classed in 363.1.

Priority of safety

Class those aspects of safety that society must deal with through investigations and programs in 363.1 or 363.3 rather than with the subject elsewhere in the social sciences, e.g., railroad safety 363.12, not 385.028. However, the public administration of safety is classed as instructed in 353.9.

363.1 vs. 620.8

Public safety programs vs. Human-factors and safety engineering

Accident investigation

Prefer 363.1 and related numbers in 363 to 620.8 and related numbers in 600 for accident investigations when the investigation implicates large, impersonal agencies (companies or governments) that should have prevented the accident by proper supervision, inspection, or regulation. For example, class a technical description of what went wrong at Three Mile Island in 621.48, but an investigation of why it took so long to find out what went wrong in 363.17.

363.11 vs. 613.6

Occupational and industrial hazards vs. Special topics [in promotion of health]

Use 613.6 for works that emphasize technical measures to be taken for promotion of industrial and occupational health. Use 363.11 for works that emphasize social and institutional arrangements. In case of doubt, prefer 363.11.

363.17

Hazardous materials

Many works on hazardous materials are not classed in 363. The material as an environmental factor affecting the natural ecology is classed in 577.27, as a cause of disease or injury in an organism in 571.9, and as a cause of injury to persons in 615.9 (for chemicals) and 616.9 (for radiation hazards).

363.17 vs. 604.7

[Social programs and services relating to] Hazardous materials vs. Hazardous materials technology

While the technology of handling hazardous materials is classed in 604.7, works on "handling" that are addressed to those responsible for monitoring or inspecting the handling, and that may be devoid of engineering considerations are classed in 363.17. If in doubt, prefer 363.17.

363.3 vs. 303.3, 791.4

Other aspects of public safety vs. Coordination and control vs. Motion pictures, radio, television

Censorship

Class in 303.3 theories of censorship and sociological studies of censorship of movies, radio, and television. Class in 363.3 censorship of movies and programs after being released or aired. Class in 791.4 censorship of films and programs as they are being produced, e.g., censorship through editing. If in doubt, prefer 363.3.

363.5, 363.6, 363.8 vs. 338

Housing [and] Public utilities and related services [and] Food supply vs. Production

363.5, 363.6, and 363.8 deal with the problems of providing the basic necessities of life. Each has economic implications; thus, a careful distinction must be made between these numbers and the economics of industries under 338. If the work deals with the effect of these topics on the economic aspects of society, or the impact of economic conditions on the availability of housing, water, fuel, or food, class it in 338. If it deals with broader social factors affecting these commodities, or with social measures to insure an adequate supply, class it in 363.5, 363.6, or 363.8. For example, class a study of the effect of a drop in farm prices on the food supply in 338.1, a study of the mismatch between the expected growth of the food supply and of the population in 363.8. If in doubt, prefer 363.5, 363.6, or 363.8.

363.5 vs. 643

Housing [in social services] vs. Housing and household equipment [in home economics]

A distinction is often made between "housing" and "houses." The term "housing" normally refers to the provision of shelter considered in the abstract, while the term "houses" normally refers to the buildings considered as physical objects. 643 is used for the home economics aspects of either housing or houses. It is also the number for interdisciplinary works on *houses* and their use. However, since works on housing often treat the social aspects of shelter, interdisciplinary works on *housing* are classed in 363.5.

363.6

Public utilities and related services

Water reports

Water supply reports concentrating on the supply of water on hand are classed in 553.7; on water used, or needed in the future, in 333.91; on the problem of treating and delivering water to consumers in 363.6; on assuring that waste waters are properly treated and on protection of natural waters in 363.72. Interdisciplinary reports on water supply are classed in 363.6.

Water quality monitoring reports serve several purposes. As tools for assuring compliance with water supply standards they are classed in 363.6; for assuring compliance with waste water pollution standards, in 363.739; for determining plant loads and technical difficulties in water treatment, in 628.1; and for checking the effectiveness of sewage treatment works, in 628.3. Those reporting the present chemical and biological status of available water, but not focusing on a specific objective, are classed as economic geology in 553.7. The most general works on monitoring "to protect water quality" are classed in 333.91, e.g., an environmentalist's alert "we must monitor our water supply."

363.73 vs. 571.9, 577.27

Pollution vs. Diseases   Pathology vs. Effects of humankind on ecology

In using 571.9 and 577.27 for studies of the effect of pollution and other deleterious agents, keep in mind that the former is part of pathology (571.9) while the latter is part of ecology (577). Therefore, use 571.9 for the pathological conditions caused by pollution and other agents in tissues of organisms. Use 577.27 or the number for the specific ecological environment (biome) in 577.3–.7 for the more generalized effects of substances upon the community of organisms, e.g., the reduction of species counts (biodiversity) and the general health and vigor of surviving species.

Use biology numbers with caution, however, for pollution studies, because the growth and decline of indicator species are often used to measure the extent and kind of pollution, and are interpreted to suggest the need for, or sufficiency of, remedial measures. Such studies are classed in 363.73, e.g., acid rain monitoring by use of indicator species 363.738.

If in doubt between 363.73 and 571.9 or 577.27, prefer 363.73; if in doubt between 571.9 and 577.27, prefer 571.9.

See also discussion at 333.7–.9 vs. 363.1, 363.73, 577.

363.8 vs. 338.1

[Social problems and services relating to] Food supply vs. [Economics of] Agriculture

363.8 encompasses the whole problem of supplying food to society, while 338.1 concerns the routine economic aspects. Economic problems like poverty and maldistribution are at the root of most food supply and nutrition problems, but most works concerning such problems focus on the resulting social problems and on the social services needed to overcome them, and therefore are classed in 363.8. Requirements of specific segments of the population are also classed in 363.8. For example, total economic demand for food in Nigeria is classed in 338.1, food requirements of the urban poor in Nigeria in 363.8, normal food trade in Nigeria in 381, distribution of food during a famine in Nigeria in 363.8. If in doubt, prefer 363.8.

363.8 vs. 613.2, 641.3

Food supply vs. Dietetics vs. Food

Class comprehensive works on personal aspects of nutrition in 613.2. However, class interdisciplinary works on food in 641.3, on nutrition in 363.8. The essential thrust of 613.2 is to help individuals meet dietary requirements and maintain optimal balanced intake without gaining or losing weight. Also included is material for dietitians in planning diets for individuals. In contrast, the emphasis in 641.3 is on the food itself, and in 363.8 it is on meeting and maintaining the needs of society in general and of various social groups. If in doubt between 363.8 and 613.2 or 641.3, prefer 363.8; if in doubt between 613.2 and 641.3, prefer 641.3.

363.9 vs. 304.6

Population problems vs. Population

Population control

Class in 304.6 the effects upon society of control efforts by its members, whether or not society sanctions such efforts. But class in 363.9 programs or policies that are discussed as population control efforts. If in doubt, prefer 363.9.

368 vs. 658.15

Insurance vs. Financial management

Risk management

Be alert to works that call themselves "risk management." Some are about insurance and belong in 368. Others treat a variety of management techniques to reduce loss or possible loss, with a goal of economic benefit to the organization; these works belong in 658.15. In the management context, risk management can include safety problems and their solutions, employee health programs, and all aspects of business security; specific topics are classed with the topic in management, e.g., safety management 658.4. If in doubt, prefer 368.

371 vs. 353.8, 371.2, 379

Schools and their activities; special education vs. Administration of agencies supporting and controlling education vs. School administration; administration of student academic activities vs. Public policy issues in education

The basic numbers for operation and activities of schools and school systems are found in 371. Most specific topics are concentrated in 371.2, the comprehensive number for school (and school-system) administration. Public administration in 353.8 is limited to the administration of national and state or provincial departments of education that regulate and support local school systems. In 379 are found the policy and debate on major policy issues in education. This number includes discussion of the role of government and the public in regulation and support of public and private school systems.

Subdivisions in 379 cover only general works on support and control of public education, and a limited selection of controversial issues in education. Public policy and debate on all other issues (that is, all issues not specifically named in 379) are classed in 370–378.

Each of the numbers is comprehensive in its own domain, but there are many works that do not quite fit in one or the other. Class works covering 371.2 and 353.8 in 371.2; and works covering both 371 and 379 in 370. If in doubt among the specific numbers, prefer them in the following order: 371, 371.2, 379, and 353.8.

371 vs. 372–374, 378

Schools and their activities; special education vs. Specific levels of education [and] Higher education

The one overriding principle of arrangement in the education schedule is that level of education is preferred over specific topics in 371.01–.8. Therefore, when looking up a topic in 371.01–.8, be sure to ask, "Does this topic apply to a specific level?" If so, class with the level.

For elementary and secondary education, most specific topics are classed in 372.1 and 373.1, respectively, under subdivisions parallel to ones given under 371. For higher education, most specific topics are classed in 378.1. For adult education, the specific topics are classed in 374. Before using 372.1, 373.1, or 378.1, however, check carefully to find out if there are exceptions applying to the topic in hand. For example, there is no provision for specific kinds of elementary schools (class them in 372.1) or colleges and universities (class them in 378). Specific kinds of secondary schools are found in 373.2.

372.24 and 373.23

Specific levels of elementary education [and] Specific levels of secondary education

There are many different ways of dividing the levels of elementary and secondary education. The Decimal Classification Division assigns individual grades (when they are treated separately) according to the 3-3-3-3 plan shown in the first table below. The other tables after the first show how the Division classifies the most common American pattern of levels.

Names often used for the specific levels, and numbers in which they are classed follow:

Grades	Number
1–3 (Primary grades)	372.24
4–6 (Intermediate grades)	372.24
7–9 (Junior high school)	373.236
10–12 (Senior high school)	373.238

The 6-6 pattern:

Grades	Number
1–6 (Elementary school)	372
7–12 (High school)	373

The six-year elementary school is often called grammar school in the United States, and primary school in the United Kingdom.

The 8-4 pattern:

Grades	Number
1–8 (Elementary school)	372
9–12 (High school)	373

The 4-4-4 pattern:

Grades	Number
1–4 (Elementary school)	372
5–8 (Middle school)	373.236
9–12 (High school)	373

Other combinations are classed with the higher level, e.g., a K–2 infant school in 372.24, unless the majority of the grades are at a lower level. Schools extending from first to ninth grade or beyond are classed in 371.

These guidelines apply only to discussion of sublevels in general, e.g., junior high schools in the United States 373.2360973. The situation in specific schools, however, tends to change so much over time that specific schools are classed in the geographic span under the general number for elementary or secondary education, or in 371.009. For example, a specific junior high school in Atlanta, Georgia, is classed in 373.758.

378 vs. 355.0071

Higher education vs. Education [in military science]

Military schools

College level military schools that are not official service academies, that is, those whose students (except in wartime) normally enter civilian occupations, are treated like other higher educational institutions and classed in 378 plus notation for the area where they are located, e.g., Virginia Military Institute (Lexington, Virginia) 378.755, The Citadel (Charleston, South Carolina) 378.757. If in doubt, prefer 378.

380

Commerce, communications, transportation

In order of preference of subjects under 330 in the Manual, commerce and transportation take the same position as production. Therefore, a work on the labor market in transportation would be classed in 331.12, but production economics of transportation 388.

Add table

09 vs. 06

Historical, geographic, persons treatment vs. Organization and management

Use notation 06 when the work discusses the corporate history of the organization, e.g., the corporate history of the Union Pacific Railroad 385.06.

Use notation 09 when the work discusses the system (facilities, activities, services) maintained by the company in a specific area, e.g., railroad transportation provided by the Union Pacific Railroad 385.0978.

If in doubt, prefer 09.

380.1 and 381, 382

Commerce (Trade) [and] Internal commerce (Domestic trade) [and] International commerce (Foreign trade)

Commercial miscellany

Commercial miscellany of specific products or groups of products is classed with the product plus notation 029 from Table 1, e.g., offers to sell tools 621.90029. Commercial miscellany of a broad range of products, however, is classed here, e.g., offers to sell products of secondary industries 380.1, department store catalogs 381, agricultural export directories 382. A noncurrent offer for sale of a broad range of products that is used primarily to illustrate customs of an earlier period is classed in 909 or 930–990.

See also discussion at 338 vs. 060, 381, 382, 670.29, 910, T1–025, T1–029.

380.1 vs. 658.8

Commerce (Trade) vs. Management of distribution (Marketing)

Class in 380.1 the economic aspects of trading and selling goods, what is traded and in what amounts. Class managerial techniques for successfully disposing of the products and services of enterprises in 658.8. If in doubt, prefer 380.1.

381 vs. 658.8

Internal commerce (Domestic trade) vs. Management of distribution (Marketing)

Retail stores

The choice of number for management of retail stores is complex. For management of a particular kind of retail store, use 658.8 if there is no emphasis on a specific kind of product. For example, class management of retail chain stores in 658.8, not 381, since chain stores are a form of management organization. Use 658.8 also for a specific aspect of managing retail stores, e.g., financial management of chain stores. However, class management of retail stores marketing a specific product, e.g., management of book stores, in 381. If in doubt whether a management work focuses on marketing a specific product, prefer 658.8.

When there is no emphasis on a specific kind of product, use 381 for economic aspects of retail stores and for interdisciplinary works on economics and management of retail stores. If in doubt whether a work is limited to management or is an interdisciplinary work with both economics and management, prefer 381.

384 vs. 791.4

Communications   Telecommunication vs. [Performing arts aspects of] Motion pictures, radio, television

Class works combining aspects of 384 and 791.4 in 384.

Class in 791.4 the various aspects of producing an individual program, e.g., arranging the various acts of a television variety show 791.45. Class in 384 the various aspects of presenting the finished program to the general public, e.g., selecting the correct day and time to broadcast a television variety show 384.55.

The history of a radio, television, or motion picture company is classed using the following criteria:

1. Class in 384, plus notation 09 from Table 1, a general history of the organization, e.g., a history of NBC (National Broadcasting Company) Radio Network 384.540973.

2. Class in 384, plus notation 06 from the add table under 380, the corporate history of the organization, e.g., the corporate history of the NBC Radio Network 384.5406.

3. Class in 384, without use of either notation 06 or 09, the history of the system (facilities, activities, services) maintained by the organization, e.g., stations broadcasting NBC radio programs 384.54.

4. Class in 791.4, plus notation 09 from Table 1, the history and critical appraisal of the products of the organization, e.g., the history of the radio programs provided by NBC 791.440973.

386 vs. 387.1

Inland waterway and ferry transportation vs. Ports

The choice between 387.1 and 386 for a specific port is based on whether the port is on tidal waters (387.1) or on nontidal waters (386), not upon either the distance from the sea or the ability to handle oceangoing ships. For example, class the port of New Orleans (110 miles from the mouth of the Mississippi River but on tidal waters) in 387.109763, the port of Chicago (which can handle oceangoing vessels but is on nontidal waters) in 386.

391 vs. 646, 746.9

Costume and personal appearance vs. Sewing, clothing and accessories, management of personal and family living vs. [Artistic aspects of] Costume

Costume, clothing, and fashion can be treated in terms of customs, home economics, or art. Customs, such as what was worn, what is fashionable, national costumes, are classed in 391. Home economics aspects, such as how to dress on a limited budget, select the best quality clothing, dress correctly for the business world, are classed in 646. Artistic aspects, such as clothing considered as a product of the textile arts, fashion design, are classed in 746.9. If in doubt between 391 and 646 or 746.9, prefer 391; between 646 and 746.9, prefer 746.9.

394 vs. 791.6

General customs vs. Pageantry

Class in 394 works that discuss traditions of pageants, processions, or parades and works that describe the event. Class in 791.6 works that discuss planning, promoting, and staging the event, including such topics as publicity and float construction. If in doubt, prefer 394.

398, 398.27 vs. 615.8

Folklore [and] Tales and lore of everyday human life vs. Specific therapies and kinds of therapies

Medical folk literature

Class a work of medical folk literature in 398.27 if the emphasis is on the story told or literary criticism of the lore; a work on the history and criticism of medical folklore in 398. Class in 615.8 only if the emphasis is on the medical practice. If in doubt, class in either 398 or 398.27.

398.2

Folk literature

There is no notation available for folk literature in 398.2 to distinguish literary forms, collections, or criticism as there is for general literature in 800. In each case, disregard these aspects in classifying, and use the most specific number available.

398.2 vs. 291.1

Folklore vs. Religious mythology, social theology, interreligious relations and attitudes

Mythology

Works on the mythology of a people or on mythologies from around the world are usually concerned with the most basic beliefs of people and with religious beliefs and practices. Such works are predominantly concerned with religion and are classed in 291.1. But mythology may refer also to beliefs and stories that can be referred to as superstitions, legends, fairy tales, etc., where the religious content or interest is not apparent. Class in 398.2 mythology having a nonreligious basis. Interdisciplinary works on mythology are classed in 398.2, since this number includes folk narratives with a broader focus than religion alone. If in doubt, prefer 398.2.

Religious myths are classed either in 398.2 or 291.1 according to content, mode of presentation, or author's or editor's intention. Mythology presented from a strictly theological point of view or presented as an embodiment of the religion of a people is classed in 291.1. However, myths or mythology presented in terms of cultural entertainment or, especially, as representatives of the early literary expression of a society are classed in 398.2, even if they are populated by gods and goddesses. Often the literary or religious focus is clear. For example, almost all Greco-Roman myths retold for a juvenile audience are classed in 398.2; but Jataka tales are usually classed in 294.3 because they illustrate the character of the Buddha.

Specific myths and legends presented as examples of a people's religion are classed with the subject in religion, e.g., legends of Jesus' coming to Britain 232.9.

398.2 vs. 398

Folk literature vs. Folklore

Class the folk tale on a specific subject and literary criticism of the tale in 398.2. Class comprehensive works on the history and criticism of the tale in 398. For example, tales of witches and wizards are classed in 398.21, a treatise on why in the tales witches are usually evil and wizards are usually good is classed in 398. If in doubt, prefer 398.2.

400 vs. 800

Language vs. Literature (Belles-lettres) and rhetoric

Many works treating both language and literature are predominantly about literature; such works are classed in 800. Comprehensive works on language and literature, giving equal attention to both, are classed in 400. If in doubt, prefer 400.

407.1, T1—071 vs. 401, 410.71, 418.0071, T4—80071

Education [in language] and [Table 1 notation for] Education vs. Philosophy and theory [of languages] vs. [Education in linguistics] vs. [Education in standard usage of language] and [Table 4 notation for education in standard usage of individual languages]

The basic distinction between prescriptive and nonprescriptive linguistics is explained in the Manual note at 410. Class in 418.0071 works on how to study or teach language using a prescriptive approach.

Class in 407.1 broad works on language education not limited to the prescriptive approach and comprehensive works on the study and teaching of both language and literature.

Class in 410.71 works on the study and teaching of linguistics.

If in doubt about 407.1, 410.71, and 418.0071, prefer 407.1.

Class in notation 80071 from Table 4 works on how to study or teach a specific language using a prescriptive approach, e.g., how to teach basic French 448.0071. In Table 4 there is no analogue to 410.71. Class with the specific language plus notation 071 from Table 1 (which is incorporated in Table 4), works on studying and teaching the linguistics of the language, broad works on studying and teaching the language that are not limited to the prescriptive approach, and comprehensive works on studying and teaching both the language and its literature. If in doubt between using T4—80071 and T1—071, prefer T1—071.

Class in 401 works on the psychology of learning language, including both the psychology of learning language informally, as a child learns from its parents, and the psychology of formal study and teaching of language.

410

Linguistics

Prescriptive linguistics is concerned with promoting standard or correct usage of language. Anyone trying to learn to speak or write like educated native users of a standard form of a language is involved with prescriptive linguistics. The various nonprescriptive approaches to linguistics (e.g., descriptive, theoretical, comparative linguistics) are concerned with describing or explaining language usage as it does or did exist, without regard to an ideal of correct usage. Most works of prescriptive linguistics are classed in 418 or with the specific language, plus notation 8 from Table 4; works of nonprescriptive linguistics are classed elsewhere in 410–490. For example, descriptive works about grammar are classed in 415 and with the specific language, plus notation 5 from Table 4; but prescriptive works about grammar are classed in 418 or with the specific language, plus notation 8 from Table 4. Dictionaries, however, are classed in 413 or with the specific language, plus notation 3 from Table 4, regardless of whether they are prescriptive or descriptive.

Comprehensive works containing both nonprescriptive and prescriptive linguistics are classed in the number for nonprescriptive approaches; for example, a collection containing both descriptive and prescriptive papers about grammar in general or the grammar of many different languages is classed in 415. If in doubt, prefer the number for nonprescriptive approaches.

General historical (diachronic) linguistics is classed in 417. Under some languages, specific early forms of the language are classed in notation 7 from Table 4, e.g., 427 Middle English. For general historical linguistics of a specific language, or for historical linguistics of a specific topic, use notation 09 from Table 1 if the work gives a history, but not if the work merely discusses the processes of change in a general way. For example, class a general discussion of grammatical change in 415, a history of grammatical changes in the English language in 425.09, a history of all kinds of changes in the English language in 420.9.

Class a comparison of two languages with the language requiring local emphasis (usually the language that is less common in the particular setting). For example, a work comparing English and Japanese is classed in 495.6 in English-speaking countries, but in 420 in Japan. If no emphasis is required, class the work with the language coming later in 420–490.

Class a comparison of three or more languages in the most specific number that will contain them all; e.g., class a comparison of Dutch, German, and English at 430 since all are Germanic languages.

If there is no number that will contain them all (e.g., a comparison of French, Hebrew, and Japanese), class the work in 410.

For comparisons of just one feature of various languages, apply the criteria given above, except do not add notation from Table 4 to the number for language families. A comparison of French, Hebrew, and Spanish grammar is classed in 415; a comparison of Dutch, German, and English grammar in 430.

See also discussion at 407.1, T1—071 vs. 401, 410.71, 418.80071, T4—80071.

410.285 vs. 006.3

Data processing   Computer applications [in linguistics] vs. Artificial intelligence

Class in 006.3 computer processing of natural human language used for computer science purposes, e.g., to allow people to communicate with computers in ordinary English instead of formalized commands. Class in 410.285 and elsewhere in 400 computer processing of natural language used for linguistics purposes, e.g., for machine translation 418. If in doubt, prefer 410.285.

420–490

Specific languages

The citation order of 420–490 is straightforward and without exception: Language + language subdivision from Table 4 + standard subdivision from Table 1.

> Russian grammar 491.75
> 491.7 + T4—5

> History of the Korean language 495.709
> 495.7 + T1—09

> Etymological dictionary of the English language 422.03
> 42 + T4—2 + T1—03

For languages with short numbers, three-digit numbers appear in the schedule that have been built with a Table 4 number added to a two-digit base number, e.g., 425 (42 + T4—5) Grammar of standard English.

Dialects

It frequently happens that one source calls a particular tongue a language, and another calls it a dialect. Consequently, it is common for a tongue to be treated as a dialect in the Dewey Decimal Classification and as a language in the work being classified, or vice versa.

Language vs. subject

Class examples and collections of "text" whose purpose is to display and study a language with the language, even if limited to a specific subject, e.g., a grammar of scientific English 425. Language analysis of a specific work is criticism and is classed with the work. If in doubt, prefer the specific subject or work.

500 vs. 001

Natural sciences and mathematics vs. Knowledge

Be careful about equating the word "science" with the natural sciences and mathematics in 500. The word is often used to cover the social sciences and the analytical aspects of other disciplines. Class a work in 001 when "science" is used without implying emphasis on "natural science," in 001.2 Scholarship and learning when used to cover disciplines outside 500, and in 500 only when it is clearly used to imply emphasis on the natural sciences. Works on scientific method and scientific research are apt to belong in 001.4 Research rather than 507. According to literary warrant, however, "history of science" more often than not relates to the natural sciences and mathematics and is classed in 509. If in doubt, class in 500.

500 vs. 600

Natural sciences and mathematics vs. Technology (Applied sciences)

The natural sciences (500) describe and attempt to explain the world we live in, while technology (600) consists of utilizing these sciences to manipulate the natural world and its resources for the benefit of humankind. Be alert, however, for certain subdivisions of 500 that consist largely of technology, e.g., surveying and cartography in 526 and celestial navigation in 527 (both of which would fit better in 620 Engineering); and certain subdivisions of 600 which consist largely of natural science, e.g., human anatomy and physiology in 611–612 (which clearly are parts of internal biological processes and structures of animals [571–573]).

Class in 500 interdisciplinary works on any science and its applications in technology. For example, a work on space science (500.5), engineering in other worlds (620), and astronautics (629.4) is classed in 500.5.

510

Mathematics

The type of mathematics presently taught in elementary and secondary schools in the United States is not usually classed in 510. The following is a list of school subjects and their numbers:

Arithmetic	513
Algebra	512.9
Geometry	516.2
Trigonometry	516.24

Use caution, however, when classifying books with "precalculus" in the title. Depending on the topics addressed, such works may be classed in 510, 512, or 515.

520 vs. 500.5, 523.1, 530.1, 919.9

Astronomy and allied sciences vs. Space sciences vs. The universe, galaxies, quasars vs. Theories and mathematical physics vs. [Geography of and travel in extraterrestrial worlds]

Outer space

The terms "space" and "outer space" are widely used in popular works on astronomy, but almost never refer to empty space devoid of matter and energy. Class works that use such terms while discussing the various interesting astronomical bodies and phenomena of the universe in 520, and works that use the terms as synonymous with the universe treated as a single unit in 523.1.

Works on exploring space or outer space may refer to either astronomical or geographic exploration. When the emphasis is on astronomical findings, class in 520 (or a specific number in 523 if the work is limited to specific bodies, e.g., the solar system 523.2). When the works refer to geographic exploration, that is, live humans going out on real or imaginary visits to the planets or stars, class in 919.9 plus notation 04 from the table under 913–919.

If a work having no particular reference to astronomical bodies refers to space sciences in general, class it in 500.5; if it refers simply to space with nothing in it, class it in 530.1, where an including note mentions space.

If in doubt, prefer a science number over 919.9, a specific space science number over 500.5, an astronomy number over 530.1, and 520 over 523.1.

520 vs. 523.1, 523.8

Astronomy and allied sciences vs. The universe, galaxies, quasars vs. Stars

Use 520 for works describing the universe in its several distinct components, e.g., as individual planets, stars, galaxies. Use 523.1 for works treating the universe as a single unit. If in doubt, prefer 520.

Stars and galaxies

When a work treats only stars and galaxies, two numbers must be considered. Use 523.8 for comprehensive works on stars and galaxies when they are treated as individual astronomical bodies. However, use 523.1 when stars are considered primarily as components of galaxies, or when stars and galaxies are considered in the context of cosmological theories. Usually in works belonging in the universe number (523.1) there is little discussion of individual stars or galaxies. When works discuss other astronomical bodies, e.g., planets and comets, as well as stars and galaxies, use 520. If in doubt between 523.8 and 523.1, prefer 523.8.

530 vs. 540

Physics vs. Chemistry and allied sciences

Class works on specific topics common to both physics and chemistry with chemistry when they relate to chemical composition, or to reactions affecting the combination of atoms in chemical processes. Class other works with physics. Clues more useful here than in most disciplines are the occupations of the authors or the fields of the sponsoring organizations, the presumption being that chemists are writing about chemistry and physicists, about physics. If in doubt, class in 530.

530 vs. 621

Physics vs. Applied physics

When the heading of an applied physics subdivision corresponds to one in physics, use the 621 number when the focus is on technology, even though much of the work is scientific background; use the 530 number when the focus is equally on science and technology. If in doubt, prefer 530.

530.12 vs. 531

Quantum mechanics (Quantum theory) vs. Classical mechanics   Solid mechanics

Quantum mechanics (530.12) is the concept that energy exists in small separate units (quanta) and is not continuous. It is contrasted with continuum or classical mechanics (531), which applies to the large scale phenomena of the solids, liquids, and gases of everyday observation. Since the two mechanics have practically nothing in common, and are fundamental to modern (sometimes called quantum) and classical physics respectively, class works covering both in 530. The word mechanics by itself is often used when only classical mechanics is being referred to; therefore, check the contents of a work on mechanics to make sure that both 530.12 and 531 are covered before placing it in 530.

541 vs. 546

Physical and theoretical chemistry vs. inorganic chemistry

The rule that physical and theoretical chemistry of specific elements or compounds is classed in 546 does not apply when one or two examples drawn from large groupings like metals or nonmetals are used primarily to study or explain a specific topic in physical or theoretical chemistry. In such cases, use the number in 541, e.g., oxidation reactions 541.3, not 546. If in doubt, prefer 541.

543 vs. 544–545

Analytical chemistry vs. [Qualitative and quantitative analysis]

The distinction between qualitative and quantitative analysis has been rendered largely obsolete by the growing sophistication of techniques. Therefore, prefer 543 over 544 or 545 for specific techniques unless qualitative or quantitative use is specifically emphasized.

549 vs. 546

Mineralogy vs. Inorganic chemistry

Chemistry and mineralogy are considered to be coordinate subjects. As a result, many topics of physical and theoretical chemistry pertaining to the structure and behavior of homogeneous crystalline solids will not be classed in 546. Use 546 for comprehensive works on the chemistry and mineralogy of specific chemical types, but if in doubt, prefer 549.

549 vs. 548

Mineralogy vs. Crystallography

The relation between crystallography and mineralogy is approximately the same as between physical and theoretical chemistry (541) and inorganic chemistry (546). The crystallography of specific minerals is classed in 549 unless used to study or explain a topic in 548, e.g. quartz and feldspar 549, but the study of crystal lattices using quartz and feldspar 548. If in doubt, prefer 549.

550 vs. 910

Earth sciences vs. Geography and travel

Geophysics (550) is the analysis of the structure of the earth and the forces shaping it; physical geography (part of geography and travel in 910) is the description of the resulting landscape. Descriptions of the results of a specific force or process are classed with the force or process in 551; the operation of all forces and processes that combine to create a specific topographic land form is classed in 551.41–.45; the operation of all the forces and processes taken as a whole in a specific area, especially if emphasizing solid geology, is classed with the area in 554–559. However, if the work treats the geographic landscape with only minor consideration of the geophysical processes, it is classed in 910 or under the specific area number in 913–919. For example, physical description of surface features in Myanmar (Burma) 915.91, geophysical processes operating in Myanmar or the geology of Myanmar 555.91, earthquakes in Myanmar 551.2209591, elevations in Myanmar 551.4309591. If in doubt, prefer 550.

Descriptions of surface features for travelers, which usually cover resort accommodations and the ambience as well as geographic features, are also classed in 910, plus notation 04 from the table under 913–919 as appropriate, e.g., tourist beaches in Myanmar 915.9104.

551.5 vs. 551.6

Meteorology vs. Climatology and weather

Meteorology analyzes and describes the properties and phenomena of the atmosphere, and thus explains climate and weather. Meteorology is also the comprehensive subject, encompassing consideration of climatology and weather. Unfortunately, however, some works on the larger subject (meteorology) may be called "climatology," "climate and weather," or simply "climate" or "weather," but must be classed in 551.5 in spite of the words used in the titles. Books so titled are classed in 551.6 only when the words are limited to four senses:

> 1. The description of phenomena of the atmosphere taken as a whole, weather usually being the short-range description, and climate the long-range description
>
> 2. The prediction of weather, climate, or specific meteorological phenomena, that is, weather forecasting and forecasts (551.63–.65)
>
> 3. The study of climate or meteorology in small areas, that is, microclimatology or micrometeorology (551.6)
>
> 4. The attempt to modify weather or any meteorological phenomena (551.68), which is actually a technology

All other aspects, including description (weather reports) of specific phenomena, remain in 551.5, regardless of the terms used in the works in hand. For example, reports of rainfall are classed in 551.57, forecasts of rainfall in 551.64, a forecast of a rainy day in Singapore 551.655957, a discussion of the factors that produce weather in 551.5.

If in doubt, prefer 551.5.

551.7 vs. 560

Historical geology vs. Paleontology   Paleozoology

Paleontology is the study of life in former geological ages through the interpretation of fossils. It utilizes the same material as historical geology (that is, the geologic record) but only as a record of life and the environment in which life evolved. Historical geology emphasizes the rocks and their strata, using paleontological facts to help date and interpret deposition, movement, erosion. If in doubt, prefer 551.7.

552 vs. 549

Petrology vs. Mineralogy

Rocks can be defined as aggregates of minerals, the minerals being homogeneous, usually crystalline grains (large and small) that give rocks their texture. Petrology encompasses the study of rocks and minerals, or of rocks alone. The homogeneous minerals studied by themselves are classed in 549. If in doubt, prefer 552.

553 vs. 333.8, 338.2

Economic geology vs. Subsurface resources vs. Extraction of minerals

For subsurface resources, class reserves in nature in appropriate subdivisions of 553, e.g., reserves of oil that have never been pumped out of the ground 553.2. The only kind of reserves that may be classed in 333.8 are reserves in storage, e.g., crude oil stored in salt caves as a strategic reserve and crude oil in tanks awaiting refinement both 333.8. Class works treating equally reserves in nature and in storage in 553. Do not class any kind of reserves in 338.2.

Class requirements (need, demand) for subsurface resources in 333.8. Do not class demand in 338.2 or 553.

Do not class development of subsurface resources in 333.8, because there is no development of subsurface resources comparable to that possible with other types of resources. New coal mines cannot be grown. What is often referred to as development is almost always some form of extraction, which is classed in 338.2.

Class interdisciplinary works on subsurface resources that include reserves in nature, requirements, and development in 553.

559.9

[Earth sciences in extraterrestrial worlds]

Use 559.9 and notation 0999 from Table 1 in 551–553 for phenomena of celestial bodies directly comparable to terrestrial phenomena. Generally the analogy with earth holds only if the bodies have distinct lithospheres; otherwise hydrosphere and meteorology are moot concepts. For example, class atmosphere of Mars (which has a lithosphere) in 551.50999, but atmosphere of stars (which do not) in 523.8, the red spot of Jupiter (a planet without a distinct lithosphere) in 523.45.

560–590

Life sciences

Summary of major units of the new schedule

The schedule for the life sciences presented in this edition has received a major overhaul. Some units have been more drastically revised than others. Parts of the old schedule that did not need to be changed have been retained. The basic outline of 560 and 580–590 remains intact. Even where revision is complete, a deliberate effort was made to avoid unnecessary reuse of numbers. In most cases, the most heavily used old numbers were sidestepped without compromising the logic of the new schedule.

560 Paleontology

Relatively few changes were made in 560 Paleontology. Protozoa were relocated from 563 to 561, and worms from 565 to 562. Dinosaurs have been changed from an including note to a class-here note in 567.9. The change means that the dinosaurs now approximate the whole of fossil reptiles, and standard subdivisions can be added, e.g., dinosaurs of North America 567.9097.

570 Life sciences   Biology

570 becomes the comprehensive number for biology as well as life sciences.

571–575 Internal biological processes and structures

The completely revised span for biological processes is the core of the new schedule. Biological processes in microorganisms, plants, and animals are now classed in this span, not with the specific organisms as in Edition 12. The processes include physiology, pathology, biochemistry, and related subjects. Anatomy and structure are placed in this sequence because they are basic to an understanding of how all internal biological processes work.

576–578 General and external biological phenomena

Biological subjects other than internal processes and structures are developed in this unit: genetics and evolution, ecology, and natural history of organisms. When these subjects refer to microorganisms, plants, or animals, they are classed with the organisms in 579–590. For these subjects, the preference in favor of organisms continues as in earlier editions. Because behavior refers only to animals, it is developed under animals in 591.5.

579–590 Natural history of specific kinds of organisms

The schedule for specific kinds of organisms retains the basic outline of earlier editions, except that microorganisms, fungi, and algae have all been brought together in 579. Plants remain in 580, animals remain in 590, and no three-digit number in 580–590 has changed its essential meaning. Worms have been relocated from 595.1 to 592, and 599 has been extensively revised to provide greater detail for mammals.

The two biologies

While preference between organism and process was reversed for internal biological processes and structures developed in 571–575, preference for organism was retained in other subjects in biology. The distinction is based upon the recognition of fundamental differences between the literature on the biology of internal processes and the literature on biology of whole organisms. The biology of internal processes is predominantly an experimental science conducted in the laboratory to find out how the parts work. The other biology is predominately a descriptive science conducted in the field to describe how organisms look, how they work as entire organisms, and what their relationships are to each other and the environment. What is true in internal processes tends to be true (with minor variations) of large classes of organisms or of all organisms, and the literature emphasizes the commonalities. In contrast, what is true in general and external biology tends to differ radically among groups of organisms, and the literature emphasizes the differences.

For the most part, the biology of processes needed the most fundamental revision. The outline of the part of the old schedule devoted to the biology of whole organisms remains recognizable in the new.

Recasting 570

570 was completely revised for two reasons: *First*, the preference previously given to specific kind of organism over biological process resulted in scattering of material that should be kept together under process. Internal biological processes and structures have been developed in 571–575, and the plant and animal materials on these subjects have been relocated from 580–590 (particularly from 581 and 591) to the new span. For example, biochemistry is now classed in 572 regardless of the plant or animal in which it is studied, and the digestive system is classed in 573.3 regardless of the animal in which it is studied.

Second, the old 570 schedule was very unbalanced, with about 80% of the material found in two subdivisions (70% in 574, and 10% in 575). Many subdivisions were left unused or scarcely used at all. The imbalance of useful notation in the old schedule makes it possible to limit the reuse of numbers in the new one. In order to help libraries implement the new schedule without requiring them to reclassify the bulk of their collections immediately, 574 and 575 through 575.2 have been left vacant.

Major changes in 579–590

The term "natural history" in the heading of this unit (Natural history of specific kinds of organisms) is shorthand for topics found in 576–578 General and external biological phenomena.

579 Microorganisms, fungi, and algae

The three minor kingdoms of organisms have been brought together in 579 by relocations from 576, 589, and 593.1. 579 was one of the least used subdivisions of 570 in earlier editions.

581 and 591 Specific topics in natural history of plants and animals

581 and 591 have been retained with much narrower meanings. For the most part, subdivisions vacated when internal biological processes and structures in plants and animals were relocated to 571–575 were not reused. 581.4 and 591.4 are exceptions; the former morphology numbers have been redefined to serve for adaptations. 581.7 and 591.7 now replace both the former ecology subdivisions (581.5 and 591.5) and the former subdivisions for biology of areas, regions, places in general (581.909–.92 and 591.909–.92). While the old plant ecology number (581.5) is not reused, 591.5 retains the behavior meaning from former editions and two of the behavior subdivisions.

592–595 Invertebrates

Worms and related animals have been relocated from 595.1 to 592, thus allowing 595 to be limited to arthropods, the largest and most important group of invertebrates. Because Protozoa were relocated out of 593, 593 has been given a heading that better describes its contents: miscellaneous marine and seashore invertebrates.

597 Cold-blooded vertebrates   Fishes

Numbers have been given to two popular kinds of fish, sharks in 597.3 and salmonids (salmon and trout) in 597.5. Amphibians, which were spread over three subdivisions in Edition 12, are now all found in 597.8.

599 Mammalia (Mammals)

Mammals were revised to provide shorter numbers for the major kinds, e.g., ungulates and carnivores. As a result, specific numbers can be given for many popular animals left in broad numbers in Edition 12. For example, dolphins and porpoises have a number in 599.53, beavers in 599.37, deer in 599.65, wolves in 599.773, and seals in 599.79.

571–575

Internal biological processes and structures

Reversal of preference between organism and process

The major change in the new biology schedule is the reversal of preference between organism and process or structure for internal biological processes and structures. The schedule in 571–575 now gives preference to the process or structure. For example, physiology of trees is classed in 571.2 (physiology of plants), not 582.16 (general biology of trees); anatomy of the rat brain in 573.8 (nervous and sensory systems), not 599.35 (general biology of rodents).

Definition and arrangement of internal biological processes

The internal biological processes encompass physiology in its broadest sense. They include biophysics; tissue biology; cell biology; biological control and secretions; reproduction, development, and growth; diseases and pathology; bio-chemistry; and physiological systems.

The specific biological processes are preceded by anatomy and morphology, and are arranged in 571–575 in the order given above. The basic order is to place first the subjects needed to explain or help one understand subjects that come later. Thus anatomy and morphology come first in 571.3 because they are considered basic to an understanding of how all biological processes work. Biophysics comes next in 571.4 because it is basic to all the other processes. The progression continues from relatively simple subjects to complex subjects that are fully explained only through the application of the subjects placed earlier in the schedule.

Three biological subjects, however, differ in their relative scale rather than in their application to each other: tissue biology, cell biology, and biochemistry. These three might be best placed together and arranged according to scale, from the visible level through the microscopic to the submicroscopic level. The first two have been so arranged, tissue biology in 571.5, followed by cell biology in 571.6.

Logically, biochemistry follows cell biology, especially since all cellular process-es are basically chemical, e.g., cell digestion and cell respiration. Because of the amount of literature on the subject, however, biochemistry has a three-digit num-ber to itself in 572, following all the other general processes in 571.

Returning to 571, biological control and secretions follow in 571.7. Next are reproduction, development, and growth in 571.8, subjects in which all the pre-viously mentioned processes come together to produce living organisms. The last general processes, diseases and pathology (in which all the aforementioned processes unravel), come in 571.9.

Specific physiological systems follow biochemistry, those of animals in 573 and those of plants in 575. (574 is left vacant because over 70% of the 570 material classed under earlier editions fell in that single main subdivision.) The arrange-ment of physiological systems in 573 for animals is generally parallel to that found in medicine under 616.1–.8, e.g., respiratory system in 573.2 and 616.2. At the end of the parallel span, 573.9 is used for miscellaneous systems and top-ics specific to animals: physiology of communication, bioelectric organs, and regional physiology and histology.

There are relatively few parallels between 573 (for animal systems) and 575 (for plant parts and systems) because the structures and the principles upon which plants and animals work are so different. The subdivisions of 575 begin with parts and move into physiological systems. Stems are found in 575.4, roots and leaves in 575.5, and flowers in 575.6. 575.6 (Reproductive organs   Flowers) is the only subdivision that parallels the corresponding subdivision for animals (573.6 Reproductive system), because only among the generative organs is there a fundamental similarity between organs in plants and organs in animals. (*For the relation between reproductive systems and organs [573.6 and 575.6] and reproduction, development, and growth in general, see discussion at 571.8 vs. 573.6, 575.6.*)

The final three subdivisions of 575 are devoted to physiological systems in plants that are only vaguely similar to systems found in animals. Plant circulation (575.7) is driven by the forces of physical chemistry, not muscular action as in animals. Transpiration follows in 575.8. The last subdivision, 575.9, covers animal-like processes in plants: movement, sensitivity, and predation by carnivorous plants.

Processes limited to kinds of organisms

Most of the span 571–572 is devoted to internal processes that are common to plants and animals, but a few topics in 571–572 are more fully developed in animals than in other organisms, e.g., immunity in 571.9. Similarly, photosynthesis, a biochemical process limited to plants and certain other organisms, is found in 572, not in 575.

Since microorganisms, fungi, and algae do not have the unique organ systems and specialized structures that require the special developments found in 573 and 575, all internal processes and structures related to them will be found in appropriate subdivisions of 571–572. For example, respiration in microorganisms is cellular respiration and is classed in biochemistry (572).

571–575 vs. 630

Internal biological processes and structures vs. Agriculture and related technologies

Physiology and pathology

The classification of physiology and anatomy differs between agricultural plants and animals. Physiology and anatomy of agricultural plants are classed in biology (571.2 and 571.3 and related numbers in 571.5–.9 and 575); physiology and anatomy of animals, in agriculture (636.089 and related numbers in 636.1–.8).

The classification of pathology and diseases is the same for agricultural plants and animals. The number for plant pathology and diseases (and for comprehensive works on plant and animal pathology and diseases in agriculture) is 632. The number for animal pathology and diseases is 636.089.

The rules given above do not apply to experimental work on basic biology that uses domestic plants and animals as models. Class such works in 571–575.

571–573 vs. 610

[Internal processes and structures in animals] vs. Medical sciences   Medicine

Class results of anatomical and physiological research with animal models in 571–573, but results of pharmacological, therapeutic, and pathological research in 615–618 if the medical relevance for humans is stated or implied. If in doubt, prefer 571–573.

571.6 vs. 571.2

Cell biology vs. [Physiology and related subjects in] Plants and microorganisms

Microorganisms

There is a significant overlap between the general physiology of microorganisms and their cell biology. Class in 571.2 works that are either limited to generalities, or discuss cell reproduction of microorganisms (571.8) as well as their general cell biology. Class in 571.6 works that go into details of internal structures, e.g., membranes and organelles, without also discussing details of reproduction. If in doubt, prefer 571.6.

571.8 vs. 573.6, 575.6

Reproduction, development, growth vs. Reproductive system [in animals and] Reproductive organs [in plants]   Flowers

Reproduction has a place in both parts of the schedule for internal biological processes and structures. In the part concerned with general processes (571–572), it is found in 571.8 linked with development and growth as a general process affecting the whole body of all kinds of organisms. In the part concerned with organ systems and specialized structures unique to either plants or animals (573–575), it is found in 573.6 (reproductive system in animals) and 575.6 (reproductive organs or flowers of plants).

573.4 vs. 571.7

Endocrine and excretory systems vs. Biological control and secretions

Hormones

571.7 is the comprehensive number for hormones, but the hormones of the endocrine system of animals are much more elaborately developed than the hormones of plants and microorganisms. Most of the literature on hormones emphasizes hormones in animals. Hence, one should use 571.7 only for the truly comprehensive works that give balanced treatment of hormones in plants and microorganisms. Use 573.4 for works that emphasize endocrine hormones while giving relatively limited treatment to hormones outside the animal kingdom. If in doubt, prefer 573.4.

576.5 vs. 572.8

Genetics vs. Biochemical genetics

The big division in genetics is between those topics that held the attention of scientists before the discovery of the double helix structure of DNA and those that emerged after the discovery. Once the basic chemical structure of genetic material was understood, topics emerged that are basically biochemical, e.g., genetic replication and errors in transcription. These are classed in 572.8. Although chromosomes and genes were known long before the structure of DNA, their operation and function cannot be explained except by studying the chemistry of the DNA they contain. Thus they are also classed in 572.8. Class comprehensive works on genetics, and discussion of topics that do not emphasize chemicals like DNA, RNA, and their components in 576.5; class those topics in which an understanding of the structure of DNA is central in 572.8. If in doubt, prefer 576.5.

576.8 vs. 560

Evolution vs. Paleontology   Paleozoology

Paleontology provides a major part of the evidence for evolution, and many works cover both fields. Class in 576.8 works that emphasize how paleontological findings are evidence for evolution and works that include significant non-paleontological evidence. Class in 560 works on the evolution of extinct organisms and works on the history of life that emphasize the description of extinct organisms and ancient environments. If in doubt, prefer 576.8.

577 vs. 578.7

Ecology vs. Organisms characteristic of specific kinds of environment

Kinds of environment treated in ecology (577) all have counterparts under the number for organisms in specific kinds of environment (578.7). Class in 578.7 descriptive accounts of organisms found in a specific kind of area; class in 577 works emphasizing the interrelationships among various elements in a specific kind of area. 578.7 is the comprehensive number for biology of specific kinds of areas, e.g., marine biology 578.77. As soon as discussion begins to emphasize interrelationships among organisms, however, consider 577. If in doubt about the emphasis, prefer 577 (even though 578.7 is the comprehensive number).

577.2 vs. 579–590

Specific factors affecting ecology vs. Natural history of specific kinds of organisms

Autecology

Use caution when classing works on autecology of dominant organisms (usually plants) of a specific environment in the span for specific kinds of organisms. For example, class the role of grass in grasslands in 577.4 (*not* 584 [the number for general biology of monocotyledons, which includes grasses]). Similarly, class the ecology of specific forest associations in 577.3, e.g., ecology of coniferous forest associations 577.3 (*not* 585).

The same principle applies for ecosystems named after animals, e.g., fishpond ecosystems. Unless the emphasis is really on the fishes in the fishpond, class in 577.6 Aquatic ecology (*not* 597 [the number for fishes]).

In summary, to be classed in 579–590, a work must emphasize the kind of organism, not an environment which takes its name from a kind of organism, e.g., it must emphasize grasses rather than grasslands in general. If in doubt, prefer 577.

578 vs. 304.2, 508, 910

Natural history of organisms and related subjects vs. Human ecology vs. Natural history vs. Geography and travel

Use 508 if a work on nature has significant emphasis on earth sciences phenomena, e.g., weather, water features, and mountains; but use 578 if the work concentrates on various living things and their settings. If the work covers the description of human settlement as well as natural phenomena, class it in 910. If the emphasis is on the relationship between natural phenomena and human institutions, class it in 304.2. If in doubt between 304.2 and 910, prefer 910. If in doubt between science (508 and 578) and nonscience (304.2 and 910) numbers, prefer 508 and 578. If in doubt between 508 and 578, prefer 578.

578.76–.77 vs. 551.46

[Aquatic environments] vs. Hydrosphere   Oceanography

While 551.46 is the number for comprehensive treatment of the hydrosphere and the biology of water bodies, works on aquatic biology and marine biology may include significant consideration of land and sea waters as part of the lives of aquatic organisms. If in doubt, prefer 578.76–.77.

579–590

Natural history of specific kinds of organisms

Nomenclature

Common English terms are preferred to scientific terms in headings when the English terms are generally accepted as covering all the organisms in the number. For example, at 598 "Birds" means the same thing as "Aves," and at 595.78 "Moths and butterflies" cover all the insects in the group called Lepidoptera; therefore, neither "Aves" nor "Lepidoptera" are named at these numbers. However, at 595.79, there is no commonly accepted name or set of names covering Hymenoptera; therefore, "Hymenoptera" is given in the heading, and ants, bees, and wasps are given in notes.

In some cases, the rule giving preference to common names leads to mixed headings, e.g., "Falconiformes, Caprimulgiformes, owls" at 598.9.

Scientific names are not usually given in notes except under headings beginning with the word "Miscellaneous," where the common names do not define all that is found in the number. Occasionally, scientific names are added in parentheses in the heading if the common term might be ambiguous, e.g., at 595.77 Flies (Diptera) and fleas, to make clear that "flies" in 595.77 do not include certain other insects called flies.

580 vs. 582.13

Plants vs. Plants noted for their flowers

The difference between flower books and books on flowering plants is analogous to the difference between a flower garden and a vegetable garden. Everything normally planted in a vegetable garden is a "flowering plant," yet a vegetable garden is rarely confused with a flower garden. Likewise, one should not confuse general works on flowering plants that cover anything from magnolias to grass with works that emphasize flowers. Class the former in 580, and the latter in 582.13. If in doubt, prefer 580.

583–585

[Spermatophytes (Seed plants)]

Interdisciplinary works

Interdisciplinary works on most plants important for food or other products are classed in technology numbers. The general rule is to prefer numbers in which a thing is used for interdisciplinary works on the thing. Therefore, prefer 641.3 for food plants, e.g., apples 641.3 (*not* 583); 635.9 for ornamental plants, e.g., lilies 635.9 (*not* 584); and 677 for textile plants, e.g., cotton 677 (*not* 583).

When there are two or more uses in technology, or one big use offset by an obvious botanical interest, the interdisciplinary number remains in botany. For example, interdisciplinary works on oaks are classed in 583 because oaks are useful as ornamental trees as well as lumber trees. Laurels are well known as ornamentals, but interdisciplinary works on laurels are classed in 583 because there are many wild species of interest to botanists and nature lovers.

If in doubt, class interdisciplinary works on specific plants in 583–585.

604.7 vs. 660

Hazardous materials technology vs. Chemical engineering and related technologies

Use 660 for consideration of hazardous chemicals during chemical engineering; prefer 604.7 for comprehensive consideration of hazardous chemicals that includes handling, transporting, and utilization outside the chemical industry.

However, for specific hazardous chemicals, the comprehensive technology number is usually found in 660, e.g., processing, transportation, utilization of natural gas 665.7.

If in doubt, prefer 604.7.

608 vs. 609

Inventions and patents vs. Historical, geographic, persons treatment [of technology]

Use 608 for works on inventions that are primarily descriptive (and usually arranged topically); 609 for works that emphasize historical factors that stimulat ed inventions, or that arrange inventions chronologically. If in doubt, prefer 608.

610 vs. 362.1

Medical sciences   Medicine vs. Physical illness

Services at 362.1 refer to societal arrangements to make sure that specific kinds of medical work are provided, e.g., services of nurses. The work actually performed is classed in 610, e.g., the work of nurses 610.73. Interdisciplinary works covering both societal arrangements for medical work and the work itself are classed in 362.1. If in doubt, prefer 610.

610 vs. 616

Medical sciences   Medicine vs. Diseases

Class in 616 comprehensive works on the diseases listed in 616–618. However, if a work contains separate treatment of health, pharmacology, and therapeutics, as well as of diseases, class it in 610.

When the whole of medicine is brought to bear on the concept of diseases in a single treatise that discusses group after group of diseases, class the work in 616. The table of contents usually offers guidance. If it reads like a summary of topics in 610.73–619, class the work in 610; if it reads like a summary of topics in 616.02–.99 or in 616–618, class the work in 616. If in doubt, prefer 610.

Standard subdivisions

Use notation from Table 1 with caution under 616 except for internal medicine or works clearly limited to the concept of diseases. Prefer 610.3 for medical dictionaries, 610.71 for medical schools, 610.92 for doctors not having a distinct specialty.

610.73

Nursing and services of medical technicians and assistants

Class here only works that emphasize what the nurse does. As the nursing profession continues to expand its responsibilities and gain recognition for those it already has, more and more works by and for nurses are about the subjects of medical science in a larger context than intended here. Class such works in other medical numbers, e.g., a survey of medical sciences for nurses 610, not 610.73; a work treating the problems and techniques of surgery written to help nurses understand the context of their duties 617, not 610.73, even if called surgical nursing.

610.9

Historical, geographic, persons treatment [of medical sciences, of medicine]

Class in 610.9 the history of three or more medical sciences. Class the history of a particular medical science with the science, e.g., the history of nursing 610.7309, of surgery 617.09, of internal medicine 616.009. Class histories of major diseases and their distribution in 614.4, and histories of medical service and medical welfare in 362.109. (*See also discussion at 362.1–.4 vs. 610.*)

Class works on former medical practices emphasizing therapy, e.g., folk remedies, in 615.8.

612 vs. 611

Human physiology vs. Human anatomy, cytology (cell biology), histology (tissue biology)

Anatomy concerns the form and structure of organs in contrast to their physiology, which deals with how they work. Sometimes works bearing the names of organs emphasize their physiology or treat physiology as well as anatomy; class these works in 612, unless they are limited to the cytological and histological level. Class treatment of anatomy, physiology, and pathology at the cytological and histological level in 611. If in doubt, prefer 612.

612.8 vs. 152

[Physiology of] Nervous functions Sensory functions vs. [Psychology of] Sensory perception, movement, emotions, physiological drives

Class in 152 works that emphasize awareness, sensation, intentions, meanings, and actions as experienced by the individual or observed and described without reference to the physics or chemistry of the nervous system, e.g., seeing colors, feeling anger. Class in 612.8 works that emphasize the physical and chemical mechanisms and pathways of sensations, emotions, movements, e.g., studies using electrodes to determine what parts of the brain process different kinds of stimuli. Class comprehensive works in 152. If in doubt, prefer 612.8.

612.8 vs. 154.6

[Physiology of] Nervous functions Sensory functions vs. [Psychology of] Sleep phenomena

Class sleep phenomena in 154.6 if the emphasis is on the overall state of sleep, on the effect of sleep on other psychological activity, or on dreams as phenomena that have meaning in themselves or in the life of the dreamer. Class sleep phenomena in 612.8 if the emphasis is on the chain of bodily activities or on other physiological activity accompanying sleep or dreams, e.g., eye movements, breathing, brain waves. If in doubt, prefer 612.8.

613 vs. 615.8

Promotion of health vs. Specific therapies and kinds of therapies

Many of the topics in 613 appear also in 615.8, e.g., breathing, diet, exercise. In each case the 613 number refers to the preventive or "staying healthy" aspects, while 615.8 refers to the therapeutic or "regaining health" aspects. Class comprehensive works in 613.

613.7 vs. 646.7, 796

Physical fitness vs. Management of personal and family living
Grooming vs. Athletic and outdoor sports and games [as recreation]

Exercise and sports activities as means of improving physical fitness are classed in 613.7, as means of improving the appearance of the body in 646.7, as recreation in 796. For example, lifting weights for physical fitness is classed in 613.7, bodybuilding contests in 646.7, weight lifting as a sport (i.e., contests to determine who can lift the most weight) in 796.41. If in doubt among 613.7, 646.7, and 796, prefer 613.7.

614.4–.5 vs. 362.1–.4

[Incidence of and public measures to prevent disease] vs. Problems of and services to persons with illnesses and disabilities

Studies of epidemics and of the incidence of physical disease (including mental retardation and physical disabilities) are classed in 614 when treated solely from the medical standpoint. Works emphasizing diseases as social problems are classed in 362.1. If in doubt, prefer 614.4–.5.

Works on the social provision of services to persons with physical illness are classed in 362.1. Works on preventive measures, however, are classed in 614.4–.5, regardless of whether the emphasis is medical or social. Thus works on social provision of immunization services are classed in 614.4, as are works on the medical aspects of immunization. Note that the public measures classed in 614.4–.5 are strictly limited to preventive ones. For example, class fluoridation and programs advising people how to avoid cavities in 614.5, but class programs to identify and treat people with cavities in 362.1. If in doubt, prefer 362.1.

Works about the incidence and prevention of mental illness, mental illness as a social problem, and social provision of services to the mentally ill, are all classed in 362.2.

614.4

Incidence of and public measures to prevent disease

Epidemiology

The term "epidemiology" sometimes refers to a research technique with application outside 614, e.g., in determining etiologies, such as smoking as a cause of cancer 616.99; in determining the dimensions of social service requirements, such as the boundaries of the mental retardation problem 362.3; in exploring the possible effectiveness of proposed preventive measures, such as in reducing traffic accidents 363.12.

615.5

Therapeutics

Use 615.5 when the discussion of general therapeutic systems is historical or theoretical, e.g., a discussion of the theory of chiropractic 615.5. When these systems are discussed in their application to therapy, class them in a therapy number, e.g., the application of chiropractic 615.8. When the therapies are applied to specific conditions, class in 616–618, e.g., chiropractic in musculoskeletal diseases 616.7.

Be careful about biography. Founders of systems are usually classed with the respective systems, e.g., a biography of Andrew Taylor Still, the founder of osteopathy, 615.5. Other practitioners of a specific system are usually classed in 610.92. Many chiropractors limit their practice to therapeutic manipulation (615.8) or to manipulation for diseases of the musculoskeletal system (616.7). For these people, the best biography number is one that emphasizes their special therapeutic system—615.5. For chiropractors who do not limit their practice, use 610.92 for biographies.

615.8

Specific therapies and kinds of therapies

Several therapies listed in 615.8 are usually applied only to certain specific types of disorders, and works on the therapies take such application for granted without highlighting it in the title. Note the unstated emphasis and class accordingly, e.g., radiotherapy emphasizing cancer treatment 616.99, music therapy emphasizing psychiatric uses 616.89.

Use 615.8 with caution for diet therapy; when a single food element is heavily emphasized, diet therapy may amount to therapy with a specific drug, which is classed at 615, e.g., a diet distinctive largely by its use of enzymes or by its use of royal jelly.

Folk medicine

Folk medicine at 615.8 is under therapy. If a work gives more than token consideration to folk theories on the causes of disease, it must be classed in 610, e.g., folk etiologies and therapies of India 610.954 (or 616.00954 when the material is arranged by class of disease as in 616.1–.9).

615.8 vs. 234, 291.3

Specific therapies and kinds of therapies vs. Salvation (Soteriology) and grace [and] Public worship and other practices

Religious and psychic therapy

In many cultures, medicine and healing involve rites and ceremonies and religious beliefs, as well as physical practices. Class a work on healing and medicine in 615.8 if it focuses on religious practices as a part of the medical practice.

Also class in 615.8 works on the use of psychic and paranormal powers in healing that do not mention a religious context.

Class in 291.3 or 234 healing as a religious practice, including such topics as religious beliefs about illness, rituals and prayers for healing, miraculous cures by charismatic leaders or saints. Often, works on this topic are also concerned with emotional or spiritual healing as well as physical healing, or in place of physical healing.

If in doubt, prefer 615.8.

616–618 vs. 615

[Diseases, surgery, other branches of medicine] vs. Pharmacology and therapeutics

Class in 615 only general works on the pharmacodynamic action of drugs and their effects on the human body. Class the use of a drug in treatment in 616–618. If in doubt, prefer 616–618.

616 vs. 612

Diseases vs. Human physiology

Class in 612 comprehensive works on physiology (612) and pathological physiology (616.07). Class in 616 comprehensive works on diseases that move from a discussion of physiology to a more general consideration of causes of disease, complications, prevention, and therapy. For example, class the normal and pathological conditions of the circulatory system in 612.1, but the physiology, pathology, and therapeutics of the circulatory system in 616.1. If in doubt, prefer 616.

616 vs. 616.07

Diseases vs. Pathology

Use 616.07 for detailed descriptions of diseased conditions, mechanisms and processes of disease, causes and manifestations, diagnostic techniques. For more general works about disease that include prevention and treatment as well as pathology, use 616.

"Clinical medicine" has two meanings. In one sense it approximates the whole of 616, i.e., the application of all branches of medicine to treatment of various diseases. However, just as often it is shorthand for the work of a clinical diagnostic laboratory, and is properly classed at 616.07.

If in doubt, prefer 616.

616 vs. 617.4

Diseases vs. Surgery by systems

617.4 is primarily limited to operative surgery of systems. Nonoperative therapies are usually classed in 616, e.g., therapeutic manipulation of muscles 616.7, not 617.4. Nonoperative therapies are classed in 617.4 only if they have some connection with operative surgery, e.g., electrotherapy by heart pacer 617.4, since the pacer must be surgically implanted. If in doubt, prefer 616.

616 vs. 618.92

Diseases vs. Pediatrics

Use caution in classing in 618.92 certain diseases that are most often treated in children, but that remain lifetime problems or threats, e.g., congenital diseases, mumps. Class these in 616 unless the work in hand is actually limited to their occurrence in children.

616.07 vs. 571.9

Pathology [in medicine] vs. Diseases   Pathology [in biology]

Immunology

Class in 616.07 and other numbers in 616–618 works emphasizing immunology in relation to diseases and problems in human beings. Class in 571.9 works emphasizing immunology in relation to diseases in general and diseases in animals. If in doubt, prefer 616.07.

616.1–.8

Diseases of specific systems and organs

When a disease of one system affects another system so strongly that it is the second system that must be the focus of concern and treatment, class the work with the affected system, e.g., retinal complications of diabetes 617.7 (*not* 616.4).

616.1–.8 vs. 616.9

Diseases of specific systems and organs vs. Other diseases

Communicable diseases

Communicable diseases that affect primarily one organ or system are most often classed with the system or organ in 616.1–.8, but there are many exceptions. For example, comprehensive works on diarrhea are classed in 616.3, but Asiatic cholera is classed in 616.9. Check the index to see where a specific communicable disease should be classed. If in doubt, prefer 616.1–.8 over 616.9 for a communicable disease affecting primarily one organ or system.

616.85

Neuroses; speech and language disorders; disorders of personality, intellect, impulse control

Homosexuality

Only works in which the author treats homosexuality as a medical disorder—or focuses on arguing against the views of those who consider homosexuality to be a medical disorder—should be classed in 616.85. Works about gay men and lesbians in relation to other topics in medicine should be classed with the topic plus notation 086 from Table 1, e.g., advice to gay men and lesbians about substance abuse problems 616.860086. Most works about gay men and lesbians are classed outside medicine, e.g., Christian social theology about homosexuality 261.8, gay liberation movement 305.9, interdisciplinary works on homosexuality 306.76, gay men and lesbians in armed forces 355.0086. If in doubt, prefer a number other than 616.85.

616.86 vs. 158.1, 248.8, 291.4, 362.29

[Medical aspects of] Substance abuse (Drug abuse) vs. [Applied psychology aspects of] Personal improvement and analysis vs. Guides to Christian life for specific classes of persons [and] Religious experience, life, practice vs. Substance abuse [as a social problem]

Recovery from addiction

Class in 616.86 self-help programs for individuals recovering from substance abuse and interdisciplinary works about recovery programs that focus on the individual's life with addiction, covering the individual's experience with both social and medical aspects. Class in 362.29 the organization providing the program, including administration of the program, and interdisciplinary works that cover both organizational and therapeutic aspects of recovery programs. Class in 248.8, 291.4, and related numbers in 292–299 religious guides and inspirational works for the recovering addict. If in doubt, class in 616.86.

As a kind of medical service, recovery programs for persons recovering from a specific kind of substance abuse are classed with the substance. No distinction is made between programs run by professionals, such as psychiatrists or clinical psychologists, and self-help programs run by laypersons; both kinds of recovery programs are classed as therapy for or rehabilitation from a medical problem.

As a kind of social service, recovery programs for those recovering from a specific kind of substance abuse are classed in 362.29. Works classed in 362.29 typically emphasize the organizational or institutional aspects of the program.

For example, interdisciplinary works on life as a recovering alcoholic and the twelve step Alcoholics Anonymous program are classed in 616.86. Comprehensive works on Alcoholics Anonymous, the organization which provides the program and places for individuals in the program to meet, are classed in 362.292. A general guide to a recovering alcoholic on how to live a religious life is classed in 291.4; a Christian life, 248.8.

Works on recovery from addiction are not classed in 158.1 Personal improvement and analysis in applied psychology because psychology applied to a medical problem is classed with the medical problem, not in 150.

616.9 vs. 616

Other diseases vs. Diseases

Communicable diseases

Do not confuse medical microbiology in 616 with the classes of communicable disease in 616.9 caused by various types of microorganisms. The emphasis in 616 is on the organism, usually as the cause of disease, while in 616.9 it is on the whole disease and its course, cure, and prevention. Each is comprehensive in its own way, 616 as the interdisciplinary number for pathogenic organisms affecting humans and domestic animals, and 616.9 for the resulting diseases. If in doubt, prefer 616.9.

617 vs. 616

Miscellaneous branches of medicine   Surgery vs. Diseases

617 contains a mixed set of nonsurgical and surgical specialties. If there is a provision in both 616 and 617 for an organ that defines a specialty, use the 617 number only for surgery. (*See also discussion at 617.5.*)

Class comprehensive works on medical treatment of persons with disabilities in 617 unless the term is clearly used to cover all disabling diseases, in which case, class in 616. If in doubt whether to class a work on persons with disabilities in 616 or 617, prefer 617.

617.5

Regional medicine   Regional surgery

Two quite different concepts are brought together here: (1) regions, which incorporate parts of several physiological systems, e.g., the abdominal region; and (2) organs, which are parts of single systems, e.g., the stomach. Since the nonsurgical treatment of specific organs is provided for with the system in 616.1–.8, 617.5 is used only for surgery of specific organs. In the case of regions, resolve doubts in favor of 617.5. In the case of organs, resolve doubts in favor of 616 numbers or numbers in 617.6–.8 for teeth, eyes, and ears.

617.6 vs. 617.5

Dentistry vs. Regional medicine   Regional surgery

Oral surgery

"Oral surgery" is a term much used in the dental profession. Do not class a work so identified in 617.5 unless it covers substantially more than procedures for which one would go to a dentist (617.6).

618.92 vs. 617

Pediatrics vs. Miscellaneous branches of medicine   Surgery

Class in 618.92 nonsurgical specialties provided for in 617.5 and 617.7–.8 when applied to children (regional medicine, ophthalmology, otology, audiology). Class surgical specialties applied to children in 617—comprehensive works in 617.9, surgery of a specific organ, system, disorder with the subject. For example, class medicine of the back for children in 618.92, but surgery of the back in 617.5.

Class both medical and surgical aspects of dentistry for children in 617.6. Also class both nonsurgical and surgical aspects of topics provided for in 617.1–.2 in 617 when applied to children, e.g., pediatric sports medicine 617.1.

618.97 vs. 617

Geriatrics vs. Miscellaneous branches of medicine   Surgery

Class in 618.97 nonsurgical specialties provided for in 617.5–.8 when applied to persons in late adulthood (regional medicine, dentistry, ophthalmology, otology, audiology). Class surgical specialties applied to persons in late adulthood in 617—comprehensive works in 617.9, surgery of a specific organ, system, disorder with the subject. For example, class medicine of the back for persons in late adulthood in 618.97, but surgery of the back in 617.5; class diseases of the teeth and gums in 618.97, but dental surgery in 617.6.

Class both nonsurgical and surgical aspects of topics provided for in 617.1–.2 in 617 when applied to persons in late adulthood, e.g., injuries in late adulthood 617.10084.

621.3841 vs. 621.3845

Amateur (Ham) radio vs. Radiotelephony

Both ham and citizens band radio are two-way systems for nonprofessionals involving reserved bandwidths not available to commercial stations. However, the word "amateur" has by tradition been reserved for long-distance (usually short-wave) communication regulated by international treaties, with stiff licensing requirements for operators. In contrast, citizens band is local (ca. 10 miles or 15 kilometers), with easier or no licensing requirements. If in doubt, prefer 621.3841.

622 vs. 662, 669

Mining engineering and related processes vs. Technology of explosives, fuels, related products [and] Metallurgy

In-situ processing, ore dressing, chemical engineering

In-situ processing involves using chemical techniques to get the target materials (or compounds containing the target materials) out of the ground. It is, therefore, usually considered as mining, and is classed in 622. However, in-situ processing of a fossil fuel usually transforms the fuel into another form. When there is such a transformation, class the processing in the chemical engineering number for the material produced, e.g., coal gasification 665.7.

Ore dressing, which refers to physical means of separating more usable ore from what has been dug out of the ground, is also classed in 622. When physical means that effect substantial chemical change are applied, the process normally becomes chemical engineering (usually metallurgy, 669). For example, magnetic separation of iron ore is classed in 622, but electrodeposition of iron from ores is classed in 669.

Since use of high temperatures causes drastic chemical changes, it is counted as chemical engineering, e.g., pyrometallurgy 669.028.

If in doubt, prefer 622.

624 vs. 624.1

Civil engineering vs. Structural engineering and underground construction

Structural engineering may be considered the "general topics" heading for civil engineering. It comprises the specific subdisciplines of civil engineering that have general applicability to all kinds of structures. Since a civil engineer is normally trained in all branches of structural engineering, basic texts on civil engineering emphasize the subject. Use 624.1 only for works that take a narrow view of structural engineering, that is, that do not discuss the various types of structures to which the engineering is applied. If in doubt, prefer 624.

624 vs. 690

Civil engineering vs. Buildings

To be classed in 690, the work must limit its discussion to habitable structures (buildings). If other structures are discussed, the work is classed in 624. Works about "building" in the sense of constructing all types of structures are classed in 624, not 690. If in doubt, prefer 624.

The word "construction" in the title usually implies that a work covers more than habitable structures. However, it is sometimes used loosely for construction of the type of buildings found in 690.

629.04 vs. 388

Transportation engineering vs. Transportation [services]   Ground transportation

Vehicles

The following guidelines help to distinguish between the vehicle numbers in 385–388 and those in 623.7, 623.8, 625.2, 629, and 688.6.

Class in 385–388:

> 1. Services provided by the vehicle, e.g., transportation of passengers by trains 385.

> 2. Operation (general) of the vehicle, e.g., duties of the ship's captain 387.5.

> 3. Economic and social aspects of the vehicle, e.g., a register of the airplanes owned by a company 387.7.

Class in 629.04 and related numbers in 600:

> 1. Description of the vehicle, e.g., steam locomotives of the 1930s 625.2.

> 2. Technology of the vehicle, e.g., design tests for ships 623.8.

> 3. Operation (technical) of the vehicle, e.g., piloting spacecraft 629.45.

> 4. Maintenance and repair of the vehicle, e.g., repairing motorcycles 629.28.

Interdisciplinary works are classed in 385–388. If in doubt, prefer 629.04 and related numbers in 600.

629.04 vs. 621.43

Transportation engineering vs. Internal-combustion engines

Several specific internal-combustion engines and propulsion systems have their greatest development as engines for a single type of transportation, e.g., spark-ignition engines in passenger automobiles, jet engines in aircraft, and rocket propulsion engines or booster rockets in space vehicles. Although 621.43 is the comprehensive number of each specific kind of engine, most works will emphasize the engine in the specific type of transportation. Therefore, if in doubt between 621.43 and a number in 629, prefer the number in 629.

A work on rocket engines that discusses both missile rockets 623.4 and space transportation rockets 629.47 is classed in 621.43, the comprehensive works number for rocket engines.

629.136 vs. 387.7

Airports vs. Air transportation

Air traffic control

Class in 629.136 works on the equipment needed, e.g., radar devices, and the duties of the air traffic controllers. Class in 387.7 works on general operational aspects, such as, determining how many controllers are needed per airport; and on economic and social aspects, such as the radio call letters of the control tower. Interdisciplinary works are classed in 387.7; however, if in doubt, class in 629.136.

629.43, 629.45 vs. 919.904

Unmanned space flight [and] Manned space flight vs. Geography of and travel in extraterrestrial worlds

Class in 629.43 and 629.45 works about getting to an extraterrestrial world and exploring it from space, e.g., Viking Mars Program 629.43. Class in 919.904 works about exploring the world once the vehicle has landed. Currently, most works that class in 919.9 are projected accounts, e.g., astronautics on Mars 919.9. If in doubt, class in 629.43 and 629.45.

Most discoveries of extraterrestrial worlds concern the "earth sciences" of the world and are classed in 550, e.g., volcanic activity of Mars 551.210999.

630 vs. 579–590, 641.3

Agriculture and related technologies vs. Natural history of specific kinds of organisms vs. Food

Interdisciplinary numbers

Numbers in 579–590 are used for interdisciplinary works on plants and animals in general, but not for domestic plants and animals, or species known almost exclusively in agriculture. Discussion of varieties not known in nature is a good indicator that the interdisciplinary number for a species is in agriculture.

The interdisciplinary numbers for species harvested in the wild, e.g., mushrooms, trees, and fishes, are usually found in 579–590 unless the species is best known for a single product, e.g., teak for lumber 674 (*not* 583). Class works that have material on where to find species in the wild but concentrate on how to grow them in 630, e.g., finding and growing wild flowers 635.9 (*not* 582.13), where aquarium fish are found and how to raise them 639.34 (*not* 597).

The interdisciplinary number for food is 641.3. Thus works that discuss the utilization and food value as well as the agriculture and biology of edible plants and animals are classed in 641.3, not in 579–590 or 630.

If in doubt, prefer numbers in 600 over 579–590, and prefer 630 over 641.3.

633–635

Specific plant crops

Certain plants are important for two or more quite different crops, and may be classed in different numbers for each. Some of the more important distinctions are:

Cereal grains versus cereal grasses (633.1 vs. 633.2)

Class in 633.1 if grown for grain (even if the fodder is an important by-product), in 633.2 if the whole plant is to be consumed (even if the grain is allowed to ripen).

Legumes (633.3 vs. 635)

Class in 633.3 if grown for either the ripened fruit or forage, in 635 if the pod is to be picked green or unripened for human consumption.

Other crops

When the difference in production techniques and the appearance of the crop produced by the farmer is minor, class the crop in the category that best fits the predominant use. For example, potatoes grown for food, feed, or starch are all grown in the same manner and look alike; therefore, they are all classed in 635. However, hemlock grown for lumber is grown in a quite different manner (and looks quite different when shipped) from hemlock grown for landscaping. The first is classed in 634.9, the latter in 635.9. If the crop described does not fit existing numbers where the plant is named or implied, class the work in the closest suitable number, e.g., a legume grown for fiber 633.5. If in doubt, prefer the first number in the schedule where the plant is named or implied.

635.9 vs. 582.1

Flowers and ornamental plants [in agriculture] vs. Herbaceous and woody plants, plants noted for their flowers

The groupings of plants in 582.1 are similar to some groupings found in floriculture. Class in 635.9 if the emphasis is on plants to be cultivated or appreciated in human-made settings, in 582.1 if the emphasis is on the plants in nature or on their biology. If in doubt, prefer 635.9.

See also discussion at 630 vs. 579–590, 641.3.

636.72–.75

Specific breeds and groups of dogs

The main groupings used are those recognized by the American Kennel Club (AKC) in *The Complete Dog Book,* 1992. The roughly corresponding groupings of the Kennel Club of England (KCE) are given in class-here notes when the names differ materially. Most, but not all, of the breeds listed in the schedule are those recognized by the AKC. Class other breeds having pedigrees recognized in other nations that fit within the AKC or KCE groupings with the groupings, e.g., European gundogs 636.752. If in doubt about a breed not named in the schedule, class it in 636.7.

643, 690, 728.7 vs. 629.226

Housing and household equipment, Buildings, [Architecture of] Vacation houses, cabins, hunting lodges, houseboats, mobile homes vs. Campers, motor homes, trailers (caravans)

Use 629.226 (which is listed under types of motor land vehicles) for what are essentially either automobiles with living accommodations, collapsible living accommodations to be used with trucks or trailers, or trailers with such limited living accommodations that they would not (even when hooked up) serve as permanent homes. Do not use 629.226 for mobile homes that must be towed and are meant to stay in one location for a long time. Use the housing numbers if in doubt, and use 643 for interdisciplinary works on movable homes.

649 vs. 613.2

Child rearing and home care of persons with illnesses and disabilities vs. Dietetics

Breast feeding

Class in 649 interdisciplinary works on breast feeding and practical mothers' guides to breast feeding. Works classed in 649 may cover a range of topics, including mother-infant bonding and the joy of breast feeding, how to position the baby to avoid nipple soreness, how to cope with an over-abundant milk supply, expressing and storing breast milk, breast feeding for working mothers. Nutrition and personal health are likely to be among the topics covered in a work that belongs in 649, but they are not the focus. Class works about breast feeding that focus on nutrition and personal health in 613.2, e.g., works emphasizing the effect of a mother's diet on the composition and volume of her breast milk, the nutritional values of human breast milk, changes in the composition of breast milk during lactation. Also classed in 613.2 are comprehensive works on medical aspects of breast feeding. If in doubt, prefer 649.

657 vs. 658.15

Accounting vs. Financial management

How to do accounting is classed in 657, use of accounting information by management in 658.15. How to prepare a financial statement is classed in 657, use of a financial statement by management to improve business performance in 658.15. Design of accounting systems in general and for outside reporting is classed in 657. Design of accounting systems with specific emphasis on increasing the internal flow of information to management is classed in 658.15. If in doubt, prefer 657.

658 and T1—068

General management [and Table 1 notation for] Management [in specific fields]

Management comprises the conduct of all types of enterprises except government agencies that do not themselves provide direct services. *(See discussion at T1—068 vs. 353–354.)* Management is not confined to "business enterprises."

Organizations to be managed may be divided in three ways. First is division by size or scope of the enterprise, which is classed in 658 for big business and 658.02 for small business. Second is division by the legal form of the enterprise, e.g., corporations, partnerships, etc., which is classed in 658. Third, and most important, is division by the kind of work the organization does: selling books, manufacturing light bulbs, carrying freight, caring for the sick, etc. Management of enterprises doing specific kinds of work is classed with the kind of work being done plus notation 068 from Table 1, e.g., management of airlines 387.7068. If there is no specific number for the kind of work, notation 068 cannot be used, e.g., management of savings and loan institutions 332.2. 658 and its subdivisions are reserved for discussions of management applicable to any type of enterprise. Comprehensive works on management of public enterprises are classed in 352.2.

For an enterprise's field of work, select if possible a straightforward number for making a product or performing a service. For example, class works on the management of automobile manufacturing in 629.222068, not 338.7, because 338.7 is for the economics of automobile manufacturing.

See also discussion at 381 vs. 658.8.

658 vs. 658.1, 658.4

General management vs. Organization and finance vs. Executive management

Class organization by legal and ownership forms (e.g., corporations, partnerships) in 658. Class in 658.1 works that focus on initiating a particular form of organization. If in doubt between 658 and 658.1, prefer 658.

In 658.4 "organization" means the internal managerial organization of an enterprise, not the form of legal or ownership organization. Internal organization is concerned with the way that authority and responsibility are apportioned. For example, in line organization a single manager exercises final authority, either directly over production workers or over several supervisors who in turn supervise workers. If in doubt between 658 or 658.1 and 658.4, prefer 658 or 658.1.

658.4 and T1—068

Executive management [and Table 1 notation for] Management [in specific fields]

Executive management concerns the work of top and middle management. Because top and middle managers deal with all aspects of management, however, many aspects of executive management are classed in other management numbers besides 658.4. The number 658.4 is limited to works that focus on the role, function, powers, or position of top and middle management; or to works that treat the topics mentioned in the including note in the entry for 658.4. Broader works are classed in 658 and T1—068. The table of contents can be a useful guide: if the chapter headings read like the topics mentioned in the entry for 658.4, class in 658.4; but if they read like the principal subdivisions of 658 (e.g., separate chapters on finance, personnel, production, and marketing), class in 658. Works on executive management applied to another branch of management are classed with the branch, e.g., executive management of marketing 658.8 and T1—068.

658.4 vs. 651.7, 808

Executive management vs. Communication   Creation and transmission of records [as an office service] vs. Rhetoric and collections of literary texts from more than one literature

Class in 651.7 such topics as the use of the telephone, techniques of dictation, how to use microcomputer software for form letters, mail-handling techniques—in short, the mechanics of communication. Do not class in 651.7 works that emphasize effective business writing style.

Class in 808 style manuals for business writing and works on how to do effective business writing, whether aimed at secretaries or executives. Class in 808 works on how to write a specific type of communication (e.g., business letters) and model collections of a specific type intended to illustrate good writing style. If in doubt between 651.7 and 808, prefer 808.

Class in 658.4 works that focus on use of communication to achieve management goals. Often these works emphasize the personal relations aspects of management communication. If in doubt between 651.7 and 658.4, prefer 658.4. If in doubt between 808 and 658.4, prefer 658.4.

658.8, T1—068 vs. 659

Management of distribution (Marketing) [and Table 1 notation for] Management [in specific fields] vs. Advertising and public relations

Marketing (658.8) is the broader concept; it includes sales management, marketing research, channels of distribution, and customer credit management (all classed in 658.8); it also includes the advertising and public relations that have been drawn off to 659. What belongs in 659 is the publicity used by an organization to present itself and its goods and services to the public. Research focused on advertising or public relations is the only kind of marketing research classed in 659; broader research is classed in 658.8. If in doubt, prefer 658.8.

670.42 vs. 670.285

Factory operations engineering vs. Data processing   Computer applications [in manufacturing]

Flexible manufacturing systems

Works on flexible manufacturing systems are classed in 670.42 if limited to computer-aided manufacture; in 670.285 if including also other computer applications in manufacturing, such as computer-aided design or computer applications in management of manufacturing. If in doubt, prefer 670.42.

671–679 vs. 680

Manufacture of products from specific materials vs. Manufacture of products for specific uses

The distinction between 671–679 and 680 cannot be drawn consistently because some manufacture by material appears in 680, e.g., leather and fur goods 685; and some products for specific uses appear in 671–679, e.g., paper plates and cups 676. In general 671–679 has primary products in contrast to the final products from a given material in 680, e.g., textiles 677, clothing 687; but that distinction is not relevant in many specific cases, e.g., brushes 679, combs 688. If in doubt, prefer 671–679.

680 vs. 745.5

Manufacture of products for specific uses vs. [Artistic] Handicrafts

Handicraft when limited to artistic work is classed in 745.5. In general usage the term "crafts" may be used for country crafts, and cottage industries and trades, such as those of the farrier, the cooper, and the thatcher. Crafts in this sense and handicrafts as the routine way of manufacturing secondary and final products are classed in 680. If in doubt, prefer 680.

690 vs. 643

[Construction of] Buildings vs. Housing and household equipment

Renovation, improvement, remodeling

The scope note at 643 reading "works for owner-occupants and renters covering activities by members of household" indicates that 643 is used for a broad range of material intended for the do-it-yourself enthusiast. Works on home renovation and remodeling for professional builders are classed in 690. If in doubt, prefer 690.

700

The arts   Fine and decorative arts

The word "arts" used without a qualifier is usually a signal that the area covered is broader than the fine and decorative arts. Literature, music, and the performing arts are the other kinds of arts most often included. A quick check each time that "art" or "arts" is used should establish the area covered.

"Computer art" usually refers to two different uses of computers in the arts. The computer can be a device employed in creating the final art work, as when the computer serves as an aid in composing music to be played on traditional instruments or as an aid in designing or engraving the plates for otherwise traditional prints. Alternatively, the computer can serve as the instrument on which music is performed, as in computer music, or as the display medium for visual art, as when computer graphics works are intended for display on a computer monitor. The computer as a device is classed with other devices using either notation 0285 from Table 1 or specific provisions in the schedule, e.g., computers and the arts 700.285, computers in the graphic arts 760.0285, computer composition of music 781.3. The computer as an instrument or display medium is classed with the type of art, e.g., history of computer art 709.04, computer graphic art 760, computer music 786.7.

700.92

Persons [in the arts]

The instructions at each major area for the classification of artists vary. Even within one division, the 730s, the treatment varies: 730.92 for a sculptor, 739.2 for a goldsmith, 730.092 for a sculptor who has also worked in one or more of the other plastic arts.

Works of an artist or artists are designated in one of two ways, either by notation 092 from Table 1 as in sculpture, or by notation for period or place as in drawing 741.93–.99.

704.9

Iconography

Prefer iconography over historical and geographic treatment, e.g., a general work on Romanesque art 709.02, Romanesque art of Normandy 709.44, but the Virgin Mary and Child in Romanesque art of Normandy 704.9. However, care should be taken in classifying schools and styles that usually are limited in subject matter, such as early Christian, Byzantine, and Romanesque schools, which usually treat religious themes. Class in 704.9 only if a point is made that iconography or one of its aspects is the focus of the work.

709.01–.05 vs. 709.3–.9

Periods of development [of fine and decorative arts] and arts of nonliterate peoples vs. Treatment by specific continents, countries, localities [of fine and decorative arts]

Class the works produced by an artistic school or in a particular style as follows:

1. From two countries, with the country coming first in Table 2 in 709.3–.9.

2. From three or more European countries, with the period when the school or style flourished in 709.01–.05.

3. From three or more non-European countries within the same continent, with the continent in 709.3–.9.

4. From three or more countries not within the same continent, with the period when the school or style flourished in 709.01–.05.

If in doubt, prefer 709.01–.05.

709.2 vs. 380.1

Persons [associated with fine and decorative arts] vs. Commerce (Trade)

Art dealers

Works about art dealers that focus on the economics of trading in art are classed in 380.1. Works that focus on the dealers as a part of the art world, e.g., the artists the dealers knew and works of art they handled, are classed in 709.2. If in doubt, class in 709.2.

721 vs. 690

Architectural structure vs. Buildings

Descriptive details of buildings erected in the past or planned for the future are classed in 721. Principles of engineering design and construction or actual instruction (e.g., for the builder) on how to put structural elements, shapes, and materials together are classed in 690. If in doubt, prefer 721.

729

Design and decoration of structures and accessories

More material is taken out of 729 by notes than is left in. Class in 729 only those general works in which the focus is specifically architectural design. Design and construction treated together are classed in 721. Construction alone is classed in

690. Decoration is classed in 729 only when the subject is being treated as an aspect of architectural decoration rather than as an art object in itself. For example, comprehensive works on murals are classed in 751.7; however, the use of murals as architectural decoration is classed in 729.

731–735 vs. 736–739

Sculpture vs. Other plastic arts

The products and techniques of the plastic arts in 736–739 are often difficult to separate from those of sculpture; if in doubt, prefer 731–735. For example, bronze figures are classed in sculpture, but a bronze figure is classed in 739.5 if it was a part (such as a finial or handle) of a larger decorative work.

741.6 vs. 800

Graphic design, illustration, commercial art vs. Literature (Belles-lettres) and rhetoric

Class illustration in general in 741.6. Class a specific type of illustration with the art form represented if the type is emphasized, e.g., etchings. If the illustrations merely accompany or enhance the literary text, class with the text in literature. If in doubt, class in 741.6.

745.1

Antiques

Class a specific type of antique with the subject in art if a number is provided, e.g., gold coins 737.4, antique New England furniture 749.214.

If there is no available number in 700–799, use the appropriate number in 600–699, e.g., antique passenger automobiles 629.222. If there is a separate technology number for the use of the object in question as opposed to the number for the manufacture of the object, prefer the use number, e.g., thimbles 646 rather than 687.

If antiques and collectibles fit in neither the art nor the technology numbers, class with the subject with which they are most closely associated, e.g., Shirley Temple collectibles 791.43.

745.5928

[Handcrafted] Models and miniatures

Class handcrafted miniatures and models as follows:

Class in 700:

1. If there is a specific number for the model, e.g., paper airplanes 745.592.

2. If there is a specific number for the subject illustrated by the model, e.g., handcrafted miniature furniture 749.022. (Note: notation 022 from Table 1 is used to indicate the model or miniature.)

3. If there is no number for the model or the subject illustrated in 600. In this case the most specific number possible is chosen.

Class in 600 if there is no specific number in 700–779 *and* either of the following conditions is met:

1. If there is a specific number in 600–699 for the model, e.g., handcrafted model airplanes 629.133.

2. If there is a specific number for the subject illustrated by the model, e.g., handcrafted miniature reciprocating steam engines 621.1.

753–758

Iconography

Prefer iconography over historical and geographic treatment, e.g., a general work on Romanesque painting 759.02, Romanesque painting of France 759.409, but the Virgin Mary and Child in Romanesque painting of France 755. However, care should be taken in classifying schools and styles that usually are limited in subject matter, such as early Christian, Byzantine, and Romanesque schools, which usually treat religious themes. Class in 753–758 only if a point is made that iconography or one of its aspects is the focus of the work.

Notation 09 from Table 1 plus notation 3–9 from Table 2 is added to show the nationality or locality of the artists rather than the location of the subject, e.g., Canadian portraits of British royalty 757.0971.

769.92

Persons

Both the printmakers who copy other artists and the artists being copied (if only prints are being discussed) are classed here, e.g., prints after Gainsborough 769.92. Prints produced by either a print workshop or a studio are classed in 769.93–.99.

778.3 vs. 621.36

Special kinds of photography vs. Applied optics and paraphotic engineering

The techniques of producing the picture as an end unto itself are classed in 778.3. The engineering technology underlying the photography and the scientific applications are classed in 621.36. Applications to a specific field of science are classed with the field, e.g., astronomy 522. If in doubt, prefer 778.3.

780.26

Treatises on music scores, recordings, texts

The meaning of 026 is different when used within 780–788 than when used with 780–788 numbers added elsewhere in the schedules. Within 780, 026 is used only for treatises about scores and recordings in order to shelve them apart from the treatises about the music. Because the formats of scores and recordings differ from that of treatises, they are normally shelved separately, and the Classification does not distinguish among them. A library that wishes to distinguish them has to apply either the optional provision or some other notational device. However, when 780–788 numbers are added elsewhere in the schedules, 026 is used for scores and recordings, as well as for treatises about them. The notation is added because the material outside 780 that concerns scores and recordings is usually bibliographic in nature and would interfile with the treatises on the shelf unless the notation distinguished them. For example:

Number	Used for
787.2	A treatise on violin music
787.2	Violin scores
787.2	Recordings of violin music
787.2026	A treatise on violin scores
787.2026	A treatise on recordings of violin music
016.7872	A bibliography of treatises on violin music
016.7872026	A bibliography of violin scores
016.7872026	A bibliography of treatises on violin scores
016.7872026	A discography of recordings of violin music
016.7872026	A bibliography of treatises on recordings of violin music.

780.92

Persons associated with music

Musicians

Comprehensive works on musicians are classed in the most specific number that describes their careers. 780.92 is used only for musicians who are equally known for both their vocal and instrumental work, e.g., Ludwig van Beethoven 780.92. Musicians known primarily for vocal music are classed in 782–783, e.g., Richard Wagner, an opera composer, 782.1092; Elvis Presley, a rock singer, 782.42166092. Musicians known primarily for instrumental music are classed in 784–788, e.g., Sir Thomas Beecham, a conductor, 784.2092; Nicolò Paganini, a violinist, 787.2092. (*See also 781.6 for discussion on musicians associated with traditions of music other than classical.*)

Composers

Notation 092 from Table 1 is used to indicate a biography, a general criticism of the composer, an analysis of a composer's contribution to the development of some aspect of music (such as Haydn's role in the development of the concerto form), critical works on the body of a composer's work (such as a critique of the piano music of Ravel), and a collection of analyses of the individual pieces of music. Criticism of an individual work by a composer does not receive notation 092 in order that a piece of music and criticism of it will fall at the same class number.

781.6

Traditions of music

Musicians

Comprehensive works on musicians are classed in the most specific number that describes their careers. Numbers in the range 781.62–.66 are used only for musicians that are equally known for both their vocal and instrumental work, e.g., Louis Armstrong, a jazz trumpeter, singer, and band leader, 781.65092. Musicians known primarily for vocal music are classed in 782–783, e.g., Ella Fitzgerald, a jazz singer, 782.42165092. Musicians known primarily for instrumental music are classed in 784–788, e.g., John Coltrane, a jazz tenor-saxophonist, 788.7.

781.62 vs. 780.89

Folk music vs. Music with respect to specific racial, ethnic, national groups

Works discussing a racial, ethnic, or national group in relation to music in general are classed in 780.89, e.g., a work about African American composers, opera singers, and jazz conductors. Works discussing music indigenous to the group, e.g., African American music, are classed in 781.62. If in doubt, class in 781.62.

781.62 vs. 781.62009

Folk music vs. Historical, geographic, persons treatment [of folk music]

The folk music of an area is usually the folk music of the racial, ethnic, or national group living in that area. Thus, 781.62 is usually used instead of 781.620093–.620099. 781.62 is used both for groups that predominate in an area and for groups that do not, and it is used for national groups that may include multiple ethnic groups, e.g., people of the United States. However, when there is no one specific ethnic group, 781.620093–.620099 is used. For example, folk music of Germany is classed in 781.62, while folk music of Europe is classed in 781.620094.

782

Vocal music

The primary characteristic of arrangement is that of *character*. Vocal music is either dramatic (782.1) or nondramatic (782.2–.4); nondramatic is either sacred (782.2–.3) or secular (782.4). (Staging dramatic music is classed in 792.5.)

For nondramatic vocal music (782.2–783) classification is determined by whether an item is a treatise or a recording, on the one hand, or a score, on the other. A person interested in reading about or listening to a singer or a piece of music will usually not know the singer's vocal range or the vocal requirements of that piece of music. In contrast, a person interested in scores will know the type of voice or voices involved, e.g., a song cycle sung by a soprano, or a mass sung by a tenor and male chorus. Therefore, treatises about and recordings of singers and nondramatic vocal forms are classed in 782.2–.4, while scores and texts are classed in 782.5–783.9.

Examples:

Soprano arias from opera [scores]	782.1
Soprano airs not from opera [scores]	783.6
Sacred songs by sopranos [recordings]	782.25
Women's soprano voice [treatise]	783.6

Vocal scores

When dealing with scores, kind of voice and size of vocal ensemble must be considered. The distinction between 782.5–.9 and 783 is based upon the number of voices per part. Class in 782.5–.9 works that treat music having several voices per part (what is usually meant by choral music). Class in 783 works that treat music having one voice per part (part songs and solos). Observe the following preference order for scores and parts of nondramatic vocal music:

Size of vocal ensemble (including solos)
Type of voice, e.g., male, high, soprano, child's
Vocal forms

Size of vocal ensemble parallels the primary division in the instrument portion of the schedule. Choral music is analogous to orchestral music (more than one voice/instrument per part in some parts); single voices in combination is analogous to chamber music (only one voice/instrument per part); and music for solo voice is analogous to music for solo instrument.

782.1 vs. 792.5

[Musical aspects of] Dramatic vocal forms   Operas vs. [Staging] Dramatic vocal forms   Operas

Class in 782.1 works that discuss dramatic vocal forms as a type of vocal music, including such topics as tempos, plots, singers, conducting. Class in 792.5 and related numbers works that discuss dramatic vocal forms as a type of stage presentation, including such topics as costumes, sets, direction. For example, operas as vocal music are classed in 782.1, staging of operas in 792.5; musical plays as vocal music in 782.1, staging of musical plays in 792.6. Works about an opera house and its productions are classed in 792.509, e.g., a history of La Scala, Milan 792.50945. If in doubt, class in 782.1.

784–788

Instruments and their music

Persons

For persons associated with an instrument and its music <u>and</u> for persons associated with the music for the instrument, add notation 092 from Table 1 directly to the number for the instrument and its music, e.g., Nicolò Paganini (a violinist and composer) <u>and</u> Isaac Stern (a violinist) 787.2092. However, for persons interested only in the instrument, do *not* add notation 092 from Table 1, e.g., Antonio Stradivari (a violin maker) 787.2.

For persons associated with a specific tradition of music other than western art music, do *not* add notation 092 from Table 1, e.g., a country music violinist 787.2. If the person is associated with more than one tradition, notation 092 from Table 1 can be added.

791.092

Persons [associated with public performances]

Class the biography of a performer with the activity with which the person's career is chiefly identified, e.g., the biography of an opera singer 782.1092. If the person's career involves more than one kind of public performance with no particular predominance, class the biography with the activity that comes first in the following table of preference:

Music	780
Dancing	792.8
Stage	792
Motion pictures	791.43
Television	791.45
Radio	791.44

For example, class the biography of a stage actor who has also done considerable work in television in 792. Activities listed in the table above take precedence over all other other activities listed in 791.

791.43 and 791.44, 791.45, 792.9

Motion pictures [and] Radio [and] Television [and] Stage productions

The text of a play is classed in the appropriate number in literature, e.g., the text of Thornton Wilder's *Our Town* 812. A production script is classed in either 791 or 792, e.g., the production script for a staged production of *Our Town* 792.9. A production script is distinguished from a literary text in that it contains a variety of directions, e.g., where the furniture is to be placed, where the actors are to stand.

A production recorded in a different medium than the original production is classed with the recording, not with the production. For example, a staged opera recorded for television is classed with television in 791.45, not with staged opera in 792.5.

791.43, 791.45 vs. 778.5

Motion pictures [and] Television vs. Cinematography, video production, related activities

Works on the technical aspects of making motion pictures and videos are classed in 778.5. Works on motion pictures and television as art forms and comprehensive works on producing them are classed in 791.43 and 791.45. For example, a work on determining what kind of lighting apparatus to use while filming in bright sunlight is classed in 778.5. A work on the use of lighting techniques to enhance the mood of the scene and a comprehensive work on lighting are classed in 791.43. If in doubt, prefer 791.43 and 791.45.

792.7 vs. 792.8, 793.3

Theatrical dancing and variety shows vs. Ballet and modern dance vs. Social, folk, national dancing

A social, folk, or national dance can be given in the theater, just as a theatrical dance can become a social dance. In addition, either kind can be a part of a ballet. A dance is classed in 792.7, 792.8, or 793.3 depending upon the focus of the work. For example, the waltz is usually treated as a ballroom dance and is classed in 793.3; but waltzes as an integral part of Balanchine's *Vienna Waltzes,* a ballet, are classed in 792.8.

793.93 vs. 794.8

Adventure games   Fantasy games vs. Electronic games   Computer games

Computer adventure games present the player with a situation and a goal (or goals). These goals may involve solving a mystery or problems and accumulating points. The player must think as opposed to making reflex actions, and is projected into an interactive story. Examples of this type are *Witness*® and *King's Quest*®. Class this type of game in 793.93.

Computer fantasy role-playing games also involve reaching a goal by solving intellectual problems. However, reflex actions are necessary because of the fighting or athletic action. Outcomes are decided by the computer. Examples of this type are *Exodus: Ultima II*® and *Wizardry: Proving Grounds of the Mad Overlord*®. Also class this type of game in 793.93.

Arcade games refer to a type of game, not just those games played in video arcades. They emphasize quick reflexes, as opposed to intellectual decisions. Among the types of these games are fighting, space flight, shooting, pinball, mazes, space shootouts, and strategy. Examples are *Robo Cop*® and *PacMan*®. Class this type of game in 794.8.

If in doubt, prefer 793.93.

795.01 vs. 519.2

Philosophy and theory [of games of chance] vs. Probabilities

"Games of chance" in the recreational sense are games in which chance, not skill, is the most important factor in determining the outcome, e.g., craps, poker, solitaire. Works discussing the probabilities, or odds, of winning these games are classed in 795.01. In the mathematical sense, "games of chance" are limited to games played by a single player to determine the optimal policy or strategy of winning the games. Because these games are a part of the theory of controlled probabilities, they are classed in 519.2. If in doubt, prefer 795.01.

796.08 vs. 796.04

History and description of sports and games with respect to kinds of persons vs. General kinds of sports and games

If the sports or games are not modified to allow participation of a specific kind of persons, class with the kind either in 796.08 or with the specific sport or game, plus notation 08 from Table 1. If the sports or games have been modified, class either in 796.04 or in the number for the type of sport without adding notation 08 from Table 1. If in doubt, class in 796.08 or in the number for the specific sport or game, plus notation 08 from Table 1. For example, a person who has lost a leg can usually play golf without a major change to the rules of golf. Thus, works for that person on how to golf would class in 796.352087. However, in order to participate in other sports, the person who has lost a leg usually requires a wheelchair. Comprehensive works on wheelchair sports are classed in 796.04. The wheelchair version of a specific sport is classed with the sport without adding notation 08 from Table 1, e.g., wheelchair basketball 796.323.

The name of a variant of the sport may give the impression that it is for only one class of person when any type can play it. For example, women's basketball before 1971 was a variant of basketball in which there are six players per team and the three forwards played in the forecourt. This variant can be played by either men or women and is classed in 796.323, not 796.323082.

Some sports and games have similar sounding names but the rules are so different as to create separate, though related, sports and games. For example, American football, Canadian football, and Australian-rules football are similar sports but they each have their own separate rules and are classed in 796.332, 796.335, and 796.33, respectively.

796.15 vs. 629.04

Play with remote-control models, kites, similar devices vs. Transportation engineering

Class in 629.04 and related numbers in the 620s the design and construction of model vehicles, e.g., building model airplanes 629.133. Class in 796.15 both play with and interdisciplinary works on remote-control vehicles, e.g., flying and building remote-control airplanes. If in doubt, class in 796.15.

Because most play with model railroads and trains does not involve remote-control vehicles, play with all types of model railroads and trains is classed in 790.1.

800

Literature [Belles-lettres] and rhetoric

In the following discussion, whenever application of principles to various literatures is being discussed, notation from Table 3 is mentioned. For example, "T3—1" is used to discuss poetry in specific literatures rather than "811, 841, etc."

Choice between literature and nonliterary subject

The aims of literature, according to Horace, are twofold: to teach and delight. The Dewey Decimal Classification holds to this precept. Works of the imagination intended to delight are classed in 800, but works that are essentially informational are classed according to subject in other parts of the schedule. The discipline of literature is restricted to: (1) works of the imagination that are written in the various literary forms, e.g., fiction, poetry; (2) literary criticism and description; (3) literary history and biography. The exclusion of informational works from the realm of belles-lettres holds regardless of the literary form of a work. Jonathan Swift's *The Drapier's Letters*, therefore, is not classed as a collection of the author's letters, rather as a work on monetary policy in 332.4.

Essays, speeches, letters, and diaries are commonly used for nonliterary purposes. If in doubt whether a work in one of these forms should be classed as literature in 800 or with a subject elsewhere in the schedule, class with the subject.

The nonfiction novel is a problem for classifiers. This kind of novel uses the techniques of fiction writing to tell the story of actual people and actual events. Class an account of a true event or series of events using the names of the people involved, not inventing characters or distorting facts to enhance an intended artistic effect, not going beyond the information available to the author from investigation and interviews, in the discipline appropriate to the facts described. Truman Capote's *In Cold Blood*, a true account of a multiple murder, has not been assigned a fiction number, but is classed in 364.15, the criminology number for murder. If, however, the author goes beyond what is learned from investigation and interviews in describing conversations, feelings, thoughts, or states of mind of the people depicted in the book, then the author is treating them as fictional persons, and the work should be classed as fiction, e.g., Norman Mailer's *The Executioner's Song* 813. In case of doubt, class as fiction.

Other kinds of fiction, and poetry and drama are sometimes used as vehicles for conveying factual information. Biographies have been written in verse, and fiction has been employed to teach the fundamentals of mathematics. Prefer 800 for poetry, drama, and fiction unless the form is purely incidental to the explanation of a specific subject, e.g., Harvey's *Circulation of the Blood* (written in Latin verse) 612.1, not 871.

An exception to the general rule is made for certain ancient works that have long been classed as literature regardless of the content of the work. For example, Hesiod's *Works and Days* is classed in 881, not 631, even though it deals with practical agriculture. These ancient works continue to be classed as literature, but new works whose major purpose is to inform are classed with the subject treated.

Class a collection of literary texts (or excerpts from literary texts) that is meant to serve as a model for studying another discipline with the discipline illustrated. For instance, class in 307 a collection meant to explain what a community is.

Class a literary study of nonliterary works, e.g., the Bible as literature, in 809.

Language

Literature always involves the use of language, and language is the basic facet for building numbers in 800.

Class literary works by language, not by country of origin. A major exception to this rule is that works in English originating in countries of the Western Hemisphere are classed in 810, not in 820 with English literature from the Eastern Hemisphere and comprehensive works on English literature.

Class literary works in the language in which they were originally written. An English translation of a work originally written in Spanish is classed with Spanish literature in 860, not with English literature in 820.

Literature of two or more languages

Works treating literature of two or more languages are usually collections or works of criticism. If two languages are involved, class the work in the number coming first in 820–890, except class Greek and Latin in 880, not 870. If more than two languages are involved, class the work in the most specific number that will contain them all. For instance, class a work including English, German, and Dutch in 830 since these are all Germanic languages. Do not class in 820–890 such a broad grouping as Indo-European literature; for example, class a work involving English, French, and Russian (all Indo-European languages) in 808 for collections, 809 for criticism, 800 for a combination of collections and criticism. Similarly, class in 800, 808, or 809 a work about literature in more than two languages when the languages are unrelated except that they belong to a broad grouping such as nonwestern or Asian languages; for example, class a collection of Arabic, Persian, and Turkish literary texts in 808, not 890. If any one language is predominant, class with that language.

Literary form

The second facet to be applied in literature is form. In literature there are two basic modes of expression: poetry and prose. Drama, whether in poetry or prose, is classed with drama in T3—2. The epigram is classed with miscellaneous writings in T3—8, regardless of mode. Works in other forms are classed with poetry in T3—1 if written in verse. Prose works are classed in T3—3 Fiction, T3—4 Essays, T3—5 Speeches, T3—6 Letters, and T3—8 Miscellaneous writings. T3—8 is used for prose literature in more than one literary form; prose literature in a specific form is classed with the form.

Though humor and satire have the number T3—7 in the span for specific forms, they are neither form nor mode; rather, they are categories of writing marked in the case of humor by a manner of expression that makes a point amusingly, in the case of satire by ridicule and derision. Literary works in a particular form (T3—1–6 and T3—8) exhibiting satire and humor are classed with the form. A collection of works by an individual author in more than one form exhibiting satire and humor is classed in T3—8.

Literary criticism

The chief rule to be observed in classing criticism is that it is always classed with the literature being criticized.

Criticism of a specific work is classed with the work, e.g., a critical analysis of Hemingway's *For Whom the Bell Tolls* is classed in 813, the same number as the work itself. Criticism of the work of an author in general is classed in the comprehensive number for the author in question, e.g., criticism of Hemingway 813.

809 and notation 09 from Table 3 and related numbers under specific forms of literature are used for criticism of all kinds of literature except the works of individual authors. Criticism of several literatures as a whole is classed in 809, criticism of fiction from several literatures in 809.3. Criticism of the English-language literature of the United States in general is classed in 810.9, criticism of fiction of the English-language United States in general in 813.009, criticism of early 20th-century American fiction in 813.

Class criticism of literature in a specific form from more than one literature in 809.1–.7. Class in 808.1–.7 critical works in which the emphasis is on the various forms of literature as such, not on the various authors and literatures that may be used as examples. If in doubt between 808.1–.7 and 809.1–.7, prefer 809.1–.7.

Class in 801 the theory and technique of literary criticism. Class the theory and technique of criticism of specific literary forms in 808.1–.7. If in doubt between 801 and 808.1–.7, prefer 801.

Appreciation of literature is classed in the same manner as other criticism.

Textual criticism of literature is classed in the same manner as other criticism except that the theory and technique of textual criticism of specific literary forms is classed in 801, not in 808.1–.7.

Criticism of criticism is classed with the criticism being criticized and hence with the original subject of criticism. Criticism of Hemingway is classed in 813. If a third person writes a criticism of the criticism of Hemingway, this also is classed in 813.

Works about critics are treated in the same manner as works about other authors, i.e., critics are classed with the kind of literature that they chiefly criticizes. Thus, a man who devoted the major part of his life to criticizing the works of Hemingway is classed in 813. A critic of Spanish literature is classed in 860.9.

It should be noted that criticism and critics are classed with the language of the literature they are criticizing, not with the language in which the criticism is written. For example, a French critic writing in French but criticizing American literature is classed in 810.9.

Adaptations

An adaptation may alter the form of a work or modify the content to such an extent in language, scope, or level of presentation that it can no longer be considered a version of the original. An adaptation is classed in the number appropriate to the adaptation, e.g., Lamb's *Tales from Shakespeare* 823. (*For translations, see 800: Language.*)

Note, however, that a prose translation of poetry (which is merely a change in mode) is not treated as an adaptation, e.g., Dante's *Divine Comedy* translated into German prose 851.

Excerpts

Treat a collection of excerpts from different literary works as a collection.

800 vs. 398.2

Literature (Belles-lettres) and rhetoric vs. Folk literature

Folk literature consists of brief works in the oral tradition and is classed in 398.2. Whatever literary individuality the folk literature may once have had has been lost to the anonymity that the passage of time brings. Anonymous classics, however, are not considered to be folk literature. Despite the fact that their authorship is unknown, such works have a recognized literary merit, are almost always lengthy, and form a part of the literary canon. Therefore, they are classed in 800, e.g., *Chanson de Roland* 841, *Cantar de mio Cid* 861, *Kalevala* 894.

Some legendary or historical events or themes, such as the search for the Holy Grail or the battle of Roland with the Saracens, appear as the basis for original works in many literatures, periods, and forms, the medieval works involving them often being anonymous. Although the theme rather than the literature is the binding thread, what is read is a literary work. Consequently, class each retelling of the event or theme with the literature, form, and period in which it was written, e.g., Mary Stewart's Merlin trilogy 823. Class works about a specific theme treated in several literatures in 809.

If in doubt, prefer 800.

800 vs. 398.24, 590, 636

Literature (Belles-lettres) and rhetoric vs. Tales and lore of plants and animals vs. Animals vs. Animal husbandry

Works about animals intended to contribute to some discipline other than literature are classed in the relevant discipline. Class animal stories in which the author's emphasis is on the habits and behavior of the animal in 590, on the care and training of the animal in 636. Class folk literature about animals in 398.24.

Literary accounts of animals are classed with the appropriate form in literature, e.g., poetry. Such accounts may be either fictional or true. A book about animals is certainly fiction if it contains conversations or thoughts of animals. Literary accounts of actual animals are often in the form of anecdotes or personal reminiscences. Such accounts are usually accommodated in T3—8 Miscellaneous writings.

If in doubt, prefer 800.

808

Rhetoric and collections of literary texts from more than two literatures

Readers (Textbooks)

Readers used in the study of composition are classed here. Readers limited to a particular literary form are classed in the rhetoric number for the form, e.g., short stories 808.3. Academic readers in a subject are classed with the subject.

808.001–.7 vs. 070.5

[Rhetoric] vs. Publishing

Three elements combine to produce the finished piece of writing: composition, preparation of the manuscript, and publishing:

1. Composition 808

2. Preparation of the manuscript 808

3. Publishing 070.5

  Class in 070.5 works limited to securing agents, submitting manuscripts, the relations of authors and publishers.

Works combining (2) and (3) are classed in the numbers for preparation of the manuscript (808, etc.) unless heavily weighted toward the publishing end:

  How to make money in free-lance writing 808

  Where to market your manuscript 070.5

If in doubt, prefer 808.001–.7.

900

Geography, history, and auxiliary disciplines

History is a record of events, their causes and effects, and of the contemporary conditions that clarify and enrich these events. When a work is the story of events that have transpired or an account of the conditions that have prevailed in a particular place or region, it is classed in 900. When it is the history of a specific subject, it is classed in the appropriate discipline, e.g., a history of political developments (such as internal developments in government) without respect to their effect upon the larger society and place where they occur 320.9; of economic events in France 330.944; of warfare 355.0209.

Political history is a strong component of history because it affects the whole of a particular society. But the history of political developments as they affect the internal activity of parties or other political groups is classed in 320.9 or in the 324 numbers for parties, campaigns, and election history.

History includes the present (situation and conditions), but not the future (projected events). Class projected events at 303.4.

Position on the map rather than political affiliation usually determines the number assigned to the history or the geography of a particular place, for while political affiliation may change, position on the earth's surface does not.

Historical events vs. nonhistorical events

Depending upon their impact, specific events are classed either in 900 or in specific disciplines in 001–899. Events that are important enough to affect the general social life and history of the place are classed with the history of the place regardless of any discipline involved. For example, the sinking of the Lusitania is classed in 940.4, the assassination of Abraham Lincoln in 973.7092, the San Francisco earthquake in 979.4.

Other specific events are classed with the history of the discipline to which they relate. For example, the history of a crime is classed in 364, e.g., the Whitechapel murders committed by Jack the Ripper 364.15. A sporting accident is classed in 796–799, e.g., a fatal accident during an automobile race 796.72.

In applying the above, the classifier should take into account the author's purpose or point of view. For instance, a work about the assassination of John F. Kennedy that is focused on the modus operandi of the crime, the detective work involved in solving it, or both, is classed in 364.15, not in 973.922092.

Works about events are more apt to emphasize social aspects than technological aspects and are usually classed in 300 rather than 600. If safety factors are stressed, the work is classed in 363, not with any other discipline involved. For example, a study of the wreck of the Andrea Doria to determine what the causes of the accident were, what preventive measures might be mandated as a result of the incident, is classed at 363.12.

Collected accounts of events are treated in the same manner, provided that they all pertain to one discipline, e.g., scientific travel 508. Class collected events without such focus in 904.

909, 930–990 vs. 320

World history [and] History of ancient world; of specific continents, countries, localities; of extraterrestrial worlds vs. Political science (Politics and government)

Political history

Political history with an emphasis on major political events typified by the "battles, kings, and dates" school of history is clearly 900. Political history with an emphasis on the mechanics of give and take of political forces and movements and on their internal development is usually classed in 320.9, but if the forces and movements come to power or bring about major changes in society, their successes or failures become general history, and should be classed in 900.

Political activities

The sum total of political activity of a specific period or place is also considered general history, and is classed in 909 and 930–990. Various subdivisions of 320 include material on important political activities when considered in terms of the discipline "political science," but whenever an activity is discussed in a manner which highlights its influence on general events 900 must be considered. The general rule is: Important events and leaders with wide-ranging responsibilities are classed in general history, unless considered primarily in the context of a specific subject. The chief problems concern three numbers: 320.9, 324, and 328.

320.9: Under political situation and conditions there can be works on habitual activities and styles of leading political figures as a group, and on the activities reflecting the adjustment of political forces or the status of political parties and movements. But when the activities are analyzed in terms of their effect on general events, use 900.

324: Party histories are classed in 324.2; and histories of nomination and election campaigns, in 324.5 and 324.9, respectively, but only when they concern largely internal events of the parties and campaigns, or report winners, losers, and votes. A history of how a party or candidate came to power (or almost did), or a discussion of how party and campaign events move nations (or other areas) in certain directions is classed in 900.

328: Histories of specific legislative bodies are classed in 328.4–.9, but only when they are largely limited to what happened within or to the bodies, without significant consideration of what the legislative body did for the political unit it served. The accomplishments of a given legislative session are normally a matter of general history and are classed in 900, but if a work concentrates on the body's internal history it is classed in 328. While the report of proceedings of a legislature (i.e., its motions, debates, actions) may constitute the raw material of history, it is not in itself general history, and remains in 328.

909, 930–990 vs. 320.4, 321, 321.09

World history [and] History of ancient world; of specific continents, countries, localities; of extraterrestrial worlds vs. Structure and function of government vs. Systems of governments and states vs. Change in system of government

Change of government

The number for changes in systems of government (321.09) is used primarily for studies of *the process* of change, rather than for works on particular changes. Prefer other numbers in 321 or subdivisions of 320.4 for works on particular systems or kinds of systems, and 900 numbers for the history of changes in government or particular coups and revolutions in specific areas.

For example, class general political treatment of a specific system of government preceding or following changes in 321 (e.g., 321.8 for new republics); class political treatment of systems of government that precede or follow changes in a specific country in 320.4 (e.g., the government of the Soviet Union after the 1917 revolution 320.447); and class general history of changes of government in specific areas and works on specific coups in 909 or 930–999 (e.g., revolutions in the 20th century 909.82, the Russian Revolution 947.084).

If in doubt, give preference in order of the numbers in the heading, that is, prefer 909 or 930–990 over 320.4 or 321, 320.4 over 321, and all other subdivisions of 321 over 321.09.

909, 930–990 vs. 910

World history [and] History of ancient world; of specific continents, countries, localities vs. Geography and travel

If a work deals with geography and civilization or travel and civilization, class it in 909 or 930–990; however, if the treatment of geography or travel is predominant, class the work in 910. If in doubt, prefer 909 or 930–990.

If the work deals with the description of the physical earth only, class it in 910 or in 913–919.

912 vs. T1—022

Graphic representations of surface of earth and of extraterrestrial worlds vs. [Table 1 notation for] Illustrations, models, miniatures

Atlases and maps

Geographic atlases and maps, i.e., atlases and maps which either do not emphasize a subject, or are devoted to any subject in 910 (general geography and travel) are classed in 912. Road atlases and maps, being primarily intended for travelers, are also classed in 912, but railroad atlases are normally devoted to transportation, thus are classed in 385.022 or (if limited to a specific place) in 385.09, e.g., a railroad atlas of Brazil 385.0981. If in doubt, class in 912.

913–919

Geography of and travel in ancient world and specific continents, countries, localities in modern world; extraterrestrial worlds

Historic sites and buildings

Works describing historic sites and buildings should be classed with the discipline emphasized.

If a building has or had a specific purpose, class the work about it with the purpose of the building unless some other discipline is emphasized, e.g., a work about a Benedictine monastery in Austria that emphasizes the history of the religious order in that place 271, a guide to the New York Stock Exchange building 332.64. Works about buildings that are associated with the life of an individual are classed with the biography number for that person, e.g., the home of Thomas Wolfe in Asheville, North Carolina 813. Works about a site that is famous for an historical event are classed with the history of the event, e.g., Gettysburg National Military Park 973.7.

A work on a building or buildings in an area that focuses on the architecture of the building or buildings is classed in 720.9 or 725–728. Works on religious buildings often fall in this category and are classed in 726. Also class in 725–728 the art history of a building and its contents, including the architecture of the building and the art works it contains.

If a work describing the buildings in an area is written for the purpose of suggesting historic preservation projects to be undertaken, see the discussion at *930–990: Historic preservation*. A work that describes the buildings in an area for the purpose of illustrating the history of the area is classed in 930–990.

If no specific purpose or discipline is evident, class the work in 913–919. For guidebooks, the discussion below under 04 Travel on *Guidebooks*.

See also discussion at 333.7–.9 vs. 508, 913–919, 933–990.

Add table

04

Travel

Use this subdivision for accounts of travel. Such accounts should emphasize events of the trip, places stopped at, accommodations, modes of transportation. If the work is purely a description of the area visited, with none, or very few, of these accompaniments, do not add subdivision 04, or class the work in 930–990 for civilization and social conditions of the place visited, as the case may be. Works of a person who has lived for several years in the area described are usually classed in 930–990.

Travel does not normally cover the whole of any given area. Class accounts according to the widest span covered. For example, travel from New York to San Francisco 917.3, from Marseilles to Paris 914.4, from New York City to Buffalo, New York 917.47.

Discovery and exploration

Use 04 for works describing excursions into previously unknown or little known areas, e.g., the Lewis and Clark expedition 917.804. However, if the initial exploration of a place forms an important part of its early history, class the work in 930–990, e.g., early exploration of North America 970.01.

Class accounts of archaeological expeditions in 930.1.

Guidebooks

A guidebook can be either a residential guidebook, i.e., a guide for either the permanent resident and long-term visitor of an area, or a tourist guidebook, i.e., a guide for the short-term visitor. The residential guidebook covers not only the tourist attractions but also the other parts of the area, such as banks, churches, grocery stores, real estate agencies, and residential neighborhoods. These guidebooks normally give a snapshot view of the history of the area and are classed in 940–990 plus the period notation for when it was written, e.g., a residential guidebook to Washington, D.C., written in 1995 975.304. Tourist guidebooks provide detailed information about the area through which the tourists travel, telling them what to see, where to stay, and where to dine. These guidebooks are classed following the instructions in the following paragraphs. If in doubt whether the book is a residential or a tourist guidebook, class it as a tourist guidebook.

Tourist guidebooks are usually classed in 913–919 plus notation 04 from the table at 913–919, e.g., guidebooks to the United States 917.304. Guidebooks written before ca. 499 are classed in 913, e.g., Pausanias' guide to Greece written ca. 130 913.804. Class modern guidebooks to ancient areas in the corresponding modern area numbers in 914–919, e.g., a 1995 guide to the ruins of Italy 914.504.

A guidebook that is limited to an aspect of the trip is classed with that aspect, e.g., a guide to London's underground rail system 388.4, lodgings for tourists in London 647.94421, restaurants of Hawaii 647.95969. In addition, guidebooks emphasizing a specific subject are classed with the subject, e.g., a guidebook to holy places in Spain 263, a skiing guide to Aspen, Colorado 796.9309788. (*For guidebooks to historic sites and buildings, see the discussion in the section above, Historic sites and buildings.*)

A guidebook to a locality that is usually visited for only one type of attraction is classed with that attraction. For example, most people go to Orlando, Florida, in order to visit its theme parks: Walt Disney World, Sea World of Florida, and Universal Studios Florida. Thus, both guidebooks to the theme parks and to Orlando in general are classed with theme parks in 791.06. However, a guidebook that covers more than one locality is usually classed in 913–919 plus notation 04 from the table at 913–919, e.g., a guide to Florida which covers not only Orlando but also Cape Canaveral, Miami, and Tampa 917.5904.

See also discussion at 333.7–.9 vs. 508, 913–919, 930–990; also at 913–919 vs. 796.51.

Biography

Use 04 for biographies of discoverers, explorers, travelers, but not for general geographers. Class biographies of general geographers in the base number for the area without further subdivision. Also use 04 for first-person accounts of travel. Do not add notation 092 from Table 1 in any case.

913–919 vs. 796.51

Geography of and travel in ancient world and specific continents, countries, localities in modern world; extraterrestrial worlds vs. Walking

Walkers' guides

Walkers' guides can be written for either the hiker or the tourist. Both types of guides give detailed instructions on how to get from point A to point B, e.g., at the fork turn left, and a general description of the route in order for the walker to choose one route over another, such as distance, what can be seen. Guides for the tourist also give detailed description of things en route, e.g., the type of rock outcropping, the history of the wayside shrine. Guides for the hiker are classed in 796.51, while those for the tourist in 913–919 plus notation 04 from the table at 913–919. Walking guides to an urban area are classed in 913–919, e.g., walking guides to San Francisco 917.94. If in doubt, class in 913–919.

A guide limited to one topic is classed with that topic, e.g., a walker's guide to the geology of Yosemite National Park 557.94, a walking tour of houses of San Francisco 728.09794.

930–990

History of ancient world; of specific continents, countries, localities; of extraterrestrial worlds

Wars

In most instances, the history of a war is classed with the history of the country or region in which most of the fighting took place, e.g., the Vietnamese War 959.704, the Napoleonic wars 940.2. However, some wars are arbitrarily assigned to either the history of one of the principal participants or to the region where the war began. For example, the Spanish-American War is classed with United States history in 973.8. World War II is classed in European history (the area where the war began) at 940.53, and not in world history at 909.82. In addition, when a war is fought within a limited portion of a country, it is classed with the history of the country as a whole, e.g., the Second Seminole War, which was fought against the Seminole Indians in Florida, is classed in 973.5, not 975.9.

Regardless of the area to which a war is assigned, specific battles or actions of a war are classed in the number for the war, not with the number of the place where the action occurred. For example, a battle occurring in the Philippines during the Spanish-American War is classed in 973.8, not 959.9; air raids on Tokyo in World War II 940.54, not 952.

There are two kinds of wartime history that are not classed in the war numbers (unless the number for the area covered coincides with the number for the war). Routine history of the everyday events of an area, even if during wartime, is classed with the number for the area, e.g., the history of Maryland during the Civil War 975.2, not 973.709752. The effect of military action on the everyday life and civilization of a place is classed with the history of the place, e.g., the effect of Civil War military actions on Maryland 975.2, not 973.709752. These two kinds of history must be carefully distinguished from the participation of an area in the war because the area's participation in the war is classed with the war, e.g., Maryland's participation in the Civil War 973.709752, not 975.2. Usually, national histories covering a time of war will emphasize the country's participation and will be classed with the war; if there is no such emphasis, the history will be classed in the appropriate national history number. For example, British participation in World War II 940.53, history of Britain during George VI's reign 941.084.

See also discussion at 333.7–.9 vs. 508, 913–919, 930–990.

Wars: Occupied countries

The history of the occupation of a country during time of war is classed with the war, e.g., occupation of countries in World War II 940.53. Military administration of the government of an occupied country during or following the war is classed in 355.4. International law with respect to occupation is classed in 341.6.

Wars: Military units

The history of specific military units in a war is classed with the history of the particular war, e.g., military units in World War I 940.4.

Class comprehensive works on specific military units and military units in peacetime in 355.3 or related numbers in 355–359.

Wars: Personal narratives

The personal narratives of participants in a war are classed in the appropriate subdivision of the history numbers for the specific war, but notation 092 from Table 1 is not added, e.g., personal narratives of American soldiers in World War II 940.54.

The narrative of a person's experiences during time of war, if it does not focus on the war as such, is classed as biography and not in the number for the war. For example, an actor's personal experiences of performing in Scotland during 1940–1942 are classed in 792.092, not 940.53.

Historic preservation

Class comprehensive works on historic preservation and lists of preservation projects to be undertaken in 363.6. However, if such a list is primarily devoted to inventorying or describing the sites, class the list in the appropriate number in 930–990, or, if primarily a description of buildings at the site, class in 720.

Class administrative annual reports of agencies promoting the preservation of historical sites in 353.7.

Class historic preservation in an architectural context in 720.28 and cognate numbers in 721–729.

See also discussion at 333.7–.9 vs. 508, 913–919, 930–990.

Biography

Notation 092 from Table 1 is added to subdivisions 01–09 for biographies of persons who lived during the historical period and of historians and historiographers of that period, e.g., biographies of Abraham Lincoln and of Bruce Catton, Civil War historian 973.7092. If the life span of the person or the time during which the person impacted upon the history of the country or locality does not approximate the whole of the period, notation 092 is not added, e.g., biography of Rajiv Gandhi 954.05. Subdivision 0099 (which is limited to collected treatment) is used *only* for works not limited to a specific period, e.g., biographies of the kings and queens of Great Britain 941.009. If subdivisions 01–09 for historical periods are not given in the schedule, do not add subdivision 009 either for collected biographies limited to a specific period or for individual biographies, e.g., biographies of the 20th-century rulers of Kuwait 953.67, not 953.67009; however, subdivision 009 is added for collected biographies *not* limited to a specific period, e.g., biographies of the rulers of Kuwait 953.67009. Biographies of historians and historiographers whose works are not limited to a specific period are classed in the number for the the history of the country as a whole, e.g., biographies of historians of British history 941.

Add table

01–09

Historical periods

When adding standard subdivisions to the historical periods, use notation 01–09 from Table 1, not 001–009 from the table under 930–990. However, subdivisions T1—089 and T1—091 are not used.

930–990 vs. 355.009

History of ancient world; of specific continents, countries, localities; of extraterrestrial worlds vs. Historical, geographic, persons treatment [of military science]

Military topics and war

Use the historical treatment standard subdivisions in 355–359 for works emphasizing military history or topics without consideration of the general course of a war, e.g., changes in tank tactics during the course of World War II 358. Use numbers in 900 for works on the military history of wars that deal with the outcome of significant events, e.g., the use of tanks on the Eastern Front and how the use affected various battles 940.54. If in doubt between 355–359 and 930–990, prefer 930–990.

Persons

Use 930–990 for comprehensive works on soldiers chiefly associated with the history of a specific war, e.g., William Tecumseh Sherman 973.73092; use 355.0092 for comprehensive works on soldiers associated with more than one war, or who had long and varied careers, e.g., Douglas MacArthur. If in doubt, prefer 930–990.

See also discussion at 930–990: Wars.

941

[History of the] British Isles

Class here works on the United Kingdom (England, Wales, Scotland, and Northern Ireland), a political entity, and on Great Britain (England, Wales, and Scotland), a geographic entity. Class in 942 only works dealing with England alone, or with England and Wales. Histories of the period since 1603 (or including this period) will seldom deal with England or England and Wales alone. Histories of the period before 1603 may deal with England or England and Wales alone. Books on the civilization of this area may deal with any combination. The following combinations of two areas will be classed in 941: England and Scotland, England and Ireland, Ireland and Wales.

970.004

North American native peoples

The principal fact to keep in mind in assigning class numbers to works on the various native American peoples is that they have moved over time from place to place and that these places are often widely scattered.

Therefore, in general, class a work on specific peoples, e.g., a general work on Cherokees, in 970.004. If, however, the focus of the work is clearly on the native peoples in a specific place, use the number for the place. For example, native peoples of Canada 971, Cherokees in North Carolina 975.6.

Policies and Procedures of the
Library of Congress Decimal Classification Division

Segmentation in Centrally Cataloged Records

One aid to reduction of the full DDC number is the segmentation provided in DDC numbers by centralized cataloging services, such as the Decimal Classification Division of the Library of Congress, the British Library, and the National Library of Canada. The segmentation is indicated by a prime mark ('), a slash mark (/), or other comparable indicators.

The segmentation provided by the Decimal Classification Division is applied according to two different principles. A segmentation mark can indicate the end of an abridged number (as found in the Abridged Edition of the DDC), or the beginning of a standard subdivision. Thus, a DDC number can consist of one, two, or three segments. For example:

324.6′23′092	A biography of Susan B. Anthony
324.6	Election systems and procedures; suffrage (the number found in the Abridged Edition)
23	Women's suffrage (the remainder of the number from the Schedules of the Unabridged Edition)
092	Persons (from Unabridged Table 1)

323′.025′73	Directory of civil rights leaders and organizations in the United States
323	Civil and political rights (the number found in the Abridged Edition)
.025	Directories (applicable standard subdivision from Abridged Table 1)
73	United States (area notation from Table 2 that can be added to the directories number [025] in Unabridged Table 1)

Bracketed DDC Numbers on LC Bibliographic Records

Libraries using cataloging data provided by the Library of Congress will notice that there are sometimes two or more DDC numbers or non-numeric notation in the DDC field. On LC printed cards, all but the first DDC number is given in brackets ([ ]). The following examples (omitting segmentation marks described above) explain the practices of the Decimal Classification Division with respect to bracketed DDC numbers:

Nonjuvenile Works

A. For works belonging to a monographic series classed as a set but analyzed in full or in part according to the decisions of the Subject Cataloging Division of the Library of Congress, the Decimal Classification Division assigns two numbers:

081 s   the number for the item if the series is kept together at one class number

[327.7]   the number for the specific item in the series

B. For biography and works primarily biographical, the Division assigns a number and the letter [B]:

780.92   the number if the item is added to the classified collection

[B]   the letter if the item is added to the biography collection

C. Brackets for a monograph in a series and for biography may both be present:

780.92 s   the number for the series

[787.66092] [B]   the number and the letter for a monograph in a series

D. For law, the Division makes the only exception to its practice of eschewing optional numbers. It supplies both the preferred number and the Option B number:

345.7308   the preferred number

[347.3058]   the Option B number

E. When works on law belong to analyzed monographic sets, four numbers are supplied. On Library of Congress catalog cards, they are usually printed two by two, with the DDC preferred numbers on the top line and the optional numbers on the bottom line:

343.41052 s   [343.410523]

344.10352 s   [344.103523]

Juvenile Works

For juvenile works, bracketed numbers and alphabetical codes (other than [B]) are assigned by the Children's Literature Section of the Library of Congress.

A. Easy books
    1. Easy books without a clearly defined topic in a recognized field of study are assigned [E], e.g., Tommy takes his first trip to the store [E].
    2. Easy books with a discernible topic in a recognized field of study are assigned both an [E] and a DDC number, e.g., Tommy takes his first trip to London 914.2 [E].
    3. Easy fiction, for children K-3 (through eight years old) is assigned [E].

B. Fiction intended for grades 4–6, or ages 9–11, is assigned [Fic]. Adult fiction that has been deemed appropriate for a juvenile and classes of children's literature that have a continuing adult audience will be assigned [Fic] as well as a class number, e.g., *Treasure Island* 823.8 [Fic].

C. Biography
    1. Without subject or disciplinary associations

        One person   [92]

        Several persons   [920]

    2. With subject or disciplinary association

        One person   509.2   [B]   [92]

        Several persons   509.22   [B]   [920]

Classifying Children's Books in the DCD

The Decimal Classification Division classifies most children's literature processed by the Children's Literature Section of the Library of Congress, except that works designated by [Fic] or [E] are normally sent on without further classification.

The 13th Abridged Edition of the Dewey Decimal Classification was designed by Lisa Hanifan of Albany, New York. The book was composed in Times Roman and Helvetica by Inforonics, Inc. of Littleton, Massachusetts and by Word Management Corporation of Albany, New York. The book was printed and bound by Hamilton Printing Company of Rensselaer, New York.